100 BANNED BOOKS

CENSORSHIP HISTORIES OF WORLD LITERATURE

NICHOLAS J. KAROLIDES,
MARGARET BALD AND DAWN B. SOVA

Introduction by
Ken Wachsberger

D0059269

Checkmark Books™
An imprint of Facts On File, Inc.

100 Banned Books: Censorship Histories of World Literature

Checkmark Books
An imprint of Facts On File, Inc.
11 Penn Plaza
New York NY 10001

Library of Congress Cataloging-in-Publication Data

Karolides, Nicholas J.
censorship histories of world literature / Nicholas J. Karolides, Margaret Bald, and
Dawn B. Sova ; introduction by Ken Wachsberger
p. cm. —
This is a one-volume abridgement containing twenty-five critiques from each of the
four volumes in the Banned books series.
Includes bibliographical references and index.
ISBN 0-8160-4059-1 (acid-free paper)
1. Censorship—United States—History—20th century.
2. Prohibited books—United States—History—20th century.
3. Censorship—History. 4. Prohibited books—History. I. Bald,
Margaret. II. Sova, Dawn B. III. Title. IV. Title: One hundred
banned books.
Z658.U5K35 1999
363.3′1—dc21   99-17140

Checkmark Books are available at special discounts when purchased in bulk
quantities for businesses, associations, institutions or sales promotions. Please call
our Special Sales Department in New York at 212/967-8800 or 800/322-8755.

You can find Facts On File on the World Wide Web at http://www.factsonfile.com

Text design by Cathy Rincon
Cover design by Catherine Lau Hunt

Printed in the United States of America.

MP FOF 10 9 8 7 6 5 4

This book is printed on acid-free paper.

There is no freedom either in civil or ecclesiastical [affairs], but where the liberty of the press is maintained.
—Matthew Tindal

If all mankind minus one were of one opinion, and only one person were of the contrary opinion, mankind would be no more justified in silencing that one person, than he, if he had the power, would be justified in silencing mankind.
—John Stuart Mill

Dare to think for yourself.
—Voltaire

CONTENTS

LITERATURE SUPPRESSED ON
RELIGIOUS GROUNDS

LITERATURE SUPPRESSED ON
SEXUAL GROUNDS

LITERATURE SUPPRESSED ON
SOCIAL GROUNDS

ACKNOWLEDGMENTS

Credit and appreciation are due to a university colleague, Marshall Toman; former students and my daughter, Mitchell Fay, Jane Graves, Alexis Karolides; Laurie Pap; and Eric P. Schmidt, who read texts, researched censorship histories and wrote fine, meaningful essays found in this volume. Their names follow their individual writings. My thanks also go to colleagues who offered advice and scholarship on individual entries: Herbert R. Cederberg, historian; Tracey L. Gladstone-Sovell, political scientist; J. Michael Norman, journalist; John R. Walker, economist; and C. B. Brohaugh, for language expertise. In addition to the librarians to whom this volume is dedicated, I applaud the cooperation of librarians and school personnel in communities across the country who have readily researched newspaper reports of censorship and school district files for me. I am particularly grateful to Inga Karolides for her advice about language clarity and nuance throughout, and to Ken Wachsberger for his expert editing. My gratitude as well goes to Doreen Cegielski for efficient and conscientious preparation of the typescript, and to Sue Voelker, who initially participated in its preparation.

—N. J. K.

Credit and thanks are due to Jonathan Pollack, for his contribution of research and writing for the entries on Charles Darwin and Roger Williams. Thank you also to Ken Wachsberger for his keen editorial eye and unflagging encouragement and enthusiasm, to Bert Holtje, Siobhan Dowd, George Calvert, Elizabeth Stuart Calvert and my colleagues in the National Writers Union. A special thanks to Jonathan Calvert for the constancy of his loving support and to my children, André MacLeod Calvert and Daniel Ian Calvert, young opponents of censorship, for their understanding and affection.

—M. B.

The long history of censorship has created many heroes, both famous and obscure, authors and publishers who have dared to defy the restrictions of their respective ages in order to reveal truth in their writings. The works of some appear in this volume, but many more were silenced and their works destroyed. To all, however, this book owes both life and purpose. Had they acquiesced to those who challenge, censor and ban books containing ideas or language that displease vocal minorities, our intellectual universe would be significantly smaller.

I am grateful for my association with Bert Holtje of James Peter Associates, Inc., whose support and advice as both literary agent and friend helped me to maintain perspective throughout this lengthy project. His insight and literate commentary helped to resolve seemingly insurmountable problems.

My sincere appreciation also belongs to Facts On File, Inc., editors Gary M. Krebs, who saw potential in the idea and courageously proposed a censorship series, and Drew Silver, who provided substance and direction to the work. Gary gave the project life, and Drew worked with me to form its personality as he guided the work to completion. I also appreciate my collaboration with Ken Wachsberger.

Actual works were used to create entries in this volume, giving this book an authenticity that the use of mere summaries could not. This often difficult to locate literature would not have been available to me without the efforts of I. Macarthur Nickles, Director of the Garfield (New Jersey) Library, a man whose professional expertise and insight have been invaluable. He has made certain that my sometimes obscure research requests are satisfied and continues to introduce innovations in my hometown library. I am also grateful to reference experts Kathleen Zalenski and Karen Calandriello, who tracked down unusual books and odd quotations, dates and notes, always persevering long after I had given up the chase.

In my personal life, no one has meant more to me than my son, Rob Gregor, who helped me to organize my thoughts, contributed insights on various works and kept me human. I appreciate greatly the continued support of my parents, Emil and Violet Sova, whose pride in my accomplishments and unwavering confidence in my abilities have always sustained me.

Finally, although I can never meet them, I appreciate the efforts of the many authors over centuries who risked their livelihoods and lives to stand strong against the oppressive efforts of those who would silence all who refuse to conform.

—D. B. S.

INTRODUCTION

I am honored to be writing this introduction to *100 Banned Books: Censorship Histories of World Literature*, but sad that this discussion is concerned less with the distant past than with current events. Unfortunately, censorship persists, even though, as Margaret Bald, author of the section on books banned for religious reasons, observes, "When you look back over centuries at censorship and see the incredible range of books and authors whose works were suppressed, you can only be struck by how absurdly ineffective and useless it has been in the long run."

The First Amendment is the greatest vision America has given to the world: it ensures the freedom of expression and of religion to all who visit or live here. My family and I visited Europe for the first time last summer. While in Germany, we happened to park on Avenue of the Jews. I didn't know if the street's name was a vestige of Nazi anti-Semitism, a memorial to victims of the Holocaust or simply a record of those who used to populate the neighborhood it traversed, but I remained disconcerted even as I visited a Jewish temple that had been rebuilt by a Christian community after being destroyed by the Nazis on Kristallnacht.

We did not travel to Iran, but it is not necessary to have done so to have heard of the *fatwa*, or religious interdict, against Salman Rushdie and his novel *The Satanic Verses*. Delivered in 1989, the *fatwa* amounted to a death sentence against the author, who has lived in hiding ever since. Even though the *fatwa* was officially lifted in 1998, religious conservatives have resolved to carry it out.

In Bangladesh, feminist columnist and author Taslima Nasrin has had bounties placed on her head for her uncompromising stand against patriarchal religious traditions that she sees as oppressive to women.

Americans live in relative freedom. Yet censorship also has been a menace throughout U.S. history, from the time of Roger Williams and other early colonial freethinkers. Southeast Michigan, where I live, recently experienced embarrassing spectacles of First Amendment repression by left- and right-wing advocates. In Ann Arbor, members of a welfare rights organization claiming to speak on behalf of liberal members of the community threw stones at members of the Ku Klux Klan. In neighboring Belleville, science teachers were forced to tear pages with references to abortion from science books.

The latter is an example of social censorship, the prohibition of ideas that make some people uncomfortable. *Anne Frank: The Diary of a Young Girl* was censored by the Alabama Textbook Commission in 1983 because it was "a real downer." Portions of the book were cut by her Dutch publisher because of references to her menstruation and a friend's growing breasts.

Many of our richest literary works—*The Adventures of Huckleberry Finn, The Grapes of Wrath, Uncle Tom's Cabin, Catch-22*—have been censored at one time or another. Advancing technology has provided more diverse targets—the record, film and television industries and the Internet—for school boards, local governments, religious fanatics and moral crusaders to take aim at as they work to restrict free expression and the freedom to read, watch and listen, in order to shield their children, and you, from original or disturbing thoughts.

100 Banned Books contains selections from Facts On File's four-volume Banned Books series, which I edited, about books banned or censored for political, religious, sexual or social reasons. Each of the 100 books is discussed individually through summaries of its contents and censorship history. While many of these books have been legally "banned"—prohibited "as by official order"—all indeed have been banned in a broader sense: targeted for removal from school curricula or library shelves, condemned in churches and forbidden to the faithful, rejected or expurgated by publishers, challenged in court, even voluntarily rewritten by their authors. Censored authors have been verbally abused, physically attacked, shunned by their families and communities, ex-commmunicated from their religous congregations, and shot, hanged or burned at the stake by their enemies. The 100 works in this volume include novels, histories, biographies, children's books, religious and philosophical treatises, poems, polemics and other forms of written expression. Their censorship histories are inspiring.

* * *

NOTE: Works whose titles appear in *SMALL CAPITAL LETTERS* have their own entries in the volume.

—Ken Wachsberger

LITERATURE SUPPRESSED ON POLITICAL GROUNDS

The phrase "suppressed on political grounds" casts a shadow of a heavy-handed government blocking its citizens from receiving information, ideas and opinions that it perceives to be critical, embarrassing or threatening. This image, unfortunately, is too often reality. It is not, however, limited to dictatorships such as those of Hitler's Nazi Germany, Stalin's communist Soviet Union and Suharto's Indonesia. The governments of democracies also participate in attempts to censor such critical material in order to protect their own perceived state security.

Further, the impression that censorship for political reasons emanates only from national governments is mistaken. The second common source of such activity is at the local community level, generated by school board members or citizens, individually or in groups, who attack textbooks and fiction used in schools or available in school libraries. In contrast to censorship challenges at the national level, challenges at the local level are aimed at the political values and images that children are receiving. Over the years, the chief targets have been socialism, communism and the portrayal of the Soviet Union. A companion concern is the portrayal of the United States. Examining flaws in American society is deemed unpatriotic to these critics, who become concerned when past and present policies of their government are questioned in school textbooks. At the center of their objections has been the fear that the Soviet Union would be viewed too positively, or the United States, too negatively.

The 25 censored titles discussed in this section vary considerably in subject and form. Some texts have extensive or impressive censorship histories. *The Grapes of Wrath* was challenged and burned within months of its publication in 1939 and has been subject to attacks for more than 50 years. The censorship of Solzhenitsyn's books by the Soviet government gained international notoriety. Other works appear to have had limited censorship exposure. However, not all objections are formalized or publicly announced; others are reported only in local newspapers. Self-censorship by teachers and librarians is common; I recall the comment of a librarian who accounted for the lack of challenges to her collection through her tactic of not ordering books that were censored elsewhere. Further, not all attacks are identified forthrightly; it is apparently more difficult to protest the politics of a text than it is to protest its offensive language. This is evident in the treatment of many of the contested books discussed in this volume. *Catch-22* by Joseph Heller, for instance, was censored for social reasons. Lee Burress, who had conducted five state and national surveys of censorship of school library and classroom materials, referred to this mask as the "hidden agenda" of censorship.

The accounts of these attacks at local levels may seem to the glancing eye diversified and transient; those at the national level may appear remote and arcane. These multiple streams of curtailed thought, however, combine to form a treacherous current. Its undertow can ensnare the mind in the tangled weeds of ignorance and irrationality. Denied both in individual incidents and en masse is the sine qua non of democracy, the right of fundamental inquiry, the ebb and flow of thought.

—Nicholas J. Karolides
University of Wisconsin–
River Falls

ALL QUIET ON THE WESTERN FRONT

Author: Erich Maria Remarque
Original date and place of publication: 1928, Germany; 1929, United States
Publisher: Impropylaen-Verlag; Little, Brown and Company
Literary form: Novel

SUMMARY

> He fell in October 1918, on a day that was so quiet and still on the whole front, that the army report confined itself to the single sentence: All quiet on the Western Front.

> He had fallen forward and lay on the earth as though sleeping. Turning him over one saw that he could not have suffered long; his face had an expression of calm, as though almost glad the end had come.

This final passage of Remarque's renowned novel enunciates not only the irony of death of this unknown soldier, but also the irony of the wartime communiques that announced that there was nothing new to report while thousands were wounded and dying daily. (The German title of the novel, *Im Westen Nichts Neues*, translates as "nothing new in the West.") The final passage also signals the irony of the title, a bitterness that pervades the entire work.

There are many unknown soldiers in the novel on both sides of the trenches. They are the bodies piled three deep in the shell craters, the mutilated bodies thrown about in the fields, the "naked soldier squatting in the fork of a tree . . . his helmet on, otherwise he is entirely unclad. There is one half of him sitting there, the top half, the legs are missing." They are the young Frenchman in retreat who lags behind, is overtaken—"a blow from a spade cleaves through his face."

The unknown soldiers are background. The novel focuses on Paul Baumer, the narrator, and his comrades of the Second Company, chiefly Albert Kropp, his close friend, and Stanislaus Katczinsky, the leader of the group. Katczinsky (Kat) is 40 years old; the others are 18 and 19. They are ordinary folk: Muller, who dreams of examinations; Tjaden, a locksmith; Haie Westhus, a peat-digger; and Detering, a peasant.

The novel opens five miles behind the front. The men are "at rest" after 14 days on the front line. Of the 150 men to go forward, only 80 have returned. A theme—and the tone of disillusionment—is introduced immediately, the catalyst being the receipt of a letter from Kantorek, their former schoolmaster. It was he who had urged them all to volunteer, causing the hesitant ones to feel like cowards.

> For us lads of eighteen [adults] ought to have been mediators and guides to the world of maturity. . . . in our hearts we trusted them. The idea of authority, which they represented, was associated in our minds with a greater insight and a manlier wisdom. But the first death we saw shattered this belief. . . . The first

3

bombardment showed us our mistake, and under it the world as they had taught it to us broke in pieces.

This theme is repeated in Paul's conversation with adults at home during a leave. They evince deep ignorance of the nature of trench warfare and the living conditions and the dying. "Naturally it's worse here. Naturally. The best for our soldiers. . . ." They argue about what territories ought to be annexed and how the war should be fought. Paul is unable to speak the truth to them.

Vignettes of the soldiers' lives pile up in the first several chapters: inhumane treatment of the recruits at the hands of a militaristic, rank-conscious corporal; the painful death of a schoolmate after a leg amputation; the meager food often in limited supply; the primitive housing; and glimpses of the fear and horror, the cries and explosions of the front. The experienced men reveal their distance from their youth, not merely the trench warfare smarts in contrast to the innocent unready replacement recruits. Gone was the "ideal and almost romantic character" of the war. They recognized that the "classical conception of the Fatherland held by our teachers resolved itself here into a renunciation of personality." They have been cut off from their youth and from the opportunity of growing up naturally; they cannot conceive a future.

After a major battle, Paul narrates: "Today we would pass through the scenes of our youth like travellers. We are burnt up by hard facts; like tradesmen we understand distinctions, and like butchers, necessities. We are no longer untroubled—we are indifferent. We long to be there; but could we live there?"

Paul experiences the depths of this alienation during his leave. Beyond recognition and a vivid yearning, he knows he is an outsider. He cannot get close to his family; of course, he is unable to reveal the truth of his terror-filled experiences, so he cannot seek their comfort. Sitting in the armchair in his room, his books before him, he tries to recapture the past and imagine the future. His comrades at the front seem the only reality.

Rumors of an offensive turn out to be true. They are accompanied by a high double-wall stack of yellow, unpolished, brand-new coffins and extra issues of food. When the enemy bombardment comes, the earth booms and heavy fire falls on them. The shells tear down the parapet, root up the embankment and demolish the upper layers of concrete. The rear is hit as well. A recruit loses control and must be forcibly restrained. The attack is met by machine-gun fire and hand grenades. Anger replaces fear.

No longer do we lie helpless, waiting on the scaffold, we can destroy and kill, to save ourselves, to save ourselves and be revenged . . . crouching like cats we run on, overwhelmed by this wave that bears us along, that fills us with ferocity, turning us into thugs, into murderers, into God only knows what devils; this wave that multiplies our strength with fear and madness and greed of life, seeking and fighting for nothing but our deliverance. If your own father came over with them you would not hesitate to fling a bomb into him.

Attacks alternate with counterattacks and "slowly the dead pile up in the field of craters between the trenches." When it is over and the company is relieved, only 32 men answer the call.

In another situation the relative anonymity of trench warfare is erased. On patrol to scout out the enemy lines, Paul becomes separated from his own troops and finds himself in French territory. He hides in a shell hole, surrounded by exploding shells and sounds of activity. He is strained to the utmost, armed with fear and a knife. When a body crashes in upon him, he automatically slashes at and then shares the shell hole with the dying Frenchman who has become a person. He tries to dress the stab wounds. He is devoured by guilt:

> Comrade, I did not want to kill you. If you jumped in here again, I would not do it, if you would be sensible too. But you were only an idea to me before, an abstraction that lived in my mind and called forth its appropriate response. It was that abstraction I stabbed. But now, for the first time, I see you are a man like me. I thought of your hand grenades, of your bayonet, of your rifle; now I see your wife and your face and our fellowship. Forgive me, comrade. We always see it too late.

There is a respite for the company, and then it is sent out to evacuate a village. During the march, both Paul and Albert Kropp are wounded, Albert seriously. Hospitalized, they fear the amputation-prone doctors; Kropp loses his leg; he does not want to live a "cripple." Paul hobbles around the hospital during his recovery, visiting the wards, increasingly aware of shattered bodies:

> And this is only one hospital, one single station; there are hundreds of thousands in Germany, hundreds of thousands in France, hundreds of thousands in Russia. How senseless is everything that can be written, done, or thought, when such things are possible. It must all be lies and of no account when the culture of a thousand years could not prevent this stream of blood being poured out, these torture-chambers in their hundreds of thousands. A hospital alone shows what war is.

Back at the front the war continues, death continues. One by one the circle of comrades is killed. Detering, maddened for home by the sight of a cherry tree in bloom, attempts to desert but is captured. Only Paul, Kat and Tjaden are alive. In the late summer of 1918 Kat sustains a leg injury; Paul attempts to carry him to a medical facility. Near collapse, he stumbles and falls as he reaches the dressing station. He rises only to discover that Kat is dead; en route he has sustained a splinter in the head.

5

In the autumn there is talk of peace and armistice. Paul meditates about the future:

> And men will not understand us—for the generation that grew up before us, though it has passed these years with us here, already had a home and a calling; now it will return to its old occupations, and the war will be forgotten—and the generation that has grown up after us will be strange to us and push us aside. We will be superfluous even to ourselves, we will grow older, a few will adapt themselves, some other will merely submit, and most will be bewildered;—the years will pass by and in the end we shall fall into ruin.

CENSORSHIP HISTORY

When *All Quiet on the Western Front* was issued in Germany in 1928, National Socialism was already a powerful political force. In the social political context a decade after the war, the novel generated a strong popular response, selling 600,000 copies before it was issued in the United States, but it also generated significant resentment. It affronted the National Socialists, who read it as slanderous to their ideals of home and fatherland. This resentment led to political pamphleteering against it. It was banned in Germany in 1930. In 1933, all of Remarque's works were consigned to the infamous bonfires. On May 10, the first large-scale demonstration occurred in front of the University of Berlin: students gathered 25,000 volumes of Jewish authors; 40,000 "unenthusiastic" people watched. Similar demonstrations took place at other universities; in Munich 5,000 children watched and participated in burning books labeled marxist and un-German.

Remarque, who had not been silenced by the violent attacks against his book, published in 1930 a sequel, *The Road Back*. By 1932, however, he escaped Nazi harassment by moving to Switzerland and then to the United States.

Bannings occurred in other European countries. In 1929, Austrian soldiers were forbidden to read the book, and in Czechoslovakia it was barred from military libraries. In 1933 in Italy, the translation was banned because of its antiwar propaganda.

In the United States, in 1929, the publishers Little, Brown and Company acceded to suggestions of the Book-of-the-Month Club judges, who had selected the novel as the club's June selection, to make some changes; they deleted three words, five phrases and two entire episodes—one of makeshift latrine arrangements and the other a hospital scene during which a married couple, separated for two years, have intercourse. The publishers argued that "some words and sentences were too robust for our American edition" and that without the changes there might be conflict with federal law and certainly with Massachusetts law. Decades later, another kind of publisher's censorship was revealed by Remarque himself. Putnam's had rejected the book in 1929 despite the evidence of its considerable success in Europe. According to the author, "some idiot said he would not publish a book by a 'Hun'."

Nevertheless, *All Quiet on the Western Front* was banned in Boston in 1929 on grounds of obscenity. In the same year, in Chicago, U.S. Customs seized copies of the English translation, which had not been expurgated. It is still identified as censored in the People for the American Way school censorship survey, "Attacks on the Freedom to Learn, 1987–1988," the charge being "offensive language." The suggestion is, however, that censors have shifted their tactics, using these charges instead of such traditional accusations as "globalism" or "far-right scare words." Jonathon Green in his *Encyclopedia of Censorship* identifies *All Quiet on the Western Front* as one of the "most often" censored books.

FURTHER READINGS

"Censorship Continues Unabated; Extremists Adapt Mainstream Tactics." *Newsletter on Intellectual Freedom* 37 (1988): 193.

Geller, Evelyn. *Forbidden Books in American Public Libraries, 1876–1939: A Study in Cultural Change*. Westport, Conn.: Greenwood Press, 1984.

Green, Jonathon. *Encyclopedia of Censorship*. New York: Facts On File, 1990.

Haight, Anne L., and Chandler B. Grannis. *Banned Books: 387 B.C. to 1978 A.D.* 4th ed. New York: R. R. Bowker, 1978.

Hansen, Harry. "The Book That Shocked a Nation." In *All Quiet on the Western Front*, by Erich Maria Remarque. New York: Heritage Press, 1969.

Tebbel, John. *A History of Book Publishing in the United States*, Vol. III. New York: R. R. Bowker, 1978.

ANDERSONVILLE

Author: MacKinlay Kantor
Original date and place of publication: 1955, United States
Publisher: The World Publishing Company
Literary form: Novel

SUMMARY

Andersonville is a novel of war—the Civil War; it does not, however, fit the stereotype of war novels, for it offers little action on the battlefield, strategies and troop movements or individual responses to such situations in the manner of Stephen Crane's *The Red Badge of Courage* or Erich Maria Remarque's *ALL QUIET ON THE WESTERN FRONT*. There are essentially two settings: Ira Claffey's Georgia plantation and Andersonville, a prison for captured Yankees.

Episodic in structure, the novel provides access to Ira's life and his emotional and intellectual reactions to the war and the prison. These episodes, interspersed among those that focus on Yankee prisoners and Confederate officers and guards, provide plot movement.

Managing his plantation from the outset of the war without the help of an overseer, Ira Claffey is perceived as capable and honest. In this the last year of the war, he nurtures his family with compassion. Only two live on the plantation with him: Veronica, his wife, and Lucy, their daughter. They are joined during this year by Surgeon Harry Elkins, formerly a comrade-in-arms of the Claffey's eldest son. This son and another have already died in battle; their third son is reported dead early in the novel. This final bereavement casts a shroud over the mind of Veronica. She gradually distances herself from the living and fades into the past. Lucy bears these burdens and the death of her fiancé with pain and anger and courage.

Ira is not a secessionist; he does not favor the war. Initially angry and embittered, he grieves for his sons. His philosophy and nature help him to acknowledge the reality of war's destruction and that families in the North also grieve for their lost sons.

Deploring cruelty, Ira treats his slaves, now totaling 12 including children, with paternalistic kindness. He will not allow them to be mistreated by the Confederate soldiers; and when he must sell them, he assures himself that they will not be mistreated. At the end of the war he informs them of their freedom and their right to leave; however, out of concern for their safety and welfare, he urges them to remain on the plantation as salaried employees. When one couple decides to leave, he gives them a mule and cart so their young children won't have to walk.

Ira's sense of compassion is intensified with the advent of the stockade. At first he disbelieves the deliberate intent, as voiced by Captain Winder, to mistreat the prisoners by providing no shelter from the elements, to cause their deaths. He is increasingly horrified by the brutality and miserable conditions. He attempts to help—protesting to the officers, joining his neighbors to bring food and clothing for the prisoners (these are rejected), traveling to Richmond to gain the ear of President Jefferson Davis, a friend from his military days—but realizes his helplessness.

Others join him in these attitudes. Chief among them is Surgeon Elkins, who, having come to investigate the health conditions, returns out of a humane sense of obligation to tend the sick. The post commander, Lieutenant-Colonel Persons, of like mind, puts his career on the line to protest the actions of Confederate brigadier-general John H. Winder and his son, Captain Sid Winder. Other inspectors follow suit; Dr. Joseph Jones concludes his highly critical report with the following:

> This gigantic mass of human misery calls loudly for relief, not only for the sake of suffering humanity, but also on account of our own brave soldiers now captives in the hands of the Federal government. Strict justice to the gallant men of the Confederate armies, who have been or who may be so unfortunate as to be compelled to surrender in battle, demands that the Confederate government should adopt that course which will best secure their health and

comfort in captivity; or at least leave their enemies without a shadow of an excuse for any violation of the rules of civilized warfare in the treatment of prisoners.

In counterpoint to these beacons of humanity are Brigadier-General Winder and Captain Winder, whose intentions are revealed in this statement by the captain in response to Surgeon Elkins's concern that there are no shelters built or trees left to shield the prisoners from the hot Georgia sun: "What the hell's the use of coddling a pen full of Yankees? I've got a pen here that ought to kill more God damn Yankees than you ever saw killed at the front." The general demonstrates a more rabid expression of these intentions.

General Winder assigns Captain Henry Wirz as superintendent of the prison. Wirz, a doctor by profession, made intensely irritable and vituperative by an arm wound, brutalizes the prisoners: they are tyrannized; their diet is insufficient in both quantity and nutrients; their living conditions are abominable. A failure as an administrator, his efforts are ineffectual. Wirz is in part victim of a situation he cannot control: the vindictiveness of the Winders; the overloading of the compound; lack or denial of food and medical supplies.

The stockade and the prisoners are, however, the core of the novel. The stockade's 27 acres, intended for some 10,000 men, held upwards of 30,000 at one time. (Of the 50,000 prisoners received there, about 16,000 died.) With no sanitation facilities, the area soon becomes putrid, its limited water supply polluted, its stench befouling the surrounding neighborhood. The Yankees die from dysentery, scurvy and polluted water; wounds, scratches and stings festered into gangrene. Others die of starvation and violence, groups of "raiders" attacking and stealing from the weak, the innocent, the unprepared among them.

Against the background of ever-increasing privation and brutality, decay and death, individual prisoners are spotlighted. Their origins and childhoods, their initial responses to the war are counterpoints to their immediate situation. How they survive—whether they survive—reveals their natures. Edward Blamey, a New England fisherman, survives, though he initially resists, by selling his extraordinary eyesight to the raider, Willie Collins, in return for protection and creature comforts. Blamey spies goods among the other prisoners that can be stolen. Collins, surly and corrupt since childhood, uses his brute strength and amorality to build a power structure in which the "raiders" within the stockade terrorize fellow prisoners. He is finally tried, condemned and hanged, along with others of his ilk by a group of prisoners, organized by Seneca MacBean and Nathan Dreyfoos, a semi-educated midwesterner and an upper-class easterner. The Iowan Eben Dolliver's childhood is filled with a consciousness of birds, with birdsong; he is driven by starvation to attack a swallow for food. At age 13, Willie Mann of Missouri had rescued several immigrant German children from a bully; subsequently he fell in love with one of them and now is sustained by dreams of returning to her. He survives because his doctor father had taught him the health value of pure water; he refuses to drink except when it rains.

A minor plot strand, the story of the poor white Tebbs family, particularly a vignette of the eldest son, brings the novel to fruition. Having enlisted at age 17, Coral returns home without a foot. Embittered, depressed, he flails at his family and at his life. While searching for a bird he has shot, he discovers an escaped prisoner lacking a hand, just about dead from starvation and weariness. Both have lost their limbs at Gettysburg. Coral on an impulse decides to help him with food and a hideout; the Yankee boy, Nazareth Strider from Pennsylvania, helps Coral in return by shaping a "peg-leg-foot" for him, with knowledge gleaned from his father's craft and tools borrowed from Ira Claffey. When Ira discovers their secret, he shocks them both by helping. Again, Ira's humanity emerges; he muses as he works on the wooden foot, "It seemed odd to be performing a service for a wounded Yankee and a wounded Confederate in the same act and in the same breath." Acts of humanity unite the two boys.

The novel continues for another 40 pages beyond this episode to encompass the defeat of the Confederacy, the release of the prisoners and the military arrest of Wirz. Two of Ira's adult slaves with their children take advantage of their freedom and leave; Coral Tebbs finds employment as their replacement. However, the crescendo of the novel is in the mutual salvation of Coral and Nazareth, and in the symbolic healing and reunification it expresses.

CENSORSHIP HISTORY

Andersonville was challenged by Laurence Van Der Oord, the father of an Amherst (Ohio) High School student in 1967. Identifying the novel as "filth," he claimed his 16-year-old daughter couldn't read it because she didn't understand the obscene words. He indicated that the book was 1 percent history and 99 percent filth, and demanded that Donald Hicks, the history teacher who had assigned the novel as an optional choice, be dismissed.

Hicks countered that the relative worth of the novel outweighed the objectionable parts; about 30 of the 795 pages contain slightly obscene language. Defense of the novel was also offered by the school board president, Mrs. Clem Rice: " . . . maybe we should not shield high school students. . . . Perhaps they should know these facts exist even though they are bad and may not exist in our community." On August 24, the school superintendent announced that he would not order the removal of the book.

In 1973, a Buncombe County, North Carolina, school board member, Edna Roberts, removed several books, including *Andersonville*, from their high school library, claiming they were "unsuitable" for school libraries because they contained objectionable language. Subsequently, she introduced a resolution to the board that would have "expunged 'unsuitable' books from school libraries." The board rejected it, reaffirming its "Policies for Selection." Mrs. Roberts's efforts were supported by the Christian Action League and Answer for America.

Buncombe County in 1981 was the scene of another controversy over classroom and library books, including, among others, *Andersonville*. The protest was initiated by a group of citizens meeting at Asheville's Owens High School in January; the meeting was led by several fundamentalist ministers, a chief spokesperson being Wendell Runion, who had organized the Concerned Citizens of Owens District group. The books on the list were labeled obscene. The group planned to file a grievance with the Buncombe County schools' administration to get the books removed. In February, an opposition group, calling itself "Books," was organized to provide an alternative perspective. On February 19, more than 1,000 residents attended a forum to air the two positions. Those opposed to the current book selection policy called for closing loopholes that "promote immorality." Pastor Randy Stone noted, "The use of God's name in vain, whether it be in a Pulitzer-prize winner or a book from an adult bookstore, is offensive to us and demands some sort of attention." Books's spokespersons included Loretta Martin, the president of the North Carolina Association of Educators, and Elsie Brumbeck, the director of educational media for the State Department of Public Instruction. Martin said, "Our schools are the only institution today that seeks to free the human mind." Brumbeck read a letter from the North Carolina Library Association in support of Buncombe County's current selection policy. Receiving the strongest accolade, however, was Pastor Fred Ohler, who, in support of the book selection policy, asked, "Why is immorality seen only as profanity and sexuality in Steinbeck, Salinger or Kantor and the larger issues of grinding poverty and social misjustice, of adult hypocrisy, of war camp atrocities never faced?" Referring to the list of quotations from the challenged books, he continued, "To read the Bible as some folks read *The Grapes of Wrath* would be like going through the Gospels and only seeing tax collectors, wine-bibers and Mary Magdalene." In March the Buncombe County Board of Education voted (5–2) to support the book selection policy.

Andersonville was withdrawn from the eleventh grade reading list at the Whitehall, Michigan, high school on December 12, 1963. An "unspecified number of unidentified complaints" were received by Superintendent of Schools Melvin Lubbers and County Prosecutor Harry J. Knudsen; the latter indicated he didn't care if the book had won 20 Pulitzer Prizes; it wasn't fit reading for high school students. One parent, Jane Moog, angry about the dropping of the book, termed the act a "violation of civil liberties." Lubbers indicated that they did not quarrel with the author's message, but it was not of "sufficient benefit to justify putting it before the young mind." Despite a defense of the book by a school board member, Evelyn Robinson, and Circuit Judge John H. Piercy, the board of education voted 6–1 in support of Lubbers.

In 1961, under the leadership of J. Evetts Haley, Texans for America, a right-wing group, supported by the Daughters of the American Revolution and the John Birch Society, attacked the language and concepts of a range of history books. They succeeded in causing the State Textbook Committee to reject 12 books opposed by the Texans for America and four opposed by the

DAR. In addition, substantial changes in their texts were required of publishers for specific books.

These textbook battles spilled over to affect library books. *Andersonville* was banned from the four Amarillo high schools and at Amarillo College. The cited reasons were its political ideas and that its author was cited by the House Un-American Activities Committee. In 1962, a committee of inquiry, instigated by a Texas House of Representatives resolution, investigated the content of school books, searching for subversion of American principles and traditions. At an Austin hearing, excerpts from *Andersonville* were read as examples of obscenity and filth.

An attempt to ban *Andersonville* was also reported in Rock County in Wisconsin in 1969.

FURTHER READINGS

Blake, Barbara. "Who Is the Rev. Wendell Runion and Why Does He Want Those Books Banned?" *Asheville Citizen* (January 31, 1981): [n.p.]).

Burress, Lee. *The Battle of the Books: Literary Censorship in Public Schools, 1950–85*, Metuchen, N.J.: The Scarecrow Press, 1989.

Campbell, John, Jr. "Concern Expressed Over Books in Schools." *Asheville Citizen* (January 23, 1981): [n.p.].

———. "Large Crowd Gathers for Sessions on Books." *Asheville Citizen* (February 20, 1981): 17.

Grisso, James L. "Amherst High Keeps *Andersonville*." *Cleveland Plain Dealer* (August 25, 1967): [n.p.].

Hoyle Bolick, Sandy. "Book Issue: Pros, Cons." *Asheville Times* (February 20, 1981): [n.p.].

Nelson, Jack, and Gene Roberts, Jr. *The Censors and the Schools*. Boston: Little, Brown and Company, 1963.

Newsletter on Intellectual Freedom 13 (1964): 14; 22 (1973): 52; 30 (1981): 74.

"Official Removes 'Objectional' Books." *St. Louis Post Dispatch* (March 28, 1973): 22A.

"Pro Books Group Is Organized in County." *Asheville Citizen* (February 14, 1981): 7.

Rock County Librarians United to Battle Would-Be Banners." *Beloit Daily News* (April 17, 1969): [n.p.].

ANIMAL FARM

Author: George Orwell
Original date and place of publication: 1945, England; 1946, United States
Publisher: Secker & Warburg; Harcourt, Brace & World
Literary form: Novel

SUMMARY

George Orwell's subtitle, "A Fairy Story," reveals that he is not focusing on reality in the traditional sense. Indeed, his characters are animals who rebel against humans and take over Manor Farm, renaming it Animal Farm. Orwell, as quoted by C. M. Woodhouse, from the *Times Literary Supplement*, in the preface to the Signet Classics 29th edition (dated August 6, 1954), wrote "Every line of serious work that I have written since 1936 has been written, directly or indirectly against totalitarianism . . . *Animal Farm* was the first book in which I tried, with full consciousness . . . , to fuse political purpose and artistic purpose into one whole."

The animals' rebellion can be traced back to old Major, the prize-winning boar who assembles the animals one night to communicate to them his strange dream. He sermonizes about the low state of animals at the hands of humans, a life of hard work for which there is no reward except bare rations and a stall; since Man consumes without producing, animals must resolve to bear enmity toward humans. Through his dream he predicts that Man will be vanquished and animals will reign in freedom.

Inspired to a new outlook, the animals secretly begin planning for a Rebellion. The pigs, deemed the cleverest, take charge, under the leadership of Snowball and Napoleon. Several months later, when Mr. Jones gets drunk and sleeps through the day, forgetting to feed the animals, they respond to their hunger and angry frustration by taking action. They gain control of the farm.

At first, all is bliss; that is, equality among the animals is practiced. Seven Commandments are identified and painted on the barn wall, expressing that "All animals are equal" and other tenets, chiefly reflecting animosity toward humans and their ways. The animals work hard together, completing farm tasks for the good of the community. Boxer, the horse, is foremost with his energy and power, establishing for himself an "I will work harder" motto. The animals also fight off, under the leadership of Snowball, a counterattack from Jones and his men. After this, an even greater spirit and sense of dedication prevail.

The bliss and equality, however, are marred: first, the pigs quietly take the daily milk for themselves; then, they commandeer the windfall apples. It seems natural that they should take charge and direct the farm's activities, and natural that they should work at organizing and planning, rather than laboring in the fields. The less clever animals accept this and are confused by the quarrels between Snowball and Napoleon.

Their disputes come to a head over the windmill proposed by Snowball. When he appears to have carried the vote, Napoleon gives a high-pitched whimper; nine enormous dogs, which he had secretly trained, dash into the barn and attack Snowball, who only barely manages to escape. Napoleon's autocratic regime is thus initiated, the troubled animals too shocked and terrified to react to the new edicts. The new code words now are "loyalty and obedience."

The animals adhere to their duties while Napoleon tightens his control, exacting more work from them, giving them less food and less relaxation time. When Napoleon establishes trade relations with the enemy, there is vague uneasiness among the animals; however, they accept the assurances made by

Squealer, Napoleon's mouthpiece. They also accept the scapegoating of Snowball for everything that goes wrong, a pattern that begins with moderate accusations but escalates to denouncing his past purposes, putting him in secret league with the enemy. At an assembly, Napoleon, surrounded by his snarling dogs, demands "confessions" of all disloyal animals; hearing these, he orders the guilty animals slaughtered on the spot by his dogs.

These indignities are suffered. The animals, frightened and disturbed, are mournful. They perceive that their dream of a "society of animals set free from hunger and the whip, all equal, each working according to his capacity, the strong protecting the weak" is somehow in jeopardy. The more astute of them, Boxer and Clover, the horses, and Muriel, the goat, note that some of the commandments seem changed—"without cause" has been added to "no animal shall kill any other animal"—but can't be certain, can't quite remember how it had originally read.

In the succeeding months, another invasion is fought off, but less successfully. Napoleon, unlike Snowball, directs the animal forces from the rear. Boxer, who is injured in the attack, continues to work but collapses from overexertion. He is presumably being taken to a veterinarian for treatment but is picked up by a truck labeled "Horse Slaughterer and Glue Boiler." This reading is forcibly denied by Squealer as "wicked rumour."

Years later, only a few of the original animals live. The Rebellion has faded in their memories; the succeeding animals don't know anything about it. Three startling events conclude the fairy story: the pigs start walking on their hind legs; only a single Commandment remains on the barn wall—"All animals are equal but some Animals are more equal than others"; Napoleon hosts a party, the guests being the neighborhood human farmers. Clover and other animals watch through the window as a farmer toasts Napoleon for his discipline over the "lower animals," for getting them to do more work yet feeding them less. Napoleon announces in his return toast the changed name of the farm, from "Animal Farm" to "Manor Farm." As the creatures outside watch, the pigs and men inside become indistinguishable—"from pig to man, and from man to pig, and from pig to man again; but already it was impossible to say which was which."

CENSORSHIP HISTORY

Animal Farm was one of 64 books of literature banned from classroom teaching at Bay and Mosley High Schools in Panama City, Florida, on May 7, 1987. The action was taken by Bay County School Superintendent Leonard Hall. Although six days later the Bay County School Board reinstated all 64 texts, the controversy did not end. The situation and issues are detailed in the censorship history discussion of *I AM THE CHEESE* by Robert Cormier.

A survey of censorship challenges in the schools, conducted in DeKalb County, Georgia, in 1982 for the period 1979 to 1982, revealed that *Animal*

Farm had been objected to for its political theories. (The survey's list does not provide details.)

A comparable study of censorship in New York State English classrooms was conducted in 1968 by the New York State English Council's Committee on Defenses Against Censorship. Its findings, based on 160 returns, identified *Animal Farm* to be high on its list of "problem books"; the reason cited was that "Orwell was a communist."

A Wisconsin survey in 1963 revealed that the John Birch Society had challenged the use of Animal Farm; it objected to the words "masses will revolt."

Under the heading "index of banned books," Jonathon Green in *Encyclopedia of Censorship* identifies *Animal Farm* as one of the "most often" censored books.

FURTHER READINGS

Burress, Lee. *The Battle of the Books: Literary Censorship in Public Schools, 1950–1985.* Metuchen, N.J.: The Scarecrow Press, 1989.
Fransecky, Roger B. "Censorship and the Teaching of English." *Newsletter on Intellectual Freedom* 17 (1968): 39–40.
Green, Jonathon. *Encyclopedia of Censorship.* New York: Facts On File, 1990.
Kegler, Sissy, and Gene Guerro. "Censorship in the South." *Newsletter on Intellectual Freedom* 35 (1986): 29, 56.
Orwell, George. *Animal Farm.* New York: New American Library, 1946.

AREOPAGITICA

Author: John Milton
Original date and place of publication: 1644, England; 1888, United States
Publisher: [s.n.]; Cassell & Company
Literary form: Nonfiction essay

SUMMARY

The title of John Milton's most famous prose work was derived from Areopagus, the hill of Ares in Athens named after Ares, one of the 12 major gods of ancient Greece. At this site the highest judicial court of ancient Athens met to debate political and religious matters. Its nearly 300 members were elected by a vote of all the freed men of the city. Identified with the glory of Athens's democratic institutions, the title *Areopagitica* reveals Milton's inclinations. The subtitle, "A Speech for the Liberty of Unlicensed Printing to the Parliament of England," identifies his intent.

In his "The Second Defense of the people of England," published in 1654, Milton noted, I wrote my *Areopagetica* in order to deliver the press from the restraints with which it was encumbered; that the power of determining what was true and what was false, what ought to be published and what to be suppressed, might no longer be entrusted to a few illiterate and illiberal individuals, who refused their sanction to any work which contained views or sentiments at all above the level of vulgar superstition.

It was specifically directed against the Order of Parliament of June 14, 1643, an ordinance requiring the licensing of all books and pamphlets in advance of publication. (It also expresses significant ideas of religious liberty, interrelated with those of freedom of the press; however, these will not be discussed here.)

Milton recognized the great concern the "Church and Commonwealth" had about the contents of books "for books are not absolutely dead things, but do contain a potency of life. . . . they do preserve as in a vial the purest efficacy and extraction of that living intellect that bred them." However, he argued that "Who kills a man kills a reasonable creature, God's image; but he who destroys a good book, kills reason itself, kills the image of God, as it were in the eye."

Milton decried censoring activities that represented what is now termed *prior restraint*; indeed, this becomes a basic tenet of his discussion. He likened the impulse to license to the prohibitory attitudes and actions of the Papal Court, which led to the Spanish Inquisition. He noted that their censoring acts spread from the heretical to any subject they found unsuitable, thus expressing a warning about the pattern of censorship. Before this "tyrannous inquisition," books were allowed to be born into the world, judgment about them reserved. Continuing this metaphor, rather than stand before a jury prior to birth to be judged in darkness without any public scrutiny, books should be examined more openly after publication.

Historical examples are used to support this position. He identifies practices in classical Athens and early Christianity, finding them free of control prior to publication and in all instances after publication except atheism, blasphemy and libel. One example is the burning of the books of Protagoras and the banishing of the author himself upon command of the judges of Areopagus; Protagoras had written that he did not know "whether there were gods, or whether not."

The value of knowledge and learning forms a cornerstone of Milton's discussion. Books enhance our understanding of the known and introduce us to the new. The Order of Parliament would "suppress all this flowry crop of knowledge . . . to bring a famine upon our minds again" and allow the people to know only what the licensers permit. He likens this to the state of ignorance to which the decree of Julian the Apostate reduced the Christians, forbidding them to study the heathen texts. Thus, licensing would greatly discourage learning by reducing access to information and discussion. Restraining the freedom to write and the liberty of printing nullifies the privilege of the people and shackles the freedom to learn.

Knowledge thrives on the mind's exercise as does the discovery and affirmation of truth. His illustrations encompass the religious and scientific, attaining the truth by examining all opinions, even errors, so they may be known and evaluated. Individuals who base their beliefs solely on what they are told by their pastors or as determined by the assembly without knowing reasons cannot be said to understand. Even if the doctrine is true in an objective sense, it is not believed in the right way. It has not been questioned or examined, thus not really understood; the belief is superficial. An unlicensed press can propose challenges to cause thinking, thus enhancing the understanding of accepted beliefs or revealing new truths. Milton proposes these concepts for both the nation and individuals.

Extending this position, Milton promotes the reading of all texts, the good as well as those of "evil substance." The latter to a "discreet and judicious reader serve in many respects to discover, to confute, to forewarn, and to illustrate." Truth and virtue are attained by including all opinions, even errors, so they may be known and reasoned. Individuals are put in positions of having to make moral choices between the good and evil that surround them.

> Since therefore the knowledge and survey of vice is in this world so necessary to the constituting of human virtue, and the scanning of error to the confirmation of truth, how can we more safely, and with less danger, scout into the regions of sin and falsity than by reading all manner of tractate, and hearing all manner of reason? And this is the benefit which may be had of books promiscuously read.

Milton drew a cause-and-effect connection between the actions of government and the nature of the populace. An "oppressive, arbitrary and tyrannous" government breeds a "brutish, formall, and slavish" people. A mild and free human government promotes liberty, the liberty of free writing and free speaking. These in the past have enlightened the spirits, enfranchised and enlarged the apprehensions of the English people, making them more capable, more knowing and more eager to pursue the truth. These attributes would be suppressed by the enforcement of this order.

The effectiveness of the order is also questioned. One aspect is the licensers themselves: they need to be above all other men to accomplish the task without bias, but are apt to be ignorant, corrupt or overworked. Another is the assumption that books themselves are the sole source of ideas and behaviors that are perceived by the authorities to be censorable. Milton refutes both of these, arguing, as summarized above, the efficacy of books, thus the requirement of unlicensed printing.

CENSORSHIP HISTORY

Licensing of books, which should be understood as the suppression of undesired publications, was a frequent policy in England. As early as 1408, confirmed by Parliament in 1414, Archbishop Arundel's constitution forbade the reading of any book that had not been examined and approved by the University of Oxford or Cambridge. Henry the VIII forbade the printing of any books concerning holy scripture unless it had been examined or approved. This was spread to the licensing of books of any kind. This policy was reasserted by the monarchs who succeeded him—Edward, Mary, Elizabeth, James and Charles.

The practice and procedures of censorship had been developed in England over the 16th and 17th centuries, including the incorporation of a Stationers Company charged with the administration of the system. In 1637, in Charles's reign, the Star Chamber decree of July 11 established a broad range of censorship measures that forbade the printing, importing or selling of seditious or offensive books; required the licensing of all books before being printed or reprinted; limited the number of master printers, specifying the number of presses and workers each might have; forbade the providing of space for unlicensed printers; and empowered the Stationers Company to search houses for such unlicensed printers.

In 1641, the Star Chamber had been abolished, an outcome of the defeat of Charles in the English Civil War. Though the Stationers Company was not abolished, its powers were diminished; for about 18 months there were no statutory restrictions on the press. Gradually, the openness was narrowed. In 1643, the Puritans through a series of regulations, preceded by a 1642 regulation mandating that every publication bear the name of the printer, reinstated censorship practices until they were in full force. A significant factor underpinning these actions was the religious toleration controversy of the time.

In this context, John Milton published in 1643 *Doctrine and Discipline of Divorce* without benefit of authorization, registration or signature, by then required. It was reprinted in February 1644, again without being authorized or registered, though it was signed. At this time the Royalists suffered a defeat, causing the Westminster Assembly (an advisory body to Parliament about reformation of the church, dominated by Presbyterians) to condemn tracts favoring toleration. A sermon on this subject, preached before Parliament, spoke against illegal books and identified *Doctrine and Discipline of Divorce* as immoral. Further, booksellers, united in a corporation, complained about illegal books to the House of Commons, denouncing Milton among others.

These were the direct catalysts of *Areopagitica*. Issued on November 23, 1644, it also was published without benefit of authorization or registration and in defiance of the restraining ordinance. (It was also delivered orally before Parliament.) On December 9, the booksellers complained to the House of Lords, but the lords took no action.

Milton's attack on licensing had no effect on Parliament's policy. Indeed, licensing was reasserted several times and continued to be practiced until 20 years after Milton's death, in 1694. Frederick Seaton Siebert notes that

Areopagitica had "very little effect" on Milton's contemporaries; it "went unmentioned by most of the writers and public men of the times."

After the execution of Charles I and the abolition of the monarchy, Oliver Cromwell, named as lord protector in 1658, condemned *Areopagitica* as did the "Little Parliament" of Protestant England which had succeeded the expelled House of Commons.

Areopagitica appeared in only one edition and was not republished until 1738. At this time it aroused public support for the concept of freedom of the mind. According to Siebert, a significant factor in this change in public opinion was the Peter Zenger trial in a colonial courtroom in New York. Zenger's acquittal of libel of the royal governor was perceived as a freedom of the press issue; the publication of the trial transcript, four editions in London in 1728, notes Siebert, "undoubtedly set on example for English juries. "

FURTHER READINGS

Green, Jonathon. *The Encyclopedia of Censorship*. New York: Facts On File, 1990.

Haight, Anne Lyon, and Chandler B. Grannis. *Banned Books: 387 B.C. to 1978 A.D.* 4th ed. New York: R.R. Bowker Company, 1978.

Hunter, William B., ed. *A Milton Encyclopedia*. Lewisburg, Pa.: Bucknell University Press, 1978.

Saillens, Emile. *John Milton: Man, Poet, Polemist*. Oxford: Basil Blackwell, 1964.

Siebert, Fredrick Seaton. *Freedom of the Press in England, 1476–1776*. Urbana: University of Illinois Press, 1965.

Sirluck, Ernest. "Preface and Notes." In *Complete Prose Works of John Milton*, Vol. II. New Haven: Yale University Press, 1959.

BLACK BOY

Author: Richard Wright
Original date and place of publication: 1945, United States
Publisher: Harper & Row
Literary form: Autobiography

SUMMARY

"My days and nights were one long, quiet, continuously contained dream of terror, tension and anxiety. I wondered how long I could bear it." So concludes chapter 13 (there are 14) of Richard Wright's autobiography, expressing the crescendo of his feelings before finally in the last chapter achieving his secret dream of escaping the South to the North.

Subtitled "Record of Childhood and Youth," the memoir begins when he is four years old and takes him into his nineteenth year. His accounts of his experiences and relationships reveal how he has been shaped and conditioned, the person he has become.

Wright's childhood was one of trauma and indignity, narrowness and poverty. The family moved frequently, first from the plantation of his birth, where his father was a sharecropper, to Memphis. Other moves resulted from his father's abandoning his wife and two sons for another woman. These moves took the family to lower-rent accommodations, to new locations in search of jobs, or to relatives where they lived on their sometimes grudging charity. Such dependence became virtually permanent after his mother at quite a young age suffered a stroke that caused paralysis of her legs.

Dominant childhood memories are of hunger, deficiency and fear. With the father's departure, there was no income until his mother was able to find work. Hunger, constant and gnawing, haunted the family; when food was available, it was insufficient in both quantity and nutrition. Often there was not enough money to heat their shack. Sometimes young Richard's mother brought the two boys to work with her; they stood in the corner of the kitchen where she was a cook, smelling the food but unable to eat. There was not enough money for clothes; ashamed of Richard's destitute appearance, his mother would not send him to school.

Beatings appear to have been "automatic" responses of adults toward children for misbehavior or stubborn resistance. Young Richard, an intractable, willful child, is often birched or strapped by his mother (before her illness) and relatives. Uncles and aunts attempt also to browbeat him into submitting to their wills. A parallel violence is evident in contacts with neighborhood gangs and in schoolyards. Richard, the new kid, the outsider, has to prove himself before he can gain entrance.

The sense of abandonment, exacerbated by being placed in an orphanage when his mother could not afford to take care of the two boys, and the feelings of loss—though perhaps not understood—were affective in forming Richard's personality. These dovetailed with his frequent outsider status; opportunities for deep and lasting relationships were thwarted by both the frequent moves and the suppressive attitudes of the significant adults. Warmth, tenderness and encouragement were lacking, except sporadically from his mother.

Religion was another source of agony and emotional browbeating, particularly during the period when he lived in his grandmother's house. Despite his young age, he resisted his grandmother's efforts to commit him to her fear-evoking religion, refusing to be bullied into submission. When his equally rigid and devout aunt, who is also his teacher, struck him across the knuckles with a ruler because she assumes he, rather than a devout classmate, is guilty of littering the floor, he vowed not to allow it a second time. When she came at him at home with a switch, he fought her off with a kitchen knife, fighting, in effect, for his sense of justice and independence.

A contrasting strand is woven through the autobiography: young Richard's curiosity, his eagnerness to learn to read and the rapidity with which he learned. He began to pick out and recognize words in his playmates' schoolbooks at age six; in about an hour's time, the coalman taught him to count to 100. He questioned about everything. His school attendance started late and was erratic; he was past 12 before he had a full year of formal schooling. But once fully enrolled, he excelled, graduating as the valedictorian of his class. Books became his salvation, both an escape from his tormenting environment and an avenue to a dreamed of future: "going north and writing books, novels." Books opened up the world of serious writing, opened up for him the life of the mind and encouraged his conviction to live beyond the constraints of the South.

Richard Wright acknowledges his limited contacts with whites during his early years. By age nine, a dread of whites had grown in him, fueled by frightening tales of repression, of the Ku Klux Klan and his family's experiences. His first jobs with whites when he is a young teenager corroborate his impressions of their meanness and mistreatment, projecting their view that blacks are children or idiots and less than human. A significant realization is his understanding that "the entire educational system of the South had been rigged to stifle" the aspirations of the black citizens.

As he gains experiences in the white world, Wright learns to keep secret his dream of going north and becoming a writer. It takes him considerably longer than his school and work acquaintances to learn appropriate obsequious mannerisms, language and tone. His ignorance causes him to lose employment and to suffer harm. Part of his "problem," as a friend notes in his sixteenth year: "'You act around white people as if you didn't know that they were white.'" Wright silently acknowledges this truth:

> . . . it was simply impossible for me to calculate, to scheme, to act, to plot all the time. I would remember to dissemble for short periods, then I would forget and act straight and human again, not with the desire to harm anybody, but merely forgetting the artificial status of race and class.

His friend continues: "You know, Dick, you may think I'm an Uncle Tom, but I'm not. I hate these white people, hate 'em with all my heart. But I can't show it; if I did, they'd kill me."

Richard Wright did learn to control his public face and voice to a greater extent, but not without a sense of shame, tension and mental strain. While the latter dissipated somewhat in the more urbane atmosphere of Memphis, he was frequently reminded of the need to be guarded. These experiences and responses reveal Wright's growth and cultural assimilation. They also reveal the survival training induced in blacks by the white threat: deception, dishonesty, lying and irresponsibility.

When contemplating his present life and his future, Wright sees four choices: rebellion, organizing with other blacks to fight the southern whites; submitting and living the life of a genial slave, thus denying that his "life had shaped [him] to live by [his] own feelings and thoughts"; draining his restlessness by fighting other blacks, thus transferring his hatred of himself to others with a black skin; and forgetting what he's learned through books, forgetting whites and finding release in sex and alcohol. In this context, he continues:

> I had no hope whatever of being a professional man. Not only had I been so conditioned that I did not desire it, but the fulfillment of such an ambition was beyond my capabilities. Well-to-do Negroes lived in a world that was almost as alien to me as the world inhabited by whites.

Finally, however, "sheer wish and hope prevailed over common sense and facts." Planning with his mother, brother and aunt, he takes the step; he boards the train bound for Chicago.

CENSORSHIP HISTORY[*]

Richard Wright was not unfamiliar with the threat of censorship. A member of the Communist Party in 1940 when *Native Son* was published, he was threatened with expulsion because at least one party leader sensed a fundamental disagreement between the party's views and those expressed in the book. Wright had been saved by its popularity and acclaim, making Wright too important a member to lose. Wright had recognized other attempts by the party to constrain his thinking. In 1940 he renounced his affiliation with the party.

The Special Committee On Un-American Activities, The Dies Committee, had investigated him and called him subversive. Wright had also been the target of a top-priority investigation of the FBI regarding his affiliation with and activities for the Communist Party. Wright knew that his neighbors had been questioned. These events had preceded the publication of *Black Boy*. In the 1950s Richard Wright was identified unfavorably before the House Un-American Activities Committee and cited by the committee as belonging to one or more "fronts." According to existing directives, his work should have been withdrawn from U.S. libraries overseas.

Black Boy as originally submitted, titled *American Hunger*, included Wright's Chicago experience. Initially accepted by Harper & Row, his editor later informed Wright that the book would be divided: the first two-thirds, the experiences in the South, would be published separately from the experiences in the North, Chicago and New York. Initially, Wright accepted this suggestion without question; Constance Webb, Wright's biographer, notes, however, that subsequently, he felt "in his whole being that his book was being censored

---

*This censorship history was augmented by the research and writing of Dawn Sova.

in some way." He considered the possibility that Harper & Row did not want to offend the communists, since the United States and the U.S.S.R. were then allies, or that the Communist Party itself was exerting some influence over the publisher. He determined to find a way to publish the omitted final segment of his manuscript.

At the time of publication, despite its being a Book-of-the-Month Club selection and achieving both broad readership and significant acclaim in reviews, Mississippi banned it; Senator Theodore Bilbo of Mississippi condemned the book and its author in Congress:

> *Black Boy* should be taken off the shelves of stores; sales should be stopped; it was a damnable lie, from beginning to end; it built fabulous lies about the South. The purpose of the book was to plant seeds of hate and devilment in the minds of every American. It was the dirtiest, filthiest, most obscene, filthy and dirty, and came from a Negro from whom one could not expect better.

The autobiography has created controversy in school districts in all regions of the United States. Most of the challenges have been of mainly local interest, while one case received national attention and created precedent. In 1972, parents in Michigan objected to the book's sexual overtones and claimed that it was unsuitable for impressionable sophomores, which resulted in the removal of the book from classroom use. In 1975, the book was removed from Tennessee schools for being obscene, instigating hatred between the races and encouraging immorality.

Complaints against five books, including *Black Boy*, were filed in November 1975 in East Baton Rouge, Louisiana, by Babs Minhinnette, chairperson of Concerned Citizens and Taxpayers for Decent School Books. This complaint emerged out of a controversy over the removal of two books, one by the school board and the other by the principal. This controversy had led to the adoption in May 1975 of a policy to handle objections. Subsequently, however, in September 1975, the school board had ordered a search for books and materials containing obscenity, filth or pornography. Teachers and librarians criticized the search order, claiming it was a reversal of the policy adopted in May. The challenge to the five books by the Concerned Citizens chairperson was perceived as an attempt to test the new review procedure. The committee voted 6–1 to reject the request to remove the books after a review conducted in late November.

A comparable situation developed in Nashua, New Hampshire, in 1978. As a result of a complaint against the use of *Black Boy* in the ninth grade of the high school in Nashua, a review committee recommended that the book be removed from this grade level and that it be used only in elective courses in grades 11 and 12. The controversy over *Black Boy* and *Ms.* magazine gave rise to questions about the appropriateness of certain textbooks in schools across the state and gave impetus to the formation of a new organization,

Concerned Citizens and Taxpayers for Better Education. This group's intention was to monitor books used in classes of several communities, from which its members were drawn, in order to safeguard "traditional Judeo-Christian values" in the schools.

In September 1987, Nebraska Governor Kay Orr's "kitchen cabinet" met with leaders of a citizens' group, Taxpayers for Quality Education. The group made recommendations to the governor regarding curriculum, strategies for teaching reading and school administration. It also indicated it would monitor books in school libraries and recommend reading lists. George Darlington, president of Taxpayers for Quality Education, identified *Black Boy* as one of the books that should be removed, asserting it had a "corruptive obscene nature" and citing the use of profanity throughout and the incidents of violence. He noted that such books "inflict a cancer on the body of education we want our children to develop." The book was removed from library shelves, then returned after the controversy abated.

The Anaheim (California) Secondary Teachers Association in September 1978 charged the Anaheim Union High School Board of Trustees with having "banned thousands of books from English classrooms of the Anaheim secondary schools." The trustees, acting on a recommendation of the district's administration, had removed more than half of the reading material available to English teachers. *Black Boy* was among the books banned from the classroom and from school libraries. The board's president, James P. Bonnell, claimed that the 270 books remaining on the grade 7 to 12 list were "adequate." Teachers were instructed to simply store the book, along with others, and cautioned that they were not permitted to provide the books for supplemental reading or to discuss the books with students. The local school board warned teachers that they risked dismissal if they taught any of the banned books. The result of the confrontation was the mounting of a recall campaign: petitions were circulated to enforce a re-election ballot for Bonnell and another trustee and "Notice of Intent to Recall" papers were served on these individuals. The recall election was successful in unseating these trustees.

In a landmark case, the autobiography was one of nine books that the school board of the Island Trees (New York) Union Free District removed from the junior and senior high school libraries in 1976; two books were removed from classrooms. The other books were *The Best Short Stories by Negro Writers, The Fixer, GO ASK ALICE, SLAUGHTERHOUSE-FIVE, Down These Mean Streets, A Hero Ain't Nothin' but a Sandwich, Laughing Boy, The Naked Ape, Soul on Ice* and *A Reader for Writers.* Condemned with broad generalizations, the books were charged with being "anti-American, anti-Christian, anti-Semitic, or just plain filthy." As entered in the court record, the specific objections to *Black Boy* concerned the use of obscenity and the anti-Semitic remarks and other ethnic slurs, in such passages as the following: "We black children—seven or eight or nine years of age—used to run to the Jew's store and shout: . . . Bloody Christ

Killers/Never trust a Jew/Bloody Christ Killers/What won't a Jew do/Red, white and blue/Your pa was a Jew/Your ma a dirty dago/What the hell is you?"

The controversy began in March 1976 when the chair of the Long Island school board, Richard J. Ahrens, using a list of "objectionable" books and a collection of excerpts compiled by Parents of New York United (PONY-U), ordered 11 books removed from the Island Trees School District High School library. Teachers indicated that two of the books, *The Fixer* and *The Best Short Stories of Negro Writers*, had been removed from classrooms, where they were being used in a literature course. The local teachers union did file a formal grievance against the board, alleging a violation of the provisions of academic freedom in the union contract. A group of residents also objected to the censorship, stating they would protest to the state commissioner of education.

In defense against the protests of parents and students, the school board appointed a committee made up of parents and teachers to review the books and to determine which, if any, had merit. The committee recommended that seven of the books be returned to the library shelves, that two be placed on restricted shelves and that two be removed from the library, but the school board in July ignored these recommendations and voted to keep all but two of the books off the shelves. It authorized "restricted" circulation for *Black Boy* and circulation without restriction for *Laughing Boy*. The others would be "removed from . . . libraries and from use in the curriculum," that is, not to be assigned as required, optional or even suggested reading, although the books might still be discussed in class. The vote was unanimous on most titles. Ahrens said, "It is not only our right but our duty to make the decision, and we would do it again in the face of the abuse heaped upon us by the media."

Five students—one junior high school and four senior high school—filed suit on January 4, 1977, against the school district, seeking an injunction to have the books returned to the library shelves. The students challenged the censorship, claiming that the school board had violated their constitutional rights under the guise of protecting their social and moral tastes.

A federal district court decision handed down in August 1979 (*Pico v. Board of Education*) favored the school board. U.S. District Court Judge George C. Pratt rejected what he termed "tenure" for a book; in effect, he ruled that school boards have the right to examine the contents of library materials in order to determine their "suitability." At the center of the controversy was the constitutional role of the school board in public education, particularly in selection of content in relation to the perceived values of the community.

> In the absence of a sharp, focused issue of academic freedom, the court concludes that respect for the traditional values of the community and deference to the school board's substantial control over educational content preclude any finding of a First Amendment violation arising out of removal of any of the books from use in the curriculum.

After a U.S. Circuit Court of Appeals decision to remand the case for trial—in a 2–1 vote—the school board requested a review by the U.S. Supreme Court, which was granted. The appellate court had concluded that the First Amendment rights of the students had been violated and the criteria for the removal of the books were too general and overbroad.

The Supreme Court justices, sharply divided in a 5–4 decision (*Board of Education, Island Trees Union Free School District v. Pico*) upheld the appeals court. The Supreme Court mandated further trial proceedings to determine the underlying motivations of the school board. The majority relied on the concept that the "right to receive ideas" is a "necessary predicate" to the meaningful exercise of freedom of speech, press and political freedom. Justice Brennan, writing for the majority (which included Justices Marshall, Stevens and Blackmun; and Justice White with qualifications), stated: "Local school boards have broad discretion in the management of school affairs but this discretion must be exercised in a manner that comports with the transcendent imperatives of the First Amendment."

Our Constitution does not permit the official suppression of *ideas*. Thus whether [school board's] removal of books from their school libraries denied [students] their First Amendment rights upon the motivation. . . . If [school board] *intended* by their removal decision to deny [students] access to ideas with which [school board] disagreed, and if this intent was a decisive factor in [school board's] decision, then [school board] have exercised their discretion in violation of the Constitution. To permit such intentions to control official actions would be to encourage . . . officially prescribed orthodoxy. . . . (emphasis in original).

[W]e hold that local school boards may not remove books from school library shelves simply because they dislike the ideas contained in those books and seek by their removal to "prescribe what shall be orthodox in politics, nationalism, religion, or other matters of opinion". . . . Such purposes stand inescapably condemned by our precedents.

In their dissenting opinion, Chief Justice Burger and Justices O'Connor, Powell and Rehnquist issued a warning as to the role of the Supreme Court in making local censorship decisions: "If the plurality's view were to become the law, the court would come perilously close to becoming a 'super censor' of school board library decisions and the Constitution does not dictate that judges, rather than parents, teachers, and local school boards, must determine how the standards of morality and vulgarity are to be treated in the classroom." Thus, in their reluctance to place the Supreme Court in the position of local censor, the conservative justices recommended that the task of setting local community standards remain in local hands.

The controversy ended on August 12, 1982, when the Island Trees school board voted 6–1 to return the nine books to the school library shelves without restriction as to their circulation, but with a stipulation that the librarian must send a written notice to parents of students who borrow books containing material that the parents might find objectionable. The board also delayed action on whether *The Fixer* by Bernard Malamud would be returned to the curriculum.

FURTHER READINGS

"ASTA Release." *Anaheim Secondary Teachers Association* (September 27, 1978 and November 15, 1979).

Attacks on the Freedom to Learn: 1980–1983. New York: People for the American Way. The New York Regional Office, November 1983.

Board of Education, Island Trees Union Free School District #26 v. Pico et al., 457 U.S. 853, 102 S.Ct. 2799, 73 L.Ed.2s 435 (1982).

Gayle, Addison. *Richard Wright: Ordeal of a Native Son.* Garden City, N.Y.: Anchor Press/Doubleday, 1980.

Graham, Maryemma, and Jerry W. Ward, Jr. "*Black Boy (American Hunger)*: Freedom to Remember." In *Censored Books: Critical Viewpoints.* Ed. Nicholas J. Karolides, Lee Burress and Jack Kean. Metuchen, N.J.: The Scarecrow Press, 1993. 109–116.

Hurwitz, Leon. *Historical Dictionary of Censorship in the United States.* Westport, Conn.: Greenwood Press, 1985.

Jenkinson, Edward B. *Censors in the Classroom: The Mind Benders.* Carbondale: Southern Illinois University Press, 1979.

Newsletter on Intellectual Freedom 24 (1975): 104, 120; 25 (1976): 34, 61–62, 85–86, 115; 26 (1977): 45; 27 (1978): 57; 28 (1979): 6, 141–145; 31 (1982): 12–13, 166, 197; and 36 (1987): 225.

North, William D. "Pico and the Challenge to Books in Schools." *Newsletter on Intellectual Freedom* 31 (1982): 195, 221–225.

Rich, R. Bruce. "The Supreme Court's Decision in Island Trees." *Newsletter on Intellectual Freedom* 31 (1982): 149, 173–186.

Simoneau, Duke. "Book Controversy Flares in Nashua." *New Hampshire Sunday News* (March 5, 1978): 1, 18.

Weathersby, Dorothy T. *Censorship of Literature Textbooks in Tennessee: A Study of the Commission, Publishers, Teachers, and Textbooks.* Ed.D. diss., University of Tennessee, 1975.

Webb, Constance. *Richard Wright: A Biography.* New York: Putnam, 1968.

BURGER'S DAUGHTER

Author: Nadine Gordimer
Original date and place of publication: 1979, Great Britain; 1979, United States
Publisher: Jonathan Cape; Viking Press
Literary form: Novel

SUMMARY

Lionel Burger is not the center-stage character in *Burger's Daughter*. Yet, the novel revolves around him as the life of his daughter, Rosa, emanates from and seems dominated by him. Lionel, a white Afrikaner from a wealthy family, is well reputed as a doctor, but has gained notoriety as a leader of the South African Communist Party and through his activities against the government's system of apartheid. He and his second wife, Cathy, have established a household that welcomes black Africans in an atmosphere of equality, a household in which social consciousness and responsibility are givens. Both parents face constantly the threat of arrest; indeed, Lionel dies of illness in prison during the third year of his life sentence, and Cathy dies of multiple sclerosis, her health damaged by imprisonment. The immediate sociopolitical context of these events is the South Africa of the March 1960 Sharpeville massacre in Rosa's childhood and the June 1976 Soweto school riots in her adulthood.

Despite the powerful presence of Lionel in the lives of this novel's characters, it is Rosa's story. Her early years are punctuated by activities that mark her parents' philosophy and expectations. Indeed, the story opens with Rosa, age 14, waiting outside a prison with a quilt and hot water bottle to deliver to her mother, who had been picked up by the police the night before and is being detained. But that act is not as revealing as the fact that she has secreted a note, seemingly innocuous in its message should it be discovered, inside the bottle cap to convey to her mother the status of her father. A few years later, at age 17, she takes on the pretense of being engaged to a political prisoner, a known associate of her father, to obtain permission to visit him in prison. At these monthly visits, she communicates information to him in the guise of a love letter and receives messages in return about the political prisoners through his vocal nuances and body language.

Rosa's early memories reveal her parents' activities and household. The evening of the Sharpeville massacre, African National Congress (ANC) leaders, Pan-African Congress people, lawyers and others gather at their house, talking through the night about the changed political situation. At the opposite extreme, celebratory events—a successful boycott or march, a leader's release from prison or Lionel found not guilty of a charge—also bring gatherings of the anti-apartheid faithful, white and black, to the house. Vivid in her memory is Boasie, a black child Rosa's age, the son of an ANC organizer, who is cared for by her family while his father travels on ANC business. She recurrently recalls their learning to swim together, fighting for "the anchorage of wet hair on Lionel Burger's warm breast in the cold swimming pool." They are separated once when both of Rosa's parents are arrested together; she does not see him again until many years later in London, a meeting that is emotionally traumatic for her.

In her recollections of her adolescent and young adult past, Rosa also reveals a note of resentment against the claim of familial relationship that enforces upon her certain situations—standing outside the prison, waiting for her mother and attending her father's trial for 217 days, both in the public eye. She expresses anger at her parents for their expectations of her playacting role as fiancée to the prisoner (for whom she really has tender feelings). After her mother's and then her father's death, the note of resentment swells at the expectations of the faithful that she will continue their activities, their social commitment. She muses:

> Even animals have the instinct to turn from suffering. The sense to run away. Perhaps it was an illness not to be able to live one's life . . . with justice defined in terms of respect for property, innocence defended in their children's privileges, love in their procreation, and care only for each other. A sickness not to be able to ignore that condition of a healthy, ordinary life: other people's suffering.

The suffering referred to is that of the black populace. This suffering is not actually visited, except in the connotations of shootings, protests and imprisonment, the oppression of pass laws and curfews. Instead, attention is given to raids that net one or another or both parents for periods of incarceration (the last leading to Lionel's trial and conviction to a life sentence) as well as others of the party. Cathy Burger and others are banned from certain occupations, and from free movement around the country, even house arrest, and from associations with particular people. There is a consciousness, too, of surveillance: the authorities' knowledge of Rosa's domiciles, her lovers, her movements, her contacts—her need to account for every visit and visitor just in case there is an interrogation.

The reader knows that the authorities are aware of her visits a year later to Pretoria; who she visits, the dates and frequency. Her purpose is to obtain a passport to leave the country (for she is forbidden access to a passport through normal channels), because, as she says, "I'd like to see Europe." After a year, Rosa is granted a passport (with understandings of where she is not to travel and with whom she is not to associate) and departs from South Africa, expecting to be stopped even as she is walking across the tarmac toward the plane. She isn't stopped, but "Surveillance watched her go in."

Book II chronicles Rosa's escape to France, first very briefly to Paris and then to the south of France to be with Lionel's first wife, whom she has never met. Katya (actually Colette), an aspiring ballerina, had been disciplined by the party for her "inactivity" and her "bourgeois tendencies to put [her] private life first." Rosa is overcome by the luminous landscape, its voluptuousness; the "pleasure of scents, sights and sounds exciting only in themselves, associated with nothing and nobody." She responds to a life lived for itself, without social mission and surveillance. Soon she has a lover; upon her impending departure for London he arranges for a rendezvous in London.

The sojourn in London does not evolve as anticipated. Her lover delayed by illness, Rosa spends relaxed hours wandering about London, chatting with people, taking a French class. She begins to think about meeting the people she had planned to avoid and does so. She goes to a gathering with other Africans in attendance, including South African revolutionaries. When she is recognized, she is introduced within the context of a speech about revolutionary heroes, particularly Lionel Burger.

Boasie is there. He seems guarded. Later that night, however, he telephones, but instead of reestablishing their childhood relationship, he rejects her, her memories and her father. He is bitter that Lionel should be ennobled as heroic, while his own father, also a victim of the struggle, is forgotten, that whites should be credited and blacks neglected. Rosa is angered, her thoughts and emotions in turmoil.

Rosa returns to South Africa and to a job as a physiotherapist in a Johannesburg hospital. She is on duty in 1976 when the Soweto school riot victims fill the wards, after the police fire machine guns against the students' stones. A student rebellion ensues against the separate system of education; most never return to school after June 1976.

In October 1977 many people are detained, arrested or banned; many organizations are banned as is the only black newspaper. Most of the banned people are black. Among the few whites is Rosa Burger, who is detained without charges. She is, however, subject to charges of collusion in a "conspiracy to further the aims of communism and/or the African National Congress. The charges would allege incitement and aiding and abetting of the students' and school children's revolt." One piece of evidence that will be identified in the indictment against her is her attendance at a leftist "rally" in London.

CENSORSHIP HISTORY

On July 5, 1979, *Burger's Daughter* was banned by the Republic of South Africa on the grounds that it "endangers the safety of the state" and that it depicts "whites as baddies, blacks as goodies." Further, the author was accused of using her central character "as a pad from which to launch a full-scale attack on the Republic of South Africa." The publications' committee cited six categories of violation of the Publications Act of 1974.

In early October, however, the censoring committee was overruled by the Publications Appeal Board. The board's ruling was made on the advice of a committee of literary experts and an expert on security measures, and despite "crudities and profanity, derogatory references to whites and a distorted picture of the political situation in South Africa."

> The state security expert found there was no threat to the state from the novel. The literary experts concluded that the original censorship committee, in banning the book, stood "convicted of bias, prejudice, and literary incompetence. It has not read accurately, it has severely distorted by quoting extensively out of context, it has not considered the work as a literary work deserves to be considered, and it has directly, and by implication, smeared the authoress [sic]."

This turnabout resulted from a change of strategy by the Directorate of Publications, which administered the censorship system in South Africa. The

1974 Publications and Entertainments Act permitted appeals of censorship decisions made by committees appointed by the Directorate; the right to appeal was granted to the Directorate itself, to persons with financial interest and to the body that had originally submitted the text for censorship consideration. The change referred to above was that the Directorate itself appealed the decision of its own committee. *Burger's Daughter* was the first banned text so appealed and the first to be reinstated. However, as Gordimer herself stated, " . . . the censorship laws remain the same."

Ironically, in 1980, Gordimer was awarded the CNA Prize, one of South Africa's highest literary awards, for *Burger's Daughter*. She also was awarded the Nobel Prize in literature in 1991.

FURTHER READINGS

Gordimer, Nadine. *The Essential Gesture: Writing, Politics and Places.* New York: Alfred A. Knopf, 1988.
Index on Censorship 6 (November/December 1979): 69; 2 (April 1980): 73.
"Latest Gordimer Novel Banned in South Africa." *The New York Times* (September 7, 1979): 8.
"South Africa Bans Two Novels." *Newsletter on Intellectual Freedom* 28 (1979): 147.
"South Africa Lifts Ban on Gordimer Novel." *The New York Times* (October 7, 1979): 79.
"South Africans Cancel Ban on Gordimer Book." *The New York Times* (October 5, 1979): 6.

DECENT INTERVAL

Author: Frank Snepp
Original date and place of publication: 1977, United States and Canada
Publisher: Random House and Random House of Canada, Ltd.
Literary form: Nonfiction

SUMMARY

An Insider's Account of Saigon's Indecent End Told by the CIA's Chief Strategy Analyst in Vietnam, this extended subtitle reveals the surface of Frank Snepp's purpose in *Decent Interval*. A large measure of his disclosure exposes aspects of strategy and battlefield encounters of both North Vietnam and South Vietnam forces. He also recounts the thinking and activities of the men who shaped these strategies. A significant focus interwoven in these accounts is the making of American policy, its operation and the chief actors in Saigon and Washington. The title's "decent interval" refers to the accusation of critics against Assistant to the President for National Security Affairs Henry Kissinger with reference to the January 1973 cease-fire agreement: "that he had never meant for the agreement to work anyway, but was merely trying through its convolutions and vagaries to assure a 'decent interval' between the American withdrawal and a final fight to the death between the two Vietnamese sides."

The author, too, is a player, as the subtitle reveals. In the text, he identifies his activities and attitudes; however, he is the on-the-spot observer and documenter, his "spot" being one of the upper floors of the United States Embassy in Saigon where the CIA had its central operation. The time period for the core of the book is from October 1972 through April 30, 1975, the date when the last evacuation helicopter pulled off.

By October 1972, American troops had largely been withdrawn from Vietnam. "Vietnamization," that is, the transfer of responsibility for managing and protecting the country to the South Vietnamese, had become the basis of United States policy. Despite this policy, the United States, through its ambassador and CIA station chief who had "manipulated and penetrated" South Vietnam President Thieu's government, was still controlling the situation.

On January 28, 1973, a cease-fire agreement went into effect. Signed in Paris for the United States by Secretary of State William Rogers, it had been negotiated by Henry Kissinger, starting in early 1969. The treaty was significantly flawed. Both political and military issues were unresolved. The problem of who would rule South Vietnam was ignored, though it did provide for a process of political evolution. Technical aspects vital to the cease-fire's enforcement were also omitted: nondesignation of control of disputed territory; an imprecise date for enacting such control; nonestablishment of "legal" limitations for providing additional supplies and reinforcement for communist troops in South Vietnam. The postwar strategy of "equilibrium," which was to lead to a stalemate and a live-and-let-live attitude on both sides, was thrown off balance from the start. "At no point did [Kissinger] seriously consider the alternative of promoting a genuine coalition arrangement. To have done so would have meant abandoning the ideal of a non-Communist South Vietnam to which he and Nixon remained committed."

Overshadowing these flaws were those of the process itself. Both Kissinger and Nixon had "continued to bombard [President] Thieu with threats and promises in a relentless effort to bring him to heel." After Thieu reluctantly agreed, Kissinger neglected to inform him of changes in the document effected subsequently. During the negotiations, Kissinger made secret commitments to both combatants: continued U.S. support to South Vietnam; suspension of U.S. reconnaissance flights over North Vietnam and withdrawal of all American technicians within a year. If either commitment had become known to the opposite combatant, or to the American people, each might have withdrawn support and questioned Kissinger's diplomacy.

As the events unfold from the maneuvering to establish a cease-fire to the final collapse of South Vietnam and the American evacuation, three individuals are portrayed in a negative light. As suggested by the discussion of the cease-fire accord, Kissinger, who was elevated to the position of secretary of state in 1973, is the first of these. Two particular traits are expressed: his "penchant for the virtuoso performance," a determination to do everything himself, which led him to fail to delegate oversight responsibilities of Vietnam activities; and his "addiction to secrecy." He was not candid or honest with Thieu and other South Vietnam officials, nor did he reveal to Congress the commitments he had made (which required congressional approval). He is shown to be impatient with CIA assessments that do not support his position and direction; in later months, against evidence to the contrary, he maintained a position that a negotiated truce with the intervention of the Soviet Union or China could be achieved. Accusing his critics of being self-serving, he is identified as being "so inflexible on so many issues—or so intolerant of debate." These attributes and this perceived goal caused significant delays in activating the evacuation procedures, leading to the chaos of the final days and the failure in meeting "moral" obligations to those Vietnamese who had worked with United States officials.

Five months after the cease-fire in June 1973, Graham Martin became Kissinger's hand-picked ambassador to Saigon. His personality and character traits combined with his perceptions and beliefs are defined as counterproductive to the operation of the embassy and handicaps to the final mission: evacuation. Supremely confident in himself, he was conscious of his status, and demanded the rights and respect of hierarchy; he was sensitive to any slight and held a grudge against any "insubordination," transferring those who questioned his opinions or judgments. He used deception with Congress and the press to further his political purposes. Fervently anticommunist, he sought additional aid to bolster the Thieu government and army while hiding their faults and weaknesses, so as to convince Congress of the worthiness of such action. Believing in the probability of a negotiated peace, along with Kissinger, he assiduously discounted increasingly persuasive evidence that questioned this view.

Thomas Polgar, the CIA section chief, Snepp's immediate superior, is also identified as falling victim to the belief that additional aid would save South Vietnam and that a negotiated peace was imminent. He, too, was blindsided, so that he put aside evidence that did not support his position. Despite his strong anticommunist beliefs, Hungarian-born Polgar was successfully duped by the Hungarian delegation to the International Commission of Control and Supervision; the communist group received information from him ostensibly in its role as intermediary with the North Vietnamese, while supplying him with false information that fed his false expectations.

The thrust of most of Snepp's book is the final offensive, in its several stages, of the North Vietnamese forces from mid-December 1974 through April 1975 and the retreat and eventual defeat of the South Vietnamese armies. In conjunction, he offers extensive details of the evacuation experiences of the Americans and their associated South Vietnamese personnel.

Two significant images are revealed. The North Vietnamese leadership carefully planned the military offensive, establishing details and options. Data gleaned from the memoirs of General Van Tien Dung, who commanded the North Vietnam army, indicate frequent and precise consultations and reassessments so as to adapt strategies to the dynamic situation. In contrast, the South Vietnamese leadership, though anticipating an attack, was in a reactive mode. Planning was global; decisions were delayed, partly because the leaders were operating under a "borrowed vision" (i.e., dependence on Americans), partly because there was limited coordination, and the choices threatened their egos and their status. Decisions seemed not to be based on analysis of the ability to accomplish selected strategies. The military situation was also handicapped by contradictory shifts in strategy in midstream. The South Vietnamese army's defeat was further encouraged by several ineffective, corrupt commanders.

Fearing that Saigon would be surrounded and isolated with his major divisions on the outlying boundaries, Thieu issued a belated order for them to withdraw to new positions. Given the conditions identified above, the result was havoc. When Dung recognized what was happening, he moved expeditiously to take advantage of the situation. Two armies were cut off; another was surrounded while attempting to defend two northeastern coastal cities. The evacuation of these cities in the area north of Saigon, especially Danang, was chaotic and in some respects disastrous. This "unraveling" occurred during March 1975.

The "ides of March," however, did not sufficiently forewarn Saigon. Anticipating that the serious situation would at last convince Congress to agree to the aid requested and that negotiations would take place to forestall the attack, Ambassador Martin stonewalled necessary arrangements for evacuation of the city. Though the war around Saigon heated up in early April, even Washington officials did not resolve their position to exert pressure on Martin to expedite the evacuation until mid-April. Martin, who had thwarted efforts to plan the evacuation, stalled further, essentially effecting the panic and chaos that resulted.

Snepp's heroes are the men who worked around these delaying orders and exerted their energies and imagination to establish an evacuation plan and to put it into motion. Among others, he applauds General Homer Smith and Colonel Bill Legro, the DAO (Defense Attache's Office) intelligence chief, and Legro's staff. Heroes also are the many men who put their energies and lives on the line to initiate (sometimes against orders) and operate the evacuation process, including officials of the embassy and other staff personnel. Praised also are the fixed-wing and, subsequently, the helo-lift pilots who flew in and out continuously under heavy pressure, and the Marines on the ground who were the last Americans to evacuate.

The book poses a pair of interlocking issues that evolve from these events. Kissinger establishes a political-moral view: He was convinced that the United States had to show some support for South Vietnam "as a surety for American prestige abroad"; he argued that if we didn't, other nations, Israel, for example, would doubt our consistency. He is quoted in a press conference: "There is also a moral question for the United States, a question of whether when an ally with whom it has been associated for ten years wishes to defend itself, it is the United States that should make the decision for it by withholding supplies."

A second issue is expressed time and again in the text: What was the responsibility of the United States to safeguard South Vietnamese who had worked closely with the embassy, the CIA and other agencies? Many, including Snepp, felt a deep moral obligation to evacuate these associates and friends—"our people"—to save them from certain abuse at the hands of the Communists. Others were unconcerned; their personnel were left to fend for themselves when the Americans departed. Still others, like Polgar, caught up in false expectations, placed their local collaborators in jeopardy by waiting too long. Indeed, this was the "real" disaster referred to earlier. While the near disaster was averted when the Americans were evacuated, many of these South Vietnamese personnel were left behind because the evacuation procedure was delayed by both Saigon and Washington officials. Time ran out.

CENSORSHIP HISTORY

In a postscript to his basic text, Snepp reveals the "cover-up and the cosmeticizing of events" by the administrations; he specifically identifies Kissinger, Polgar and Martin in this regard. He is directed to "fill out an affidavit which in effect attributed the breakdown of the evacuation to 'local enemy action.'" He refused to sign it. Having been denied an opportunity to prepare a "damage assessment," criticized for presenting a "full-fledged commentary on what had taken place," realizing that the agency's precensorship would contravene his intention of revealing what had actually happened in Vietnam, Snepp made a critical decision:

> Because of its continued assaults on my integrity, and its reluctance to deal candidly with the Vietnam issue.... I also resolved not to submit my manuscript to the agency for clearance and censorship, as all former employees-turned-author are required to do. In my view, if the CIA could officially leak to the press to whitewash its role in Vietnam, it had forfeited the right to censor me in the name of security or national interest.

The preparations to publish *Decent Interval* were conducted in an atmosphere of secrecy; it was issued in November 1977.

In February 1978, the United States Department of Justice filed a civil suit in the federal district court against Frank Snepp, asserting a breach of contract, that is, the agreement signed by all CIA employees to "not . . . publish . . . any information or material relating to the agency, its activities or intelligence activities generally, either during or after the term of employment . . . without specific prior approval by the agency." A concurrent factor is the requirement of nondisclosure of any classified information related to the agency. The U.S. Justice Department sought an injunction requiring prepublication review of future writing and damages, that is, a constructive trust—the confiscation of all royalties from the sale of the book. Snepp, in response, filed papers that the suit violated his First Amendment rights, a case of "prior restraint on protected speech."

During the trial, government lawyers argued that trust and confidence in the CIA had been undermined by Snepp's publishing without permission. Further, in response to Snepp's claim that there was no violation of security, the government claimed that it, not the individual, had the right to decide whether there was such a violation. Snepp's claim of nonviolation of security was not contested.

U.S. District Court (Eastern Division of Virginia) Judge Owen R. Lewis in June 1978 found that Snepp had "willfully, deliberately and surreptitiously" breached his position of trust with the CIA and the secrecy agreement. Publication of his book had "caused the United States irreparable harm and loss." He enjoined future breaches of this secrecy agreement and imposed a constructive trust on Snepp's royalties (estimated as $60,000 by Robert L. Bernstein, president of Random House). Thus, the contract factor superseded the issue of revelation of classified information, emphasizing the agency's prepublication right to review.

The Fourth Circuit Court of Appeals (Judges Harrison L. Winter, J. Dickson Phillips and Walter Hoffman) in March 1979 concurred with the findings of the district court with regard to the breach of contract and the CIA's prepublication right to review; it upheld the injunction against future violations of this obligation. However, the appellate court rejected the constructive trust, asserting that the confiscation of all of Snepp's royalties was improper punishment. Such damages would have been proper only if he had disclosed classified information. "In other words, the court thought that Snepp's fiduciary obligation extended only to preserving the confidentiality of classified material."

The United States Supreme Court in February 1980, having been asked by Snepp to review the ruling of the U.S. Court of Appeals that upheld the validity of the CIA contract, responded to the case with an unsigned opinion; it did not formally grant a review or hear arguments. The restraints on CIA employees were upheld: The secrecy agreement is a judicially enforceable contract that applies to classified and unclassified information. Snepp "deliberately and surreptitiously violated his obligation to submit all materials for prepublication review"; a former agent cannot rely on his own judgment about what information is detrimental against the "broader understanding [of the CIA] of what may expose classified information and confidential sources. . . ." Further, it reversed the court of appeals and upheld the district court with regard to the constructive trust of all of Snepp's royalties.

The dissenting opinion written by Justice John Paul Stevens (concurred in by Justices William J. Brennan, Jr., and Thurgood Marshall) argued that the purpose of the secrecy agreement was "not to give the CIA power to censor its employees' critical speech, but rather to ensure that classified, nonpublic information is not disclosed. . . ." Further he argued that granting to the government a constructive trust over Snepp's profits was "unprecedented and drastic relief." Justice Stevens noted that the rule of law the court announced with this ruling was not supported by statute, by the contract, or by the common law.

> The Court has not persuaded me that a rule of reason analysis should not be applied to Snepp's covenant to submit to prepublication review. Like an ordinary employer, the CIA has a vital interest in protecting certain types of information; at the same time, the CIA employee has a countervailing interest in preserving a wide range of work opportunities (including work as an author) and in protecting his First Amendment rights. The public interest lies in a proper accommodation that will preserve the intelligence mission of the Agency while not abridging the free flow of unclassified information. When the Government seeks to enforce a harsh restriction on the employee's freedom, despite its admission that the interest the agreement was designed to protect—the confidentiality of classified information—has not been compromised, an equity court might well be persuaded that the case is not one in which the covenant should be enforced.

This case was the first to make it illegal for an American intelligence official to publish any information, secret or otherwise, that had been gleaned from official sources.

Subsequent to the ruling of the Supreme Court, Snepp petitioned for a rehearing so that arguments could be presented. This appeal was denied in April 1980. On August 21, 1980, Anthony Lewis reported that Snepp had paid a fine of $116,658.15 to the government—all that he had earned. He still owed $24,000, which he had promised to pay as soon as he could borrow it.

On March 3, 1980, not quite a month after the Supreme Court's decision against Frank Snepp, the Justice Department sued John R. Stockwell for the profits obtained from his book, *In Search of Enemies, a CIA Story*. Its text accuses the CIA of lying to Congress and the public about its covert military activities in Angola in 1975–76. Stockwell, a former CIA employee, had been chief of the agency's task force in Angola. The book was published in 1978.

Given the Supreme Court judgment against Snepp, on July 25 Stockwell agreed to pay any profits from future sales. The government allowed Stockwell to keep past earnings of about $40,000, which he had already spent. Stockwell, who did not admit to violating his secrecy agreement, agreed to submit future manuscripts for prepublication review by the CIA.

The CIA also targeted Philip Agee by seeking profits from two of his books, *Dirty Work: The CIA in Western Europe* and *Dirty Work II: The CIA in Africa*. (Agee's *Inside the Company: CIA Diary* was not included in this suit.) The Justice Department in mid-February attempted to halt the publication of *Dirty Work II* before realizing it was already for sale in several Washington bookstores.

FURTHER READINGS

Carmody, Dierdre. "Ex-Aide Challenges CIA's Secrecy Suit." *The New York Times* (March 9, 1978): 19.

Eder, Richard. "Why Decisions in Snepp Case Disturbs Publishers." *The New York Times* (March 11, 1980): III 5.

"Ex-CIA Agent and U.S. Settle Suit Over Profits from Book." *The New York Times* (June 28, 1980): 14.

Green, Jonathon. *Encyclopedia of Censorship*. New York: Facts On File, 1990.

"High Court Backs CIA in Curb on Articles Its Employees Write." *The New York Times* (February 20, 1980): 1.

"High Court Ends Snepp's Fight to Keep Royalties." *Publishers Weekly* 217 (April 25, 1980): 18, 23.

Hurwitz, Leon. *Historical Dictionary of Censorship in the United States*. Westport, Conn.: Greenwood Press, 1985.

"Judge Rules Snepp Violated Contract and Must Forfeit Profits on Book." *The New York Times* (July 8, 1978): 8.

Kaplan, Steven H. "The CIA Responds to Its Black Sheep: Censorship and Passport Revocation—The Cases of Philip Agee." *Connecticut Law Review* 13 (Winter 1981): 317–96.

Lewis, Anthony. "The Price of Secrets." *The New York Times* (August 21, 1980): A27.

Morro, Anthony. "Judge Says He Thinks Ex-Official of CIA Violated Secrecy Pact." *The New York Times* (June 22, 1978): 12.

———. "Reporters' Notebook: Alarums and Explosions at Ex-Agent's Trial." *The New York Times* (June 23, 1978): 8.

———. "Trial Over CIA Book Raises Rights Issues." *The New York Times* (June 19, 1978): 15.

———. "Turner, Testifying in Snepp Case, Says Book by Ex-Agent Has Hurt CIA." *The New York Times* (June 21, 1978): 15.

Newsletter on Intellectual Freedom 27 (1978): 67, 100, 124; 28 (1979): 81, 110; 29 (1980): 48, 53–54.

Oliver, Malcolm. "Appeals Court Upholds CIA Secrecy Pact in Snepp Case." *Publishers Weekly* 215 (April 2, 1979): 24, 26.

Snepp, Frank. "On CIA Secrecy, News Leaks and Censorship." *The New York Times* (March 3, 1978): 25.

———. "Postscript." *Decent Interval*. New York. Random House, 1977.

Snepp v. United States. 444 U.S. 507. Supreme Court 1980.

"Stockwell Settles with CIA to Keep Profits from Book." *Publishers Weekly* 218 (July 11, 1980): 16, 18.

"Third Ex-CIA Agent Sued by U.S. for Profits." *The New York Times* (March 4, 1980): 13.

Weaver, Warren, Jr. "Justice Department to Sue Author of CIA Book." *The New York Times* (February 15, 1978): 21.

DOCTOR ZHIVAGO

Author: Boris Pasternak
Original date and place of publication: 1957, Italy; 1958, United States

Publisher: Giangiacomo Feltrinelli Editore; Pantheon Books
Literary form: Novel

SUMMARY

Doctor Zhivago spans the life of its title character until his death before age 40. It spans also a vital period in Russia's history from just after the turn of the century, through the 1917 revolution, the civil war and up to the terror of the 1930s. An epilogue given during World War II (after Zhivago's death) affords a glimpse of the future as well as closure to the past.

Yurii Andreievich Zhivago is orphaned at a young age. His father, a rich industrialist who abandoned the family even before the early death of his mother, has squandered the family fortune. Yurii is brought up in the home of a cultured, intellectual family in Moscow. He studies to become a physician, earning esteem as a diagnostician, and marries Tonia, the daughter of his "adoptive" parents. A child is born, but their lives are sundered with Zhivago's induction into the military during World War I.

During this military service, Zhivago meets Lara—Larisa Feodorovna Antipova (nee Guishar), the daughter of a Russianized, widowed French-woman. He had encountered her twice during adolescence. Trained as a nurse, she is searching for her husband, Pasha—Pavel Pavlovich Antipov—who is rumored to have been injured or slain in battle. Lara carries with her the weight of a past bereavement—the loss of her innocence and purity, having been seduced during adolescence by the lecher Komarovsky, her mother's lover. Yurii and Lara gradually become friends before she departs for her home in Yuriatin in the Ural region and he to his family in Moscow.

> "Big news! Street fighting in Petersburg! The Petersburg garrison has joined the insurgents! The revolution!"

This announcement closes part one of the text and ushers in dramatic changes in the lives of the protagonists and of Russia.

Upon his return, Yurii finds Moscow disordered and depressed. Fuel and firewood are scarce. Maintaining subsistence is challenging and enervating. Yurii attempts to re-establish his medical practice and his social circle, but he finds himself feeling alienated from associates and friends. He begins to recognize the dangers to the family in the new political environment because of their past status.

After a brutal winter, Tonia and her father, with the help of Yurii's half brother, Evgraf, convince Yurii they must escape Moscow to Varykino, Tonia's grandfather's estate, a dangerous choice because it identifies them with its past. The long train ride in a freight car is itself dangerous; they must endure frequent searches. Along the way within sight of Yuriatin, Zhivago briefly meets the infamous Strelnikov, the fanatic officer of the Red Army. (He is in reality Lara's missing husband, who has taken the rumors of his death as an opportunity to change his identity.)

The Zhivagos' life at Varykino takes on an aura of peace and obscurity. Yurii's sense of peace, however, is broken by two events: his love affair with Lara, upon whom he chances in the Yuriatin library—he is tormented by this egregious betrayal of Tonia, whom he also loves; and his being conscripted at gunpoint by the Red partisans, the Forest Brotherhood, to replace their slain surgeon. This imprisonment lasts over a year before he is able to escape on his fourth attempt.

After a six-week walk, Yurii, black with grime, emaciated and weak, arrives in Yuriatin to find Lara. He learns his family has returned to Moscow and, later, that they have been exiled from Russia. However, because she is the wife of Strelnikov, he and Lara are not safe. They disappear to Varykino. Their paths separate when she escapes to a Pacific province, expecting him to follow. He stays behind, deceiving her for her safety, determined to go to Moscow. Before he leaves, Strelnikov arrives, seeking his wife and a hideout. The next day, anticipating capture, he shoots himself.

In Moscow again, Yurii seems unable to commit himself to either his work or his writing. Even his efforts to obtain an exit permit seem halfhearted. He deteriorates physically and intellectually. At last, with the help of his half brother, Evgraf, he takes initial steps toward revitalizing himself. He dies, however, of a heart attack, en route to a new hospital position.

Among those gathered for the wake is Lara. She has come to Moscow on an urgent mission–apparently to locate her and Yurii's lost child; for memory's sake she had come to visit her husband's student apartment, the very one in which Yurii had last lived. After the funeral, she stays to help Evgraf with Zhivago's papers—and then disappears.

> One day Larisa Feodorovna went out and did not come back. She must have been arrested in the street at that time. She vanished without a trace and probably died somewhere, forgotten as a nameless number on a list that afterwards got mislaid, in one of the innumerable mixed or women's concentration camps in the north.

Within this plot, Pasternak introduces an array of characters from all walks of life and portrays their life situations. He provides vignettes of personal and sociopolitical events to evoke the historical and human landscape. In the prewar, prerevolutionary period, the prosperity and charm of upper-class life is contrasted with that of the working class—musical evenings and a Christmas party of dancing, feasting and card playing in opposition to an angry railroad strike and Cossack dragoons attacking and massacring a group of peaceful demonstrators.

In contrast to the Varykino interlude, a creative haven of happiness found in family, the rewards of work and the beauty of nature, there is the surrounding devastation—the shelled and burned villages viewed from the train, caught between the crossfire of the White and Red armies or destroyed because of uprisings. The peasants live in misery, their lives disrupted, their sons taken as soldiers.

Yurii's initial response to the revolution anticipates the "promises of a new order" as it had been expressed in the idealized revolutionary thought of 1905 and 1912–14; he had been cognizant of the oppression in czarist Russia. Subsequently, he is provoked by less familiar ideas growing out of the reality of a savage and ruthless war and the upheaval of the "soldiers revolution led by those professional revolutionaries, the Bolsheviks." While en route to Moscow, a train companion, a revolutionary, counters Zhivago's suggestion that the country must return to "relative peace and order" before embarking on "dangerous experiments":

> "That's naive. . . . What you call disorder is just as normal a state of things as the order you're so keen about. All this destruction—it's a natural and preliminary stage of a broad creative plan. Society has not yet disintegrated sufficiently. It must fall to pieces completely, then a genuinely revolutionary government will put the pieces together and build on completely new foundations."

Zhivago resists this siren song; as the train approaches Moscow, to him the war and the revolution seem empty and meaningless while his home, intact and dear, is meaningful.

Episodes of the revolution in process provide glimpses within the surface devastation and deprivation and cast a shadow over the occasional political rhetoric of revolutionaries. A village is gratuitously shelled from an armored train because it is adjacent to another that had refused to adhere to the party line. Another is raided and burned to the ground for withholding food from the army, food supplies needed by the villagers. The second stage of the revolution is characterized as one of suspicion and intrigue informers acting on hatred and envy, ready to destroy individuals in the "name of higher revolutionary justice."

Yurii, too often outspoken for his own safety, expresses his antagonism:

> "But, first, the idea of social betterment as it is understood since the October revolution doesn't fill me with enthusiasm. Second, it is so far from being put into practice, and the mere talk about it has cost such a sea of blood, that I'm not sure that the end justifies the means. And last—and this is the main thing—when I hear people speak of reshaping life it makes me lose my self-control and I fall into despair."

In another passage, he questions marxism and its leaders:

> "Marxism a science? . . . Marxism is too uncertain of its ground to be a science. Sciences are more balanced, more objective. I don't know a movement more self-centered and further removed from the facts than Marxism. Everyone is worried only about proving himself in practical matters, and as for the men in power, they are so anxious to establish the myth of their infallibility that they do their utmost to ignore the truth. Politics doesn't appeal to me. I don't like people who don't care about the truth."

At the height of his energy and power, Yurii dreams of living his life wholly and individually, "living by the sweat of [his] brow." He responds to "man's eternal longing to go back to the land." He embraces the beauty around him and loves to experience and express. He wants his freedom expanded, not diminished; he struggles to protect his privacy and the personal basis of his life. Zhivago maintains these values, though his lust for life and his life ebb away.

The epilogue set during World War II in 1943 features two of Zhivago's childhood friends. They have been in Soviet penal camps but are now officers in the army. They mull over their past, the atrocities they have experienced. One of them comments on an important aspect of the Soviet system:

> "I think that collectivization was an erroneous and unsuccessful measure and it was impossible to admit the error. To conceal the failure people had to be cured, by every means of terrorism, of the habit of thinking and judging for them-selves, and forced to see what didn't exist, to assert the very opposite of what their eyes told them. This accounts for the unexampled cruelty of the Yezhov period, the promulgation of a constitution that was never meant to be applied, and the introduction of elections that violated the very principle of free choice. And when the war broke out, its real horrors, its real dangers, its menace of real death were a blessing compared with the inhuman reign of the lie, and they brought relief because they broke the spell of the dead letter."

CENSORSHIP HISTORY

After the death of Stalin during the Khrushchev period when the Kremlin eased its censorship policy in 1953, Pasternak began writing *Doctor Zhivago*. He had been silent during the Stalinist period, which had "muted creative individual-ism and exacted conformity to party dictates from all writers." Upon submitting it to the State Publishing House and receiving a positive reaction, the author sent a copy to Giangiacomo Feltrinelli Editore, a publisher in Italy. Sub-sequently, the State Publishing House had second thoughts and condemned the book; its "cumulative effect casts doubt on the validity of the Bolshevik Revolution which it depicts as if it were the great crime in Russian history." Pasternak was required to request the book's return from the Italian publisher for "revisions." The publisher refused.

When Boris Pasternak was awarded the Nobel Prize for literature in 1958, he was forced to refuse the award: "[I]n view of the meaning given to this honor in the community in which I belong, I should abstain from the undeserved prize that has been awarded me."

The Soviet Union denounced the award—and the Swedish judges—as a "hostile political act for recognizing a work withheld from Russian readers which was counter-revolutionary and slanderous." Further, Pasternak was expelled from the Soviet Union of Authors and deprived of the title "Soviet writer."

In 1986, reflecting the Gorbachev open policies, issues of censorship and bureaucratic interference in literature were debated at the Eighth Soviet Congress of Writers. A reform-oriented slate was elected to the leadership position of the Writers' Union. Its chief announced that the state publishing agency was considering the publication of *Doctor Zhivago*. It was at last published in 1988.

In the United States in 1964, a Larchmont, New York, bookstore owner revealed that a man, who identified himself as a member of the John Birch Society, had telephoned to protest the great number of "subversive" books on the shelves. The titles identified were *Doctor Zhivago*, *Inside Russia Today* by John Gunther and *Das Kapital* by Karl Marx; he also mentioned a book by Nabokov and a Russian-English dictionary. He threatened that if these and other "un-American" books were not removed from view, the society would organize a boycott of the bookstore. The editor of the *Newsletter on Intellectual Freedom* advised the bookseller, "Don't take any guff from a self-appointed censor." Presumably, the bookstore owner did not.

Jonathon Green, under the heading "index of banned books," identifies *Doctor Zhivago* as one of the "most often" censored books.

FURTHER READINGS

Chalidze, Valery. *To Defend These Rights: Human Rights and the Soviet Union*. New York: Random House, 1974.

Conquest, Robert. *The Pasternak Affair: Courage of Genius*. Philadelphia: J.B. Lippincott Company, 1962.

Haight, Anne Lyon, and Chandler B. Grannis. *Banned Books: 387 B.C. to 1978 A.D.* 4th ed. New York: R.R. Bowker Company, 1978.

Newsletter on Intellectual Freedom 13 (1964): 81; 35 (1986): 196 97, 36 (1987): 72.

Payne, Robert. *The Three Worlds of Boris Pasternak*. Bloomington: Indiana University Press, 1961.

Rowland Mary F., and Paul Rowland. *Pasternak's Doctor Zhivago*. Carbondale: Southern Illinois University Press, 1967.

Salisbury, Harrison E. "Triumph of Boris Pasternak." *Saturday Review* 41 (November 8, 1958): 22.

Simmons, Ernest J. "Russia from Within." *The Atlantic Monthly* 202 (September 1958): 67–68, 72.

THE GRAPES OF WRATH

Author: John Steinbeck
Original date and place of publication: 1939, United States
Publisher: The Viking Press
Literary form: Novel

SUMMARY

Set during the Great Depression in Oklahoma and California—the dust bowl and the verdant promised land—and the long road in between, *The Grapes of*

Wrath expresses the travail of the Joad family in their journey to find a place for themselves. The dust claimed the land and destroyed their crops year after year; the people living on it are stranded. Hope, generated by handbills proclaiming the job opportunities in California and emblazoned by images of verdant and fruited lands, lures the divested westward.

The Joad family is one of thousands of the dispossessed. They take to the road in a decrepit car turned into a truck with a precariously low supply of money. They number 12, in addition to Casy, a former preacher, who joins them. Chief among them are Ma and Pa; Tom, just released on parole from prison, where he'd served time for murdering a man who had knifed him; 16-year-old Al, who is a capable driver and mechanic; and Rose of Sharon, who is pregnant.

The journey from Oklahoma is hazardous. Reminiscent of pioneer westbound travelers, they face problems of supplies and water, transportation and challenging landscape. Not unexpectedly, the car breaks down; tires give out. Al's alertness and skill, with help from Tom, salvage these exigent situations before disaster strikes. Their meager savings dwindle—gas, car repairs, food—so diet and health suffer. However, the Joads do make it.

Unfortunately, Grandpa Joad dies at the first encampment, and his wife, in a state of emotional collapse and physical exhaustion, dies while crossing the desert. The eldest son, Noah, decides to leave the family when they arrive in Needles, California; he is captivated by its river. Rose of Sharon's husband abandons her and the family when he realizes he will not have easy access to a job and personal advancement that he had expected. At the end of the novel, Rose of Sharon delivers a stillborn, apparently malnourished baby.

The promise of California proves to be barren. Before the journey, Ma Joad had said apprehensively, "I hope things is all right in California," and there are forewarnings along the way from returning emigrants that the handbill advertisements are a false lure, that the land is pretty but unavailable. There are two deceits: the jobs and the welcome. The handbills have lured thousands of workers for relatively few seasonal jobs. The Joads learn the script quickly. Out of food and money, they accept the first available work, picking peaches for five cents a box. They're ushered into the ranch area by police on motorcycles through throngs of striking men. They, too, had been offered five cents a box.

> "Lookie, Tom," [Casy] said at last. "We come to work, there. They says it's gonna be fi'cents. They was a hell of a lot of us. We got there an' they says they're payin' two an' a half cents. A fella can't even eat on that, an' if he got kids—So we says we won't take it. So they druv us off. An' all the cops in the worl' come down on us. Now they're payin' you five. When they bust this here strike—ya think they'll pay five? . . . We tried to camp together, an' they druv us like pigs. Scattered us. Beat the hell outa fellas . . . We can't las' much longer. Some people ain't et for two days. . . ."

The Joads and others hired with them are paid as promised, but as soon as the strike is broken, the wage is reduced to two and a half cents a box.

The living conditions add to the migrants' misery and dehumanization. Instead of the neat white house that Ma Joad and Rose of Sharon dream of, they find "Hooverville" [a reference to President Hoover's failed aid program] camps, a collection of some 40 tents and shacks: "The rag town lay close to water; and the houses were tents, and weed-thatched enclosures, paper houses, a great junk pile." These are scattered randomly, some neatly maintained, others surrounded by the debris of travel. Sanitary facilities do not exist, nor are there hot water and any other amenities.

The rare alternative is Weedpatch, the camp established by the government. Limited in the number of families it can house, it is a cooperative enterprise, operated and maintained by its residents, who establish its rules of order, conduct and cleanliness through elected committees. The camp provides sanitary facilities—toilets, showers and sinks, clothes-washing basins and other amenities such as wood for fires. Equally meaningful to the Joads, who find space in the camp for a time, are the community relationships and support, the sense of being treated as human beings, the unity and mutual protectiveness.

The government camp is perceived by the landowners as a "red threat" [a reflection of the fear of socialism] to the status quo they wish to maintain. When Tom Joad asks about the availability of hot water at the peach ranch camp, he is treated contemptuously. A guard remarks,

> "Hot water, for Christ's sake. Be wantin' tubs next." He stared glumly after the four Joads.
>
> . . ."It's them gov'ment camps," he said. "I bet that fella been in a gov'ment camp. We ain't gonna have no peace till we wipe them camps out. They'll be wantin' clean sheets, first thing we know."

While the Joads are at the government camp, the local landowners and police indeed attempt to instigate a fight within the campgrounds to give them an excuse to send in a riot squad to destroy it.

The physical miseries are compounded by the attitude reflected in the hiring policies and the actions taken by police. The migrants are bullied and beaten, charged and jailed as vagrants for any resistance, even verbal. One "vagrant," who complains about the dishonest promises of pay rates, is labeled a "red": "He's talkin' red, agitating trouble." Other migrants are warned: "You fellas don't want to listen to these goddamn reds. Troublemakers. . . ." Hooverville communities are burned as well for such small infractions. The people themselves are judged by their surface condition: their poverty and hunger, their grime and tatters. They are condescendingly called "Okies": "Well, Okie use' ta mean you was from Oklahoma. Now it means you're a dirty son-of-a bitch. Okie means you're scum. Don't mean nother itself, it's the way they say it."

Two interlocking strands reveal aspects of the political-philosophic underpinnings of the novel. One strand signals the destruction of the family farm and the farmer; the second focuses on the tractor and other machinery that displace men and their animals, making them extraneous.

The family farm and farmer are victims of owners and banks, of companies with extensive acreage. In Oklahoma, when crops fail again and again, the owners, the Company, the Bank moved in. Eventually, the farmer is forced from the land. But the owners go one step further: "One man on a tractor can take the place of twelve or fourteen families." The tractor destroys the concept of the family farm and the farm itself: keeping "the line straight," it drives through the dooryard, turns over buildings, tramples fences. The novel frequently refers to the farmers being "tractored off."

In California, the operation is essentially the same. The great owners and companies dominate: they control the land. The small landowner is pressured into line by the Farmers Association run by the Bank, which "owns most of this valley, and it's got paper on everything it don't own." They set the low wages and the cutthroat policies. Since this isn't enough to satiate their greed, a great owner buys a cannery, then sells the fruit to the cannery at a low price and the canned goods to consumers at a high price, ensuring a profit. The little farmer is squeezed out of business.

In direct contrast, the sharing ethic is evidenced among the migrants. From the outset when the Joads graciously welcome Casy as a travel companion despite the overcrowded vehicle, to the closing scene when Rose of Sharon readily nurses the starving man discovered in the barn, there is consistent expression of the need to help and to accept help without becoming a burden. Ma crystallizes the ethic and the contrast: "I'm learnin' one thing good. . . . Learnin' it all a time, ever' day. If you're in trouble or hurt or need—go to poor people. They're the only ones that'll help—the only ones."

Two opposing forces converge to climax the action and issues of the novel. The men, hungering for work until they are hired to pick peaches or cotton, wonder how they'll manage when all the picking seasons are over. "Fella had a team of horses, had to use 'em to plow an' cultivate an' mow, wouldn' think a turnin' 'em out to starve when they wasn't workin'." The deprivation and desperation of the migrants brings them together; they begin to unite to create a solid front, culminating in a spontaneous strike. The owners, feeling the status quo threatened by the "reds" and needing to maintain control against a perceived insurrection, develop a counterforce of the police and citizen. The latter themselves feel threatened in their status and livelihood.

The clash of forces at the strike leads to Casy's death—he's the strike leader—and Tom's becoming a wanted man for battering Casy's murderer. While in hiding, Tom determines his future role: to take on Casy's mission, to unite his people, to help them to achieve their goal—"to live decent and bring up their kids decent."

> "I been thinkin' a hell of a lot, thinkin' about our people livin' like pigs, an' the good rich lan' layin' fallow, or maybe one fella with a million acres, while a hundred thousan' good farmers is starvin'. An' I been wonderin' if all our folks got together an' yelled, like them fellas yelled, only a few of 'em at the Hooper ranch—"

In the concluding chapters, the Joads, having helped Tom escape, are trapped by a flood, unable to leave their boxcar "home" because Rose of Sharon is delivering her stillborn child. When the birthing is over and the floodwaters have receded slightly, the three remaining adults carry Rose of Sharon and the two children through the chest-deep waters to higher ground where they find refuge in a barn. It is occupied, they discover, by a boy and his starving father; he had given all their food to his son. The Joads have found a temporary haven. Like their pioneer forebears, however, they have not found the promised land of opportunity.

CENSORSHIP HISTORY

The Grapes of Wrath faced censorship challenges within months after it was published, April 1939, and fairly consistently over the years to the present. National, regional and state surveys attest to this, as well as to the novel's rating among the "most frequently" challenged books. Lee Burress in his five national surveys of librarians or schoolteachers/administrators reports multiple cases: 1966—five challenges (tied for fourth most frequently); 1973—four (tied for third); 1977—eight (second place); 1982—six (tied for sixth); 1988—two challenges. Surveys conducted by James Davis in Ohio (1982) and Kenneth Donelson in Arizona (1967) identify challenges as do those of Georgia (1982, 1984), North Carolina (1983), Minnesota (1991) and People for the American Way (1992). (Other titles reported by Burress among the top 25 most censored and included in this volume are *1984*, *SLAUGHTERHOUSE-FIVE*, *BLACK LIKE ME* and *JOHNNY GOT HIS GUN*.)

Specifically documented attacks on the novel in its first year occurred in widely separate parts of the country: Kansas City, Kansas, where the board of education on August 18, 1939, voted 4–2 to order copies of the novel removed from the 20 public libraries for reasons of indecency, obscenity, abhorrence of the portrayal of women and for "portray[ing] life in such a bestial way"; Buffalo, New York, where Alexander Galt, head librarian of the city libraries, barred it from being purchased because of its "vulgar words"; Kern County, California, where the county board of supervisors, voting 4–1 on August 21, 1939, "requested that the use, possession, and circulation of [the novel] be banned from the county's libraries and schools"; East St. Louis, Illinois, where five of nine library board members voted unanimously on

November 15, 1939, to have three copies of the book burned on the courtyard steps (within a week, by a 6–2 vote, the board rescinded its burning order in response to the "national commotion it had aroused"; it placed the three copies on the "Adults Only" shelf); Greene County, Ohio, where in late November the library board members voted 4–3 to ban the novel as "unsuitable" for circulation among its patrons; and the U.S.S. *Tennessee*, where the chaplain removed it from the ship's library.

These challenges occurred as *The Grapes of Wrath* was becoming a best-seller: 360,000 copies were in print, including a new printing of 50,000. The East St. Louis burning order occurred in 1939 during the week the novel had its largest sales order to date, 11,340 copies. A record 430,000 copies were sold by the end of the year. The East St. Louis librarian indicated that the waiting list for the novel was the largest of any book in recent years; a Greene County librarian noted that her library's five copies had been on reserve since it came out, the waiting list of 62 names in November stretching to March; there were 50 men on the waiting list of the U.S.S. *Tennessee*. In Kern County, with 60 books in circulation at the time of the ban, 112 persons were on the several waiting lists.

Kern County, California

Of these challenges, the Kern County, California, event was the most organized in its opposition. Kern County is in the center of the agricultural region featured in *The Grapes of Wrath*. Though there had not been any registered complaints at the local libraries nor any articles or editorials debating the merits of the book, the board of supervisors—which also had not previously discussed the issue—passed the banning resolution proposed by Supervisor Stanley Abel on August 21, 1939. It read in part: "*The Grapes of Wrath* has offended our citizenry by falsely implying that many of our fine people are a low, ignorant, profane and blasphemous type living in a vicious, filthy manner." Another section objected to Steinbeck's choosing to ignore the education, recreation, hospitalization, welfare and relief services made available by Kern County. In addition to the banning of the book from the county libraries and schools, the resolution requested that Twentieth Century-Fox Film Corporation not complete its motion picture adaptation that was then in production. County Librarian Gretchen Knief wrote immediately to Supervisor Abel. An excerpt follows:

> If that book is banned today, what book will be banned tomorrow? And what group will want a book banned the day after that? It's such a vicious and dangerous thing to begin and may in the end lead to exactly the same thing we see in Europe today.
>
> Besides, banning books is so utterly hopeless and futile. Ideas don't die because a book is forbidden reading. If Steinbeck has written truth, that truth will survive. If he is merely being sensational and lascivious, if all the "little words"

are really no more than fly specks on a large painting, then the book will soon go the way of all other modern novels and be forgotten.

The offended citizens appear to have been the Associated Farmers of Kern County. Led by its president, Wofford B. Camp, a prominent rancher, it had sent a telegram of praise to Kansas City. Camp called Steinbeck's novel "propaganda of the vilest sort" and claimed, "We are defending our farm workers as well as ourselves when we take action against that book." Camp and two other men "ceremoniously burned" a copy of the book; a photograph of this act appeared in *Look* magazine.

The Associated Farmers group also organized a statewide action plan to suppress the book, to "remove the 'smear' to the good name of Kern, the state of California and agriculture." They urged all organizations in the San Joaquin Valley to approve a measure comparable to that of Kern County. Camp declared:

> We are angry, not because we were attacked but because we were attacked by a book obscene in the extreme sense of the word and because our workers with whom we have lived and worked for years are pictured as the lowest type of human life when we know that is not true.

> You can't argue with a book like that, it is too filthy for you to go over the various parts and point out the vile propaganda it contains. Americans have a right to say what they please but they do not have the right to attack a community in such words that any red-blooded American man would refuse to allow his daughter to read them.

Established in 1933 through the joint efforts of the California Farm Bureau Federation and the state Chamber of Commerce with the financial backing of the Canners League and large landholders, the Associated Farmers' original purpose was to organize local citizen committees to pass anti-picketing regulations so as to derail farm workers' strikes and unionizing activities; strikebreaking efforts were a second phase of the organization's purposes.

During the ensuing week the battle lines were drawn. Supported, perhaps, by a series of articles and editorials that had appeared early in August in the *Bakersfield Californian*, which noted the irreconcilability between Steinbeck's fiction and the facts of assistance to migrants, adherents argued for even stronger action than a ban. Pro-America, a national women's organization, which was meeting in San Francisco, denounced the book as a "lie promoting class hatred" and indicated that the "farmworkers of California are better paid and better housed than agriculture workers anywhere else in the world."

Denunciations of the banning by the American Civil Liberties Union were joined by protests of several local unions—Oil Workers Union, Hod Carriers Union, Butchers Union and the Brotherhood of Engineers—and the Workers Alliance, an organization of relief recipients, as well as library clients. The debate centered on the abridgement of constitutional rights; it also included discussion of the ethics of the supervisors' action and their "hidden motivation," that is, the influence of the Associated Farmers of Kern County.

Editorials and articles in newspapers throughout the Central Valley were highly critical of the censorship. In response to the endorsement of the banning by Pro-America, the *Selma Irrigator* editorialized about the politics of special interest groups:

> As for the meeting in San Francisco at which Mr. Steinbeck's book was denounced, wasn't it significant that the men and women who have read the book but don't want others to read it assembled in one of San Francisco's most luxurious hotels far from the San Joaquin cotton fields.

John Raymond Locke of the *Dinuba Sentinel* wrote:

> It is absolutely foolish to try and deny the conditions pictured, whether of the Dust Bowl West or of our own California. Here in our own state most of the pioneers have been "run off" the land they brought into bearing. Look over files of the *Sentinel* for the past 20 years and see the hundreds that have been foreclosed.

The board of supervisors' meeting on August 28 was crowded. Pickets carried banners urging the rescinding of the ban in front of the courthouse meeting room. The discussion was heated and lasted an entire day. R. W. Henderson of the ACLU argued that book censorship "could lead to partisan coloration of the library's contents"; Reverend Edgar J. Evans, in reaction to a supervisor's claim, after citing selected passages, that the "book was lewd," questioned whether it was language that was objected to, suggesting that instead it was "the exposure of a sociological condition." Supervisor Stanley Abel, the resolution's sponsor, admitted that the local Chamber of Commerce secretary had written the resolution. He pursued the morality issue for the most part, but at one point claimed that he was trying to bring national attention to the migrant workers in hopes of improving their lot. Despite the efforts of anti-ban partisans, the vote to rescind failed on a 2–2 vote, the chairperson being absent on vacation.

Some attempts to have the ban lifted were made at the following meetings of the board, but no action was taken until January 27, 1941, when such a vote did succeed. The books were returned to the Kern County library shelves. In the 1940 November election, Stanley Abel had been defeated.

1970s

In April 1972, in Herman, New York, a petition from 100 residents, led by Rev. Barber, argued for the removal from the library and curriculum of books "containing profanity or descriptions of a sexual nature which arouse sexual desire" or those with "references and dialog that condone immorality or references that promote disrespect or defiance of parental or other constituted authority." Among the 10 books identified were three by Steinbeck—*The*

Grapes of Wrath, OF MICE AND MEN and *In Dubious Battle*—as well as THE CATCHER IN THE RYE by J. D. Salinger and TO KILL A MOCKINGBIRD by Harper Lee. Three committees were established, one to re-evaluate the named books and one each to evaluate the high school and elementary school collections. In Richlands, Virginia, representatives of 17 churches complained in February 1973 about *The Grapes of Wrath* being in the Richland High School library; they characterized it as "pornographic, filthy, and dirty." In Buncombe, North Carolina, two challenges were issued, the first in the fall of 1973, the second in February 1981. The complaints: passages were objectionable to parents; the book was morally [in]decent to the community. The books in both cases were *The Grapes of Wrath*, *The Catcher in the Rye* and ANDERSONVILLE by MacKinlay Kantor; Steinbeck's *Of Mice and Men*, Eldridge Cleaver's *Soul on Ice* and Gordon Parks's *The Learning Tree* were also included the first time. The board of education rejected the resolution, reaffirming its "Policies for Selection," in both instances. (See Censorship History for ANDERSONVILLE.) In Scituate, Rhode Island, in June 1975, after they had been denied their request to censor *The Grapes of Wrath* (and *Of Mice and Men*, *The Catcher in the Rye*, *Lord of the Flies* by William Golding, *The Art of Loving* by Erich Fromm and *Listen to the Silence* by David Elliott) a group of ministers and other citizens protested by distributing leaflets with excerpts that would have "caused the devil to blush." Farmville, North Carolina, in 1977 established written guidelines for the classroom and library use of books like *The Grapes of Wrath*, *The Catcher in the Rye* and *Of Mice and Men*. They were placed on restricted shelves, available only with written parental permission.

Kanawha, Iowa

The challenge to *The Grapes of Wrath* in Kanawha on February 11, 1980, emerged as a language issue. Marvin E. Stupka, the vice president of the bank and father of a tenth grader, read the first 11 pages of the novel assigned to his son's English class and "became incensed with the book's language." He concluded after reading "scattered portions" that the book is "profane, vulgar and obscene" because "it takes the Lord's name in vain dozens of times" and features a preacher who is an immoral hypocrite. He and others complained to Superintendent Leroy Scharnhorst, who ordered the books collected and stored until the school board could decide the issue. At its February 11 meeting, the board voted 5–0 to permanently remove the books from two sophomore English classes. Teachers could not require it, but might recommend it to their students; copies of the novel would remain in the school library.

While none of the parents told school officials they objected to the novel's message, School Board President Wayne Rietema commented that the United States was "going pell mell downhill" morally and the Kanawha community had a chance to act and reverse that trend by banning the book from the classes. "This is the backbone of America—the small town." He added, "We do not intend to become a censoring committee," but he urged nevertheless that the board act to control the book. The attempt of one reporter to interview residents of Kanawha found them reluctant to be quoted, some out of fear of reprisals. However, letters and commentary in the Des Moines *Register* were entirely critical of the school board's action. One predictable result was that *The Grapes of Wrath* became a best-seller in surrounding communities' bookstores and libraries; the Kanawha Public Library borrowed a dozen copies to supplement its own single volume so as to meet reader demand.

In his discussion/analysis of the censoring of *The Grapes of Wrath*, Lee Burress points to the coincidence that in this instance a banker in Iowa should attack the novel for its language, ignoring the Jeffersonian agrarianism that permeates the book and Steinbeck's "charge that capital [of banks] is used to buy big tractors and drive the farmers off the land." He further notes:

> It is an interesting coincidence that approximately at the same time the book was removed from use in the English class at Kanawha, the Sioux City Diocese of the Roman Catholic Church issued a report concerning land ownership patterns in Iowa after two years of study. The report stated that in the 14 northwestern counties of Iowa, 77% of the land was owned by absentee owners.

Vernon, New York
Censorship of seven books from reading lists for junior and senior high students was demanded by Rev. Carl Hodley in February 1980. He labeled them "filthy, trashy sex novels." In addition to *The Grapes of Wrath*, his list included *Of Mice and Men* and *The Red Pony* by John Steinbeck, *A Separate Peace* by John Knowles, *It's Not the End of the World* by Judy Blume, *To Kill a Mockingbird* by Harper Lee and *A Farewell to Arms* by Ernest Hemingway. The Vernon-Verona-Sherill school district refused to adhere to his request.

Buncombe County, North Carolina
The Grapes of Wrath was among the books challenged by a group led by several fundamentalist ministers. This censorship history is detailed in the discussion of *ANDERSONVILLE*.

Richford, Vermont
In early fall 1981, five parents, led by Claire Doe, complaining *The Grapes of Wrath* contained immoral and offensive material, requested the book be banned from the high school library and dropped from the junior year American literature class. Objections centered on the image of the former minister, who describes how he used to "take advantage" of young women when he was a preacher, and on "the Lord's name being taken in vain." Doe, whose 16-year-old son was in the class, said that it was a good book for adults but not for children.

Following the school district's procedures, Superintendent Forest Farnum appointed a nine-member committee, made up of teachers, parents and church leaders, to study the book. Its chairperson, Edward Wilkins, an elementary school principal from a neighboring town, advised the members to consider historical value, literary merit and religious symbolism. The committee heard the objections of Doe's group and reactions of some 25 parents who supported the book. The committee recommended to the school board that Steinbeck's novel be retained for classroom and library use without restrictions. The school board concurred.

> Carroll Hull, principal of Richford High School, said, "The decision reaffirms our right to require what we feel is necessary for a child's education. . . . In some cases, we allow students an alternative if the parents object to the material. But some works, like *The Grapes of Wrath*, we consider essential."

Barry Steinhardt, executive director of the ACLU in Vermont, had indicated that legal action would be taken if the book was banned.

Anniston, Alabama

In the fall of 1982, a group of about 50 ministers together with church members, representing the "Moral Majority," a fundamentalist conservative faction, targeted seven school library books, including *The Grapes of Wrath*, for removal. They labeled the books "ungodly" and "obscene" and circulated petitions to be presented to the Calhoun County Board of Education on October 18. They also planned to ask permission to form a church-assigned committee to review books on the library shelves as well as new selections. The other books were *Doris Day: Her Own Story*, Steinbeck's *East of Eden*, J. D. Salinger's *The Catcher in the Rye*, Anthony Burgess's *A CLOCKWORK ORANGE*, Barbara Beasley Murphy's *No Place to Run* and Frances Hanckel and John Cunningham's *The Way of Love*.

Before the school board met to hear the request, two principals ordered the removal of books. Principal Grover Whaley, of Alexandria High School, caused Steinbeck's books to be withdrawn because of some language in *Of Mice and Men* he found to be vulgar and profane; he had not been contacted by the ministers but had talked with one parent who disapproved of the book. He had received a few telephone calls protesting his action. Principal Wayne Wigley removed *Doris Day: Her Own Story* from the Pleasant Valley High School library upon a parent's complaint.

On a unanimous vote on November 16, the board of education returned all of the books to the library shelves but on a restricted basis. A 10-person committee consisting of Calhoun County Superintendent Dan Henderson and school representatives so recommended after being advised by the board's counsel, H. R. Burnham, that comparable attempts to censor school library books around the country had failed in the courts. The ministers' request to screen library books was also rejected. Alternatively, a five-person committee to include a school administrator, teacher, librarian and two parents was to be appointed at each county school to select and screen books, undertaking the function of the school's librarians.

Burlington, North Carolina

"The book is full of filth. My son is being raised in a Christian home and this book takes the Lord's name in vain and has all kinds of profanity in it," complained Robert Wagner in March 1986. Though not formalized, his complaint about his son's 11th-grade literature class reading led to the assignment of an alternative text.

Carthage, North Carolina

A similar but formalized complaint about the use of the book in an 11th-grade class at Pinecrest High School by Marie Mofield on August 5, 1986, led the Moore County school system to appoint a study committee to evaluate whether *The Grapes of Wrath* should be required reading or banned per her request. The committee, led by Peggy Olney, the head librarian, met with Mofield, who subsequently withdrew her banning request, being satisfied that her 11th-grade child would not be required to read it.

Greenville, South Carolina

The purpose for the January 29, 1991, petition signed by 864 people and submitted to the Greenville County school board was the removal of five books from the approved reading list. The basis: They used the name of God and Jesus in a "vain and profane manner along with inappropriate sexual references." The school district's materials review committee had already approved the books' retention on the reading list; however, the instruction committee of the school board voted to conduct its own review. In addition to *The Grapes of Wrath*, the books objected to were *Second Heaven* by Judith Guest, *My Brother Sam Is Dead* by James L. Collier and Christopher Collier, *The Water Is Wide* by Pat Conroy and *East of Eden* by John Steinbeck.

The argument was joined at a second board meeting with 13 speakers supporting the books, asserting, "It is vital that along with American pride, we have humility and show all aspects of American life"; and one speaker favoring the ban because "Under the definitions you have given tonight, we would have to approve *Playboy* and *Hustler*, too." At a third meeting on April 9, the school board affirmed by a 4–2 vote the district policy that allowed administration-appointed panels to review books about which parents raise concerns. The policy also authorized the parental option of refusing to have their children read a given book. A proposal from a school board trustee to provide reading lists with potentially offensive books identified was labeled as censorship by Pat Scales, a librarian:

> "[I]f the district does that, it might as well remove the books. Labeling books
> in any way is censorship. I do in my heart believe parents should be able to
> select reading material for their children. But our calling attention to [the fact
> the book may offend some] relieves them of that responsibility."

Union City, Tennessee

A somewhat more complex controversy emerged from Bobby Pegg's December 1993 objection to his daughter's 11th-grade advanced placement English class assignment of *The Grapes of Wrath*. His formal request of the Union City school board was for an alternative selection for his daughter without penalty to her grade. His claim: "Reading this book is against my daughter's religious beliefs." His request led to parental voices of support for the class and the book as well as parental opposition to the book; the latter individuals called for the book's being "outlawed and banned," citing "offensive and vulgar material" and language as being inappropriate for high school students. An eight-member ad hoc review committee denied Pegg's basic request for an alternative book assignment; the school board heard his appeal on January 10, 1994. The committee reviewed the book on specific criteria, including its appropriateness, content and authenticity. Pegg had itemized the number of offensive passages: God's name taken in vain—129 times; vulgar language—264 times; and references to sex—31 times. After a two-hour debate the school board voted unanimously in support of the committee's recommendation of maintaining the reading list for the AP English class, which was not a required class. In opposition to the "moral consciousness of the student" and alternative-selection arguments, proponents of the book argued for the maintenance of standards of the AP national course requirements and resisting exceptions, reasoning that one would potentially lead to many. A selected spokesperson, Glenda Candle, said:

> There were books that could be deemed offensive by spokesmen for any number of religious, political, sexual and racial agenda. But does that capacity to offend mean these books should be ignored for their ultimate value and thus removed from the list of required reading? . . . I must respectfully suggest that if she wishes to continue as a student in the AP English program, she should be required to complete the work as assigned by her teacher.

FURTHER READINGS

"Anniston Coalition Targets 'Obscenity'." *Tuscaloosa News* (October 9, 1982): [n.p.].

Bixler, Paul. "Book Banned by Greene County Libraries, Is Offered to Public by Antioch College." *The Steinbeck Newsletter* (Winter 1993): 10–11.

Bowden, Kevin. "Community Split on Steinbeck Novel." *Union City Daily Messenger* (December 13, 1993): 1, 2.

———. "Request For Alternate Book Denied." *Union City Daily Messenger* (January 11, 1995): 1, 2.

Burress, Lee. "*The Grapes of Wrath*: Preserving Its Place in the Curriculum." In *Censored Books: Critical Viewpoints*. Ed. Nicholas J. Karolides, Lee Burress and John M. Kean. Metuchen, N.J.: Scarecrow Press, 1993. 278–87.

Cowperthwait, Richard, and Alan Abbey. "Richford Parents Fermenting Over *Grapes of Wrath*." *Burlington Free Press* (November 11, 1981): 1–2B.

"Fifty Years of *Wrath*." *Newsletter on Intellectual Freedom* 38 (1989): 121–23.

Gehrke, Donna. "Kanawha Bans Classic Book from Classes." *Des Moines Register* (February 12, 1980): 1A.

———. "School Board May Ban *Grapes of Wrath*." *Des Moines Register* (February 10, 1980): 1B.

Hollobaugh, Dix. "The Wrath of Kanawha." *Des Moines Sunday Register* (February 24, 1980): 1A, 5A.

Jarvis, Richard. "Let Parents See Reading Lists, Trustee to Urge." *Greenville Piedmont* (April 10, 1991): 3.

Kappel, Tim. "Trampling Out the Vineyards—Kern County's Ban on *The Grapes of Wrath*." *California History* (Fall 1982): 210–21.

Karolides, Nicholas J., and Lee Burress, eds. *Celebrating Censored Books*. Racine, Wisc.: Wisconsin Council of Teachers of English, 1985.

"K.C. Libraries Ban *Grapes of Wrath*." *The Bakersfield Californian* (August 18, 1939): [n.p.].

May, Lucy. "Group Wants Five Books Off Schools List." *Greenville News* (January 30, 1991): 1C.

———. "Proposal to Ban Some Books Draws Crowds to Board Meeting." *Greenville News* (March 13, 1991): 2.

———. "School Board Affirms Policy Allowing Panel to OK Books." *Greenville News* (April 10, 1991): 2.

McVicar, D. Morgan. "Disputed Books Go to Reserve Shelves." *Anniston Star* (November 17, 1982): 1, 5A.

Mutter, John. "*Grapes of Wrath* Survives Banning Attempt in Vermont Town." *Publishers Weekly* 220 (December 11, 1981): 9.

Newsletter on Intellectual Freedom 21 (1972): 103–04; 22 (1973): 88, 146; 24 (1975): 139; 30 (1981): 74; 31 (1982): 18, 58, 59–60; 32 (1983): 7, 37; 35 (1986): 210; and 36 (1987): 32–33.

Rintoul, William T. "The Banning of *The Grapes of Wrath*." *California Crossroads* (January 1963): 4–6.

———. The Banning of *The Grapes of Wrath*. *California Crossroads* (February 1963): 26–28.

Roos, Jonathan. "Kanawha's Ban Turns Novel Into Best-seller." *Des Moines Register* (March 6, 1980): 1A, 4A.

"Support of *Grapes* Ban Is Urged by Farmers Group." *The Bakersfield Californian* (August 22, 1939): [n.p.].

Tebbel, John. *A History of Book Publishing in the United States*, Vol. III. New York: R.R. Bowker Company, 1978.

Veon, R. J. Kern County Clerk and Clerk of the Board. Letter to Gretchen D. Knief, County Librarian. January 27, 1941.

THE GULAG ARCHIPELAGO 1918–1956
An Experiment in Literary Investigation

Author: Aleksandr Solzhenitsyn
Original dates and place of publication: 1973–1974, France; Volume I–1974, Volume II–1975, Volume III–1978, United States

Publisher: YMCA Press; Harper & Row
Literary form: Nonfiction

SUMMARY

Aleksandr Solzhenitsyn's purpose in his three volumes of *The Gulag Archipelago* is to document and reveal a great holocaust in the Soviet Union—exceeding that of Germany against the Jews and others during World War II. Tens of millions of Soviet citizens were imprisoned, savagely mistreated and often murdered by their own government. The "archipelago" of the title refers to the forced-labor camps, "thousands of islands," scattered across the country geographically "from the Bering Strait almost to the Bosporus" but "in the psychological sense, fused into a continent—an almost invisible, almost imperceptible country inhabited by the zek people [prisoners]." "Gulag," an acronym, designates the Soviet penal system. Solzhenitsyn uses the background of his own prison experiences from 1945 to 1953; these are supplemented with reports by, memoirs of and letters by 227 other eyewitnesses.

An early chapter in Volume I, "The History of Our Sewage Disposal System," establishes the origins and continuity of government repression from 1917 to 1956, in effect rejecting the Soviet government's acknowledged purges during Stalin's regime as being limited in time and scope. The text otherwise provides an internal structure from scenes of arrest to confinement and interrogation, then to first cell. Subsequently, the reader travels cross-country with the prisoner to the "ports," the prisons of the archipelago. The destinations are forced labor camps. Each chapter is illustrated with the experiences of individual prisoners, thus providing verifying detail. Another quartet of chapters expresses the shift in the Soviet government's laws and "justice"—attitudes and procedures, including the initial rejection of capital punishment to its massive, seemingly capricious utilization.

A significant assertion is that the arrests and imprisonments did not begin and end with the three biggest "waves" of repression. Of these the acknowledged purges in 1937 and 1938 of "people of position, people with a Party past, educated people" were not the main wave, nor were they accurately represented. Assurances that the arrests were chiefly of communist leaders are not supported by the fact that about 90 percent of the "millions arrested" were outside this circle. "The real law underlying the arrests of those years was *the assignment of quotas* . . . to every city, every district, every military unit. . . ." Before this, the wave of 1929 and 1930 "drove a mere fifteen million peasants, maybe more, out into the taiga and the tundra" and afterward the wave of 1944 to 1946 "dumped whole *nations* down the sewer pipes, not to mention millions and millions of others who . . . had been prisoners of war, or carried off to Germany and subsequently repatriated."

The chronology of purges begins with V. I. Lenin's edict in late 1917 and connects with those of Stalin, who refined and enlarged Lenin's tactics. Arrests encompassed a broad segment of the populace: tens of thousands of hostages; peasants revolting against the taking of their harvests without compensation; students for "criticism of the system"; religious practitioners and believers who were "arrested uninterruptedly"; workers who had not met quotas; and nationalist groups in central Asia. Soviet soldiers who had been prisoners of war were also arrested and sent to labor camps, even those who had escaped and joined the resistance forces.

> It would appear that during the one thousand one hundred years of Russia's existence as a state there have been, ah, how many foul and terrible deeds! But among them was there ever so multimillioned foul a deed as this: to betray one's own soldiers and proclaim them traitors?

The presumption was that the soldiers had become traitors or had "acquired a very harmful spirit living freely among Europeans."

The Criminal Code of 1926, specifically Article 58, defined the crimes against the state. Operative for many years, the code's basic tenet was that any action—or any absence of action—directed toward the weakening of state power was considered to be counterrevolutionary. Along with armed rebellion, espionage and suspicion of espionage or unproven espionage, the list of criminal activities included subversion of industry, transport and trade; propaganda or agitation containing an appeal, including face-to-face conversation between friends and spouses, private letters and preparation of literary materials; failure to make a denunciation of any action and conscious failure to carry out defined duties or intentionally careless execution of them.

The charges against victims were unanswerable. Indeed, "interrogations under Article 58 were *almost never* undertaken to elicit the truth" but rather to induce a confession to an alleged crime or to draw the individual into statements that could be interpreted as self-incriminating. The burden of proof of innocence was upon the victims, who were given little opportunity to provide proof, nor were they apprised of their rights. Interrogation by torture was practiced:

> . . . that prisoners would have their skulls squeezed within iron rings; that a human being would be lowered into an acid bath; that they would be trussed up naked to be bitten by ants and bedbugs; that a ramrod heated over a primus stove would be thrust up their anal canal (the "secret brand"); that a man's genitals would be slowly crushed beneath the toe of a jackboot; and that, in the luckiest possible circumstances, prisoners would be tortured by being kept from sleeping for a week, by thirst, and by being beaten to a bloody pulp. . . .

Psychological torture was also employed, including interrogations at night, foul language, intimidation accompanied by false promises, threatening harm to loved ones and being placed in a box without being informed of charges.

"The more fantastic the charges were, the more ferocious the interrogation had to be in order to force the required confession."

Once condemned, the prisoners' miseries continued on the transport railroad cars, cattle cars or barges. Subjected to severely overcrowded and underventilated conditions, at extreme temperatures and with insufficient food, they were brutalized by both the common criminals with whom they traveled and the guards.

A pervasive commentary of *Gulag Archipelago I* is of corruption not merely of top officials but of men and women at all levels of officialdom, who had been corrupted by power and, often, a justifiable fear that if they acted otherwise they would become victims. At base, Solzhenitsyn maintains that the destruction of millions of innocent people is derived from the Bolshevik revolution and the Soviet political system.

The author provides ironic counterpoints, such as the comparison of the Soviet and tsarist practices. For example, during a 30-year period of revolutionary agitation and terrorism from 1876 to 1904, executions were rare—17 people a year for the whole country. In contrast, during the 1937–38 wave, a half-million political prisoners and almost a half-million thieves were executed in a year and a half; another source cited for the period identifies the execution figure as 1.7 million. Another counterpoint: the direct victims in the Soviet Union number between 15 and 25 million people; those of Nazi Germany number between 10 and 12 million.

The brutality of life and death in the "destructive-labor camps," or slave labor camps, is the focus of Volume II. During Stalin's reign, 10 to 15 million men, women and children over age 12 were imprisoned in these "extermination factories" in any one year. Solzhenitsyn distinguishes between the prisons where a human being is able to confront "his grief face to face . . . to find space within himself for it" and the slave labor camps where survival, often at the expense of others, demanded every energy. The lives of the imprisoned consisted of "work, work, work; of starvation, cold, and cunning." Solzhenitsyn provides a brief capsule enumerating the range and types of work and expressing its exhausting, debilitating effects: back-breaking, hand-wearing labor with picks and shovels on the earth, in mines and quarries, in brickyards, tunnels and on farms (favored for the food to be grabbed from the ground); lumberjack work in the forests. The workday in the summer was "sometimes sixteen hours long." The hours were shortened during the winter, but workers were "chased out" to work in cold lower than 60 degrees below zero in order to "prove it was possible to fulfill" quotas.

> And how did they feed them in return? They poured water into a pot, and the best one might expect was that they would drop unscrubbed small potatoes into it, but otherwise black cabbage, beet tops, all kinds of trash. Or else vetch or bran, they didn't begrudge these.

In several chapters Solzhenitsyn scrutinizes the relationship between the penal system—the Gulag—and the Soviet economy "when the plan for super-industrialization was rejected in favor of the plan for supersupersuperindustrialization . . . with the massive public works of the First Five-Year Plan. . . ." Slave labor allowed Stalin to industrialize the nation cheaply. The laborers were expendable: The victims were sent to isolated regions and worked brutally without concern for their well-being and safety to construct railroads, canals, highways, hydroelectric stations and nine cities. The laborers were not paid: "[F]orced labor should be set up in such a way that the prisoner should not earn anything from his work but that the state should derive economic profit from it." This system was termed "correction through labor."

The system didn't work; corruption and thievery were rampant. Construction materials were stolen; machinery was damaged. The prisoners were not dutiful workers, nor did their weakened conditions make for efficient and effective work.

As with Volume I, examples of individuals caught in the mesh provide details to reveal the extent of villainy. A particularly affective chapter details the fate of children who are bereft as a result of the war or the imprisonment of their parents. They are swept up and sent away to be mistreated in colonies or workhouses. From the age of 12 they can be sentenced under the Criminal Code and end up in the Archipelago. "In 1927 prisoners aged sixteen (they didn't count the younger ones) to twenty-four represented 48 percent of all prisoners."

Solzhenitsyn enumerates and explains the "traits of *free* life," which were determined by the ever present threat of the Archipelago: constant fear—of arrest, purges, inspections, dismissal from work, deprivation of residence permit, expulsion or exile; servitude; secrecy and mistrust; universal ignorance; squealing; betrayal as a form of existence; corruption; the lie as a form of existence; and cruelty.

Volume III turns away from the brutality and suffering of slave labor to focus on resistance within the camps. In Part V, "Katorga" (hard labor), Solzhenitsyn recounts the attempted escapes by individuals and small groups. An extended pair of chapters explores the reactions and behaviors of "a *committed* escaper," one who "never for a minute doubts that a man cannot live behind bars." The exploits of this individual, who does successfully escape, but is recaptured because he refuses to kill innocent people, and the plans and procedures of others attest to the energy and determination of those who had not resigned themselves.

Particularly in the Special Camps, which had been established to separate the "socially irredeemable" political prisoners from the others, did the idea of rebellion begin to take shape and spread. Avengers emerged from the formed comradeships to murder informers. Though only a relatively few got the knife, the result was extensive: informers stopped informing, and the air was "cleansed of suspicion." Insurrections occurred with varying days and degrees of success; military power was used to quell the major revolts. In May 1954, the prisoners of Kengir gained control of the camp for 40 days. Without any outside support, having been encircled by troops and deceived by an announcement that their demands had been accepted, the prisoners were crushed, literally (by tanks) and politically. More than 700 were killed.

Exile or banishment—the Soviet euphemism was "deportation"—was another instrument of power borrowed from the tsars. The "export of undesirables" started shortly after the revolution; in 1929 a system of exile to remote localities in conjunction with forced labor was developed. The exile system grew steadily in capacity and importance in the World War II and postwar years, particularly from the "liberated" (occupied) territories and the western republics. The crimes for which a citizen was punished by exile or banishment included "belonging to a criminal nationality [including both whole nations and, as in the case of the Baltics, special categories of citizens]; a previous term of imprisonment in the camps [prisoners were "released into exile" in perpetuity]; and residence in a criminal environment." All these deportations, "even without the exiled peasants, exceeded many times over the figure of 500,000 exiles which was all that Tsarist Russia, the prison house of nations, could muster in the whole course of the nineteenth century."

With Stalin's death there came a political thaw and some reprieve for the prisoners. Indeed, many were released. However, Solzhenitsyn points out that in the 40 pre-Khrushchev years, release meant "the space between two arrests." Even when the prisoner was rehabilitated, after being found to be falsely accused, the villains escaped judgment and punishment. Equally profound is the recognition that the camps, approved by the party, continued to exist; there are "still millions inside, and just as before, many of them are helpless victims of perverted justice: swept in simply to keep the system operating and well fed."

Solzhenitsyn specifically reveals his own error, the degree to which he had been deceived. He had let himself be persuaded by the state's authorization to publish *One Day in the Life of Ivan Denisovich* and by the "complacent mainland" that the relaxation was real. He writes, "But I (even I) succumbed and I do not deserve forgiveness."

CENSORSHIP HISTORY

Solzhenitsyn's works were barred from publication in the Soviet Union after Nikita Khrushchev lost power in 1964; previously under the Khrushchev regime, *One Day in the Life of Ivan Denisovich* had been approved for publication. J. M. Coetzee cites Dina Spechler's analysis of "permitted dissent" in the U.S.S.R. from the death of Stalin in 1953 to 1970. Given the twists and turns of Soviet political life, Khrushchev, reacting to the "nagging resistance from the Party and bureaucracy, used *Novy mir* [which first published *One Day in the Life of Ivan Denisovich* in 1962] as a vehicle to 'expose and dramatize problems and reveal facts that demonstrated . . . the necessity of the changes he proposed.'"

In February 1974, Aleksandr Solzhenitsyn was arrested; he lost his Soviet citizenship and was deported, that is, exiled from Russia. A Russian-language edition of *Gulag Archipelago I* had been published in Paris in September 1973. The American edition, which should have appeared immediately after the Russian, was delayed for six months, a delay to which the author attributes his arrest and exile, according to his memoir, *The Oak and the Calf*. He believes that "if all America had been reading *Gulag* by the New Year," the Soviets would have been hesitant to move against him.

The events leading to the publication significantly reflect the text. It had been completed in June 1968; a microfilm of the manuscript had been secretly and at great peril sent to the West, but the author had postponed its publication. The decision to publish was forced upon him in August 1973 when a Leningrad woman to whom Solzhenitsyn had entrusted the manuscript revealed the hiding place of a copy after having been terrorized through five sleepless days of interrogation by the K.G.B. (Released after the manuscript was located, she hanged herself.) The author understood that he had no alternative but to authorize publication immediately: The book contained the names of several hundred people who had provided him with information.

The underlying reason for the action against Solzhenitsyn with the publication of this volume was the rejection of the then-current Russian orthodoxy, that is, that "the abuses of justice under Stalinism were the direct consequence of the personality of the dictator." His data insist that the tyranny began with Lenin and continued under Nikita Khrushchev.

In contradiction of the United Nations Universal Declaration of Human Rights, which binds members to uphold the dissemination of ideas and information "through any media and regardless of frontiers," *Gulag Archipelago* was removed from two Swiss bookshops operating on United Nations premises. It was reported that the removal was instigated by the Soviet Union. Secretary-General Kurt Waldheim, at a July 1974 press conference, indicated a policy of giving "guidance" to the bookshops, that is, as indicated by Geneva Director-General Vittorio Winspeare-Guicciardi, telling them it was their "duty" to avoid "publications *à caractère outrageant pour un Etat Membre*" [publications of an insulting character for a Member Nation]. The press conference was held in response to the protest of the books' removal by more than 250 UN employees.

Solzhenitsyn's works were barred from publication in the Soviet Union after Nikita Khrushchev's death in 1964.

FURTHER READINGS

Blake, Patricia. "*The Gulag Archipelago*." *The New York Times Book Review* (October 26, 1975): 1, 18–21.

Burg, David, and George Feifer. *Solzhenitsyn*. New York: Stein and Day, 1972.

Chalidze, Vallery. *To Defend These Rights: Human Rights and the Soviet Union*. New York: Random House, 1974.

Coetzee, J. M. "Censorship and Polemic: The Solzhenitsyn Affair." *Pretexts* 2 (Summer 1990): 3–26.

Conquest, Robert. "Evaluation of an Exile." *Saturday Review* (April 20, 1974): 22–24, 30.
"*Gulag* at the UN." *Newsletter on Intellectual Freedom* 23 (1974): 162.
Kramer, Hilton. "The Soviet Terror Continued." *The New York Times Book Review* (June 18, 1978): 1, 28–29.
Rubenstein, Joshua. "*The Gulag Archipelago*." *The New Republic* 170 (June 22, 1974): 21–22.
Solzhenitsyn, Aleksandr. *The Oak and the Calf.* New York: Harper & Row, 1980.
Steiner, George. "The Forests of the Night." *The New Yorker* 50 (June 16, 1974): 78–87.

THE HOAX OF THE TWENTIETH CENTURY

Author: Arthur R. Butz
Original date and place of publication: 1975, Great Britain
Publisher: Historical Review Press
Literary form: Nonfiction

SUMMARY

The "hoax" of the title of *The Hoax of the Twentieth Century* refers to Germany's "murderous outburst during World War II," specifically to features of the Holocaust. Arthur R. Butz in his foreword establishes his position in response to potential questions about his qualifications: "If a 'scholar,' regardless of his specialty, perceives that scholarship is acquiescing, from whatever motivation, in a monstrous lie, then it is his duty to expose the lie, whatever his qualifications." Butz defines his purpose with reference to specific features: "The subject of this book is the question of whether or not the Germans attempted to exterminate the European Jews. We are not concerned with considering in any detail the general question of alleged brutalities of all sorts or with presenting a complete picture of the functioning of German camps." Further, "The thesis of this book is that the story of Jewish extermination in World War II is a propaganda hoax."

Questions are raised about the "war crimes trials," which were "precedent shattering in their scope and in the explicitness of the victorious powers' claims to some sort of legal jurisdiction in respect of laws or understandings which did not exist at the time they were allegedly broken by the Axis powers." This "disregard of European honor conventions which had been respected for centuries" was further compounded by judicial prejudgment: the judges had previous to the trials talked about the obvious guilt of the defendants.

A basic argument disputes the claim that six million Jews were exterminated. The statistics of the demographics of Jewish population in the world are attacked. "The 1948 *World Almanac* (p. 249) also gives the American Jewish Committee estimate for 1938 [sic], 15,688,259, while the 1949 *World Almanac* (p. 204) reports new figures from the American Jewish Committee which were developed in 1947–1948: 16,643,120 in 1939 and 11,226,600 in 1947." This last figure is immediately countered by citing military expert Hanson Baldwin's 1948 *New York Times* article's data of 15 to 18 million world Jewish population. This contention of erroneous population figures is furthered by questioning United States Jewish population statistics given by the Jewish Statistical Bureau, identified as a subsidiary of either the American Jewish Conference or the Synagogue of America: 1,770,647 in 1937 and 5.3 million in 1959. The author proposes two conservative estimates of Jewish population growth in the United States, both of which approximate a figure of 1 million to 1.5 million in excess of that of the Jewish Statistical Bureau's figure.

> Moreover, in the demographic argument for a five or six million drop in world Jewish population, the sources and authorities for the figures used are Communist and Jewish and thus, by the nature of the problem we are examining, must be considered essentially useless. In addition, the post-war figures for the United States are demonstrably too low by a significant amount.

To counter the "extermination mythology" as an explanation for any drop in Jewish population, Butz builds a case for deportations and deaths resulting from disease and starvation. Before the war, the "German Government had used all means to encourage the emigration of Jews from Germany and most German Jews had left before the outbreak of the war." The difficulty of arranging for other countries to take the Jews was solved by the German army's easterly movement. A resettlement program got under way in autumn of 1941 to move European Jews, most of whom were within the German sphere of influence, to the East. It was only partially carried out.

> . . . of course, nowhere near six million Jews were involved. Excluding Polish and Rumanian Jews, perhaps 750,000 Jews were resettled, primarily in the Ukraine, White Russia and Latvia. Not all Polish Jews fell under German domination. Apart from those who managed to flee before or after the German occupation, several hundred thousand or perhaps a million Jews had been deported from Poland by the Russians in 1940 and had been dispersed in the Soviet Union. For the most part, the Polish Jews who came into German hands were crowded into ghettoes in eastern Poland (1939 boundaries).

> What happened to all of these people can be established only in a very general way, because all of the territory that the Jews had been resettled onto became Soviet territory after the war, and because the victorious powers engaged in considerable suppression of the data. However there is sufficient evidence to permit us to see approximately what happened. Although it is very likely that a fair number perished in the disorderly and chaotic conditions that accompanied the German retreats, it is established that a large number of Jews, predominantly of pre-war Polish nationality,

were absorbed into the Soviet Union, and the remainder of the Jews who had been uprooted ultimately resettled in Palestine, the U.S., Europe and elsewhere.

Disease, specifically typhus, plagued the German concentration camps since early in the war. A typhus epidemic at the Belsen camp, for example, is cited as the major cause of deaths, resulting from a "total loss of control" at the end of the war, not a "deliberate policy." Butz suggests that scenes of "a large number of unburied bodies" were repeated in other German camps for the same reasons. The epidemic caught the Auschwitz authorities with inadequate crematory facilities. ("It was German policy to cremate the bodies of camp inmates who died.") Epidemics were also "common in the ghettos," according to German attribution, because of a "lack of discipline on the part of the Jews."

Among the many types of German camps, only 13 were "concentration camps" and only six were "alleged" to be "extermination camps." Only two camps, Auschwitz and Lublin, fit into both of these categories. The number of inmates in the entire German concentration camp system was "224,000 in August 1943 and 524,000 a year later."

Butz focuses on Auschwitz because of its notoriety. Actually a collection of neighboring camps, it was a huge industrial operation, including a hydrogenation and a "Buna" synthetic rubber plant, employing both free and prison labor. Birkenau was an important satellite camp with the largest number of deportees and prisoners. Typical inmate strengths for these two camps were 20,000 and 35,000 respectively (30 to 60 percent women), making it thus the largest complex of camps in the German system. Besides discussing the operation and labor functions of these camps, Butz examines the claim that at Berkinau "a program of mass killings of Jews via gas chamber was in operation, the Jews having been transported to Auschwitz primarily for this purpose."

In discrediting the "extermination legend" Butz disputes the data by pointing to "inconsistencies and inplausibilities." Among these are the inconsistencies of the figures of the exterminated, ranging from 750,000 to seven million. Colonel Rudolf Hoess, commandant of Auschwitz from May 1940 to late 1943, admits in his affidavit to 2.5 million victims, which Butz discredits. Butz also rejects the existence of gas chambers for extermination purposes, asserting they were used for disinfecting clothing in order to destroy all lice, which were carriers of typhus. The gas chambers allegedly disguised as showers were indeed showers: "all 'survivor literature', sincere or inventive, . . . report the same basic procedure involved in entering a German camp: disrobe, shave hair, shower, dress in new clothes or in old clothes after disinfection." Hoess refers to this procedure as an attempt to fool the victims. In contrast, Butz states:

> In any case Birkenau was, in a very real sense, a "death camp"; dead, dying and sick people were sent there and, after the crematoria were built, the dead were

disposed of in them. If one is to claim an "extermination camp" when there is none, what better choice is there but a "death camp"?

To substantiate his claims about the exaggerated figures of Jewish deaths, Butz demonstrates in detail the insufficient numbers of crematoria to accommodate the alleged numbers of bodies.

The text is not limited to discourse about the events and situation at Auschwitz. Information about other camps is also included for supporting detail. An entire chapter focuses on the Hungarian Jews, that is, the alleged deportation of approximately 400,000 persons by rail to Birkenau, where they were killed. Further discussion of the trials focuses on the defendants with an analysis of their responses in relation to their anticipation of the trials' purpose and outcome.

A consistent assertion within the text relates to the origins and promotion of the hoax: Zionist Jews are the source of the propaganda. "The claims of exterminations of Jews have their origin not in Allied intelligence information but in the operations of the World Jewish Congress . . ." Butz traces the six-million figure to Rabbi Israel Goldstein's December 13, 1942, declaration, printed in the *New York Times*, that there were "authenticated reports" of two million Jews slain "and plans for the total extermination of all Jews" by the Nazis. By December 20, 1942, a second figure of five million "in danger of extermination" had been added to the original number. Several pages of excerpts of stories from the *New York Times*, from June 14, 1942, to April 25, 1943, each story expressing the tyranny of the Nazis against the Jews, are presented to support the allegation of a propaganda buildup. Subsequently, the World Jewish Congress supplied the figure of 5,721,800 "missing" Jews to the International Military Tribunal at Nurenberg.

The Americans and British adopted these atrocities as the "propaganda basis for their war," then fed the fire with additional data and enraged reactions. Butz points to individuals of considerable rank in the American government who mobilized energy and attitudes in this regard. He particularly cites the influence of Secretary of the Treasury Henry Morgenthau Jr. (in conflict with Department of State leaders), who interfered in foreign policy as part of his "long crusade against Germany." He is linked with Zionist causes; his name and department are joined in the text with the World Jewish Congress and its leader, Rabbi Stephen S. Wise. One accomplishment of this group was to convince President Franklin D. Roosevelt to establish the War Refugee Board, "an instrument of Wise and other Zionists," which subsequently issued its "most consequential propaganda achievement," a booklet, *German Extermination Camps: Auschwitz and Birkenau*. The booklet is identified as the "formal birth of the 'official' thesis of extermination via gas chamber at Auschwitz."

> Of course the WRB report failed to change the opinions of the State Department people who had scoffed at the extermination propaganda from the very beginning. In private with [Josiah] DuBois, they were blunt in their opinion of the WRB report: "Stuff like this has been coming from Bern ever since 1942. . . . Don't forget, this

is a Jew telling about the Jews." . . . "This is just a campaign by that Jew Morgenthau and his Jewish assistants."

CENSORSHIP HISTORY

Challenges to *The Hoax of the Twentieth Century* have taken several forms. One of these occurred in November 1984 at the California Library Association (CLA) convention and earlier, in 1983, at the Torrance City Library, California. The two incidents are parallel and interrelated; both involve David McCalden, director (in 1985) of Truth Missions and former director of the Institute for Historical Review.

McCalden was denied access to exhibit space in 1983 during the Torrance City Library's Banned Book Week event. Its librarian, James Buckley, indicated that McCalden's intent was to display books that "presented one-sided views by obscure authors." In addition to *The Hoax*, other titles included *The Diary of Anne Frank* and *Did Six Million Really Die?* by Richard Harwood. The chair of the Southern California Coalition for Intellectual Freedom, Jeffrey Selth, a librarian at the University of California, Riverside, suggested the CLA annual convention as an alternative venue for McCalden's exhibit. Selth felt that McCalden had been unfairly treated.

In late spring, CLA's executive director, Stefan Moses, himself a Jewish refugee from the Nazis, approved McCalden's application both for exhibit space and for a meeting room to offer discussion about revisionist history to include "an overview . . . of the severe censorship and intellectual terrorism which inhibits any objective, open discussion of this controversial topic." When, in September 1984, several council members discovered this potential forum under CLA's auspices, the protests began. One ex-officio council member, "as a matter of conscience," informed the American Jewish Committee. Feeling pressured by the "threat" of organized Jewish demonstrations and the ruination of CLA's and his own "good name," Moses canceled McCalden's contract. When McCalden indicated he would sue for breach of contract, the contract was reinstated. On November 13, Moses said, "I just keep thinking of the same quote over and over again . . . 'I may not agree with what you say, but I'll defend with my life your right to say it,' and the fact is, whether you agree with him or not, as a publisher, McCalden has rights."

On November 16, however, Moses and CLA "caved in" under pressure to "strenuous objections" from California Assembly Speaker Willie Brown, Los Angeles Mayor Tom Bradley and the Los Angeles City Council. The city council voted unanimously to direct the Los Angeles Public Library to withdraw from CLA if the contract was not rescinded. A Los Angeles Police Department official's stated concern for Moses' safety at the hands of members of a militant Jewish organization added to the pressure on Moses along with the threatened demonstration and boycott of the conference.

The contract's cancellation was disavowed by Bernard Krussman, the president of CLA (who is Jewish), and Carol Sobel, associate director of the

ACLU of Southern California, respectively on intellectual freedom and free speech grounds.

Another challenge removed the book itself from the University of Calgary (Canada) library by the Royal Canadian Mounted Police customs and excise division on August 8, 1984. Canada had banned the book under a Canadian law that barred import of materials considered seditious, treasonable, immoral or indecent; so-called hate crime is included in these categories. The inclusion of *The Hoax of the Twentieth Century* on the barred list resulted from a complaint by B'nai B'rith against its distribution. The University of Calgary library had purchased *The Hoax* before its import was barred under the law. The then director of libraries at Calgary, Alan MacDonald, and the Library Association of Alberta condemned the seizure. MacDonald noted the "responsibility of the university . . . to make available all materials of an intellectual nature regardless of their viewpoints." The League of Human Rights of B'nai B'rith national chair David Matas agreed that it is inappropriate to take books from university libraries because they are not "really a source of propaganda and hatred if it means the propaganda could be refuted."

Supported by President Norman Wagner, the university decided to fight the seizure. A comprehensive brief was filed against the action of the customs department. According to Tom Eadie, current director of libraries, and Mac-Donald, the two copies of *The Hoax of the Twentieth Century* were returned to the library on September 17, 1984. The "technicality" that the books had been purchased prior to the law barring importation was the rationale for the return.

MacDonald has identified two other events in Canada. In January 1995, a copy of *The Hoax of the Twentieth Century* was seized from the rural Didsbury public library. It was shredded on the same day. In 1983, James Keegstra was dismissed from his teaching position because he had introduced Holocaust-denial materials in his curriculum, including the use of this book. After an extended trial over a period of years, Keegstra lost his case.

Protests on the campus of Northwestern University where Arthur R. Butz is a faculty member brought the third challenge. One incident occurred in January 1977. A controversy on the campus and in the community was sparked by a news report in *The Daily Northwestern*, the student newspaper, which revealed the existence of the book and expressed the nature of its contents. Petitions signed by faculty members and students were circulated to, in effect, censure the author. The petitions warned that the book gave "academic legitimacy to anti-Semitic propaganda" and criticized the administration for not "expressing any personal outrage over the book's allegations. Both the university president and the provost responded by noting that Butz had the right of any private citizen to publish what he chose.

A comparable incident at Northwestern University in 1994 caused the cancellation of a "fireside on Holocaust revisionism," a scheduled presentation by Butz. The Public Affairs Residential College (PARC), through its student academic chair, Dan Prosterman, had invited Butz to speak. In the ensuing emotional debate about the upcoming event among the dormitory residents, some advocated Butz's right to speak, while others, feeling personally offended, objected to providing a forum. The fireside speech was specifically canceled after the vice president for student affairs, Peggy Barr, informed the residents that they would be required to pay for security for the event, a fee of $1,500 for 11 security officers. When an anticipated source for this money was denied, the cancellation became inevitable. Despite the cancellation, about 120 demonstrators rallied against Holocaust revisionism. Other students—Prosterman and some PARC residents—expressed being "extremely upset" because the university administration had not been "up front" about the use of funds and had acted so late. Professor Charles Thompson, PARC's master, was quoted as saying that the financial qualification was part of Northwestern University's "campaign of intimidation" against Butz's presenting his views. Butz himself said that "this was the closest" he'd gotten to doing so.

Another academic freedom–free speech controversy developed during the fall semester of 1996 when Sheldon Epstein, a part-time lecturer at Northwestern University's School of Engineering, discovered that Butz had created a home page on Northwestern's World Wide Web site. Epstein criticized Butz's home page and the university's role in a classroom lecture, in a course on engineering design and entrepreneurship; it was deemed an "inappropriate" topic by the dean of the School of Engineering, Jerome Cohen, who warned Epstein. Epstein maintained that his course included a "segment on ethics and social responsibility in engineering"; he gave his students a research assignment on the Holocaust. These actions led to Epstein's contract not being renewed. Cohen argued that if Epstein were allowed to continue, then Butz could demand the right to espouse his views in class; he added, "This is an engineering school, not a political battleground." Northwestern University President Henry Bienen cited the university's policy of open access to the Internet for any purpose that is not illegal as rooted in traditional principles of free speech and academic freedom. Should he "draw the line" on Butz's access to the university's Web site, what, he pondered, would be next? In a statement on the Web, Northwestern called Butz's views a "contemptible insult" to the Nazis' victims and their families, but "we cannot take action based on the content of what Mr. Butz says regarding the Holocaust without undermining the vital principle of intellectual freedom that our policy serves to protect."

In a telephone interview in March 1996, Butz revealed that the German translation of his book is X-rated, that is, not suitable for use, in Germany. Restrictions are so heavy that they amount to censorship: The book cannot be displayed or advertised; mail order purchases are severely constrained.

The Canadian law referred to above led to a parallel barring of *Did Six Million Really Die?* by Richard Harwood. Publisher Ernst Zundel, an immigrant from West Germany, was sentenced in 1985 to 15 months' imprisonment, placed on three years' probation and prohibited during that time from publishing anything connected with the Holocaust. He was found guilty by a district court of "knowingly publishing false information likely to cause social and racial intolerance" and which also "dismisses the slaughter of Jews in the Second World War as a Hoax and a Zionist conspiracy designed to extract reparations from Germany."

FURTHER READINGS

"Calgary, Canada." *Newsletter on Intellectual Freedom* 34 (1985): 15–16.
"CLA Cancels 'Holocaust Hoax' Publisher." *Newsletter on Intellectual Freedom* 34 (1985): 1, 30–31.
Eadie, Tom. Director of Libraries, University of Calgary. Telephone interview. February 12, 1997.
"Index Index." *Index on Censorship* 14 (1985): 48.
King, Seth S. "Professor Causes Furor by Saying Nazis Slaying of Jews Is a Myth." *The New York Times* (January 28, 1977): 10.
Landy, Heather. "Protestors Condemn Butz, Holocaust Revisionism." *The Daily Northwestern* (May 10, 1994): 4.
MacDonald, Alan. Director of Information Services, University of Calgary. Telephone interview. February 11, 1997.
McRae, Lorie. "Seized Book Is Back." *Feliciter* (October 30, 1984): 1.
"Northwestern Is Thrust into Debate over Academic Freedom." *Minneapolis Star Tribune* (January 10, 1997): A9.
Schwendener, P. "The Holocaust Didn't Happen." *Reader* 12 (February 1983): 8–14.
"Seizing Anti-Semitic Book Wrong—Jews." *Edmonton Journal* (September 14, 1984): B3.
Stadtmiller, Amanda. "PARC Cancels Controversial Fireside after NU Intervention." *The Daily Northwestern* (May 10, 1944): 4.
Winer, Todd. "Tangled Web: NU Professor and the Holocaust." *The Chicago Jewish News* (October 25–31, 1996): [n.p.].
Witteles, Ron. "PARC Bureaucrats: 'We Know What's Best For You.'" *Northwestern Chronicle* (May 13, 1944): 1.

I AM THE CHEESE

Author: Robert Cormier
Original date and place of publication: 1977, United States
Publisher: Pantheon Books
Literary form: Novel

SUMMARY

Two disparate alternating components—a narrative adventure and a series of transcripts of taped interviews—provide the structure and build the plot and ideas of *I Am the Cheese*. Adam Farmer, in the first, is journeying on his old-fashioned bicycle from Monument, Massachusetts, to Rutterberg, Vermont, to visit his father in the hospital. It is an adventure with a purpose, but Adam is afraid. The taped interviews between Adam and Brint, identified as a psychiatrist, an identity that is doubted by Adam and made suspect in the text, reveal an attempt to help Adam regain his memory; these tapes are supported by third-person narrative accounts of past events that fill in the memory "blanks." These two components gradually intertwine, the tension mounting, the clues and bits of evidence fitting together to reveal what has happened and is happening to Adam Farmer.

Adam Farmer is really Paul Delmonte. He doesn't know this, however, until he is 14 when his father tells him the truth (the reader doesn't learn this until midway through the book). When Adam/Paul was young, his father, an energetic investigative reporter, had uncovered documents in the Albany, New York, State House that were damaging, indeed irrevocably ruinous, to both state and federal officials. The evident corruption involved links of government to criminal syndicates. After testifying in Washington in strict secrecy, under promises of protected identity, he returned home to resume his life. Two attempts on his life change that.

A "Mr. Grey" enters their lives. An agent of the U.S. Department of Re-Identification—a precursor of the Witness Re-Establishment Program—he provides the Delmontes with new identities and histories, new situations, even a newspaper article about their deaths by automobile accident. He causes them to be relocated to begin life anew. Mr. Grey remains in their lives, visiting their home once or twice a month for private conversations with David (Delmonte) Farmer in a sealed basement room.

But that is the past. In the present, Adam is on his bicycle pedaling toward Rutterberg, Vermont. He doesn't tell anyone. He is fearful because it is his nature to be so, he says, but this is a striking foreshadowing. Remembering his father's singing, Adam tries to mimic his joyous rendering of "The Farmer in the Dell" to give himself courage. He is, however, terrified by a dog that tears after him and, subsequently, three men in a lunchroom. Although they do threaten him, he manages to escape from them temporarily. They follow him in a car, mockingly passing him, returning and passing him again and again, closer and closer until they knock him over the side into a gully. Adam is rescued and taken as far as Hookset, Vermont. There his bicycle is stolen by Junior Varney, but Adam is able to reclaim it after a tussle.

Two other incidents provide clues of wonder and suspense. Adam tries to telephone his best friend, Amy Hertz. But after calling the familiar number twice, he is told by a stranger who answers that he has had the number for three years. The information operator tells him there is no Hertz in Monument, Massachusetts. When Adam reaches Belton Falls, he goes to the Rest-A-While Motel, where he and his parents had happily stayed the year before, only to discover it is closed. The gas station attendant across the street tells him it has been closed for "two or three years . . . at least."

At last arriving at the hospital in Rutterberg, Adam is greeted by a doctor who walks with him. They pass Whipper, Dobbie and Lewis, the three troublemakers from the lunchroom; he hears the growl of a ferocious dog and watches for the lurking Junior Varney. Adam is taken to his own room where he sings "The Farmer in the Dell." He doesn't respond to the name "Paul," nor does he recall his other name. But he knows who he is; "I am the cheese," he says. He stands alone.

The interviews are also in the present, conducted in a confinement facility. The interviews unpeel the shrouds, sheet by sheet, over Adam's memory. These conversations help Adam remember the past, starting from an earliest memory of a stealthy trip when he was four, moving through the first clues to his first questions and suspicions, leading to the revelations about the changed identity and situation of his family. Adam also raises doubts about where he is—it doesn't seem like a hospital to him—and who Brint really is. Brint seems something more or other than a psychiatrist; his questions seem to reach beyond a search for Adam's personal life, but rather to a search for certain specifics, secrets. He seems at times "a predator, an enemy. . . ." Despite his constantly drugged condition, Adam suspects Brint and resists his inquiries, maintaining a slight degree of self-protective will.

Mr. Grey, always dressed in gray, is an important figure of the past. He does not merely protect the Delmontes by re-establishing them. He watches over them and maintains surveillance over them. He determines the options at every stage; he controls the family's movements and life. It is his "emergency" call that sets the stage for the demise of the family.

Mr. Grey had called, saying that their identities may have been discovered, that they had to leave town for a few days so that his men could check for any suspicious developments. The Farmers take this enforced holiday, staying the first night at the Rest-A-While Motel, enjoying each other and their escape. The next day, David Farmer notices a car following them. When they stop and get out of their car to admire a distant view and stretch their legs, a car hurtles toward them and crashes into them.

Adam remembers. In slow motion he remembers himself flying through the air, twisting and trembling. He remembers seeing his mother die instantly. He remembers a voice saying that his father, hurt, had run away but that "They'll get him—they never miss." He remembers the men coming toward him, looming over him: "Grey pants. Him. Hearing his voice again: 'Move fast. Remove her. The boy—check him. He may be useful. Fast now, fast.'"

The novel concludes with the annual report, filed presumably by Brint. It summarizes the third annual questioning of Subject A, Adam Farmer, establishing that he "discloses no awareness of data provided Department 1-R by Witness #599-6" (David Delmonte). It indicates that these results are consistent with the two previous interrogations and that "Inducement of medication . . . plus pre-knowledge interrogation failed to bring forth suspected knowledge. . . ."; also, it notes that "deep withdrawal" occurs when these topics are approached and "complete withdrawal accompanies recapitulation of termination of Witness #599-6 and affiliate (spouse)."

The report includes three advisories: 1) that the policy, which does not allow termination procedures by Department 1-R be eliminated; 2) that the suspension of Personnel #2222 (Mr. Grey) be discontinued, granting him full reinstatement (the suspension had resulted from suspected complicity of Mr. Grey in the termination of Witness #599-6; the evidence of his contacting the Adversaries and revealing the location of the witness was only circumstantial); 3) that Subject A's confinement be continued, since he is "final linkage between Witness #599-6 and File Data 865-01," until "termination procedures are approved" pending revision of policy, or his "condition be sustained" until he "obliterates."

The closing paragraph of the novel is identical to the opening paragraph: Adam is on the bicycle, pedaling, pedaling.

CENSORSHIP HISTORY

The challenge in Panama City, Florida, against *I Am the Cheese* (winner of three awards—best young adult book by *Newsweek*, the *New York Times* and the *School Library Journal*— and critical acclaim) was initiated by a formal complaint in April 1986 (which also included *About David* by Susan Beth Pfeffer). It eventually resulted in a federal court case (*Farrell v. Hall*) that was adjudicated on July 18, 1988; the situation was not finally resolved for another three years.

A preliminary pair of letters preceded the formal complaint. Marion Collins, grandmother of a student at Mowat Junior High School, complained by letter in fall 1985 to Leonard Hall, superintendent of the Bay County School District; she objected to vulgar language and advocacy of humanism and behaviorism. Hall immediately ordered Mowat's principal, Joel Creel, to ban the book. In follow-up letters to Hall and Creel, Collins further complained that the book was still in use.

The formal complainant was Claudia Shumaker, Collins's daughter and mother of a seventh grader in ReLeah Hawks's accelerated English class. Her complaint was filed upon the suggestion of Superintendent Hall after Hawks, anticipating the Shumaker complaint, had informed parents of her intent to teach *I Am the Cheese* and to offer an alternative text to students whose parents objected; she had received 88 favorable permission slips and only four declinations. Shumaker wanted the book banned altogether, noting her daughter would be ostracized.

Both *I Am the Cheese* and *About David* were withdrawn immediately from classroom use, pending consideration of the district review committee. That committee in a month's time recommended the reinstatement of *I Am the Cheese*. (It did not act on *About David* because it was not scheduled for classroom use.) However, Superintendent Hall did not act on the recommendation, thus effectively preventing Hawks and other teachers from using it in their classrooms.

Thereupon, the controversy heated up. Claudia Shumaker had protested that *I Am the Cheese*'s theme is "morbid and depressing," its language "crude and vulgar" and the "sexual descriptions and suggestions are extremely inappropriate." The offending words were "hell," "shit," "fart" and "goddam"; the sexual descriptions included a scene of teens kissing, a description of breasts as "large" and "wonderful" and a reference to a supermarket display of Kotex. Her father, Charles E. Collins, who had served on the Bay County school board from 1954 to 1970, in a May 22, 1986 letter mailed to all the parents of Mowat students, protested in addition the novel's "subversive theme . . . which makes the 'government agents' out to be devious and 'hit teams' that killed the boy's parents, and now must kill the boy because he knows too much about the government's activities." In the letter and in an advertisement in the *Panama City News Herald*, he asked for telephone calls and mail-in coupons. M. Berry, M.D. in a letter to the editor, complained that the novel "slyly casts doubt on the U.S. government, parental authority and the medical profession."

The teachers called a public meeting on May 27, inviting students, teachers and parents to discuss the issue. On that morning, Hall instructed the teachers not to discuss the First Amendment or the book controversy with their students; he also ordered them to tell the students not to attend the meeting and that their exclusion was the teachers' idea. About 300 parents attended the meeting; approximately two-thirds of them indicated support for the teachers and the English program.

Hall, on June 5, rejected the review committee's recommendation and ruled against use of *I Am the Cheese*. He argued that the book had never been officially adopted by the school board. In a later statement, however, he expressed a negative reaction to an idea he inferred from the novel: "You know what happens at the end? The mother and father are exterminated by the United States government. What does that tell you? I mean do you ever trust government again?" He said further that students should not be taught that a government agency might be corrupt and untrustworthy.

Beyond rejecting *I Am the Cheese* because the school board had not approved it, Hall added that any other materials that had not been approved, except state-approved textbooks, would also have to be approved by a five-step procedure: 1) The teachers would submit a detailed rationale for each book to be included in the curriculum and the classroom library; 2) The principal would either reject the rationale or send it to the county instructional staff; 3) The staff would either reject it or send it to the superintendent; 4) The superintendent would either reject it or send it to the school board; 5) The board would make the final decision. Rejection at any stage would terminate the procedure; teachers would not be allowed to appeal. An additional procedure allowed citizens who objected to an approved book to appeal its inclusion; a procedure for a citizen to appeal a decision to reject a book was not included. This had the effect of eliminating classroom libraries and most classroom novels. Further, if a book was approved and then challenged, it would be withdrawn until judged by a series of review boards.

The proposed policy was debated at an extended school board meeting in August 1986. Parents and teachers who opposed Hall's proposed policy "protested that it was ham-fistedly authoritarian and heavily biased toward excluding, rather than including, material." Of the 25 citizens attending the meeting, 17 spoke against the proposal. Collins, however, submitted a stack of anti-obscenity petitions, containing by his account 9,000 signatures. (An enterprising television journalist, Cindy Hill, discovered in the fall that there were actually only 3,549 signatures.) The school board voted to approve Hall's policy, changing it only to add a one-year grace period for books that had been taught in 1985–86. This still denied teachers and students access to *I Am the Cheese* and *About David*.

Gloria T. Pipkin, chair of the English department, filed a request to teach *I Am the Cheese* to her advanced eighth-grade English class. Creel, having consulted Hall, rejected her request. Pipkin revised the rationale and sent it to Hall, who responded that the principal's rejection terminated the procedure. Pipkin then asked to be placed on the school board agenda; the chair at first attempted to prevent her from speaking, reminding her that "as a Mowat employee, she was subject to Creel's authority." Granted the right to speak, Pipkin asserted, "Make no mistake about it, *I Am the Cheese* has been banned in the Bay County school system because the ideas it contains are offensive to a few: no ruse can obscure that fact." Her request that the board go on record to restore the book to the classroom was ignored.

As the time arrived for the receipt of a rationale for teaching non-state approved books, Hall added another step to the review process; he required senior high school teachers to categorize their books: Category I—no vulgar, obscene or sexually explicit material; Category II—very limited vulgarity and no sexually explicit or obscene material; Category III—quite a bit of vulgarity or obscene and/or sexually explicit material.

When the review procedure was completed, Hall had eliminated 64 classics from Bay County classrooms. They included the following:

"Banned" from Bay High School: *A Farewell to Arms* by Ernest Hemingway; *The Great Gatsby* by F. Scott Fitzgerald; *Intruder in the Dust* by William Faulkner; *Lost Horizon* by James Hilton; *Oedipus Rex* by Sophocles; *The Red Badge of Courage* by Stephen Crane; *A Separate Peace* by John Knowles; *Shane* by Jack Schaefer; and *Three Comedies of American Life* by Joseph Mersand.

"Banned" from Mosley High School: *Adventures in English Literature*; *After the First Death* by Robert Cormier; *Alas, Babylon* by Pat Frank; *Animal Farm* by George Orwell; *Arrangement in Literature*; *The Autobiography of Benjamin Franklin* by Benjamin Franklin; *Best Short Stories*; *Brave New World* by Aldous Huxley; *The Call of the Wild* by Jack London; *The Canterbury Tales* by Geoffrey Chaucer; *The Crucible* by Arthur Miller; *Death Be Not Proud* by John Gunther; *Deathwatch* by Robb White; *Desire Under the Elms*, *The Emperor Jones*, and *Long Day's Journey Into Night* by Eugene O'Neill; *Exploring Life Through Literature*; *Fahrenheit 451* by Ray Bradbury; *The Fixer* by Bernard Malamud; *Ghosts* [sic] and *Miss Julie* by August Strindberg; *The Glass Menagerie* by Tennessee Williams; *Great Expectations* by Charles Dickens; *The Great Gatsby* by F. Scott Fitzgerald; *Growing Up*; *Hamlet, King Lear, The Merchant of Venice* and *Twelfth Night* by William Shakespeare; *Hippolytus* by Euripides; *In Cold Blood* by Truman Capote; *The Inferno* by Dante (Ciardi translation); *The Little Foxes* by Lillian Hellman; *Lord of the Flies* by William Golding; *Major British Writers* (shorter edition); *The Man Who Came to Dinner* by George S. Kaufman and Moss Hart; *The Mayor of Casterbridge* by Thomas Hardy; *McTeague* by Frank Norris; *Mister Roberts* by Thomas Heggen; *Oedipus the King: The Oedipus Plays of Sophocles*; *Of Mice and Men* and *The Pearl* by John Steinbeck; *The Old Man and the Sea* by Ernest Hemingway; *On Baile's Strand* by W.B. Yeats; *The Outsiders* by S. E. Hinton; *Player Piano* by Kurt Vonnegut; *The Prince and the Pauper* by Mark Twain; *Prometheus Unbound* by Percy Bysshe Shelley; *Tale Blazer Library: A Raisin in the Sun* by Lorraine Hansberry; *The Red Badge of Courage* by Stephen Crane; *A Separate Peace* by John Knowles; *To Kill a Mockingbird* by Harper Lee; *Watership Down* by Richard Adams; *Winterset* by Maxwell Anderson; and *Wuthering Heights* by Emily Brontë.

These exclusions engendered public protest and ridicule, including resolutions from the Chamber of Commerce. A letter of protest, signed by almost 2,000 county residents, was submitted to the school board on May 13. Hundreds of high school students wearing black arm bands packed the boardroom in protest.

On May 12, 1987, a suit was filed by 44 Bay County parents, teachers and students against Hall, Creel and the school board. The suit, labeled *Farrell* (after a student, Jennifer Farrell, whose name headed the list of plaintiffs) *v. Hall*, went forward despite the school board's reactive effort to revise the review policy by permitting the inclusion of books used in 1986–87 that were recommended by the school principal. This "revision," while reinstating the 64 titles, maintained the Hall policy and the banning of *I Am the Cheese*, *About David* and *Never Cry Wolf*, which had been barred in the interim. (The offense: one phrase shouted by a dogsled driver to his barking dogs—"FURCHRSAKE-STOPYOUGODAMNSONSABITCHES!")

The plaintiffs' case asked that *I Am the Cheese* and other young adult novels be restored to the curriculum; further, it asserted that the review policy denied students their First Amendment rights to receive information and be educated according to their parents' wishes and denied teachers their rights of free speech and academic freedom as well as placing an undue burden upon them in the preparation of rationales for every book taught and placed in their classroom libraries. At the core, the plaintiffs argued that Hall had acted counter to the First Amendment by using his position as superintendent of schools to reject books whose ideas violated his religious or political beliefs rather than because of their language. The defendants argued that the revised policy answered the plaintiffs' complaints and that the courts should not interfere in educational matters.

On July 18, 1988, Judge Roger Vinson of the United States District Court for the Northern District of Florida gave neither side a clear victory. He denied motions to dismiss the case. On behalf of the plaintiffs he noted in reference to Hall:

> [He] accepts as true . . . [that his] actions were motivated by his personal beliefs which form the basis for his conservative educational policy. Hall believes that his duty as superintendent is to restore Christian values to the Bay County school system. He thinks that one vulgarity in a work of literature is sufficient reason to keep the book from the Bay County school curriculum. Hall's opposition to *I Am the Cheese* arises solely from his personal opposition to the ideas expressed in the book. He believes that it is improper to question the trustworthiness of the government. Thus, students should not be presented with such ideas.

With regard to the accusation that books had been removed because of disagreement with the ideas they contained, he ruled:

> Local school officials may establish and implement the curriculum to transmit community values, a task which requires decisions based on the social and ethical values of the school officials. . . . On the other hand, the discretion of state and local school authorities must be exercised in a manner that comports with the first amendment. Local school officials may not suppress ideas simply because they disagree with those ideas so as to create a "pall of orthodoxy" in the classroom.

Thus, he supported the claims about the removal of *I Am the Cheese* and other works in order to suppress their ideas.

However, Judge Vinson did not support the plaintiffs' complaint relating to language; he asserted that rejecting books because of one vulgar word is within the school board's authority. So, too, the review policy was acceptable to the court because school boards have the right to approve books by whatever process they choose. The significant factor in this context is that board *decisions* may be challenged if deemed illegal or arbitrary. This applies also to books selected for school and classroom libraries.

Judge Vinson also ruled that federal courts, when First Amendment issues are involved, are obligated to intervene in educational matters.

The case was eventually settled out of court, after Hall decided not to run for re-election. Upon the request of his successor, Jack Simonon, to be given time to try to resolve the situation, a 60-day suspension of the trial was granted. The suspension lasted three years, during which time the People for the American Way organization negotiated on behalf of the teachers with the school board attorney to achieve a book review policy that was acceptable to all. Key features of this policy included time limits set for each stage of the review procedure; detailed procedures for handling challenges for existing materials; procedures established for the appeal of negative decisions; and provisions made to inform parents whose children would be affected of any complaint against a book so they could support or oppose the complaint.

Two additional challenges are recorded by the *Newsletter for Intellectual Freedom*, one in Cornwall, New York, in October 1984, and one in Evergreen, Colorado, in November 1993. In the former, Mrs. Oliver F. Schreiber objected to the contents of two of Robert Cormier's books: *I Am the Cheese* and *The Chocolate War*; her complaint described the books as humanistic and destructive of religious and morals beliefs and of national spirit. No action was taken on this complaint since, according to Superintendent R. Lancaster Crowley, Schreiber's son was not required to read the novel and had been excused from class discussion.

The second incident was more complicated. Principal Larry Fayer removed 42 books from the Wilmot Elementary School Media Center after 10 parents objected to foul language and violence in six titles; *I Am the Cheese* was among them. The removal was appealed by librarian Theresa March. During the review procedure, Fayer agreed to display the books for parental inspection and to return to the shelves all those that were not challenged. Thirty-one of them met this criterion, including *I Am the Cheese*. When the challengers of the remaining 11 discovered that their complaints would become public information, the challenges were withdrawn, and they, too, were reshelved.

FURTHER READINGS

Carlson, Peter. "A Chilling Case of Censorship." *The Washington Post Magazine* (January 4, 1987): 10–17, 40–41.

Collins, Charles E. Letter to Parents, Mowat Middle School, Panama City, Florida. May 22, 1986.

Collins, Marion. Letter to Joel Creel, Principal, Mowat Middle School, Panama City, Florida. February 3, 1986.

DelFattore, Joan. *What Johnny Shouldn't Read: Textbook Censorship in America*. New Haven: Yale University Press, 1992.

Foerstal, Herbert N. *Banned in the U.S.A.: A Reference Guide to Book Censorship in Schools and Public Libraries*. Westport, Conn.: Greenwood Press, 1994.

Gallo, Donald R. "Reality and Responsibility: The Continuing Controversy Over Robert Cormier's Books for Young Adults." In *The VOYA Reader*. Ed. Dorothy M. Broderick. Metuchen, N.J.: Scarecrow Press, 1990.

Linn, Jennifer. "Censorship Fight Has Just Begun." *Panama City News-Herald* (May 15, 1987): 1A, 2A.

———. "Lawsuit Filed Against Hall, School Board." *Panama City News-Herald* (May 13, 1987): 1A, 2A.

———. "Leonard Hall Bans 64 Books." *Panama City News-Herald* (May 8, 1987): 1A, 2A.

May, Greg. "Hall Challenged: City Protests Categories." *Panama City News-Herald* (May 13, 1987): 1B, 7B.

Newsletter on Intellectual Freedom 34 (1985): 45; 35 (1986): 209–10; 36 (1987): 52, 126–28, 168–69, 224; and 43 (1994): 97.

"One Arbitrary Policy Doesn't Justify Another." *Panama City News-Herald* (May 13, 1987): 6A.

Peyser, Andrea. "Battles Over Book-Bans Getting Dirty." *Tampa Tribune* (May 17, 1987): 1B, 10B.

Pipkin, Gloria. "Confessions of an Accused Pornographer." *Arizona English Bulletin* (1994): 14–18.

IN THE SPIRIT OF CRAZY HORSE

Author: Peter Matthiessen
Original date and place of publication: 1983, United States
Publisher: The Viking Press
Literary form: Nonfiction

SUMMARY

Prefatory comment: As the censorship history will detail, two major libel suits against the author and publisher challenged *In the Spirit of Crazy Horse*. The plaintiffs in these suits, William Janklow, then governor of South Dakota, and FBI Special Agent David Price, will be given some prominence in this summary to provide a context for the cases.

While spotlighting the tensions and events of the 1970s on the Sioux reservations in South Dakota, *In the Spirit of Crazy Horse* provides in Book I a brief history of this nation from 1835 to 1965 as well as the origins (1968) and growth of the American Indian Movement (AIM). Four major issues emerge from the text: the loss and despoiling of Indian lands; the quest for sovereignty; FBI (Federal Bureau of Investigation) and BIA (Bureau of Indian Affairs) interference and brutality on the reservations; and the severe schism and distrust within the Sioux nation. These issues are represented through two major confrontations—Wounded Knee in 1973 and the Oglala shoot-out on June 26, 1975—as well as the subsequent manhunt for witnesses and fugitives, particularly Leonard Peltier, and their trials.

One of the major treaties of the Midwest region, the Fort Laramie Treaty of 1868, is at the heart of the claims of the Sioux (also designated Lakota) nation, which include the Teton tribes from the western plains of North and South Dakota; and the Dakota, Santee and Yankton tribes from the prairies of Minnesota and eastern North and South Dakota. This treaty guaranteed

> absolute and undisturbed use of the Great Sioux Reservation. . . . No persons
> . . . shall ever be permitted to pass over, settle upon, or reside in territory

described in this article, or without consent of the Indians pass through the same. . . . No treaty for the cession of any portion or part of the reservation herein described . . . shall be of any validity or force . . . unless executed and signed by at least three-fourths of all the adult male Indians, occupying or interested in the same.

The lands so guaranteed, which included the sacred Black Hills area, were gradually taken away. As early as 1876, the Black Hills were invaded by miners seeking gold; they were supported by government troops. The forced sale of this sacred area along with 22.8 million acres of surrounding territory followed. The resident tribes were resettled elsewhere on the reservation lands, but were "forbidden to trespass on the 40 million acres of unceded land that was supposedly still a part of the Great Sioux Reservation." During President Benjamin Harrison's administration in 1889, the original reservation tract was dismantled and the seven reservations that exist today were established.

In subsequent years, a series of "reforms," some of them well intentioned, further reduced the Indian lands: the General Allotment Act of 1887 broke down the Indians' communal attitude toward land by parceling it out; the Indian Claims Commission of 1946 in effect eliminated existing and potential land claims by monetary compensation; the termination legislation enacted in the 1930s, by relocating Indians off the reservations and giving them "independence" from tribal dependent status, made Indian reservation lands available to whites. Further, the BIA's land-tenure rules required that each family's allocation of land be equally divided among heirs, which created parcels too small to support a family.

A particular example illustrates the land mass lost:

By 1942, nearly 1 million of the 2,722,000 acres assigned to Pine Ridge when the reservation was created in 1889 had passed into other hands, and by the 1970s, over 90 percent of reservation lands were owned or leased by white people or people with a low percentage of Indian blood, not because these people were more able but because the dispossessed traditionals had no money or means to work their land.

In recent years, the forests already having been stripped off and other minerals removed, the push to gain access to the uranium and coal fields on reservation lands had further threatened the reservations. However, resistance of the tribes had also mounted, accompanied by attempts to reclaim the lost lands.

The issue of sovereignty of Indian nations and the revalidation of Indian treaties is concomitant with the land claims. Two statements illustrate the opposing viewpoints. In the first, Judge Warren Urbom, a trial judge in some of the Wounded Knee cases, who dismissed 32 cases before trial, noted that, despite the "ugly history" and the "treaties pocked by duplicity," the Lakota claims to sovereignty were "squarely in opposition" to law and Supreme Court rulings, as developed in "an unbroken line." Judge Urbom pointed out that treaties were placed "by the Constitution of the United States on no higher plane than an Act of Congress, so if a self-executing treaty and an Act of Congress be in conflict, the more recent governs." In summary, he said, "the law is that native American tribes do not have complete sovereignty, have no external sovereignty, and have only as much internal sovereignty as has not been relinquished by them by treaty or explicitly taken by act of the U.S. Congress." The second statement is from Darrelle Dean (Dino) Butler's opening remarks at his trial for the murder of the two FBI agents at Oglala:

> We are members of a sovereign nation. We live under our own laws, tribal and natural. We recognize and respect our own traditional and elected leaders. The treaties that were made between Indian nations and the United States government state that we have the right to live according to our own laws on the land given to us in the treaties. That the laws of the United States government shall not interfere with the laws of our nations.

The conflict of these views of sovereignty is expressed in the behavior of United States official personnel, who presumed a proprietary status, and the reactions of the members of the Sioux nation. The overt conflict surfaces in the Wounded Knee episode, reported in Book I, and resurfaces in the Oglala shoot-out, detailed in Book II.

FBI and BIA agent intervention in reservation affairs is highlighted in the Wounded Knee and Oglala episodes, but it does not begin or end there. The agents of these bureaus are portrayed as vehemently antagonistic to AIM leaders and activities and, along with police, are frequently identified with injustice, harassment and brutality. These range from intimidating and beating Indians, notably suspects or potential witnesses, to invasion of private property, presumably in search of suspects:

> Under cross-examination by the defense, [Wilford] "Wish" Draper [a young Navaho visitor] acknowledged without hesitation that he had lied to the grand jury in January and also as a prosecution witness in this trial; that when he had been apprehended in Arizona in January, he had been thrown against a car, then handcuffed and strapped for three hours in a chair while being threatened with a first-degree murder charge, until he finally agreed to supply useful testimony about the killings; that before the trial, he had told the defense attorneys that Peltier, Robideau, and Butler were all in camp when the shooting started; . . . and that most of his damning testimony on this subject was based on instruction from the FBI agents at the time of the grand-jury hearing, and also by Assistant U.S. Attorney Robert Sikma.

> That morning of September 5, an air-land-and-river operation had descended at daybreak on the Crow Dog and Running properties, in a massive racketing

of helicopters that swept in over the dawn trees. More than fifty FBI agents in combat dress, with four large helicopters, military vehicles, trucks, vans, cars, and even rubber boats—presumably to prevent aquatic escapes down the narrow creek called the Little White River—surrounded the houses and tents, shouting, "This is the FBI! Come out with your hands up!" No one was given time to dress—Crow Dog himself was marched out naked—and even the small frightened children were lined up against walls as the agents ransacked and all but wrecked every house, tent, cabin, and car on both properties.

At the conclusion of the Dennis Banks–Russell Means conspiracy trial, Federal Judge Alfred Nichols severely criticized the FBI for its manipulation and unethical behavior. He had at first seemed sympathetic to the government's case and had indicated he had "revered" the FBI.

The FBI was also accused of fomenting discord among Indian factions on the reservations and promoting violence. Dino Butler, an AIM leader, is quoted as saying:

> The stories that go out from the reservations look like Indian versus Indian—you know, Dick Wilson and his goons versus the American Indian Movement. But we know different. The Federal Bureau of Investigation, the CIA, and the BIA, and all these different organizations working for the government—they are the ones causing all the trouble. They give Dick Wilson and his goons money. . . . When AIM gathers, the FBI buys ammunition and booze and stuff for these goons so that they will start drinking. That's how they get their courage.

Dick Wilson, the tribal chairman, and his "goon squad" (an acronym for Guardians of the Oglala Nation), identified in the book as Wilson's private police force, represent one faction. As accused by Butler, they are depicted as drunkenly brutal and repressive, holding the "traditionals" hostage, in effect. Outrageously corrupt, they milk the tribal coffers for their own benefit. The AIM organization is perceived as their enemy; thus, Wilson and his men are in league with the FBI, apparently to protect their privileges. The antagonism is decidedly bloody. These combined negative forces are evident in the Wounded Knee and Oglala incidents.

Judge Nichols was not the only judicial officer who started out with an anti-Indian bias, but not all changed their attitudes. Another legal officer, the attorney general of South Dakota during the Oglala episode, William Janklow, is quoted as having said, "The only way to deal with Indian problems in South Dakota is to put a gun to the AIM leaders' heads and pull the trigger." Janklow had taken his first job after law school as head of the legal services program on the reservation; he was serving effectively. In 1967, however, a 15-year old girl accused Janklow of raping her. (He was her legal guardian.) "The hospital records included evidence, suggesting that an attack had occurred." Janklow was not prosecuted at the time after the FBI "smoothed over" the incident. In

September 1974, during the Banks–Means trial, the charges resurfaced. "The would-be Attorney General refused to answer his summons, the BIA refused to deliver the subpoenaed file, and the FBI refused to cooperate in any way. Nevertheless, Janklow was charged by Judge Mario Gonzales with 'assault with intent to commit rape, and carnal knowledge of a female under 16.'" Janklow denied the charges and refused to appear in court; the charges were rejected repeatedly by the FBI, and the government did its best to thwart the investigation. In March 1975, the victim died as a result of a hit-and-run accident on a deserted road.

The siege at Wounded Knee began as a gesture of protest against injustices and the presence of federal officers on the reservation. The Oglala Sioux Civil Rights Organization (OSCRO) allied itself with AIM; on February 28, 1973, several hundred men, women and children drove in caravan to Wounded Knee and took over the community. They issued a public statement demanding hearings on their treaty and an investigation of the BIA. Wounded Knee was surrounded the next day by an armed force consisting of the FBI, the U.S. Marshal Service and the BIA police, supported by Dick Wilson's men. On May 9, after several attempts to negotiate and after exchanged gunfire that led to the death of a young Indian male, it was over. "The few Indians still left in the settlement submitted themselves to arrest by the U.S. government."

The Wounded Knee trials, particularly that of Dennis Banks and Russell Means, from January to September 1974, gained widespread notoriety. The prosecution, "dismissing past wrongs as irrelevant to this case, portrayed the two leaders as common criminals who had invaded, terrorized and looted a helpless community." At the end of this eight-and-a-half-week trial, the prosecution produced a surprise witness, former AIM member Louis Moves Camp, who "filled in every gap in the prosecution's case." Moves Camp had been assigned to FBI Agent David Price, who, with his partner, had met daily with him from August 5 through August 10 and then had accompanied him from August 13 to 16, the day of his testimony. Moves Camp's testimony and the role played by Price were significantly questioned.

> More serious than Louis Moves Camp's lies was the all but inescapable conclusion that Agent Price and perhaps Agent Williams had knowingly prepared this man to give false testimony; or, at the very least, they had found his story so convenient that they had not bothered to find out if it was true.

There was a further assertion that Price was implicated in an "alleged cover-up of a disputed rape" committed by Moves Camp in River Falls, Wisconsin, on August 14. One of the Indians' legal aides is quoted as recalling: "Price can be friendly when he feels like it, and he can look you in the face and lie and know you know he's lying—and *still* not show a damned thing in his eyes."

Both Banks and Means were acquitted; others had charges dismissed, while a few received minor sentences for related charges. Of the leaders, only Crow

Dog served any jail time—a few months—on charges directly related to Wounded Knee.

A little more than two years later, on June 26, 1975, the shoot-out at Oglala, specifically the Jumping Bull property, occurred. The firing erupted suddenly, catching the Indians off guard. Two special agents who had driven onto the property were wounded in the firefight, one seriously; subsequently, they were killed by shots at close range. One young Indian was also killed when a bullet struck him in the forehead. Federal reinforcements had arrived seemingly, to the Indians, almost immediately and set up roadblocks. Nevertheless, all but one—the dead Indian—had managed to escape.

What followed was a massive "reservation murders" investigation into the deaths of the two officers; the shooting death of the Indian was not considered. Public statements, printed in major newspapers, by FBI spokesmen and South Dakota Attorney General William Janklow (who was subsequently reprimanded by Governor Richard Kniep for his inflammatory statements) that the agents' bodies had been "riddled with bullets" and that their cars had also been "riddled by machine-gun bullets" turned public opinion against AIM. (Each agent had actually been struck three times.) Outraged FBI officers "ransacked . . . house[s] without a warrant," harassed, coerced and bribed witnesses, and, in the words of the U.S. Civil Rights Commission, overreacted so that the investigation took on "aspects of a vendetta . . . a full-scale military-type invasion." Special Agent David Price is identified as a member of some of these groups.

The activities of the fugitive Indians are also followed, from one camp or hideaway house to another. Some who had not been on the Jumping Bull property that fateful morning were pursued as AIM members. One of them, Anna Mae Aquash, died in a strange, questionable, hit-and-run accident. Eventually, four individuals were indicted on two counts of first-degree murder: James Theodore Eagle, Darrelle Dean Butler, Robert Eugene Robideau and Leonard Peltier. Initially, Peltier was not yet in custody; he was later located in Canada, extradited to the United States with falsified documents and tried separately.

The trial of Butler and Robideau was transferred from Rapid City, South Dakota, to Cedar Rapids, Iowa, based on the successful argument of anti-Indian prejudice. The trial opened on June 7, 1976, and concluded on July 16, 1976, with their acquittal on all counts. In addition to the significant testimony of a prosecution witness to defense cross-examination (quoted above relative to FBI manipulation of witnesses), the following argument to the court by a defense attorney regarding David Price's testimony was revealed:

> Mr. William Kunstler: We want to show this man fabricated testimony. That he has suborned perjury with witnesses in Indian trials involving A.I.M. people before. That he was the principal agent that produced witnesses they don't dare use now, produced witnesses that were to be used in this trial. John Stewart, Myrtle Poor Bear, Marvin Bragg, who was one they didn't produce on the stand, and that this man is notorious for producing fabricated evidence. They

have put a witness like [James] Harper [a white man who had shared a cell with Dino Butler] on the stand and we are permitted to show, I think, under the rules of evidence that this is the way they prepare and work on witnesses, that they deliberately suborn perjury and use perjurious witnesses.

The case against James Theodore Eagle was abandoned as a result of the Cedar Rapids decision, but that of Leonard Peltier was pursued in Fargo, North Dakota. It ended on April 18, 1977, when the jury brought in a verdict of guilty on two counts of murder in the first degree. (The author comments that had Peltier been tried in Cedar Rapids, "it seems almost certain that he would have been acquitted" since there was "no good evidence that his actions had differed in a meaningful way. . . ."

Book III details Peltier's escape from prison, his recapture and life in federal penitentiaries. Two chapters—one significantly titled "Forked Tongues"—investigate and analyze the evidence against Peltier. A third chapter, which includes a telephone interview with Special Agent David Price, investigates the situation of a potential prosecution witness, Myrtle Lulu Poor Bear, whom Price had been implicated in manipulating. There are also chapters on the "real enemy" of the Indians, that is, "the corporate state," that "coalition of industry and government that was seeking to exploit the last large Indian reservations in the West"; and on the attempt of the Indians in April 1981 to reassert their ownership of the Black Hills, the sacred Paha Sapa, by occupying sections of it.

CENSORSHIP HISTORY

The author and publisher of *In the Spirit of Crazy Horse* faced two libel suits two months after the book was published in 1983. The first plaintiff was William J. Janklow, then governor of South Dakota; the second was David Price, an FBI special agent. Peter Matthiessen, in his epilogue in the second edition, which came out after the trial, indicates that he assumed that the "FBI itself had sponsored [Price's] suit in order to lend some sort of credibility to the suit by Janklow" because Price himself "had assured me in our lengthy interview that he never made a move without the approval of his superiors, and since an FBI agent's salary could never pay for the very expensive attorneys he retained." There were altogether eight court decisions in eight years of litigation.

In April 1983, Governor Janklow called bookstores in Rapid City and Sioux Falls (he indicated he was attempting to call all bookstores in South Dakota) asking them to remove *In the Spirit of Crazy Horse* from their shelves because it was libelous and contained passages critical of him. "Nobody has the right to print lies and injure me or my family." While Janklow indicated he was acting as a private citizen, three of the booksellers reported that he had called from his office; one call was made by his secretary. Some stores removed the books; others did not. The disclosure of the governor's actions caused the sales of the book to increase.

Janklow filed a suit on May 19, 1983, asking $24 million in damages, against Viking Press, Peter Matthiessen and three bookstores. Janklow alleged that the book portrayed him as "morally decadent, a drunkard," "a racist and bigot" and "an antagonist of the environment." He claimed that Matthiessen's recounting of historical charges that he had raped a teenage Indian girl in 1967 and accusations against him by the American Indian Movement were "prepared either with a reckless disregard for truth or with actual malice for plaintiff." The defendants had edited all references to him and disregarded contrary evidence "in order to present a false and defamatory picture." His suit said that three federal investigations had determined that the rape charges were unfounded.

An attempt by the defendants for a change of venue from a state court in South Dakota to a federal court was denied on September 2, 1983, by U.S. District Court Judge John B. Jones. The defendants had argued that Janklow had deliberately included the booksellers in his suit so that the case would be heard in the state courts. There was a presumption of bias in Janklow's favor at the state level.

On February 6, 1984, the booksellers' attorneys filed a joint memorandum asking Judge Gene Paul Kean of the Circuit Court of the Second Judicial Circuit in Sioux Falls to dismiss the case. The attorneys argued that courts had never required booksellers to investigate the accuracy of the books they sell. Further, a ruling to prove that the identified passages were indeed libelous had not been made, nor had it been shown that the booksellers knew of the libel.

In support of the booksellers, the Freedom to Read Foundation on February 23 filed an *amicus curiae* brief in which they argued that if Janklow's

> contention were to be accepted, every bookseller, librarian, and other passive distributor of information would be confronted with a Hobson's choice: they would either have to review every potentially controversial book for factual accuracy and be prepared to defend such review in court, or accept at face value every claim made by a disgruntled reader who alleges that a particular work defames him and suppress all further distribution until such time, if ever, that the claim is resolved.

> It requires no prescience to recognize which choice must and will be made. Booksellers and librarians simply do not have the resources to undertake an in-depth review of every publication they are asked to distribute.... [therefore] the only way in which booksellers, librarians and other passive distributors of literary materials could minimize their risk of litigation and liability under plaintiff's theory would be to categorically reject for distribution all works which address public controversy....

> Plaintiff's theory of bookseller liability is not only insupportable under the First Amendment but also unconscionable in a society founded on the rule of law.... The hazard of self-censorship can be avoided only by equating "responsibility" with "authority." The remedy for libel must rest against the person responsible for it and by whose authority it was published.... To hold defendant booksell-

ers proper defendants in this case would thus render their defense of First Amendment rights the very source of their liability for libel.

A society which permits its legal process to become an instrument of coercion cannot long preserve the rule of law. And, as Justice Brandeis noted, silence coerced by law is the argument of force in its worst form. The defense of plaintiff's name does not require the "argument of force" he demands. The remedy for libel does not require the right to close the marketplace of ideas at will.

The booksellers were successful in their motion to have the suit against them dismissed. On June 25, 1986, Judge Kean granted the defendants' motion. Having noted the author's reputation as neither a sensationalist nor a scandalous writer and the like reputation of the publisher, he stated:

The calling up of booksellers and book distributors and expressing a view that something in the book may be false is not adequate. . . . If anyone who felt that he was libeled in written material could stop distribution in such fashion it would have a "chilling" effect on book distributors and book publishers.

Janklow did not appeal this decision.

Meanwhile, on July 13, 1984, Judge Kean issued an opinion granting Viking's and Matthiessen's motion to dismiss Janklow's entire case. He found Matthiessen's reporting of the historical charges to be fair, balanced and protected as "neutral reportage." (This is an "evolving First Amendment doctrine that affords protection to reporting of charges.") Judge Kean stated further: "To force a writer to determine the responsibility of an organization or an original speaker at the risk of substantial liability would undoubtedly have a chilling effect on the dissemination of information." He also said that Matthiessen had the right to criticize Janklow in the book, which dealt with a longstanding public controversy.

Janklow's appeal of Judge Kean's decision was upheld on December 11, 1985, when the Supreme Court of South Dakota reversed the dismissal. It refused to adopt the principle of neutral reportage in South Dakota since the U.S. Supreme Court had not yet adopted the neutral reportage privilege. It remanded the case for summary judgment, requiring Judge Kean to rule on whether there was any evidence of wrongdoing by Viking and Matthiessen.

The Circuit Court of the Second Judicial Circuit in Sioux Falls again dismissed Janklow's case on June 2, 1989. Judge Kean ruled that "By no means are the statements concerning Janklow . . . a reckless publication about a public official. Defendants have provided evidence to support the statements in a lengthy affidavit by Matthiessen, accompanied by several exhibits totaling over 1,200 pages." Janklow's appeal to the South Dakota Supreme Court was rejected in a 4–1 decision, the majority citing First Amendment requirements.

This suit was formally ended in late October 1990 when Janklow allowed the 90-day deadline for appeal to the United States Supreme Court to lapse.

FBI Special Agent David Price filed his complaint of libel in January 1984 in state court in Rapids City, South Dakota, asking damages of $25 million. Price contended that he had been defamed by Matthiessen's charges that he and other FBI agents had engaged in illegal conduct in the events leading up to a gunfight between FBI agents and a few members of AIM living on the Pine Ridge Reservation. Specifically, he objected to allegations "that agents induced witnesses to commit perjury, and obstructed justice in the Peltier case . . .; that they were racist and killers; and that they were 'corrupt and vicious' in their treatment of Indians on the reservation." He tried to impugn Matthiessen's sources by declaring that the AIM members among them had been convicted of criminal acts resulting from the Wounded Knee episode. Price also questioned the book's conclusion that Peltier's conviction had been a miscarriage of justice resulting from FBI misconduct.

In February 1985, South Dakota State Circuit Court Judge Merton B. Tice Jr. ruled that FBI Agent Price's case against Viking Press and Matthiessen was not appropriate to South Dakota jurisdiction because Viking did not do enough business in South Dakota to establish the necessary "contact"; thus, if Price was harmed, it was not in South Dakota.

At the federal level, Judge Diana Murphy of the U.S. federal district court in Minneapolis in late January 1986 dismissed three of four counts in Price's suit. A significant rejection was Price's allegation of "group libel," that is, passages critical of the FBI had thereby defamed him personally. Judge Murphy's dismissal indicated that under these circumstances "the context of publication [must raise] a reasonable presumption of personal allusion." With regard to the remaining claims, Judge Murphy allowed Price two years of investigation. Thereafter, on January 13, 1988, she granted a motion for summary judgment and dismissal of the remaining claims. Judge Murphy upheld the right of an author "to publish an entirely one-sided view of people and events." Further, she noted that statements alleged by Price as defamatory were opinion and entitled to constitutional protection. With regard to factual statements about Price, the judge did not find that many were false; she also ruled that minor factual errors were not motivated by malice or negligence.

"The book deals with historical events, but does so from a very pointed perspective. The book's tone and style suggest the statements in question are opinion"; it seeks to persuade readers of the justice of a cause. She wrote, "The conduct of [FBI] agents in exerting their Federal authority is a matter of legitimate public interest" and noted that many statements of opinion were criticisms of government: "*In the Spirit of Crazy Horse* concerns speech about government officials, and it is this form of speech which the framers of the Bill of Rights were most anxious to protect. Criticism of government is entitled maximum protection of the First Amendment." She also pointed out that "Viking recognized that responsible publishing companies owe some duty to the public to undertake difficult but important works."

Price appealed the federal district court ruling. The unanimous decision of the U.S. Court of Appeals for the Eighth Circuit on August 7, 1989, granted summary judgment to Viking and Matthiessen, affirming all of Judge Murphy's rulings. The court, in effect, ruled that the challenged statements were constitutionally protected either as opinion or as "neutral reportage" in which the author transmits the views of others. Judge Gerald Heaney, writing for the three-judge panel, cited a 1964 precedent, *The New York Times v. Sullivan* decision of the Supreme Court. He wrote:

> The motivating factor in the Court's analysis was protection for criticism of public officials and speech regarding issues of political concern. The *New York Times* standard was constructed in light of three truths about public speech. First, false statements would necessarily occur in the course of a vigorous public debate. Second, absent protection for even false statements, destructive self-censorship would result. *Third, the legal standards for defamation must protect defendants from the self-censorship imposed by threats of litigation.* The Court felt that debate on matters of public concern "should be uninhibited, robust, and wide-open . . . [though] it may well include vehement, caustic, and sometimes unpleasantly sharp attacks on government and public officials. [Emphasis added by Martin Garbus, defense attorney for Viking Press and Matthiessen]

While Price had relied on the previously accepted law that repeating a false accusation, even against a government official, could be libelous, Matthiessen had argued that some of the accusations he had printed were true and that reporting the historical fact that an accusation had been made was necessary to show the Indians' views. Further, the distinction between responsible critics and those whom Price labeled as leftists, that is, "good" and "bad" sources, was not accepted.

In conclusion, Judge Heaney reiterated Judge Murphy's sense that even if a government official could be injured by critical reports, to suppress them would unduly inhibit debate on issues of public significance:

> Sometimes it is difficult to write about controversial events without getting into some controversy along the way. In this setting, we have decided that the Constitution requires more speech rather than less. Our decision is an anomaly in a time when tort analysis increasingly focuses on whether there was an injury, for in debating this case we have searched diligently for fault and ignored certain injury. But there is a larger injury to be considered, the damage done to every American when a book is pulled from a shelf, as in this case, or when an idea is not circulated.
>
> In its entirety, *Crazy Horse* focuses more on public institutions and social forces than it does on any public official. The sentiments it expresses are debatable. We favor letting the debate continue.

Price made two separate applications to the U.S. Supreme Court to reverse the appellate court ruling. In his appeal for review, Price argued that the appeals court had created an "insurmountable hurdle" for plaintiffs in libel cases. "Any author with even a modicum of cleverness can publish purposely false allegations of criminal wrongdoing . . . or include clever and meaningless qualifiers to his defamatory allegations . . . he is absolutely protected by the opinion doctrine." In both instances, the Supreme Court refused to hear the appeal, thus leaving intact the appeals court ruling. The latter Supreme Court rejection occurred in January 1990.

Except for the initial printing of 35,000 copies, *In the Spirit of Crazy Horse* had been unavailable since the first lawsuit was filed in 1983. It was republished in 1991.

FURTHER READINGS

"Court Dismisses Janklow Suit Against Viking and Matthiessen." *Publishers Weekly* 235 (June 16, 1989): 14.

"Crazy Horse Suit Ends; Viking to Publish New Edition in 1991." *Publishers Weekly* 237 (November 9, 1990): 12.

Fields, Howard. "High Court Rejects Libel Appeal Against Viking." *Publishers Weekly* 237 (January 26, 1990): 310, 312.

Garbus, Martin. "Afterword." In *In the Spirit of Crazy Horse*, by Peter Matthiessen. New York: Viking, 1991: 589–96.

Greenhouse, Linda. "Reviving Affirmative Action Issue, Court Will Decide." *The New York Times* (January 9, 1990): A1, 18.

"Libel Suit Against Viking Dismissed." *The New York Times* (June 21, 1984): III 17.

Mitgang, Herbert. "Crazy Horse Author Is Upheld in Libel Case." *The New York Times* (January 16, 1988): II 5.

Newsletter on Intellectual Freedom 32 (1983): 112; 33 (1984): 18, 75–76, 116, 148; 34 (1985) 34; 35 (1986): 52, 91; 37 (1988): 99; and 40 (1991): 55.

"South Dakota Governor Calls Stores to Ask Book's Removal." *The New York Times* (May 1, 1983): I32.

"Viking and Matthiessen Prevail in Libel Suit." *Publishers Weekly* 233 (January 29, 1988): 314.

"Viking, Matthiessen Win in Price Libel Suit." *Publishers Weekly* 236 (September 1, 1989): 8.

JOHNNY GOT HIS GUN

Author: Dalton Trumbo
Original date and place of publication: 1939, United States
Publisher: Lippincott
Literary form: Novel

SUMMARY

Johnny Got His Gun is divided into Book I, "The Dead" and Book II, "The Living." "The Dead" is structured with chapters alternating from present to past as the protagonist, Joe Bonham, attempts to come to grips with what has happened to him. "The Living" concentrates on the present, though there are occasional reflections of the past. The novel is written in first person, an extended monologue—the mind, memories and hallucinations of the protagonist.

> He was the nearest thing to a dead man on earth.
> He was a dead man with a mind that could still think. He knew all the answers that the dead knew and couldn't think about. He could speak for the dead because he was one of them.

These thoughts toward the close of Book I reflect Joe's realization and attitude. He has come far from the dull confusion and semiconsciousness of the first chapter. He begins to realize that he has been badly hurt and that he is deaf, but he is alive and in a hospital. In subsequent chapters, he next realizes that he has lost one arm and then the other and then both legs. At last, he knows he has no mouth or tongue, no nose, and that he is blind.

The trauma and terror of these discoveries are like a bad dream; at times, Joe thinks he's dreaming or doesn't know when he's awake and when he's asleep. The nightmares shake him but being awake shakes him, too.

The balancing chapters, Joe's recollections of the past, reveal Joe's *everyman* background—the normality of his life and love of his family; the buoyant adolescence and emerging manhood. His memories encompass the everyday: his mother's wordless singing while canning or making jelly; the smell and taste of freshly cooked hamburgers; camping-fishing holidays with his father; kissing and loving his sweetheart. By the close of Book I, Joe has established his sensibility and his stability of character. As his memories unravel and clarify, he establishes his sanity.

An antiwar element materializes in Book I. It is introduced in Chapter 2—"He lay and thought oh Joe Joe this is no place for you. This was no war for you. This thing wasn't any of your business. What do you care about making the world safe for democracy?" In Chapter 10 an extended stream-of-consciousness essay denounces fighting for empty words: freedom, liberty, honor, death before dishonor. The dead renounce these, for they died "yearning for the face of a friend . . . moaning and sighing for life." Joe knows for he's "the nearest thing to a dead man on earth."

In Book II, Joe tries to maintain control of his memory and gain cognizance and control of his environment. He works his mind, starting with recollections of numbers, quotations, and books; he tries to establish time, the passage of time. During a quite poignant moment, Joe solves this problem when he realizes he has identified the coming of dawn and opens up his memory bank of sunrise. He marks time, counting the days into years.

He works also on space and the message of vibrations until he can tell who is with him and what is being done. He is at first bewildered by a group of visitors in the fourth year of his hospitalization and then intensely angered when he realizes that he has been awarded a medal. His anger leads him to recall his use of a wireless set years before; he initiates efforts to communicate by tapping the Morse code "SOS" on his pillow.

Months later, a young substitute nurse recognizes the code, and Joe's attempt to communicate. His joy at being acknowledged a live man with a mind is a "new wild frantic happiness." When he answers her question, "What do you want?" the answer is, "What you ask is against regulations."

What did he want? He wants, of course, his life back—his senses, his limbs. He asks to be let out, to be released from the hospital "prison." He longs for air, sensations on his skin, to be among people. His mind runs ahead of his tapping, revealing his desire to make an exhibit of himself to show ordinary people—parents, schoolchildren—and legislators: "Here is war."

The text concludes in emotional antiwar rhetoric.

CENSORSHIP HISTORY

In his 1959 introduction to *Johnny Got His Gun*, Dalton Trumbo recounts the book's "weird political history." "Written in 1938 when pacifism was anathema to the American left and most of the center, it went to the printers in the spring of 1939 and was published on September third—ten days after the Nazi-Soviet pact, two days after the start of World War II." Subsequently, serial rights were sold to *The Daily Worker* of New York City, becoming for months a rallying point for the left.

During World War II, the United States Army initiated a program of distributing books to soldiers overseas. From 1941 to 1943, three million books had been shipped. Subsequently, the army invited the Council on Books in Wartime, an organization formed by the publishing industry to assist the war effort, to help in this program. In the next three years 1,080 separate titles, accounting for more than 122 million books, were made available to servicemen.

There was an underlying censorship stance involved in the book selection, that is, the rejection prior to 1943 of magazines and newspapers of Axis propaganda. In addition, three books were banned by the Special Services Division, two of them "by direction from higher authority." One of these was *Johnny Got His Gun*, presumably because of its pacifist message.

During World War II, after the book went out of print, Dalton Trumbo himself resisted requests to have it reprinted; his publishers agreed. These requests came from the extreme American right who wanted a negotiated peace and who perceived the novel, according to Bruce Cook, to be "useful as propaganda . . . as the Axis fortunes began to fall" because of the antiwar message. "Anti-Semitic and native Fascist groups put on a big push for an early peace, demanding that Hitler be offered a conditional peace." Individuals of these persuasions claimed that Jews, Communists and international bankers had suppressed the novel. Trumbo was distressed that his book was being so used by these groups; he had shifted from the antiwar attitude of *Johnny Got His Gun* to "militant support for the war effort."

In 1947, Trumbo was blacklisted as one of the Hollywood Ten. He had joined the Communist Party in 1943 (he left the party in 1948) when the United States and the Soviet Union were allies and had been active representing his views. As such, he was an obvious recepient of a subpoena to appear before the House Committee on Un-American Activities in Washington, D.C., on October 23, 1947. The hearings focused on the "Communist Infiltration of the Motion Picture Industry": the presumption was that Communist dogma and propaganda had been written into film scripts. The Ten perceived the essential question to be one of freedom of speech. Because of Trumbo's refusal to answer questions about his membership in the Screen Writers Guild and the Communist Party, he was "voted in contempt of the House of Representatives of the United States" by the members of the committee then present. All 10 individuals cited for contempt of Congress served prison terms; Trumbo, sentenced to a year, served 10 months, starting on June 7, 1950.

Despite disclaimers that they would do anything so un-American, the motion picture industry prepared in November 1947 the notorious Waldorf Agreement which, in effect, declared the Hollywood Ten and others like them to be "no longer employable in the motion picture industry." The Ten did bring suit on their contracts, but they lost when on November 14, 1949, the Supreme Court turned down their petition and refused to hear the case. Trumbo refers to this situation as a domestic manifestation of the cold war that was then developing: "We are against the Soviet Union in our foreign policy abroad, and we are against anything partaking of socialism or Communism in our internal affairs. This quality of opposition has become the keystone of our national existence."

Before and after his imprisonment, Trumbo wrote for the movie black market under pseudonyms or under the cover of other screenwriters' names. In 1957, he won the Oscar for the Best Motion Picture Story for *The Brave One* under his pseudonym Robert Rich; this award "marked the beginning of the end of the black list," according to Cook, which by this time affected any writers implicated in the Joe McCarthy witchhunt. Cook quotes Trumbo as remarking that because there were so many screenwriters working in the movie black market under false or borrowed names "no record of credits between 1947 and 1960 can be considered even remotely accurate." Cook also credits Trumbo with the dissolution of the blacklist in 1960: It was "a coordinated and deliberate personal campaign in the media . . . a crusade, a vendetta."

Johnny Got His Gun has been challenged and/or censored in schools: in the Midwest (1973) for vulgarity of incidents and language; in Michigan (1977) for too much profanity, too gruesome details of a human being, expressing unpatriotic and anti-American ideas, and sexual passages; in Wisconsin (1977) for too much profanity; in Texas (1977) as unpatriotic and anti-American; in

Colorado (1977) for the description of the main character after he had been maimed in the war; in California (1977) for the language and for several passages describing sexual encounters; in Wisconsin (1982) as antiwar; in Vermont and Illinois (1982) as too violent.

FURTHER READINGS

Cook, Bruce. *Dalton Trumbo*. New York: Charles Scribner's Sons, 1977.

DeMuth, James. *"Johnny Got His Gun*: A Depression Era Classic." In *Censored Books: Critical Viewpoints*. Ed. Nicholas J. Karolides, Lee Burress and John M. Kean. Metuchen, N.J.: Scarecrow Press, 1993. 331–37.

Jamieson, John. *Books for the Army: The Army Library Service in the Second World War*. New York: Columbia University Press, 1950.

Leary, William M., Jr. "Books, Soldiers and Censorship during the Second World War." *American Quarterly* 20 (1968): 237–45.

Trumbo, Dalton. "Introduction." In his *Johnny Got His Gun*. New York: Bantam Books, 1983.

LAND OF THE FREE: A HISTORY OF THE UNITED STATES

Authors: John W. Caughey, John Hope Franklin and Ernest R. May
Original date and place of publication: 1965, United States
Publisher: Benziger, Incorporated
Literary form: Textbook

SUMMARY

The opening inscription by Adlai E. Stevenson and a series of contrasting features about the United States set the tone and direction of *Land of the Free*, a social studies textbook.

> When an American says that he loves his country, he means not only that he loves the New England hills, the prairies glistening in the sun, the wide and rising plains, the great mountains, and the sea. He means that he loves an inner air, an inner light in which freedom lives, and in which a man can draw the breath of self-respect.

The contrasts are seen in the political and the environmental realms. Excerpts from the Constitution's high aims and Abraham Lincoln's Gettysburg Address—"government of the people, by the people, and for the people"—"are arrayed against American practice [that] has not always measured up to the ideal of 'government of the people'": the initial limitation of the right to vote to men of property; not granting this right to women until 1920 and even later to Indians; denying slaves voting rights and barring or discouraging them from voting for more than a hundred years after slavery's end.

The United States, symbol of freedom, boldly represents itself in terms of "liberty and justice for all"; these are guaranteed by the Bill of Rights. But "promises of equal rights have not always been kept—or, worse yet, have been kept for some Americans but not for others." Cited are discrimination in the job market for African Americans as well as in access to housing and education.

The beauty of the American landscape and the rich resources of the land are extolled. These features are contrasted with examples of waste and damage from the pioneers who destroyed timber stands to later overuse of resources and the "sprawl" of housing, industry and highways. Mounting pollution ranges from "cities . . . in danger of being buried under their own trash and garbage" to the spoiling of the earth and sea with chemicals and other wastes.

The text begins with a standard unit, "Earliest America," that discusses explorations and their background, provides a 14-page glimpse of the "first Americans" and describes the first colonies. The glimpse of the first Americans is superficial but differentiation is made among broadly grouped tribes of the regions of the country. One page is devoted to the plight of the Indians: "These first Americans were the first to have their lands taken from them, the first to be segregated, the last to get the vote, and the last to share in the rewards of the American system." Justification by the settlers for the first of these actions is that the "Indians were a barrier to progress and should be eliminated by force or negotiation."

The developmental stage of the English colonies leading to the founding of a nation represents expansionist actions: land takeover (English kings, claiming title, exercised their prerogative to grant lands from sea to sea); increased trade, agriculture and industry; and wars among the European powers until the English gained control. The population was diversified; it included enslaved Africans as well as people from non-English origins. Emerging tensions are evident: the banishment of Anne Hutchinson and Roger Williams from the Massachusetts Bay Colony for religious heresy and political criticism; the quarrel about freedom of the press; protest against slavery. Tensions also developed between the colonists and England, resulting in large measure from taxation without representation, which led to the impulse for independence and war, followed by the Declaration of Independence. That the Americans were divided among themselves is carefully noted. "Some were patriots, some were loyalists, some were undecided. With the changing fortunes of war, many shifted from one camp to another."

During the war and after victory the leaders of the states did not come to an easy solution in the establishment of a union. In framing the Constitution, compromise was the key to resolution, particularly in the nature of representation in the houses of Congress and the powers of the central government over the states.

The first decades of the new nation were developmental and precedent setting in establishing principles and practice. An important principle emerged from the "revolution of 1800" when Thomas Jefferson was elected. Instead of leading a political overthrow, Jefferson acted to calm the populace and the politicians; he appealed to all Americans: "Let us then, fellow citizens, unite with one heart and one mind. We are all Republicans, we are all Federalists." In the succeeding years, however, sectional rivalries were prominent: The slavery issue separated the South; although an 1807 law ended the slave trade, slaves were still smuggled into the South. The status of slavery in the western territories as they achieved statehood increased sectional rancor.

Two great issues of the 19th century were westward expansion and the Civil War. Westward expansion represented the territorial growth and political definition of the nation as now known. It also represented a rise of democracy in government: The new states granted suffrage to every white male adult and some eastern states followed suit. However, westward expansion also meant annexing land: by purchase—Louisiana from France; by conquest; by persuading Indians to release land for settlement; by making and breaking treaties—some settlers ignored them; and by removing all Indians from the area east of the Mississippi through treaty and enforced requirement. Most of the estimated 100,000 Indians living east of the Mississippi River were moved out.

In discussing the tragedy of the Civil War, the authors illustrate slavery's inhumanity and effects.

> Constantly watched and subject to complete control by the master, a slave was never allowed to forget that he was a slave. . . . Most of the slaves endured what they had to. If they loafed on the job, it was often a form of protest. Slaves pretended to be ill and unable to work. Sometimes they destroyed tools or other property or damaged the crops. A few slaves were so desperate that they cut off their own hands or committed suicide.

Abolitionists, passionate and unequivocal, demanded immediate emancipation. Slave owners defended slavery as necessary to their operations and to keep the South prosperous.

> Glancing through history, the southern apologist for slavery found other arguments. Every progressive society, he argued, was built on slavery. The Egyptians had slaves; the Greeks held slaves; the Romans held slaves. "In all social systems," the governor of South Carolina said, "there must be a class . . . to perform the drudgery of life." With Negroes as slaves, he said, the southern whites had the leisure to become more cultivated.

After President Abraham Lincoln's Proclamation of Emancipation, the end of the bloody war and the murder of the president, the freed slaves found their problems had just begun. Unprepared for freedom and for citizenship, without employment and education, they were easily abused. Every former Confederate state enacted a Black Code that treated the freedmen unjustly. The codes denied the rights to vote and to an education, and instituted segregation. The Ku Klux Klan "terrified, tortured and often killed Negroes and their white sympathizers."

In contrast, partly in response to the actions of the former Confederate states, Congress acted to thwart these actions. They imposed reforms, the formula being "less forgiveness to Confederate leaders and more participation by the freedmen." During this period the Thirteenth, Fourteenth and Fifteenth Amendments to the Constitution were ratified. These ended slavery and granted citizenship to Negroes, guaranteeing due process of law, equal protection of law and the right to vote. After 1877, however, the southern states enacted a battery of Jim Crow laws that separated the races by treating "Negroes" as inferior.

In the discussion of succeeding decades the authors take three major tacks: the developmental progress of the United States; the social and political problems and issues, often outgrowths of progress; and the attempts to achieve reform and broader humanity. The first of these encompasses major inventions and industrialization, the transcontinental railroad, mining bonanzas of the far West and the industrial revolution. Cities with skyscrapers developed as business and industrial centers, offering new opportunities for leisure and learning. Later advances in science became triumphs with achievements in space and medicine. At the turn of the century, the United States "acquired an empire," an extension of expansionist urges. Alaska was purchased from Russia; additional territory was taken through war with Spain and then annexation. In the 20th century, the United States became a world power.

While industrialization resulted in progress, especially for millionaires concerned with profits, it also resulted in crowded cities whose residential districts near town center were stifling and unhealthy and created a "runaway problem of crime." Laborers' working conditions were mean; their long hours were filled with drudgery, their lives destitute. The waves of immigrants from Asia and from eastern and southern Europe faced hardships and language problems, but also unfair treatment and intolerance. Indians were gathered on reservations: "One purpose was to teach them to farm, thereby releasing most of the hunting area on which they had lived." Intolerance and violence against "Negroes" accelerated. During World War II, "Americans of Japanese ancestry . . . were treated as one great security risk, which they were not. With no questions asked, and no allowance for positive evidence of loyalty, they were hustled off to detention camps. . . . they were deprived of protections that the Constitution otherwise would have given them against arrest, detention, forced removal, and implication of lack of loyalty. They also had the embarrassment of being put where they could do little for the war effort."

Reform efforts were manifested in the workplace, in the community, in business and in government. Labor unions were formed; strikes yielded successes and failures. As labor unions grew in strength and gained higher wages, fewer hours and better working conditions, employers organized against them, hiring strikebreakers and using publicity and the courts to defeat them. A resurgence of union power in the 1930s helped to ensure prosperity for millions of workers. Muckraking newspapers, social activists like Jane Addams and progressive governors like Robert LaFollette of Wisconsin acted to ease the conditions of the poor; laws were enacted to control child labor. At the federal level, such laws also controlled women's labor as well as abuses of "big business," drug manufacturers and monopolies and trusts. A conservation program was launched. Attacks on corruption in government ranged from the eradication of the spoils system, replaced by a professional civil service, to the ratification of the Seventeenth Amendment, which provided for the popular election of senators.

The closing pages of the text juxtapose "Panic about Security" in response to the fear of communism with the civil rights movement for "Equal Rights and Fair Treatment." The former alludes to loyalty oaths, widespread suspicion and the terrorizing of the State Department and many persons in government by Senator Joseph R. McCarthy. The latter expresses the denunciation of segregation in 1954 by the Supreme Court and the expansion of the civil rights movement from schools to buses, restaurants and voting rights. Strong support for these civil rights measures was won among whites and blacks in all parts of the country.

> The drive also drew savage resistance from local police, the White Citizens Council, the Ku Klux Klan; and mobs and assassins. Seeing the Negroes set upon with police dogs, fire hoses, cattle prods, gas, whips, and clubs roused the nation. So did the bombing of Negro homes and churches and the assassination of literally dozens of persons, white and black, who were working for civil rights.

The demonstrations led to the Civil Rights Act of 1964 and the Voting Act of 1965.

CENSORSHIP HISTORY

The challenges to *Land of the Free* were multi-staged, coming from varied sources. The first occurred at the state level, from California's state assembly and the superintendent of public instruction, Max Rafferty. The controversy apparently began in May 1966 when State Assemblyman John L. E. Collier identified the book as "very distasteful, slanted and objectionable" and said he would attempt to block appropriation of the text. Joining Collier in objecting to the text were Assemblyman Charles Conrad and State Senator John G. Schmitz. The text was criticized for stressing a one-world government, quoting accused communists, portraying the United States as a bully, distorting history and putting American forefathers in a bad light. The Textbook Study League, Inc., formerly the National Anti-Communist League of America, charged that the book exercises "thought control" rather than providing information.

Of particular notoriety was a criticism of Superintendent Rafferty that the text is "slanted in the direction of civil rights," a judgment based on a critique of the text prepared by his "longtime advisor, Emery Stoops, a professor of educational administration at the University of Southern California." In contrast, Assemblyman Collier is cited as having said that the book is slanted politically in references to "Negroes," never mentioning their positive accomplishments. John Caughey, professor of history at the University of California at Los Angeles, specifically disputed this claim by providing evidence from the text of references to "Negroes" and their significant activities.

In a detailed critique published in *The Tablet*, a Catholic newspaper of the Brooklyn, New York, diocese, Assemblyman Conrad quarreled with the lack of balance in the book. "The authors virtually ignore whole periods of our nation's history, apparently because the authors dislike the political philosophy of those times. On the other hand, whole pages are devoted to trivia." He complained against the elimination of facts about the Harding, Coolidge and Hoover administrations and their depiction as having done little while in office; he claimed that "school children have the right to know that these men believed the federal government should act only in times of emergencies, that during periods of prosperity we should reduce taxes and attempt to pay off the national debt." Comparably, Conrad found lack of balance in the amount of representation of the Eisenhower administration and its misrepresentation in its response to communism. The treatment of communism was questioned as well; it was presented not as negatively as fascism, both in the sympathetic treatment of accused communists in the United States and the absence of identification of Russian atrocities in Hungary, its invasion of Finland and its seizure of Poland. "This is the current liberal line that, of course, Stalin was a tyrant, but that Communism, at least Russian Communism has changed its image and can now be trusted." Conrad asserted that this treatment "doubtlessly reflects the feelings of . . . Caughey." In this context, he referred to the fact that author Caughey had refused to sign the California regents loyalty oath in the 1950s, for which he was dismissed from teaching at UCLA for two years until he signed the so-called Levering Oath. Conrad also objected to the omission of American deaths at Pearl Harbor while listing the casualties at Hiroshima and devoting more than a page to the Japanese sent to "detention camps."

Because of "public pressure," the state Curriculum Commission convened a panel of noted historians to review the book and the criticisms. The panel's list of suggested revisions was forwarded to the authors. Rafferty indicated he would ask Governor Ronald Reagan "to withhold the money for its distribution" if the recommended corrections were not made.

In December 1966, after the requested changes were made, Max Rafferty supported the approval of the book for use in California schools. The state board of education unanimously approved it. Its use was to begin in eighth-grade classes in the fall of 1967.

A tangential censorship incident occurred at the United Republicans of California (UROC) convention in May 1967. The UROC's board of governors ordered the excision of the last two pages of a book being sold outside the convention hall. The 60-page pamphlet, *The Story Behind the "Land of the Free"* by Ford Sammis, was critical of the book itself as well as Superintendent of Public Instruction Max Rafferty. The last two pages made unflattering allusions to Rafferty, who was supported by many delegates as a prospective 1968 candidate for the U.S. Senate. Rafferty's shift in position from hostile criticism to praise is noted; he is quoted as saying, "I almost singlehandedly succeeded in getting this book so extensively changed. The book is 500 percent better than a year ago, largely due to my efforts." (Telephone conversations with the text's two living authors, John Hope Franklin and Ernest R. May, reveal that there were "not many" and "very few" changes. Some were resisted, such as the request to identify W. E. B. Du Bois as a communist.") With the two pages of Sammis's book excised, permission for the book's sale was granted despite the presence of comparable criticism of Rafferty on other pages of the text.

Sammis's criticism of the *Land of the Free* refers particularly to its statements about "civil rights and Negro affairs." The treatment of these matters was deemed slanted as were those of liberalism and patriotism.

Despite the approval of the California state board of education and the ruling of the state attorney general that the book must be used, opposition to the text continued in the fall of 1967. The Charter Oak school trustees on August 7 went on record in opposition to the book, while the school administration scheduled a meeting of the teachers using the text to discuss the book and district policy "laid out as to its use." (The Charter Oak staff described the book as "highly readable, colorfully illustrated and [able to] serve as an excellent teaching instrument if carefully used and industriously supplemented.")

Challenges to the book appeared in other California school districts. The Paso Robles school district voted to use *Land of the Free* under protest; Downey school district refused to order the textbooks, despite being subject to losing state appropriations; Arcadia school district considered similar action and the Tuolumne (Sonora) County Board of Education voted to oppose the use of the text. Richard Pland of the Sonora county board objected to the book as "negative. It's designed to build a segment of the country at the expense of the rest of the country. . . . it tears down instead of building up . . . like they are trying to instill a guilt complex in us." Altogether 14 school districts declined to order this text, but by mid-December only three—Downey, Los Angeles County; Fruitvale, Kern County; and Allensworth, Tulare County—were holding out. By January only Downey had not done so; its school trustees voted unanimously on January 8, 1968, to reaffirm their rejections of the state-required textbook. One of the board's objections to this textbook was to its interpretive level: "Eighth-graders aren't ready for interpretations of history—particularly biased interpretations, be they liberal or conservative." They also objected to the content, for example, "down-grading our heroes":

Nathan Hale and Davey Crockett are not mentioned, nor are the military exploits of Generals George Patton or Omar Bradley. A speech of Patrick Henry is called a "tirade," and the Boston Tea Party is described as a "mob scene . . . hijacking British ships." On December 14, 1967, the state board of education decided to insist on the book's use; in mid-January, the Downey Unified School District board voted to challenge in court the right of the state board of education to force the use of the book. It contended that the state education code did not prescribe mandatory textbooks in junior high school.

Parent groups and individuals also expressed objections. The Concerned Parents of Rialto on August 23, 1967, objected to the "numerous inaccuracies" and the failure to emphasize what they viewed to be significant events in history. In Wheatland-Chili, three residents asked for a replacement book because in their view *Land of the Free* "runs America down." The Santa Paula school district also received "several calls . . . from concerned parents." The Rialto parents were told that the school district had no choice about books to be used in the eighth grade; the Wheatland-Chili residents' request was denied by the trustees because they trusted the judgment of the book selection committee of teachers.

A citizens group, *Land of the Free* Protesters, was formed to seek expulsion of the controversial text from Orange County classrooms. The group had circulated petitions and were ready in June 1968 to submit "200 to 300" signatures to one of four school boards. The goal of the group was 10,000 signatures. Their specific charges claimed that the text

> fails to develop the great traditions of America, e.g., love of country, strong individualism, worship of God and private enterprise . . . and places undue emphasis on minor historical people, indoctrinates toward collectivism, mocks American justice, projects negative thought models and promotes propaganda alien to the American Ideal.

Individual parents expressed their objections to the textbook by preventing their children from attending the class in which it was being used. Their objections charged that it was "not a true portrayal of the history of this country" and that it presented a "slanted version of history and ridicules religious beliefs held in our home." The child of each set of parents was expelled because of the parents' refusal to allow class attendance; a criminal complaint was filed against the parents by each school district. In April 1968, one couple was found guilty of violating the state education code and was sentenced to a $10 fine or five days in jail. The verdict in effect ordered the parents to allow their son to return to school. (The outcome of the second case is not available.)

Although David Shaw asserts in his account that *Land of the Free* is "being used virtually without protest in Cleveland, Denver, Philadelphia, Kansas City, Detroit, Washington and Milwaukee," Gerald Grant identifies a specific case outside of California in Columbus, Ohio. The book was a target of the Let

Freedom Ring group, which attacked it as unpatriotic and communist inspired because one of the authors had once refused to take an academic loyalty oath. They also charged that the textbook teaches "guilt and shame" about America's past, and they found it unthinkable that there was no picture of Betsy Ross sewing the American flag.

In January 1968, the National Education Association reported, based on questionnaire responses of 1,700 educational leaders, that *Land of the Free* received the most criticism from private groups and the public. The report also listed groups that ranked high in handing out "destructive criticism," that is, criticism that caused difficulty rather than helping. The John Birch Society and teachers' unions were first and second, respectively.

Seventeen California teachers contributed to a 45-page document, *Land of the Free and Its Critics*, in which they reviewed the credentials of the major critics of *Land of the Free*—only one was a historian, but he was an Irish and European history specialist—and analyzed the questions raised about the book. The teachers quoted specific passages in the text that belied the criticisms, either in the language used, the data presented, or both. Several examples follow:

- In response to a "soft on communism" charge: "upgrades radicals and communists, treats American documents carelessly, promotes world government." Authors write: "Communism *seemed* more idealistic than Fascism or Nazism. Its apparent aim was to ensure everyone a fair share; its benefits *supposedly* would go to workers rather than an elite or master race. But Communism *attached no value to any freedom* except freedom from want. The Communist leaders believed *they alone knew* what was good for the people. *All other parties were suppressed.* So were all churches. *Speech and writing were controlled. Critics were jailed or killed.* Every effort was made to force all the people to accept Communism and *obey* the party leaders *unquestioningly.* In practice, Communist Russia was as *brutal a police state as Mussolini's Italy or Hitler's Germany.*" (Emphasis added in the document.)

- In response to criticism that patriots are omitted: "Perhaps this is why another of his [Patrick Henry] legendary sayings, 'Give me liberty or give me death!' is buried without credit in a Lyndon Johnson speech. . . ." Authors' wrote: "Discussion of the meaning of liberty came to a high point in the 1760's and 1770's." ". . . Other efforts by individuals included . . . Patrick Henry's 'GIVE ME LIBERTY OR GIVE ME DEATH!'"

- In response to the accusation that historical events are sullied: Critics quote: "This mob scene, showing the hijacking of the British ships in Boston Harbor, has come down in history under the more cheerful name, The Boston Tea Party." Research is cited: ". . . a mob disguised as Mohawk Indians and Negroes rushed down to the waterfront and emptied 342 big chests of precious tea into the harbor." Samuel Eliot Morison, *Oxford History of the American People* (New York, 1965).

FURTHER READINGS

Allen, Shirley, et al. *Land of the Free and Its Critics.* Millbrae, Calif.: California Council for the Social Studies, 1967.

Conrad, Charles. "*Land of Free* Skimpy with Facts." *The Tablet* (July 28, 1966): [n.p.].

Franklin, John Hope. Co-author of text. Telephone interviews. November 1996.

Grant, Gerald. "Radical Rightists Try to Suppress Texts Sympathetic to Minorities." *The Washington Post* (December 11, 1996): A1, 6.

Hasegawa, Ann. "*Land of Free* Causes Delay in State Budget." *UCLA Daily Bruin* (May 18, 1966): [n.p.].

"History Texts Declared 'Sick.'" *Sonora* [California] *Union-Democrat* (March 12, 1968): 1, 6.

May, Ernest R. Co-author of text. Telephone interview. October 1996.

Newsletter on Intellectual Freedom 16 (1967): 14, 67; and 17 (1968): 15, 20, 22, 52, 55, 63.

"Rafferty Finds Two Dirty Words." *San Francisco Chronicle* (May 13, 1966): 43.

Shaw, David. "History 'Interpretation' Stirs Tempest in Downey." *Long Beach* [California] *Press-Telegram* (February 19, 1968): B1, 4.

"Textbook Issue Causes Suspension of Morongo Student." *Riverside* [California] *Enterprise* (February 13, 1968): [n.p.].

"Tuolumne Education Board Opposes History Text." *Stockton* [California] *Record* (March 12, 1969): [n.p.].

MANIFESTO OF THE COMMUNIST PARTY

Authors: Karl Marx and Friedrich Engels
Original date and place of publication: 1848, Great Britain; 1872, United States (English translation)
Publisher: Communist League; Woodbull and Claflin's Weekly
Literary form: Nonfiction

SUMMARY

In the "Preface to the English Edition of 1888," Engels noted that "the history of the *Manifesto* reflects, to a great extent, the history of the modern working-class movement" and identified it as the most international of all socialist literature. Yet, he acknowledged significant differences between the socialists of 1847, "adherents of the various Utopian systems," and communists, "Whatever portion of the working class had become convinced of the insufficiency of mere political revolutions and had proclaimed the necessity of a total social change. . . ."

This definition lends itself to a central issue of section I: class struggle. Such struggle between the oppressor, or the bourgeoisie, and the oppressed, or the proletariat, has existed throughout history and existed in the mid- and late 19th century. The bourgeoisie, equated with capital, developed in the same proportion as the proletariat developed. The latter is defined as "a class of laborers, who live only so long as they find work, and who find work only so long as their labor increases capital."

The bourgeois class developed from the feudal economic system, which was replaced by a manufacturing system to meet the demands of new markets that kept expanding, even establishing world markets. Politically oppressed by the feudal nobility in the pre-existing system, the manufacturing middle class, itself revolutionized by the advance of industrialization, had achieved the position of power and control. "The executive of the modern state is but a committee for managing the common affairs of the whole bourgeoisie."

Beyond gaining political supremacy and massively altering the forms and extent of production, the bourgeoisie changed the face of society. By expanding the means of communication, all nations, even the most primitive, were drawn into civilization. The towns came to dominate the country, with significant increases in urban populations. The outcome of this was the creation of patterns of dependence: rural regions dependent on towns and cities; the primitive countries dependent on the developed ones. Also, the bourgeoisie destroyed the feudal patriarchal relations, "stripped of its halo every occupation, . . . and reduced the family relation to a mere money relation."

> It has resolved personal work into exchange value, and in place of the numberless indefeasible chartered freedoms, has set up that single, unconscionable freedom—Free Trade. In one word, for exploitation, veiled by religious and political illusions, it has substituted naked, shameless, direct, brutal exploitation.

Another outcome of centralized production was the concentration of property in a few hands and the creation of "more colossal productive forces than all preceding generations together." This means of production and its control are equated with social-political power. These movements of change are identified as constant, the "revolt of modern productive forces against modern conditions of production" leading to commercial crises during which existing products and previously created forces are destroyed. "The weapons with which the bourgeoisie felled feudalism to the ground are now turned against the bourgeoisie itself." The men who will wield the weapons of destruction are the modern working class, the proletarians.

Industrialization caused the work of proletarians to lose all its individual character. As a mere appendage of a machine, the worker's value is decreased, equal essentially to the cost of production, subsistence for his maintenance and for the propagation of his race.

As privates of the industrial army they are placed under the command of a perfect hierarchy of officers and sergeants. Not only are they slaves of the bourgeois class, and of the bourgeois state; they are daily and hourly enslaved by the machine, by the over-looker, and, above all, by the individual bourgeois manufacturer himself. The more openly this despotism proclaims gain to be its end and aim, the more petty, the more hateful and the more embittering it is.

The worker is further exploited, beyond the factory, by other members of the bourgeoisie—the landlord, the shopkeeper—who take his wages from him.

In 1848, the proletariat was not yet organized in the worker's own behalf. Its struggle with the bourgeoisie was scattered and individualized or by factory, locale or trade; it was misdirected against the instruments of production rather than the bourgeois conditions of production. However, the predicted change, given the development of industry—thus, the concentration of masses of workers and the equalization of life within the workers' rank and of wages at the same low level—was that the workers would unify.

The unifying force: communism. Defined as not forming a separate party in opposition to other working-class parties and as having no interests "separate and apart from those of the proletariat as a whole," the communists' immediate aims are the formation of the proletariat into a class, the overthrow of bourgeois supremacy and the conquest of political power by the proletariat. Marx and Engels saw the Communist Party as the only one that had as its purpose the advancing of the true interests of the proletariat as a class.

The "abolition of private property" was central in the theory of the communists. This abolition focused on bourgeois property, "the final and most complete expression of the system of producing and appropriating products that is based on class antagonisms, on the exploitation of the many by the few." (The "hard-won, self-acquired, self-earned property . . . of the petty artisan and of the small peasant" was perhaps excluded from this abolition; the issue was sidestepped by the view that such property had already been destroyed by the development of industry.)

Wage-labor does not create property for the laborer; it creates capital—"the kind of property which exploits wage-labor, and which cannot increase except upon condition of begetting a new supply of wage-labor for fresh exploitation." The solution to this antagonism between capital and wage-labor, given that capital is not a personal but a social power, was to convert capital into common property. The intention, further, was to change the "miserable character" of the "personal appropriation of the products of labor" so as "to widen, to enrich, to promote the existence of the laborer."

The proletariat will use its political supremacy to wrest, by degrees, all capital from the bourgeoisie, to centralize all instruments of production in the hands of the state, i.e., of the proletariat organized as the ruling class; and to increase the total of productive forces as rapidly as possible.

The "Communist revolution is the most radical rupture with traditional property relations . . . [and] with traditional ideas." *The Communist Manifesto* is a call to arms, to revolutionary activity.

While recognizing the variation of this undertaking in different countries, the following goals were identified as generally applicable:

1. Abolition of property in land and application of all rents of land to public purposes.
2. A heavy progressive or graduated income tax.
3. Abolition of all right of inheritance.
4. Confiscation of the property of all emigrants and rebels.
5. Centralization of credit in the hands of the state, by means of a national bank with state capital and an exclusive monopoly.
6. Centralization of the means of communication and transport in the hands of the state.
7. Extension of factories and instruments of production owned by the state; the bringing into cultivation of waste lands, and the improvement of the soil generally in accordance with a common plan.
8. Equal obligation of all to work. Establishment of industrial armies, especially for agriculture.
9. Combination of agriculture with manufacturing industries; gradual abolition of the distinction between town and country, by a more equitable distribution of the population over the country.
10. Free education for all children in public schools. Abolition of child factory labor in its present form. Combination of education with industrial production.

The concluding pages of the text define and differentiate between communism and several socialism movements. Three broad categories of socialism are discussed: reactionary socialism, including feudal socialism, petty-bourgeois socialism and German or "true" socialism; conservative or bourgeois socialism; and critical-utopian socialism. Each of these socialist movements is dismissed as inadequate, focusing on the dethroned aristocrat or the petty bourgeois; the preservation of the present state of society; the "redressing of social grievances, in order to secure the continued existence of bourgeois society" and the rejection of political and revolutionary action, seeking to improve conditions through appeals to society at large, chiefly the ruling class.

CENSORSHIP HISTORY

Censorship of Karl Marx's works began before the publication of *Manifesto of the Communist Party*. The political and social journal, *Rheinische Zeitung*, was suppressed in 1843, one year after Marx became editor. He was exiled in Paris and Brussels. He was expelled from France about 1845 for contributing to the radical magazine, *Vorwarts*. In 1849, the *Neue Rheinische Zeitung*, edited by

Marx, advocated nonpayment of taxes and armed resistance against Emperor Frederick William. The journal was suspended, and Marx was tried for treason; though acquitted by a middle-class jury, he was expelled from Germany.

Action to ban the *Manifesto* in Germany occurred in 1878. It grew out of two assassination attempts—on May 11 and June 2—on the life of Emperor William I, the second of which wounded him seriously. Chancellor Otto von Bismarck exploited the fact that the first assassin had once belonged to the Social Democratic Party and caused a bill to be drafted against the "socialists and their press." It failed because of opposition from the National Liberal Party. Though there was no evidence that the second assassin was a socialist, Bismarck again "conjured up the red peril" and dissolved the Reichstag. The next election gave him a stronger conservative party base, which easily passed his anti-socialism bill, the "Exceptional Law." In addition to limiting rights to form associations and organizations in support of social democratic, socialist or communist activities which "are designed to subvert the existing political order in ways that threaten the public order and particularly the harmony of the social classes," the law forbade the publication of newspapers or books, including the *Communist Manifesto*.

The Catholic Church undertook its anticommunist stance in the 19th century—"since *The Communist Manifesto* first appeared in 1848." Donald Crosby S.J. points out, "[T]he popes taught that communism was essentially atheistic and irreligious," representing the very Antichrist. They regarded the communists as "anarchistic, violent and opposed to what was best for man," and their materialism as contrary to "the heart of the church, the world of God and of the spirit." The savage persecution of Russian Catholics after the Bolshevik Revolution intensified the church's hostility. The *Communist Manifesto* during this time was listed in the *Index Librorum Prohibitorum*.

In the United States in the late thirties, Catholics identified anticommunism as demonstrating compatibility with American patriotism and the greater American society. The anticommunism of the church's leaders did not waver and was indeed solidified by the "martyring" of Archbishop Aloysius Stepinac of Yugoslavia and Joseph Cardinal Mindszenty of Hungary. Two positions of anticommunism emerged, particularly evident in the post–World War II period: a militant, conservative effort that allied with Senator Joseph McCarthy in zealous pursuit of subversives and "fellow travelers" in government and other aspects of society; and a liberal effort that, while equally opposed to communism, believed the answer was not "an extension of Red hunts and repressive legislation but an expansion of social programs designed to end hunger, disease, deficient housing and other social and economic ills that drove men into the hands of the Marxists." This group vehemently opposed Senator McCarthy and his tactics.

Given this historic position and current attitudes, the revelations of a poll of libraries in 30 cities, reported in the *New York Times* in 1953, are understandable. While public institutions did not curb books by communists—texts by Marx, Lenin and Stalin could be borrowed without restriction—some private religious education institutions did limit their availability. Roman Catholic universities such as Loyola University in New Orleans, Creighton University in Omaha and Marquette University in Milwaukee placed these texts under restricted access. Students could borrow them if related to assignments or if being used for reference under direction when studying the theories of communism for thesis work. At Marquette, the instructors submitted the names of students who borrowed these books; the list was subsequently turned over to the archbishop. The Marquette University spokesperson indicated as explanation for the restricted access of the *Manifesto* that it was listed in the Index.

The 1950–53 period in the United States was one of extensive criticism of Marx's works as well as other communist writings. The period was dramatically punctuated by the activities and accusations of Senator Joseph McCarthy and of the House Committee on Un-American Activities. It included such disparate situations as a 1950s report before the Illinois legislature's Seditious Activities Investigation Committee in 1950 that urged limiting access of many books by Marx in the public library. "They develop the subject at length and by so doing put in the young mind a yearning for that." At another level in 1953, after students in Brooksfield, Florida, who were working on papers about Russia, reported finding materials favoring that country, Paul B. Parker, a retired colonel and a library board member, set himself up as a one-person censorship committee. He removed an unspecified number of books and magazines from the nearby Brooksville public library because they were "communist propaganda." These included the *Manifesto of the Communist Party*, *Mission to Moscow* by Joseph E. Davies, former United States ambassador to Russia, and both *The New Republic* and *Reporter* magazines. Mayor Howard B. Smith demanded their return despite Parker's threat to label him a "fellow traveler." With the library board also insisting on the return of the material and further rejecting Parker's motion that the books and magazines be stamped "Propaganda," some were returned. One exception: *Manifesto of the Communist Party*.

The Boston Public Library came under attack on September 23, 1952, when the *Boston Post*, recently purchased by John Fox, revealed that it subscribed to the pro-Soviet monthly *New World Review* and to Russian newspapers, *Pravda* and *Izvestia*; it also disclosed it had a lobby display of the *Manifesto* and "thousands" of communist publications. The *Post* argued: "We believe that pro-Soviet literature should be suppressed in our public libraries. . . ." This position was counterargued by the director of the library, Milton E. Lord, who was supported by the *Boston Herald*. Lord was quoted: "It is essential that information in all aspects of the political, international and other questions be available for information purposes in order that citizens of Boston be informed about the friends and enemies of their country." Supporters of the *Post* included the American Legion and the Veterans of Foreign Wars; joining the *Herald* were the *Pilot*, a Catholic diocesan paper, and the *Christian Science Monitor*. On October 3, the Boston Public Library board voted 3–2 to maintain their collection of communist materials.

The idea of "branding" books emerged in San Antonio, Texas, in 1953. Mayor Jack White suggested to the city council that it "consider branding all communist-written volumes in the library," that is, books whose authors had been accused of affiliation with subversive organizations. The organizer of the San Antonio Minute Women, Myrtle Hance, provided a list of 600 titles by authors whose names had been gleaned from congressional investigation testimony. After the 15-member library board protested vehemently and the public's negative reaction to the proposal emerged, the branding idea was dropped.

During 1953, international repercussions resulted from the national debate. Senator McCarthy attacked the overseas libraries of the International Information Agency (IIA), claiming that there were some "30,000 volumes subversive of American interests" by 418 authors whose loyalty to the United States was suspect. The purpose of the libraries in the postwar period was to provide a balanced view of the opinion and thinking of the United States, to provide books that were nonpolitical in nature to accurately portray the American scene—without regard to the politics of the authors. The idea was to demonstrate the free marketplace of ideas to contrast and combat, in Germany, for example, the intellectual stagnation of the Nazi period. However, in practice during this period, according to David Oshinsky, "The rule of thumb, then, was to include 'controversial' books while excluding blatantly pro-communist or anti-American propaganda." The State Department, under its secretary, John Foster Dulles, reacted to McCarthy's attack by directing, with some confusion, the removal of all books by controversial authors—"communists, fellow-travelers, leftists, et cetera"—and books critical of U.S. policies. Even books without any political content were barred, including, for instance, the mysteries of Dashiell Hammett. In Australia and Singapore, the overseas library staffs actually burned books.

In his address to the graduating class of Dartmouth College on June 14, 1953, President Dwight D. Eisenhower spoke out against censorship: "Don't join the book-burners." He defended reading Marx and others as a way of maintaining awareness of the world crisis and the purposes of the Soviets; he defended the retention of "merely controversial" books in American libraries and overseas. However, at a subsequent press conference he objected to books advocating the overthrow of the United States and agreed to the elimination of books written by communists, while recommending books written by anticommunists about communism.

Censorship on the international scene was prevalent. As Jonathon Green summarizes, while there is not consistency, "it may be generally assumed that those governments pursuing right-wing totalitarianism or dictatorial policies are keen to ban the founder of communism." In this vein, a 1950 survey reported in the *New York Times* listed 16 countries as having outlawed the

Communist Party, "legally or otherwise, and have taken steps in that direction." The list included Greece, Turkey, Lebanon, Syria, Korea, Burma, Indonesia, Indo-China, Malaya, Portugal, Spain, Peru, Bolivia, Chile, Brazil and Venezuela. Other nations that then were considering such action included South Africa, Australia, Egypt and Denmark.

Anne Haight identifies the attempts of the Nationalist Government of China in 1929 to stop the reading of the *Manifesto* and *Das Kapital*. Karl Marx's works were among those 25,000 volumes publicly burned in Berlin, Germany, in 1933 in a large-scale "symbolic" bonfire demonstration. The destruction of books by the Nazis continued until World War II: in Austria, Vienna (1938) and Salzburg were notable sites; in Czechoslovakia, the education minister ordered all "unpatriotic" books, particularly by patriots, to be removed from public libraries and destroyed.

In 1946, the coordinating council of the American military government in Germany ordered the destruction of Nazi memorials in order to eliminate the "spirit of German militarism and Nazism as far as possible." Darkly ironic, the "placement of books by Hitler, Goebbels, Mussolini and Karl Marx on restricted lists in libraries, or in some instances pulped," was ordered on the 11th anniversary of the Nazi book-burning demonstration.

On two occasions, October 18, 1988 and March 8, 1989, customs officials in Grenada confiscated boxes of books being shipped by Pathfinder Press, a publisher of political, historical and academic books based in New York. The *Manifesto of the Communist Party* was one of the confiscated books. Other notable books barred include *One People, One Destiny: The Caribbean and Central America Today* by Don Rojas, *The State and Revolution* by V. I. Lenin, *The Struggle Is My Life* by Nelson Mandela, *Maurice Bishop Speaks: The Grenada Revolution 1979–83* by Maurice Bishop, *Malcolm X Speaks* by Malcolm X and *Nothing Can Stop the Course of History: An Interview with Fidel Castro* by Congressman Mervyn Dymally and Jeffrey M. Elliott.

FURTHER READINGS

"Book Burning." *The New Republic* 128 (June 29, 1953): 7–17.
"Branding of Books Stirs Texas Battle." *The New York Times* (June 7, 1953): 61.
Cook, Fred J. *The Nightmare Decade: The Life and Times of Senator Joe McCarthy*. New York: Random House, 1971.
Crankshaw, Edward. *Bismarck*. New York: Viking Press, 1981.
Crosby, Donald F., S.J. *God, Church, and the Flag: Senator Joseph R. McCarthy and the Catholic Church, 1950–1957*. Chapel Hill, N.C.: University of North Carolina Press, 1978.
"Firefighting." *The New Republic* 129 (September 7, 1953): 5.
Green, Jonathon. *The Encyclopedia of Censorship*. New York: Facts On File, 1990.
Haight, Anne Lyon, and Chandler B. Grannis. *Banned Books 387 B.C. to 1978 A.D.* 4th ed. New York: R.R. Bowker Company, 1978.

Importation of Publications (Prohibition) Order. Grenada. Statutory Rules and Orders No. 6 of 1989. Gazetted April 14, 1989.

Inter-American Commission on Human Rights. Report No. 2/96, Case 10, 325 Grenada. Washington, D.C.: Organization of American States, March 1, 1996.

Kipp, Lawrence J. "Report from Boston." *Library Journal* 77 (1952): 1,843–46, 1,887.

Oshinsky, David M. *A Conspiracy So Immense: The World of Joe McCarthy*. New York: Free Press, 1983.

Pathfinder Press Releases. New York: October 19, 1988; March 10, April 5 and April 27, 1989.

"Poll of Libraries Shows Free Choice." *The New York Times* (June 16, 1953): 22.

"St. George's, Grenada." *Newsletter on Intellectual Freedom* 38 (1989): 141–42.

"16 Countries Outlaw Reds, Survey Shows." *The New York Times* (May 16, 1950): 20.

MEIN KAMPF

Author: Adolf Hitler
Original date and place of publication: 1925, Germany; 1933, United States
Publisher: Eher Verlag, Germany; Houghton Mifflin, United States
Literary form: Biography

SUMMARY

Tormented and impoverished as a youth, optimistic yet often disappointed as an adolescent, determined and ultimately revered as a young man, Adolf Hitler's life echoes his work's title, which translates as *My Struggle*. In spite of the victories attained while rising to power and during his reign as fuhrer, he met many failures; his success can be attributed to sheer determination and will to see a "dream" fulfilled, even though for most it was and will always be a nightmare.

Hitler was born in 1889 on Easter Sunday in Braunau, a small Austrian border town on the Inn River that was highly concentrated with people of German heritage. Depending on whose viewpoint one believes, Hitler's childhood was either an exercise in the development of discipline or pure hell. Charles B. Flood, author of *Hitler: The Path to Power*, paints a macabre beginning for the man who would one day rule the German empire. Alois Hitler, Adolf's father, was labeled "a small-town Henry VIII" for his exploits with women. Before Adolf he produced two children by two different women. The first was a widow who bore him a daughter. They would marry and be together for seven years until she filed for separation because Alois had moved on to a 19-year-old kitchen maid in the hotel where they were living. After his estranged first wife died, he and the kitchen maid had a son, Alois Jr. They married, but she too died, which allowed Alois to marry Klara Polzl, the children's nursemaid, 23 years younger than he. She was Adolf's mother. According to Alois Jr., Hitler's half brother, Alois Sr., would at times beat

Junior unmercifully, and when he moved out at 14, the father's abusive behavior was shifted toward seven-year-old Adolf. Young Adolf bore many beatings by his father until one day he decided not to cry. After a total of 32 strikes with a stick, his father ceased, never to beat him again. This example of childhood misery, which some say worked to forge hard the mind of Hitler, goes unmentioned in the opening pages of *Mein Kampf*, due to the fact that, according to Otto D. Tolischus, reviewer for the *New York Times Magazine*, one of Hitler's primary goals was that the book be a tool of propaganda, not a solely biographical depiction highlighting, among other topics, his imperfect upbringing. This would explain Hitler's view of his father, which is very different from the account given by Flood. *Mein Kampf* has Hitler revering his father as "a gentleman . . . whose most ardent desire had been to help his son forge his career, thus preserving him from his own bitter experience (which had been growing up poor and without direction)." After his mother passed away, when Adolf was 18, his father having died when he was 13, Adolf said that "I honored my father, but my mother I had loved."

Mein Kampf is a work consisting of two volumes. The first, "A Reckoning," describes the period of Hitler's life when his thoughts on politics and the German Fatherland were combined to form his tenet of National Socialism; the second, "The National Socialist Movement," expands many of the ideas presented in the first volume. Those ideas stemmed from feelings and experiences of a young ambitious Hitler trying to forge a way of life for himself other than his father's suggestion of becoming a civil servant. Hitler's first love was art, which was squelched by his nonacceptance into the Academy (few thought as highly of Hitler's work as he). As a result, he turned his attention to architecture, but because of his intolerance for study at the Realschule, this also became an unfulfilled dream.

As his misfortune grew, he began making connections with other Austrian Germans, noting many shortcomings that he and they shared. He sensed a lack of pride toward the German heritage, not only from other Germans, but from all with whom he came into contact, as though somehow Germans were second-rate. He felt misplaced along with many other Austrian Germans, as if they were removed from a righteous existence. He saw the prevalence of Social Democrats in positions of power, positions that undermined the dignity of the working class, keeping the masses in line, obedient and helplessly stuck in positions of servitude.

Hitler learned to despise Jews because, in his viewpoint, they were the Social Democrats who made life miserable for Hitler and other Austrian Germans in the working class. Slowly, he began to notice that the most prominent members of the Social Democratic movement, the authors of the press, those who protested against restraints upon business, and those against whom he argued about the policies of marxism, the tool he directly related to Social Democracy, were all Jews. His greatest revelation in all of this was that these people were not of the Austrian nation or the German nation, but were foreigners who had come to take total control. They had no nation really. Even if a Jew had been born in Austria or Germany and was a citizen of either country, it made no difference to Hitler. His goal and the goal of all Germans would be to fight against the people whose purpose, according to Hitler, was the defilement of all humanity and destruction of all established cultures and nations. He reasoned that if the German nation was preserved and advanced by self-propagation, then that was upholding the work of nature and performing the will of God: "By defending myself against the Jew, I am fighting for the work of the Lord."

Not only did his experience in Vienna further sour his feelings toward Jews and marxism, he also saw other inadequacies that shifted him into a career in politics where his involvement with the National Socialist movement blossomed. In Austria, Hitler viewed Parliament as a self-serving system that totally neglected the working masses. If a problem or need arose that could not be remedied by the governing body, there seemed to be no blame placed upon anyone from within. Hitler could not recognize good government in a bureaucracy that did nothing but advance its own idleness and satisfaction of the status quo. Hitler was further infuriated with how the Parliament continued to maintain power by lulling the people into a status-quo satisfaction which, especially before times of election, seemed to ice any chance of change or revolution, which he desperately desired.

Upon his arrival in Austria in 1904, Hitler became involved in the Pan-Germanic movement. He idolized Georg von Schonerer and Dr. Karl Lueger, who both worked to save the German people from ruin and to destroy the Austrian state. However, the movement ultimately failed. According to Hitler, the movement lost all momentum because 1) the social problem had an unclear conception, 2) the tactics of trying to win support from within Parliament had failed and 3) the public lacked the will to see the revolution take place. Each of these elements brought the movement to a standstill. However, these elements would not be forgotten by Hitler, who saw each as direct opposition to what must happen in order for all German people to one day be reunited and prosper over all of Europe and ultimately the world.

Hitler returned to Munich shortly before the outbreak of World War I, which he called the happiest time in his life. He immediately requested in writing to be enlisted, and was given permission via King Ludwig III to don the tunic of the Bavarian regiment, in which he served for six years. This experience led Hitler to another key discovery in terms of his personal philosophy. Throughout the war Hitler noticed that propaganda was a tool keenly utilized by the enemy, who portrayed the Germans as fierce, bloodthirsty fighting machines—but not by his own government. He claimed this as one of the factors that led to Germany's hard loss. He saw propaganda, when properly utilized, as one of the most effective tools of war, a means by which the masses are uniformly persuaded: simple, true in essence and proven in methodology and message. He stored what he learned from this failure for certain future use.

Because the fall of the Reich happened so quickly, the defeat was recognized and immediately put aside, which according to Hitler provided more time for the rebuilding mentality to rapidly set in and grow. Building upon the earlier aims of the failed Pan-Germanic movement from his time in Austria, Hitler's focus became the full development of National Socialism, rallying a lost nation around the concept of strength through a united Germany. Within this goal was the operating premise that only those of pure German heritage were worthy of citizenry; all others were deemed expendable for the good of the nation.

> Any crossing between two beings of not quite the same high standard produces a medium between the standards of the parents. That means: the young one will probably be on a higher level than the racially lower parent, but not as high as the higher one . . . if it were different, every further development towards higher levels would stop, and rather the contrary would happen . . . just as little as Nature desires a mating between weaker individuals and stronger ones, far less she desires the mixing of a higher race with a lower one, as in this case her entire work of higher breeding, which has perhaps taken hundreds of thousands of years, would tumble at one blow . . . The result of any crossing, in brief, is always the following: (a) Lowering of the standard of the higher race; (b) Physical and mental regression, and, with it, the beginning of a slowly but steadily progressive lingering illness. To bring about such a development means nothing less than sinning against the will of the Eternal Creator.

Hitler's observations in youth came to represent the foundations of Nazi Germany. To him the Aryan, Hitler's master race, was the strong, powerful and culturally creative prototype of an ideal human being, the building block for humanity that reverberated the philosophy of the National Socialist Party. Diversity among races was a liability, not an asset; one race must rise above all others and claim absolute control. Only when Germans stood alone as the elite rulers of the world would his vision be complete. Until then, Hitler would use any tactic and force to attain that position.

The years leading up to World War II saw the most intense scrutiny of *Mein Kampf*, due to the fact that much of the world by now was certain that the text was a blueprint for Hitler's plan of world domination. Otto D. Tolischus, reporting for the *New York Times Magazine*, stated, "In content *Mein Kampf* is ten percent autobiography, ninety percent dogma, and one hundred percent propaganda. Every word in it . . . has been included . . . solely for the propagandist effect. Judged by its success, it is the propagandistic masterpiece of the age." The "masterpiece" also contains representations of Hitler's values: He recognized the futility of a government that was too large to uphold accountability and solve problems effectively; he identified one downfall of education as information taught yet never utilized while he promoted the Greek ideal of a balance between the development of mind and body as one; and he identified merit and strength in a nation bound by patriotism and the will to succeed.

CENSORSHIP HISTORY

Mein Kampf had many challenges from the time of its publication to the height of World War II. Jonathon Green in *The Encyclopedia of Censorship* identifies *Mein Kampf* as one of the "most often" censored books. But perhaps the most documented history comes courtesy of James and Patience Barnes's text, *Hitler's Mein Kampf in Britain and America*, which highlights not only the publication wars in the United States, but also key censorship cases that both directly and indirectly were brought on by *Mein Kampf.*

The first U.S. publication in this country was in 1933 by Houghton Mifflin in Boston; that version was published in London the same year by Hurst & Blackett. The translator for the text was E. T. S. Dugdale. A side note to the text's translation: In 1928 Curtis Brown Limited was given the translation rights from Eher Verlag, the German publisher. However, Cherry Kearton, a former Curtis Brown employee who shifted over to work for rival Hurst & Blackett, had left the text when he transferred companies, figuring that nothing would ever come of Hitler's position. When Hitler's chancellorship was announced, Kearton tried to obtain the copy of the text in hopes of beating out his former firm with the publication. However, Curtis Brown now demanded a hefty sum for just the untranslated text, a move that made the decision to purchase it more difficult. That was when Dugdale stepped in and offered his translated version to Kearton and Hurst & Blackett gratis. They accepted and went ahead with publication.

In August of that same year, the *American Hebrew and Jewish Tribune* cried foul against Houghton Mifflin for the upcoming publication, citing, "We charge these publishers with an attempt to cash in on the misery and catastrophe of an important section of the human family." An article from the August 18, 1933, edition of the *New York Times* quoted an editorial from the *American Hebrew and Jewish Tribune* that stated "that if Houghton Mifflin Company is bent on publishing Hitler's book 'they would do well to print the text in red, as symbolic of the blood that has dripped from Nazi bludgeons in the Third Reich . . .'" David Brown, publisher of the Jewish periodical, stated, "We protest emphatically against the publication, sale and distribution of the English translation of Hitler's *Mein Kampf* in the United States."

Reactions similar to those of the *American Hebrew and Jewish Tribune* also began to surface, and not just for the text itself, but against the publisher. A group of concerned New York City residents petitioned the New York City Board of Education, citing their efforts to discontinue the use of school textbooks that had been published by Houghton Mifflin. The residents charged that Houghton Mifflin was guilty of aiding in the spread of "propaganda of a common gangster." In rebuttal, Edward Mandel, associate superintendent of education, stated that the text must be placed so all "may see whether the book is worthy or is an exhibition of ignorance, stupidity, and dullness." The annual report for 1934 of the American Jewish Committee also issued a statement to counteract the publication of the text. Private citizens wrote to President Roosevelt, as well as to newspaper publishers. One letter to the *Chicago Israelite* stated, "It is the utterance of venomous untruths about a large law-abiding peoples and I was wondering if there was not some way to stop the publication of this book." In response to the public outcry, Roger L. Scaife, an officer with Houghton Mifflin, stated:

> In confidence I may add that we have had no end of trouble over the book—protest from the Jews by the hundreds, and not all of them from the common run of shad. Such prominent citizens as Louis Kirstein and Samuel Untermeyer and others have added their protest, although I am glad to say that a number of intellectual Jews have also written complimenting us upon the stand we have taken.

The pre-publication challenges did not succeed.

As domestic complaints were high in number, so, too, did the banning of *Mein Kampf* begin to happen more frequently on a global level. Three incidents occurred in the latter part of 1933. The first occurred in Prague, Czechoslovakia, on September 18, when Hitler's book was banned from sale or circulation, along with two other Austrian monarchist books of propaganda. The government was targeting not only Hitler, but a number of other National Socialist publications.

The second incident happened not a week later in Munich, Germany, where it was reported that the one millionth copy of the book had been put into circulation. Part of that article stated that Hitler's response to the apparent crushing of the National Socialist movement at the time he was thrown into Landsberg prison for his involvement in the famous "putsch" of 1923 was, "Give me five years after I am out of this and I shall have the party restored."

The third event occurred on October 1, 1933, when the court at Katowice in Warsaw, Poland, banned Hitler's book for being "insulting." German booksellers had previously protested a court-ordered confiscation of the work, but the court upheld its prior decision. Hitler's response to the ban was that the Poles had not been sufficiently Germanized before the world war.

Three years later, and on the eve of World War II, the Soviets began to increase their armaments significantly, fearing that an attack from Germany was imminent. Premier Vyacheslaff M. Molotoff [Molotov], speaking before the Congress of the Central Executive Committee, stressed that "Hitler, in *Mein Kampf*, states it is necessary for Germany to acquire new territory, and he points to Russia and the Baltic Region"; therefore, he urged that it was essential to make marked increases in the military budget. Whether the book was ever banned by the Soviets is not identified.

One year later, Germany and Austria came to an agreement concerning a press truce, so that *Mein Kampf* and German newspapers were permitted in Austria so long as they weren't used for propaganda against the German government.

116

In Germany, *Mein Kampf* was responsible for the banishment of the Bible. In 1942, Dr. Alfred Rosenberg, a key supporter of the "new national church," released a 30-point doctrine of the National Reich Church, which outlined the plan for all churches to be transformed into instruments of the state and for Christianity to be systematically eliminated from all facets of religious existence. Seven of the 30 points specifically refer to the banishment of the Bible, which is to be subsequently replaced by *Mein Kampf*:

13) The National Reich Church demands the immediate cessation of the printing of the Bible, as well as its dissemination, throughout the Reich and colonies. All Sunday papers with any religious content also shall be suppressed.

14) The National Reich Church shall see that the importation of the Bible and other religious works into Reich territory is made impossible.

15) The National Reich Church decrees that the most important document of all time—therefore the guiding document of the German people—is the book of our Fuehrer [sic], *Mein Kampf*. It recognizes that this book contains the principles of the purist ethnic morals under which the German people must live.

16) The National Reich Church will see to it that this book spread its active forces among the entire population and that all Germans live by it.

17) The National Reich Church stipulates that the future editions of *Mein Kampf* shall contain its present number of pages and contents unmodified.

18) The National Reich Church will remove from the altars of all churches the Bible, the cross and religious objects.

19) In their place will be set that which must be venerated by the German people and therefore is by God, our most saintly book, *Mein Kampf*, and to the left of this a sword.

Today only one version of *Mein Kampf* is easily attainable in the United States. Copyrighted in 1971, published by Houghton Mifflin and translated by Ralph Manheim, it represents the work of, as the translator labels Hitler, "a half-educated writer, without clear ideas, [who] generally feels that to say a thing only once is rather slight." He also states that Hitler's style attempts to come off as highly educated and cultured, which marks his style at best redundant and without an edge.

FURTHER READINGS

Barnes, James J., and Patience P. Barnes. *Hitler's Mein Kampf in America.* Cambridge, Mass.: Cambridge University Press, 1980.

Cohen, Carl, ed. *Communism, Fascism, and Democracy*, 2nd ed. New York: Random House, 1972.

"Czechs Ban Hitler's Book." *The New York Times* (September 19, 1933): 12.

Flood, Charles Bracelen. *Hitler: The Path to Power*. Boston: Houghton Mifflin Company, 1989.

Green, Jonathon. *The Encyclopedia of Censorship*. New York: Facts On File, 1990.

Haight, Anne Lyon, and Chandler B. Grannis. *Banned Books: 387 B.C. to 1978 A.D.*, 4th ed. New York: R.R. Bowker Company, 1978.

"Hitler Book Is Banned as 'Insulting' in Poland." *The New York Times* (October 1, 1933): 4:2.

"Millionth Copy of Book by Hitler Off the Press." *The New York Times* (September 28, 1933): 16.

"Nazi State Church Plan Proposes to Oust Other Faiths and Ban Bible." *The New York Times* (January 3, 1942): 1.

"Publisher Scored for Hitler's Book." *The New York Times* (August 18, 1933): 16.

"Reich and Austria Reach Peace Truce." *The New York Times* (July 13, 1937): 15.

Sabine, George H., and Thomas L. Thorson. *A History of Political Theory*. 4th ed. Hinsdale, Ill.: Dryden Press, 1973.

"Soviets to Increase All Arms, Fearing Reich and Japan." *The New York Times* (January 11, 1936): 1.

Tolischus, Otto D. "The German Book of Destiny." *The New York Times Magazine* (October 28, 1936): 1–2, 23.

—Eric P. Schmidt

1984

Author: George Orwell
Original date and place of publication: 1949, London; 1949, United States
Publishers: Secker and Warburg; Harcourt Brace Jovanovich
Literary form: Novel

SUMMARY

The time after World War II was one of great turmoil. Although the immediate danger was over, many feared that the communist ideologies that had taken over the U.S.S.R. and parts of eastern Europe would spread throughout the world, meaning an end to the democracy and capitalism under which the United States and many other countries flourished. *1984* is a novel that took these fears to their furthest point, projecting a future world that is entirely totalitarian and describing in-depth the problems of humanity in such a world.

Winston Smith lives in London on the landmass known as Airstrip One in the country Oceania. The 39-year-old man is sickly and balding with a bleeding open sore on his ankle that never heals. Every day he must climb the seven floors to his apartment, for the elevator never works. His main subsistence is the stale bread and pasty stew with unidentifiable meat that he can get for lunch at work. In order to keep sane, he drinks a lot of Victory Gin, which makes his eyes water as it painfully slides down his throat, and smokes many Victory Cigarettes, which he must always remember to hold carefully so the tobacco does not fall out. He is constantly surrounded by the lies his government tells, forced to listen to them at all hours from the telescreens blaring away in every room. He is one of the few aware that what is heard are lies, for he works as a fact-changer at the Ministry of Truth, which is responsible for all publications, propaganda and entertainment for Oceania.

> What happened in the unseen labyrinth to which the pneumatic tubes led, he did not know in detail, but he did know in general terms. As soon as all the corrections which happened to be necessary in any particular number of the *Times* had been assembled and collated, that number would be reprinted, the original copy destroyed, and the corrected copy placed on the files in its stead. This process of continuous alteration was applied not only to newspapers, but to books, periodicals, pamphlets, posters, leaflets, films, sound tracks, cartoons, photographs—to every kind of literature of documentation which might conceivably hold any political or ideological significance. Day by day and almost minute by minute the past was brought up to date. . . . In no case would it have been possible, once the deed was done, to prove that any falsification had taken place.

At the same time as history is being revised, statistics are being faked so they are in accordance with the image the Party wishes to project:

> But actually, he thought as he readjusted the Ministry of Plenty's figures, it was not even forgery. It was merely the substitution of one piece of nonsense for another. . . . For example, the Ministry of Plenty's forecast had estimated the output of boots for the quarter at a hundred and forty-five million pairs. The actual output was given as sixty-two millions. Winston, however, in rewriting the forecast, marked the figure down to fifty-seven millions, so as to allow for the usual claim that the quota had been overfilled. In any case, sixty-two millions was no nearer the truth than fifty-seven millions, or than a hundred and forty-five millions. Very likely no boots had been produced at all. Likelier still, nobody knew how many had been produced, much less cared. All one knew was that every quarter astronomical numbers of boots were produced on paper, while perhaps half the population of Oceania went barefoot.

In addition to the faking of statistics, historical facts are changed. Besides Oceania, the only other countries in the world are Eastasia and Eurasia. If Oceania is at war with one of these, it has always been at war with it. So, when the country changes allies and begins warring with a different nation, all of the past newspaper articles detailing the war must be changed to fit into this new world order. Then every individual must change the past in his or her mind, known as doublethink, and forget that anything other than this new truth was ever known.

It is this kind of deception that has Winston questioning his entire upbringing. He has always been told that Big Brother, the leader of the Party, saved the country from the terrible oppression of the capitalists. But he looks around him at the lack of many necessities and substandard quality of others and wonders if it has always been this way. If the Party lies about war, could it not also lie about saving society?

He has decided to begin consciously fighting the Party and attempting to discover the truth by keeping a diary of his thoughts, most of which are against Big Brother. He is careful to point out, though, that his first act of defiance began long ago. When one thinks about defying Big Brother, he or she has already committed a crime against him, known as thoughtcrime, which in and of itself is punishable by death. For this reason, Winston thinks he may as well go as far as possible in his defiance because he is essentially already dead.

Some day the Thought Police will catch him and he will die. Every room has a telescreen that simultaneously broadcasts Party news and monitors whatever is happening in the room for the Thought Police. People he knows could turn him in to save themselves. He has already reconciled himself to the fact that he will be caught someday and has given up any hope for his future. But he wants to find out the truth before he is discovered.

Winston's journey to discover this truth while rebelling against the Party encompasses many levels. The first is his fascination with the past. Winston frequents an antique shop where many relics of the age of capitalism are present—things that have no real purpose other than beauty, such as a blown glass paperweight filled with coral. He purchases the paperweight and takes the opportunity to talk with the proprietor about the time before Big Brother took over. The man does not know much, but he gives some credence to Winston's idea that the world was better before the reign of Big Brother.

A second level of rebellion is sexual. The Party does not like people to bond in that way, fearing that they may love one another more than they love the Party, and has set up many anti-sex leagues to promote its view. Winston is approached one day by a beautiful, young woman named Julia, who also works at the Ministry of Truth. After many difficult encounters where they attempt to hide from the telescreens, they agree to meet in a clearing in the woods. Here they are able to be free with one another and have sex for the first time. They do it because they have been told not to, and the more rebellious they are, the better they like it. After a few more such meetings Winston gets the proprietor of the antique store to rent them the furnished room above his shop. There they have many encounters, which are more than just sex, but a sharing of feelings and desires.

The third level is a more active form of rebellion against Big Brother. Julia and Winston decide to attempt to join the underground organization called the Brotherhood. Winston has always felt a special comradeship with a member of the Inner Party who works in his building, O'Brien. In the hall one day, O'Brien tells him how much he admires his work and to stop by his house for a new edition of the dictionary of Newspeak, the official language of Oceania. Winston and Julia take the chance that this is a secret message and arrive at O'Brien's house together in order to proclaim their hatred of Big Brother and their alliance with the Brotherhood. O'Brien, after questioning them, agrees to let them join, and gets a copy of the book that details the truth about Big Brother and the formation of Oceania.

The book, entitled *The Theory and Practice of Oligarchical Collectivism*, was written by the man on whom most of the anger and hatred of the Party members is focused, Emmanuel Goldstein. It appears that years before he was a highly influential charter member of the Party, but as its views changed, he was eliminated and has now become the scapegoat for all of the problems of Oceania. During the Two Minutes Hate, a daily ceremony in which all members are required to participate, his face is constantly shown so it can be insulted. The book discusses the truth behind the three Party slogans—"Ignorance is Strength," "War is Peace" and "Freedom is Slavery." For instance, war is peace because the constant preparation for war allows the economy to remain steady by using up surplus goods. Although battles rarely take place, war is a socially acceptable excuse for constant rationing. It also keeps the citizens in the state of fear, which makes them believe they need the protection of the government.

After receiving the book and reading it, Julia and Winston are caught in their room above the antique shop. A picture falls down to reveal the telescreen, which has been monitoring them the whole time. Then the proprietor, who has removed his disguise, is seen in his true form, a member of the Thought Police. They are brought to the Ministry of Love and put in separate jail cells. After much physical torture and starvation, which is standard procedure for all criminals, Winston begins his special sessions with O'Brien, who, along with the Thought Police, had been monitoring Winston for seven years. During these sessions O'Brien uses a type of shock therapy to get Winston to realize the power of the Party and the futility of opposing it. Winston holds firm to his belief that the Party cannot take the truth from him, believing there are certain truths that cannot be controlled. For instance, he thinks that 2+2=4, and there is no other way to think. O'Brien, though, gets him to believe that 2+2=5, which proves the end of his resistance and final acceptance of everything the Party tells him.

After he is released from the Ministry of Love, Winston is a pitiful shell of what he once was. He doesn't really work anymore, but spends his time drinking at a cafe and playing chess with himself. He sees Julia once, but their desire to be together has been taken from them, and both accept the Party's truth. He knows one day, when he is not paying attention, he will be shot in the back of the head. But he believes that he has discovered the ultimate truth of Big Brother and has been saved, so he is ready. The final lines of the novel show his ultimate acceptance of that which he vehemently denied his entire life.

He gazed up at the enormous face. Forty years it had taken him to learn what kind of smile was hidden beneath the dark mustache. O cruel, needless misunderstanding! O stubborn, self-willed exile from the loving breast! Two ginger-scented tears trickled down the sides of his nose. But it was all right, everything was all right, the struggle was finished. He had won the victory over himself. He loved Big Brother.

CENSORSHIP HISTORY

Many attempts have been made to rid school libraries of *1984* in the nearly 50 years since its publication. Jonathon Green identifies the novel as one of "those books that have been most often censored." In his introduction to *Celebrating Censored Books*, Lee Burress identified the 30 most frequently challenged books from a compilation of data from six national surveys of censorship pressures on American schools (1965–82); *1984* ranked fifth. This was especially true in the sixties and seventies, when the nation was gripped in fear over the possibility of nuclear war with the Soviet Union, whose mere existence as a successful communist country threatened the United States and its democratic ideals. As such, the novel was frequently called into question.

More often than not, though, these claims surround the immorality and profanity of the novel. The sexual explicitness was often called inappropriate for adolescents or for any age group. Some did object to the study of the book because of its communistic ties. In the Lee Burress study of censorship in Wisconsin schools conducted in 1963, the John Birch Society is cited as objecting to the book for its "study of communism." A 1966 national survey completed by Burress, which does not cite specific names or places, identifies a principal who thought the novel "shows communism in a favorable light." A parent on the same survey complained that the "socialistic state shows utopia which is wrong." While in the latter case the request was denied, the principal's objection prevented the book from being purchased.

In a case cited in Jack Nelson and Gene Roberts's *The Censors and the Schools*, a teacher in Wrenshall, Minnesota, refused to remove *1984* from his reading list, leading to his dismissal. He was reinstated, though, after arguments "that the book 'illustrates what happens in a totalitarian society.'"

Nelson and Roberts also discuss the censoring of *1984* as a consequence of the "textbook battles" of the 1960s in Texas. Ten novels were removed from the libraries of the four Amarillo high schools and Amarillo College, including MacKinlay Kantor's *ANDERSONVILLE*, Aldous Huxley's *BRAVE NEW WORLD*, John Steinbeck's *THE GRAPES OF WRATH* and Oliver La Farge's *Laughing Boy*. (Please refer to the censorship history discussion of *ANDERSONVILLE*.) According to Nelson and Roberts, most objections were raised because of obscenities in the novels, but some charges were due to the books' "political ideas or because the authors had once belonged to groups cited by the House Un-American Activities Committee."

As late as 1981, similar complaints were still being lodged. A Baptist minister in Sneads, Florida, Rev. Len Coley, attempted to have the book banned from school use on numerous occasions, often claiming the support of other church groups who later denied involvement. He said it was pro-communist and contained explicit sexual material. As cited in the *Newsletter on Intellectual Freedom*, though, on January 13, 1981, the Jackson County school board voted unanimously to retain the novel as a "parallel reading text in a course on 'anti-communism' offered at Sneads High School."

Many cases do not turn out so well, however. Many objections to the novel end with its removal from the classroom or the library or with it not being purchased. The continual objections to the novel are well evidenced by the fact that in a national survey completed by Burress in 1966, although the book was already considered a classic by many critics, it was only present in 43 percent of school libraries.

FURTHER READINGS

Burress, Lee. *Battle of the Books: Literary Censorship in the Public School, 1950–1985.* Metuchen, N.J.: Scarecrow Press, 1989.
———. *Censorship Report.* Unpublished: 1966.
———. "The Pressure of Censorship on Wisconsin Public Schools." *Wisconsin English Journal* 6 (October 1963): 6–28.
Green, Jonathon. "Index of Banned Books." *The Encyclopedia of Censorship.* New York: Facts On File, 1990.
Karolides, Nicholas J., and Lee Burress, eds. *Celebrating Censored Books.* Racine, Wisc.: Wisconsin Council of Teachers of English, 1985.
Nelson, Jack, and Gene Roberts, Jr. *The Censors and the Schools.* Boston: Little, Brown and Company, 1963.
Newsletter on Intellectual Freedom 30 (1981): 73.

—Jane Graves

THE PRINCE (IL PRINCIPE)

Author: Niccolò Machiavelli
Original date and place publication: 1532, Italy; 1640, England
Publishers: Antonio Blado; R. Bishop
Literary form: Nonfiction

SUMMARY

Dedicated to Lorenzo de' Medici (though initially to Giuliano de' Medici, his uncle, who died in 1516), *The Prince* was written in 1513–14, against a backdrop of 15th-century Italian intrigue, strife and political upheaval. Machiavelli had been a casualty of this upheaval when the republican government of Florence in which he had been a civil servant, chiefly in the diplomatic corps, fell and the Medici family returned to power. (Three generations of Medicis had ruled prior to the formation of the republican government in 1494.)

Machiavelli's purpose in this treatise on politics, at least on the surface, is to offer advice on successful governance, including gaining and maintaining control of territories. Ultimately, he wanted a "strong state, capable of imposing its authority on a hopelessly divided Italy" and the expulsion of foreign powers. Underlying his analysis is a basic tenet: "the real truth of things rather than an imaginary view of them," favoring political realism and rejecting idealist views of human behavior, including rulers and the ruled, with regard to political practice and response. In this context of politics, Machiavelli subordinated morals to political expediency.

Having minimized the problems of princes of hereditary states in maintaining control of their territory—"it is simply a matter of not upsetting ancient customs, and of adjusting them instead to meet new circumstances," for the people have grown accustomed to their prince's family—Machiavelli turns his attention to the greater difficulties of "mixed principalities," that is, a new territory grafted onto the old states, and of new states. These difficulties increase when the language, customs and laws of the new possession differ from those of the conquering prince.

One of the chief difficulties is the conquered, some of whom may have welcomed the opportunity to change masters but are fickle in their friendship when they discover that their expectations of bettering their lives have not been borne out. Additionally, those who have been harmed in the power seizure become enemies. Machiavelli recommends extinguishing the family line of the previous prince but maintaining the old way of life and customs, laws and taxes, thus earning the good will of the people, so as to incorporate the new territory into the old in the shortest possible time.

For new possessions, Machiavelli recommends that the new prince go to the new territory to live; troubles may be spotted and dealt with before they expand. Another tactic is to establish colonies rather than maintain any army because fewer are hurt and they are poor and scattered.

> All the others remain untouched, which is a persuasion to keep quiet; yet they also become fearful of making a mistake and suffering like those who have already been despoiled. . . . And in this connection it should be remarked that men ought either to be caressed or destroyed, since they will seek revenge for minor hurts but will not be able to revenge major ones. Any harm you do to a man should be done in such a way that you need not fear his revenge.

Further, the conqueror should become the protector of his weak neighbors, should act to weaken his strong neighbors and should fight an invading force of a powerful foreigner. In this vein, Machiavelli asserts, using the Romans as his example, that war should not be avoided: " . . . wars don't just go away, they are only postponed to another's advantage." A critical error in this regard is to allow or assist another state to become powerful. "From this we can draw a general rule, which never fails or only rarely: the man who makes another powerful ruins himself."

Machiavelli distinguishes between those princes who acquire territories through chance or good fortune and those who acquire territories through their own arms and energy. While the latter may endure more problems in gaining and securing power; they will more easily hold power because of the strength of character they exhibited. "Such men meet with great difficulties in their rise to power; all their dangers are on the way up, and must be overcome by their talents (*virtù*) but once they are on top, once they are held in veneration, and have destroyed all their envious rivals, they remain powerful, secure, honored, and happy." In contrast, men who achieve new states with other people's arms and by good luck are at a loss because they are dependent on the good will and good fortune of those who elevated them. They cannot command because they lack capability and do not have their own loyal troops unless they corrupt them.

Cesare Borgia exemplifies one who became established through the power of his natural father, Pope Alexander VI, and his troops. However, Cesare, a man of shrewdness and ambition, solidified his position by attacking neighboring cities. Having taken control of the Romagna, and realizing the people had been plundered by their former masters and had become lawless, he created peace and obedience by establishing good government based on absolute authority and cruelty. When his ends were achieved, he caused his agent, the man held responsible for the excessive harshness, to be publicly and savagely murdered, thus removing the onus of blame from himself. Machiavelli does not condemn Cesare but offers him as a model for those who rise to power through the fortune and arms of others.

While he credits their courage and their ability to overcome adversity, Machiavelli does not acknowledge as excellent those who come to power by crime. It is a factor neither of fortune nor of virtue to "murder his fellow citizens, betray his friends, to be devoid of truth, pity, or religion."

In discussing empowerment to rule in a civil princedom, Machiavelli identifies two forces: the nobles, who desire to command and oppress the people; and the people, who desire not to be dominated and oppressed. Becoming a prince with the help of the nobles is more difficult than with the help of the people. The nobles claim equality, so he cannot command or manage them; also, the nobles are apt to be self-interested and independent and, thus, not dependable in times of adversity. If the people have selected him, the prince needs only take them under his protection and provide benefits for them; he should do this even if they did not select him in order to gain their support and obligation. This is all the more important when it is recognized that a prince cannot make himself safe against a hostile people; there are too many of them. He can, however, safeguard against hostile nobles who are few. "And because men, when they receive benefits from a prince whom they expected to harm them, are especially obligated to him, such a prince's subjects may feel more warmly toward him than if he had risen to power with their help."

Several chapters focus on character and behavior attributes of princes that lead to praise or blame. In introducing these, Machiavelli identifies basic generalizations: "I know everyone will agree that among these many qualities a prince certainly ought to have all those that are considered good. But since it is impossible to have and exercise them all, because the conditions of human life simply do not allow it, a prince must be shrewd enough to avoid the public disgrace of those vices that would lose him his state." These also reveal a practical imperative: success of the enterprise.

Machiavelli compares several key virtues and vices. Among these are generosity and stinginess; he opts for the latter because by being stingy a prince can save his resources to support the defense of his state and to engage in wars and ventures without taxing his people. Generosity is not recognized unless it is so ostentatious as to deplete his funds, causing him to raise money through taxes. Princes can afford to be generous with what belongs to strangers.

While being thought merciful is preferable, princes will find cruelty advantageous. Cesare Borgia used cruelty to unify, to restore order and obedience. Cruelty can also compel loyalty and respect, particularly among soldiers. However, such behavior should be tempered with humanity to avoid being hated. For a prince to be feared is more advantageous than to be loved. Men—"ungrateful, fickle, liars and deceivers, fearful of danger and greedy for gain"—don't worry about offending a man who makes himself loved when it is to their advantage; fear, however, involves dread of punishment from which there is no escape. To avoid being hated, though feared, a prince should refrain from taking the property of his subjects and citizens and from taking their women. "Cruelty is badly used when it is infrequent at first, but increases with time instead of diminishing."

Comparably, Machiavelli argues that a crafty, cunning, manipulative prince is more successful than one who keeps his word. A prince needs to be flexible in this regard to suit his interests. He cites Pope Alexander VI as a master at such deception; while appearing virtuous, convincing in his assertions and solemn in his oaths and using these characteristics, when possible, he was ready for the contrary when the situation warranted. Men judge by appearances. The prince's task is to "win victories and uphold his state."

By avoiding contempt and hatred, by demonstrating in his actions that he isn't fickle or frivolous, that he is courageous, sober and strong, the prince will be highly esteemed. This respect and the good will of his people whom he keeps satisfied will avert internal subversion against which the prince must be on guard. Conspirators will not act against him if they know the people will be outraged and will not support them. The prince must also be on guard against foreign powers. This defense is secured by good weapons and good friends; "if he has good weapons, he will never lack for good friends."

The Prince concludes with an impassioned "exhortation to restore Italy to liberty and free her from barbarians," a plea seemingly connected to his dedication. The times are propitious; the country is ready to be released from "cruel insolence of the barbarians." He calls particularly on the House of the Medici to raise a citizen army to disperse and defeat the invaders.

Machiavelli's name has become synonymous with unscrupulous political behavior. He has been identified as an agent of Satan and charged with "deliberately advocating evil." Segments quoted out of context, as exemplified by the Gentillet publication (see Censorship History), effectively illustrate Machiavelli's iniquity. Such interpretations still obtain, as exemplified by the opinion of Leo Strauss: "If it is true that only an evil man will stoop to teach maxims of public and private gangsterism, we are forced to say that Machiavelli was an evil man."

A more modern interpretation focuses on Machiavelli's intent to express the reality of political action based on analysis of history in contrast to the ideal behavior. J. R. Hale infers that Machiavelli "was concerned only with *il vero*, the true picture of what actually happened, and that he only talked about politics in terms directly deduced from the way in which men had behaved and did behave." An extension of this position, as identified by numerous critics, is Machiavelli's low esteem of men, evident in *The Prince* in his derisive language and attitude describing the populace, the nobles and the rulers themselves.

Robert M. Adams relates a 180-degree variation in the 20th century, that is, "tradition [which] has emphasized the idealistic, enthusiastic, patriotic, and democratically minded Machiavelli." In this context he acclaims Machiavelli as "a great moral conscience"; "he resurrects . . . the undying worm of man's bad conscience at pretending to rule his fellow men."

CENSORSHIP HISTORY

Despite Antonio Blado's having received permission from Pope Clement VII (Giulio de' Medici) to publish Machiavelli's writing, in 1559 all of Machiavelli's works were placed on the Index of Prohibited Books, the Index of Paul IV, in the "banned absolutely" category. Compiled by the Holy Inquisition in Rome at the urging of Pope Paul IV (described as "implacably anti-heretical"), the Index forbade Catholics to read the works, including *The Prince*, or even own copies. The prohibition resulted from the Council of Trent, meeting from 1545 to 1563 in order to strengthen the discipline of the Roman Catholic Church against Protestantism. Pope Paul IV, a lifelong inquisitor and mortal enemy of heresy, widened the scope of the Index to include, beyond heresy, morality and manners in general. This was the first appearance of Machiavelli on an Index list.

This censorship system was finally abandoned in 1966; the last Index, the Index of Leo XIII, had been published in 1881 with supplements in 1884, 1896 and 1900. Books previously banned but published prior to 1600 were removed from the Index, "although," as Jonathon Green points out, "they are to be considered as much condemned today as they ever were."

The 1572 massacre of some 50,000 French Huguenots by Catholic leaders, beginning on Saint Bartholomew's night and extending for several weeks, was blamed on Machiavelli by the Protestants. This was because Catherine de' Medici, the queen mother and power behind the throne of her 22-year-old son, was a reader of Machiavelli; she was hated as an Italian and a Medici and as a secret and treacherous person. The irony of the accusation against Machiavelli is that the Catholics were at this time forbidden to read him.

In 1576, a French Huguenot, Innocent Gentillet, published (in French) *A discourse on the meanes of evel governing and maintaining in good peace, a kingdome, or other principalitie: Divided into three parts, namely, the counsele, the religion, and the policie, which a prince ought to hold and follow. Against Nicholas Machiavelli, the Florentine*. It was translated and published in English in 1602. Gentillet, who held Machiavelli directly responsible for the Saint Bartholomew massacre, used selected maxims to attack *The Prince*. His text was considerably influential since translation of *The Prince* itself into the languages of Protestant countries was delayed for many years. The English translation was published in 1640 when the episcopal censorship broke down. (See Censorship History discussion of *AREOPAGITICA* by John Milton.) The Elizabethans' understanding of and hostility to *The Prince* derived from Gentillet's book.

In his *Encyclopedia of Censorship*, Jonathon Green lists Machiavelli's *Il Principe* as one of the "most often" censored books.

Two alternative scenarios: In 1935, Benito Mussolini, Fascist dictator of Italy, encouraged the distribution of *Il Principe*, thereby demonstrating Italy's need for an all-powerful dictator supported by a national army. And shortly after Fidel Castro overthrew the Batista government in Cuba in 1959, a newspaper reported that *The Prince* was on his revolutionary reading list.

FURTHER READINGS

Adams, Robert M. "The Interior Prince, or Machiavelli Mythologized" and "The Rise, Proliferation, and Degradation of Machiavellism: An Outline." In *The Prince*. Ed. Robert M. Adams. New York. W.W. Norton & Company, 1977. 238–50.

Bull, George. "Introduction." In *The Prince*. Trans. by George Bull. Baltimore: Penguin Books, 1961. 9–26.

Green, Jonathon. *The Encyclopedia of Censorship*. New York: Facts On File, 1990.

Haight, Anne Lyon, and Chandler B. Grannis. *Banned Books 387 B.C. to 1978 A.D.* 4th ed. New York: R.R. Bowker, 1978.

Hale, J. R. "The Setting of *The Prince*." In *The Prince*. Ed. Robert M. Adams, New York: W.W. Norton, 1977. 141–52.

Magill, Frank N., ed. *Masterplots*. Rev. ed. Englewood Cliffs, N.J.: Salem Press, 1976.

Strauss, Leo. "Machiavelli the Immoralist." In *The Prince*. Ed. Robert M. Adams, New York: W.W. Norton, 1977. 180–85.

THE RIGHTS OF MAN

Author: Thomas Paine
Original date and place of publication: 1791 (1st part), 1792 (2nd part), United States; 1791 (1st part), 1792 (2nd part), England. The first part was also serialized in New York City in the summer of 1791.
Publisher: Graham, United States; serialized by the *Daily Advertiser*; Jeremiah Samuel Jordan, England
Literary form: Nonfiction

SUMMARY

In the latter part of the 1700s, as England saw its prized colony slip away from control and witnessed revolution in France, it attempted to suppress the flow of ideas from America, whose independence served as an inspiration to others who would fight for liberty and was seen as a danger to the Crown. Much of the efforts centered on the works of Thomas Paine. *The Rights of Man* was among the most prosecuted books in the 1790s in England. Most often it was prosecuted on the charge of seditious libel.

Paine began writing *The Rights of Man* within two days of the publication of Edmund Burke's 1790 book, *Reflections on the Revolution in France*. Burke, who bitterly denounced the French Revolution, had heretofore been much admired by Paine, but Paine turned on what he saw as flaws in Burke's writings as well as the inherent evil of the English government.

Paine's writing style is recursive. In addition, many of his ideas focus on the history of his time, but the historical data were not what got Paine into trouble with the censors.

Paine begins by refuting Burke's assertion that the ascension of William and Mary in 1689 bound the nation of England in fealty forever to the monarchy. Paine claimed that it was absurd to believe that today's generation could be bound by the promises of earlier generations. The living must have precedence over the dead, and the Parliament that gave the oath of loyalty had no power to do so; hence, the actions of that earlier generation are not binding on those people living in the present.

Paine also argues against the notion of hereditary superiority. "Man" is the highest title that one can receive or need. As there is no inherent quality in a title, such titles are merely meaningless nicknames, but a "unity of man" stems from the natural rights of all human beings. As all people are equally children of God, so all are equal in rights to each other.

Among the natural rights that humans have simply because of existence are intellectual rights, which include liberty to read and hear, to speak and to think.

The rights of the mind also include spiritual rights. Paine forcefully argues that freedom of religion is not simply tolerance. Humans have no right or power to simply "tolerate" another religion; to speak of tolerance would be tantamount to a deliberative body passing a law allowing God to receive the worship of the Jew or to prevent God from doing this. Clearly, no earthly power exists that could pass such a measure. To God, all beliefs are equal and one. Besides intellectual rights, humans have the right to act in the interests of their own happiness, so long as the pursuit of happiness is not injurious to the rights of others.

Out of these natural rights are derived civil rights. To exist in society requires a certain sacrifice of some portion of natural rights. But this sacrifice must be a part of a social compact; no government can summarily take these rights from its people. People enter into society in order to ensure enjoyment of civil rights, which individuals acting on their own might not be able to guarantee.

Paine then builds on these ideas of rights by examining the ways in which a government may rule. Governments can exist through superstition and be led by priests; they can exist through the force of power and be led by conquerors; or they can be based on rights and rule through reason and the will of the people. The last is the only government that deserves to exist. By contrast, an aristocracy is equal to tyranny for several reasons: As there is no heredity of ability, there is no justice in passing power within a particular family from one generation to another; aristocratic classes are not accountable to the people and thus are inherently unjust; the aristocracy is based on power instead of rights; the aristocratic class (in part due to rules of primogeniture) necessarily degenerates over the course of time.

In contrast to England, Paine presents France. Much of the first part of *The Rights of Man* is devoted to countering claims of tyranny and excess in the French Revolution. Unfortunately for Paine, only a few years would pass before such tyranny would occur and he himself would become one of the victims of it, a prisoner in France after the revolution. But France, says Paine, is superior to England because it has a real constitution and because its legislature is responsive to the people. Where the government can claim to "reform itself," there is no real chance for reform, because there is no accountability. Paine asserts that everything about the government of England is the opposite of what it should be.

The second part of *The Rights of Man* was published in 1792. Again, it was well received by the reading public. Paine explains why representative government is best. Using America as a model and harbinger of change, Paine demonstrates that monarchies are, by their nature, militaristic. In addition, their quest for further conquest represents a drain on the nation's finances through taxation and debt. To end this despotism, Paine calls for the liquidation of the monarchy and for the monies of England to be distributed among the poor and to promote employment of those who are currently unemployed. In addition, these monies would promote new marriages and the raising of children.

After showing the problems of monarchism, Paine distinguishes between the possible types of government, and tells us that the "more perfect civilization is, the less occasion has it for government." Furthermore, government should be "nothing more than a national association acting on the principles of society." But a monarchy acts in the best interests of the monarch; an aristocracy acts in the best interests of the aristocratic class. It is only a republic, such as found in America, that acts in the best interests of the welfare of the people.

To develop this argument in greater detail, Paine takes his readers through the development of the Constitution of Pennsylvania, the Articles of Confederation and the Constitution of the United States of America. He ends with the optimistic thought that revolution, and the desire for the freedom that a representative democracy can bring, might spread throughout Europe and could mean an end to war and tyranny.

CENSORSHIP HISTORY

While most of Paine's *The Rights of Man* seems, to modern Americans, a basic and accepted part of political beliefs, it presented a clear challenge to England. Although essentially free of the censor's ire in our time, Paine himself was persecuted in his lifetime; in fact, this book has also made Jonathon Green's list of works "most often" censored.

In 1791, Charles James Fox introduced a bill to the House of Commons that would allow juries to decide what was and was not libelous. Although it was thrown out by the House of Lords, in 1792 Fox's Libel Act survived attacks by Lord Kenyon and his cronies to become law. Although judges were still allowed to give their opinions to the juries, juries were now empowered to disregard judges' advice. At the same time, an increasing number of books and newspaper articles had attacked the monarchy; some suggested that Prime Minister William Pitt was using the king's madness as an excuse to take over the government.

In this situation, Paine's publication was like holding a match to tinder. The first printing of *The Rights of Man* was discontinued in February 1791. The printer, known today variously as Johnson and Chapman, decided that the book exhibited a "dangerous tendency" and ceased his work. The next month in England, Jeremiah Samuel Jordan released the book to the public with a much larger printing. The initial printing of 10,000 copies sold out overnight in London. However, in the summer of 1792, Jordan was arrested and pled guilty to a charge of seditious libel for printing the second part of *The Rights of Man*. By some estimates, the first part of *The Rights of Man* may have sold as many as two million copies within its first year and was available at low cost.

William Pitt agreed that Paine was probably correct in many of his attacks, but asserted that his writing could cause "a bloody revolution" if not checked. Although he did not take the drastic step of burning all copies of *The Rights of Man*, Pitt is reported to have paid demonstrators five shillings a man to take to the streets and denounce Paine. On a single night in February of 1792, Paine was burned in effigy in four separate places in

London. He was hanged in effigy in London, Worcester, Canterbury and elsewhere. When the English discovered that the American version of Paine's book restored a section that had been left out of the English one, the charge that government in England was in every way the opposite of what it should be, Pitt took more extreme action.

An initial summons on the charge of seditious libel was made against Paine on May 21, 1792; on June 8, he appeared in trial, but the actual court date was postponed until December. Paine did not relent in his attacks, but as time went on, his friends began to fear for his life. Legend has it that the poet William Blake urged him to flee the country. One step ahead of a warrant for his arrest and imprisonment without bail, Paine fled England for France on September 18. Unfortunately, he was later imprisoned while in France because of his hostility to the Jacobins and his efforts to prevent the execution of Louis XVI.

Thomas Erskine, the attorney-general to the Prince of Wales and an advocate for freedom of the press, served as Paine's spokesman at the trial over *The Rights of Man*. Erskine argued against using passages out of context as grounds for finding a book to be seditious. He was often successful in winning acquittals for those charged with libel, and frequently published on the subject of press freedom. He would even invite juries to set aside the laws as written. Although Thomas Erskine agreed to take on Paine's case, not everyone was happy with his decision, including Lord Loughborough, who was to become the lord chancellor.

The trial, held on December 18, 1792, was presided over by the same Lord Kenyon who had led the fight against the Fox Libel Act. While Erskine objected to the prosecution's reading of a letter from Paine as evidence (Erskine contended that the charges were brought against Paine for *The Rights of Man* and not for any other private correspondence), Kenyon overruled. Facing a hostile jury, Erskine argued for three hours and 40 minutes that the book should be viewed as a whole, without items taken out of context. He stated that Paine was not guilty because he had not attempted to incite his readers to break the law. Writers, he argued, have a right and a duty to point out error by the government. However, the jury was so keen to convict that they had lost the patience to hear Erskine's summing up. Under British law, seditious libel meant that if the words could topple the established order, their truth or falsity had no bearing on the case. On December 20, Paine was found guilty, not only of libel, but of high treason. He was forbidden, on pain of death, to set foot in England ever again.

After Paine's trial, a spate of prosecutions for seditious libel resulted, including against the works of Paine. Jonathon Green notes that *The Rights of Man* was "regularly seized and burned in succeeding years." However, in June 1793, a jury found Daniel Isaac Eaton guilty only of publishing *The Rights of Man;* they denied that Eaton was guilty of criminal intent. This was the verdict in a like suit against him in July 1793 for publishing *Letter Addressed to the Addressers on the Late Proclamation*, although in early 1793, the publisher Henry Delaney Symonds was sentenced to a year in prison and fined 100 pounds for selling the same pamphlet. And in 1819, Richard Carlile was found guilty of publishing *THE AGE OF REASON*, incurring a fine of 1,000 pounds and two years' imprisonment. Still, despite *The Rights of Man* and *The Age of Reason* being condemned by the courts, comments Donald Thomas, "throughout the first quarter of the nineteenth century there was no shortage of willing martyrs prepared to go . . . to Newgate [prison] for six months or a year, in order that the philosophy of Thomas Paine should not go unread or unheard." Erskine himself was allowed to print an account of the trial of Paine. Samuel Taylor Coleridge and Jeremy Bentham would later join the cause for the free press. Coleridge asked, "How many of Thomas Paine's hundreds of thousands of readers have been incited to acts of political violence by reading him?" He averred that few, if any, had been so moved. In the 19th century, England largely came to agree with Erskine's argument that sedition existed only when an author actually attempted to incite readers to violence against the government.

But because Paine never hesitated to speak his mind, by the end of his life he had become an outcast in America, England and France. Although he spent his final years in America, he was ostracized and shunned as an atheist and as a traitor to the cause of freedom. He survived a murder attempt, was stripped of his right to vote and was labeled a blasphemer. The man who may have done more than any other to promote the causes of the American Revolution and liberty died on June 8, 1809, in relative obscurity. Even long after his death, Teddy Roosevelt called Paine "a filthy little atheist." Robert B. Downs notes, "He was none of these . . . few figures in American history are as controversial as Thomas Paine and few made contributions as notable as his toward the beginning of the United States as a nation."

FURTHER READINGS

Downs, Robert B. *Books That Changed America*. London: MacMillan Company, 1970.
Edward, Samuel. *Rebel! A Biography of Tom Paine*. New York: Praeger, 1974.
Green, Jonathon. *The Encyclopedia of Censorship*. New York: Facts On File, 1990.
Thomas, Donald. *A Long Time Burning: The History of Literary Censorship in England*. New York: Praeger, 1969.

—Mitchell Fay

SLAUGHTERHOUSE-FIVE; OR THE CHILDREN'S CRUSADE
A Duty Dance With Death

Author: Kurt Vonnegut Jr.
Original date and place of publication: 1969, United States

Publisher: Delacorte Press
Literary form: Fiction

SUMMARY

Many years after World War II, Kurt Vonnegut visited Bernard V. O'Hare, a friend from the war, to discuss the destruction of Dresden. The Allied forces annihilated Dresden with so much firepower that it resembled the ruins one might imagine seeing after an atomic bomb had been dropped. Vonnegut and other American prisoners of war (POWs) survived the ordeal in "Schlachthof-funf," Slaughterhouse-Five, a cement fortress originally used as a stockyard killing shed. The two men later returned to Dresden, which, along with personal experience, provided Vonnegut with material to write his "famous book about Dresden."

Billy Pilgrim, the protagonist, was born in Ilium, New York, in 1922. He served in the army as a chaplain's assistant. After his father is accidentally killed in a hunting accident, Billy returns from furlough and is assigned as an aide to a regimental chaplain whose assistant has been killed. However, the chaplain is killed in the Battle of the Bulge, leaving Billy and three other Americans lost and wandering deep in German territory. One of the other Americans, Roland Weary, is an antitank gunner who has been plagued throughout his life by being the unpopular person everyone likes to ditch. More than once Weary pushes Billy out of the line of enemy gunfire, but Billy is so exhausted and in such poor condition that he does not realize his life has been spared. This attitude infuriates Weary, who "had been saving Billy's life for days, cursing him, kicking him, slapping him, making him move." Weary and the other two in the quartet, both scouts, have become "The Three Musketeers" in Weary's mind. However, as Weary's obsession to keep the hallucinating Billy alive grows, the scouts' contempt of Billy and Weary also grows, and they ditch Billy and Weary. Weary is set on destroying Billy, but just as he is about to send his heel crashing through Billy's exposed spine, the two are discovered by a band of German soldiers and taken as prisoners of war.

Billy and Weary are searched, deprived of their weapons and valuables and paraded away to a cottage that has been transformed into a holding place for POWs. The men are placed with about 20 other Americans. For a propagandist technique, Billy is singled out and photographed as an example of how the American army prepares its men for the war. The Germans and the POWs travel on and meet with more POWs until they form a human river. They arrive at a railyard and are separated by rank, privates with privates, colonels with colonels, and so on. Billy and Weary are separated, but Weary's continuous testimony of how Billy was responsible for the breakup of "The Three Musketeers" eventually spreads to the car where Billy is being held, causing a general feeling of hatred from the occupants of the car toward Billy. On the ninth day of their journey, Weary dies of gangrene. On the 10th day the train finally stops and the occupants are released into a prison camp. Billy is the next to last to leave his car. A corpse stays behind.

The men are stripped, they shower and their clothes are sanitized. Among them is Edgar Derby, a middle-aged man whose son is fighting in the Pacific theater, and Paul Lazzaro, a tiny shriveled-up man who is covered with boils. Both men were with Weary when he died; Derby cradled his head, and Lazzaro promised to enact revenge upon Billy. The men are given their clothes and dogtags, which they must wear at all times. They are led to a shed that houses a number of middle-aged Englishmen who had been POWs since near the beginning of the war. Unlike their American counterparts, however, the Englishmen have made the most of their imprisonment by keeping themselves in shape and properly groomed. They have also cleverly hoarded enough rations that they can afford to trade with the Germans for supplies like lumber and other building materials that they use to maintain their shed.

In poor condition and in a hallucinatory state, Billy is billeted in the hospital portion of the British compound, which is in reality six beds in another room of the shed. Here he is injected with morphine and watched by Derby, who reads *The Red Badge of Courage* to pass the time. Billy awakens from his morphine-induced sleep, not knowing where he is or what year it is. Derby and Lazzaro are sleeping in adjacent beds. Apparently Lazzaro's arm has been broken for stealing cigarettes from an Englishman, and he is now lecturing Billy and Derby on how he will someday enact revenge for that and for Weary's death, for which he holds Billy responsible.

The Americans are informed by the head Englishman that they will be "leaving this afternoon for Dresden—a beautiful city. . . . [they] needn't worry about bombs. . . . Dresden is an open city. It is undefended, and contains no war industries or troop concentrations of any importance." The Americans arrive to find that what they have been told is true. They are led to a cement fortress that had been a slaughterhouse of livestock and is now their dwelling place "Schlachthof-funf." The Americans are assigned to work in a factory that produces malt syrup enriched with vitamins and minerals, to be used by pregnant German women.

Four days later, Dresden is destroyed. Billy, some Americans and four German guards are safe in the underground slaughterhouse while the entire city is fire-bombed. As they emerge the next afternoon, "the sky was black with smoke. The sun was an angry little pinhead. Dresden was like the moon now, nothing but minerals. The stones were hot. Everybody else in the neighborhood was dead." The soldiers order the Americans to line up in fours, and they all march away until they come to a country inn that is far enough removed from Dresden to not have been affected.

Two days after the war ends, Billy and five other Americans ride back to Dresden, looting through abandoned homes and taking as many souvenirs as they please. The Russians come along soon afterward and arrest the Americans, who are sent home on the *Lucretia A. Mott* two days later.

Throughout his war experience, Billy Pilgrim is a time traveler. His trips stem from a few incidents, namely, when he is near death or when he is on drugs. As he is being pushed along by Weary, he travels in time forward and backward. For example, he goes back to when he was a boy, when he and his father were at the YMCA. His father wanted to teach Billy how to swim by using the "sink-or-swim" technique. Pushing him into the deep end, Billy ended up "on the bottom of the pool, and there was beautiful music everywhere. He lost consciousness, but the music went on. He dimly sensed that somebody was rescuing him. [He] resented that." From the pool he goes forward in time to 1965 to visit his mother in Pine Knoll, a rest home; then he returns to 1958 to his son's little league banquet; from there he goes ahead to a New Year's Eve party in 1961, where he is caught cheating with another woman; finally he is back in the German outland being shaken against a tree by Weary.

While under the morphine-induced sleep in the British-run prison camp, Billy travels through time to 1948, to the veterans' hospital near Lake Placid. He is being introduced by Eliot Rosewater, a former infantry captain, to the works of Kilgore Trout, a little-known science fiction writer who will become Billy's favorite author and whom Billy will meet some years later. Billy also goes ahead to a time when he is 44 years old and a captive in the zoo on Tralfamadore. The Tralfamadorians, telepathic beings who live in four dimensions and have a firm understanding of the concept of death, have captured Billy and put him into a "human exhibit," where he is naked in a setting consisting of furniture and appliances from the Sears & Roebuck warehouse in Iowa City, Iowa. Not long after Billy is captured, the Tralfamadorians capture a female earthling, Montana Wildhack, a 20-year-old motion picture star whom they hope will mate with Billy. In time she gains Billy's trust and they mate, much to the awe and delight of the Tralfamadorians.

Not long after their sexual experience, however, Billy wakes up. It is 1968, and he is sweating profusely because his electric blanket is on the highest setting. His daughter had laid him in bed upon his return from the hospital, where he had been placed after being the lone survivor in a plane crash in Vermont, en route to an optometrists' convention in Canada. His wife, the former Valencia Merble, is the daughter of a well-to-do optometrist, who had placed Billy in charge of his business in Ilium, thus making Billy a wealthy man. She died while rushing to visit Billy in the hospital after the plane crash, apparently from carbon monoxide poisoning.

Billy Pilgrim drives to New York City the next day, hoping to be on a television show so he can tell the world about the Tralfamadorians. Instead, he ends up on a radio talk show where the topic is "Is the novel dead or not?" Billy speaks of his travels, Montana, the Tralfamadorians, multiple dimensions and so on, until "He was gently expelled from the studio during a commercial. He went back to his hotel room, put a quarter into the Magic Fingers machine connected to his bed, and he went to sleep. He traveled back in time to Tralfamadore." Billy Pilgrim dies on February 13, 1976.

CENSORSHIP HISTORY

As one of the most censored books of the past 25 years according to Lee Burress, *Slaughterhouse-Five* can boast dozens of cases when students, parents, teachers, administrators, librarians and members of the clergy have called for the removal or destruction of the Vonnegut novel for one or many of the following reasons: obscenity, vulgar language, violence, inappropriateness, bathroom language, "R-rated" language, un-Godliness, immoral subject matter, cruelty, language that is "too modern" and an "unpatriotic" portrayal of war.

June Edwards focuses on the charge of parents and the religious right: "The book is an indictment of war, criticizes government actions, is anti-American, and is unpatriotic." This charge defies the reason why Vonnegut wrote the novel, which was to show that "there is nothing intelligent to say about a massacre." Edwards supports this position by also countering the final two arguments: "Young people may refuse to serve in future combats after reading about the horrors of war in novels like *Slaughterhouse Five* . . . , but this does not make them un-American. They do not want their country to engage in violence, to exterminate whole populations, but to find other ways to resolve conflicts."

Nat Hentoff reports that Bruce Severy, the only English teacher in North Dakota's Drake High School in 1973, used *Slaughterhouse-Five* in his classroom as an example of a "lively contemporary book." Severy submitted the text to the superintendent for review and, after receiving no response, went ahead and taught it. A student's objection citing "unnecessary language" led to a school board meeting where the text was denounced and labeled "a tool of the devil" by a local minister. The school board decided that the novel would be burned, even though no board member had read the entire book. Severy, after discovering his contract would not be renewed, stated, "A few four-letter words in a book is no big deal. Those students have all heard these words before; none learned any new words. I've always thought the purpose of school was to prepare these people for living in the 'big, bad world,' but it evidently isn't so." Severy, with help from the American Civil Liberties Union, sued the school district; the following verdict was reached in an out-of-court settlement: 1) *Slaughterhouse-Five* could be used by teachers in Drake High School in connection with the teaching of English in grades 11 and 12; 2) Severy's performance could not be in written or oral terms deemed unsatisfactory; and 3) Severy was awarded $5,000.

The Librarians Guide to Handling Censorship Conflicts gives a detailed account of the suits and countersuit of *Pico v. Board of Education*, Island Trees Union Free School District cases of 1979, 1980 and 1982. It is noted for being the first case of school library censorship to have reached the Supreme Court. The case stemmed from the actions of school board members attending a meeting in 1975 of Parents of New York United (PONY-U), where one of the issues concerned "the control of textbooks and library books in the schools." Using a list that contained books considered objectionable in other high school libraries, Richard Ahrens, then president of the school board, along with board member Frank Martin, descended upon the school library one evening to see which listed books were shelved there. They discovered nine, including *Slaughterhouse-Five*. At a subsequent meeting in February 1976 with two high school principals, the board decided to remove the nine books, along with two others from the junior high school. That decision prompted a memo from Superintendent Richard Morrow, who stated, "I don't believe we should accept and act on someone else's list. . . . we already have a policy . . . designed expressly to handle such problems." At the March 30 meeting, President Aherns disregarded the memo and ordered the books removed from the district's libraries. After the media got word of the brewing controversy, the board wrote a rebuttal that stated:

> This Board of Education wants to make it clear that we in no way are BOOK BANNERS or BOOK BURNERS. While most of us agree that these books have a place on the shelves of the public library, we all agree that these books simply DO NOT belong in school libraries where they are so easily accessible to children whose minds are still in the formulative [sic] stage, and where their presence actually entices children to read and savor them. . . .

Superintendent Morrow responded that it was "wrong for the Board—or any other single group—to act to remove books without prolonged prior consideration of the views of both the parents whose children read these books, and the teachers who use these books to instruct . . . and to by-pass the established procedure for reviewing the challenged books." On April 6 the board and Morrow voted to appoint a review committee of four parents and four teachers to review the books and make recommendations concerning their future status. In the meantime, Morrow requested that the books be returned to the shelves until the review process was completed. They were not. In subsequent meetings, the review committee determined that six of the 11 books, including *Slaughterhouse-Five*, should be returned to the school shelves. Three were not recommended, and two others couldn't be decided upon. However, on July 28, the board in an open meeting voted to return only one book, *Laughing Boy*, to the shelves without restrictions and one, *BLACK BOY*, with restrictions despite the committee's stance. Aherns stated that the other nine books could not be assigned as required, optional or suggested reading, but could be discussed in class.

A lawsuit was filed on January 4, 1977, by Stephen Pico and other junior and senior high school students, who were represented by the New York Civil Liberties Union. Pico claimed that First Amendment rights had been violated via the board's removal of the books.

As entered in the court record, the school board condemned the books as "anti-American, anti-Christian, anti-Semitic, and just plain filthy"; it cited passages referring to male genitalia, to sexuality, to lewd and profane language and to sacrilegious interpretations of the Gospels and of Jesus Christ. According to Leon Hurwitz, "A federal district court gave summary judgment for the board, but an appellate court remanded the case for a trial on the students' allegations." The Supreme Court to which the school board appealed this decision, in a 5–4 decision, upheld the appellate court, rejecting the idea that "there are no potential constitutional constraints on school board actions in this area." The case came full circle on August 12, 1982, when the school board voted 6–1 to return the books to the school library shelves, with the stipulation that the librarian send a notice to the parents of any student who might check out a book containing objectionable material. (For further discussion of this case, refer to the censorship history of BLACK BOY.)

Many other incidents have occurred throughout the seventies, eighties and nineties concerning *Slaughterhouse-Five*. According to *Banned Books: 387 B.C. to 1987 A.D.*, an unidentified Iowa town's school board in 1973, the same year as the Drake burning, ordered 32 copies burned because of objectionable language. The teacher who assigned the text had his job threatened. In McBee, South Carolina, a teacher using the text was arrested and charged with using obscene materials.

Newsletter on Intellectual Freedom reports that a review committee in Lakeland, Florida, in 1982 voted 3–2 to ban *Slaughterhouse-Five* from the Lake Gibson High School library, citing explicit sexual scenes, violence and obscene language. The complaint originated from a board member and was backed by then Polk County Deputy School Superintendent Cliff Mains, who stated that the book review policy maintained the decision's legal validity.

On May 27, 1984, in Racine, Wisconsin, William Grindeland, the district administrative assistant for instructional services, barred the purchase of *Slaughterhouse-Five*, stating, "I don't believe it belongs in a school library." Unified school board member Eugene Dunk countered, "Denial of quality reading materials for our youngsters is criminal." This stirred up a heated controversy, which was compounded by the board's banning of five textbooks, three in social studies and two in home economics, on June 12. Board member Barbara Scott proposed that a "reserved list" be developed that contained books for which written parental permission would be required for students to check them out. Meanwhile, the Racine Education Association threatened to take legal action and file a lawsuit in federal court against the Unified school board if the book was banned. REA Executive Director Jim Ennis said the suit's goal would be to "prevent the school board from excluding 'contemporary and relevant literature' from Unified libraries and courses." On June 14, a committee of administrators did recommend that the school district purchase a new copy of *Slaughterhouse-Five*, and also recommended a new library book selection policy, which called for the formation of a committee consisting of parents, librarians and directors of instruction, who together would be responsible for the selection of new library materials. This news prompted the REA to hold off on any legal action against the school district.

On May 15, 1986, Jane Robbins-Carter, president of the Wisconsin Library Association, wrote to inform the Racine Unified School District that a resolution of censure had been developed "due to the conflict between the policies and practices of the District as they relate to library materials selection and purchase and the principles of intellectual freedom as supported by the Library Bill of Rights of the American Library Association." The charges stemmed from the actions undertaken by William Grindeland, which allowed him "the authority to delete orders for library materials 'not in keeping with the standards of the selection policy,'" to use "vague and subjective criteria" in choosing what materials could be used and to refer "requests for materials of a highly controversial nature . . . to the public library, local bookstores or newsstands." Robbins-Carter added that "the censure will remain in effect until such time as the Board of Education adopts a revised Library Materials Selection and Purchase Policy." The Racine Unified School District adopted a policy in June 1985; on December 9, the Racine Unified School District's Library Materials Review Committee voted 6–2 to place *Slaughterhouse-Five* under limited access to students with parental permission. Grindeland, a member of the committee that reviewed the book, said, "I objected to the book being in a school library, and I still do. But restricting it is a good compromise."

In October 1985, in Owensboro, Kentucky, parent Carol Roberts filed a complaint stating that *Slaughterhouse-Five* was "just plain despicable," referring to the passages about bestiality, Magic Fingers and the sentence, "The gun made a ripping sound like the opening of the zipper on the fly of God Almighty." She had also prepared a petition with the signatures of over 100 parents. In November, a meeting consisting of administrators, teachers and parents voted unanimously that the text remain on the school library shelves. Judith Edwards, director of the city schools' department of instruction, commented that the committee "felt the book was meritorious." In April 1987, in LaRue, Kentucky, the LaRue County Board of Education refused to remove *Slaughterhouse-Five* from the school library shelves despite numerous complaints citing foul language and deviant sexual behavior. Principal Phil Eason defended the book, stating that it "show[s] the obscenity of war," and "We don't make them [the people opposing the text] read them [books in the library]."

In August 1987, in Fitzgerald, Georgia, school officials decided that a policy used to ban *Slaughterhouse-Five* from all city schools would also offer the same protection against other "objectional" materials. The book was permanently banned by a 6–5 vote after Farise and Maxine Taylor, whose daughter had brought the book home, filed a formal complaint in June, citing that "[I[f we don't do anything about it, they're putting that garbage in the classroom and we're putting our stamp of approval on it."

In February 1988, in Baton Rouge, Louisiana, school board member Gordon Hutchinson stated that he wanted to ban *Slaughterhouse-Five*, and all books like it, which he described as being "a book of dirty language." The complaint was brought to his attention by parent Brenda Forrest, whose daughter had selected the book from a suggested reading list at Central High School. Baton Rouge District PTA President Beverly Trahan commented, "You can get into some very serious problems with book bans." Dick Eiche, executive director of the East Baton Rouge Association of Educators, echoed Trahan's view supporting the book. School Board President Robert Crawford, a Vietnam veteran, agreed with Eiche and Trahan's views when he stated, "I think it's dangerous to start banning books. We could clean out the libraries if we wanted to." In March, Superintendent of Schools Bernard Weiss said a committee would be formed to evaluate the book. The 12-member committee voted 11–0 with one abstention to retain the book. Community member Bill Huey stated, "I can hardly believe this community . . . is even discussing removing a book from library shelves. I don't want to live in a community that sanctions bingo and bans books."

Banned in the U.S.A.: A Reference Guide to Book Censorship in Schools and Public Libraries cites an attack against *Slaughterhouse-Five* that occurred in 1991 in Plummer, Idaho. Parents objected to the books's use in an 11th-grade English class, citing profanity. Because the school had no policy in effect to deal with the challenge, an official ordered that the book be removed from the school and that the teacher using the book throw away all copies.

FURTHER READINGS

Board of Education, Island Trees Union Free School District #26 v. Pico et al., 457 U.S. 853, 102 S. Ct. 2799, 73 L. Ed. 2s 435 (1982).
"Board Reverses Censorship Stand." *Racine Journal Times* (June 22, 1984): [n.p.].
"Book Banning." *Racine Journal Times* (June 13, 1984): [n.p.].
Burress, Lee. "Introduction." In *Celebrating Censored Books!* Ed. Nicholas J. Karolides and Lee Burress. Racine, Wis.: Wisconsin Council of Teachers of English, 1985.
Edwards, June. *Opposing Censorship in the Public Schools: Religion, Morality, and Literature.* Mahwah, N.J.: Lawrence Erlbaum Associates, Publishers, 1998.
Foerstel, Herbert N. *Banned in the U.S.A.: A Reference Guide to Book Censorship in Schools and Public Libraries.* Westport, Conn.: Greenwood Press, 1994.
Haight, Anne Lyon, and Chandler B. Grannis, *Banned Books: 387 B.C. to 1978 A.D.*, 4th ed. New York: R.R. Bowker Company, 1978.
Hentoff, Nat. *The First Freedom: The Tumultuous History of Free Speech in America.* New York: Delacorte Press, 1980.
Hurwitz, Leon. *Historical Dictionary of Censorship in the United States.* Westport, Conn.: Greenwood Press, 1985.
Jenkinson, Edward B. *Censors in the Classroom: The Mind Benders.* Carbondale: Southern Illinois University Press, 1979.
Jones, Frances M. *Defusing Censorship: The Librarian's Guide to Handling Censorship Conflicts.* Phoenix, Ariz.: Oryx Press, 1983.

Newsletter on Intellectual Freedom 23 (1974): 4; 29 (1980): 51; 31 (1982): 155, 197; 33
    (1984): 158; 35 (1986): 9–10, 57, 114; 36 (1987): 51, 224; 37 (1988): 86–87, 139–40.
"OK for *Slaughterhouse Five.*" *Racine Journal Times* (June 14, 1984): [n.p.].
"Unified Bans 5 Books." *Racine Journal Times* (June 12, 1984): [n.p.].
"Unified Lifts Book Ban." *Racine Journal Times* (June 19, 1984): [n.p.].
"Unstocking the Shelves." *Racine Journal Times* (May 27, 1984): [n.p.].

—Eric P. Schmidt

SPYCATCHER

Author: Peter Wright
Original date and place of publication: 1987, Australia; 1987, United States
Publisher: William Heinemann, Australia; Viking
Literary form: Autobiography

SUMMARY

Subtitled "The Candid Autobiography of a Senior Intelligence Officer," *Spy-catcher* reveals the activities of MI5, the "Security Service" of Great Britain, while focusing on the role of Peter Wright. MI5's central function is domestic counterintelligence in contrast to the foreign intelligence mission of MI6, alias the "Secret Service." The MI stands for "Military Intelligence" but MI5 is operated entirely by civilians.

Wright entered the service initially prior to 1955 as a research scientist and worked as an agent for MI5 from 1955 to 1976. Wright's first appraisal was that the services were woefully out of date technologically, needing new techniques of eavesdropping that did not require entry to premises. His first project, a sensitive microphone, established the underpinnings of his reputation. This success was followed by the development of other devices. He describes the early 1950s as "years of fun," detailing a series of spysearching and eavesdropping incidents that illustrate technological inventiveness.

The saga continues through the 1960s, but the tone begins to change with the appointment of Roger Hollis as director-general of MI5 in 1956. Clearly, Wright doubts Hollis's ability to lead the Security Service and questions his negation of or hesitation to pursue active measures. Nevertheless, targets were pursued, among them the Egyptian government. Wright was able to develop a method of determining the settings of the cipher machines in the Egyptian embassies, thus enabling the British to decode the cipher. This ability was significantly helpful during the Suez Crisis.

In the context of the Suez conflict, Wright also mentions that MI6 developed a plan to assassinate Gamel Abdel Nasser, the president of Egypt. Two alternative plans, he claims, had been approved by Prime Minister Anthony Eden. Another revelation is that MI5 had gone beyond attempting to bug the avowed cold war enemy, Russia, but had also bugged the embassies of Britain's ally, France. This intelligence eavesdropping occurred during the 1960–63 interval when Great Britain was attempting to enter the Common Market.

A persistent, sometimes overriding concern relates to the infiltration of the British intelligence operations at the hands of an elaborate "Ring of Five" spy group. A Russian defector had so identified a conspiracy group. Double agents Guy Burgess, former executive officer of the British Foreign Service, and Donald Maclean, British diplomat, had defected to Russia in 1951. Harold "Kim" Philby, a high-level British diplomat and senior intelligence officer, was cleared after interrogation by MI6; however, Philby's reinterrogation by MI5 in 1962 led to his confession that he, too, was a double agent. He defected to Russia in 1963. In 1964, Sir Anthony Blunt, about whom there had been suspicions for years, also confessed to being a Russian spy. Wright, at the heart of these investigations, provides extended details of them along with his efforts to track down the fifth man. He reveals evidence that MI5's plans and procedures had often been leaked; he is sure that the culprit is in a high-level position. He and a colleague narrow down the choices to the director himself, Roger Hollis. Wright time and again asserts his belief in this finding even after Hollis is cleared after he has retired in 1965.

With regard to these revelations Wright reports considerable dismay and embarrassment within the intelligence community and the government. The revelations cast doubt on the effectiveness of the services, in particular their ability to maintain secrecy.

Another major operation, which may have grown out of fervor to track down subversives in government, is directed against Prime Minister Harold Wilson. Wilson came under suspicion, a suspicion, according to Wright, fed by James Angleton, chief of counterintelligence of the CIA, who would not reveal his source. Wilson's office was bugged while he was prime minister. Wright claims that MI5 had enough information to cause "a political scandal of incalculable consequences" that would have led to Wilson's resignation. He further states that he was approached by a group of MI5 officers to participate in a plot to leak information to "contacts in the press and among union officials ... that Wilson was considered a security risk." The purpose was to bring down the government.

The book closes with Wright's retirement. He reiterates in the last chapter his conviction that Hollis was the "fifth man" and that "fear of scandal" became the most important consideration affecting everyone for the "turmoil of the 1960s." Throughout the book he asserts his own devotion to the cause represented by MI5 and acknowledges his many efforts on behalf of that cause.

CENSORSHIP HISTORY

The censorship challenge of *Spycatcher* emerged on two fronts: the publication of the book and the publication of excerpts and reports of its contents in newspapers. The government of Prime Minister Margaret Thatcher argued that publication would cause loss of confidence in MI5's ability to protect classified information, would damage national security and would violate secrecy oaths taken by intelligence officers.

The Book

In September 1985, having learned of the planned publication of *Spycatcher* in Australia, thus avoiding litigation in Britain (the publisher had sent an advance copy to the attorney general, suggesting he could remove offensive passages, but a review of the text had determined that the book should be totally suppressed), the British government began legal action to suppress release of the book. It sought and was granted a temporary injunction by an Australian court, blocking publication until a trial had settled the legal issues.

The civil suit was tried in the New South Wales Supreme Court, Sydney, in November 1986, having been preceded by pretrial hearings. Essentially two major arguments emerged, those of national security and those of Wright's violation of his lifetime agreement to maintain secrecy about his MI5 activities. The defense argued that a previous publication, *Their Trade Is Treachery* by Chapman Pincher, published in 1981, had already revealed the information in *Spycatcher* (Wright had been an unnamed consultant to Pincher) and that the government had not taken action to prevent its publication. Thus Wright was not violating the secrecy code. The government claimed that Pincher the journalist was different from Wright the public official. The five-week trial ended on December 20, 1986, with Justice Philip Powell questioning the veracity of British Cabinet Secretary Sir Robert Armstrong, the chief witness for the Thatcher government.

Justice Powell announced his ruling on March 13, 1987. In a 286-page document, he rejected the claim of the government that *Spycatcher* would be harmful to British security and denied the request for a permanent injunction. He reasoned that the material in Wright's book was either harmless or already disclosed. He agreed that the government had the right to expect intelligence agents to keep secrets. However, two general reasons were offered why the British government could not claim that right in this instance: Earlier books and other publications had not been banned; disclosure to the public should be permitted when intelligence officers conducting secret operations break the law.

Within days, the British attorney general announced that the ruling would be appealed. The appeal hearing began on July 27, 1987, and the verdict on that appeal was announced on September 24, 1987. The New South Wales Court of Appeals rejected the government's request on a 2–1 vote. The court allowed the injunction against publication for three days. The government then appealed this decision that would have allowed publication to the High Court, Australia's highest judicial body. It was denied on September 27, 1987, allowing publication of the book in Australia. (About 240,000 copies of *Spycatcher* were sold in Australia after the lower court had ruled in favor of publication.)

The appeal to the High Court went forward, scheduled for March 8, 1988. The High Court's seven judges announced their unanimous decision on June 2, 1988, rejecting the government's attempt to ban further publication. These judges also accepted Britain's reasoning that Wright was bound by his lifetime oath to remain silent. They indicated, however, that the Australian court had no jurisdiction to enforce a British security regulation.

The Newspapers

In June 1986, the British government obtained legal rulings barring two newspapers, the *Guardian* and the *Observer* from publishing leaks of Wright's allegations. The two newspapers had already each published an article in relation to the Australia trial. The newspapers appealed on the grounds that the information was already in the public domain and in the public interest since serious wrongdoing of the secret service was alleged. The appeal was denied: if the original publication was unauthorized, then republication would also be unauthorized.

Three different newspapers published articles on April 17, 1987. The *Independent* first included a full front-page summary of Wright's allegations with verbatim quotes from his book; the *Evening Standard* and the *Daily News* followed suit. The attorney general charged them with criminal contempt of court, citing the existing ban on the first two newspapers. The initial verdict supported the newspapers on the grounds that one newspaper was not bound by an injunction on another. However, on July 15, the appellate court overturned this verdict, in effect setting wide-ranging restrictions on any newspaper that published any material that another had been prevented from publishing.

Meanwhile, the *Sunday Times* on July 12, 1987, had begun a serialization of *Spycatcher*. This series, however, was stalled by a temporary injunction by the government on July 16.

In the succeeding week, the *Sunday Times*, the *Guardian* and the *Observer* appealed the injunction. Days later, a High Court judge sided with the newspapers by dismissing the injunction. However, the government's appeal to the court of appeals resulted in a decision favorable to the government, but modified: Extracts were disallowed, but publication of Wright's allegations were legitimate news. Both parties appealed to the law committee of the House of Lords, the "Law Lords," Britain's highest appellate body. Its decision, a 3–2 ruling, on July 30, 1987, not only favored the government, but extended the original ruling to include any evidence or arguments from the Australian court hearings. The Law Lords stated in their written opinions, issued in mid-August, that their ruling was temporary, pending a full trial. Further publication would destroy the government's case in advance of a trial. The minority opinion, calling attention to the release of *Spycatcher* in the United States and its availability in Britain, indicated that the claim of confidentiality was an empty one since it had already been lost; another point noted that the attempts to insulate the British public were "a significant step down the very dangerous road of censorship."

In the interim between ruling and opinions, the newspapers had violated the ban: the *Guardian* had reported the Australian court's hearings; the *News on Sunday* printed excerpts from *Spycatcher*. The attorney general announced it would prosecute the *News on Sunday* for contempt of court. Prime Minister Margaret Thatcher indicated the fight was a matter of principle because of the violation of a lifelong vow. Editor Brian Whitaker's reaction: "It is unacceptable that in a democracy like ours the British press should not be allowed to print stories concerning this country which are appearing in other newspapers throughout the world."

The trial to determine whether the injunctions should be permanent began in late November 1987; it concluded on December 21, 1987, when the High Court judge found in favor of the newspapers, rejecting a permanent injunction. Justice Richard R. F. Scott was critical of the government: The duty of the press to inform the public had "overwhelming weight" against potential government embarrassment because of scandal. "The ability of the press freely to report allegations of scandal in government is one of the bulwarks of our democratic society. . . . If the price that has to be paid is the exposure of the Government of the day to pressure or embarrassment when mischievous or false allegations are made, then . . . that price must be paid."

The court of appeals, to which the government had immediately appealed, ruled unanimously in favor of the newspapers in February 1988. The ban on press publication remained in effect while the government appealed to the House of Lords. In October, that body unanimously upheld the court of appeals, lifting the temporary injunctions barring the newspapers from printing news about and excerpts from Wright's book and the trial. The government lost a two-and-a-half-year struggle.

The language of the ruling did not express a legal right to publish. Rather, the finding in favor of the newspapers was based on the reality of the information no longer being secret. In the majority opinion, Lord Keith declared, "[G]eneral publication in this country would not bring about any significant damage to the public interest beyond what has already been done."

United States Publication
With regard to the publication of Spycatcher in the United States, letters dated between March 6 and July 5, 1987, and published in London's *Independent* revealed that Assistant Treasury Solicitor David Hogg suggested to Viscount Blankenham, chair of Pearson—owner of Pearson, Inc. in the United States whose subsidiary, Viking Penguin, was considering publishing *Spycatcher*—that Blankenham could "remove the directors of the American subsidiaries" if they persisted in their plans. Blankenham, while admitting his sympathy for the government's position, nevertheless stated:

"[P]redisposition to sympathy [cannot] lead—in an international publishing group—to any insistence by Pearson . . . that overseas publishing houses in the group acknowledge and act on that sympathy." It is not open to an English court, he said, to control the exercise of power arising in the internal management of a foreign company.

Spycatcher was published in the United States in July 1987.

FURTHER READINGS

"British Official Suggests Ousting Viking Board to Stop *Spycatcher.*" *Publishers Weekly* 232 (August 7, 1987): 311.
Clines, Francis X. "*Spycatcher* Judge Rules Against Thatcher." *The New York Times* (December 22, 1987): 16.
Fysh, Michael, ed. *The Spycatcher Cases*. London: European Law Centre, 1989.
Kirtley, Jane E. "The Law Lords Take a Detour: Chapter Two of the *Spycatcher* Saga." *Government Information Quarterly* 7 (1990): 53–58.
———. "A Walk Down a Dangerous Road: British Press Censorship and the *Spycatcher* Debacle." *Government Information Quarterly* 5 (1988): 117–35.
Newsletter on Intellectual Freedom, 36 (1987): 229.
Pincher, Chapman. *The Spycatcher Affair*. New York: St. Martin's Press, 1988.
———. *Their Trade Is Treachery*. London: Sidgwick & Jackson, 1981.
Turnbull, Malcolm. *The Spycatcher Trial*. Topsfield, Mass.: Salem House Publishers, 1989.

THE UGLY AMERICAN

Authors: William J. Lederer and Eugene Burdick
Original date and place of publication: 1958, United States
Publisher: W.W. Norton & Company
Literary form: Fiction

SUMMARY

The Ugly American begins with a note from the authors stating the story is fiction but based on fact. They write, "The names, the places, the events, are our inventions; our aim is not to embarrass individuals, but to stimulate thought—and, we hope, action."

Louis Sears is the American ambassador to Sarkhan, a fictional country in Southeast Asia near Burma and Thailand. For 18 years, Sears was a United States senator. While awaiting an appointment as a federal judge, he is offered the ambassadorship to Sarkhan. Sears does not know anything about the country; in fact, he is not even sure where it is located. Accepting the appointment in the early 1950s, he goes to Sarkhan, but he never learns anything about its culture or language. He considers the natives "damned little monkeys" and manages to alienate and offend most of them with his rudeness and his assuming ways.

Russian Ambassador Louis Krupitzyn arrives in Sarkhan one week after Sears. He and his wife have rigorously studied the culture for the past two years. Krupitzyn knows how to read and write the language. He has molded himself into the ideal man by Sarkhanese standards: He lost 40 pounds, he took ballet lessons, he read Sarkhanese literature and drama, he became a skillful player of the nose flute and he regularly attended lectures on Buddhist religion and practices. The day after his arrival in Sarkhan, Krupitzyn goes to the great monastery to pay his respects to the chief abbot, the leader of all Buddhists in the area, to whom he speaks with reverence in classical Sarkhanese.

Sears and Krupitzyn are in competition to win the favor of the Sarkhanese government and people, although Sears does not understand the full implications. The Russians, primarily due to Krupitzyn's knowledge and skill, are moving toward their goal of turning Sarkhan to communism within 30 months. Krupitzyn and his staff are victorious in portraying the Russian government as more helpful and supportive than the American government.

Reading of the threat of communism in Sarkhan in 1952, John Colvin, former Office of Strategic Services (OSS) agent in Sarkhan during the war, writes many letters to his congressman, explaining Sarkhanese culture and offering suggestions for helping the people. He decides to aid the situation himself when he receives inadequate replies from the government. His plan is to introduce powdered milk into the culture and eventually bring in Texas cattle that could feed on the useless grasses found throughout the country. He will support the initial investment of the venture, but he plans to turn the operations and revenues over to the native peoples who help him run the business.

Colvin, in Sarkhan for two weeks selling powdered milk, is beaten by his former friend and military associate Deong, now a communist, who accuses him of trying to poison the people. A group of women beat, kick and scratch him; they drop him naked on the embassy sidewalk with a note pinned to his bare chest saying he raped a native woman. Ambassador Sears does not believe Colvin's version of the events.

In 1952, Father Finian is assigned to Burma as overseer of Catholic missions. In his quest to help the Burmese people fight communism, Father Finian lives among the natives, learns their language and suffers through weeks of severe dysentery in order to eat their food and drink their water. He gathers eight native men and facilitates a plan to help them rid the countryside of communism. They publish a newspaper called *The Communist Farmer*, which exposes communist doctrine and illustrates the truth about the Communist Party to the people. Through the efforts of the "nine friends," the communists are run out of the Burmese countryside. Father Finian plans to move to Sarkhan next and begin a similar operation.

In a letter to a State Department official in Washington, Louis Sears writes,

> We got another crackpot here, too—Father Finian. This priest has to be handled with kid gloves. I don't want to get into a beef with the Roman Catholics. But this Finian has just come from Burma where he started a small revolution; now he's organizing here in Sarkhan way up north, and the local papers are beginning to raise hell. If Cardinal Spellman is for him, I can tolerate him, I suppose. But if the Catholic bigshots are down on him, I'll get him shipped back to the States.

After several major political blunders, Sears is awarded his judgeship earlier than expected and immediately leaves Sarkhan. Before leaving the country, he takes three courses of action: He refuses to extend protection to Father Finian; he advises the Sarkhanese government to refuse a visa to John Colvin; and he writes a letter to the State Department, noting his accomplishments in Sarkhan.

Gilbert MacWhite, a recognized expert on Soviet theory and practice, is the new ambassador. Excited about his new appointment, MacWhite learns the Sarkhanese language and reads about Sarkhan's history and political life. MacWhite is determined to destroy the communist stronghold in Sarkhan. His complex plan, however, is revealed to the communists by two trusted Sarkhanese servants. MacWhite decides to go to the Philippines and Vietnam to learn how they deal with the communists and to gain a better understanding of Asian peoples. During his travels, he invites several Americans to Sarkhan to help improve the situation.

Homer Atkins, an engineer, and his wife, Emma, move to a small village in Sarkhan. Homer employs the help of the villagers in the designing, building and selling of pumps that will move water from the rivers up the hillsides to the rice paddies. Emma, who notices that all of the old people have stooped backs caused by sweeping with short-handled brooms, locates a tall natural reed and uses it to construct a longer broom handle, thus helping the villagers. James Wolchek, an army paratrooper who has learned to adapt communist tactics in battle, comes to Sarkhan to instruct recruits in guerrilla tactics. U Maung Swe, a well-known and respected Burmese journalist, tells MacWhite that John Colvin was framed by the communists; he recommends that Colvin be brought back to continue his work.

When U Maung Swe is asked about American prestige in Southeast Asia, he responds, "Poor America. It took the British a hundred years to lose their prestige in Asia. America has managed to lose hers in ten years. And there was no need for it. In fact, she could get it all back in two years, if she wanted to." He explains that Americans in foreign countries isolate themselves socially, live pretentiously, and they are loud and ostentatious.

The chair of the Senate Foreign Affairs Committee, Senator Brown, decides to tour Asia and the Far East. His plan is to visit as many countries as possible, talk to the natives and low-ranking employees and find out what is really happening in these countries. The ambassador to Vietnam, Arthur Alexander Gray, forewarned of the senator's arrival, plans to keep him away from the truth about the situation in Vietnam. He hires an interpreter to "make sense" out of what the natives say to the senator. He instructs his staff to stay at the embassy, working until at least eight o'clock at night, to ride bicycles instead of driving their cars, to stay out of the French restaurants and cafes and to generally prove their "sense of drive and dedication." The plan to keep Brown from learning too much is successful, and Senator Brown returns to the United States pleased with his positive interactions abroad.

Ambassador Gilbert MacWhite is an honest man. His reports to the United States government directly conflict with the reports of Senator Brown, a discrepancy that results in a reprimand from the secretary of state. In response, MacWhite writes that he was not prepared for "the silent desperation with which the battle between the communist world and our world is being fought here." He states that the Russians have not suffered a major defeat since the end of World War II and advises the United States government and its representatives to engage in moral acts in the real interest of the people. "To the extent that our foreign policy is humane and reasonable, it will be successful. To the extent that it is imperialistic and grandiose, it will fail."

In the final section of MacWhite's letter, he requests that every American sent to Sarkhan be able to speak and read Sarkhanese; that no dependents be allowed to come to Sarkhan unless the American employee is willing to serve there for at least two years; that the American commissary and PX be withdrawn with no supplies for Americans except toilet articles, baby food, canned milk, coffee and tobacco; that Americans not be allowed to bring their own automobiles to Sarkhan; and that Americans coming to Sarkhan be well read in books by communist leaders. MacWhite indicates that if these requests are not met he will resign his position. Three weeks later, all requests are denied for being "highly impractical," and MacWhite is requested to return to the United States.

In the final chapter of the book, "A Factual Epilogue," the authors again state that the book is based on fact. They substantiate the characters and stories in the book with real-life individuals and instances from their time in Southeast Asia. Finally, they offer their own statement about United States foreign policy in that part of the world:

> We have been offering the Asian nations the wrong kind of help. We have so lost sight of our own past that we are trying to sell guns and money alone, instead of remembering that it was the quest for the dignity of freedom that was responsible for our own way of life.

CENSORSHIP HISTORY

In 1953, Senator Joe McCarthy led an investigation of the Overseas Library Program. The libraries, overseen by the International Information Agency

(IIA), existed with the objective of providing a balanced view of United States beliefs to people in foreign countries. Books were chosen "based on content without regard to authorship." Controversial books were included, while blatantly anti-American or pro-communist books were excluded from the library shelves. McCarthy and his team planned to "investigate the way in which controversial books were allowed to reach" the libraries. Carl McArdle, assistant secretary for public affairs, in response to the investigation, stated, "no material by any controversial persons, Communists, fellow travelers, etc., will be used by the IIA."

The repercussions of this new policy were far-reaching. After testimony before the House Un-American Activities Committee, a list, published in 1953, named those who had been mentioned unfavorably throughout the hearings. Many respected individuals had their works removed from libraries. (Please refer to the censorship discussion of *MANIFESTO OF THE COMMUNIST PARTY* for more details.)

Immediately after publication, *The Ugly American* was temporarily censored by George V. Allen, director of the United States Information Agency, previously the IIA. The agency had an information media guaranty program in which booksellers abroad were given dollars for local currencies derived from the sale of American books. Allen, undoubtedly influenced by McCarthy's investigation five years earlier, felt that permitting the book to be sent abroad under this program "would not be in the interests of the United States." In December 1958, Allen changed his mind. An agency spokesperson said, "One facet in Mr. Allen's decision to approve the book for the program was his desire not to create any impression of 'another Pasternak' case by 'censorship at home.'" He was referring to the Soviet Union's ban on *DOCTOR ZHIVAGO* by Boris Pasternak.

Senator J. W. Fulbright, Arkansas Democrat and chair of the Senate Foreign Relations Committee, criticized the novel from the Senate floor in 1959. He was upset by the portrayal of Americans overseas as "boobs or worse," while Russian diplomats were portrayed as "talented, dedicated servants of communism." He said the book had "misled a number of gullible Americans, including a few Senators," into thinking it was an accurate portrayal of American personnel abroad.

The Ugly American is listed in Lee Burress's 1963 survey of censored books completed by Wisconsin English Department chairpersons and school administrators. The teachers who reported felt that some objectors had hidden motives; the objectors professed to object to the language in the books they attacked, but they were actually objecting to the ideas found within the pages. It was believed that those who objected to ideas found more support for their objections by attacking the morality and/or language of those books. *The Ugly American* falls into this category, according to the survey.

According to the same survey, a Wisconsin teacher and a group of parents objected to the *The Ugly American* because of its critical pictures of Americans abroad. This same group also objected to what they deemed immorality and obscenity. The unpublished 1966 National Survey of Objections to Books by Lee Burress cites three further challenges to the book based on its "filthy language and references to sex" and its profane and vile language. These requests for censorship were denied.

FURTHER READINGS

Burress, Lee. *Battle of the Books: Literary Censorship in Public Schools.* Metuchen, N.J.: Scarecrow Press, 1989.

———. "The Pressure of Censorship on Wisconsin Public Schools." *Wisconsin English Journal* 6 (October 1963): 6–28.

"Fulbright Attacks '*The Ugly American.*'" *The New York Times* (May 20, 1959): [n.p].

Oshinsky, David M. *A Conspiracy So Immense: The World of Joe McCarthy.* New York: Free Press, 1983.

"A Special New Republic Report on Book Burning: Who Are the Book Burners? What Happened in San Antonio, St. Cloud and Boston? Senate Transcript—McCarthy vs. Conant." *The New Republic* 128 (June 29, 1953): 7–9.

"U.S.I.A. in Reversal on '*Ugly American.*'" *The New York Times* (December 6, 1958): [n.p.].

—Laurie Pap

UNCLE TOM'S CABIN

Author: Harriet Beecher Stowe
Original date and place of publication: 1852, United States
Publishers: John P. Jewett
Literary form: Novel

SUMMARY

When Harriet Beecher Stowe wrote *Uncle Tom's Cabin,* her main goal was to paint a picture of slavery so heartrending as to cause white people to rise up against it. Her goal was not one of political change, however, for she believed that change that did not include a change of heart would not last. She thought the only way to effect a proper change was through conversion of the entire nation to Christianity. If everyone not only believed in an equality ordained by God, but practiced it, the slaves would necessarily be set free and everyone would be able to go to Heaven. As such, every plot line focuses on a character who is a model of acceptance of Christianity, or a character whose faith is tested.

Whether characters are good or evil depends upon their religious nature more than their deeds.

One plot line tells of the slave Eliza, her husband, George, who lives on another plantation, and their son, Harry. When Eliza discovers that her owner, Mr. Shelby, has sold her son to pay off a debt, she decides her only option is to run away. Her husband has already done so, as he is afraid his master will not allow his marriage to Eliza to continue, but will instead force him to live with another woman on his plantation. George feels his only hope is to run away to Canada and earn enough money to buy his wife and child. Once Eliza decides to escape, she realizes that her only hope, too, lies in Canada. She runs with her child toward the river that separates her home state of Kentucky from the free state of Ohio. With the slave trader Haley about to capture her, she has few choices; she crosses the ice-covered Ohio River, baby in her arms and no shoes on her feet, and arrives on the free side, tired and full of gashes. Unfortunately, due to the Fugitive Slave Law of 1850, being in a free state means relatively little. The new law forbids the people of the free states from helping runaway slaves and requires the slaves to be captured and returned to their proper owners. Quakers, notorious for their hatred of slavery, reject this law, becoming her main assistants, offering her food and shelter and reuniting her with her husband. The family is still in danger, however, as the slave trader has hired two men to find and capture Eliza and Harry, and they have set up a posse toward that end. The family attempts its escape to Canada, then is cornered by the posse, but George is unwilling to give up easily and begins shooting, wounding one of the group and scaring the others away.

Eliza and George are virtuous Christians, while Haley and the men he has hired are not. Eliza has faith that God will do what is best, as shown by her belief that He will help her across the river. George's faith, however, is tested. He feels that he and all blacks have been deserted by God. According to the beliefs of the narrator, George must accept Christianity as a necessary part of becoming a good man. This acceptance comes when, at the home of a Quaker with his wife and son, George is treated as an equal for the first time. The narrator says that "a belief in God, and trust in His providence, began to encircle his heart, as, with a golden cloud of protection and confidence, dark, misanthropic, pining, atheistic doubts, and fierce despair, melted away before the light of a living Gospel. . . ." George has converted in his soul, and thus is saved; Haley and the two slave trackers, however, are seen as evil, not because they sin daily by treating humans as property, but because they are not Christians. The narrative makes clear that their lack of Christian virtue will most certainly be dealt with harshly on Judgment Day.

The second major plot line follows the journeys of a virtuous man, Uncle Tom. He was also sold to Haley, but unlike Eliza, he is not willing to run away. He believes that he must do what his master says in this life and in the next. The plantation owner has put his trust in Tom, and Tom feels he cannot disobey. More important, Tom believes that whatever is to happen is ordained by God, and he will not risk becoming wicked by breaking His laws. While Tom has a wife and several children, he passively allows himself to be taken away and is soon found on a ship going down the Mississippi River. Also aboard is a young girl, little Eva. Tom is drawn to befriend her because she is angelic and pure. When he saves her life after she falls into the river, her father, Augustine St. Clare, agrees to purchase him.

Tom is brought to his new home in New Orleans, where the reader is introduced to a variety of characters. Eva's mother, Marie, is an extremely selfish hypochondriac who cares more for her own fabricated illnesses than the real illness of her child. St. Clare, on the other hand, cares deeply for his child and for his slaves. He believes slavery is wrong, but does not see any way he can stop it. He believes it is his own fault if his slaves misbehave because being slaves has made them immoral. St. Clare also does not care much for religion because, as he says, religious slave owners are hypocritical, and he does not want to attend a church where the ministers tell the owners what they want to hear instead of the truth. Miss Ophelia is St. Clare's cousin from Vermont, whom he has engaged to run his household while his wife is "sick." She is hypocritical in a different way because she is religious and believes slavery is wrong, but she cannot stand to think of black people as her moral or intellectual equals.

St. Clare, while himself against slavery, details why his brother, Alfred, is in favor of it. Alfred, an "aristocrat," gives several arguments in defense of slavery by comparing it to other political systems.

> ". . . . 'the American planter is only doing, in another form, what the English aristocracy and capitalists are doing by the lower classes;' that is I take it, *appropriating* them, body and bone, soul and spirit, to their use and convenience. . . . there can be no high civilization without enslavement of the masses, either nominal or real. There must, [Alfred] says, be a lower class, given up to physical toil and confined to an animal nature; and a higher one thereby acquires leisure and wealth for a more expanded intelligence and improvement, and becomes the directing soul of the lower."

Eva is the ideal type of person Stowe wanted everyone to become—purely Christian and not hypocritical. Even in death, Eva remains pure, for she welcomes the opportunity to see her savior and converts others to the path of righteousness. Unlike her mother, she does not use the Bible to prove that God made slavery for a reason. Unlike Ophelia, she practices love and kindness. Unlike her father, she believes ending slavery is possible and that it is her mission to change the feelings of those around her so they feel compelled to free their slaves. She accomplishes this goal through her death. Her father is so moved that he becomes more religious and begins the paperwork necessary to free Tom, while Topsy, a mischievous and self-proclaimed "wicked" young slave girl, becomes good, and Ophelia begins to think of Topsy as a human, capable of loving and being loved.

Unfortunately, the papers that would give Tom his freedom have not been completed by the time St. Clare is stabbed trying to break up a fight—the ultimate act of Christian selflessness—so Tom is sold by Marie. He is bought at an auction by Simon Legree, a man who uses constant beatings to keep his slaves in line and drives them until they die, then buys new ones. More than his lack of respect for human life, his desire to make Tom give up his religion makes him a villain; when he finds Tom's hymnbook while rooting through his belongings, he says, "'Well, I'll soon have *that* out of you. I have none o' yer bawling, praying, singing niggers on my place; so remember. Now, mind yourself . . . *I'm* your church now! You understand,—you've got to be as I say.'" When Tom refuses Legree's order that he beat another slave, Legree becomes incensed. He tells Tom that he owns him, body and soul, but Tom responds:

> "Mas'r Legree, as ye bought me, I'll be a true and faithful servant to ye. I'll give ye all the work of my hand, all my time, all my strength; but my soul I won't give up to mortal man. I will hold on to the Lord, and put his commands before all,—die or live; you may be sure on't. Mas'r Legree, I an't a grain afeard to die. I'd as soon die as not. Ye may whip me, starve me, burn me,—it'll only send me sooner where I want to go."

This attitude forces Legree into a state of fear because he knows himself to be wicked and that, in the end, he will go to Hell. This fear manifests itself in a hatred of Tom so strong that he eventually beats him to death. Tom is another exemplary Christian who would rather accept his own death than inflict pain on another. His death causes the conversion of Cassy, an older slave woman who has turned away from God because she believes He has turned away from her. He also converts Sambo and Quimbo, Legree's slaves, who run the plantation and willingly beat their fellow slaves; when he dies, they realize the wrongs they have done to him and others and repent. Finally, Tom's death causes a different kind of conversion, when George Shelby, son of Tom's old owner, frees all of his slaves.

CENSORSHIP HISTORY

Uncle Tom's Cabin, from the moment it was published, was extremely controversial. The topic of slavery lay at the ideological heart of America and caused a great split, for how could a nation founded on principles of equality support a system in which five million of its populace were degraded and forced into submission? For this reason, the novel spurred many debates. Many in the North wanted to know if the stories were true; not living in slavery and seeing it firsthand, they could not believe that it was so cruel. That is why at the end Stowe included a chapter entitled "Concluding Remarks," in which she vouches for the truth of each incident she details, including the flight of Eliza across the icy Ohio River and the sad tales of familial separation on the auction block. Despite the controversy surrounding the novel and the fact that, as Joseph Conlin says in his book *Our Land, Our Time*, it "was banned in the South," the novel quickly became a bestseller, with three million copies in print before the Civil War. In addition to responding to censorship, a dialogue was created between the proslavery and antislavery activists of both the North and the South. Those who disagreed with Stowe's conclusions countered them with criticism of her novel and with what John Tebbel calls "'anti-Uncle Tom' books," such as *Aunt Phillis's Cabin; or, Southern Life as It Is.*

Uncle Tom's Cabin was not only potentially dangerous to the American system of slavery, however. The idea of equality offended many others. Anne Haight notes that in 1852 it was "banned under the 'censorship terror' of Nicholas I." Censorship was a large part of Russian history, not just of books, but also of periodicals, plays, music and other forms of expression. This trend was started long before Nicholas became tsar, but his reign reinforced and extended the prohibitions. According to the statute on censorship of 1828:

> Works of literature, science, and art are to be banned by the censorship: (a) if they contain anything that tends to undermine the teachings of the Orthodox Greco-Russian church, its traditions and rituals, or in general the truths and dogmas of the Christian faith; (b) if they contain anything infringing upon the inviolability of the supreme autocratic power or upon the respect for the imperial house, or anything contradicting basic government legislation.

Uncle Tom's Cabin was seen as a threat to both of these conditions and was, therefore, censored. The system of aristocracy that Stowe criticizes as inhumane existed in Russia as well. The tsar and other nobles prospered, while the lower classes worked very hard for relatively little. The free circulation of such ideas was understood as dangerous to the tsar, so the novel was censored. Similar censorship took place for many other authors.

Also based on the statute of 1828, the novel was censored for undermining religious ideals. While the novel is extremely pro-Christian, it often takes sides against the church and the clergy. Both St. Clare and Stowe herself discuss the hypocrisy of the Christian church, which twists scripture to the advantage of slaveholders. When Marie tells how a sermon discussed scripture that showed how slavery was properly ordained by God, St. Clare scoffs at the idea: "'This religious talk on such matters,—why don't they carry it a little further, and show the beauty, in its season, of a fellow's taking a glass too much, and sitting a little too late over his cards, and various providential arrangements of that sort, which are pretty frequent among us young men; we'd like to hear that those are right and godly, too.'" Stowe, in her final paragraph, says, "Both North and South have been guilty before God; and the *Christian Church* has a heavy account to answer. . . ." She believed that it was the church's responsibility to teach the Christian virtues of kindness and equality, not to help support the unkind and unequal system of slavery.

The belief that the church allows so unjust a system to continue was also the reason behind papal censorship of this novel. Haight notes that in Italy and all papal states in 1855 "the sale of the volume was prohibited, though not listed on the index." The Index of Prohibited Books listed the works Catholics were forbidden to read, due to their blasphemous nature.

In addition to censorship in other countries, the novel was often protested and censored in the United States in later years by people who felt it was racist. Haight writes that in Bridgeport, Connecticut, in 1955, "a dramatized version . . . was protested by blacks as a caricature of reality." Stowe's novel, in fact, presents a stereotypical view of blacks and whites. For example, while Aunt Chloe is delightedly describing a dinner she made, she compares herself to her mistress, and several implicitly racist statements are made:

> "I and Missis, we come pretty near quarreling about dat are crust. . . . and, finally, I got kinder sarcy, and, says I, 'Now Missis, do look at dem beautiful white hands o' yourn, with long fingers . . . and look at my great black stumpin' hands. Now, don't ye think dat de Lord must have meant *me* to make de pie-crust, and you to stay in de parlor?'"

Remarks like these, found throughout the narrative, upset readers. Elsewhere in the story, Stowe paints a picture of blacks who are so happy as slaves that when George Shelby gives them their freedom, they refuse it. She also ends the plot of George and Eliza by sending them to Liberia, a colony in Africa set aside for freed slaves, making it obvious that educated, free blacks are not welcome in America. Also, many felt the character of Tom to be overly passive and unwilling to fight for his own life and freedom or that of his family. As Haight points out, during the 1950s, "'Uncle Tom' was becoming a derogatory phrase implying submissiveness."

In 1984, in Waukegan, Illinois, the book was protested by Alderman Robert B. Evans Sr., along with Mark Twain's *ADVENTURES OF HUCKLEBERRRY FINN*, Harper Lee's *TO KILL A MOCKINGBIRD* and Margaret Mitchell's *Gone With The Wind*. As Lee Burress points out, students and parents joined the protest in objection of "'racism' and 'language.'" Specifically, as the *Newsletter on Intellectual Freedom* says, Evans objected to the books' use of the word "nigger" and requested that they be removed from the curriculum: "There are no books in the district that talk about 'honkies,' 'dagos,' 'spics,' 'polacks,' or 'Hymies.' Just like people of those nationalities are offended by use of those words, black folks are offended by use of the word 'nigger.'" Since only *Huckleberry Finn* was required reading, the result was removal of this novel from the required reading list.

FURTHER READINGS

Burress, Lee. *Battle of the Books: Literary Censorship in Public Schools*, 1950–1985. Metuchen, N.J.: Scarecrow Press, 1989.

Conlin, Joseph R. *Our Land, Our Time: A History of the United States*. San Diego: Coronado Publishers, 1985.

Haight, Anne Lyon, and Chandler B. Grannis. *Banned Books: 387 B.C. to 1978 A.D.* 4th ed. New York: R.R. Bowker, 1978.

Monas, Sidney. *The Third Section: Police and Society in Russia under Nicholas I*. Cambridge, Mass.: Harvard University Press, 1961.

Newsletter on Intellectual Freedom 33 (July 1984): 105.

Tebbell, John. *The Creation of an Industry: 1630–1865*. New York: R.R. Bowker, 1972. Vol. III of *A History of Book Publishing in the United States*.

Vernadsky, George, ed. *A Source Book for Russian History from Early Times to 1917*. Vol. II. New Haven, Conn.: Yale University Press, 1972.

—Jane Graves

UNITED STATES VIETNAM RELATIONS, 1945–1967 (The "Pentagon Papers")

Commissioned by: United States Department of Defense
Original date and place of publication: 1971, United States
Publisher: United States Government Printing Office
Literary form: Nonfiction

SUMMARY

The publishing history of the "Pentagon Papers" deserves detailing. Initially, it was an extensive Defense Department study commissioned by Secretary of Defense Robert S. McNamara on June 17, 1967, and completed on January 15, 1969, a narrative of about 3,000 pages and about 4,000 pages of documents, totaling 47 volumes. On June 13, 1971, the *New York Times*, having secretly received a copy, began printing a series of nine sets of articles and supporting documents; interrupted by an extended court restraining order, the series was completed on July 5, 1971. Other newspapers, principally the *Washington Post*, but also the *Boston Globe*, the *Chicago Sun-Times*, the *St. Louis Post-Dispatch* and the *Christian Science Monitor*, also published articles during this time.

On June 29, U.S. Senator Mike Gravel of Alaska attempted to read portions of the Pentagon study into the *Congressional Record* from the Senate floor. When this tactic was unsuccessful because of a parliamentary maneuver, he achieved his goal through the Senate Subcommittee on Public Buildings and Grounds, of which he was chair.

The New York Times *Series—A Summary*

While the government's challenge involved the entire set of narratives and documents in its attempt to retrieve the materials and retain their "top secret" designation, the immediate catalyst was the publication of summaries of portions of the study and related documents by the *New York Times*.

June 13, 1971: Two front-page pieces introduce the series. One describes the "Vietnam Archive," summarizes the broad conclusions of the study, from the initial involvement of the Truman administration to the build-up of American political, military and psychological stakes leading to open warfare in 1965. The second details the origins and development of the report itself.

The substantive articles relate to the Tonkin Gulf destroyer incident of August 1964. "The Covert War" reveals that for six months prior to the August incident, the United States government had operated an elaborate program of covert military operations, sabotage, commando raids and destroyer patrols in the gulf against the state of North Vietnam. The intent was to force the Hanoi government to order the withdrawal of guerrillas through substantial destruction and psychological harassment. Prior to its onset, both the intelligence community and the Joint Chiefs of Staff gave this program little chance of success.

The progressive build-up of a take-charge and war mentality is expressed. These were fed by the perceived failure and inability of the South Vietnam government to control the Vietcong rebellion, which persisted in gaining strength. Administration leaders reacted strongly against a negotiated compromise political settlement or "neutralization" because either would signify a communist victory and signal the destruction of the American position in South Vietnam. President Johnson is revealed as "pushing his Administration to plan energetically for escalation while . . . continually hesitating to translate these plans into military action." At the same time, he is perceived as "calculating international and domestic political conditions before making any of his moves in public." The underpinnings of these policy decisions were the "domino" theory, which predicted the fall of all Southeast Asia to communism one country at a time unless it was stopped; the threat of China; and the fear of loss of prestige and U.S. world dominance.

The planning of the bombing strategy and the government's political and psychological maneuvering blended in with the chain of events leading to the Tonkin Gulf incident. Public statements at the time by Secretary of State Rusk and Secretary of Defense McNamara obscured United States involvement in pre-incident attacks against North Vietnam. A significant outcome of the Tonkin event and the congressional and public discussions that ensued was the preparation of the American public for escalation, a major recommendation of a strategy conference the previous June.

June 14, 1971: The consensus to bomb North Vietnam was reached at a White House strategy meeting in September 1964 in concert with the emerging view that the war needed to be escalated if the situation was to be saved. Publicly

Johnson (at the height of the presidential election contest) took a position of restraint, against enlarging the war. However, there is evident relentless progress toward a war mentality, expressed by the concept of "provocative strategy," provoking a response that would allow a retaliatory air attack. Evident also is a hardening of options: the elimination of "extreme withdrawal" and "fall back" positions; the rejection of tactics like a selective bombing campaign, which would lead to negotiations.

In late November a bombing strategy of "progressively more serious air strikes" was designed, yet the president was reassuring the press at a news conference that "speculating and taking positions" about expansion of the war were premature. Both the Joint Chiefs of Staff and the intelligence agencies dissented from this decision, the former advocating a willingness to apply unlimited force, the latter pessimistically not giving the plan "very strong chances for breaking the will of Hanoi." Reluctant to even hint at the existence of the plans as late as January 3, 1965, Secretary Rusk ruled out "either a U.S. withdrawal or a major expansion of the war." Two reprisal air strikes occurred on February 8 and 11. The order to begin sustained bombing was given on February 13.

June 15, 1971: The third set of articles expresses the decision of April 1, 1965, to launch a ground war using American troops. This decision was tied to the recognition that the bombing strategy was not going to work. President Johnson ordered that this decision be kept secret, that subsequent increases in military support forces, initially 18–20,000 men, not receive premature publicity and that the "appearance of sudden changes in policy" be minimized. On July 17, "swiftly and in an atmosphere of crisis," President Johnson approved the deployment of 200,000 troops, as requested by General William C. Westmoreland.

These decisions were not without warnings of failure and recommendations against committing ground forces. Under Secretary of State George W. Ball "proposed that the United States 'cut its losses' and withdraw from South Vietnam." Director of Central Intelligence John A. McCone also warned against committing ground troops and becoming mired in jungle combat. On the other side were the many voices advocating a tough stand. President Johnson was responding to these and to the advice of General Westmoreland. The president publicly took a posture of compromise, but the offered conditions for peace were "more akin to a 'cease and desist' order," perceived by the North Vietnam government as a demand for surrender.

July 1, 1971: The focus of this day's articles dips back to the Kennedy administration, 1961–63. The study indicates that Kennedy shifted the direction and involvement of the Vietnam strategy from the "limited-risk gamble" of the Eisenhower administration to one of "broad commitment." The underlying objective was to prevent communist domination of South Vietnam. While Kennedy resisted pressures to commit ground-combat units, the number of troops was increased, initially by 500 on May 11, 1961, but up to 16,000 by the end of his 34 months in office; he also approved of covert operations involving American military advisers. These commitments were not disclosed to the public. In taking these steps, Kennedy ignored the advice of the intelligence community, which was "conspicuously more pessimistic (and more realistic)" than other senior advisers. The Joint Chiefs of Staff, advocating a range of combat operations, estimated "a good chance of . . . *arresting* things and giving Diem a chance to do better and clean up. . . ."

According to the Pentagon's study, the Kennedy administration, despite its disavowal, "knew and approved of plans for the military coup d'etat that overthrew" the government of President Ngo Dinh Nhu on November 1–2, 1963. The study indicates that "Our complicity in his overthrow heightened our responsibilities and our commitment." There was internal friction in the administration—at least two officials recommended disengagement; however, the decision was made largely in recognition of the failures of Diem to control the country, manage the war effort and achieve popular support through political, economic and military reforms. Further, Washington was upset that Diem's promise of conciliatory actions toward Buddhists who protested religious persecution was repudiated by repeated brutalities. The study acknowledges that this was a "watershed" period for the United States when the Vietnam policy could have been reconsidered, even to the point of disengagement. Apparently, the direction chosen was a greater commitment to maintaining a noncommunist South Vietnam.

July 2, 1971: The mid-1965 to late 1966 period represented a rapid expansion of American forces, jumping incrementally from 175,000 men in June 1965 to 542,000 in June 1966. Neither the requests for troops nor the approvals of all but the last by President Johnson were made public. The build-up was based on a "colossal misjudgment" about the effect of the bombings on both the North Vietnam military capabilities and morale; it did not consider the "escalation reactions" of North Vietnam. The American military commanders were confident of victory, General Westmoreland pinning his expectations on "search-and-destroy strategy," taking "the war to the enemy, denying him freedom of movement anywhere in the country. . . ." A program of expanding the bombing, targeting oil tanks, was urged by the Joint Chiefs and, against a negative recommendation of the CIA, approved by President Johnson on June 22, 1966. However, civilian leaders, including Secretary of Defense Robert McNamara, began to reveal doubts as early as fall 1966 about both the effectiveness of the bombings and the ground war. By summer's end it was clear that, though the major oil storage capacity of North Vietnam had been destroyed, the enterprise had failed in its ultimate purposes: The bombing had not persuaded Hanoi to negotiate, nor had it limited Hanoi's ability to infiltrate men and supplies to the south.

July 3, 1971: The schism in the Johnson administration with regard to the conduct of the war deepened in the October 1966 to May 1967 period. The study identified three groups: the "disillusioned doves," the McNamara group, which tried to set limits on the war and then reduce it; the military group, urging the widening of the war; and, in the middle position, President Johnson along with senior civilian White House officials. Early in this period, McNamara, having recognized the failure of United States policy to produce both the necessary reforms and morale in South Vietnam and the military-psychological reversals to North Vietnam, recommended cutting back the bombing and seeking a political settlement; in May 1967, he advocated that the United States stop trying to guarantee a noncommunist South Vietnam and be willing to accept a coalition government to include the Vietcong. He wrote: "(1) Our commitment is only to see that the people of South Vietnam are permitted to determine their own future. (2) This commitment ceases if the country ceases to help itself." When General Westmoreland requested an additional 200,000 troops, President Johnson resisted, authorizing a 55,000-man increase, drawing the line at mobilization of reserve forces and reflecting on the concomitant increase in North Vietnam's forces. Johnson did side with the military in escalating the bombing. A proposal to reduce bombing did not reemerge until March 1968, several days after Secretary McNamara left office, opening the way toward the May negotiations in Paris.

July 4, 1971: The Tet offensive occurred in February 1968. The turmoil at the front—for this North Vietnam offensive took the White House and Joint Chiefs by surprise (though this was denied)—was matched by the turmoil of the debate in February and March among advisers and among the public. According to the study, the president himself was severely shocked and disappointed because he had discounted negative analyses and attended to optimistic reports. The military's renewed requests for more troops to meet the offensive were heavily resisted by civilian advisers—only a 10,500-man contingent was authorized. A review of United States policy, led by Clark M. Clifford, secretary of defense-designate, concluded that sizable troop increases would not alter the course of the war; the group's recommendation, however, was a compromise. In conjunction, the CIA indicated that a bombing halt could result in Hanoi's offer to negotiate.

In his speech to the American people on March 31, 1968, President Johnson gave evidence that he had reversed the decisions to send 30,000 additional troops and to continue the bombing. He also announced he would not be a candidate for his party's nomination for president. The president's new strategy signaled a turn in policy on the road to peace; two considerations had fueled the decision: 1) additional troops "would not make a military victory any more likely; and 2) a deeply felt conviction of the need to restore unity to the American nation."

July 5, 1971: This final article returns to the 1945–60 period to reveal early policy decisions that set the stage and the commitments of the United States to Vietnam. The Truman administration initially rejected assistance to both the French and the Vietminh in their conflict but, on December 30, 1949, decided, after the takeover of mainland China by the communists, to provide military aid to the French against the communist-led Vietminh. Subsequently, the Eisenhower administration pledged to abide by the Geneva Accords of 1954 (though it had termed them a "disaster"); however, it approved actions, including the introduction of American troops, that had "a direct role in the ultimate breakdown of the Geneva settlement." Secret operations were already being conducted during the Geneva conference. Further, despite the recognition of the instability of Premier Diem's regime, his lack of support and his ineffectual measures to help the peasants, a decision was made to back him. The U.S. role in blocking the elections scheduled in the Geneva Accords or in being responsible for Diem's refusal to hold them is also questioned. The fear was that elections would lead to unification of the two Vietnams under Ho Chi Minh. But American aid (almost entirely for security with minimal funds for community development, social welfare, health and education) did not curb the North Vietnam insurgency.

CENSORSHIP HISTORY

The first articles and documents of the Pentagon study—what came to be known as the "Pentagon Papers"—were published by the *New York Times* on Sunday, June 13, 1971. There was no immediate reaction, but on the next day Attorney General John Mitchell requested that the *Times* voluntarily stop publishing and return the materials. The *Times* declined to accede to the request.

On Tuesday, July 15, the *Times*, upon the request of the government, was ordered by Federal District Court Judge Murray I. Gurfein to halt publication for four days. (The third set of articles had appeared on this day.) The hearing on the government's civil suit to permanently enjoin the *Times* from further publication was set for Friday, June 18. On the succeeding day, Judge Gurfein refused to order the *Times* to return the report immediately; he indicated that temporary harm to the *Times* "far outweighed" the "irreparable harm that could be done to the interests of the United States." The *Times* had argued that the release of the documents would cause their source to be identifiable, because the copying machine could be traced, as could some handwriting. Instead, on July 17, a list of descriptive headings was submitted to the Justice Department.

At this stage, the gist of the government's argument was that the *Times* had violated a statute that made it a crime for persons who had unauthorized possession of government documents to disclose their contents when such disclosure "could be used to the injury to the United States or to the advantage of any foreign nation." The *Times* claimed that this antiespionage law was not intended by Congress to be used against newspapers; and that this was a classic case of censorship of the press, forbidden by the First Amendment.

On Friday, June 18, the Justice Department requested a restraining order against the *Washington Post*, which had initiated its series of articles on sections of the "Pentagon Papers" on the previous day. However, Judge Gerhard Gesell of the Federal District Court of the District of Columbia refused to grant even a temporary restraining order, claiming there was no evidence of a threat to national security. However, this decision was reversed on June 19 by a 2-1 circuit court of appeals vote that ordered Judge Gesell to hold a hearing on the government's request. The two judges supporting the government indicated that they had acted on the belief that "freedom of the press, important as it is, is not boundless." The third judge objected to the decision as a "suppression of one of our most important freedoms."

In the *New York Times* case, on June 18, Judge Gurfein extended the restraining order another day so he could come to a decision. At the hearing, the government argued that the *Times* had violated the law and presidential orders; by publishing secret documents the *Times* had declassified them, and thus had "compromised our current military and defense plans and intelligence operations and [had] jeopardized our international relations." The *Times*'s position was that the government overclassified documents to hide embarrassing information and that the First Amendment forbids the executive and judicial branches of the government to use "national security" as a reason for censoring articles, except as they might reveal troop movements.

On June 19, Judge Gurfein announced his decision: He refused to enjoin the *Times* from publishing further articles based on the Pentagon study. His finding was that the government had failed to show harm to the national security to justify prior restraint. He noted, "The security of the nation is not on the ramparts alone. Security also lies in the value of our free institutions." However, Judge Irving Kaufman of the Court of Appeals of the Second Circuit extended the injunction against further publication, pending the government's appeal of the decision.

The *Washington Post* case also moved to the Court of Appeals of the District of Columbia after Judge Gesell's ruling on Monday, June 21, that the *Post* could resume publication. As had Judge Gurfein, he also found that the government had failed to show "an immediate grave threat to national security, which in close and narrowly defined circumstances would justify prior restraint on publication." He added, "it should be obvious that the interests of the Government are inseparable from the interests of the public, and the public interest makes an insistent plea for publication."

On June 22, the Justice Department requested and received a restraining order from Federal District Judge Anthony Julian against the *Boston Globe*, which had published materials from the Pentagon study on this date.

Wednesday, June 23 was a day of conflicting decisions. Having first on June 21 decided in New York that the cases were too significant to be heard by the usual three judge team, the full complement of court of appeals judges—eight in New York, nine in Washington—held hearings. However, while the District of Columbia Court of Appeals ruled on a 7–2 vote that the *Washington Post* had the "Constitutional right to publish," the Second Circuit Court of Appeals on a 5–3 decision permitted the *Times* to publish, but only those materials cleared by the government as not being dangerous to national security. The three dissenting judges voted to approve the decision of the district court. In this case, Judge Gurfein was instructed to hold hearings to determine which documents would "pose such grave and immediate danger to the security of the United States as to warrant their publication being enjoined."

The *Chicago Sun-Times* started publishing articles on June 23 based on the Pentagon study. However, the Justice Department did not take action to enjoin this newspaper, claiming the materials used had been declassified.

President Richard M. Nixon announced on June 23 that 47 volumes of the Pentagon study would be made available to Congress, but that the secret classification must be maintained, pending review of the documents by the executive branch. When delivered, the documents were placed in a vault.

After the *New York Times* and the Justice Department appealed their respective negative decisions on June 24, the Supreme Court agreed on June 25 to hear arguments. Four justices—Hugo L. Black, William O. Douglas, William J. Brennan, Jr. and Thurgood Marshall—dissented from this decision, voting instead to allow publication without a hearing.

The *New York Times* indicated it would not resume publishing under the authorized circumstances because its case was pending. To print articles defined as acceptable by the government would in effect be submitting to censorship. The *Washington Post* also indicated it would not resume publishing until the case was adjudicated. Chief Justice Warren E. Burger placed both papers on equal publication restraint, using the Second Circuit Court of Appeals ruling as the basis.

Though eight of 11 newspapers in the Knight Newspapers group (a newspaper chain mainly in the eastern third of the country) along with the *Los Angeles Times* began publishing features of the Pentagon study on June 24, the Justice Department did not attempt to enjoin them. The *St. Louis Post-Dispatch* was restrained by court order on June 26 after it initiated an article series. However, the *Christian Science Monitor* series, initiated on June 29, was not enjoined.

On Wednesday, June 30, the Supreme Court issued its 6–3 decision, upholding the right of the two newspapers to publish materials from the Pentagon study. The restraining orders against the *Boston Globe* and the *St. Louis Post-Dispatch* were immediately dissolved.

Within the broad assertion that any attempt to ban news articles prior to publication bears "a heavy presumption against its constitutionality. . . . the

Government has not met that burden," the justices' opinions fell into three groups:

1. The absolutists (Hugo L. Black, William O. Douglas and Thurgood Marshall)—The First Amendment forbids any judicial restraint: Justice Black indicated that a paramount responsibility of the free press "is the duty to prevent any part of the Government from deceiving the people and sending them off to distant lands to die of foreign fevers and foreign shot and shell. . . . far from condemnation [the newspapers] should be commended for serving the purpose that the Founding Fathers saw so clearly." Beyond this, Marshall argued that Congress had twice (1917 and 1957) considered and rejected such power for the courts; the Supreme Court would be "enacting law" if it had imposed restraint.

2. The middle position (William J. Brennan Jr., Potter Stewart and Byron White)—The press could not be blocked except to prevent direct, immediate and irreparable harm; this material did not pose such a threat. White added, however, that he "would not have any difficulty in sustaining convictions" under the law even if the security threats did not justify prior restraint.

3. The dissenters (Warren E. Burger John M. Harlan and Harry E. Blackmun)—The courts should not refuse to enforce the executive branch's decision that the materials were confidential, affecting foreign policy; they also agreed with Justice White's position regarding convictions.

This case was significant beyond the immediate decision related to these documents and these two (or four) newspapers. It was the first time in the nation's history that a newspaper had been restrained by a court from publishing an article; it was, further, the first time the Supreme Court had ruled on a case of prior restraint of a newspaper by the government.

FURTHER READINGS

Butterfield, Fox. "Pentagon Papers: Eisenhower Decisions Undercut the Geneva Accords." *The New York Times* (July 5, 1971): 1, 13.

Graham, Fred P. "Court Denies U.S. an Injunction to Block *Times* Vietnam Series." *The New York Times* (June 20, 1971): 1, 26.

———. "Court Restrains the *Times* Again; A Hearing Today." *The New York Times* (June 22, 1971): 1, 18.

———. "Judge, at Request of U.S., Halts *Times* Vietnam Series Four Days Pending Hearing on Injunction." *The New York Times* (June 16, 1971): 1.

———. "*Times* Asks Supreme Court to End Restraint on Its Vietnam Series." *The New York Times* (June 25, 1971): 1, 12.

———. "*Times* Case Heard, Restraint Extended; U.S. Action Halts a *Boston Globe* Series." *The New York Times* (June 23, 1971): 1, 22.

———. "*Times* Series Is Delayed Again; Paper to Appeal to High Court." *The New York Times* (June 24, 1971): 1, 16.

———. "*Times* Series Still Held Up Pending Court Ruling Today." *The New York Times* (June 19, 1971): 1, 11.

———. "Supreme Court Agrees to Rule on Printing of Vietnam Series, Arguments to Be Heard Today." *The New York Times* (June 26, 1971): 1, 10.

———. "Supreme Court, 6-3 Upholds Newspapers on Publication of the Pentagon Papers." *The New York Times* (July 1, 1971): 1, 15–19.

———. "U.S. Asking Court for Order to See *Times* Documents." *The New York Times* (June 17, 1971): 1, 18.

———. "U.S. Fails to Get Immediate Court Order to Force *Times* to Turn Over Documents." *The New York Times* (June 18, 1971): 1, 14.

Halloran, Richard. "Ruling for *Post.*" *The New York Times* (June 22, 1971): 1, 27.

Naughton, James N. "Panel Backs *Washington Post.*" *The New York Times* (June 24, 1971): 1, 16.

———. "*Post* Case Opinion." *The New York Times* (June 20, 1971): 1, 27.

———. "U.S. Loses in Move to Curb *Post.*" *The New York Times* (June 25, 1971): 1, 13.

———. "*Washington Post* Restrained: Appeals Court Reversed Decision Favoring Paper." *The New York Times* (June 19, 1971): 1, 11.

New York Times Co. *v.* United States, 403 U.S. 713: Supreme Court 1971.

Salter, Kenneth W. *The Pentagon Papers Trial.* Berkeley, Calif.: Justa Publications, 1975.

Shapiro, Martin. *The Pentagon Papers and the Courts.* San Francisco: Chandler Publishing Company, 1972.

Sheehan, Neil, Hedrick Smith, E. W. Kenworthy and Fox Butterfield. *The Pentagon Papers.* New York: Bantam Books, 1971.

Turner, Robert F. *Myths of the Vietnam War: The Pentagon Papers Reconsidered* (Southeast Asian Perspectives, #7). New York: American Friends of Vietnam, 1972.

Ungar, Sanford J. *The Papers and the Papers.* New York: E.P. Dutton & Co., 1972.

United States *v.* Washington Post Co., 403 U.S. 713: Supreme Court 1971.

LITERATURE SUPPRESSED
ON RELIGIOUS GROUNDS

In 1989 an edict from Tehran brought a shocking reminder of religious censorship, regarded by many as a spectre from the distant past of the Inquisition and the burning of heretics. The Ayatollah Khomeini's death decree against author Salman Rushdie and the widespread banning of Rushdie's novel, *The Satanic Verses*, for blasphemy against Islam was a startling example of a phenomenon that is as old as history and, with the current wave of religious fundamentalism, as recent as today's headlines.

Censorship has existed in every society to protect the prevailing moral and social order. Book censorship in Western culture can be traced to the earliest years of Christianity, when the church began to suppress competing views as heretical. In the second century, the Council of Ephesus burned superstitious works and prohibited the *Acta Pauli*, a history of St. Paul, and in the fifth century, the pope issued the first list of forbidden books.

The flood of unauthorized Bible translations and religious tracts that followed the invention of the printing press in 1450 and the rise of religious dissent during the Protestant Reformation motivated the church to expand its censorial functions. In 1559 Pope Paul IV published the first *Index Librorum Prohibitorum* (Index of Forbidden Books). The Index, sometimes referred to as the Roman Index, was administered by the Roman Inquisition. It was binding on all Roman Catholics, who represented most of the population of continental Europe, and was enforced by government authorities. At the same time, similar Indexes were also prepared by theological faculties in Paris and Louvain and by the Spanish Inquisition.

As church and state in Europe began to separate in the 16th century, national monarchies instituted their own mechanisms of religious and political censorship to supplement or substitute for that of the church. In the areas where they had political control, the new Protestant faiths began to ban the writings of Catholics or dissenters.

From the earliest times religious orthodoxy and politics have been intimately connected. To be a heretic was often to be considered a traitor, subject to punishment by secular authorities. And manipulation of religious sensibilities for political purposes has a long and sordid history, with recorded examples dating to the trial of Socrates, in 399 B.C.

As Europe became more politically fragmented and means of communication more sophisticated, state censorships were rarely thorough enough to prevent forbidden books from circulating. By the 18th century, the proliferation of underground publishing, as France's book censor Malesherbes said, meant that "a man who had read only books that originally appeared with the formal approval of the government would be behind his contemporaries by nearly a century."

It is impossible to discuss religious censorship of books without referring to the Index of Forbidden Books, described as the most successful censorial device of modern times, undoubtedly the most enduring. When it was finally abolished by the Vatican in 1966 after four centuries of existence, however, it had outlived its effectiveness. The church had long before lost the authority to enforce it and the list was widely viewed as anachronistic.

In the 42nd and final Index issued in 1948 and in print until 1966, of total of 4,126 books were still prohibited to Catholics: 1,331 from the 17th century or earlier, 1,186 from the 18th century, 1,354 from the 19th and 255 from the 20th century. Though many were obscure theological titles or works that were controversial in their day but had been forgotten for centuries, literary and philosophical classics by dozens of authors representing a Who's Who of Western thought were also included, among them, Bentham, Bergson, Comte, Defoe, Descartes, Diderot, Flaubert, Gibbon, Hobbes, Hume, Kant, Locke, Mill, Montaigne, Montesquieu, Pascal, Rousseau, Sand, Spinoza, Stendhal, Voltaire and Zola. Rather than banning books, the church's post-Index book censorship has focused primarily on sanctioning dissident Catholic theologians for their writing or pressuring the occasional Catholic author to hew to orthodoxy.

Though the First Amendment prevents government authorities from practicing religious censorship in the United States, individuals and organized religious fundamentalist have successfully pressed to remove books viewed as anti-Christian from public and school libraries and curricula. The majority of these instances have focused on perceived immorality, profane language or treatment of sexuality, rather than religious content per se. Their targets have included textbooks that teach evolution without presenting the alternative theory of "creationism," books said to promote the religion of "secular humanism" and, in a growing trend, material with references to Eastern religions, "New Age" thought, witchcraft or the occult.

Although Rushdie's *Satanic Verses* is the most notorious international case of book censorship in this century, it is not unique. Authors in Muslim countries face increasing threats to their freedom of expression and their safety both from governments that censor or prosecute those whose writing is offensive to Islamic religious authorities and from unofficial militant Islamic groups.

Egyptian intellectual Farag Fouda and Algerian novelist and journalist Tahar Djaout, among scores of Algerian intellectuals, were murdered during the 1990s by fundamentalist terrorists. In 1994, the Egyptian Nobel laureate Naguib Mahfouz was stabbed and seriously wounded. Other writers, such as Taslima Nasrin of Bangladesh, have been driven into exile by death threats or, like Egyptian novelist Alaa Hamed, sentenced to prison for blasphemy. The writing of feminists such as Nasrin, Nawal El Saadawi of Egypt and Fatima Mernissi of Morocco, who challenge interpretations of Islamic dogma that restrict women, has particularly angered both governments and Islamist fundamentalists.

The books discussed in this section represent a sampling of the thousands that have been targets of religious censorship over the centuries. They include texts of the world's major religions, novels and classic works of philosophy and science representing the intellectual heritage of Western civilization. They also include contemporary works that offended church authorities, governments or Christian or Muslim fundamentalists. A few entries—Dickens's *Oliver Twist*, for example—chronicle censorship attempts in the United States that were ultimately unsuccessful but that merit attention because they involved legal challenges.

Many of these books were branded with the charge of heresy. Heresy is defined as opinion or doctrine that is at variance with orthodox religious teaching, or, as religious historian David Christie-Murray observed, "the opinion held by a minority of men which the majority declares is unacceptable and is strong enough to punish." Others were tarred with the brush of blasphemy, speaking in a profane or irreverent manner of the sacred. All were censored because they were seen as dangerous—to orthodoxy, to faith and morals or to the social and political order.

The history of censorship is one of inhumanity, of lives and livelihoods lost, talent or genius snuffed out, work unfinished, withheld, deleted or destroyed. Literary history and the present are dark with silences, Tillie Olsen has written. It is also a history of rebellion, of defiance in the face of mortal danger and perseverance against harassment, discouragement and disdain.

Yet to review the censorship of the books discussed in this section is to be struck by the futility of religious censorship. As historian Leonard W. Levy observed, the verdicts of time mock judgments and alter sensibilities. Insurgent faiths become established and revolutionary ideas lose their power to shock. For centuries censorship has created best-sellers because as Montaigne said, "To forbid us anything is to make us have a mind for it." Like water leaking slowly through a dike to become a steady trickle or a flood, words and ideas inexorably elude the censor's grasp.

"A book cannot be killed," commented Moroccan writer Nadia Tazi on Rushdie's censorship, "it lives and dies on its own. Once the 'vases' are 'broken,' the fragments of life spread throughout the world; voices escape, going their adventurous ways; and there are always encounters, mutations, and festivals of the spirit."

—Margaret Bald

THE AGE OF REASON

Author: Thomas Paine
Original date and place of publication: 1794–95, France
Literary form: Philosophical treatise

SUMMARY

The Anglo-American political theorist, writer and revolutionary Thomas Paine was one of the greatest pamphleteers in the English language. *The Age of Reason*, an uncompromising attack on Christianity based on the principles of rationalism, became the most popular deist work ever written.

The son of an English Quaker, Paine emigrated to America in 1774 and became active in the independence movement. His pamphlet, *Common Sense*, published in January 1776, called for the founding of an American republic and galvanized the public toward independence.

In 1787 Paine returned to England, where he published in 1791–92 THE RIGHTS OF MAN, a work defending the French Revolution and attacking social and political inequities in Britain. It was to sell an estimated half-million copies in the next decade and become one of the most widely read books in England. Indicted for seditious libel by the British government for *The Rights of Man*, Paine fled to Paris, where he participated in the French Revolution as a member of the National Convention. For 10 months in 1794, during the Reign of Terror, he was imprisoned by Robespierre and the Jacobins before being rescued by the American ambassador to France, James Monroe.

On his way to prison Paine delivered to a friend the manuscript of part one of *The Age of Reason*, which was published in Paris in 1794. After his release from prison he completed part two, which appeared in 1795. During his stay in France, Paine became convinced that popular revulsion against the reactionary activities of the French clergy, who plotted against the revolution in alliance with the forces of aristocracy and monarchy, was leading the French people to turn to atheism. In *The Age of Reason*, Paine resolved to rescue true religion from the Christian system of faith, which he regarded as a "pious fraud" and "repugnant to reason."

Paine, in common with many prominent American and European intellectuals, such as Benjamin Franklin, Thomas Jefferson, Voltaire and Rousseau, was a deist. Deism, a religious expression of scientific rationalism, proposed that the existence of God could be inferred from the order and harmony of creation. Deists saw formal religion as superfluous and scorned claims of supernatural revelation as a basis for belief. God's creation, deists believed, was the only bible.

In *The Age of Reason*, Paine popularized deism, removed it from the sphere of the intellectual elite and made the philosophy accessible to a mass audience. Though the book was described as "the atheist's bible" by the book's critics,

Paine repudiated atheism. He opened the book with a profession of faith: "I believe in one God, and no more; and I hope for happiness beyond this life."

Paine's declared objective in all his political writings, beginning with *Common Sense*, was to rescue people from tyranny and false principles of government. *The Age of Reason* was written in the same vein. "Of all the tyrannies that affect mankind," Paine wrote, "tyranny in religion is the worst; every other species of tyranny is limited to the world we live in; but this attempts to stride beyond the grave, and seeks to pursue us into eternity." Organized religion was set up to "terrify and enslave mankind, and monopolize power and profit." The only true theology was "natural philosophy, embracing the whole circle of science."

Paine criticized insincere claims of belief as "mental lying." Every national church or religion claims some special mission from God, communicated to certain individuals, and every church proclaims certain books to be revelation or the word of God. "It is a contradiction to call anything a revelation that comes to us second-hand, either verbally or in writing," Paine wrote.

Paine believed that mystery, miracle and prophesy were three frauds and that the Old and the New Testaments could not be attributed to revelation. "I totally disbelieve that the Almighty ever did communicate anything to man . . . other than by the universal display of Himself in the works of the creation, and by that repugnance we feel in ourselves to bad actions, and the disposition to do good ones." It was the "Bible of Creation," not the "stupid Bible of the Church," to which men should turn for knowledge. "My own mind is my own church," he proclaimed.

While in part one of *The Age of Reason* Paine disputed in general terms the tenets of Christianity, in part two he attacked both the Old and the New Testaments in tones of ridicule and sarcasm. Challenging the authenticity of the five books of Moses, Paine asserted that they had not been written in the time of Moses; rather, they represented an "anonymous book of stories, fables and traditionary or invented absurdities, or of downright lies." He described the Old Testament as being full of "obscene stories, the voluptuous debaucheries, the cruel and tortuous executions . . . a history of wickedness that has served to corrupt and brutalize mankind; and for my part, I sincerely detest it as I detest everything that is cruel."

Criticizing the New Testament, Paine wrote that the Gospels, having appeared centuries after the death of Christ, were not written by the apostles. He admitted that Jesus was a virtuous and honorable man, but denied that he was God. He took offense at the Christianity of the church, "a religion of pomp and revenue" contradictory to the character of Jesus, whose life was characterized by humility and poverty. He described the story of the Immaculate Conception as "blasphemously obscene." He deplored the depiction of miracles for "degrading the Almighty into the character of a showman."

Of all the systems of religion that ever were invented, none is "more derogatory to the Almighty, more unedifying to man, more repugnant to reason, and more contradictory in itself, than this thing called Christianity," Paine wrote. "As an engine of power, it serves the purpose of despotism; and as a means of wealth, the avarice of priests; but so far as respects the good of man in general, it leads to nothing here or hereafter."

As Christianity worships a man rather than God, it is itself a species of atheism, a religious denial of God, Paine contended. "The creation is the Bible of the Deist. He there reads, in the handwriting of the Creator himself, the certainty of his existence and the immutability of His power, and all other Bibles and Testaments are to him forgeries."

CENSORSHIP HISTORY

The Age of Reason was written in an accessible, easy-to-read style and was distributed free of charge or at low cost in America and Europe by deistic organizations. In America, in the mid-1790s, Paine's book went through 17 editions, selling tens of thousands of copies. *The Age of Reason* became the bible of American deists, Paine their hero and deism a mass movement allied with republicanism.

However, the book also aroused the hostility of clergy and believers on both sides of the Atlantic—a hostility that endured even long after Paine's death. A century later, for example, Theodore Roosevelt referred to Paine as "a filthy little atheist." *The Age of Reason* outraged the leaders of the religious establishment. But it also angered religious reformers who shared Paine's critique of religious conservatism but who parted company with him when he rejected the Bible and all forms of Christianity.

Like its seditious predecessor, *The Rights of Man*, *The Age of Reason* was regarded by the British government as genuinely dangerous, because it appeared in the context of mass unrest stirred by the French Revolution. Though Paine was out of reach of British law in France and America, his publishers and booksellers in Britain were not. They were relentlessly prosecuted and imprisoned by the British government over a period of more than 25 years.

In 1797, Thomas Williams of London was tried by a special jury before the Court of King's Bench and found guilty of the crime of blasphemy for having published *The Age of Reason*. The prosecution contended that Paine's book, by subverting the truths of Christianity, undermined the government and the Constitution, both of which rested on Christianity. Further, *The Age of Reason* robbed the poor by depriving them of a belief in a happier afterlife. Williams was sentenced to a year at hard labor and a £1,000 fine.

In 1812, the British Crown prosecuted publisher Daniel Isaac Eaton for blasphemy for publishing and selling a new edition of *The Age of Reason*. Eaton had earlier been imprisoned for publishing *The Rights of Man*. "Our civil and religious institutions are so closely interwoven together," the prosecutor told the jury, "that they cannot be separated—the attempt to destroy either is fraught with ruin to the state." Eaton was sentenced to stand in the pillory and to serve 18 months in Newgate Prison. Upon his release from prison he again defied authorities by publishing *The Age of Reason*; once again, he was prosecuted and convicted of blasphemy. However, because of his age and poor health, he was not sentenced.

The highest price for the defense of Paine's right to publish his ideas was paid by publisher Richard Carlile, a radical exponent of freedom of the press, who between 1817 and 1835 served more than nine years in prison for publishing *The Age of Reason* and other deist tracts. In 1818, he read *The Age of Reason* for the first time and became a deist. He decided to republish the book knowing that its previous publishers had been imprisoned for blasphemy. Indicted for blasphemy, Carlile defiantly kept selling the book. He was brought to trial in October 1819 and in his own defense read the entire book to the jury, taking 12 hours the first day of the trial. By reading it into the court proceedings, he ensured that the work would be republished as part of the public record. It sold 10,000 copies in this form thanks to publicity surrounding the trial.

Carlile was found guilty of blasphemy and sentenced to two years in prison and a £1,000 fine for publishing *The Age of Reason*, and a year in prison and a £500 fine for publishing Elihu Palmer's deist book, *The Principles of Nature*. Within an hour of his conviction, government officers seized the contents of his shop and closed it down. Carlile was bankrupted and spent six years in prison, as he could not pay his fines. His wife, his sister and more than 20 of his workers were also prosecuted and jailed in the years that followed for continuing to publish *The Age of Reason* and other material judged blasphemous.

Rather than succeeding in suppressing Paine's work, Carlile's prosecution aroused interest in it. Four years later more than 20,000 copies were in circulation in England. According to the philosopher John Stuart Mill, writing in 1824, "as among the poorer classes it is notorious that there are several readers to one purchaser, it may be estimated that at least one hundred thousand persons have been led to the perusal of that work under circumstances highly favourable to its making an impression on their minds."

FURTHER READINGS

Foner, Eric. *Tom Paine and Revolutionary America*. London: Oxford University Press, 1976.

Levy, Leonard W. *Blasphemy: Verbal Offense Against the Sacred, from Moses to Salman Rushdie*. New York: Alfred A. Knopf, 1993.

Paine, Thomas. *The Age of Reason*. Intro. by Philip S. Foner. Secaucus, N.J.: Citadel Press, 1974.

THE BIBLE

Literary form: Religious text

SUMMARY

The Bible is a collection of books containing the sacred writings of the Jewish and Christian religions. Both religions regard the Bible as inspired by God. The Christian Bible has two parts: the Old Testament, which includes the Hebrew Bible that is sacred to Jews, and the NEW TESTAMENT, which includes specifically Christian writings. The Hebrew Bible is divided into three sections: the Law, or Torah (also known as the Pentateuch), consisting of the first five books—Genesis, Exodus, Leviticus, Numbers and Deuteronomy; the Prophets, books of history and prophecy; and the Writings, containing prayers, poems and maxims.

The books of the Bible were written over centuries by many different authors. The authorship of the Old Testament was traditionally attributed to great Jewish leaders, among them Moses, Samuel, David, Solomon and various prophets. Modern scholars, however, have concluded that many of the books are later compilations of early traditions and writings. Scholars believe that the earliest books of the Bible began as oral literature and were first written down following the reign of King David, after 1000 B.C. The Book of Genesis, for example, contains passages that may date to the 10th century B.C., but the entire book was probably not written down in its present form until the fifth century B.C. The whole Torah, or first five books of the Bible, was in use by about 400 B.C.

The Old Testament—written in Hebrew, with some sections in Aramaic—tells the story of Creation and provides information on pre-Israelite times and the history and religious life of ancient Israel from about 1300 B.C. to the second century B.C. Christians and Jews regard the Old Testament as the record of a covenant or testament made by God with man and revealed to Moses on Mount Sinai.

The canonical books of the Old Testament and their order vary within the Jewish, Catholic and Protestant religions. The Hebrew Bible revered by Jews consists of 24 books. The Christian Old Testament divides some of the books, increasing their number to 39. The Catholic Bible also includes as authentic seven books of the Old Testament that Protestants consider to be of doubtful authority and refer to as the Apocrypha.

The 27 books of the New Testament, sacred only to Christians, chronicle the years from the birth of Jesus Christ to about A.D. 100, and comprise the earliest documents extant on the life and teaching of Jesus and the establishment of the Christian church. Christians believe that Jesus Christ proclaimed a new covenant or new testament that both fulfilled and superseded the covenant revealed to Moses.

177

The New Testament is divided into four sections: the Gospels or biographies of Jesus; the Acts of the Apostles; the Letters or Epistles of the apostles; and Revelation, a book of prophecy. Written in Greek between A.D. 70 and 100, the New Testament was compiled in the second century. Although the New Testament is traditionally considered to have been written by the apostles and disciples of Jesus, modern scholars have questioned the apostolic authorship of some of the books.

Both the Old and New testaments were translated into Latin by Saint Jerome in about A.D. 400 and compiled as the standard and definitive text in the sixth century. His translation, known as the Vulgate, was designated as the authorized Bible of the Roman Catholic Church and remained so for 1,000 years, up to the time of the 16th-century Reformation. The first book printed in Europe, the famous Gutenberg Bible of 1456, was an edition of the Vulgate.

CENSORSHIP HISTORY

"Both read the Bible day and night, But thou read'st black where I read white." These words of the poet William Blake aptly describe the origins of censorship of the Bible over the centuries. Battles over the correct version of the Bible began in the early years of Christianity, when many of the church's first decrees established certain books as acceptable parts of the Bible and disclaimed others. Throughout the later Middle Ages, the Catholic Church discouraged translation of its official Latin Vulgate edition for fear that the text might be corrupted or misinterpreted. In the late 14th century, in defiance of the church's restrictions, the first complete translation of the Vulgate into English appeared, the work of the scholar and reformer John Wycliff and his followers.

Wycliff, whose treatise *On Civil Lordship* was condemned for heresy, maintained that all people had the right to read the Gospel "in that tongue in which they know best Christ's teaching." Reading the Wycliff Bible was forbidden in England except by ecclesiastical permission. In 1409, the Synod of Canterbury at Saint Paul's in London issued a decree forbidding translation of the Scriptures or the reading of any new translations without a special license, under penalty of excommunication. Although Bible translations were undertaken in other European countries, no others appeared in England until the Protestant Reformation. Despite the ban, the Wycliff Bible was frequently copied and some portions of it were later adopted by William Tyndale, the first of the Reformation translators.

The 16th-century Protestant reformers held that, because God speaks directly to human beings through the medium of the Bible, it is the right and duty of every Christian to study it. They either sponsored or undertook themselves translations of the Bible into their own languages. By 1522, when Martin Luther's German translation was published, or shortly thereafter, there were already 14 printed German Bibles, and vernacular versions had appeared in France, Italy, Spain, Portugal, Bohemia, the Netherlands and Scandinavia.

Protestant reformers believed that the Bible should be understood literally and historically by readers without interpretation by church authorities. This doctrine, *sola scriptura* (the Bible alone), was seen as threatening by the Catholic Church, faced with a widespread loss of its authority as the Protestant revolt spread throughout Europe. Catholic censorship focused on the burgeoning number of Protestant vernacular versions of the Bible, notably Martin Luther's in Germany, William Tyndale's in England and Robert Estienne's in France. Protestants also censored biblical material, banning titles by dissenting Protestants as well as by Catholics. But Protestants could only censor within their own political boundaries. Because of the fragmentation of Protestant Europe, Protestant censorship was not as comprehensive as that of the Catholic Church.

The most violently suppressed Bible translation was Tyndale's. He was the first person to translate the Bible into English from its original Hebrew and Greek, and the first to print it in English. His translation of the New Testament, printed in Cologne and Worms, Germany, in 1524–26, was smuggled into England, where it was banned and publicly burned by the church. His translations of the Pentateuch in 1530, the book of Jonah in 1531 and a revised New Testament in 1534 were also prohibited and burned. Despite the bans, many reprints of Tyndale's translations were smuggled into the country and circulated.

In a plot masterminded by English authorities, Tyndale was arrested by authorities in Antwerp, Belgium, tried for heresy and strangled and burned at the stake near Brussels in 1536 with copies of his Bible translation. Despite its repression, Tyndale's translation survived to form a considerable portion of later Bibles, including the Authorized or King James Version published in 1611.

Miles Coverdale, Tyndale's colleague, produced a complete English Bible in 1535. Because it could not be licensed to be printed in England, it was published in Germany. The popular demand for the Bible in English and the growing difficulty of suppressing its publication led King Henry VIII to name an authorized version, Matthew's Bible, based on Tyndale's and Coverdale's work. It appeared in 1537 with prefaces and annotations by John Rogers, who used the pseudonym John Matthew. Rogers was a Catholic priest who converted to Protestantism and a friend of Tyndale. Matthew's Bible was the first in English to be licensed by the government. But on the accession of the loyal Catholic queen Mary I, Rogers was among the first of 300 martyrs to be imprisoned and burned as heretics in 1554.

Bans on new Bible versions were not confined to England. In 1539, Henry VIII issued his own Great Bible, a revision by Coverdale of his earlier work, which was to be the official version in the newly reformed Church of England. When he decided to print it in Paris, authorities moved to stop it. Regnault, the famous Parisian printer of English books, was seized by the Inquisition and imprisoned. Sheets of the Great Bible were smuggled out of France in hats and taken to every church in England with the king's directive that each man should interpret Scripture for himself.

In 1546, the doctors of theology at the Sorbonne secured the condemnation in the Louvain Index of Forbidden Books of a Bible edition printed by the renowned humanist Robert Estienne, the official printer of King Francis I. The king responded by prohibiting the printing or circulation in France of the Louvain Index and ordering the withdrawal of strictures on the Estienne Bible. With the death of the king in 1547, however, the prohibition was renewed and Estienne had to move his press to Geneva. But Protestant Geneva, under the authority of the Protestant reformer John Calvin, was not a bastion of religious toleration. The Calvinists also condemned the Estienne Bible.

Spain under the Inquisition moved to suppress Bible editions influenced by Protestantism. In 1551, the Index of Valladolid listed 103 editions condemned because of errors and heresies to suppression, correction or cancellation.

The restoration of papal authority, ecclesiastical courts and the laws against heresy in England under the Catholic regime of Mary I reconfirmed the ban on Protestant Bibles. In 1555, a royal proclamation commanded "that no manner of persons presume to bring into this realm any manuscripts, books, papers . . . in the name of Martin Luther, John Calvin, Miles Coverdale, Erasmus, Tyndale . . . or any like books containing false doctrines against the Catholic faith." Protestants from England who took refuge in Frankfurt and Geneva published the Calvinist "Breeches Bible" in 1560. Although its use was forbidden in churches in England, it went into 140 editions between 1560 and 1644.

In 1546, the Catholic Church's Council of Trent declared the Latin Vulgate of Saint Jerome to be the sole canonical text of the Bible. In opposition to the Protestant reformers, the council decreed that dogma is transmitted through the church's teaching, whose authority is equal to that of the Bible, and forbade the reading of any unapproved translation. The first English version approved for Catholics was a translation of the New Testament from the Vulgate by church scholars published in Rheims in 1582 and printed in 1610 with an approved Old Testament as the Rheims-Douay version.

In 1631, the word "not" was inadvertently omitted from the seventh commandment, "Thou shalt not commit adultery," in an edition of 1,000 copies of the Bible printed in England by R. Barker. The printers were heavily fined and the edition, known as the "wicked Bible," was so vigorously suppressed that few copies have survived.

Because the copyright of the Authorized (King James) Version was held by the British Crown, the right to print it in England in the 17th century was held by the royal printers. Only the universities of Oxford and Cambridge were exempt from the restriction. This meant that no authorized Bible could be printed in the American colonies until after their independence. The first Bible printed in America was not the King James Version, but the *Up-Biblum God*, John Eliot's Bible translation for the Algonquian Indians, published in 1661–63. The Bible in English was probably not published in the United States until 1782 in Philadelphia, though historians have found evidence that a Bible may have been secretly printed in Boston about 1752.

The prudish sensibilities of the Victorian period in England and the United States produced a new kind of censorship of the Bible—the publication of expurgated editions. *The Holy Bible, Newly Translated*, by John Bellamy, a Swedenborgian, was published in 1818. Declaring that no major biblical figure could have committed actions he found unacceptable, Bellamy decided that the translation from Hebrew must be at fault, and he revised passages he considered indecent. *The New Family Bible and Improved Version*, by Dr. Benjamin Boothroyd, a Congregationalist who wanted to circumvent "many offensive and indelicate expressions" in the Bible, was published in several editions beginning in 1824. That year, in *The Holy Bible Arranged and Adapted for Family Reading*, John Watson, a Church of England layman, replaced offensive sections with his own writing and dropped the numbering of traditional chapters and verses so that it was difficult for readers to notice what had been cut. In 1828, William Alexander, a Quaker printer, published *The Holy Bible, Principally Designed to Facilitate the Audible or Social Reading of the Sacred Scriptures*. He changed words and passages "not congenial to the views and genius of the present age of refinement."

The first expurgated Bible in America was published in 1833 by the lexicographer Noah Webster, who made thousands of alterations in material he considered indecent. Although his Bible was adopted by the state of Connecticut in 1835, endorsed by Yale and widely used in Congregational pulpits for about 20 years, Webster's desire to make changes even in "decent" parts of the Bible met with criticism. The third edition, published in 1841, was the last.

Twentieth-century government censorship of the Bible has been most widespread in socialist countries. In 1926, the Soviet government instructed libraries throughout the U.S.S.R. to remove all religious books such as the Bible. It was allowed to remain only in the country's largest libraries. Its importation was forbidden and it was not printed again in the Soviet Union until 1956. In China, during the Cultural Revolution of the 1960s and 1970s—a campaign to destroy "the four olds" of culture, thinking, habits and customs—Bibles were burned and all places of Christian worship were closed.

A 1986 government-authorized printing of a Bible used by the Baptist church in Romania marked the first time since 1951 that the Bible had been printed there. The socialist military government of Ethiopia in 1986 banned several books of the Bible as "contrary to the ongoing revolution." A shipment of more than 45,000 Bibles destined for a church in Ethiopia was held indefinitely in customs.

Many attempts to censor the Bible have been recorded in the United States. Parents or religious groups who denounced the teaching of the Bible as comparative literature or believed it should be taught only as the sacred word of God from their own perspective and interpretation have attempted to remove it from school libraries or curricula. Challenges to the Bible have also often been based in misunderstanding of Supreme Court decisions prohibiting prayer in the public schools. In 1963 in *District of Abington Township v. Schempp*, the U.S. Supreme Court prohibited devotional exercises in public schools. The court, however, did not forbid the study of the Bible as literature, or of religion in historical or social studies. In its decision the court declared, "In addition, it might well be said that one's education is not complete without a study of comparative religion or the history of religion and its relationship to the advancement of civilization. Nothing we have said here indicates that such study of the Bible or of religion, when presented objectively as part of a secular program of education, may not be effected consistently. . . ."

In an early challenge to the Supreme Court decision, a conservative religious organization sued the University of Washington for having offered an elective course on the Bible as literature. It argued that such a course could not be offered in a public institution and that the approach taken conflicted with its religious views. The Washington state courts upheld the inclusion of the course in a broad curriculum.

A 1982 study of 17 surveys conducted of school libraries during the previous two decades found that the presence or use of the Bible in schools had been challenged by students, parents or teachers who thought it was illegal or who objected to the interpretation used. Similar challenges were reported during the 1980s and 1990s. For example, in 1989 an elementary school student in Omaha, Nebraska, was forbidden to read the Bible in school or to have it on the premises. In a settlement of a suit in Federal District Court that never came to trial, it was agreed that the student could read the religious literature of his choice at school during his free time. In 1991, a library patron who believed that public funds could not be expended on religious books challenged the presence of the *Evangelical Commentary on the Bible* and the *Official Catholic Directory* in the Multnomah, Oregon, public library. The books were retained by the library. In May 1981, Christian fundamentalists burned copies of The Living Bible in Gastonia, North Carolina.

A spate of attempts during the 1990s to restrict access to the Bible, reminiscent of Victorian-era attempts to bowdlerize it, have been motivated by the view that it contains indecent material. In 1992 in the Brooklyn Center, Minnesota, independent school district, an atheist "seeking to turn the tables on the religious right" challenged use of the Bible, declaring that "the lewd, indecent, and violent contents of that book are hardly suitable for young children." In 1993, the Bible was challenged as "obscene and pornographic," but retained, at the Noel Wien Library in Fairbanks, Alaska. Near Harrisburg, Pennsylvania, protestors attempting to remove it from the West Shore schools cited "more than 300 examples of obscenities in the book" and objected that it "contains language and stories that are inappropriate for children of any age, including tales of incest and murder."

Though the Bible is among the most censored books in history, it has been translated more times and into more languages than any other and has outsold every book in the history of publishing. In the English language alone, 450 different editions are in print. The long history of Bible censorship has had little impact on its availability and influence today.

FURTHER READINGS

Burress, Lee. *Battle of the Books: Library Censorship in the Public Schools, 1950–1985.* Metuchen, N.J.: Scarecrow Press, 1989.

Daniell, David. *Let There Be Light: William Tyndale and the Making of the English Bible.* London: British Library, 1994.

———. *William Tyndale: A Biography.* New Haven: Yale University Press, 1994.

Doyle, Robert P. *Banned Books 1996 Resource Guide.* Chicago: American Library Association, 1996.

Haight, Anne Lyon. *Banned Books: 387 B.C. to 1978 A.D.* Updated and enlarged by Chandler B. Grannis. New York: R. R. Bowker, 1978.

Hentoff, Nat. *Free Speech for Me, but Not for Thee.* New York: HarperCollins, 1992.

Jenkinson, Edward B. "The Bible: A Source of Great Literature and Controversy." In *Censored Books: Critical Viewpoints.* Ed. by Nicholas J. Karolides, Lee Burress and John M. Kean, 98–102. Metuchen, N.J.: Scarecrow Press, 1993.

Lofmark, Carl. *What Is the Bible?* Buffalo, N.Y.: Prometheus Books, 1992.

Manguel, Alberto. *A History of Reading.* New York: Viking, 1996.

New York Public Library. *Censorship: 500 Years of Conflict.* New York: Oxford University Press, 1984.

O'Neil, Robert M. "The Bible and the Constitution." In *Censored Books: Critical Viewpoints.* Ed. by Nicholas J. Karolides, Lee Burress and John M. Kean, 103–8. Metuchen, N.J.: Scarecrow Press, 1993.

Perrin, Noel. *Dr. Bowdler's Legacy: A History of Expurgated Books in England and America.* Anchor Books, 1971.

Putnam, George Haven. *The Censorship of the Church of Rome.* Vol. 1. New York: G. P. Putnam's Sons, 1906–7.

Tinguet, Margaret. "Ethiopia: Destroy the Muslims." *Index on Censorship* 16:4 (April 1987): 33–35.

THE BLOUDY TENENT OF PERSECUTION

Author: Roger Williams
Original date and place of publication: 1644, England
Literary form: Religious text

SUMMARY

Roger Williams, a founder of the Massachusetts Bay Colony, brought a radical liberty of conscience to the shores of New England. In *The Bloudy Tenent of Persecution* he espoused the ideas of religious toleration and intellectual freedom under both secular and ecclesiastical governments. The trajectory of Williams's life represented the dissenting currents in British Protestant thought. Born into a family that belonged to the Church of England, he became a Puritan while at Cambridge in the 1620s and was a Separatist Puritan by the time he joined the Massachusetts Bay Colony in 1631.

In 1635, his disenchantment with the Separatists in Massachusetts led to his exile to Rhode Island, at that time a wilderness between the British colonies of Massachusetts and Connecticut. Williams was dissatisfied with the way churches began as fundamentalist, back-to-basics movements and gradually developed their own orthodoxies. His desire for a pure church led him to question the idea of an official church decreed by a political entity, such as a local or colonial government.

In the summer of 1643, Williams returned to England to persuade Parliament to grant him a charter for Rhode Island, which would establish it as an official colony, free to govern its own affairs. England in this period was racked with religious controversy, particularly over the boundaries between church and state authority and individual liberty. By the spring of 1644, Williams had made a name for himself arguing for a balance of church, state and individual interests that would favor individual conscience. Observing the proliferation of new Protestant sects, he believed that no church or state power could control this impulse toward fragmentation. Liberty of conscience, which Williams defined as the freedom to worship as one saw fit, should not be restricted.

Williams published his ideas in *The Bloudy Tenent of Persecution*, officially a rebuttal to John Cotton, the most powerful Puritan minister in Massachusetts and a skillful politician who wanted to curry favor with Parliament. Cotton had endorsed new legislation that increased the church's power in civil affairs. Williams's book argued against the right of Parliament to demand and enforce conformity in interpretation and practice of scriptural principles. He claimed that the Massachusetts Puritans were trying to build a modern state based on the Ten Commandments. He criticized the idea that the abstract and absolute principles of Moses could be used to govern society thousands of years later.

Williams had his own religious and philosophical reasons for opposing Cotton's ideas. Williams believed that the British government's enforcement of the First Commandment, that there is one God to be obeyed, was offensive to Christian tradition, because the New Testament superseded Mosaic law; Williams also objected because, as he put it, prayer offered insincerely "stinks in God's nostrils."

The Bloudy Tenent of Persecution continued in this vein, offering copious evidence from religious and secular history that the state and the church had separate realms. Williams denounced the philosophy and practice of religious repression. The earth has been "made drunk with the bloud of its inhabitants," he wrote, slaughtering each other with indiscriminate zeal as each sect seeks to aggrandize itself at the expense of others. "Those churches cannot be truly Christian . . . which either actually themselves, or by the civil power of kings and princes . . . doe persecute such as dissent from them or be opposite against them." Unless reason and charity prevail, the result will be the ruin of the church and the devastation of civil society.

Williams was all too familiar with the power of an official church. In *The Bloudy Tenent* he stated that his exile to Rhode Island was a result of his campaigning for liberty of conscience and that the Puritans sent him to a remote outpost to silence him. The example of his own life, he hoped, would persuade readers of the harm of religious doctrine enforced through civil punishment.

Williams wrote *The Bloudy Tenent* in the form of a dialogue between Peace and Truth, as a parable about his fight with the established churches of his day. He was particularly troubled by the role of nonbelievers in English and colonial society. He wondered what was to be gained in forcing someone who was not a sincere Protestant to mouth the words of Protestant doctrine. Williams believed that the salvation of nonbelieving individuals would come from their own conversion experiences, rather than through the commands of a religious orthodoxy.

To Williams, religion was primarily an inner belief, as opposed to the outward expression of religion practiced by most Puritans in Massachusetts and Presbyterians in the English Parliament. Official religion, state celebration of religious holidays and courts empowered to enforce religious doctrine offended his religious sensibilities. Mixing the private religious sphere and the public governmental sphere resulted in a cheapening of religion: religious doctrine came straight from divine sources, while political leaders were merely appointed or elected by other humans. This latter idea offended King Charles I, who still clung to the idea that his power could be traced to divine origins.

Williams's ideas in *The Bloudy Tenent*, as they attacked the relationship between church and state—which most Britons took for granted—became infamous. But his inflammatory language won few converts to his ideas. However, his book did not hinder his achieving another goal. One month after its publication, he returned to the wilderness of Rhode Island with the charter in hand that established Rhode Island as a British colony.

CENSORSHIP HISTORY

Upon its publication in July 1644, *The Bloudy Tenent of Persecution* failed to persuade Parliament and the British reading public of the importance of separating religious doctrine from civil policy. Given the imperative that Parliament placed on religious conformity, it is hardly surprising that Parliament ordered all copies of Williams's 400-page book to be burned publicly in August 1644.

Williams's style of organization was partly to blame as well. He had composed his book in fits and starts over nearly 25 years. This gradual formation of a religious philosophy showed up in the muddled prose of the original work. It is unlikely that most members of Parliament, or anyone else, read far enough into the book to be persuaded by Williams's defense of his ideas through painstaking analysis of scriptural passages.

Hostility toward this book may also have been generated by its subtitle: "for cause of Conscience." Liberty of conscience was a radical concept in England at this time. When members of such dissenting sects as the Quakers were jailed for their beliefs and Catholics and Jews faced more violent suppression, a plea for complete religious tolerance was unlikely to be persuasive.

By the time Williams's book was burned, he was on a ship bound for New England. He never faced jail or other personal punishment for writing *The Bloudy Tenent of Persecution*. He did, however, have to answer attacks on his ideas. In 1647, his old nemesis John Cotton wrote *The Bloudy Tenent, Washed, and Made White in the Bloud of the Lamb*, in which he denied that Williams had been expelled from Massachusetts for religious reasons. He contended, rather, that Williams had spoken against the Boston government, preaching sedition, and had to be punished. Explicit in Cotton's argument was the idea that there was no separation between religious and civil authorities, that a dispute with the religious practice of civil leaders was tantamount to a civil dispute and this constituted advocating rebellion. Cotton attacked Williams as self-serving, and dismissed Williams's claims that he was persecuted for his religious beliefs.

Five years after Cotton's rebuttal, Williams published *The Bloudy Tenent yet More Bloudy: by Mr. Cotton's endeavour to wash it white in the Bloud of the Lambe*. Williams stood by his original principles, especially the scriptural justification for religious tolerance. In his opinion, forcing people to worship in churches against their will resulted in the sin of hypocrisy. Thus, the Massachusetts authorities were requiring their citizens to sin. Forcing nonmembers to attend a church was to Williams a greater sin than was lack of belief in Christianity.

While Parliament's burning of *The Bloudy Tenent of Persecution* did not stop Roger Williams from publishing his ideas or from prospering in his colony of Rhode Island, this censorship signaled the beginning of an era of religious intolerance in both England and New England. Respect for Williams's belief in freedom of conscience grew, however, over the following 150 years. His philosophy of religious tolerance inspired the rights to "life, liberty, and the pursuit of happiness" in the Declaration of Independence, as well as the Constitution's First Amendment guarantees of freedom of religion and speech. In 1936, 300 years after Williams's exile to Rhode Island, the state of Massachusetts pardoned him for his offense.

FURTHER READINGS

Covey, Cyclone. *The Gentle Radical: A Biography of Roger Williams*. New York: Macmillan Co., 1966.
Gaustad, Edwin S. *Liberty of Conscience: Roger Williams in America*. Grand Rapids, Mich.: Wm. B. Eerdmans Publishing Co., 1991.
Green, Jonathon. *The Encyclopedia of Censorship*. New York: Facts On File, 1990.

Haight, Anne Lyon. *Banned Books: 387 B.C. to 1978 A.D.* Updated and enlarged by Chandler B. Grannis. New York: R. R. Bowker, 1978.

Jordan, W. K. *The Development of Religious Toleration in England.* Vol. 3. Gloucester, Mass.: Peter Smith, 1965.

Morgan, Edmund S. *Roger Williams: The Church and the State.* New York: Harcourt, Brace & World, 1967.

Polishook, Irwin H. *Roger Williams, John Cotton, and Religious Freedom: A Controversy in New and Old England.* Englewood Cliffs, N.J.: Prentice-Hall, 1967.

CHILDREN OF THE ALLEY

Author: Naguib Mahfouz
Original date and place of publication: 1959, Egypt; 1988, United States
Original publisher: *Al-Ahram* newspaper; Three Continents Press
Literary form: Novel

SUMMARY

The Egyptian author Naguib Mahfouz, awarded the Nobel Prize in literature in 1988, is the most celebrated contemporary Arab writer, with 35 novels and more than a dozen collections of stories to his credit over the last half century. Many of Mahfouz's richly detailed novels portray life in Cairo's teeming working-class neighborhoods. Among them are the three novels of his masterpiece *The Cairo Trilogy*, written between 1945 and 1957, chronicling the fortunes of three generations of a Cairo family.

Children of the Alley (also known by the title *Children of Gebelawi*) is the history of an imaginary Cairo alley and a retelling in allegorical form of the lives of Adam and Eve, Cain and Abel, and Moses, Jesus and Muhammad. The novel can be read on many levels. It is an evocative account of the vanished world of Mahfouz's childhood in the alleys of Gemalia in Cairo and an engrossing fictional narrative. It is also a fable that echoes the history of Judaism, Christianity and Islam, as well as a critique of religious intolerance and political and economic repression.

Narrated by an unnamed resident of the alley who is a professional writer, the story begins in the shadow of the mansion of Gabalawi, master of the estate at the foot of Muqattam mountain. Gabalawi, whose despotic presence looms over generations of his descendants, represents God, or as Mahfouz has said, a certain idea of God that people have created.

Gabalawi's son, Adham, and Adham's wife, Umaima, tempted and tricked by Adham's dissolute brother, Idris, are permanently expelled by Gabalawi from the mansion and its fragrant gardens for seeking a look at his forbidden book. One of their two sons, Qadri, kills the other, Humam, in a fight. Qadri marries Hind, the daughter of Idris. They have several children and from these ancestors all the people of the alley descend.

Gabalawi shuts himself away in his mansion and is not seen again. The management of his estate subsequently becomes a source of conflict. Though the estate's overseer at first follows the good example of Gabalawi, sharing its benefits with all the descendants, greed eventually gets the better of him and he exploits the poor. The neighborhood is run by young gangsters in the overseer's employ, who extort protection money from its hard-working inhabitants.

The first to rise up and rebel against injustice in the alley is the snake charmer Gabal, who defeats the gangsters and takes over leadership of the quarter. Gabal, who applies eye-for-an-eye justice, is honest and upright and shares the estate revenues equally, but he is also feared. He is a symbol of justice and order, but after his death, the era of the dishonest overseers and their threatening gangsters returns.

In another generation, a new leader—Rifaa, the carpenter's son—comes forth to preach against violence and materialism. He calls on Gabal's followers to trust him so that he can deliver them from evil spirits. Rifaa is murdered by the overseer and his gangsters, who see him as a threat to their social order.

A third leader, Qassem, eventually emerges from among the Desert Rats, the poorest and most wretched people of the neighborhood. He says that the people of the alley are all equally Gabalawi's children and the rule of gangsters must end. Following Rifaa's example, he ushers in an era of brotherhood and peace among the followers of Gabal, Rifaa and his own disciples. He proclaims that no neighborhood is more closely related to Gabalawi than any other and that the estate belongs to everyone.

But those who succeed Qassem as overseer return to the old system of violence and exploitation. The alley is again divided against itself, with separate quarters for the followers of Gabal, Rifaa and Qassem. "Gabalawi," the old man Shakrun cries out facing the mansion, "how long will you be silent and hidden? Your commandments are ignored and your money is being wasted. . . . Don't you know what has happened to us?"

Arafa, a magician, resolves to liberate the alley from the overseer's tyranny. He wants to find Gabalawi's book, the cause of Adham's exile, believing that it holds the magic secret of Gabalawi's power. When he breaks into the mansion to search for the book, he kills a servant. Having come in a quest for power to use against evil, he has turned into an evildoer.

In murdering a servant, Arafa indirectly kills Gabalawi, who dies from the shock of the murder in his house. The followers of Gabal, Rifaa and Qassem squabble over where Gabalawi should be buried, each group believing they have a closer relationship with their ancestor. The overseer instructs the storytellers to sing the story of Gabalawi, emphasizing how he died at the hands of Arafa. But the people favor Arafa and his magic, exalting his name above those of Gabel, Rifaa and Qassem. Gabalawi is dead, the people of the alley say: "We have nothing to do with the past. Our only hope lies in Arafa's magic, and if we had to choose between Gabalawi and magic, we'd choose magic."

The final line of the book looks to the future with hope: "Injustice must have an end, as day must follow night. We will see the death of tyranny, and the dawn of light and miracles."

CENSORSHIP HISTORY

Children of the Alley was serialized in 1959 in the semiofficial Cairo newspaper *Al-Ahram*. Devout Muslims took to the streets in protest, demanding a ban because Mahfouz had suggested in allegorical fashion that the God of Adam, Moses, Jesus and Muhammad might be dead. It was only upon the intervention of Egypt's president, Abdul Nasser, a friend of *Al-Ahram*'s editor, Mohammed Heikal, that the serialization was published uncut to the end. However, the scholars of Cairo's powerful government-recognized religious authority, Al-Azhar University, banned *Children of the Alley*, condemning it as "blasphemous," and calling its author a heretic for causing offense to the prophets of Islam and for misrepresenting the character of Muhammad.

Since that time, militant Islamic groups have sustained a relentless campaign against the book and its author, which successfully ensured its banning for over three decades. *Children of the Alley* was passed from hand to hand in its newspaper version until 1967, when a pirated edition of the novel was published in Beirut, Lebanon, in slightly expurgated form. Smuggled into Egypt, it was sold under the counter at some Cairo bookstores.

In 1979, Mahfouz again incurred the wrath of Islamic fundamentalists in Egypt and elsewhere in the Arab world when he was among the first to support the peace treaty between Egypt and Israel. His novels were banned for several years in many Arab countries.

In 1988, Mahfouz won the Nobel Prize. Fundamentalists, who had never forgiven him for writing *Children of the Alley*, renewed their attacks, fearing that the prize would be used as a pretext to remove the book from the proscribed list. "The novel had basically been forgotten for a period of 30 years," Mahfouz said in a 1989 interview, "but following the prize it was subjected to very heavy attack in all the Islamicist-oriented newspapers and magazines. So the idea of publishing it here isn't even a topic for discussion."

Bolstered by Egyptian President Hosni Mubarak's statement that the novel should be published and the fact of its availability in much of the rest of the Arab world, renewed attempts were made to lift the ban on the book. But when the Egyptian monthly *Al-Yasar* began to serialize it in 1989, the Islamic press campaigned so virulently against it that Mahfouz himself asked the magazine to stop the serialization.

Mahfouz again ran afoul of militants that same year when he spoke out against Iran's Ayatollah Khomeini's edict calling for the death of British author Salman Rushdie for having written *THE SATANIC VERSES*. Sheikh Omar Abdel Rahman, the Egyptian fundamentalist leader of the militant Gamaat Islamia sect (who was later convicted in a plot to blow up New York City landmarks and assassinate U.S. political leaders), issued a statement calling on both Mahfouz and Rushdie to repent. "If they do not, they will be killed," he said. "If this sentence had been passed on Naguib Mahfouz when he wrote *Children of the Alley*, Salman Rushdie would have realized that he had to stay within certain bounds."

In June 1992, Islamist terrorists in Cairo shot and killed Farag Fouda, a prominent Egyptian secular writer, who, like Mahfouz, had spoken out against violent censorship. Shortly after Fouda's slaying, the Egyptian government uncovered a death list including Mahfouz and several other leading writers and intellectuals. Mahfouz was offered but declined police protection.

In early 1994, the weekly magazine *Rose el-Youssef* published extracts from several banned works, including *The Satanic Verses* and *Children of the Alley*, accompanied by a statement in defense of freedom of expression. Most Arab countries, with the exception of Egypt and Kuwait, banned the magazine's distribution. In October 1994, Mahfouz was stabbed several times in the neck as he sat in a car outside his Cairo home. (Two Islamic militants were convicted of attempted murder and executed, and others received lesser sentences.) Mahfouz has not regained full use of his right arm and hand since the assault and dictates his writings.

Shortly thereafter, the government's minister of information, speaking from Mahfouz's hospital bed, said the government did not support a ban on any of his works. His statement was interpreted as ending the official prohibition of *Children of the Alley*. As Egyptian newspapers rushed to serialize the novel, Mahfouz asked that publication come at a later time, fearing that his life would be further endangered. "The issue is diverting attention from a crime against my life to whether this novel is, or is not, against religion," he said. But his request was ignored. A few weeks after the attack, the novel was published in the Egyptian press for the first time in 35 years. As of mid-1997, however, the novel had not been published in book form in Egypt.

FURTHER READINGS

Appignanesi, Lisa, and Sara Maitland, eds. *The Rushdie File*. Syracuse, New York: Syracuse University Press, 1990.
Pipes, Daniel. *The Rushdie Affair*. New York: Carol Publishing Group, 1990.
Weaver, Mary Anne. "The Novelist and the Sheikh," *The New Yorker* (January 30, 1995): 52–59.

CHRISTIANITY RESTORED

Author: Michael Servetus
Original date and place of publication: 1552, France
Literary form: Theological treatise

SUMMARY

The Spanish theologian and physician Michael Servetus earned his reputation for religious deviationism at the age of 20. During his law studies at Toulouse, France, he had discovered in the Scriptures the historical person of Jesus of Nazareth, leading him to reject traditional formulations of the nature of Christ and the relationship of the three persons of the Trinity.

Servetus believed that Protestant reformers Luther, Calvin and Zwingli were not revolutionary enough, because they accepted the doctrine of the Trinity, which he viewed as incomprehensible. Failing to convince the reformers in Basel and Strasbourg of his ideas, Servetus decided to write a book that would persuade all Christians of the truth of his discoveries.

In 1531, he published *On the Errors of the Trinity*, a treatise asserting that traditional Scholastic theology introduced Greek philosophical terms and non-biblical concepts into the definitions of the Trinity that were abstract, speculative and unrelated to the living God. "Not one word is found in the whole Bible about the Trinity, nor about its Persons, nor about an Essence, nor about a unity of the Substance, nor about one Nature of the several beings," he wrote. Orthodox Catholics and many Protestants viewed Servetus's theology as having revived the fourth-century heresy of Arianism, which denied the doctrine of the Trinity by teaching that Jesus as the Son of God was neither equal to nor eternal with God the Father.

In 1552, Servetus recast his earlier tracts in a new book, *Christianity Restored*. It contained a revised edition of *On the Errors of the Trinity* and new material, including 30 letters on theology that he had sent to John Calvin. In *Christianity Restored* Servetus challenged the established churches, both Catholic and Protestant, to return Christendom to the purity of its origins: "A calling of the whole apostolic church to make a fresh start, restored completely in the knowledge of God, the faith of Christ, our justification, regeneration, baptism, and the Lord's Supper. Our restoration finally in the kingdom of heaven, with the loosing of the captivity of ungodly Babylon and Antichrist and his own destroyed."

In the new work he claimed that Christianity had failed because it had become corrupted in the early fourth century by pagan doctrines and by the church's acquisition of temporal power. He attacked the definition of the Trinity established by the church's Council of Nicaea in the fourth century, as well as the practice of infant baptism, which he termed as unchristian. He accepted the heretical Anabaptist tenet that baptism should be deferred until maturity, when a sinner has experienced Christ and repented. Christ himself was not baptized until he was an adult, Servetus wrote, and becoming a Christian meant sharing a spiritual communion that an infant could not understand.

CENSORSHIP HISTORY

The publication in 1531 of *On the Errors of the Trinity* made Servetus notorious and a hunted man, threatened by both the French and Spanish Inquisitions and the Protestants, who banned his book and closed cities to him. In 1532, the Inquisition in Toulouse issued a decree ordering his arrest. He went underground in Paris and assumed a new identity, adopting the name of Michel de Villeneuve, from the family home of Villanueva, Spain. Fear of persecution in Paris drove him to Lyons, where he worked as a printer's editor, eventually settling in 1540 in the Lyons suburb of Vienne.

Using his own name, Servetus began to correspond with Protestant reformer John Calvin in Geneva, instructing him on theology. In all he sent 30 epistolary discourses to Calvin. Calvin sent him a copy of his *Institutes of the Christian Religion*, which Servetus boldly returned annotated with criticisms. Servetus also presented Calvin with a manuscript copy of part of *Christianity Restored*, apparently hoping that Calvin would view it favorably.

A thousand copies of *Christianity Restored* were printed anonymously and in secret in Vienne by the publishers Arnoullet and Guéroult in 1552 after publishers in Basel refused to have anything to do with the book. Some copies were sent to the Frankfurt book fair and others to a bookseller in Geneva. There a copy came into the hands of Calvin's colleague, Guillaume Trie, who forwarded the first four leaves of the book to a Catholic cousin in Lyons, revealing Villeneuve's identity and location in Vienne. The cousin placed the material in the hands of the Inquisition, which began an investigation.

Servetus and his publisher Arnoullet denied any knowledge of the book. But at the request of the Inquisition, Trie provided the investigators the manuscript copy of the book sent by Servetus to Calvin, implicating Servetus. Servetus was arrested and held for trial, but escaped. In June 1553, the civil tribunal of Lyons condemned him in absentia for heresy, sedition, rebellion and evasion of prison, fining him 2,000 livres and sentencing him to be burned. In his absence, bales of copies of his books were incinerated with his effigy. His publisher was imprisoned.

In August, on his way to seek refuge in Italy, Servetus passed through Geneva, Calvin's stronghold. There he was recognized and, on Calvin's orders, arrested. Charged with 39 counts of heresy and blasphemy, for more than two months he stood trial before the judges of the Geneva city council. The verdict of the council was that the book Servetus had secretly printed in Vienne had spread "heresies and horrible, execrable blasphemies against the Holy Trinity, against the Son of God, against the baptism of infants and foundations of the Christian religion." The Geneva authorities consulted the magistrates of all the Swiss cantons, who unanimously agreed on the verdict.

Servetus was sentenced to be burned to ashes with his book for trying "to infect the world with [his] stinking heretical poison." The verdict stated further, "And so you shall finish your days and give an example to others who would commit the like." Servetus's last request was to see Calvin. "I told him to beg the pardon of the son of God, whom he had disfigured with his dreams . . .," Calvin reported. "But when I saw that all this did no good I did not wish to be wiser than my Master allows. So following the rule of St. Paul, I withdrew from the heretic who was self-condemned."

Servetus asked to die by the sword, rather than by burning. Although Calvin supported this request for mercy, it was denied by the magistrates. "He asked forgiveness for his errors, ignorance and sins, but never made a full confession," wrote Calvin's colleague, Guillaume Farel. "But we could never get him openly to admit his errors and confess that Christ is the eternal son of God." On October 27, 1553, Servetus was burned at the stake.

Calvin urged the destruction of *Christianity Restored* in Protestant countries, as it contained "prodigious blasphemies against God." Only three copies survived. In part the tragic result of a power struggle between Calvin and his opponents, Servetus's execution damaged Calvin's reputation. As church historian Roland H. Bainton wrote, Servetus had "the singular distinction of having been burned by the Catholics in effigy and by the Protestants in actuality." Servetus was the first person to be executed as a heretic on the authority of a reformed church. His martyrdom came to have a significance greater than any other in his century, as it marked the first important controversy over the issue of toleration within Protestantism.

The movement on behalf of toleration, reflected in Sebastian Castellio's 1554 defense of toleration *Concerning Heretics and How They Are to Be Treated*, was galvanized by widespread revulsion at Servetus's punishment. Yet the systematic repression of *Christianity Restored* minimized Servetus's posthumous influence on religious thought. Almost two centuries later, Richard Mead, the physician to the king of England, tried to publish Servetus's work. In 1723, the government seized and burned the whole printing and imprisoned Mead and his printer.

FURTHER READINGS

Bainton, Roland H. *Hunted Heretic: The Life and Death of Michael Servetus.* Gloucester, Mass.: Peter Smith, 1978.

Christie-Murray, David. *A History of Heresy.* Oxford: Oxford University Press, 1989.

Haight, Anne Lyon. *Banned Books: 387 B.C. to 1978 A.D.* Updated and enlarged by Chandler B. Grannis. New York: R. R. Bowker, 1978.

Levy, Leonard W. *Blasphemy: Verbal Offense Against the Sacred, from Moses to Salman Rushdie.* New York: Alfred A. Knopf, 1993.

Parker, T. H. L. *John Calvin.* Batavia, Ill.: Lion Publishing Corporation, 1975.

Smith, George H. *Atheism, Ayn Rand, and Other Heresies.* Buffalo: Prometheus Books, 1991.

Spitz, Lewis W., ed. *The Protestant Reformation.* Englewood Cliffs, N.J.: Prentice-Hall, 1966.

CHURCH: CHARISM AND POWER: LIBERATION THEOLOGY AND THE INSTITUTIONAL CHURCH

Author: Leonardo Boff
Original date and place of publication: 1981, Brazil; 1985, United States

Original publisher: Editora Vôzes; Crossroad
Literary form: Theological essays

SUMMARY

The Brazilian Catholic theologian Leonardo Boff is among the leading exponents of liberation theology, an interpretation of Christian faith drawn from the experience of the poor. *Church: Charism and Power*, a collection of essays, speeches and lecture notes, contains some of the sharpest criticisms of the Roman Catholic church to come from Latin America. Boff argues from his experience with the poor in Brazilian base communities—grassroots, Catholic communities led by laity. He urges institutional reform of Catholicism and its transformation into a "liberation Church," not simply *for* the poor, but *of* the poor. Criticizing abuse of hierarchical power, he calls for a return to the collegial structure of early church communities, in which both clergy and laity exercised power.

Boff's central thesis is that the struggle for justice and human rights cannot be separated from a similar struggle within the church itself. The preferential option for the poor demands shifts within Catholicism. The institutional church must move away from its reliance on power and coercion and toward a democratic model of openness and tolerance, the original model upon which Christ founded the church. Boff contends that the church hierarchy took its form only after Jesus' death. When Christianity became the official religion of the Roman Empire, the church began to reflect the empire's feudal structure of authority, including its institutions, laws and bureaucratic centralization.

Boff distinguishes between two kinds of power: *exousia*, the power of love employed by Jesus, and *potestas*, the power to dominate and rule that characterized Roman officialdom. He describes the exercise of *potestas* by the clergy and the division between the clergy and the laity as a cancer within the church. The charismatic essence of the church, in which everyone has a charism, or gift, to offer, has been extinguished. "Christianity is not against power in itself," Boff writes, "but its diabolical forms which show themselves as dominion and control." Using marxist terminology, Boff refers to the "gradual expropriation of the spiritual means of production from the Christian people by the clergy."

The church must contain charisms, such as teaching, serving, preaching and administering, as well as power. The papacy does have a special position within the church in maintaining doctrinal unity based on the emerging consensus of the community. Power can be a charism, Boff believes, as long as it serves everyone and is an instrument for building justice in the community.

CENSORSHIP HISTORY

Boff's orthodoxy already had been investigated by the Vatican in 1976 and again in 1980 on suspicion of doctrinal deviation. The 1980 investigation centered on his book *Jesus Christ, the Liberator*. But the Vatican had been generally willing to leave the question of orthodoxy of individual Latin American theologians to their own bishops.

When *Church: Charism and Power* was published in Brazil, Spain and Italy in 1981, it was not expected to spark widespread debate. It was a further development of ideas expressed in Boff's doctoral thesis and in a previous book on ecclesiology, or the study of the structure of the church. Boff was not optimistic that the book, a loosely connected collection of disparate writings and talks rather than a comprehensive analysis, would find an audience.

Almost immediately, however, the book provoked an unusual amount of discussion. Boff had applied the insights of liberation theology, previously directed at the reform of secular society, to the church itself. His choice of the words "symbolic violence" to refer to the Vatican's methods for discouraging dissent and his use of quasi-marxist terminology to analyze the church's structure angered critics.

In the book, he quotes at length a Brazilian Catholic who makes a point-by-point parallel between Kremlin and Vatican styles of governance. In another highly controversial passage, he writes: "It is strange to see that the Church institution has developed into exactly that which Christ did not want it to be."

Boff had earlier described the Vatican's Congregation for the Doctrine of the Faith as relying on procedures that are unacceptable in civil society, a "Kafkaesque process wherein the accuser, defender, the lawyer and judge are one and the same." In 1982, a similar process was initiated to investigate Boff's views.

In February 1982, Boff, who knew that his critics had already complained to the Vatican, mailed to Rome as a courtesy a copy of some negative reviews of his book and a response by Father Urbano Zilles of Brazil. Three months later, he received a letter from Joseph Cardinal Ratzinger, Prefect of the Congregation for the Doctrine of the Faith, asking him to respond to criticisms. He wrote a response and published it.

In May 1984, Boff received a six-page letter from Ratzinger criticizing Boff's views as expressed in the book and saying they "did not merit acceptance." The letter referred to Boff's theological method, his analysis of church structure, his concepts of dogma and revelation and his description of the exercise of power in the church. It criticized his "ecclesiastical relativism" and his "sociological" analysis. Ratzinger accused Boff of using language that was "polemic, defamatory and pamphleteering, absolutely inappropriate for a theologian," drawing on "ideological principles of a certain neo-Marxist inspiration," proposing "a certain revolutionary utopia which is foreign to the church" and holding a "relativizing conception" of church structure and doctrine.

Boff replied with a 50-page document, insisting that he wrote "only to right the balance in the direction of the experience of the laity, the poor, and the contributions of the social sciences." He concluded, "Of one thing I am sure:

I prefer to walk in the church than go it alone with my theology. The church is a reality of Faith that I assume. Theology is a product of reason that I discuss."

Rather than going through the Brazilian bishops, who would have supported Boff, Ratzinger summoned him to Rome for a "colloquy" in September 1984. Boff took with him to Rome petitions signed by 50,000 Brazilians and was accompanied by two Brazilian cardinals, who came to show their support. Although Boff would not have selected *Church: Charism and Power* to fully represent his ideas, the colloquy turned out to be a full-scale interrogation on his views as expressed in the book.

In March 1985, the congregation published a Notification, making public the letter Ratzinger had sent the previous year and labeling it an official public notification approved by the pope. The congregation stated that its reservations about his book "had not been substantially overcome" and that Boff was guilty of three errors: his statement that the church borrowed societal characteristics from contemporary Roman and later feudal society; his relativistic interpretation of dogma as good for specific circumstances and times; and his statements that clergy had expropriated spiritual means of production from the laity. "The options of Leonardo Boff analyzed herein endanger the sound doctrine of the Faith which this congregation has the task of promoting and safeguarding," the Notification concluded.

In May 1985, Boff received an official notice from the congregation ordering him to begin immediately to observe an "obedient silence" for an unspecified period of time. The notice stated that the period of silence "would permit Friar Boff a time for serious reflection." It required him to abstain completely from writing and publishing, from his duties as editor of the *Revista Ecclesiastica Brasileira*, the most influential theological journal in Brazil, from his work as editor of books on theology at the publishing house Editora Vôzes and from teaching or lecturing. Boff submitted to the silencing, saying, "As a Christian, Franciscan friar and theologian, it is for me to listen and adhere."

Ten Brazilian bishops, who viewed the Vatican's attack on one of liberation theology's most prominent figures as an unwelcome intrusion of Rome into Latin American matters and a threat to the right of Catholics to think and write freely, took the highly unusual step of publicly criticizing the Vatican's treatment of Boff. Senior Brazilian bishops met with Pope John Paul II in Rome during March 1986. That month, after 10 months of the silencing, Boff's punishment was lifted. Boff said he received the news "as an Easter present" and was sure that it was a gesture of good will on the part of the Vatican toward the bishops of Brazil.

In 1991, Boff published a series of articles calling for change in the church's prohibition against marriage for priests. When church officials denied approval for publication of his next manuscript, he resigned from the priesthood. In an open letter to his followers he wrote, "I am leaving the priestly ministry, but not the church. . . . I continue to be and will always be a theologian in the

Catholic and ecumenical mold, fighting with the poor against their poverty and in favor of their liberation."

FURTHER READINGS

Cox, Harvey. *The Silencing of Leonardo Boff: The Vatican and the Future of World Christianity.* Oak Park, Ill.: Meyer Stone Books, 1988.

Sigmund, Paul E. *Liberation Theology at the Crossroads: Democracy or Revolution?* New York: Oxford University Press, 1990.

DIALOGUE CONCERNING THE TWO CHIEF WORLD SYSTEMS

Author: Galileo Galilei
Original date and place of publication: 1632, Italy
Literary form: Scientific monograph

SUMMARY

The work of the great Italian astronomer, mathematician and physicist Galileo had a profound effect on the development of science and philosophy, laying the foundations for modern experimental science and enlarging human understanding of the nature of the universe. Although the Polish astronomer Copernicus had argued in *On the Revolution of Heavenly Spheres*, published in 1543, that the sun was the center of the universe and the earth a planet that moved, belief in the geocentric Ptolemaic system (named for the second-century astronomer Ptolemy) remained prevalent in the early 17th century. The Ptolemaic theory placed the earth motionless at the center of the universe, with the sun, the moon and the five planets moving around it in complex circular motions.

When Galileo, a professor of mathematics at the University of Pisa, first gazed at the sky through the refracting telescope he had designed, it had been a half-century since Copernicus introduced his theory of a heliocentric, or sun-centered, universe. For the first time, however, actual observations of the heavens through a telescope seemed to confirm Copernicus's hypothesis. In 1610, Galileo published *The Starry Messenger*, a 24-page pamphlet reporting his astronomical observations of the moon and the planets. Galileo recounted his discovery of four previously unknown heavenly bodies moving around the planet Jupiter, proof that Copernicus's theory was correct. He also noted that the moon was not a self-luminous body, but was lit by the sun.

The Venetian senate granted Galileo a salary for his discoveries, and he was appointed mathematician to the Duke of Tuscany. In 1613, he published *Letters on the Solar Spots*, in which he declared his belief in the Copernican theory. Galileo was convinced that "the Book of Nature is written in mathematical symbols," and that in observation and quantification lay the science of the future. In 1632, Galileo published the work which was to mark a turning point in the history of science, *Dialogue Concerning the Two Chief World Systems, Ptolemaic and Copernican*.

In this dialogue in the Platonic tradition, Galileo allowed arguments for and against the Copernican system to emerge from a conversation among three friends: a Florentine who believes in the Copernican system, an Aristotelian supporter of the geocentric theory and a Venetian aristocrat for whose benefit they propose their arguments. Galileo wrote in Italian for the nonspecialist, rather than in Latin, the language of scholars and intellectuals.

In structuring the *Dialogue*, Galileo complied with the church's orders that the heliocentric theory be discussed as a useful mathematical hypothesis, rather than as a representation of physical reality. But the views he expressed in the *Dialogue* were clearly supportive of the Copernican system. Galileo found that the earth, like the other planets, rotated on its axis, and that the planets revolved around the sun in elliptical paths determined by gravity. The idea of a finite universe bounded by an outer sphere of unchanging perfection was rejected. By showing that the earth was not the center of creation but, rather, an insignificant part of it, Galileo overturned the medieval system of cosmology based on Aristotelian theories of the motion of bodies.

Galileo expressed two principles in the *Dialogue* that have become the guiding principles of modern science. First, statements and hypotheses about nature must always be based on observation, rather than on received authority; and second, natural processes can best be understood if represented in mathematical terms.

CENSORSHIP HISTORY

In 1616, the system of Copernicus was denounced as dangerous to the faith and Galileo, summoned to Rome, was warned by Pope Paul V not to "hold, teach or defend" Copernican theories. Galileo promised to obey the papal injunction and returned to Florence. Similar theories, published by the German astronomer Johannes Kepler in *The New Astronomy* were banned by the pope in 1619. According to the papal bull accompanying these bans, teaching or even reading the works of Copernicus and Kepler was forbidden.

In 1624, Galileo went to Rome again to pay his respects to the newly annointed Pope Urban VIII. Despite the prohibition of 1616, he requested papal permission to publish a book comparing Ptolemaic and Copernican doctrines. The pope refused his request.

Despite warnings by the Vatican, which had cited numerous corrections required before any of Copernicus's theories might be promulgated, in 1632 Galileo published *Dialogue Concerning the Two Chief World Systems*. He attempted to satisfy the authorities by including a preface by a leading Vatican theologian describing Copernican theory as merely an interesting intellectual exercise. But the pope was unconvinced. The book had attracted the attention of all of Europe. The rising threat of Protestantism spurred the pope to respond aggressively to preserve the integrity of the church's dogmas.

Further, Galileo's enemies at the Vatican implied that by publishing the book under the colophon of three fishes—the usual imprint of the Florentine press of Landini—Galileo had made a libelous reference to Pope Urban VIII's three incompetent nephews, whom he had promoted to the church hierarchy. They further suggested that one of the characters in the dialogue, Simplicio, the conservative defender of the geocentric view of the universe, was meant to be a caricature of the pope himself.

In February 1633, Galileo was summoned to Rome. Although he was gravely ill in Florence and his doctors warned that a journey in the dead of winter might prove fatal, the pope threatened to forcibly remove him in chains if he did not appear. The grand duke of Florence provided a litter to carry Galileo to Rome, where he was imprisoned. In June he was put on trial for heresy.

The trial focused on technicalities regarding what church authorities had told him during his visit to Rome in 1616 and on how clearly he had understood the papal disapproval of Copernican doctrines. The Inquisition's verdict was that Galileo was "vehemently suspected of heresy, namely of having believed and held the doctrine which is false and contrary to the sacred and divine scriptures that the sun is the center of the world and does not move from East to West and that the earth moves and is not the center of the world and that an opinion may be held and defended as probable after it has been declared and defined to be contrary to Holy Scripture. . . ."

Galileo was sentenced to prison for an indefinite period and required to make a public and formal abjuration. On the morning of June 22, 1633, at the age of 70, Galileo knelt before the court and declared, "With sincere heart and unpretended faith I abjure, curse, and detest the aforesaid errors and heresies and also every other error and sect whatever, contrary to the Holy Church, and I swear that in the future I will never again say or assert verbally or in writing, anything that might cause a similar suspicion toward me. . . ." "And yet it [the earth] moves," he is said by legend to have muttered after his recantation.

In 1634, the *Dialogue* was formally condemned and banned along with all of Galileo's works. Galileo was confined to a secluded house in Arcetri, outside Florence, where he was allowed no visitors except with the permission of the pope's delegate. During his confinement Galileo was able to complete a new work, *Dialogue Concerning Two New Sciences*, which was smuggled out of Italy and published by the Protestants in Leiden in 1638, four years before his death. During the last four years of his life, Galileo was blind. Eventually the pope allowed him the companionship of a young scholar, Vicenzo Viviani. Still in seclusion, Galileo died on January 8, 1642, a month before his 78th birthday.

The Index of Forbidden Books of 1664 confirmed the condemnation of the works of Copernicus and Galileo and of all other writings affirming the movement of the earth and the stability of the sun. In 1753, the Index of Benedict XIV omitted the general prohibition covering books that teach the heliocentric theory.

However, it was not until 1824, when Canon Settele, a Roman astronomy professor, published a work on modern scientific theories, that the church finally announced its acceptance of "the general opinion of modern astronomers." In the next papal Index of 1835, the names of Galileo, Copernicus and Kepler were removed. On October 31, 1992, Pope John Paul II formally rehabilitated Galileo—359 years, four months and nine days after Galileo had been forced to recant his heresy that the earth moved around the sun.

FURTHER READINGS

Boorstein, Daniel J. *The Discoverers: A History of Man's Search to Know His World and Himself.* New York: Random House, 1983.
Collinson, Diané. *Fifty Major Philosophers: A Reference Guide.* London: Routledge, 1988.
Garraty, John A., and Peter Gay. *The Columbia History of the World.* New York: Harper & Row, 1972.
Green, Jonathon. *The Encyclopedia of Censorship.* New York: Facts On File, 1990.'

ESSAYS

Author: Michel de Montaigne
Original date and place of publication: 1580, France
Literary form: Essays

SUMMARY

Michel de Montaigne was the originator of the personal essay as a literary form and the inventor of a new form of autobiography. In his *essais*, or "trials," he set out to test his judgment on a wide range of subjects of interest to him, revealing his inner life and personality. Written over a period of 20 years, beginning in 1571 when Montaigne was 38 until his death in 1592, the 94 essays trace the evolution of Montaigne's thinking as he added to and changed his earlier writings. Books one and two were published in 1580. Revised and enlarged editions of the first two books appeared with book three in 1588; a final complete edition was published posthumously in 1595.

The earliest essays, which began as notes on Montaigne's reading, are mainly compilations of anecdotes with brief commentary. Over the years the essays became longer and more personal. His most influential philosophical essay was the book-length "Apology for Raymond Sebond," composed in 1576. Montaigne's skepticism, summed up in his famous motto "*Que Scay-je?*" (What do I know?), is revealed in this essay, a sustained argument on the impotence and vanity of presumptuous human reason. In the later essays his self-portrait emerges as the central theme.

Essays opens with Montaigne's preface, "To the Reader," in which he sets the conversational, personal and modest tone that is characteristic of his writing: "This book was written in good faith, reader. It warns you from the outset that in it I have set myself no goal but a domestic and private one. I have had no thought of serving either you or my own glory. . . . If I had written to seek the world's favor, I should have bedecked myself better, and should have presented myself in a studied posture. I want to be seen here in my simple, natural, ordinary fashion, without straining or artifice; for it is myself that I portray."

Drawing on his own recollections, conversations with neighbors and friends, readings in classical literature and the narratives of historians and ethnographers, the essays range over a vast array of subjects, from cannibalism to education, politics, friendship, nature and death. Montaigne reveals himself as intellectually curious, tolerant, skeptical and unafraid to contradict himself. His aim is to provide an unvarnished picture of his experience and attitudes, for if a man does not know himself, what does he know?

"My sole aim is to reveal myself," he writes, "and I may be different tomorrow if some new lesson changes me. . . . Contradictions of opinion, therefore, neither offend nor estrange me; they only arouse and exercise my mind."

Through his quest for self-knowledge, Montaigne is led to recognize common human traits and values. In his last essay, "On Experience," he concludes, "It is an absolute perfection and virtually divine to know how to enjoy our being rightfully. We seek other conditions because we do not understand the use of our own, and go outside of ourselves because we do not know what it is like inside. . . . The most beautiful lives, to my mind, are those that conform to the common human pattern, with order, but without miracle and without eccentricity."

CENSORSHIP HISTORY

The first attempt to censor the *Essays* took place in 1580–81, shortly after the first publication of books one and two, when Montaigne traveled to Germany, Switzerland and Italy. Upon his entry into Rome, as Montaigne recounted in his *Travel Journal*, his baggage was thoroughly examined by customs. Although he had passed through Germany and "was of an inquiring nature," he carried no forbidden books. Nevertheless, all the books he had, including a copy of the *Essays*, were confiscated for examination. They included a prayer book (suspect only because it was published in Paris, rather than Rome) and "also the books of certain German doctors of theology against the heretics, because in combatting them, they made mention of their errors."

Though Montaigne had been cordially received by Pope Gregory XIII, he was later summoned to the Vatican's Holy Office and advised that some passages in his *Essays* should be changed or deleted in future editions. The papal censor, theology professor Sisto Fabri, who did not read French, discussed with Montaigne various errors that had been identified upon the report of a French friar. The censor objected to the overuse of the word "fortune"; the defense of the fourth-century Roman emperor Julian, who abandoned Christianity; the praise of heretical poets; the idea that one who prays should be free from evil impulses; the critical comments on torture ("All that is beyond plain death seems to me pure cruelty"); and the recommendation that children should be fit to do either good or evil so that they may do good through free choice. Though Fabri was "content with the excuses I offered," Montaigne commented, "on each objection that his Frenchman had left him he referred it to my conscience to redress what I thought was in bad taste."

Montaigne responded that these were his opinions, which he did not feel were erroneous, and suggested that perhaps the censor had improperly understood his thoughts. He did promise, however, to consider some revisions. Ultimately, he made none of the recommended revisions in the essays.

In 1595, an unauthorized, expurgated edition was published in Lyons by Simon Goulart. Produced for Calvinist consumption, a number of chapters were suppressed and passages critical of Protestants were omitted. In its complete edition, as edited by Montaigne's literary executor Marie de Gournay and published in 1595, *Essays* remained a best-seller in France into the mid-17th century and was reprinted every two or three years. The book was considered a classic and Montaigne a standard author.

Though Montaigne's writing had been forbidden by the Spanish Inquisition in 1640, it was not until 84 years after Montaigne's death, when the *Essays* had been circulating for close to a century, that it was condemned by the Vatican. In 1676, it was placed on the Index of Forbidden Books with the specification "in whatever language they may be printed." It remained on the Index for almost 300 years.

Montaigne was a faithful Catholic, but he felt that the spheres of faith and reason should be separate. He believed that when faith and reason are contradictory, faith must prevail in religious matters. Not even the most important church dogmas, such as the existence of God and the immortality of the soul, can be proven. They must, rather, be accepted on faith. Theology and philosophy were thus separated, and modern scientific discoveries, such as the new astronomy combatted by the church, could be accepted as a matter of reason without challenging religious doctrine.

"No proposition astounds me, no belief offends me," Montaigne wrote, "however much opposed it may be to my own." Montaigne's skepticism, tolerance and mistrust of dogmatic systems of belief reflected an open-minded humanistic spirit. This attitude was still possible in Montaigne's day while the liberal philosophy of Renaissance humanism prevailed. But as the Counter-Reformation gained strength and church traditions were secured against the innovations of Protestant theology, Montaigne's views on the separation of faith and reason were attacked as the heresy of "fideism." The placement of the *Essays* on the Index in 1676 is thought to be the result of criticisms by theologians influenced by the rationalism of Descartes, which declared that faith could appeal to reason.

FURTHER READINGS

Boase, Alan M. *The Fortunes of Montaigne: A History of the Essays in France, 1580–1669.* New York: Octagon Books, 1970.

Frame, Donald M., trans. and intro. *The Complete Works of Montaigne.* Stanford: Stanford University Press, 1967.

————, trans. and intro. *The Complete Essays of Montaigne.* Stanford: Stanford University Press, 1958.

Montaigne, Michel de. *Essays.* Ed. and intro. by J. M. Cohen. Middlesex, England: Penguin Books, 1958.

Tetel, Marcel. *Montaigne: Updated Edition.* Boston: Twayne Publishers, 1990.

Toulmin, Stephen. *Cosmopolis: The Hidden Agenda of Modernity.* Chicago: University of Chicago Press, 1990.

THE GUIDE OF THE PERPLEXED

Author: Moses Maimonides
Original date and place of publication: 1197, Egypt
Literary form: Philosophical text

SUMMARY

Maimonides (Moses ben Maimon), the most important Jewish medieval philosopher, was born in Córdoba, Spain, where his father was a judge and rabbi. When Córdoba fell in 1148 to the Almohads, a fundamentalist Islamic regime from North Africa, Maimonides and his family were forced as Jews to flee Spain. They moved to Morocco, then to Palestine, and eventually settled in Egypt. Maimonides became a physician in the court of Saladin and attained wide recognition as a jurist, a philosopher and the leader of Egypt's Jewish community.

Maimonides's writings include works on law, logic, medicine and theology. His greatest legal study, the *Mishnah Torah*, an attempt to organize all of Jewish law into a single code, is regarded as one of the most important Jewish works ever written. In his principal philosophical work, *The Guide of the Perplexed*, written in 1197 in Arabic and translated in 1204 into Hebrew, Maimonides sought to reconcile Judaism with the teachings of Aristotle, explaining in a logical way all that could be known about metaphysical problems. He was considered among the most distinguished philosophers of the Islamic world to apply the methodology of Aristotle to difficult conceptual issues.

The Guide was written not for average readers, but for select contemporaries who had studied classical science and philosophy, as well as Jewish scholarship. It was addressed to a pupil of Maimonides who found it difficult to reconcile the letter of Jewish law with the discoveries of natural science and Aristotelian philosophy. The purpose of *The Guide* was, Maimonides wrote, "to give indications to a religious man for whom the validity of our Law has become established in his soul and has become actual in his belief." His aim was to guide such "perplexed" individuals to a deeper insight into philosophical truths without compromising their religious commitments.

Maimonides criticized the lack of logical rigor in the arguments of theologians addressing metaphysical problems. He viewed the world as a complex but comprehensible system of necessary laws. Exploring questions of the immortality of the soul, the basis of morality, the creation of the world, the nature of prophecy and the concept of God, Maimonides contended that Judaism and its traditions could be presented as a rational system. Yet the perplexity of the believer could not be resolved by reason alone.

Basic to Maimonides's thought in *The Guide* was the gap between our limited perspective as human beings and that of God, whose apprehension is unlimited and perfect. He was skeptical of attempted dissolutions of this gap by theologians and philosophers, but searched nevertheless for bridges to span the great divide. Maimonides claimed: "He, however, who has achieved demonstration, to the extent that it is possible, of everything that may be demonstrated; and who has ascertained in divine matters, to the extent that that is possible, everything that may be ascertained; and who has come close to certainty in those matters in which one can only come close to it—has come to be with the ruler in the inner part of the habitation."

Maimonides believed that the requirements of religion are both intellectual and moral. Believers should not simply pursue religious rituals and regulations without attempting to investigate and understand their purposes and, ultimately, the divine purpose implicit in the structure of the world. "If however, you pray merely by moving your lips while facing a wall," Maimonides wrote, "and at the same time think about your buying and selling, or if you read the Torah with your tongue while your heart is set upon the building of your habitation and does not consider what you read . . . you should not think that you have achieved the end." Maimonides concluded that we must be content to speculate about the nature of what lies beyond our experience and limit ourselves to deriving conclusions from propositions that can be established only as possible, rather than as actual.

CENSORSHIP HISTORY

Maimonides was recognized as a leading figure in Jewish thought as well as one of the most radical philosophers of the Islamic world. *The Guide of the Perplexed* also exerted profound influence on Christian thinkers. It had been translated into Latin and was well known to medieval Scholastics. However, soon after his death in 1204, *The Guide of the Perplexed* sparked furious controversy. Orthodox Jewish opponents objected to Maimonides's sympathy for Aristotelian thought, which was considered fundamentally incompatible with Hebrew tradition. They stressed the incompatibility of being both a believer and a philosopher, contending that the religion proscribed theoretical inquiry. Teaching infected by Greek philosophy and attempts to reconcile Scripture and secular rationality were condemned as heresy.

In 1232, in Montpellier, France, the learned Talmudist Solomon ben Abraham led an attack on *The Guide* and obtained the support of the rabbis of France and some of the important scholars of Spain. The work was banned from Jewish homes under penalty of excommunication. The rabbis of France approached the Catholic Dominican friars, known for an unexcelled record in "burning your heretics," and appealed to them for help in destroying the study of philosophy among Jews. If the church would burn the books of Maimonides, it would deliver "a warning to the Jews to keep away from them." The monks obligingly confiscated copies of *The Guide* and in 1233 burned them as heretical works. Maimonides is thought to be the first Jewish scholar to have his works officially burned. Three hundred years later *The Guide* was again condemned by the Yeshiva of Lublin, Poland. The work still faced bans as late as the 19th century.

FURTHER READINGS

Aronsfeld, C. C. "Book Burning in Jewish History." *Index on Censorship* 11.1 (February 1982): 18.

Gerber, Jane S. *The Jews of Spain: A History of the Sephardic Experience*. New York: Macmillan, 1992.

Green, Jonathon. *The Encyclopedia of Censorship*. New York: Facts On File, 1990.

Leaman, Oliver. *Moses Maimonides*. Cairo: American University in Cairo Press, 1993.

THE HIDDEN FACE OF EVE: WOMEN IN THE ARAB WORLD

Author: Nawal El Saadawi
Original date and place of publication: 1977, Lebanon; 1980, United States
Original publisher: al-Mu'assassat, Zed Books
Literary form: Sociological text

SUMMARY

A medical doctor, sociologist, novelist and author of nonfiction essays and books on Arab women's issues, Nawal El Saadawi is one of the most widely translated Egyptian writers and an outspoken feminist. In this personal and often disturbing account, the author exposes the hidden abuses of girls and women in the Muslim world and the ideologies she holds responsible for their oppressed condition.

Covering a wide range of topics, from female genital mutilation and sexual abuse of girls, to prostitution, sexual relationships, marriage and divorce, El Saadawi advances the thesis that the problems of Arab women stem not from the substance and values of Islam, but rather from an economic and political system based on male domination. One of the primary weapons used to keep back the revolt of women against patriarchy and its values is the misuse of the doctrines of Islam, the exploitation of religion for social and political ends.

The oppression of women in any society is an expression of an economic structure built on landownership, systems of inheritance and parenthood and the patriarchal family as a social unit, El Saadawi contends. Arab cultures are not exceptional in having transformed women into commodities. In the very essence of Islam, the status of women is no worse than it is in Judaism or Christianity.

El Saadawi recounts her own genital mutilation at the age of six, a prevalent custom for Egyptian girls when she was growing up. "Society had made me feel, since the day that I opened my eyes on life, that I was a girl, and that the word *bint* (girl) when pronounced by anyone is almost always accompanied by a frown." Recalling her experiences as a doctor working in rural areas of Egypt, she analyzes the psychological and physical damage of genital mutilation, which is aimed at denying sexual pleasure to women in order to insure their virginity before marriage and chastity throughout.

Society, as represented by its dominant classes and male structure, El Saadawi contends, realized at an early stage the power of female sexual desire. Unless women were controlled and subjugated, they would not submit to moral, legal and religious constraints, in particular those related to monogamy. An illicit intimacy with another man could lead to confusion in succession and inheritance, since there was no guarantee that another man's child would not step into the line of descendants.

El Saadawi also discusses another taboo subject, sexual molestation of girls by male family members. She cites a study she conducted in 1973, involving 160 Egyptian girls and women from different social classes, including educated and uneducated families. One of her findings showed that sexual molestation of female children by men was a common occurrence. The increasing number of men unable to marry for economic reasons, the segregation of the sexes, the lack of sexual outlets for men, the convenient proximity of female family members or young domestic servants and the low status of women are all contributing factors to the problem.

El Saadawi systematically analyzes other abuses against women, including marriage customs and laws that transform women into merchandise to be bought in exchange for dowry and sold for the price of alimony; laws that punish a woman for committing adultery; prohibitions on abortion in most Arab countries that result in maternal deaths from illegal abortions; and marriage regulations giving the husband the right to refuse his wife permission to leave the house to work or travel.

Looking back into Egyptian history, she finds in the predominance of the female goddesses of Pharaonic Egypt a reflection of the high status of women before the advent of the systems characterized by the patriarchal family, land ownership and division into social classes. In Islamic history, she points to one of Muhammad's wives, Aisha, as an example of a liberated woman known for her strong will, eloquence and intelligence. Aisha did not hesitate to oppose or contradict the Prophet; she fought in several wars and battles, and was actively involved in politics and cultural and literary activities. The complete emancipation of women, whether in the Arab countries or elsewhere, El Saadawi says, can only occur when humanity does away with class society and exploitation and when the structures and values of the patriarchal system have been erased.

CENSORSHIP HISTORY

Nawal El Saadawi has long been a thorn in the side of Egyptian religious and political authorities, whom she has angered by her unyielding demands for women's rights, daring writings on gender and sexuality and questioning of the religious and secular foundations of patriarchal authority.

She was the first feminist in the Arab world to publicly confront issues such as female genital mutilation, prostitution, incest and sexual abuse of Arab girls and women. Her first study of Arab women's problems and their struggle for liberation, *Women and Sex*, published in Egypt in 1972, was a best-seller, but it offended religious and government leaders. As a direct result of the publication of the book, she was dismissed from her post as director general of health education in the Ministry of Health. She also lost her job as editor of the journal *Health*, and was removed as assistant general secretary of the Medical Association. Her publisher was ordered to recall all copies of *Women and Sex* and put them in storage.

The 1977 publication of *The Hidden Face of Eve* in Arabic and its subsequent translation into several languages brought her international attention but also further harassment in Egypt. During the presidency of Anwar Sadat from 1970 until 1981, despite the absence of official censorship, emergency laws allowed the prime minister to withhold printing permits for publications. When a permit was denied for *The Hidden Face of Eve*, El Saadawi had it published in Beirut, Lebanon. The book was prohibited from entry to many Arab countries, including Egypt, where Egyptian customs and excise authorities barred it under the Importing of Foreign Goods Act. "Islamicists considered its critical examination of the links between the Middle East's three social taboos—religion, sex and the ruling establishment—blasphemous," El Saadawi wrote. "A disobedient woman writer is doubly punished," she contended, "since she has violated the norm of her fundamental obligation to home, husband and children."

When the Center for New Ideas in Tehran, Iran, translated the book into Farsi in 1980, Islamic extremists among followers of the Ayatollah Khomeini burned the book and its publishing house. Despite the bannings, the book, smuggled from Lebanon and sold surreptitiously, has been widely read in Egypt and in many of the other Arab countries where it is prohibited.

El Saadawi's writings and her left-wing political views—she opposed the 1979 Camp David peace treaty between Egypt and Israel—led to her arrest and imprisonment in 1981 under the Sadat regime. Along with many other Egyptian intellectuals, she was jailed for three months for alleged "crimes against the state" and released after Sadat's assassination.

Only in the early 1980s was she able to publish a book in Egypt, though she remained blacklisted from Egyptian television and radio. After her release from prison she founded the Arab Women's Solidarity Association, an international Arab women's network to support women's rights and secularism. In July 1991, the Egyptian government under President Hosni Mubarak banned the Egyptian branch of the association and also closed down its feminist magazine.

El Saadawi has been the target of numerous death threats by Muslim fundamentalists. Sheik Mohammed al-Ghazzali, a well-known faculty member at Al-Azhar University, Egypt's state-funded religious establishment, has called her "an animal." In June 1992, the government posted armed guards outside her home to protect her. "I never trusted them," says El Saadawi. "I did not believe that those in power were so concerned about my life. I also knew that political currents which were concealed behind the screen of religion killed intellectuals and writers in the name of God. . . . These religio-political currents were part of Egypt's ruling system, part of the network of power and authority. . . ." In 1993, she left Egypt, fearing for her life, and moved to the United States, where she is a visiting university professor.

FURTHER READINGS

El Saadawi, Nawal. "Defying Submission." *Index on Censorship* 19.9 (October 1980): 16.
———. *The Hidden Face of Eve: Women in the Arab World*. Preface by Nawal El Saadawi. Trans. by Sherif Hetata. London: Zed Books, 1980.
———. *The Hidden Face of Eve: Women in the Arab World*. Foreword by Irene L. Gendzier. Boston: Beacon Press, 1982.
Malti-Douglas, Fedwa, and Allen Douglas. "Reflections of a Feminist." In *Opening the Gates: A Century of Arab Feminist Writing*. Ed. by Margot Badran and Miriam Cooke, 394–404. Bloomington: Indiana University Press, 1990.

INFALLIBLE? AN INQUIRY

Author: Hans Küng

Original date and place of publication: 1970, Germany; 1971, United States

Original publisher: Benzinger Verlag; Doubleday & Company

Literary form: Theological analysis

SUMMARY

To err is human. To err is also ecclesiastical and papal, contends Catholic theologian Hans Küng, a professor at the University of Tübingen in Germany. Küng's rejection of the doctrine of papal infallibility, as expressed in *Infallible? An Inquiry*, embroiled him in conflict with Vatican authorities.

Infallibility is defined by the Roman Catholic Church as exemption from the possibility of error, bestowed on the church by the Holy Spirit. Infallibility is vested in the pope when he speaks as the head of the church on matters of faith and morals. Definitive pronouncements resulting from an ecumenical council, when ratified by the pope, are also held to be infallible. In *Infallible? An Inquiry*, Küng examines papal encyclicals and statements, conciliar pronouncements, Scripture and church history, and concludes that there is no such thing as an infallible proposition. No church teaching is automatically free from error, because the church is composed of human beings. God alone is a priori free from error in detail and in every case.

Küng believes the dogma of papal infallibility should be discarded, as it has been disproved by historical and biblical research. He suggests that it be replaced by the notion of "indefectibility"—the perpetuity of the whole church in the truth of God's word despite the possible errors of any of its parts. In the long run, he believes, in spite of errors by the teaching authority of the church, the truth of the message of God in Jesus Christ will prevail.

Küng contends that the Second Vatican Council (1962–65), for which he served as a theological consultant, despite its efforts to renew the church by broadening ecumenical understanding and opening out toward the modern world, did not go far enough in reforming church structures. The ecclesiastical teaching office is still conceived by the pope and the hierarchy in a preconciliar, authoritarian way.

"The conception of continuity, authority, infallibility of the Church and the Church's teaching has led the Catholic Church into a dangerous tight corner," Küng writes in *Infallible*. He lists numerous and indisputable past errors of the ecclesiastical teaching office, now largely recognized by the church, including the condemnation of Galileo and the excommunication of the Greek church. "A close scrutiny of the Index of Forbidden Books would be particularly revealing in this respect," he adds, "yet the teaching office found it difficult to admit these errors frankly and honestly."

Küng raises doubts about the authority of Pope Paul VI's 1968 encyclical on birth control, *Humanae Vitae*, which reaffirmed the church's traditional prohibition of contraception. In this encyclical, Küng contends, the ecclesiastical teaching office counts for more than the gospel of Christ and papal tradition is placed above Scripture. Jesus himself did not found a church, Küng says, but rather his life and death set in motion a movement which over the course of time took on increasingly institutional forms.

Küng calls for a new age of leadership, one in which "the pope exists for the Church and not the Church for the pope," in which the pope's primacy is not one of ruling, but of service. Küng writes that he remains for all his criticism a convinced Catholic theologian. But because he is deeply bound to his church, he claims the right and the duty in full awareness of his own human inadequacy and fallibility to raise a protest.

CENSORSHIP HISTORY

When *Infallible? An Inquiry* first appeared in 1970, on the centennial of the First Vatican Council's enunciation of the doctrine of papal infallibility, it sparked immediate controversy and an international debate that was unprecedented in more recent theology. The assertion of infallibility of the teaching office in the Catholic Church has long been unacceptable to non-Catholic theologians. But Küng was the first major Catholic theologian to question dramatically and forcefully the most basic concept of church authority. The divergence on this issue by a theologian as distinguished as Küng represented the extent to which the doctrine had become questionable.

In his preface to *Infallible? An Inquiry*, Küng wrote: "It is true that the Index has been abolished and another name given to the Roman Inquisition. But there are still inquisitional processes against troublesome theologians. . . ." Küng himself became subject to such processes for his dissident views. In obvious reaction to Küng's ideas, the Vatican's Congregation for the Doctrine of the Faith issued on June 24, 1973, a "Declaration Against Certain Errors of the Present Day," which reiterated Catholic teaching on the infallibility of the church and the pope and declared that the pope and bishops are indeed guaranteed immunity from error when they define doctrine.

Küng's best-selling 1974 book, *On Being a Christian*, an effort to make the traditional articles of faith intelligible to modern believers, raised further doubts within the hierarchy about his orthodoxy. In 1975 the Vatican admonished Küng not to advocate two theses drawn from his 1967 book *The Church* and from *Infallible? An Inquiry*: that in case of necessity, the Eucharist might be consecrated by an unordained person and that propositions defined by the church might be erroneous. In addition, church authorities instituted an official process to examine the orthodoxy of his views. They requested repeatedly that he come to Rome for discussions. Küng called for due process, demanded the right to see the full dossier on his case before submitting to any inquiry and asked to choose his own defense counsel. In 1968, 1,360 theologians had signed a statement calling for such due process for theologicans in cases where authorities in Rome objected to their teachings. Claiming he would not receive a fair trial, Küng refused to come to Rome.

When Pope John Paul II succeeded Paul VI in 1978, he moved to confront dissident theologians. On December 18, 1979, the Congregation for the Doctrine of the Faith withdrew Küng's *missio canonica*, barring him from teaching "in the name of the Church." The Congregation accused him of "causing confusion" among the faithful by casting doubt in his writing and teachings on the dogma of papal infallibility and questioning the doctrine of Christ's divinity. Küng was informed that he could no longer be considered a Catholic theologian. He was forbidden to teach Catholic doctrine and Catholic institutions were prohibited from employing him.

Küng remained a Catholic priest, however, as well as a tenured professor at the University of TÜbingen, a position protected by German law. He is professor of ecumenical theology and director of the Institute for Ecumenical Research and has continued to write and publish.

FURTHER READINGS

Bokenkotter, Thomas S. *A Concise History of the Catholic Church*. Garden City, N.Y.: Doubleday and Co., 1977.

Küng, Hans. *Infallible? An Unresolved Inquiry*. Preface by Herbert Haag. New York: Continuum, 1994.

THE KORAN

Original date and place of publication: Seventh century A.D., Arabia
Literary form: Religious text

SUMMARY

The Koran, or Qur'an (Recitation), is the earliest and the finest work of classical Arabic prose and the sacred book of Islam. Muslims believe that it was revealed by God to the Prophet Muhammad, transmitted over time by the angel Gabriel, beginning in A.D. 619 until the Prophet's death in A.D. 632. To Muslims, the Koran is an unalterable reproduction of original scriptures that are preserved in heaven. Originally committed to memory and recited by Muhammad's followers, the Koranic revelations were written down during the Prophet's lifetime on palm leaves, stones, bones and bark. The verses of the Koran were collected by the caliph Umar and the canonical text was established in A.D. 651–52 under the caliph Uthman by Arabic editors following the instructions of the Prophet's secretary.

The Koranic revelations are divided into 114 *suras*, or chapters, each beginning with the phrase, "In the Name of Allah, the Compassionate, the Merciful." Excepting the brief first chapter that is included in Muslim daily prayers, the *suras* are arranged generally by length, with the longest first and the shortest last. The longest *suras* relate to the period of Muhammad's role as head of the community in Medina. The shorter ones, embodying mostly his ethical teachings, were revealed earlier during his prophethood in Mecca.

The Koran preaches the oneness of God; God's omnipotence and omniscience are infinite. He is the creator of heaven and earth, of life and death. The Koran also emphasizes God's divine mercy and compassion. As his omnipotence is tempered with justice, he is forgiving to the sinner who repents. In the Koran, God speaks directly in the first person and makes known his laws. The Koran provides the basic rules of conduct fundamental to the Muslim way of life. Believers must acknowledge and apply both beliefs and acts in order to establish their faith as Muslims. The religion took on the title of Islam because Allah decreed in the Koran: "Lo the religion with Allah is *al-Islam* (the Surrender) to His will and guidance."

Duties in Islam are incumbent on all the faithful, regardless of status in society. "Verily there is no preference for any of you except by what ye enjoy in good health and your deeds of righteousness," says the Koran. The most important duties for the believer, known as the Five Pillars of Islam, are the profession of faith in Allah and his apostle, daily prayer at appointed hours, almsgiving, fasting in the month of Ramadan, and, if possible, the pilgrimage to Mecca. "Lo! Those who believe and do good works and establish worship and pay the poor-due, their reward is with their Lord and there shall no fear come upon them, neither shall they grieve," the Koran says.

For Muslims, the Koran is the living word of God, "the Scripture whereof there is no doubt," and, as such, contains not only eternal Truth but also the most perfect representation of literary style.

CENSORSHIP HISTORY

An early translation of the Koran into Latin was made around 1141 by Peter the Venerable, the abbot of Cluny. During the period of the medieval Crusades, Christian hostility toward Arabs and their religion mounted. The church fathers regarded Islam as a heresy, Muslims as infidels and Muhammad as a "renegade bishop, an imposter" who rebelled against the central mission of Christ. By 1215, the church had introduced legislation severely restricting Muslims in Christendom.

The Arabic text of the Koran was not published in Europe until 1530, in Venice. The pope ordered the burning of this edition. Latin translations of the Koran were prohibited by the Spanish Inquisition, a ban that remained in effect until 1790.

In 1541 a printer in Basel, Switzerland—Johannes Oporinus—began printing Robert of Ketton's 12th-century Latin translation of the Koran. City authorities confiscated the entire edition. Martin Luther argued that the edition should be released because knowledge of the Koran would work to "the glory of Christ, the best of Christianity, the disadvantages of the Moslems, and the vexation of the Devil." The edition was allowed to appear in 1542 with prefaces by both Luther and Protestant reformer Melanchthon.

The first English edition of the Koran and a new Latin translation were produced in the 17th century. The Koran had still not been printed in the Islamic world. It could be reproduced only in the original handwritten format used by the Prophet's disciples. In the late 17th century, a Turkish printer in Istanbul, Ibrahim Müteferrika, secured the sultan's permission to set up the first printing press in a Muslim country. In 1727, despite protests by calligraphers, he was granted an imperial edict to print books. But the printing of the Koran itself was still expressly forbidden. It was not until 1874 that the Turkish government gave permission to print the Koran, but only in Arabic. In modern times an English translation was tolerated. In the rest of the Muslim world, printing of the Koran was still prohibited.

The first printed edition of the Koran in Egypt appeared in 1833 under Muhammad Ali Pasha, credited with having laid the foundations of modern Egypt. His Bulaq Press became the first and most distinguished publisher in the Arab world. But on his deathbed religious leaders persuaded his successor, Abbas Pasha, to lock up all printed copies and ban their circulation. Only under Said Pasha, who ruled from 1854 to 1863, were they released.

The first official printed version of the Koran was published by the Egyptian government in 1925. But this version and other late 20th-century editions of the Koran published in other Muslim countries were reproduced in block printing or lithography, considered closer to handwritten script, rather than movable type. Although Islamic law prohibits only the liturgical use of the Koran in a language other than Arabic, some Muslim theologians today believe that it is a sacrilege to translate the Koran because Allah declared to Muhammad, "We have revealed unto thee an Arabic Koran." But despite such objections, unauthorized translations have been made into 43 different languages.

In 1995, *Bacaan*, a Malay translation of the Koran by Othman Ali, published in Singapore, was banned by the government of Malaysia. The banning was part of an official policy aimed at outlawing "deviant" Islamic sects. *Bacaan* was labeled as "deviational" because it offered an interpretation that differed from the official government-approved version and did not include the original text in Arabic.

Modern government censorship of the Koran has been recorded in socialist countries. In 1926 in the Soviet Union, government directives to libraries stated that religiously dogmatic books such as the Gospels, the Koran and the Talmud could remain only in large libraries, accessible to students of history, but had to be removed from the smaller ones. Such restrictions were lifted after a *modus vivendi* was worked out between Muslims and the state during World War II.

In China during the Cultural Revolution of the 1960s and 1970s, study of the Koran was forbidden and its reading in mosques prohibited. The Koran had been printed in China since the 19th century and translated into Chinese since the 1920s. The communist government had published an authorized Chinese translation in 1952.

In 1986 in Ethiopia, under the socialist military government, it was reported that copies of the Koran were destroyed or confiscated by the army, Koranic schools and mosques were closed or razed, Muslims were prohibited from praying and some were ordered to convert to Christianity and burn the Koran. Ethiopia's ruling military council, the Derg, feared that a resurgence of Islamic fundamentalism would provide moral and financial aid to Muslims who opposed the Marxist-Leninist revolution.

The Koran is today the most influential book in the world after the Bible and is, with the Bible, the most widely read of sacred texts. More portions of it are committed to memory than those of any other similar body of sacred writings.

FURTHER READINGS

Boorstein, Daniel J. *The Discoverers: A History of Man's Search to Know His World and Himself.* New York: Random House, 1983.

Dawood, N. J., trans. and intro. *The Koran.* Baltimore, Md.: Penguin Books, 1968.

Farah, Caesar E. *Islam: Belief and Observances.* New York: Barron's Educational Services, 1987.

Lippman, Thomas W. *Understanding Islam: An Introduction to the Muslim World.* New York: Penguin Books USA, 1990.

Nugent, Philippa. "Of Such Is Reputation Made." *Index on Censorship* 25.2 (March/April 1996): 160.

LAJJA (SHAME)

Author: Taslima Nasrin
Original date and place of publication: 1993, Bangladesh; 1994, India
Original publisher: Ananda Publishers Pvt. Ltd.; Penguin Books
Literary form: Novel

SUMMARY

Taslima Nasrin, a physician, poet, novelist and journalist, is an outspoken feminist from Bangladesh and the author of 21 books. *Lajja* (Shame) is a documentary novel about the plight of a Hindu family in Bangladesh persecuted by Muslim fundamentalists during an outbreak of anti-Hindu violence in 1992. On December 6, 1992, Hindu extremists demolished the Babri Masjid, a 16th-century mosque in Ayodha, India. The incident set off weeks of mob violence in India during which more than 1,200 people were killed. In Bangladesh, Hindus were terrorized and Hindu temples, shops and homes were ransacked and burned in retaliation. Hindus are a minority in Bangladesh, which has an Islamic constitution.

The novel traces the events of 13 days in the life of a fictional family, the Duttas—Sudhamoy Dutta, a physician, his wife, Kironmoyee, and their grown children, Suranjan and Maya—in the aftermath of the razing of the Babri mosque. It also reflects Hindu complaints of persistent violation of their rights.

Many Hindu friends of the Dutta family crossed the border into India to settle with relatives, particularly after a 1990 wave of anti-Hindu violence. But Sudhamoy, now an invalid, had long ago moved from the countryside to the capital, Dhaka, after being forced from his house and land. He chooses to stay, though his wife wants to flee to India.

Sudhamoy, an atheist who fought for the independence of Bangladesh from Pakistan, believes with a naive mix of optimism and idealism that his country will not let him down. His son, Suranjan, rebels against the prospect of having to flee his home as they had in 1990 when the family took shelter in the home of Muslim friends.

"After independence the reactionaries who had been against the very spirit of independence had gained power," Suranjan thinks, "changed the face of the constitution and revived the evils of communalism and unbending fundamentalism that had been rejected during the war of independence." Unlawfully and unconstitutionally, Suranjan recalls, Islam became the national religion of Bangladesh.

Suranjan catalogs the hundreds of violent incidents representing the heavy toll that communalism—chauvinism and prejudice based on religious identity—and religious fundamentalism have taken in Bangladesh over the years. He remembers the looting and burning in Hindu communities in October 1990. Women were abducted and raped, people were beaten and thrown out of their houses and property was confiscated. Suranjan is critical of the failure of the government to protect Hindus.

"Why don't we work to free all State policies, social norms and education policies from the infiltration of religion?" he asks. "If we want the introduction of secularism, it does not necessarily mean that the Gita must be recited as often as the Quran is on radio and TV. What we must insist on is the banning of religion from all State activities. In schools, colleges and universities all religious functions, prayers, the teachings of religious texts and the glorifying of lives of religious personae, should be banned."

The terror finally reaches the Dutta family when a group of seven young men invade the house and abduct 21-year-old Maya. Suranjan and his Muslim friend, Haider, search the streets of Dhaka for Maya but can find no sign of her. Maya is never found and is presumed dead. In the end Suranjan and his family decide to flee to India, their lives and their hopes for their country in ruins. "There was absolutely no one to depend upon," Nasrin writes. "He was an alien in his own country."

CENSORSHIP HISTORY

Taslima Nasrin is an uncompromising critic of patriarchal religious traditions that she sees as oppressive to women, and an outspoken advocate of women's social, political and sexual liberation. In her crusading syndicated newspaper columns, which have been collected and published in two books, she protested religious intolerance and increasing incidents of violence against women by local *salish*, or Islamic village councils, as well as the failure of the government to take adequate measures to stop them. According to Amnesty International, *salish* have sentenced women to death by stoning, burning or flogging for violating the councils' interpretation of Islamic law.

The newspaper columns, Nasrin's bold use of sexual imagery in her poetry, her self-declared atheism and her iconoclastic lifestyle aroused the fury of fundamentalist clerics. By early 1992, angry mobs began attacking bookstores that sold her works. They also assaulted Nasrin at a book fair and destroyed a stall displaying her books. That year, en route to a literary conference in India, her passport was confiscated by the Bangladeshi government, ostensibly because she listed her employment as a journalist rather than a doctor. (In addition to being a writer, Nasrin is also a gynecologist and at the time was employed by the ministry of health.)

Lajja (Shame) was published in Bangladesh in the Bengali language in February 1993, three months after the razing of the Babri mosque in India that touched off a wave of violence against Hindus in Bangladesh. Nasrin states in a preface to the English-language edition of the novel that she wrote the book in seven days soon after the demolition of the mosque because "I detest fundamentalism and communalism. . . . The riots that took place in 1992 in Bangladesh are the responsibility of us all, and we are to blame. *Lajja* is a document of our collective defeat."

During the first six months after its publication, the novel sold 60,000 copies in Bangladesh. Though panned by some critics as a didactic political tract, it was a commercial success in both Bangladesh and neighboring Bengali-speaking Calcutta. Pirated copies of the novel were widely circulated in India by militant Hindus. In 1994, the novel was published in English in New Delhi. (It was published in the United States in October 1997.)

After protests by Muslim fundamentalists in Bangladesh, in July 1993 the Bangladeshi government banned *Lajja* on the grounds that it had "created misunderstanding among communities." On September 24, 1993, Nasrin opened the daily newspaper and saw a prominently displayed notice calling for her death. A *fatwa*, or death decree, had been issued by a *mullah*, or Muslim cleric, of the Council of Soldiers of Islam, a militant group based in Sylhet, Bangladesh. It called for her execution for blasphemy and conspiracy against Islam.

The group offered a $1,250 bounty for her death. In the following weeks, additional bounties were promised. Thousands of Muslim fundamentalists attended mass rallies and marched through the streets of Dhaka, hanging and burning Nasrin in effigy. Nasrin was only able to obtain police protection after suing the government, which, in response to international pressure, posted two police officers outside her home.

The International PEN Women Writers' Committee organized a campaign on Nasrin's behalf, enlisting the support of human rights and women's organizations around the world. It called on Bangladesh's government to protect Nasrin, prosecute those who sought her death, lift the ban on her book and restore her passport. The governments of Sweden, Norway, the United States, France and Germany lodged official protests. Sweden and Norway ultimately threatened to cut off all economic assistance.

Almost overnight, Nasrin, who was unknown outside Bangladesh and India, became a symbol in the Western world of freedom of expression and women's rights. The government of Bangladesh returned Nasrin's passport, but no arrests were made, even though making a death threat and offering a reward for it is a crime in Bangladesh.

At the time, Bangladesh was governed by the Bangladesh Nationalist Party under Prime Minister Begum Khaleda Zia, the widow of President Ziaur Rahman, an army general assassinated in 1981. Prime Minister Zia was elected with the support of the Muslim party, Jamaat-e-Islami, which held 20 seats in Parliament. Critics of the government contended that she capitulated to fundamentalist demands in the Nasrin case to preserve her electoral coalition.

In April 1994, after the return of her passport, Nasrin traveled to France, where she spoke at a meeting marking International Press Freedom Day. Returning to Bangladesh through India, she gave an interview to the English-language daily, the *Calcutta Statesman*, which quoted her as saying, "the Koran should be revised thoroughly." In an open letter to the Bangladeshi and Indian press, Nasrin denied making the reported remarks, but in her denial she wrote that "the Koran, the Vedas, the Bible and all such religious texts" were "out of place and out of time."

In Bangladesh, fundamentalists took to the streets by the tens of thousands in daily demonstrations calling for her death. The offices of newspapers that showed sympathy for her were attacked; bookstores carrying her books were ransacked; and religious groups pressed the government for her arrest. On June 4, 1994, the Bangladeshi government brought charges against her under a rarely used 19th-century statute dating from the era of British colonialism that proscribes statements or writings "intended to outrage the religious feeling of any class by insulting its religion or religious believers." The crime carries a maximum penalty of two years in prison.

When a warrant was issued for her arrest, Nasrin left her apartment and went underground. In an interview given just before going into hiding, Nasrin explained, "So many injustices are carried out here in the name of Allah. I cannot stop writing against all these simply to save my own skin. . . . The Koran can no longer serve as the basis of our law. . . . It stands in the way of progress and in the way of women's emancipation. . . . The problem is the intolerance of the fundamentalists. I fight with my pen, and they want to fight with a sword. I say what I think and they want to kill me. I will never let them intimidate me."

On August 3, after protracted negotiations among her legal advisers, Western ambassadors and the government of Bangladesh, Nasrin was granted bail and ordered to appear for trial at a later, unspecified date. She fled to Stockholm, Sweden, and remained in exile in Europe and the United States. (In 1998 she returned to Bangladesh to care for her critically ill mother and was again forced to go into hiding because of threats and demonstrations against her.)

"The mullahs who would murder me will kill everything progressive in Bangladesh if they are allowed to prevail," Nasrin wrote in her preface to *Lajja*. "It is my duty to try to protect my beautiful country from them and I call on all those who share my values to help me defend my rights. . . . I am convinced that the only way the fundamentalist forces can be stopped is if all of us who are secular and humanistic join together and fight their malignant influence. I, for one, will not be silenced."

FURTHER READINGS

Crossette, Barbara. "A Cry for Tolerance Brings New Hatred Down on a Writer." *The New York Times* (July 3, 1994): 7.

Riaz, Ali. "Taslima Nasrin: Breaking the Structured Silence." *Bulletin of Concerned Asian Scholars* 27.1 (January–March 1995): 21–27.

Tax, Meredith. "Taslima Nasrin: A Background Paper." *Bulletin of Concerned Asian Scholars* 25.4 (October–December 1993): 72–74.

Weaver, Mary Anne. "A Fugitive from Justice." *The New Yorker* (September 12, 1994): 47–60.

Whyatt, Sara. "Taslima Nasrin." *Index on Censorship* 23.4–5 (September/October 1994): 202–207.

THE LAST TEMPTATION OF CHRIST

Author: Nikos Kazantzakis
Original date and place of publication: 1953, Greece; 1960, United States
Original publisher: Athenai; Simon & Schuster
Literary form: Novel

SUMMARY

The Last Temptation of Christ by the Greek novelist, poet, dramatist and translator Nikos Kazantzakis, best known for his novel *Zorba the Greek*, retells the life story of Jesus of Nazareth, imagining the human events of the gospel accounts in a vivid mosaic colored by extravagant imagery. Kazantzakis's Jesus is not the self-assured son of God following a preordained path, but a Christ of weakness, whose struggles mirror those of human beings who face fear, pain, temptation and death. Though Jesus is often confused about the path he should choose, as the story proceeds his sense of mission becomes clear. When he dies it is as a hero who has willed his own destiny.

Though the story follows the gospel narrative, its setting and atmosphere derive from the peasant life of Kazantzakis's native Crete. The novel was written in the rich, metaphor-laden vocabulary of demotic Greek, the everyday language of modern Greece.

In the 33 chapters of *The Last Temptation of Christ*, corresponding to the number of years in Jesus' life, Kazantzakis portrays what he describes as "the incessant, merciless battle between the spirit and the flesh," a central concern explored in his novels and philosophical writings. Jesus is tempted by evil, feels its attractiveness and even succumbs to it, for only in this way can his ultimate rejection of temptation have meaning.

The novel opens with the scene of a young man in the throes of a nightmare, dreaming that hordes are searching for him as their Savior. Jesus of Nazareth, the village carpenter, has been gripped since childhood by strange portents and has felt the hand of God clawing at his scalp. He shrinks from these signs and visions, hoping that, if he sins, God will leave him alone.

Jesus has loved Mary Magdalene, the daughter of the village rabbi, since childhood. He had wished to marry her, but had been mercilessly forced by God to reject her. She has become a prostitute in order to forget Jesus. Overwhelmed by remorse, Jesus seeks refuge in a desert monastery. A reluctant Messiah, he cries out to God, "I love good food, wine, laughter. I want to marry, to have children. . . . Leave me alone . . . . I want Magdalene, even if she's a prostitute. I want you to detest me, to go and find someone else; I want to be rid of you! . . . . I shall make crosses all my life, so that the Messiah you choose can be crucified."

During his stay in the desert, Jesus finds the courage and determination to embark upon his public ministry. The central chapters of the novel trace the familiar episodes of the Gospel, leading to the moment of the Crucifixion, where the last temptation comes to Jesus in his delirium on the cross in the form of a dream of erotic bliss and of a worldly life. His guardian angel had snatched him away from the Crucifixion. He had taken the smooth, easy road of men and had at last married Magdalene. Upon Magdalene's death he married Martha and Mary, the sisters of Lazarus, and fathered children. Now, as an old man, he sits on the threshold of his house and recalls the longings of his youth and his joy to have escaped the privations and tortures of the cross.

He comes face to face with his former disciples, led by Judas, who accuses him of being a traitor, a deserter and a coward. "Your place was on the cross," he says. "That's where the God of Israel put you to fight. But you got cold feet and the moment death lifted its head, you couldn't get away fast enough." Jesus suddenly remembers where he is and why he feels pain. A wild joy takes possession of him. Though temptation had captured him for a split second and led him astray, he had stood his ground honorably to the end. The joys of marriage and children were lies, illusions sent by the devil. He has not betrayed his disciples, who are alive and thriving, proclaiming his gospel. "Everything had turned out as it should, glory be to God."

CENSORSHIP HISTORY

Kazantzakis's unorthodox portrait of Jesus was recommended by critics as a powerful and important novel, an extraordinary and original work of art, which in the deepest sense celebrates the spiritual struggles of humankind. It was widely acknowledged, however, that, from an orthodox point of view, his interpretation might be considered as heretical or blasphemous.

Kazantzakis's primary motive in writing *The Last Temptation of Christ* was not, however, to disagree with the church. He wanted, rather, to lift Christ out of the church altogether, to portray Jesus as a figure for a new age, in terms which could be understood in the 20th century. In a 1951 letter, Kazantzakis explained his intentions: "It's a laborious, sacred creative endeavor to reincarnate the essence of Christ, setting aside the dross—falsehoods and pettiness which all the churches and all the cassocked representatives of Christianity have heaped up on His figure, thereby distorting it."

"That part of Christ's nature which was profoundly human helps us to understand him and love Him and pursue his passion as if it were our own," Kazantzakis wrote in the prologue of the novel. "If he had not within him this warm human element, he would never be able to touch our hearts with such assurance and tenderness; he would not be able to become a model for our lives. . . . This book was written because I wanted to offer a supreme model to the man who struggles; I wanted to show him that he must not fear pain, temptation or death—because all three can be conquered, all three have already been conquered."

Kazantzakis was excommunicated in 1954 from the Eastern Orthodox Church as a result of the publication in Greece of *The Last Temptation of Christ*. Kazantzakis wrote, "The Orthodox Church of America convened and damned *The Last Temptation* as extremely indecent, atheistic and treasonable, after admitting they hadn't read it. . . ." Kazantzakis wrote to Orthodox church leaders, quoting the third-century Christian thinker Tertullian: "At Thy

Tribunal, Lord, I make my appeal," adding, "You have execrated me, Holy Fathers; I bless you. I pray that your conscience may be as clear as mine and that you may be as moral and as religious as I am."

The same year the novel was also placed on the Catholic Church's Index of Forbidden Books. Kazantzakis commented, "I've always been amazed at the narrow-mindedness and narrow-heartedness of human beings. Here is a book that I wrote in a state of deep religious exaltation, with a fervent love of Christ; and now the Pope has no understanding of it at all. . . ."

The furor over the novel, however, had the result of increasing sales of the book. "I have ended up by becoming famous in Greece," Kazantzakis wrote in 1955. "All the newspapers, except two, have declared themselves on my side, and from all over Greece telegrams are being sent in protest over the priests' wanting to seize my books. . . . And the books are sold out the moment they are printed and certain booksellers buy up a number of copies and sell them at very high black market rates. What a disgrace! How medieval!"

Ultimately the Greek Orthodox Church was forced to halt its anti-Kazantzakis campaign. Princess Marie Bonaparte read the book and recommended it to the queen of Greece. The queen "kept the Greek Orthodox church from making itself ridiculous," wrote Helen Kazantzakis in her biography of her husband.

In 1962–65 in Long Beach, California, the novel, in the company of Jessica Mitford's *The American Way of Death* and poetry by Langston Hughes, was the target of a three-year campaign by a right-wing group aimed at removing it from the public library. The campaign was unsuccessful.

A 1988 film of the novel directed by Martin Scorsese caused worldwide controversy and was banned in several countries mainly because of the sequence drawn from the novel in which a delirious Jesus on the Cross imagined that he had loved, married and fathered children. Scorsese and the director of the Venice Film Festival were prosecuted for blasphemy in Rome, but were acquitted. In the U.S., the film was criticized by Roman Catholic authorities as blasphemous. Three Republican congressmen introduced a resolution to force the withdrawal of the film. The Dallas, Texas, city council passed a resolution condemning it. A national video rental chain, Blockbuster Video, announced that it would not carry the film. In Escambia County, Florida, the board of county commissioners voted for an ordinance to prohibit the showing of the movie in the county at risk of 60 days in jail and $500 fine or both. U.S. District Court Judge Roger Vinson issued a restraining order against the ban as an unconstitutional violation of the First Amendment.

Director Scorsese's response to the film censorship echoed that of Kazantzakis 34 years earlier. "My film was made with deep religious feeling. . . . It is more than just another film project for me. I believe it is a religious film about suffering and the struggle to find God." In December 1988, the novel was banned in Singapore as a result of pressure from fundamentalist Christians related to the controversy over the film.

FURTHER READINGS

Heins, Marjorie. *Sex, Sin, and Blasphemy: A Guide to America's Culture Wars*. New York: New Press, 1993.

Kazantzakis, Helen. *Kazantzakis: A Biography Based on His Letters*. Trans. by Amy Mims. New York: Simon & Schuster, 1968.

Kazantzakis, Nikos. *The Last Temptation of Christ*. Trans. and afterword by P. A. Bien. New York: Simon & Schuster, 1960.

Levy, Leonard. *Blasphemy: Verbal Offense Against the Sacred, from Moses to Salman Rushdie*. New York: Alfred A. Knopf, 1993.

Thompson, David, and Ian Christie, eds. *Scorsese on Scorsese*. London: Faber and Faber, 1989.

THE NEW TESTAMENT

Translator: William Tyndale
Original date and place of publication: 1526, Germany
Literary form: Religious text

SUMMARY

The English Protestant reformer and linguist William Tyndale was the first person to translate the Bible into English from the original Greek and Hebrew and the first to print the Bible in English. Many scholars consider his influence on English literature comparable to Shakespeare's.

In 1524, when Tyndale, an Oxford graduate and Catholic priest, resolved to translate the Bible, England was the only European country without a printed vernacular version. The 1408 synod of Canterbury had forbidden translation into English of any portion of the Scriptures by an unauthorized individual. Only the fifth-century Latin Vulgate edition of the Bible translated by Saint Jerome was considered acceptable.

Translation of the Bible into the vernacular remained illegal in England for fear that anarchy and schism would be brought about by the spread of Lutheranism. Lutheran books had been publicly burned in Cambridge and London in 1520. Martin Luther's doctrine of *sola scriptura*, the Bible alone, which emphasized the ability of believers to read and understand the Bible themselves without church intervention, was considered to defy church authority. Scripture could be interpreted only by the infallible pope and the hierarchy.

Tyndale could find no religious authority in London who would support his work. "And so in London I abode for almost a year, and marked the course of the world. . .," he later wrote, "and saw things whereof I defer to speak at this time and understood at the last not only that there was no room in my lord of London's palace to translate the New Testament, but also that there was no place to do it in all England, as experience doth now openly declare."

In 1524, Tyndale left England for Germany. The following year in Cologne, he began printing his translation of the New Testament from the Greek. The printing had reached Matthew 22 when it had to be suspended. His translation was violently opposed by the clergy, who, fearing Lutheranism, saw it as "pernicious merchandise." When the Cologne authorities moved to arrest him and his assistant and impound their work, they fled to Worms, where publication of the 700 pages of the New Testament was completed clandestinely and anonymously at the press of Peter Schoeffer in 1526. Six thousand copies of Tyndale's New Testament were smuggled into England the following year and widely distributed. For the first time, all 27 books of the New Testament were available in clearly printed portable form in a language that every reader could understand.

The primary source for Tyndale's New Testament was the original Greek, although he drew from both the Latin Vulgate and Martin Luther's German translation. Because he believed that the word of God should speak directly to the reader in an understandable way, his first aim was clarity, to write in everyday spoken English. "If God spare my life, ere many years, I will cause a boy that driveth a plough shall know more of the Scripture than thou dost," he told a learned man before leaving England.

His ability to write in simple, direct and rhythmic prose and, as his contemporary biographer David Daniell says, "to create unforgettable words, phrases, paragraphs and chapters, and to do so in a way that . . . . is still, even today, direct and living" had an indelible impact on both the language of the Bible and English prose.

"Am I my brother's keeper?" "Blessed are the pure of heart; for they shall see God." "No man can serve two masters." "Ask and it shall be given to you." "There were shepherds abiding in the fields." These and hundreds of proverbial phrases such as "the signs of the times," "the spirit is willing" and "fight the good fight" come from Tyndale's New Testament.

Tyndale's 1534 revision of the New Testament, published in Antwerp under his own name, was carried forward into later Renaissance Bibles and formed the basis of the Authorized or King James Version of the Bible published in 1611.

Living in concealment in the Low Countries, Tyndale also translated the first half of the Old Testament from the original Hebrew. His masterly translation of the Pentateuch appeared in 1530, beginning with Genesis: "In the beginning God created heaven and earth. . . . Then God said: let there be light and there was light." The Book of Jonah was completed in 1536. Tyndale's Old Testament books were published in pocket volumes and smuggled into England. His Old Testament was also adopted in large part into the King James Version of the Bible.

CENSORSHIP HISTORY

Tyndale's 1526 edition of the New Testament was immediately denounced by church dignitaries in England. In the summer of 1526, the English bishops met and agreed that "untrue translations" should be burned, "with further sharp corrections and punishment against the keepers and readers of the same." The English ambassador to the Low Countries was instructed by Catholic cardinal Thomas Wolsey, who controlled domestic and foreign policy for Henry VIII, to act against printers or booksellers involved in the production and distribution of the English New Testament. Tyndale's New Testament was the first printed book to be banned in England. Wolsey ordered Tyndale to be seized at Worms, but Tyndale found refuge with Phillip of Hess at Marburg.

Although Henry VIII was to break with Rome in the early 1530s, he had no sympathy with Protestant views and saw Tyndale's New Testament as Lutheran in its influence. Tyndale had translated the Greek word *ekklesia*, for example, as "the congregation," which is the body of Christ, rather than "the church." The English bishops saw this as among the heretical aspects of the translation, in that the word *congregation* implied equality of the gathering of believers. They believed that this idea was Lutheran and denied the church's authority. Copies of the books were publicly burned at Saint Paul's Cathedral in 1526. In May 1527, church authorities ordered all copies to be bought up and destroyed. But despite the ban, reprints continued to be distributed, many imported clandestinely from the Low Countries.

Tyndale, in hiding in Antwerp, continued to publish polemics from abroad in defense of the principles of the English reformation, including *The Obedience of a Christian Man* and *The Parable of the Wicked Mammon* in 1528, an exposition of the New Testament teaching that faith is more important than works. When *Wicked Mammon* began to circulate in England, the church, viewing it as containing Lutheran heresies, moved to suppress it. Those who were found with it were arrested and severely punished. *Wicked Mammon*, like the New Testament translation, was widely read, nevertheless, and continued to be influential, even years later when it was still prohibited.

The English ambassador to the Low Countries was instructed to demand that the regent extradite Tyndale and his assistant William Roye to England, but they could not be found. In 1530, Tyndale further enraged King Henry VIII by publishing *The Practice of Prelates*, which condemned the king's divorce. In May 1535, Tyndale, working in Antwerp on his translation of the Old Testament, was arrested as the result of a plot masterminded by English authorities. He was imprisoned in Vilvoorde Castle near Brussels, charged with Lutheran heresy and disagreeing with the Holy Roman Emperor. Tyndale was put on trial, formally condemned as a heretic, degraded from the priesthood and handed over to the secular authorities for punishment. In early October 1536, he was strangled at the stake and his dead body burned with copies of his Bible translation. His last words were: "Lord, open the king of England's eyes."

At the time of Tyndale's death, about 50,000 copies of his Bible translations in seven editions were in circulation in England. A small portion of Tyndale's translation was included in a complete English Bible published illegally in Germany by his colleague Miles Coverdale. In 1537, Matthew's Bible appeared in England under the pseudonym of John Matthew. Its editor, John Rogers, was a Catholic priest who converted to Protestantism, and a friend of Tyndale's. Two-thirds of Matthew's Bible printed Tyndale's translations unchanged.

Matthew's Bible was the first Bible in English to be licensed by the government. Despite its inclusion of Tyndale's translations, it was approved by Henry VIII. His break with the Catholic Church had been completed by the Act of Supremacy in 1534, which established the Church of England. Tyndale's and Coverdale's translations were also included in Henry VIII's Great Bible of 1539, which was declared the official Bible of the Church of England.

In 1546, the Catholic Church's Council of Trent said that the Latin Vulgate of Saint Jerome was the sole canonical text of the Bible. Catholics were forbidden to read any translation such as Tyndale's without special permission of the pope or the Inquisition. This restriction remained in effect until the late 18th century.

During the reign of the Catholic queen Mary I in England from 1553 to 1558, the ban on Protestant Bibles was reinstated. In 1555, a royal proclamation commanded "that no manner of persons presume to bring into this realm any manuscripts, books, papers . . . . in the name of Martin Luther, John Calvin, Miles Coverdale, Erasmus, Tyndale . . . . or any like books containing false doctrines against the Catholic faith."

The committee assembled in 1604 by King James I to prepare the Authorized Version of the Bible—often acclaimed as the greatest work ever produced by a committee and ranked in English literature with the work of Shakespeare—used as its basis Tyndale's work. Nine-tenths of the Authorized Version's New Testament is Tyndale's. Many of its finest passages were taken unchanged, though unacknowledged, from Tyndale's translations.

The tragedy of Tyndale's execution at the age of 42 is compounded by the knowledge that he was cut down before having completed his life's work. Tyndale was unable to go on to translate the poetic books and prophecies of the Old Testament or revise again his New Testament translation. As his biographer, Daniell, laments, it is as though Shakespeare had died halfway through his life, before his greatest tragedies had been written.

FURTHER READINGS

Daniell, David. *Let There Be Light: William Tyndale and the Making of the English Bible.* London: British Library, 1994.
———. *William Tyndale. A Biography.* New Haven: Yale University Press, 1994.

Haight, Anne Lyon. *Banned Books: 387 B.C. to 1978 A.D.* Updated and enlarged by Chandler B. Grannis. New York: R. R. Bowker, 1978.

NINETY-FIVE THESES

Author: Martin Luther
Original date and place of publication: 1517, Switzerland
Literary form: Theological tract

SUMMARY

Martin Luther, a German monk of the Augustinian order, was the founder of the Protestant Reformation in Europe. He was a doctor of divinity and town preacher of Wittenberg, where he taught theology at the university. A visit to Rome had convinced him of the decadence and corruption of the Catholic pope and clergy. In 1516, he began to question the efficacy of indulgences in a series of sermons.

In 16th-century Roman Catholic doctrine, the pope could transfer superfluous merit accumulated by Christ, the Virgin Mary or the saints to an individual sinner in order to remit temporal penalties for sin later to be suffered in purgatory. Such transfers of indulgences could benefit both the living and the dead. Luther's evangelical emphasis on the complete forgiveness of sins and reconciliation with God through God's grace alone led him to question the doctrine of indulgences and the pervasive ecclesiastical practice of selling them.

The following year, Tetzel, a Dominican monk, hawked indulgences to pay a debt that Albert of Brandenburg had incurred to purchase the Bishopric of Mainz and to help pay for the new basilica of Saint Peter in Rome. Luther resolved to voice his pastoral concern about the spiritual dangers of indulgences as an obstacle to the preaching of true repentance and interior conversion.

On October 15, 1517, Luther challenged his academic colleagues to debate the subject. Luther issued his challenge in the traditional manner—by posting a placard written in Latin on the door of the Castle Church in Wittenberg. Luther's notice contained his 95 theses on indulgences. To his surprise, the theses were circulated in Latin and German throughout Germany and within a few weeks to much of Europe, unleashing a storm of controversy that was to lead to the Protestant Reformation.

In his *Ninety-Five Theses or Disputation on the Power and Efficacy of Indulgences,* Luther argued that the pope could remit only those penalties he had imposed himself, and denied the pope's authority to remit sin. Luther rejected the idea that the saints had superfluous merits or that merit could be stored up for later use by others.

The pope has no control over the souls in purgatory, Luther asserted. "They preach only human doctrines who say that as soon as the money clinks into the money chest, the soul flies out of purgatory." If the pope does have such power, Luther asked, "why does not the pope empty purgatory for the sake of holy love and the dire need of all the souls that are there if he redeems an infinite number of souls for the sake of miserable money with which to build a church?"

He branded indulgences as harmful because they gave believers a false sense of security. By implying that the payment of money could appease the wrath of God, the sale of indulgences impeded salvation by diverting charity and inducing complacency. "Christians should be taught that he who gives to the poor is better than he who receives a pardon. He who spends his money for indulgences instead of relieving want receives not the indulgence of the pope but the indignation of God." Those who believe that their salvation is assured because they have indulgence letters will face eternal damnation, "together with their teachers," who preach unchristian doctrine.

Luther objected to the church's intent to raise money for a basilica by sale of indulgences. "Why does not the pope, whose wealth is today greater than the wealth of the richest Crassus, build this one basilica of St. Peter with his own money rather than with the money of poor believers?" Luther asked. Luther believed that to repress by force the objections of the laity to the sale of indulgences, rather than resolving them reasonably, "is to expose the church and the pope to the ridicule of their enemies and to make Christians unhappy."

Luther's theses were directed toward church reform. He did not see them as an attack on the pope's authority or as the beginnings of a schism. But the church's response to Luther's proposals pushed him toward a more radical stance that led ultimately to a break with Rome and the founding of a new church.

CENSORSHIP HISTORY

At first Pope Leo X did not take serious notice of Luther's theses, viewing them instead as a reflection of the rivalry between Luther's Augustinian order and the Dominicans, who were Luther's most vociferous critics. But the theses, rapidly distributed in Germany, found active support among the peasantry and civil authorities, who objected to Rome's siphoning of local funds. The hierarchy became convinced that the abuses of indulgences should be corrected and Luther silenced.

In 1518, the pope asked Hieronymus, bishop of Ascoli, to investigate Luther's case. Luther was summoned to Rome to answer charges of heresy and contumacy, or insubordination. Frederick III of Saxony stepped in to demand that Luther's hearing be held on German soil. When the hearing before the papal legate was transferred to Augsburg, where the imperial diet (the legislative assembly) was unsympathetic to papal claims, Luther refused to retract any of his theses. In a debate in Leipzig in 1519 with the German professor Johannes Eck, Luther argued that because the authority of the pope was of human origin, rather than rooted in divine right, he could be resisted when his edicts contravened the scriptures.

Johannes Froben of Basel had published the *Ninety-Five Theses* in an edition with Luther's sermons. In February 1519, Froben reported that only 10 copies were left and that no book from his presses had ever sold out so quickly. Taking full advantage of the new potential of the printing press, the book had been distributed not only in Germany, but in France, Spain, Switzerland, Belgium, England and even in Rome. The same year the theological faculties of the Universities of Louvain and Cologne ordered copies of the theses to be burned for heresy.

The pope appointed commissions to study Luther's writings. On June 15, 1520, the pope proclaimed in a papal bull, *Exsurge Domine*, "Rise up O Lord and judge thy cause. A wild boar has invaded thy vineyard." The bull pronounced 41 errors of Luther as "heretical, or scandalous, or false, or offensive to pious ears, or seductive of simple minds, or repugnant to Catholic truth, respectively." In his preface the pope wrote, "Our pastoral office can no longer tolerate the pestiferous virus of the following forty-one errors. . . . The books of Martin Luther which contain these errors are to be examined and burned. . . . Now therefore we give Martin sixty days in which to submit." It was forbidden to print, distribute, read, possess or quote any of Luther's books, tracts or sermons.

Then in August, October and November of 1520, Luther published three revolutionary tracts that dramatically raised the stakes of his disagreement with the church: *Address to the Christian Nobility of the German Nation*, which attacked the claim of papal authority over secular rulers; *The Babylonian Captivity of the Church*, which rejected the priesthood and the sacraments; and *The Freedom of Christian Man*, which reiterated his doctrine of justification by faith alone. The first edition of 4,000 copies of the *Address* sold out within a week. Riding the crest of a wave of public support, Luther in his sermons, debates and writings proposed a radical alternative to the Catholic Church.

On October 10, the papal bull reached Luther in Germany. Luther wrote a stinging reply to the bull: *Against the Execrable Bull of Antichrist*. "They say that some articles are heretical, some erroneous, some scandalous, some offensive," Luther wrote. "The implication is that those which are heretical are not erroneous, those which are erroneous are not scandalous, and those which are scandalous are not offensive." Calling on the pope to "renounce your diabolical blasphemy and audacious impiety" he concluded, "It is better that I should die a thousand times than that I should retract one syllable of the condemned articles."

Luther's books were burned in Louvain and Liège during October, and the following month in Cologne and Mainz. On December 10, 1520, Luther and his followers publicly burned the papal bull at Wittenberg, along with copies of canon law and the papal constitutions. "Since they have burned my books, I burn theirs," Luther said. In January 1521 the pope issued a new bull, *Decet*

Romanum Pontificum, which affirmed the excommunication of Luther and his followers and the burning of his works.

Luther's enormous popularity, bolstered by his appeal to German nationalist objections to Roman intervention in their affairs, saved him from the fate of other heretics. Elector Frederick III of Saxony, Luther's temporal ruler, refused to give him over for trial to Rome. The only power in Europe capable of suppressing Luther was the Holy Roman Emperor Charles V, a devout Catholic determined to root out the heresy.

On April 18, 1521, Luther was called before the Diet of Worms. Before the emperor and the assembled princes of the empire he refused to recant or disown his writings. "Should I recant at this point," he said, "I would open the door to more tyranny and impiety, and it will be all the worse should it appear that I had done so at the instance of the Holy Roman Empire." He continued, "Unless I am convicted by Scripture and plain reason—I do not accept the authority of popes and councils, for they have contradicted each other—my conscience is captive to the Word of God."

On May 26, 1521, Charles V decreed in the Edict of Worms that Luther was "a limb cut off from the Church of God, an obstinate schismatic and manifest heretic. . . . no one is to harbor him. His followers are also to be condemned. His books are to be eradicated from the memory of man." The edict included a Law of Printing, which prohibited printing, sale, possession, reading or copying Luther's work or any future works he might produce.

Though the emperor had persuaded most of the princes of Germany to sign the condemnation, few strongly supported it. Though the edict called for Luther's arrest, his friends were able to harbor him at the castle in Wartburg of Elector Frederick III of Saxony. There he translated the New Testament into German and began a 10-year project to translate the entire Bible. He returned to Wittenberg in March 1522 at considerable risk to his life and spent the rest of his life spreading his new gospel.

Censorship of Luther's writing was pervasive throughout Europe. His works and those of his disciples were destroyed and banned in England, France, Spain and the Netherlands. In 1524 the Diet of Nürnberg declared that "each prince in his own territory should enforce the Edict of Worms in so far as he might be able." As the edict implied, it could not be enforced in most of northern Germany. Cities in southern Germany and elsewhere in northern Europe joined the Lutheran reform. "Lutheran books are for sale in the marketplace immediately beneath the edicts of the Emperor and the Pope who declare them to be prohibited," a contemporary commented.

In 1555, Charles V signed the Peace of Augsburg, giving up further attempts to impose Catholicism on the Protestant princes. The peace allowed each prince to choose the religion of his state and declared that people could not be prevented from migrating to another region to practice their own religion. Lutheranism had taken hold.

Luther's works remained on the Vatican's Index of Forbidden Books until 1930, when they were omitted from the list. They were still prohibited, however, according to the church's canon law barring Catholics under penalty of mortal sin from reading books "which propound or defend heresy or schism."

FURTHER READINGS

Bainton, Roland H. *Here I Stand: The Life of Martin Luther*. New York: Penguin Group, 1995.
Bokenkotter, Thomas S. *A Concise History of the Catholic Church*. Garden City, N.Y.: Doubleday and Co., 1977.
Christie-Murray, David. *A History of Heresy*. Oxford: Oxford University Press, 1989.
Haight, Anne Lyon. *Banned Books: 387 B.C. to 1978 A.D.* Updated and enlarged by Chandler B. Grannis. New York: R. R. Bowker, 1978.
Putnam, George Haven. *The Censorship of the Church of Rome*. Vol. 1. New York: G. P. Putnam's Sons, 1906–7.
Spitz, Lewis W., ed. *The Protestant Reformation*. Englewood Cliffs, N.J.: Prentice-Hall, 1966.
Wilcox, Donald J. *In Search of God and Self: Renaissance and Reformation Thought*. Boston: Houghton Mifflin Company, 1975.

OLIVER TWIST

Author: Charles Dickens
Original date and place of publication: 1838, England
Literary form: Novel

SUMMARY

The publication of *Oliver Twist*, Dickens's second novel, the story of an orphan who falls into the hands of a group of thieves in the slums of London, firmly established the literary eminence of its 25-year-old author. Within a few years Dickens was the most popular and widely read writer of his time. Beginning in 1837, *Oliver Twist* appeared in monthly installments in a London magazine. The following year it was published in three volumes in book form. *Oliver Twist* offers the first glimpse of the genius of Dickens that would reach full flower in his later novels. It is among the most powerful works of fiction portraying the misery of daily life for the urban poor and the uncaring bureaucracies that sustain an oppressive system.

When Dickens was 12, his father was taken to debtors' prison. While the rest of the family accompanied his father to the workhouse, Dickens was sent to paste labels on bottles in a blacking factory. This experience left him with a bitter and passionate opposition to child labor and inhumane treatment of the poor and is reflected in the biting sarcasm that animates the early chapters of *Oliver Twist.*

When Oliver's destitute mother, found lying in the street, dies giving birth to him in a nearby workhouse, the infant becomes the ward of the local parish overseers. He is dispatched to a parish institution where he and other orphans are brought up under cruel conditions, "without the inconvenience of too much food or too much clothing."

At age nine Oliver is returned by the parish to the workhouse by Mr. Bumble, the unctuous parish beadle. The workhouse boys are fed three meals of thin gruel a day, with an onion twice a week and half a roll on Sunday. "Please, sir, I want some more," Oliver says. In punishment for the "impious and profane offence of asking for more," Oliver is ordered into instant solitary confinement.

He is then apprenticed by Mr. Bumble to the undertaker, Mr. Sowerberry, where he lives and works in mean circumstances. After fighting with his bullying coworker Noah, Oliver is beaten and runs away to London. There he unwittingly falls into the hands of Fagin, the nefarious leader of a gang of thieves, whose other chief members are the burglar Bill Sikes, Sikes's companion Nancy, and the pickpocket known as the Artful Dodger. When the Dodger picks the pocket of an elderly gentleman, Oliver is caught and brought to the police magistrate. Injured and ill, Oliver is rescued by the benevolent Mr. Brownlow, who takes him into his household. But Nancy finds Oliver and brings him back to the gang. When Oliver is made to accompany Sikes on a burgling expedition and is shot and wounded, he comes into the hands of Mrs. Maylie and her protégée, Rose, who treat him kindly.

A sinister person named Monks, who is known to Fagin, appears to have a special interest in Oliver. Nancy, who overhears a conversation between Fagin and Monks, goes to Rose and reveals to her that Monks is Oliver's older half brother, knows the secret of Oliver's parentage and wishes all proof of it destroyed. When Nancy's betrayal is discovered by the gang, she is brutally murdered by Sikes.

While trying to escape capture by a mob, Sikes accidentally hangs himself. Fagin is arrested and sentenced to execution. Monks confesses that he pursued Oliver's ruin so that he could retain the whole of his late father's property. Upon the death of his mother, Oliver was to have inherited the estate, as long as he had in his minority never stained the good name of his family. Fagin had received a reward from Monks for turning Oliver into a thief. It turns out that Rose is the sister of Oliver's late mother. In the end Oliver is adopted by Mr. Brownlow. Mr. Bumble ends his career as a pauper in the very same workhouse over which he formerly ruled.

In Dickens's preface to the third edition of the novel, he wrote, "I wished to show, in little Oliver, the principle of Good surviving through every adverse circumstance and triumphing at last." All ends happily in *Oliver Twist*, yet the haunting memory of the evils that beset Oliver in the poorhouses and streets of London remains.

CENSORSHIP HISTORY

"The walls and ceiling of the room were perfectly black with age and dirt. . . . Some sausages were cooking; and standing over them, with a toasting fork in this hand, was a very old shriveled Jew, whose villainous-looking and repulsive face was obscured by a quantity of matted red hair." The sinister and evil Fagin is introduced to readers of *Oliver Twist* with an archetypal anti-Semitic image dating back many centuries in Western culture, that of the Satanic and fiendish Jew. Dickens's caricature of Fagin has been the object of protest and debate since the time of the novel's publication.

The character of Fagin, referred to as "the Jew" hundreds of times throughout the novel, is shaped according to a traditional pattern commonly employed to portray Jews in literature and on the stage in the 19th century. Fagin's red hair and beard were commonly associated with ancient images of the devil. He has a hooked nose, shuffling gait, a long gabardine coat and broad-brimmed hat and is a dishonest dealer in second-hand clothes and trinkets. Fagin is portrayed, like Satan, as serpent-like, gliding stealthily along, "creeping beneath the shelter of the walls and doorways. . . . like some loathsome reptile, engendered in the slime and darkness through which he moved. . . ."

Though literary critics believe that Dickens did not intend to defame or injure Jews in his creation of the character of Fagin, Dickens was a product of the anti-Semitic culture of his time. Reflected in laws, public discourse, literature and popular entertainment, prejudice against Jews was a part of the early Victorian heritage. In the 1830s, Jews were barred from owning stores within the city of London, could not work as attorneys, receive a university degree or sit in Parliament. Because they were confined to certain occupations, the majority of England's 20,000 to 30,000 Jews made their living by buying and selling old clothes, peddling and moneylending.

In a letter to a Jewish woman who had protested the stereotypical treatment of Fagin, Dickens wrote, "Fagin is a Jew because it unfortunately was true, of the time to which the story refers, that class of criminal almost invariably was a Jew." The 1830 trial of Ikey Solomons, a Jewish fence, who, like Fagin, dealt in stolen jewelry, clothing and fabrics, had been extensively publicized and was one of the influences on Dickens's portrayal of Fagin.

The years 1830 to 1860 saw a rise in the status of Jews in England. Legal barriers and commercial restrictions were removed, Jews were elected to posts in local and national government and many became socially prominent. Social attitudes also changed, reflected in Dickens's increased awareness of and sensitivity to anti-Semitism in the years that followed the initial publication of *Oliver Twist*. "I know of no reason the Jews can have for regarding me as inimical to them," Dickens wrote in 1854.

In 1867–68, a new edition of Dickens's works was published. Dickens revised the text of *Oliver Twist*, making hundreds of changes, most in relation to Fagin. He eliminated the majority of the references to Fagin as "the Jew," either cutting them or replacing them with "Fagin" or "he." Nevertheless, "Fagin remains 'the Jew,'" literary critic Irving Howe commented, "and whoever wants to confront this novel honestly must confront the substratum of feeling that becomes visible through Dickens's obsessive repetition of 'the Jew.'" A critical reading of the novel can lead to a better understanding of the anti-Semitic stereotypes that were part of the popular culture of early 19th-century England. "There is nothing to 'do' [about Fagin]," wrote Howe, "but confront the historical realities of our culture, and all that it has thrown up from its unsavory depths."

In 1949, a group of Jewish parents in Brooklyn, New York, protested that the assignment of *Oliver Twist* in senior high school literature classes violated the rights of their children to receive an education free of religious bias. Citing the characterization of Fagin in *Oliver Twist* and Shylock in Shakespeare's play *The Merchant of Venice*, they sued the New York City Board of Education. They asked that both texts be banned from New York City public schools "because they tend to engender hatred of the Jew as a person and as a race."

In *Rosenberg v. Board of Education of City of New York*, the Kings County Supreme Court decided that the two works should not be banned from New York City schools, libraries or classrooms, declaring that the Board of Education "acted in good faith without malice or prejudice and in the best interests of the school system entrusted to their care and control, and, therefore, that no substantial reason exists which compels the suppression of the two books under consideration."

In denying the plaintiffs' bid to ban the books, the presiding judge stated, "Except where a book has been maliciously written for the apparent purpose of fomenting a bigoted and intolerant hatred against a particular racial or religious group, public interest in a free and democratic society does not warrant or encourage the suppression of any book at the whim of any unduly sensitive person or group of person, merely because a character described in such book as belonging to a particular race or religion is portrayed in a derogatory or offensive manner." Removal of the books "will contribute nothing toward the diminution of anti-religious feeling," the court said.

FURTHER READINGS

Dickens, Charles. *Oliver Twist*. Intro. by Irving Howe. New York: Bantam Books, 1982.

Doyle, Robert P. *Banned Books 1996 Resource Guide*. Chicago: American Library Association, 1996.

Kaplan, Fred, ed. *Oliver Twist: A Norton Critical Edition*. New York: W. W. Norton & Co., 1993.

Veidmanis, Gladys. "Reflections on 'the Shylock Problem.'" In *Censored Books: Critical Viewpoints*. Ed. by Nicholas J. Karolides, Lee Burress and John M. Kean, 370–78. Metuchen, N.J.: Scarecrow Press, 1993.

ON THE INFINITE UNIVERSE AND WORLDS

Author: Giordano Bruno
Original date and place of publication: 1584, France
Literary form: Philosophical treatise

SUMMARY

The Italian philosopher Giordano Bruno entered the Dominican order at a young age and was expelled in 1576 at the age of 28 when he was charged with heresy. He traveled throughout Europe for 15 years, one step ahead of the censors, teaching at Toulouse, Paris, Oxford, Wittenberg and Frankfurt. In *On the Infinite Universe and Worlds*, his major metaphysical work, published in 1584, he refuted the traditional cosmology of Aristotle and its limited conceptions of the universe. Instead, Bruno asserted that the physical universe is infinite and includes an indefinite number of worlds, each with its own sun and planets. He pictured the world as composed of individual, irreducible elements of being, called monads, governed by fixed laws of relationship.

Bruno's philosophy prefigured modern cosmic theory. He accepted Copernicus's hypothesis that the sun, rather than the earth, is the center of our world. But he went further than Copernicus in arguing that the sun is simply one star among others. All judgments about position are relative, since there are as many possible modes of viewing the world as there are possible positions. Therefore, no one star or planet can be called the center of the universe. Human beings cannot conclude that they are unique, because the presence of life, even that of rational beings, may not be confined to earth. There is no absolute truth and there are no limits to the progress of knowledge.

The infinite universe is the product of a pantheistic infinite divine power or cause whose work is manifest in human beings and in all of nature. "The Divine one extols his own glory and sets forth the greatness of his sway, not in one sun, but in uncountable suns; not in one earth, but in words without end."

Because God's power is infinite, his creation must also be infinite. The agent would be imperfect if his works did not fulfill his power. Bruno believed that understanding of the universe as the manifestation of God would free the human spirit. "[It] opens the senses, contents the soul, enlarges the mind and brings true blessed news to man. . . . For deeply considering the Being and substance in which we are fixed, we find that there is no such thing as death, not for us alone, but for the truce substance.

CENSORSHIP HISTORY

"I wish the world to possess the glorious fruits of my labor," Bruno wrote in *On the Infinite Universe and Worlds*, "to awaken the soul and open the understanding of those who are deprived of that light, which, most assuredly, is not mine own invention. Should I be in error, I do not believe I willfully go wrong."

In the view of his contemporaries, Bruno had indeed gone wrong. His assault on Aristotelian views of the universe and his construction of a "new philosophy" challenged the Scholasticism that dominated the universities. It ran counter to the beliefs held by all the ecclesiastical institutions, whether Catholic, Lutheran or Calvinist. His speculation about an endless number of celestial worlds was viewed as heretical pantheism.

In 1577, the Inquisition in Naples initiated proceedings against him and Bruno fled Italy. In 1592, he rashly returned and, denounced by a Venetian nobleman, was delivered to the Inquisition in Venice. He was imprisoned and tried on charges of blasphemy, immoral conduct and heresy. On May 26, 1592, the Holy Tribunal met to consider his case. Bruno told the judges: "I have ever expounded philosophically and according to the principles of Nature and by its light . . . although I may have set forth much suspicious matter occasioned by my own natural light . . . never have I taught anything directly contrary to the Catholic religion. . . ." When asked whether he believed that the Father, Son and Holy Spirit were one in essence but distinct persons, he admitted "I have never been able to grasp the three being really Persons and have doubted it. . . ." Bruno offered to submit to all church doctrines, but he refused to abjure his philosophy.

Bruno remained in prison for months awaiting the decision of the Venetian Inquisition. Because he was regarded as a "hesiarch," an originator and leader of heresy, the chief inquisitor at the Holy Office in Rome demanded that he be delivered there for trial. He was extradicted to Rome and on February 27, 1593, was imprisoned for seven years. He was allowed neither books nor writing material, and his only visitors were officials of the Inquisition and priests sent to urge him to repent. In 1559, several cardinals interrogated him regarding heresies extracted from his books. At a final interrogation he declared he would recant nothing. In January 1660, at a meeting presided over by the pope, it was decreed that he would be burned at the stake for "many various heretical and unsound opinions." He was executed in Rome on February 17, 1600.

On August 7, 1603, all of Bruno's writings were placed on the Index of Forbidden Books, where they remained through the last edition of the Index, in effect until 1966. Cardinal Robert Bellarmino, who had overseen Bruno's trial and punishment, was declared a saint by the Catholic Church in 1930. Bruno's works had never been popular in England or on the Continent and were scarce in Catholic countries because of their suppression. John Toland, the 17th-century English deist and author of *Christianity Not Mysterious*, recognized Bruno as a forerunner of the freethinkers of his own era; Toland translated part of *The Infinite Universe and Worlds* and wrote an account of the book. Bruno's philosophy also had an important influence on the philosophers Spinoza and Leibnitz.

FURTHER READINGS

Boulting, William. *Giordano Bruno: His Life, Thought and Martyrdom.* New York: Books for Libraries Press, 1972.

Copleston, Frederick. *A History of Philosophy.* Vol. 3, *Late Medieval and Renaissance Philosophy.* New York: Doubleday, 1993.

George, Leonard. *Crimes of Perception: An Encyclopedia of Heresies and Heretics.* New York: Paragon House, 1995.

Green, Jonathon. *The Encyclopedia of Censorship.* New York: Facts On File, 1990.

Jaspers, Karl. *The Great Philosophers.* Vol. 3. New York: Harcourt Brace & Company, 1993.

Levy, Leonard W. *Blasphemy: Verbal Offense Against the Sacred, from Moses to Salman Rushdie.* New York: Alfred A. Knopf, 1993.

ON THE ORIGIN OF SPECIES

Author: Charles Darwin
Original date and place of publication: 1859, England
Literary form: Scientific text

SUMMARY

The British naturalist Charles Darwin published his groundbreaking work, *On the Origin of Species*, 22 years after he initially wrote it, in response to competition from other scientists who were preparing to publish similar ideas. In this book, Darwin outlines the observations he made while sailing around South America on the H.M.S. *Beagle* from 1831 to 1836.

Darwin believed in "descent with modification," that generations of organisms changed over time and those that best withstood climatic and other changes were most likely to survive and multiply. Darwin stated that these changes occurred through natural selection, controlled by the organisms themselves, over millions of years. *On the Origin of Species* discussed these broad concepts through specific examples of evolution in pigeons and ants, as well as in discussion of embryology and morphology. Though his theory was based on careful measurements and observations, Darwin understood that it would be seen as radically at odds with prevailing ideas about the design of nature. Attempting to head off criticism, Darwin acknowledged that "nothing at first may be more difficult to believe than that the more complex organs and instincts should have been perfected . . . by the accumulation of innumerable slight variations, each good for the individual possessor."

Most readers of Darwin's book had been taught that God created the world according to an orderly plan, placing humans on earth with dominion over nature. Darwin's ideas provided much less certainty than traditional, biblical-based explanations of nature. Popular impressions of Darwinism, however, differed from Darwin's actual writings. Social scientists summed up his concept of descent with modification through natural selection as "survival of the fittest" and used this term to explain relations between social classes. To so-called social Darwinists, wealthier, more powerful people deserved to hold on to their advantages because they were the "fittest" human beings. Under social Darwinism, any aid to the disadvantaged became an unnatural act, needlessly prolonging the lives and traits of the "unfit." Social Darwinists shortened Darwin's ideas by using the term "evolution" and added a belief that evolution always resulted in progress.

Darwin never intended this linear approach to the study of nature. He was most interested in the mutations that occurred over generations of organisms, whether the mutations resulted in progress or not. Further, Darwin never wished to explore his theories in the realm of human behavior and social organization. When he discussed his ideas in relation to humans, he focused on the development of organs and systems in the body, not in society.

Darwin was part of a movement in science toward reliance on empirical data. He was a contemporary of scientists like John William Draper, author of *History of the Conflict Between Religion and Science*, who questioned religious-based models for scientific observation. While Darwin was careful not to attack religion directly, as Draper did, his quiet, measured arguments did not include any mention of a divine power ordering the universe.

CENSORSHIP HISTORY

Historians of science believe that one of the reasons why Darwin delayed publishing his work for so long was his fear that his ideas were too radical for the time and would be greeted with hostility. Seeing himself as a scientist, he refused to comment on the wider importance of his ideas. Near the end of his life, after publishing several other works in which he affirmed his belief in natural selection, he continued to think only in terms of advancing science and hoped that his quiet example would win people to his ideas.

On the Origin of Species by means of Natural Selection, or the Preservation of Favoured Races in the Struggle for Life was published on November 24, 1859, in an edition of only 1,250 copies by the reluctant John Murray, who did not anticipate much interest in the book. The first edition was sold out on the day of publication and a second edition of 3,000 copies soon after. The book appeared in six editions through 1872. An American edition appeared in May 1860 and was greeted with widespread controversy.

"Sixteen thousand copies have now (1876) been sold in England," Darwin wrote in his autobiography, "and considering how stiff a book it is, it is a large sale. It has been translated into almost every European tongue. . . ." He counted more than 265 reviews and numerous essays. Darwin's ideas gained wide currency in academic scientific circles almost immediately and became the foundations of modern evolution theory.

However, the publication of *On the Origin of Species* also unleashed one of the most dramatic controversies of the Victorian era. Darwin was accused of "dethroning God," as one critic put it, by challenging the literal interpretation of the book of Genesis. Clergy railed against him from pulpits all over Britain. His book was barred from Trinity College at Cambridge, even though Darwin was a graduate. Darwin, referring to occasions when he was "contemptuously criticised," declared that "I could not employ my life better than in adding a little to natural science. This I have done to the best of my abilities, and critics may say what they like, but they cannot destroy this conviction."

Unlike *Zoonomia*, a scientific treatise written by Darwin's grandfather, Erasmus Darwin, in the late 18th century, which was banned by the Catholic Church because it expressed a theory of evolution, *On the Origin of Species* was never placed on the Index of Forbidden Books.

A resurgence of opposition to Darwinism began in the 1920s in the United States. By the early 20th century, American high school science textbooks had begun to incorporate Darwinian evolution in discussing human origins and biology. In 1919, the World Christian Fundamentals Association (WCFA) was founded to oppose teaching of evolution in American public schools. Local school boards and state boards of education in areas with large fundamentalist Christian populations were pressured to reject the new textbooks and legislatures around the country were lobbied to pass antievolution resolutions. More than 20 state legislatures considered such measures.

In 1925, in the most famous example of antievolutionary sentiment, Tennessee passed a law prohibiting teachers from teaching the theory of evolution in state-supported schools. A combination of factors compelled the Tennessee state legislature to pass such a sweeping measure. The 1920s were an era of pleasure-seeking in popular culture, especially among teenagers; at the same time, fundamentalist religion and nativism were on the increase as a reaction to these "modern" ideas. Fundamentalist Christians feared that a materialistic philosophy such as natural selection would send a damaging, nihilistic message to schoolchildren. They believed that schools would produce more orderly students if they taught the biblical account of creation, with a God designing nature according to a set plan. Local leaders in the small town of Dayton, Tennessee, welcomed the chance to put their town on the map in the context of this battle.

John T. Scopes, a science teacher in Dayton, volunteered to be the test case for Tennessee's antievolution law. Representing the state was William Jennings Bryan, a populist leader and three-time Democratic presidential candidate who had served as Woodrow Wilson's secretary of state and was popular among fundamentalists for his biblically inspired rhetoric and his devotion to maintaining traditional, rural ways of life. Clarence Darrow, a noted defense lawyer and avowed agnostic, defended Scopes, arguing that academic freedom was being violated and that the legislation violated the separation of church and state. Members of the American Civil Liberties Union, at that time a new organization devoted to defending free speech, also contributed to Scopes's side.

The Scopes "monkey trial," as it became known, was an event of national importance during the summer of 1925. Newspapers from around the country sent correspondents to Dayton to cover the proceedings and Dayton merchants sold souvenirs of the trial, including stuffed monkeys to represent the idea that Darwin claimed humans were descended from apes. Reporters from big-city newspapers reported on the trial with amusement, while fundamentalist observers saw the proceedings as a crucial battle against the forces of modernism.

Both sides claimed victory. Scopes was found guilty of violating Tennessee's statute prohibiting the teaching of evolution. As a state employee, the judge ruled, Scopes could not disobey state laws. His backers were also pleased, as the decision gave them the chance to appeal the matter to a higher court, where the case for evolution and freedom of expression could get even more publicity. The Scopes case, however, was thrown out on a technicality. In the original case the judge, rather than the jury, had fined Scopes $100. This procedural error reversed the verdict that found Scopes guilty.

Antievolution efforts did not end with the conclusion of the Scopes trial. The Tennessee antievolution law remained on the books until 1967 and grassroots fundamentalists in the United States launched efforts to remove Darwin's ideas from public school textbooks. In 1968, the U.S. Supreme Court considered a case similar to Scopes's. Susan Epperson, a high school biology teacher, challenged the constitutionality of the Arkansas Anti-Evolution Statute of 1928, which provided that teachers who used a textbook that included Darwin's theory of evolution could lose their jobs. The Supreme Court ruled that the law was unconstitutional and conflicted with the First and Fourteenth Amendments. Government power could not be used to advance religious beliefs.

Having been defeated in the courts, antievolutionists shifted their focus to requiring instruction in "creationism" as an alternative to evolutionary theories. They defined creationism as the theory that all life forms came into existence instantaneously through the action of a single intelligent creator. In the early 1980s, Arkansas and Louisiana state boards of education required the teaching of both creationism and evolution in public schools. These laws were ruled unconstitutional in 1987 by the U.S. Supreme Court in *Edwards v. Aguillard* as advocating a religious doctrine and violating the establishment clause of the First Amendment. However, battles about the teaching of evolution still rage on, especially at the local school board level.

In 1935, *On the Origin of Species* was prohibited in Yugoslavia and in 1937 it was banned under the right-wing Metaxas regime in Greece. But unlike other cases of book censorship, the book was generally not removed from bookstore or library shelves in the United States. It was, rather, the ideas expressed in the book that were censored.

FURTHER READINGS

Boorstein, Daniel J. *The Discoverers: A History of Man's Search to Know His World and Himself.* New York: Random House, 1983.

Delatorre, Joan. *What Johnny Shouldn't Read: Textbook Censors in America.* New Haven: Yale University Press, 1992.

Demac, Donna A. *Liberty Denied: The Current Rise of Censorship in America.* New York: PEN American Center, 1988.

Gould, Stephen Jay. *Ever Since Darwin: Reflections on Natural History.* New York: W. W. Norton and Company, 1977.

Larson, Edward J. *Trial and Error. The American Controversy Over Creation and Evolution.* New York: Oxford University Press, 1985.

Numbers, Ronald L., ed. *Creation-Evolution Debates.* New York: Garland Publishing, 1955.

Rogers, Donald J. *Banned! Book Censorship in the Schools.* New York: Julian Messner, 1988.

POPOL VUH

Original date and place of composition: ca. 1000–1550, Guatemala
Literary form: Religious text

SUMMARY

The Popol Vuh, the sacred book of the Quiché Maya, is the most important text in the native languages of the Americas and the greatest Mesoamerican mythological work. It is considered to be among the world's masterpieces of religious writing. Blending myth, legend and history, it recounts the cosmology, migratory tradition and history of the Quiché Maya of Guatemala's highlands. The Quichés, who number over a half million today, live in the same land and among the same landmarks whose ancient history is described in the Popol Vuh or "Council Book," consulted by the lords of Quiché when they sat in Council.

The narrative in part one of the Popol Vuh begins in the primeval darkness before creation, in an empty world of only sky and sea and the gods who live in the waters. The Heart of Sky (a tripartite being also called Hurricane) and the Sovereign Plumed Serpent, who resides in the primordial sea, resolve to create the world. They say "Earth" and it suddenly comes into being, rising like a cloud or a mist. The gods begin their efforts to create human beings. On the first try they create beings who can only squawk, chatter and howl. Because they cannot speak properly to worship their gods, they are condemned to be killed for food. Their descendants are the birds and animals.

A second experiment creates a being of mud that dissolves into nothing, incapable of speaking or worshipping. Before their third attempt, the younger gods consult the elderly divinities—the matchmaker, Xpiyacoc, and the midwife, Xmucane, both daykeepers or diviners who can interpret the auguries of the calendar cycle. They approve the creation of human beings made of wood. Because the wooden manikins are empty-headed, with no memory of their creators, Heart of Sky brings a great flood down upon them. They are crushed and destroyed and their only descendants are the monkeys of the forests.

Before telling of the fourth attempt to create human beings, the narrators recount in parts two and three the three-part cycle of the exploits of the hero twins. First Hunahpu and Xbalanque, the twin grandsons of Xpiyacoc and Xmucane, in a series of adventures, vanquish Seven Macaw (the Big Dipper) and his offspring Zipacna and Earthquake.

Then the story flashes back to an earlier story of the exploits in Xibalba, the underworld, of another set of twins—One Hunahpu and Seven Hunahpu, the father and uncle of Hunahpu and Xbalanque and the sons of Xpiyacoc and Xmucane. They are summoned to the underworld and fail a series of tests and traps set by their hosts. They are sacrificed in Xibalba by the lords of death.

The final segment relates the adventures in the underworld of the first set of hero twins, Hunahpu and Xbalanque. They are successful in escaping from the traps that had caused the demise of their father and uncle and plan a way to die that will allow them to come back to life. The twins then ascend from Xibalba into the heavens to become the sun and the moon.

The stage is now set for the fourth creation. In part four, as the sun, moon and stars are about to rise, Xpiyacoc and Xmucane find yellow and white corn in a mountain. Xmucane grinds it together nine times. Mixed with water, the corn provides the material for the first human beings: Jaguar Quitze, Jaguar Night, Mahucutah and True Jaguar, the first mother-fathers of the Quiché people. But as the new men are too perfect, the gods worry that their creations will compete with them in greatness. The gods weaken the men's eyes so that they can see only nearby things clearly, limiting their powers of knowing and understanding. Then the gods make a wife for each new man and the leading Quiché lineages descend from these pairs. Finally, after much sacrifice and prayer, the sun appears for the first time. "There were countless peoples, but there was just one dawn for all tribes."

The creation myth recounted in the Popol Vuh is an actual map of the sky that replays creation in the pattern of its yearly movements. The actions of the gods, the heroes and their enemies correspond to the movements of the sun, moon, planets and stars. Creation is not a single act but a process through which the essence of divinity continually creates and maintains life. The Popol Vuh concludes in part five with a lengthy migration story that recounts episodes comprising the mythological and actual history of the Quiché people and their Mayan neighbors. It lists the names of 14 generations of the rulers of Quiché up to the time when this version of the Popol Vuh was written. In the 12th generation, the names of Three Deer and Nine Dog are followed by two sentences. "And they were ruling when Tonatiuh (Pedro de Alvarado) arrived. They were hanged by the Castilian people."

CENSORSHIP HISTORY

The Popol Vuh was originally written in Mayan hieroglyphics by Quiché Maya nobles during the Postclassic period (A.D. 1000 to 1500) and was in use by the Quiché at the time of the Spanish conquest in the 16th century. Illustrations on painted pottery and inscriptions carved on stone monuments indicate that the myths and legends told in the Popol Vuh are much older, dating at least to the Classic period (A.D. 250 to 900), the time of the highest flourishing of Mayan art and culture.

After 1523, when the Spanish conquistador Pedro de Alvarado was sent by Hernán Cortés to subdue the Mayan peoples of Guatemala, thousands of hieroglyphic books were burned by Spanish missionaries. The original Popol Vuh is assumed to have been among them. Hieroglyphic books were regarded as superstitious works of the devil. Their destruction was a part of a sustained campaign to eradicate Mayan religion and culture and impose European Catholicism.

In the 1550s, a text of the Popol Vuh was secretly rewritten in the Roman alphabet in the town of Santa Cruz del Quiché, Guatemala, by descendants of the lordly lineages who once ruled the Quiché Kingdom. Its anonymous authors had been taught by missionaries to write their language in the alphabet. In 1701–3 the book was translated into Spanish by a Dominican friar, Francisco Ximénez, the parish priest of the nearby town of Chichicastenango, who was shown the document and recognized its importance. He also made what is now the only copy of the Quiché Maya text.

The original Popol Vuh would have been fully illustrated, a folding screen manuscript painted on bark paper thinly coated with lime plaster. It would have included astrological tables and ritual almanacs used for divination, similar to the pages of the only four Mayan hieroglyphic books or fragments, called codices, that survived the depredations of the Spanish conquest. Three codices from Yucatán, Mexico, were taken to Europe in colonial times and bear the names of the cities where they were found in museums or libraries: the Dresden, Paris and Madrid codices. A fourth fragment, known as the Grolier Codex, now in Mexico City, was found in a cave in Chiapas, Mexico, in 1971. The Popol Vuh of the 16th century presented an expanded version of the original hieroglyphic book, telling the full story behind the charts and pictures.

According to the writers of the alphabetic version, the hieroglyphic codex was among the most precious possessions of the Quiché rulers because "they knew whether war would occur; everything they saw was clear to them. Whether there would be death or whether there would be famine. . . . [T]hey knew it for certain, since there was a place to see it, there was a book." The

"Council Book" allowed the Quiché lords to recover the vision lost by the first four humans.

The highly praised first unabridged English-language translation of the Popol Vuh by Dennis Tedlock, published in 1985, incorporates the insight of a contemporary Quiché Maya daykeeper and head of his patrilineage, Andrés Xiloj. It is engaging and readable, despite the complexity of the mythology it contains, and has brought the Popol Vuh to a larger audience.

FURTHER READINGS

Freidel, David, Linda Schele and Joy Parker. *Maya Cosmos: Three Thousand Years on the Shaman's Path*. New York: William Morrow and Company, 1993.

Gallenkamp, Charles. *Maya: The Riddle and Discovery of a Lost Civilization*. New York: David McKay and Company, 1976.

Markman, Roberta, and Peter Markman. *The Flayed God: The Mythology of Mesoamerica*. New York: HarperCollins, 1992.

Stuart, Gene S., and George E. Stuart. *Lost Kingdoms of the Maya*. Washington, D.C.: National Geographic Society, 1993.

Tedlock, Dennis, trans. *Popol Vuh: The Definitive Edition of the Mayan Book of the Dawn of Life and the Glories of Gods and Kings*. New York: Simon & Schuster, 1985.

THE RED AND THE BLACK

Author: Stendhal (Marie-Henri Beyle)
Original date and place of publication: France, 1831
Literary form: Fiction

SUMMARY

Stendhal—the pseudonym of Marie-Henri Beyle—was among the greatest French novelists of the 19th century. *The Red and the Black*, the story of Julien, an ambitious small-town youth who is executed for shooting his wealthy mistress, is regarded as one of the most boldly original masterworks of European fiction.

In *The Red and the Black*, Stendhal portrays a vivid tableau of French society and politics during the 1820s, the final years of the Restoration of the Bourbon monarchy. "Everywhere hypocrisy, or at least charlatanism, even among the most virtuous, even among the greatest," says Julien, echoing Stendhal's view of the times. The ultraroyalist partisans of absolute monarchy, found among the nobility, the wealthy and the clergy, had from 1815 waged a struggle to restore the ancien regime, the political state that existed before the 1789 revolution. Upon his accession to the throne in 1824, Charles X initiated antiliberal, pro-Catholic policies which, after 20 years of exile, returned the government and the army to the control of the nobility and passed measures increasing the power of the clergy.

Hostility aroused by his policies culminated in the July Revolution of 1830, which ended the rule of the elder branch of the Bourbons.

The subject of the novel was also provided by a newspaper article about a young man, Antoine Berthet, who was guillotined in 1828 for an attempt to kill his former mistress, Madame Michoud, whose children he had tutored. The story of Julien Sorel closely parallels the Berthet case. Verrières, the fictional town in which the story takes place, is much like the provincial city of Grenoble, where Berthet lived and where Stendhal spent his childhood.

Julien Sorel is an intelligent young man of peasant origins who is eager to attain a social position beyond his station in life. Under the rule of Napoleon, his most likely path to success would have been through the military. Now that the country is at peace under Bourbon rule, which has restored the political influence of the clergy, the road to advancement leads him to the Catholic Church. Julien studies Latin and theology to prepare for entrance into a seminary and attains a position as a tutor for the children of Monsieur de Rênal, the wealthy mayor of Verrières.

He becomes involved in an affair with the mayor's wife, a relationship that for Julien is fueled by the thrill of conquering a woman of a higher social class, rather than by affection. When Rênal receives an anonymous letter exposing the affair, Julien leaves the household and enters the seminary at Besançon. The seminary proves, however, not to be a refuge from the provincial life of Verrières, which Julien sees as mired in greed and petty politics. The church's institution for training future leaders is a haven of hypocrisy and mediocrity, rife with political intrigue as sordid as that of the outside world. The motivation of the young seminarians is neither spiritual nor intellectual, but, rather, strictly economic.

"Almost all were the sons of peasants," Stendhal writes, "who preferred to gain their daily bread by repeating a few Latin words instead of swinging a pickax." Their religious vocation is based in the desire to have a good dinner and a warm suit of clothes in winter. "Learning counts for nothing here," Julien observes. "The church in France seems to have understood that books themselves are its real enemy. In the eyes of the church, inward submission is all. . . ."

Julien admires two of the priests at the seminary—the elderly Curé Chélan and the seminary's director, the devout Jansenist Abbé Pirard, who is finally ousted by the pro-Jesuit faction led by the vice principal. When Pirard resigns, he takes Julien with him to Paris, where he becomes private secretary to a nobleman, the Marquis de la Mole. Julien embarks on an affair with the marquis's daughter, Matilde, who is fascinated by Julien's daring and ambition. When Matilde becomes pregnant, her father reluctantly consents to her marriage to Julien and agrees to provide him with a private income and a title. But when the marquis makes inquiries about Julien in Verrières, he receives a denunciatory letter from Madame de Rênal, dictated by her confessor. After the marquis cancels the wedding plans, Julien shoots and wounds Madame de Rênal as she kneels at church attending Mass. He is immediately arrested.

Julien is put on trial but refuses to defend himself. Despite attempts by the local clergy to manipulate the jury on his behalf, he is convicted. As Julien awaits death by the guillotine, he searches for meaning, finding it only in his belated affection for Madame de Rênal. "My word, if I find the God of the Christians, it's all up with me," he thinks. "He's a despot and, as such, full of vengeful ideas; his Bible talks of nothing but frightful punishments. I never liked him; I never could believe that anyone sincerely loved him. He is merciless (and he recalled several scriptural passages). He will punish me in some abominable way . . . I have loved truth. . . . Where is it?"

CENSORSHIP HISTORY

Stendhal's literary reputation was slow to develop. His contemporaries found the detachment and psychological realism of his novels difficult to comprehend, as his work did not fit any of the literary stereotypes of the day. Some readers were scandalized by what was viewed as Stendhal's indifference to morality and his unapologetic and understanding portrayal of a character who was seen as an unscrupulous monster. "I have been ambitious, but I have no intention of blaming myself for that; I was acting in those days according to the code of the times," Julien explains from his prison cell.

Stendhal said that he wrote "for the happy few" and correctly predicted that he would not be appreciated until 50 years later. Indeed, only one edition of *The Red and the Black* was published during his lifetime. The complete absence of a religious worldview in his novels, his portrayal of the God of the Bible as a "petty despot" and his anticlericalism led the Catholic Church to censor his writing. Stendhal's anticlericalism reflected the intellectual inheritance of the antireligious spirit of Voltaire. It also had its origins in his unhappy childhood education at the hands of Jesuit priests.

The church portrayed in *The Red and the Black* is torn between two factions—the Jesuits, the wily and worldly agents of international reaction and proponents of the ancien regime, and the austere Jansenists. Stendhal's bitterly critical attitude toward the Jesuits was common to many in France at the time. The Jesuits had been banished from the country in 1764, but continued to function in secret until 1814. Under the Bourbon regime their influence was restored. In *The Red and the Black*, Stendhal portrays the political manipulations of a powerful secret Jesuit society known as the Congregation (patterned after an organization of the time called the Knights of Faith), dedicated to advancing ultraroyalist views and the agenda of the Vatican to the detriment of France's sovereignty and the liberal agenda.

The Red and the Black and all of Stendhal's "love stories" were placed by the Vatican in 1864 on the Index of Forbidden Books and confirmed by the Index of Pope Leo XIII in 1897. They remained on the list through the last edition compiled in 1948 and in effect until 1966. In Russia, *The Red and the Black* was banned in 1850 by Czar Nicholas I, whose motto in a campaign to suppress liberal thought was "autocracy, orthodoxy, and nationality." In a similar campaign in Spain in 1939, the novel was purged from Spanish libraries by the dictatorship of Francisco Franco.

FURTHER READINGS

Brombert, Victor, ed. *Stendhal: A Collection of Critical Essays*. Englewood Cliffs, N.J.: Prentice-Hall, 1962.
Haight, Anne Lyon. *Banned Books: 387 B.C. to 1978 A.D.* Updated and enlarged by Chandler B. Grannis. New York: R. R. Bowker, 1978.
Stendhal. *Red and Black: A Norton Critical Edition*. Trans. and ed. by Robert M. Adams. New York: W. W. Norton & Company, 1969.
Talbot, Emile J. *Stendhal Revisited*. New York: Twayne Publishers, 1993.

RELIGION WITHIN THE LIMITS OF REASON ALONE

Author: Immanuel Kant
Original date and place of publication: 1793, Prussia
Literary form: Philosophical treatise

SUMMARY

The philosophical system of Immanuel Kant, one of the most important philosophers in Western culture, was designed to lay a firm foundation for the entire range of scientific, moral and aesthetic experience. In *The Critique of Pure Reason*, published in 1781, Kant offered a radical new approach to fundamental issues of epistemology and metaphysics. Mediating between rationalist claims of knowledge of what lies beyond sense perception and the opposing philosophy of skepticism, which denied the possibility of any real knowledge, Kant defined the boundaries of valid thought.

Kant's philosophy of religion is principally contained in *Religion within the Limits of Reason Alone*. Kant asserts that the existence of God can neither be affirmed nor denied on theological grounds and that all proofs derived from pure reason are invalid. Religion is outside the province of reason, as the divine cannot be an object of thought and knowledge is limited to the world of phenomena.

Kant nevertheless supports the legitimacy of religious belief. Though the existence of God cannot be scientifically demonstrated, Kant's moral philosophy shows the necessity of God's existence. For Kant, religion resides "in the heart's disposition to fulfill all human duties as divine commands." Kant's conception of religion can be described as ethical theism. He argues that moral law requires that people should be rewarded in proportion to their virtue. Since this does not always occur, he infers that there must be another existence where they are rewarded. This leads him to the conclusion that there is an eternal life and a God.

For Kant, a valid religious belief can derive only from the implications of moral principles and the nature of the moral life. Morality, however, does not require the idea of a supreme being and "thus in no way needs religion for its own service . . . but in virtue of pure practical reason, it is sufficient unto itself." In contrast to religious systems that relate doing good to securing a reward, the basis of religion should be the doing of good for its own sake.

Kant divides all religions into those that are "*endeavors to win favor* (mere worship) and *moral religions*, i.e., religions of *good life-conduct*." In the first type, Kant declares, "man flatters himself by believing either that God can make him eternally happy (through remission of his sins) without his having *to become a better man*, or else, if this seems to him impossible, that God can certainly *make him a better man* without his having to do anything more than to *ask* for it. Yet since, in the eyes of a Being who sees all, to ask is no more than to *wish*, this would really involve doing nothing at all; for mere improvements to be achieved simply by a wish, every man would be good."

According to Kant, man's moral growth begins not in the improvement of his practices, but rather in the transformation of his cast of mind and in the grounding of character. Kant describes as a peculiar "delusion of religion" that man supposes that he can do anything, apart from the good actions of his life, to become acceptable to God. "Man *himself* must make or have made himself into whatever, in a moral sense, whether good or evil, he is or is to become. Either choice must be an effect of his free choice; for otherwise he could not be held responsible for it and could therefore be *morally* neither good nor evil."

CENSORSHIP HISTORY

As the Prussian state moved to prosecute the battle against the freethinkers of the 18th-century Enlightenment, censorship of printed matter was increased. A government edict allowed toleration of views divergent from Lutheranism "so long as each quietly fulfills his duties as a good citizen of the state, but keeps his particular opinion in every case to himself, and takes care not to propagate it or to convert others and cause them to err or falter in their faith."

Because Kant was a prominent author who enjoyed the confidence of the king, his earlier works of critical philosophy, such as *The Critique of Pure Reason*, not intended for the general reader, were spared censorship. In 1791, a proposal to prohibit Kant's literary activity was submitted to the king by the high ecclesiastical councillor, but was not acted upon.

In 1792, Kant's essay "On the Radical Evil in Human Nature," which was to become the first part of *Religion within the Limits of Reason Alone*, was approved by the government censor for appearance in the publication *Berlin-*

ische Monatsschrift. But because it dealt with biblical matters, the continuation of Kant's treatise, "On the Struggle of the Good Principle with the Evil for Mastery over Mankind," was handed over for approval to a theological censor, who refused permission to publish.

Kant supplemented the two essays with two additional pieces and prepared a book, *Religion within the Limits of Reason Alone*, which he brought for approval to the theological faculty of the University of Königsberg, where he was a professor. The theologians at Königsberg regarded the book as being outside their purview to censor because it did not deal with biblical theology. Kant received, instead, an imprimatur from the philosophical faculty at the University of Jena and the book was published in 1793.

In October 1794, King Frederick William II (successor to Frederick the Great on the throne of Prussia), who was offended by the book, wrote to Kant accusing him of having "misused" his philosophy over a long period of time and of "the destruction and debasing of many principal and basic teachings of the Holy Scripture of Christianity." He warned Kant not to write or publish any similar works on religion, or "otherwise you can unfailingly expect, on continued recalcitrance, unpleasant consequences." *Religion within the Limits of Reason Alone* was banned by the Lutheran Church in Prussia.

Kant wrote to the king in his own defense that his book was not directed toward the general public, but rather exclusively intended for discussion among scholars, and that, further, it could not have contained a "debasing of Christ and the Bible, for the reason that the sole theme was the evolution of pure rational religion, not the critique of historical forms of belief."

Though Kant refused to retract his opinions, he promised "thus to prevent even the least suspicion on this score . . . cheerfully to declare myself Your Royal Majesty's most faithful subject: that I will refrain entirely in the future from all public discourse concerning religion, natural or revealed, in lectures and in writing alike." Kant kept his promise to the king, but considered it binding only during the king's lifetime. After the king's death, in 1798 Kant published *The Conflict of the Faculties*, in which he discussed the relation between theology and the critical reason and made public his correspondence with the king about the censorship of *Religion within the Limits of Reason Alone*.

Kant's philosophy did not attract the attention of the Catholic Church until 1827, when an Italian translation of *The Critique of Pure Reason* was published. Kant's contention that the existence of God can be neither confirmed nor denied through the use of reason caused the book to be placed on the Index of Forbidden Books, where it remained through the last edition in effect until 1966.

Religion within the Limits of Reason Alone, although it offered a more direct critique of institutionalized religion that conflicted with the church's doctrine, was never banned by the Vatican. It was, however, prohibited in the Soviet Union in 1928, along with all of Kant's writing, presumably because the metaphysical and transcendental themes of Kant's works were thought to conflict with Marxist-Leninist ideology. All of the works of "such disgraceful writers" as Kant and Goethe were also purged from the libraries of Spain under the Franco dictatorship in 1939.

FURTHER READINGS

Appelbaum, David. *The Vision of Kant*. Rockport, Mass.: Element Books, 1995.
Cassirer, Ernst. *Kant's Life and Thought*. Trans. by James Hader. Intro. by Stephan Korner. New Haven: Yale University Press, 1981.
Collinson, Diané. *Fifty Major Philosophers: A Reference Guide*. London: Routledge, 1988.
Copleston, Frederick. *A History of Philosophy*. Vol. 6, *Modern Philosophy: From the French Enlightenment to Kant*. New York: Doubleday, 1994.
Green, Jonathon. *The Encyclopedia of Censorship*. New York: Facts On File, 1990.
Kant, Immanuel. *The Philosophy of Kant: Immanuel Kant's Moral and Political Writings*. Ed. and intro. by Carl J. Friedrich. New York: Modern Library, 1993.
Popkin, Richard, and Avrum Stroll. *Philosophy Made Simple*. New York: Doubleday, 1993.

THE SATANIC VERSES

Author: Salman Rushdie
Original date and place of publication: 1988, England; 1989, United States
Original publisher: Penguin Books; Viking Penguin
Literary form: Fiction

SUMMARY

The Satanic Verses, by the Indian-born British author Salman Rushdie, holds a unique place in the history of literary censorship. In 1989 Iran's leader, Ayatollah Ruhollah Khomeini, condemned the book for blasphemy against Islam and issued an edict calling for its author's execution. The death threat drove Rushdie into hiding, and the furor over the novel escalated to become an unprecedented event of global dimensions.

Rushdie's complex and challenging novel is a surreal and riotously inventive mixture of realism and fantasy. In a cycle of three interconnected tales set in present-day London and Bombay, an Indian village and seventh-century Arabia, it explores themes of migration and dislocation, the nature of good and evil, doubt and loss of religious faith. "It is a migrant's-eye view of the world," Rushdie explained, commenting on the intentions of his novel. "It is written from the experience of uprooting, disjuncture and metamorphosis (slow or rapid, painful or pleasurable) that is the migrant condition, and from which, I believe, can be derived a metaphor for all humanity."

The novel opens at 29,000 feet in the air as two men fall toward the sea from a hijacked jumbo jet that has blown up over the English Channel. The two—both Indian actors—mysteriously survive the explosion and wash up on an English beach. Gibreel Farishta, formerly Ismail Najmuddin, is a legendary star of Indian movies; Saladin Chamcha, formerly Salahuddin Chamchawala, is an urbane Anglophile who makes a successful living in London doing voiceovers for television commercials.

As Rushdie describes his protagonists, *"The Satanic Verses* is the story of two painfully divided selves. In the case of one, Saladin Chamcha, the division is secular and societal; he is torn, to put it plainly, between Bombay and London, between East and West. For the other, Gibreel Farishta, the division is spiritual, a rift in the soul. He has lost his faith and is strung out between his immense need to believe and his new inability to do so. The novel is 'about' their quest for wholeness."

To their surprise and puzzlement, Gibreel and Saladin find after their fall from the sky that they have undergone a metamorphosis, acquiring characteristics alien to their own personalities. Gibreel, the womanizer, develops a halo, assuming the appearance of the Archangel Gibreel (Gabriel), while the mild and proper Saladin grows horns, hooves and a tail in the image of Satan. The fantastic adventures in England and India of these two walking symbols of good and evil form the central thread of the narrative.

The second tale, told in alternating chapters, evokes the historical origins of Islam in narratives dealing with the nature and consequences of revelation and belief. It takes place in the dreams of Gibreel Farishta, in which he becomes the archangel Gibreel, and in a film based on his imaginings in which he plays the role of the archangel. The dream-film sequences, which parallel the story of the Prophet Muhammad in Mecca, tell the story of Mahound (a derogatory medieval name for Muhammad). He is a businessman turned Prophet of Jahilia, the city of sand, who receives divine revelation through the intercession of the angel Gibreel and founds a religion called Submission (the literal English translation of the Arabic word *Islam*).

In the third tale, also dreamed up by Farishta, a charismatic holy woman cloaked in butterflies leads the faithful of a Muslim village in India on a pilgrimage to Mecca. As they walk toward Mecca, they perish when the waters of the Arabian sea do not part for them as expected.

The parts of the novel recounting Gibreel's painful visions, set in Mahound's city of Jahilia, are the primary focus of the controversy about the book. They allude to a legendary episode in the Prophet's life in which Muhammad added verses to the Koran that elevated to angelic status three goddesses worshipped by the polytheistic citizens of Mecca. Later, Muhammad revoked these verses, realizing that they had been transmitted to him not by Allah but by Satan posing as the angel Gabriel.

In contrast to the version of the incident recounted in Islamic history, Gibreel in his dream says that he was forced to speak the verses by "the overwhelming need of the Prophet Mahound," implying that Mahound, rather than Satan, put the false verses into Gibreel's mouth for opportunistic reasons. "From my mouth," Gibreel says, "both the statement and the repudiation, verses and converses, universes and reverses, the whole thing, and we all know how my mouth got worked."

In another dream passage alluding to an incident drawn from Islamic historical accounts, a scribe called Salman alters the text of the book dictated to him by Mahound. "Mahound did not notice the alterations," the scribe says, "so there I was, actually writing the Book, or re-writing anyway, polluting the word of God with my own profane language. But, good heavens, if my poor words could not be distinguished from the Revelation by God's own Messenger, then what did that mean?" Salman notices that the angel Gibreel's revelations to Mahound are particularly well timed, "so that when the faithful were disputing Mahound's views on any subject, from the possibility of space travel to the permanence of Hell, the angel would turn up with an answer, and he always supported Mahound."

Another provocative episode from Gibreel's dreams is a cinematic fantasy about a brothel in Jahilia called The Curtain (a translation of the Arabic word *hijab*, the Muslim women's veil), where business booms after 12 prostitutes assume the names and personalities of Mahound's 12 wives. A line of men awaiting their turns circles the innermost courtyard of the brothel, "rotating around its centrally positioned Fountain of Love much as pilgrims rotated for other reasons around the ancient Black Stone."

Hearing the news of the prostitutes' assumed identities, "the clandestine excitement of the city's males was intense; yet so afraid were they of discovery, both because they would surely lose their lives if Mahound or his lieutenants ever found out that they had been involved in such irreverences, and because of their sheer desire that the new service at The Curtain be maintained, that the secret was kept from the authorities."

Rushdie prefaces the story of the brothel with a statement that proved to be prescient in view of the events that engulfed his novel: "Where there is no belief, there is no blasphemy." Only because the men of Jahilia had accepted the tenets of their new faith could they find illicit pleasure in patronizing a brothel serviced by prostitutes impersonating the wives of the Prophet.

As the novel ends, Saladin Chamcha has become reintegrated into Indian society. He has completed a process of renewal and regeneration in his embrace of love and death and his return to his roots in India. Gibreel Farishta, tormented by his epic dreams and visions of doubt and skepticism, has lost his faith and failed to replace it by earthly love. Unable to escape his inner demons, he is driven mad and commits suicide.

CENSORSHIP HISTORY

The Satanic Verses was published in the United Kingdom on September 26, 1988. Rushdie's eagerly awaited fourth novel received laudatory reviews in the British press. It was hailed as "a masterpiece," "truly original" and "an exhilarating . . . extraordinary contemporary novel . . . a roller coaster ride over a vast landscape of the imagination."

Even before its publication, however, the controversy about the novel had already begun. Syed Shahabuddin and Khurshid Alam Khan, two Muslim opposition members of India's Parliament, alerted to the book's content by articles in Indian publications, launched a campaign to have it banned.

"Civilization is nothing but voluntary acceptance of restraints," Shahabuddin wrote in defense of censorship. "You may hold whatever private opinions you like but you do not enjoy an absolute right to express them in public." Expressing a view that was echoed by many opponents of the book as the controversy continued, Shahabuddin admitted that he had not read *The Satanic Verses* and did not intend to. "I do not have to wade through a filthy drain to know what filth is," he declared.

India's government, fearing civil disorder among the country's Muslim population, was the first to censor the book. On October 5, 1988, only nine days after its publication in Britain, the importation of the British edition was prohibited under a ruling of the Indian Customs Act. Muslims in India contacted Islamic organizations in Britain, urging them to take up the protest campaign. Two London publications sponsored by the Saudi Arabian government prominently featured stories denouncing the novel. At his home in London, Rushdie began to receive death threats.

The U.K. Action Committee on Islamic Affairs released a statement demanding withdrawal and destruction of the book, an apology and payment of damages to an Islamic charity. "The work, thinly disguised as a piece of literature," the statement read, "not only greatly distorts Islamic history in general, but also portrays in the worst possible colours the very characters of the Prophet Ibrahim and the Prophet Mohamed (peace upon them). It also disfigures the characters of the Prophet's companions . . . and the Prophet's holy wives and describes the Islamic creed and rituals in the most foul language."

The British-based Union of Muslim Organizations called for Rushdie's prosecution under rarely enforced British laws prohibiting blasphemy against the doctrines of the Church of England. The British government declined to consider expansion of the laws to include transgressions against the Islamic faith. On November 11, Prime Minister Margaret Thatcher announced that "there are no grounds on which the government could consider banning the book." On November 21, the grand sheik of Egypt's Al-Azhar, the mosque and university that is considered the seat of Islamic authority, called on all Islamic organizations in Britain to join in taking legal steps to prevent the book's distribution.

In the United States, where the novel had not yet appeared, its publisher, Viking Penguin, received bomb threats and thousands of menacing letters. On November 24, 1988, *The Satanic Verses* was banned in South Africa, even though it had not yet been published there. A planned visit by Rushdie was cancelled when its sponsors feared that his safety could not be guaranteed. Within weeks, the book was also banned in several countries with predominantly Muslim populations: Pakistan, Saudi Arabia, Egypt, Somalia, Bangladesh, Sudan, Malaysia, Indonesia and Qatar.

That month in England, *The Satanic Verses* received the Whitbread literary prize for best novel. In December and again in January, Muslims in Bolton, near Manchester, and in Bradford, Yorkshire, held public book burnings. A large group of demonstrators marched in London to protest the book. The Islamic Defence Council in Britain presented a petition to Penguin Books, demanding that the publisher apologize to the world Muslim community, withdraw the book, pulp the remaining copies and refrain from printing future editions.

The petition listed as insulting to Muslims the fact that Abraham was referred to in the book as "the bastard"; that the Prophet Muhammad was given the archaic medieval name of Mahound, meaning devil or false prophet; that the text states that revelations the Prophet received were well timed to suit him when "the faithful were disputing"; that the Prophet's companions were described in derogatory terms and the namesakes of his wives were depicted as prostitutes; and that the Islamic holy city of Mecca was portrayed as Jahilia, meaning ignorance or darkness.

Penguin Books refused to comply with the petitioners' demands. On January 22, 1989, Rushdie published a statement in defense of his novel. *The Satanic Verses* is not an antireligious novel, he said. "It is, however, an attempt to write about migration, its stresses and transformations, from the point of view of migrants from the Indian subcontinent to Britain. This is for me, the saddest irony of all; that after working for five years to give voice and fictional flesh to the immigrant culture of which I am myself a member, I should see my book burned, largely unread, by the people it's about, people who might find some pleasure and much recognition in its pages."

Rushdie's repeated efforts throughout the controversy to clarify the intentions and meaning of his book had little impact on the fervent opposition to it. Few of those who protested against the book had read it and, for many, the very title of the novel, which seemed to imply that the Koranic verses were written by the devil, was sacrilegious and sufficient to condemn it.

It is never stated within Gibreel Farishta's dreams that Satan wrote the sacred book. However, the passages in which Gibreel claims to have received the verses directly from Mahound, rather than from God, imply that the book was written without divine intervention. Attributing the Koran to human composition is considered blasphemous in Muslim belief.

Rushdie explained that Gibreel's blasphemous visions were intended to dramatize the struggle between faith and doubt, rather than to insult the Muslim religion. "Gibreel's most painful dreams, the ones at the center of the controversy," Rushdie wrote, "depict the birth and growth of a religion something like Islam, in a magical city of sand named Jahilia (that is 'ignorance,' the name given by Arabs to the period before Islam). Almost all of the alleged 'insults and abuse' are taken from these dream sequences. The first thing to be said about these dreams is that they are *agonizingly painful to the dreamer*. They are a 'nocturnal retribution, a punishment' for his loss of faith. . . . The first purpose of these sequences is not to vilify or 'disprove' Islam, but to portray a soul in crisis, to show how the loss of God can destroy a man's life."

The tale of the brothel was frequently cited by the novel's would-be censors as particularly offensive to Muslims. Rushdie pointed to a distinction often ignored by his critics, that the prostitutes only take the names of the Prophet's wives. The real wives are "living chastely in their harem." "The purpose of the 'brothel sequence,' then," Rushdie explained, "was not to 'insult and abuse' the Prophet's wives, but to dramatize certain ideas about morality; and sexuality, too, because what happens in the brothel . . . is that the men of 'Jahilia' are enabled to act out an ancient dream of power and possession. . . . That men should be so aroused by the great ladies' whorish counterfeits says something about *them*, not the great ladies, and about the extent to which sexual relations have to do with possession."

Rushdie's use of the name "Mahound," the Satanic figure of medieval Christian mystery plays, for the Muhammad-like character of the novel, was also noted as evidence of his invidious intentions. Rushdie described his choice of the name as an example of how his novel "tries in all sorts of ways to reoccupy negative images, to repossess pejorative language." "Even leaving aside the obvious fact that my Mahound is a dream-prophet and not the historical Muhammad," Rushdie wrote, "it may be noted that on page 93 of the novel there is this passage: 'Here he is neither Mahomet nor Moehammered; has adopted, instead, the demon tag the farangis hung around his neck. To turn insults into strengths, whigs, tories, blacks all chose to wear with pride the names that were given in scorn. . . .'"

Rushdie's view that "there are no subjects that are off limits and that includes God, includes prophets" was clearly not shared by those who urged banning of the novel. "The use of fiction was a way of creating the sort of distance from actuality that I felt would prevent offence from being taken," Rushdie declared. "I was wrong."

On February 12, 1989, during violent demonstrations against the book in Islamabad, Pakistan, six people died and 100 were injured. The next day in Srinigar, India, rioting led to the death of another person and the injury of 60. On February 14, Iran's leader, the Ayatollah Khomeini, issued a *fatwa*, or religious edict, against the book.

Khomeini's edict stated: "I inform all zealous Muslims of the world that the author of the book entitled *The Satanic Verses*—which has been compiled, printed, and published in opposition to Islam, the Prophet, and the Qur'an—and all those involved in its publication who were aware of its contents, are sentenced to death. I call on all zealous Muslims to execute them quickly, wherever they find them, so that no one else will dare to insult the

Islamic sanctities. God willing, whoever is killed on this path is a martyr. In addition, anyone who has access to the author of this book, but does not possess the power to execute him, should report him to the people so that he may be punished for his actions."

The 15 Khordad Foundation, an Iranian charity, offered a reward for Rushdie's murder: 1 million dollars was promised if the assassin were non-Iranian and 200 million rials (approximately $750,000) for an Iranian. The reward was later raised by the foundation to 2.5 million dollars. During the days following Khomeini's *fatwa*, several Middle East terrorist organizations sponsored by the Iranian government publicly declared their determination to execute Rushdie. Demonstrations were held outside the British embassy in Tehran, and all books published by Viking Penguin were banned from Iran.

On February 16, Rushdie went into hiding under protection of the British government. Two days later, he issued a public statement regretting that some Muslims might have been offended by his book. "As author of *The Satanic Verses*," he said, "I recognize that Muslims in many parts of the world are genuinely distressed by the publication of my novel. I profoundly regret the distress that the publication has occasioned to sincere followers of Islam. Living as we do in a world of many faiths, this experience has served to remind us that we must all be conscious of the sensibilities of others." Khomeini responded with a statement refusing the apology and confirming the death sentence. "Even if Salman Rushdie repents and becomes the most pious man of [our] time," he declared, "it is incumbent on every Muslim to employ everything he has, his life and his wealth, to send him to hell."

On February 22, *The Satanic Verses* was published in the United States. Hundreds of threats against booksellers prompted two major bookstore chains temporarily to remove the book from a third of the nation's bookstores. On February 28, two independently owned bookstores in Berkeley, California, were firebombed.

Violent demonstrations continued to occur in India, Pakistan and Bangladesh during the month after Khomeini's edict. On February 24, 12 people died during rioting in Bombay. Nonviolent protests against the book also took place in Sudan, Turkey, Malaysia, the Philippines, Hong Kong and Japan. On March 7, Britain broke off diplomatic relations with Iran. Later that month, two moderate Muslim religious leaders in Belgium who had publicly expressed opposition to the death sentence against Rushdie were shot dead in Brussels.

In mid-March, the Organization of the Islamic Conference, while it refused to endorse the death threat, voted to call on its 46 member governments to prohibit the book. Most countries with large Muslim populations banned the sale or importation of *The Satanic Verses*. The Revolutionary Government of Zanzibar, for example, threatened a sentence of three years in prison and a fine of $2,500 for possession of the book. In Malaysia, the penalty was set at three years in prison and a fine of $7,400. In Indonesia, possession of the book was punishable by a month in prison or a fine. Turkey was the only country with a predominantly Muslim population where it remained legal. Several countries with Muslim minorities, including Papua New Guinea, Thailand, Sri Lanka, Kenya, Tanzania, Liberia and Sierra Leone, also imposed bans.

In some cases, countries with negligible Muslim populations took steps to suppress the book. In Venezuela, owning or reading it was declared a crime under penalty of 15 months' imprisonment. In Japan, the sale of the English-language edition was banned under threat of fines. The governments of Bulgaria and Poland also restricted its distribution. Many countries banned the circulation of issues of magazines, such as *Time, Newsweek, Asiaweek* and *Far Eastern Economic Review*, that had published articles about the controversy.

Despite the bannings, the book was imported and circulated clandestinely in countries where it was forbidden, such as Kuwait, Senegal, Egypt, India and even Iran, where a few copies were smuggled in and passed from hand to hand. As a result of its notoriety, *The Satanic Verses* became a best-seller in Europe and the United States. By the end of 1989, more than 1.1 million copies of hardcover English-language editions had been sold.

On June 3, 1989, the Ayatollah Khomeini died. The edict against Rushdie, however, remained in force, reaffirmed by Iranian government officials. Acts of terrorism related to protests against the book continued to occur. During 1990, five bombings targeted booksellers in England. In July 1991, in separate incidents, Hitoshi Igarashi, the Japanese translator of *The Satanic Verses*, was stabbed to death and its Italian translator, Ettore Capriolo, was seriously wounded. In October 1993, William Nygaard, its Norwegian publisher, was shot and seriously injured. Rushdie has remained in hiding under the protection of Scotland Yard. Though his public appearances have increased in number and he has been able to travel outside Britain, he is still under around-the-clock protection by British government security services. In 1998 the Iranian government, headed by President Syed Mohammad Khatami, publicly disassociated itself from the *fatwa* against Rushdie. But religious conservatives confirmed their resolve to carry out the *fatwa*, and the 15 Khordad Foundation in Iran raised the reward for Rushdie's murder by $300,000.

FURTHER READINGS

Appignanesi, Lisa, and Sara Maitland, eds. *The Rushdie File.* Syracuse, N.Y.: Syracuse University Press, 1990.

Barnes, Julian. "Staying Alive." *The New Yorker* (February 21, 1994): 99–105.

For Rushdie: Essays by Arab and Muslim Writers in Defense of Free Speech. New York: George Braziller, 1994.

Harrison, James. *Salman Rushdie.* New York: Twayne Publishers, 1992.

Levy, Leonard W. *Blasphemy: Verbal Offense Against the Sacred, from Moses to Salman Rushdie.* New York: Alfred A. Knopf, 1993.

Pipes, Daniel. *The Rushdie Affair: The Novel, the Ayatollah, and the West.* New York: Carol Publishing Group, 1990.

Rushdie, Salman. *Imaginary Homelands: Essays and Criticism 1981–1991.* New York: Penguin Books, 1991.

Ruthven, Malise. *A Satanic Affair: Salman Rushdie and the Wrath of Islam.* London: Hogarth Press, 1991.

Weatherby, W. J. *Salman Rushdie: Sentenced to Death.* New York: Carroll and Graf Publishers, 1990.

THE SORROWS OF YOUNG WERTHER

Author: Johann Wolfgang von Goethe
Original date and place of publication: 1774, 1787, Germany
Literary form: Novel

SUMMARY

The Sorrows of Young Werther is the first novel of the great German poet, playwright and novelist Johann Wolfgang von Goethe. This epistolary romance about a hopeless love affair and a young man's suicide achieved immediate and lasting success and won fame for its 25-year-old author. First published in German in 1774 and translated into every major European language soon after, it was one of the literary sensations of the century. The novel's romantic sensibilities struck a chord among the youth of Europe, who admired it with a cult-like fervor.

The story is told in the form of letters sent by a young man named Werther to a friend, Wilhelm, over the 18 months between May 1771 and December 1772. Book One collects Werther's letters over an idyllic spring and summer in the rural hamlet of Wahlheim. He describes his pleasure at the natural beauties of the area, his peaceful existence in a secluded cottage surrounded by a garden and his delight in the simple folk he meets.

"I am experiencing the kind of happiness that God dispenses only to his saints," he writes on June 21. At a ball he has met a young woman named Charlotte (Lotte), the beautiful and charming daughter of a judge. Though he realizes that she is engaged to be married to Albert, who is away, Werther becomes deeply infatuated with Lotte, to the point of obsession. He visits her daily and begins to object to the time she spends with other acquaintances. At the end of July, Albert returns and the joyous idyll with Lotte must come to an end.

He spends a miserable six weeks in the couple's company in the throes of a hopeless and frustrating passion. In August he writes: "My full, warm enjoyment of all living things that used to overwhelm me with so much delight and transform the world around me into a paradise has been turned into unbearable torment. . . ." In early September he leaves the area to escape the tensions of the situation.

THE SORROWS OF YOUNG WERTHER

Book Two covers the remaining 13 months of Werther's life. He becomes a secretary to an ambassador whom he dislikes. Expressing his boredom at the social aspirations of the "horrible people" with whom he must associate, he chafes at the responsibilities of his position. When he hears the news that Lotte and Albert have married, he resigns his post to become companion to a prince at his country estate, but remains discontented. Returning to Wahlheim, he begins to see Lotte and Albert again. His letters become more depressed, speaking of feelings of emptiness and the wish that he might go to sleep and not wake up again.

After Werther's letter of December 6, 1772, an unnamed editor takes over to fill in the account of the last weeks in Werther's life, referring to letters and notes left behind. Werther had become more depressed, exhausted and anxious. Lotte suggested that he visit her less frequently. One night when Albert was away, Werther went to Lotte's house. After he seized her in a wild embrace she fled in fear and locked herself in her room. The next day he sent his servant to Albert to borrow a brace of pistols to take on a journey. After writing in a final letter to Lotte that "it has been given to only a few noble beings to shed their blood for those they love, and by their death to create a new life a hundred times better for their friends," Werther shot himself in the head. He died the next day without regaining consciousness. The workmen of the village carried his body to its resting place under the trees at Wahlheim and "no priest attended him."

Goethe once remarked on the autobiographical nature of much of his fiction, saying that all his works were "fragments of a great confession." *The Sorrows of Young Werther* was inspired by two incidents in Goethe's life. Werther's relationship with Lotte is based on Goethe's unhappy infatuation with Charlotte Buff, the fiancée of his friend G. C. Kestner. Suffering from depression over the unfulfilled relationship with Charlotte, Goethe was also deeply affected by the suicide of Karl Wilhelm Jerusalem, a friend from Wetzlar who was secretary to the Brunswick ambassador. Snubbed by aristocratic society and in love with the wife of a colleague, Jerusalem shot himself.

Goethe wrote in his memoirs, *My Life: Poetry and Truth*, "Suddenly I heard of Jerusalem's death and hot upon the general rumors, an exact and involved description of the entire incident. In that moment, the plan of Werther was found, the whole thing crystallized, like water in a glass that is on the point of freezing and can be turned to ice immediately with the slightest motion." Goethe said that he breathed into the work all the passion that results when there is no difference between fact and fiction.

CENSORSHIP HISTORY

Upon its publication in 1774, *The Sorrows of Young Werther* was greeted with enthusiasm by readers throughout Europe. The 20th-century German writer Thomas Mann, whose novel *Lotte in Weimar* was based on the central situation of *The Sorrows of Young Werther*, wrote, "As for Werther, all the riches of [Goethe's] gift were apparent. . . . The extreme, nerve-shattering sensitivity of the little book . . . evoked a storm of applause which went beyond all bounds and fairly intoxicated the world." It was "the spark that fell into the powder keg causing the sudden expansion of forces that had been awaiting release."

By proclaiming the rights of emotion, the book expressed the creed of youth protesting against the rationalism and moralism of the older generation. Goethe became the spokesman for his generation. The novel was a grand expression of the spirit of the Age of Sentiment and the first great achievement of what would later be called confessional literature.

The knowledge that Goethe's story was based on real events, particularly the suicide of young Karl Wilhelm Jerusalem, added to the "Werther fever" that swept the continent and was to last for decades after the novel's publication. There were sequels, parodies, imitations, operas, plays, songs and poems based on the story. Ladies wore Eau de Werther cologne, jewelry and fans. Men sported Werther's blue dress jacket and yellow vest. Figures of Werther and Lotte were modeled in export porcelain in China. Within 12 years, 20 unauthorized editions were issued in Germany. In England, by the end of the century there were 26 separate editions of a translation from French. Napoleon told Goethe that he had read the novel seven times. Pilgrims came from all over Europe to visit Karl Wilhelm Jerusalem's grave, where they made speeches and left flowers. A 19th-century English travel book guided visitors to the spot.

Werther's suicide inspired some young men and women in Germany and France to take their own lives, with copies of Goethe's novel in their pockets. Though it is not clear whether the suicides would have occurred anyway in the absence of Goethe's novel, Goethe was assailed by critics who saw the novel as having a corrupting influence and encouraging a morbid sensibility. Clergy preached sermons against the book. The Leipzig theological faculty applied for a ban of the novel on the grounds that it recommended suicide. Within two days, the city council imposed the prohibition. In Denmark in 1776, a proposed translation was forbidden as not being in accordance with Lutheran doctrine, established by the Crown as the orthodox faith of the nation.

Goethe wrote of the novel in his memoirs: "I had saved myself from a situation into which I had been driven through my own fault. . . . I felt like a man after absolute confession, happy and free again, with the rights to a new life. But just as I had felt relieved and lighthearted because I had succeeded in transforming reality into poetry, my friends were confusing themselves by believing that they had to turn poetry into reality, enact the novel and shoot themselves! What actually took place among a few, happened later *en masse*, and this little book that had done me so much good acquired the reputation of being extremely harmful!"

During the years 1783–87, Goethe revised the novel. In the definitive text of 1787 he added material intended to emphasize Werther's mental disturbance and dissuade readers from following Werther's example of suicide. The note to readers that precedes Book One reads "And you, good soul, who feel a compulsive longing such as his, draw consolation from his sorrows, and let this little book be your friend whenever through fate or through your own fault you can find no closer companion."

The Sorrows of Young Werther was censored again 163 years after its publication. In 1939, the government of Spanish dictator Francisco Franco ordered libraries purged of works by "such disgraceful writers as Goethe."

FURTHER READING

Friedenthal, Richard. *Goethe: His Life and Times.* New York: World Publishing Co., 1963.
Goethe, Johann Wolfgang von. *The Sorrows of Young Werther.* Trans. and intro. by Michael Hulse. London: Penguin Books, 1989.
————. *The Sorrows of Young Werther and Selected Writings.* Trans. by Catherine Hutter. Foreword by Hermann J. Weigand. New York: New American Library, 1962.
————. *The Sufferings of Young Werther.* Trans. and intro. by Bayard Quincy Morgan. New York: Frederick Ungar Publishing Co., 1957.

THE TALMUD

Original date and place of composition: Palestine and Mesopotamia, ca. A.D. 200–500
Literary form: Religious text

SUMMARY

The Talmud, a collection of teachings set down by the Jewish scholars of antiquity, is the compendium of the oral law and tradition of Judaism. The word *Talmud* comes from the Hebrew word meaning "instruction." The collection has two main components: the Mishnah, the book of law written in Hebrew, and the commentaries on the Mishnah, known as the Talmud or Gemarah, written in Aramaic. Talmudic sages believed that God revealed two Torahs to Moses. One was the Scriptures, or written books. The other, the Mishnah, was preserved in oral traditions handed down through many centuries and compiled toward the end of the second century. The material of the Mishnah is arranged in six groups, called orders, that deal with agriculture, the sabbath and festivals, marriage, civil and criminal law, ritual sacrifices and cleanliness. The orders are subdivided into 63 tracts or books.

Oral explanations and commentaries that developed around the Mishnah over the centuries were later put into written form and called the Gemarah. The Mishnah serves as text and the Gemarah as a series of comments and notes. Two versions of the Gemarah exist: one compiled in the fourth century by the scholars of Palestine, and the other in the fifth century by the scholars of Babylonia, which became the authoritative work. The Talmud is considered, with the Hebrew Bible, as a central pillar of Judaism and the most important book in Jewish culture. It is the accepted religious authority among all Orthodox Jews.

CENSORSHIP HISTORY

The history of suppression of the Talmud is many centuries long. Early attempts to ban it date at least to the seventh and eighth centuries. During the Middle Ages, with the revival of learning and the appearance of books of theological speculation, the Catholic Church began to adopt a more severe attitude toward suspect books. It began to examine Jewish literature and the Talmud more intensively.

In 1144 in Paris, the Talmud was burned by the Catholic Church on charges of blasphemy and immorality. Other incidents of censorship were recorded during the next hundred years. The anti-Talmudic campaign reached its height in 1239, when Pope Gregory IX ordered all Jewish books to be burned. He acted on allegations of heresy in the Talmud brought by Jewish converts to Christianity. Gregory sent letters to the kings and prelates of England, France, Navarre, Aragon, Castile and Portugal, ordering that on a sabbath during the following Lent, while Jews worshiped in their synagogues, the books should be seized and delivered to the mendicant friars for examination, and that these books deemed heretical should be destroyed. The order was carried out fully only in France.

In 1244, Pope Innocent IV ordered Louis IX of France to burn all copies of the Talmud. This order was repeated in 1248, when 20 wagonloads of books were burned in Paris, and again in 1254. In 1264 in Rome, Pope Clement IV appointed a committee of censors to expunge all passages from the Talmud that appeared derogatory to Christianity, allowing Jews to keep only expurgated versions. Three years later, Clement IV instructed the king of Aragon to force Jews to deliver Talmuds to inquisitors.

Numerous instances of official burnings of the Talmud were recorded in France in the 14th century, as the anti-Jewish polemic continued. In 1415, Pope Benedict XII ordered all copies of Talmudic books delivered to bishops for preservation subject to papal instructions. Jews themselves were forbidden to possess copies of any material considered antagonistic to Christianity, and could not ready or study the Talmud. A church synod in Basel in 1431 reaffirmed the stringent ban.

Because so many copies of the Talmud had been lost over the centuries, there was great interest among Jews in the new 15th-century technology of the printing press. The first printed edition of the Talmud appeared in Guadalajara, Spain, in 1482. But the Talmud soon became a target of the Spanish Inquisition. In 1490 in Spain, the Grand Inquisitor Torquemada burned Hebrew books by order of Ferdinand and Isabella; he later conducted at

Salamanca an auto-da-fé, or burning, of more than 6,000 volumes described as books of magic or infected with Jewish errors. When the Jews were expelled from Spain and Portugal, all Jewish books were confiscated.

In 1509, Johannes Pfefferkorn, a priest and Jewish convert to Christianity, advocated destruction of Hebrew books in all countries under the rule of the Holy Roman Emperor. Emperor Maximillian requested the opinion of another priest, Johann Reuchlin. Reuchlin, who had published the first Hebrew grammar for Christians, argued that to understand the Old Testament it was necessary to collect and study Hebrew manuscripts rather than destroying them. He suggested that Jews be required to furnish books for the universities and that chairs of Hebrew learning be instituted in every university in Germany. His recommendation was met by intense opposition, to which he responded in *Augenspiegel* (Mirror of the Eye) in 1511. He distinguished anti-Christian polemics from classical works in Hebrew, which he believed should be preserved. A sustained controversy developed between the humanists who supported Reuchlin and the clerics and leaders of the Inquisition who supported Pfefferkorn. In 1521, the Roman curia suppressed Reuchlin's writings against Pfefferkorn.

In 1520, Pope Leo X gave permission for the publication and printing of the Talmud in Venice, and several editions appeared in the next few decades. In the 1530s, Martin Luther, convinced that Christians in Moravia were being induced to convert to Judaism, urged that Jews be deported to Palestine, forbidden to practice usury, their synagogues burned and their books destroyed. German principalities expelled Jews from certain localities and suppressed their books. In other German cities, such as Frankfurt and Worms, Jews were tolerated.

As the Counter-Reformation and the church's battle against heresy and the power of the printing press intensified, Pope Julius III in 1553 halted the printings of the Talmud allowed by Pope Leo X. In 1555, the houses of Jews were searched, and Jews were ordered under pain of death to surrender all books blaspheming Christ. Princes, bishops and inquisitors were instructed to confiscate the Talmud. The books were collected and burned on the first day of Rosh Hashanah, the Jewish New Year. Christians were forbidden under threat of excommunication to possess or read Jewish books or to aid Jews by producing copies in script or by printing. Jewish books, including rare rabbinic manuscripts, were burned by the thousands in Italian cities. Some 12,000 volumes of Hebrew texts were burned after the inquisitor Sixtus of Siena destroyed the library of the Hebrew school at Cremona. The Talmud was not published again in Renaissance Italy.

The harshness of Julius III's decree was somewhat alleviated by Pope Pius IV in 1559, who allowed distribution of the Talmud only if those sections that offended Christianity were erased. As a result of this decision, a truncated and expurgated edition was printed in Basel under the supervision of Catholic monks. Subsequent editions were often similarly expurgated. In many European countries, where the Talmud could be printed only with official permission, licensing was confined to Christian printers.

The church's first Index of Forbidden Books in 1559 included the Talmud. Under the revised Index prepared by the Council of Trent in 1564, all works of Jewish doctrine were banned, except those permitted by the pope after the Jewish community offered a substantial financial "gift."

In 1592, Pope Clement VIII issued a bull forbidding either Christians or Jews from owning, reading, buying or circulating "impious talmudic books or manuscripts" or writings in Hebrew or other languages that "tacitly or expressly contain heretical or erroneous statements against the Holy Scriptures of the Old Law and Testament." Any such work, whether expurgated or not, was to be destroyed. In 1596, this ruling was modified when the publication of the Machsor, the basic Hebrew prayer book, was permitted, but only in Hebrew.

Active suppression of the Talmud by the Catholic Church lasted through the 18th century. In 1629, an Italian cardinal boasted of having collected 10,000 outlawed Jewish books for destruction. As late as 1775, Pope Clement XIV confirmed the prohibitions of previous papal bulls. No Hebrew books could be bought or sold until examined and approved by the church.

In the 20th century, the most extensive censorship of the Talmud was reported in Europe under the Communist Party in the Soviet Union and under the Nazis during the Holocaust. In 1926, the government of the Soviet Union ordered that religiously dogmatic books such as the Talmud could be left in the large libraries but must be removed from the small ones. Virtually no printing of the work was allowed after that time. A Russian translation, the first in any language to be permitted since the 1917 revolution, was recently undertaken under the sponsorship of the Russian Academy of Sciences. In 1939, most of the schools of Jewish learning in Europe were totally destroyed by the Nazis. Innumerable copies of Jewish religious texts were lost during the Holocaust.

For Western Christianity, a change in attitudes toward the Talmud was brought about by the Second Vatican Council in 1965, which deplored anti-Semitism and the persecution of Jews, emphasizing the church's biblical connection to Judaism and the common religious heritage of Christians and Jews.

FURTHER READINGS

Bainton, Roland. *Here I Stand: A Life of Martin Luther*. New York: Penguin Group, 1995.

Burman, Edward. *The Inquisition: Hammer of Heresy*. New York: Dorset Press, 1992.

Green, Jonathon. *The Encyclopedia of Censorship*. New York: Facts On File, 1990.

Haight, Anne Lyon. *Banned Books: 387 B.C. to 1978 A.D.* Updated and enlarged by Chandler B. Grannis. New York: R. R. Bowker, 1978.

Hertzberg, Arthur. "Swimming without Drowning: New Approaches to the Ocean of the Talmud." *The New York Times Book Review* (March 27, 1994): 12–14.

Lea, Henry Charles. *History of the Inquisition of the Middle Ages*. Vol. 1. New York: Russell & Russell, 1955.

Levy, Leonard W. *Blasphemy: Verbal Offense Against the Sacred, from Moses to Salman Rushdie*. New York: Alfred A. Knopf, 1993.

Peters, Edward. *Inquisition*. New York: Free Press, 1988.

Putnam, George Haven. *The Censorship of the Church of Rome*. Vol. 1 New York: G. P. Putnam's Sons, 1906–7.

Steinsaltz, Adin. *The Essential Talmud*. New York: Basic Books, 1976.

LITERATURE SUPPRESSED ON SEXUAL GROUNDS

Changing social mores have moved many books formerly forbidden because of explicit sexual content out of locked cabinets and onto the open shelves in libraries and bookstores. Many such books have also entered high school and college classrooms to be read by students who little realize their notorious pasts.

A changed society has taken literary criticism out of the courts. In 1961, the United States Supreme Court pondered if D. H. Lawrence's *Lady Chatterley's Lover* was lewd or literary. By 1969, the novel was required reading in college literature courses. The same is true of other works, such as James Joyce's *Ulysses*, Vladimir Nabokov's *Lolita*, Henry Miller's *Tropic of Cancer* and Voltaire's *Candide*, all once banned and considered indecent. When did the "obscene" and the "pornographic" become the "erotic" and the "classic?"

Dirty words alone are not enough to make a work erotic, although many books in the 19th and early 20th centuries were banned simply for that reason. Similarly, many books have been banned because they discussed or alluded to such familiar social phenomena as prostitution, unwed pregnancy and adultery, among them Thomas Hardy's *Jude the Obscure* and Nathaniel Hawthorne's *Scarlet Letter*. Neither can reasonably be termed an erotic or pornographic work, yet both books were banned for their sexual content.

In 1957, the U.S. Supreme Court changed its definition of obscenity to refer to works that had sexual content but no "redeeming social importance." This redefinition sent Americans in search of works both erotically interesting and socially redeeming, and thus legally sexually titillating. Anonymous Victorian novels, the underground pornography of their day, joined art books with lavish reproductions of Japanese and Indian erotic painting and sculpture and explicit psychological case studies of sexually "abnormal" behavior as the standard middle-class erotica of the early to mid-20th century. During that time, American courts tried obscenity cases and pondered the literary merits of *Fanny Hill, or Memoirs of a Woman of Pleasure, Lady Chatterley's Lover, Ulysses* and *Tropic of Capricorn.*

By 1970, the barriers were down and the Report of the United States President's Commission on Obscenity noted that "Virtually every English language book thought to be obscene when published, and many similar books translated into English, have been reissued by secondary publishers. The entire stockpile of 'classic erotic literature' (e.g., *The Kama Sutra,* Frank Harris, de Sade, etc.) published over centuries has thus come onto the market."

As formerly banned works gained acceptance, many novels published in the last two decades have benefited and freely include sexual detail and gratuitous sex scenes. Society's view of sex has changed and many books that would once have been condemned as pornographic or obscene now become best-sellers. Even cheaply produced "adult" books that do not pretend to any purpose other than sexual arousal are now easily available to willing buyers through direct mail and retail stores. The legal line between pornography and erotica has disappeared, and the differences are now defined more according to aesthetic appeal than to content.

But, how is "erotic" different from "pornographic?" Nineteenth-century booksellers coined the term *erotica* to describe risqué writing found in such classics as the poems of Catullus, the satires of Juvenal and love manuals such as the *Kama Sutra,* as well as that perennial favorite, *Fanny Hill, or Memoirs of a Woman of Pleasure* (1748–49), the subject of the first U.S. obscenity trial in 1821. These early works bore no resemblance to the cheaply produced, and cheap-looking, books of the mid-20th century. The market catered to men of means who could well afford the lavishly illustrated deluxe editions that satisfied what was termed their "curious" tastes. Patrons paid handsomely for their pleasure.

The growth of mass demand for erotica required mass production, and cheaply produced pulp novels with lurid covers and plotless texts appeared in great number. These contrasted strongly in appearance with the lavishly illustrated and expensively produced gentlemen's erotica of the 19th century, but they were identical in purpose. Price was the primary distinguishing factor. The differences became so blurred that the 1970 Report of the United States President's Commission on Obscenity struggled and failed to define what was obscene and pornographic, and thus illegal.

The definitions were no clearer in 1986, when the Attorney General's Commission on Pornography (often called the Meese Commission) revealed that its findings were inconclusive regarding the dangers of pornography. Although the Commission recommended intensified enforcement against child pornography and material showing sexual violence, the Commission members hedged in their recommendations regarding all-text materials. The panel recommended "extraordinary caution" in regard to prosecuting those who distributed materials that contained no photographs, pictures or drawings.

"The written word has had and continues to have a special place in this and any other civilization." Designating as among the "least harmful" types of pornography "books consisting of the printed text only," the Commission observed that such text might not always meet its criteria for pornography, that it be "sexually explicit and intended primarily for the purpose of sexual arousal."

The century and a half of obscenity trials regarding literature came to a halt, and the old argument was invalidated. Those who could read could indulge themselves in the provocative power of words that arouse, stimulate and titillate—they were consumers of "erotica." The less literate, more likely to view X-rated videos or picture magazines that arouse, stimulate and titillate, were indulging in "pornography." The appeal of the categories is the same, but their audiences differed as did the assumed consequences.

The goal of this section of works censored on grounds of sexual content is neither to deride nor defend either the mainstream erotica or the pulp pornography that has been published over the centuries. Instead, it is to illuminate changing cultural attitudes toward the erotic, through a survey of the legal fate of classic and representative works in centuries past as well as in the 20th century.

—Dawn B. Sova, Ph.D

AN AMERICAN TRAGEDY

Author: Theodore Dreiser
Original date and place of publication: 1925, United States
Original publisher: Boni & Liveright
Literary form: Novel

SUMMARY

An American Tragedy is a fictionalized version of the Chester Gillette murder case that was tried in 1906. The story examines the manner in which one man's fate is determined by his background, personality and environmental conditions that lead him to desire luxuries and perquisites beyond his reach. The novel was originally published in two volumes, a first part that recounts events that lead to a death and a second part that relates the story of the murder trial.

Clyde Griffiths is the son of street evangelists whose skid-row mission income cannot provide him with the fine clothes, high social status and sophisticated friends that he craves. As a bellhop in an expensive Kansas City hotel, he comes into contact with wealthy people who have everything that he wishes to possess. He also explores his sexual needs in his infatuation with Hortense Briggs, on whom he spends his salary. After he accidentally kills a pedestrian in an automobile accident, Clyde leaves Kansas City and travels to Lycurgus, New York, where his uncle gives him a job as a supervisor in the family collar factory. Clyde also makes his first visit to a brothel in a scene that describes both the interior of the brothel and the variety of girls available to him. His chosen partner leads him upstairs to a room and "calmly, and before a tall mirror which revealed her fully to herself and him, began to disrobe."

Wishing for a "free pagan girl of his own," Clyde becomes sexually involved with Roberta Alden, a factory worker who believes that he loves her. Although their sexual activity is not graphically described, the reader is clearly aware that their relationship is not platonic as they struggle "in vain against the greater intimacy which each knew that the other was desirous of yielding to, and eventually so yielding, looked forward to the approaching night with an eagerness which was a fever embodying a fear." The affair proceeds, but Clyde becomes infatuated with and hopes to marry the daughter of a wealthy factory owner. When he tries to break off his relationship with Roberta, he learns that she is pregnant. Despite his efforts to arrange an abortion through visits to pharmacists and a doctor, Roberta remains pregnant and insists that Clyde honor his promise to marry her. They take a day trip into the Adirondack mountains, and Roberta drowns in an isolated lake when their boat tips and she tumbles overboard. Clyde fails to save her, and the author leaves unclear whether or not he had even tried. Although Clyde runs away, he is caught and placed on trial. Eventually convicted, he is sentenced to die in the electric chair, but up until his death he remains unsure whether or not he committed a murder.

CENSORSHIP HISTORY

In 1929, *An American Tragedy* was suppressed in Boston after a jury declared New York publisher Donald Friede guilty of violating the Massachusetts antiobscenity statute by selling the novel. In the case of *Commonwealth v. Friede*, Mass. 318, 171 N.E. 472 (1930), the attorney for the Watch and Ward Society read various passages in the courtroom, and neither the judge nor the members of the jury read the entire novel. After reading the passage regarding the scene in the brothel when the girl begins to undress, the prosecuting attorney stated to the all-male jury: "*Well*, perhaps where the gentleman who published this book comes from it is not considered obscene, indecent, and impure for a woman to start disrobing before a man, but it happens to be out in Roxbury where *I* come from."

When Friede's attorney Arthur Garfield Hays and Dreiser asked the court to consider the entire book rather than merely specific passages, the judge refused. The defense also brought in noted trial attorney Clarence Darrow, whose main role consisted of reading passages from the book aloud. Hays had intended to question Dreiser in a way that would allow the author to show that he had never intended to write an indecent or obscene book, but Dreiser was denied that opportunity as the judge excluded all of the defense attorney's questions. Friede was convicted of selling an "impure and obscene" book, although he received no sentence. In May 1930, the publisher appealed the case but the Massachusetts Supreme Court upheld the conviction in *Commonwealth v. Friede*, 271 Mass. 318, 171 N.E. 472, 69 A.L.R. 640 (Sup. Jud. Ct. 1930) and forced Friede to pay a fine of $300. The trial judge refused to allow the entire book to be read in court, ruling that it would have been impractical to read the whole book to the jury and observing that omission of the allegedly obscene passages would have eliminated nothing essential from the novel. The court also overruled the appeal of the bookseller, who had been entrapped into selling the book. The irony is that, while the trial was in progress, the novel was required reading across the Charles River in a Harvard University English course.

The public outcry over *An American Tragedy* motivated the Massachusetts legislature to reform the laws regarding censorship. Of several bills that were proposed, a law that would have required the whole book rather than excerpts to be considered in court was defeated on April 1, 1929, in the Massachusetts Senate in a vote of 15 to 13. The bill was submitted a second time and again defeated, this time with a vote of 20 to 17.

FURTHER READING

Boyer, Paul S. "Boston Book Censorship in the Twenties." *American Quarterly* 15 (Spring 1930): 3–24.

Bullard, F. Lauriston. "Boston's Ban Likely to Live Long." *New York Times* (April 28, 1929): Sec. 3: 1, 7.

Gilloti, Chris F. "Book Censorship in Massachusetts: The Search for a Test of Obscenity." *Boston University Law Review* 42 (Fall 1962): 476–91.

Grant, Sidney S., and S. E. Angoff. "Recent Developments in Censorship." *Boston University Law Review* 10 (November 1930): 488–509.

Markmann, Charles L. *The Noblest Cry: A History of the American Civil Liberties Union.* New York: St. Martin's, 1965.

"More of the Same: Massachusetts Supreme Court and Dreiser's *American Tragedy*." *Outlook* 155 (June 11, 1930): 214.

Schriftgiesser, Karl. "Boston Stays Pure." *New Republic* 58 (May 8, 1929): 327–29.

THE ARABIAN NIGHTS or THE THOUSAND AND ONE NIGHTS

Translator: Sir Richard Burton
Original date and place of publication: 1881, England; 1885–88, Switzerland
Original publisher: Worthington Book Company; The Kama Shastra Society
Literary form: Collected folktales

SUMMARY

Long considered merely children's entertainment, the tales of *The Arabian Nights* were familiar to English readers through such stories as "Sinbad the Sailor," "Aladdin and His Lamp" and "Ali Baba and the Forty Thieves." Of Persian, Indian and Arabic folk origin, the tales were first collected in Cairo around 1450 and known as *The Book of a Thousand and One Nights*. The French translation by Antoine Galland, published privately from 1707 to 1717, brought the tales to the attention of Europeans, and countless adaptations were published in England and the United States in the 18th and 19th centuries.

All editions have followed the same story framework. The storyteller is Shahrazad (Scheherazade in other translations), who begins the tales as a means of staying alive. After ordering beheadings of his queen and 10 favorite concubines who had cuckolded him, the Sultan Shahryar (Schahriah in other translations) marries each night for three years a new wife who is strangled at daybreak. When his country protests the depletion of available young women to become queen for a night, he marries Shahrazad, who asks that her sister Dinarzade remain with her. Shahrazad begins a story for her sister one hour before daybreak on her wedding night. Shahryar also listens and becomes intrigued, but Shahrazad stops midstory at daybreak. Because Shahryar wants to know how the story ends, he spares her life and asks her to continue the story that evening. Cunning Shahrazad continues her story but ends midstory each daybreak for 1,001 nights, by the end of which she has borne three children, told 270 tales, and earned her husband's trust and love.

Edward William Lane published privately the first English translation in 1840 and John Payne's *The Arabian Nights* appeared in 1881, but Sir Richard Burton's translation remains the most complete and alone captures the tone of the original, although it has generally remained unavailable. Lane translated fewer than half of the tales and omitted sexual references. Payne translated substantially more tales and many of the tales lack sexual incidents while other tales contain metaphoric sexual references: "She did off her clothes and I had a lover's privacy of her and found her an unpierced pearl and a filly no man had ridden." Animal-human intercourse is reported and thighs, breasts and buttocks are frequently mentioned.

Burton, whose translation includes even more explicit sexual detail, wrote in his foreword that he translated the tales into language "as the Arab would have written in English." Thus, they are exuberant, earthy and unembarrassed tales of lust, lesbianism, sodomy, bestiality, male transvestism, pederasty, incest and sexual mutilation. His sexually willing slave girls, nubile virgins, omnipresent eunuchs, lecherous old women and wine-induced lust entice the reader. Although most of the descriptions of sexual behavior are tastefully presented with euphemisms, the sexual nature of the actions is clear. One story details a porter's carousing with three ladies who admire and toy with his "prickle" while he teases about "thy slit, thy womb, thy coynte, thy clitoris." Several seductions begin as a man and a woman "warm with wine" embrace with "kisses and murmurs of pleasure and amorous toyings," after which they indulge in "hot lust" before having "abated her maidenhead."

Included in Burton's translation is the lengthy "Terminal Essay," which devotes one-quarter of its 166 pages to analyzing, describing and evaluating on a country-by-country basis the variations of pederasty and sodomy with which he had become familiar in his years of travel. Written in the language of the social anthropologist and quoting the writings of travelers, historians and medical experts, he identifies known homosexual liaisons from history and describes the practices as well as the social roles of pederasts and homosexuals in history and in the 19th century.

CENSORSHIP HISTORY

The Obscene Publications Act was passed in 1857 with the express purpose of suppressing sexually explicit material, and fear of prosecution made Burton cautious. Although he did not expurgate his work, he did modify greatly the manner in which it was published. He had 1,000 copies of the work printed in Benares, India, at his own expense and named the Kama Shastra Society, of which he and fellow author Foster Fitzgerald Arbuthnot were founders and sole members, as the publisher. The first printing was sold to subscribers for the equivalent of $200 in today's currency. The books were financially successful, and Burton made a profit of 10,000 guineas ($25,000 in 1890s currency).

Burton claimed that *The Arabian Nights* was meant only for men and particularly for male scholars who wished to increase their understanding of other cultures. As Rice reports, Burton was denounced in the *Edinburgh Review* as "a man who knows thirty-five languages and dialects, especially that of pornography" and an authority on "all that relates to the bestial element in man." His lengthy work was called by another reviewer "an extraordinary agglomeration of filth."

After Burton's death, abridged forms of his work were published, but the full unexpurgated version remained unavailable to the public—and was banned by U.S. Customs—until after 1931. When Burton died, his wife, Lady Isabel, destroyed all of his private papers, as well as the original notes and manuscript for *The Arabian Nights*. She also entrusted William Coote, secretary of the National Vigilance Association, to burn books and papers after her death to remove all remaining "indecencies."

Payne's translation was one of a number of expensive editions of literary classics, including Boccaccio's THE DECAMERON, Queen Margaret of Navarre's *The Heptameron*, Rabelais's *Gargantua and Pantagruel*, Fielding's *History of Tom Jones*, Rousseau's CONFESSIONS and Ovid's THE ART OF LOVE (*ARS AMATORIA*), involved in the civil case *In re Worthington Company*, 30 N.Y.S. 361(1894). In 1894, the New York Society for the Suppression of Vice, under the zealous leadership of Anthony Comstock, brought civil proceedings against the bankrupt Worthington Book Publishing Company that sought the right to sell off assets. The receiver for the company asked the court to allow sale of the books, expensive volumes of world-renowned literary classics. Comstock appeared in the court record as opposing the sale.

In stating the decision of the court, Judge Morgan J. O'Brien stated that "a seeker after the sensual and degrading parts of a narrative may find in all these works, as in those of other great authors, something to satisfy his pruriency," but he added that to simply condemn an entire literary work because of a few episodes "would compel the exclusion from circulation of a very large proportion of the works of fiction of the most famous writers of the English language." The court decision characterized the specific editions as being "choice editions, both as to the letter-press and the bindings . . . as to prevent their being generally sold or purchased, except by those who would desire them for their literary merit, or for their worth as specimens of fine book-making." In short, even though the text remained the same as that in cheaper editions, Judge O'Brien determined that the "very artistic character, the high qualities of style, the absence of those glaring and crude pictures [set these books] entirely apart from such gross and obscene writings as it is the duty of the public authorities to suppress."

The United States Customs Office continued to ban the import of Burton's unexpurgated translation until 1930, when the Tariff Act removed the ban on acknowledged literary classics.

FURTHER READING

"Anthony Comstock Overruled." *Publishers Weekly* 45 (June 30, 1894): 942–43.

Bercovici, Alfred. *That Blackguard Burton!* Indianapolis, Ind.: Bobbs-Merrill, 1962.

Brodie, Fawn M. *The Devil Drives: A Life of Sir Richard Burton.* New York: Norton, 1967.

Rice, Edward. *Captain Sir Richard Francis Burton.* New York: Scribner's, 1990.

Thomas, Donald. *A Long Time Burning: The History of Literary Censorship in England.* New York: Praeger, 1969.

THE ART OF LOVE (ARS AMATORIA)

Author: Ovid (Publius Ovidius Naso)
Original date and place of publication: ca. A.D. 1, Rome; 1926, England
Original publisher: John Lane Co. (England)
Literary form: Poetry collection

SUMMARY

The Art of Love is a guide to attracting and holding a member of the opposite sex, and it is composed in three parts. The first part gives wise advice to men concerning how to win a mistress; the second part advises men how to retain the interest of the mistress and the third part tells women how they can satisfy the sensual desires of men. Ovid provides suggestions regarding the care of the body and the face, the ways of flattery and the advantages of selecting a mature mistress. Critics have noted parallels between advice given by Benjamin Franklin in "Advice on Choosing a Mistress" and passages from *Ars Amatoria*, such as

> Let me see my girl with eyes that confess her excitement;
> Let her, after she comes, want no more for a while.
> What does youth know of delight? Some things ought not to be
> hurried.
> After some thirty-odd years, lovers begin to learn how.

Ovid also gives women advice regarding how to make the most of their good points, including the ways in which to pose themselves in various situations.

> Lie on your back, if your face and all of your features are
> pretty.
> If your posterior's cute, better be seen from behind
> . . . .
> If the breasts and thighs are lovely to look at,
> Let the man stand and the girl lie on a slant on the bed.

The advice to men is geared toward grooming them to be effective predators, and his advice for women prepares them to be desirable prey.

CENSORSHIP HISTORY

The Art of Love appears to have created difficulties for Ovid in A.D. 8, when Augustus banished Ovid from Rome for political reasons, but historians note that the erotic content of the poems provided a contributing factor. In 1497, in Florence, Italy, *The Art of Love* was burned with the works of Dante for their "immoral" content in Fra. Girolamo Savonarola's Bonfire of the Vanities. In 1564, the work was added to the list of books banned by the Tridentine Index in Rome, for "treating of lascivious or obscene subjects."

In 1892, *The Art of Love* was involved in the litigation of the Worthington Book Publishing Co., which was in financial difficulty. The receiver wanted to sell some of the company stock, including Burton's translation of *THE ARABIAN NIGHTS*, Fielding's *History of Tom Jones*, Boccaccio's *THE DECAMERON*, Queen Margaret of Navarre's *Heptameron*, Rabelais's *Gargantua and Pantagruel* and Rousseau's *CONFESSIONS* to pay off creditors, but Anthony Comstock stepped in to oppose the sales. He demanded of the court that the books be officially burned. (See *THE ARABIAN NIGHTS*.)

In 1926, United States Customs officers in San Francisco held up a new English edition of the *Love Books of Ovid*, illustrated by Jean de Bosschere, published by John Lane Company. The edition had been limited to only 300 copies and was already sold out. The work was banned from importation until the passage of the 1930 amendment to the Tariff Act eased restrictions on foreign classics.

FURTHER READING

Craig, Alec. *Suppressed Books: A History of the Conception of Literary Obscenity*. New York: World Publishing, 1963.
Hurewitz, Leon. *Historical Dictionary of Censorship in the United States*. Westport, Conn.: Greenwood, 1985.
Loth, David. *The Erotic in Literature*. New York: Dorset, 1961.

THE BLUEST EYE

Author: Toni Morrison
Original date and place of publication: 1970, United States
Original publisher: Holt, Rinehart and Winston
Literary form: Novel

SUMMARY

The Bluest Eye is a sad and tragic novel that recounts the abuse and destruction of Pecola Breedlove, a young African-American girl whose mother knew that her very dark baby would grow into an unattractive young girl. The novel, which takes place in 1940, is narrated by Claudia MacTeer, two years younger than Pecola and her only friend. Black in a white-dominated world, Pecola begins to believe that life would be prettier and better if she were white, and she views blue eyes as symbolic of whiteness. She watches her father, Cholly Breedlove, become increasingly violent as his shattered dreams and constant humiliations as an African American heighten his frustrations, and her mother, Pauline, escapes into the clean and orderly life of working as a maid in a white family's home.

Pecola is raped by her father one spring afternoon when he returns home drunk and the two are alone. She becomes pregnant after he rapes her a second time. Traumatized by the attacks, she drifts further from reality and visits fraudulent minister Micah Elihue Whitcomb, known commonly as Soaphead Church, to ask him to give her blue eyes. For a fee, Soaphead claims that he can help her, but she must perform a task for him. He has wanted to rid himself of an old, sick dog, so he gives Pecola poisoned meat to feed the dog but tells her only that feeding the dog will result in a sign regarding her wish. Pecola is horrified as she watches the dog stagger around the yard, then die.

The combination of the rapes and this incident drives Pecola mad, leading to her complete loss of touch with reality. Pecola believes that she does have blue eyes and invents an imaginary friend who is always nearby for reassurance that her eyes are the bluest in the world.

CENSORSHIP HISTORY

Several incidents in the book have sparked controversy. The two rapes of Pecola have been criticized for being too graphic in description, and the novel describes the sounds that Pecola hears of her parents having sex in the room next to hers. Another incident that is specifically described is Cholly's first sexual encounter, during which he is surprised by three white hunters who focus a flashlight on the young people and force them to conclude their sexual act.

The Bluest Eye has been challenged in several school districts because of its "vulgar" and "obscene" language as well as for its "graphic sexual description." In 1994, the novel was removed from the 11th-grade curriculum at Lathrop High School in Fairbanks, Alaska, after parents complained that the language was "obscene" and that it contained explicit sexual episodes. School administrators ordered the book taken off the required reading list and stated as their reasons that "it was a very controversial book; it contains lots of very graphic descriptions and lots of disturbing language."

That same year, the novel was challenged in the West Chester, Pennsylvania, school district and at Morrisville (Pennsylvania) Borough High School. Parents in both districts complained to the school board of education about the "sexual content" of the novel and its "objectionable language." After reviewing the complaint and the book, the boards in both districts rejected the parents' request to remove the book from the school libraries and readings lists.

FURTHER READING

Butler-Evans, Elliott. *Race, Gender and Desire: Narrative Strategies in the Fiction of Toni Cade Bambara and Toni Morrison.* Philadelphia: Temple University Press, 1989.
Kuenz, Jane. "*The Bluest Eye*: Notes on History, Community and Black Female Subjectivity." *African American Review* 27 (Fall 1993): 421–31.
Newsletter on Intellectual Freedom (May 1994): 86; (January 1995): 25; (March 1995): 44–45.
Tirrell, Lynne. "Storytelling and Moral Agency." *Journal of Aesthetics & Art Criticism* 48 (Spring 1990): 115–26.
Weinstein, Philip M. *What Else but Love? The Ordeal of Race in Faulkner and Morrison.* New York: Columbia University Press, 1996.

CANDIDE

Author: Voltaire (François-Marie Arouet)
Original date and place of publication: 1759, Switzerland
Original publisher: Gabriel and Philibert Cramer
Literary form: Satire

SUMMARY

Candide, originally *Candide, ou l'optimisme*, is a satire of optimism and of the belief that "the world is the best of all possible worlds and everything in it is a necessary evil," a theory attributed to the philosopher Gottfried Leibniz. Voltaire refused to accept the philosopher's assertion that evil and death are part of a universal harmony, and he structured *Candide* to show the ridiculous nature of such thought. Voltaire hid his identity when publishing the book, noting that it was "translated from the German of Doctor Ralph with the additions which were found in the Doctor's pocket when he died at Minden in the Year of Our Lord 1759."

The work recounts the adventures of Candide, a young man educated by the optimist philosopher Pangloss to believe that the world in which he lives is "the best of all possible worlds." He lives at the castle of Baron Thunder-ten-tronckh and falls in love with the baron's beautiful daughter, Cunegonde. Caught kissing the young woman, Candide is ejected from the castle and begins to roam the world, penniless and hungry. He is witness to natural and social catastrophes, including the great earthquake of Lisbon and the terror of the

Inquisition, in which numerous people suffer. On his journey, Candide becomes reacquainted with Cunegonde, who has her own adventures as the favorite of a series of men. Candide becomes, in turn, a captain in the army, a Jesuit priest, a sheepherder in South America and a philosopher in Paris, where he also enjoys a love affair. When he finally finds Cunegonde once again, she has suffered several instances of rape and abuse, and she is now a servant. They settle on a farm with the string of characters who have joined Candide on his journey, but they soon become bored. To their good fortune, the group meets an old man who advises them to find contentment in cultivating their own garden.

CENSORSHIP HISTORY

In 1821, *Candide* was among the works to which Etienne Antoine, bishop of Troyne, referred when he wrote a pastoral letter to all clergy in France in which he reaffirmed all censorship orders previously issued by the clergy of France and the individual orders issued by the archbishops of Paris:

> in which these works were condemned as godless and sacrilegious, and as tending to undermine morals and the States. We prohibit, under canonical law, the printing or sale of these books within the territory of this diocese, and we charge the vicar-generals to enforce this regulation and to see to the carrying out of the necessary penances for all who make confession of disobedience to these regulations.

The authority of the Catholic Church in France appears to have been considered sufficient for control of the matter, and no application was made to have the work placed on the Roman Index. Nonetheless, as a means of establishing authority, Pope Pius VII had placed *Candide* on the list of prohibited books of the Roman Index of 1806 and later renewed the prohibition.

In 1893, the American Library Association for the first time offered a 5,000-title book guide for small popular libraries and branches, calling it a collection that "one could recommend to any trustee." Geller observes that no works by Voltaire were included on the list because several of his works might prove to be "offensive" to some readers. Unlike Rousseau, whose biography, but not his works, the ALA at least included in the guide, no mention was made of Voltaire.

Candide was being studied by universities worldwide, was available in libraries and appeared on college reading lists when United States Customs seized a shipment of the imported edition of the novel in 1928 and declared it obscene. The shipment was ordered by a professor of French at Harvard as assigned reading for his students. Relying on a previous ruling, a Customs official in Boston seized the shipment because the edition was unexpurgated. The professor and his Harvard colleagues contacted officials in Washington, demanding an explanation, and were told that Voltaire was on the list of banned works and that the Customs officer had acted correctly in confiscating the shipment. After the intercession of several influential politicians, the shipment was later released for use in the classroom. U.S. Customs recognized, after a major setback in the 1933 litigation of ULYSSES, that a more discriminating appraisal of books was needed. The appointment of Baltimore attorney Huntington Cairns to assess the problems of Customs censorship resulted in new procedures which, by 1937, deprived Customs collectors and their deputies of their decision-making power. This ended the confiscation of accepted literature, such as *Candide*, in most cases, unless the editions contained illustrations that were "too vulgar or erotic," according to Customs bureau standards.

FURTHER READING

Ayer, Alfred Jules. *Voltaire*. New York: Random House, 1986.
Besterman, Theodore. *Voltaire*. New York: Harcourt Brace & World, 1969.
Geller, Evelyn. *Forbidden Books in American Public Libraries, 1876–1939*. Westport, Conn.: Greenwood, 1984.
Paul, James C. N. *Federal Censorship: Obscenity in the Mail*. New York: Free Press, 1961.
Putnam, George Haven. *The Censorship of the Church of Rome and Its Influence upon the Production and Distribution of Literature*. Vol. 2. New York: Putnam, 1906.

CONFESSIONS

Author: Jean-Jacques Rousseau
Original date and place of publication: 1884, Switzerland; 1891, England
Original publisher: Waltham; Worthington
Literary form: Memoir

SUMMARY

Jean-Jacques Rousseau's *Confessions* was published posthumously, but he had completed the work just before his death in 1778. In this extensive journal of his life, Rousseau recreates the age in which he lived and brings to life the politics and society of 18th-century France. He also suffers from what one biographer refers to as "moral exhibitionism" and appears obsessed with revealing "the indecent and puerile details of his sex life." The work deals openly with his relationship with Therese Levasseur, his mistress for 16 years whom he "always treated like a wife." The two had five children, all sent to the foundling hospital. Rousseau admits that he was so disinterested in the children that he did not even keep records of their identities or dates of birth.

Several specific passages in *Confessions* have motivated attempts at censorship. Rousseau traces his sexual development to when he was aged eight and the 30-year-old baby-sitter, the sister of a parson, spanked his bare bottom. He says that this act had the effect to "determine my tastes, my desires, my passions, my very self, for the rest of my existence . . . these strange tastes which persisted with a depraved and insane intensity." Several passages speak openly of Rousseau's addiction to masturbation, to the point that he risked his health and believed himself to be epileptic, "seduced by the vice which shame and timidity find so convenient . . . I set about destroying my sturdy constitution."

When he resides at a Roman Catholic hospice in Turin, after fleeing Protestant Geneva, the 16-year-old Rousseau condemns the sister converts at the hospice as being "the greatest set of sluttish, abandoned whores that had ever contaminated the Lord's sheepfold." The brother converts are no less lustful, particularly one who "frequently kissed me with an ardour which I found most displeasing. . . . He wanted to come into my bed . . . and finally took the most revolting liberties and, by guiding my hand, tried to make me take the same liberties with him." Rousseau claims to have been ignorant of the other young man's true intent.

Not only is the reader treated to a thorough discussion of Rousseau's sex life, but his prostate problems in later life are also detailed in *Confessions*. As Rousseau advanced in age, he found the need to urinate frequently, but the respected writer and philosopher usually found himself cornered at social events and unable to reach even a convenient corner of a courtyard in which to relieve himself. He relates, "In short, I can usually urinate only in full view of everybody and on some white-stockinged leg."

CENSORSHIP HISTORY

Rousseau's lengthy *Confessions* has been banned mainly for its sexual content and for his open discussion of life with his mistress of 16 years. In 1821, *Confessions* was among the works to which Etienne Antoine, bishop of Troyne, referred when he wrote a pastoral letter to all clergy in France in which he reaffirmed all censorship orders previously issued by the clergy of France and the individual orders issued by the archbishops of Paris:

> in which these works were condemned as godless and sacrilegious, and as tending to undermine morals and the States. We prohibit, under canonical law, the printing or sale of these books within the territory of this diocese, and we charge the vicar-generals to enforce this regulation and to see to the carrying out of the necessary penances for all who make confession of disobedience to these regulations.

The authority of the Catholic Church in France appears to have been considered sufficient for control of the matter, and no application was made to have the work placed on the Roman Index. Nonetheless, as a means of establishing authority, Pope Pius VII had placed *Confessions* on the list of prohibited books of the Roman Index of 1806 and later renewed the prohibition because of the sexual adventures that Rousseau recounted.

In 1892, Rousseau's *Confessions* was involved in the litigation of the Worthington Book Publishing Company, which was in financial difficulty. The receiver wanted to sell some of the company stock, including *THE ARABIAN*

NIGHTS, *The History of Tom Jones, THE ART OF LOVE, The Heptameron, Gargantua and Pantagruel,* Boccaccio's *THE DECAMERON* and *Confessions* to pay off creditors, but Anthony Comstock stepped in to oppose the sales. He demanded of the court that the books be officially burned. The court disagreed. (See *THE ARABIAN NIGHTS.*)

A year later in 1893, the American Library Association for the first time offered a 5,000-title book guide for small popular libraries and branches, calling it a collection that "one could recommend to any trustee." No works by Rousseau were included on the list, yet a biography of the author was included. Based upon this observation, Geller notes, "This discrepancy between a writer's reputation and the acceptance of his work is a good indicator of censorship: exclusion on grounds other than significance."

United States Customs banned the book from entry in 1929, claiming that it was "injurious to public morals." Customs reversed the ban the following year.

FURTHER READING

Cranston, Maurice. *The Noble Savage: Jean-Jacques Rousseau.* Chicago: University of Chicago, 1991.
Geller, Evelyn. *Forbidden Books in American Public Libraries, 1876–1939.* Westport, Conn.: Greenwood, 1984.
Huizinga, J. H. *Rousseau: The Self-Made Saint.* New York: Grossman, 1976.
Putnam, George Haven. *The Censorship of the Church of Rome and Its Influence upon the Production and Distribution of Literature.* Vol. 2. New York: Putnam, 1906.

THE DECAMERON

Author: Giovanni Boccaccio
Original date and place of publication: 14th century, Italy; 1921, England
Original publisher: Privately printed; The Navarre Society
Literary form: Collection of tales

SUMMARY

The Decameron is one of the oldest fictional works to have been charged as "obscene" in the United States. The premise of the collection of tales is that 10 young men and women, secluded for a time to escape the plague, divert themselves by telling stories on a variety of topics. Each must tell one story per day on a specific theme, for a total of 100 tales. Of the total, only eight tales are purely erotic while the remainder deal with social criticism, the outwitting of one person by another and the criticism of nuns and priests.

In some of the tales, references to adultery or fornication are brief or oblique. In others, references are suggestive but not explicit. The stories contain figures of speech that replace explicit sexual description. Breasts and genitalia are spoken of metaphorically, and numerous metaphors are drawn from sowing, plowing and reaping. Thus, a wife complains that her husband has neglected "tilling of my poor field." A lover boards his mate in the way that "the unbridled stallions . . . assail the mares of Parthia." Even common implements such as the mortar and pestle become metaphors for sexual activity, as in the story in which a man complains that "if she will not lend me her mortar, I will not lend my pestle."

Of the eight largely erotic tales, four are based upon a trick or joke. In one, the 10th story told on the ninth day, a priest persuades a man that changing his wife into a mare will help the man in his peddling business. Thus, the wife dutifully strips and stands on all fours, as the priest carefully explains to the husband that putting on the mare's tail is the most difficult part of the process. The wife waits patiently as the priest pretends to turn her various body parts into the body of a mare. He then engages in the sexual act that will make the mare's tail, but it is described through the use of metaphor:

> Ultimately, nothing remaining to do but the tail, he pulled up his shirt and taking the dibble with which he planted men, he thrust it hastily into the furrow made therfor and said, "And be this a fine mare's tail."

The 10th story of the third day contains the lengthiest description of an act of sexual intercourse, and it was rarely translated until recent years. In this story, a friar persuades a naive young girl that she is serving God by submitting to him, because he has a "devil" in him that can only be subdued if he places it into her "hell." Even this story is humorous, for the girl outpaces the friar in showing her enthusiasm in serving God, as she tires the friar with her ardor.

CENSORSHIP HISTORY

The Decameron was first placed on the Roman Index of prohibited books in 1559, by the order of Pope Paul IV, and the prohibition was confirmed in 1564. The objections centered on the "offensive sexual acts" in which clerics, monks, nuns and abbesses in the work engaged. However, due to popular demand, in the form of an "urgent requirement" from the public, the Giunti of Florence, Italy, printed an expurgated edition in 1573, which contained a special authorization from Manrique, grand inquisitor, as well as one from de Pise, inquisitor-general of Florence. Revised under the authority of Pope Gregory VIII, the sexual activity and innuendo remained, but the religious characters were replaced by citizens, nobles and bourgeoisie. Pope Sixtus V did not find the expurgation satisfactory and the book was again placed on the Index, but the demand for copies by readers, ecclesiastics and others was so great that Sixtus authorized another expurgated edition, with orders to remove more of the sexual activity and crude innuendo. This version was printed in 1588, but the new edition did not satisfy Pope Sixtus V, and the book remained on the Index. Yet, it continued to be available in general reading and the authorities closed their eyes to this particular instance of disobedience, mainly because popular demand was so strong.

In a report entitled "How to Make a Town Library Successful," published in 1876, Frederick Beecher Perkins, assistant librarian of the Boston Public Library, recommended censorship of the collection:

> It should exclude such books as Rabelais, *The Decameron, The Heptameron*, the *Contes drolatiques* (*Droll Stories*) of Balzac, . . . all of which are sold in English translations for money by otherwise respectable American publishers. Few, indeed, are those who will object to this exclusion of ribald and immoral books from public circulating libraries.

In 1892, *The Decameron* was involved in the litigation of the Worthington Book Publishing Company, which was in financial difficulty. The receiver wanted to sell some of the company stock, including THE ARABIAN NIGHTS, *The History of Tom Jones*, THE ART OF LOVE, *The Heptameron, Gargantua and Pantagruel*, Rousseau's CONFESSIONS and *The Decameron* to pay off creditors, but Anthony Comstock stepped in to oppose the sales. He demanded of the court that the books be officially burned. (See THE ARABIAN NIGHTS.)

One year later, the American Library Association offered for the first time a 5,000-title book guide for small popular libraries and branches, calling it a collection that "one could recommend to any trustee." No works by Boccaccio were included on the list. When the American Library Association released its *Catalog* in 1904, works by Boccaccio were still excluded, leading Geller to characterize the situation as censorship by omission. In 1894, the U.S. Supreme Court applied the Hicklin rule, imported from England, to rule that standard works of high literary quality were not obscene. The first case involved editions of *The Arabian Nights, The History of Tom Jones, The Decameron, The Heptameron* and *The Art of Love*.

In 1903, the Boston Watch and Ward Society began a campaign of harassment against four area booksellers who were openly advertising and selling *The Decameron* and *Gargantua and Pantagruel* despite the request from the society that they refrain from doing so. Rather than acquiesce as in the past, the four met with other Boston booksellers and with publisher Little, Brown and Company to organize a resistance to this attempt at censorship. Booksellers, including the Old Corner, N. J. Bartlett, George E. Littlefield, Charles E. Goodspeed and six others, joined Little, Brown to raise money for a legal defense fund. The case went to Boston municipal court, and the booksellers won judgment against the society.

The Decameron was declared to be an "obscene, lewd and lascivious book of indecent character" by a jury in Cincinnati, Ohio, in 1906. Edward Stiefel, president and general manager of the Queen City Book Company, was indicted by a grand jury for sending a copy of the book through the mail to Crawfordsville, Indiana. Stiefel gathered a strong defense, calling as witnesses a well-known judge, a member of the Cincinnati Board of Education and a well-respected newspaper editor to testify to the status of the work as a classic. In addition, Stiefel offered into evidence library catalogs, catalogs from booksellers all over the world and catalogs from public auctions of books in New York and Boston, all listing *The Decameron*. Despite the evidence, the jury deliberated only an hour and 15 minutes before finding Stiefel guilty of sending "obscene" materials through the mail. The judge, who appeared less punitive, only fined the defendant $5 and court costs.

In 1927, United States Department of the Treasury officials in Washington, D.C., rendered an opinion that reversed a ruling by New York Customs inspectors and admitted 250 copies of the work, imported by A. & C. Boni, thus ending forever the banning of this classic in the United States.

FURTHER READING

Boyer, Paul S. *Purity in Print: The Vice-Society Movement and Book Censorship in America.* New York: Scribner's, 1968.

Geller, Evelyn. *Forbidden Books in American Public Libraries, 1876–1939.* Westport, Conn.: Greenwood, 1984.

Putnam, George Haven. *The Censorship of the Church of Rome and Its Influence upon the Production and Distribution of Literature.* Vol. 2. New York: Putnam, 1906.

Tebbel, John. *A History of Book Publishing in the United States.* Vol. 2. New York: Bowker, 1975.

FANNY HILL, OR MEMOIRS OF A WOMAN OF PLEASURE

Author: John Cleland
Original date and place of publication: 1748, England; 1821, United States
Original publisher: G. Fenton; Peter Holmes
Literary form: Novel

SUMMARY

Fanny Hill, or Memoirs of a Woman of Pleasure was written while John Cleland was incarcerated in a London debtor's prison. The story of an orphaned 15-year-old country girl who moves to London to find employment as a household worker but who instead enters a brothel is primarily composed of descriptions of her sexual experiences and those that she observes. Her first job is with a brothel keeper who trains Fanny for her future profession as a woman of pleasure. Those who have sought to ban the novel over the course of more than two centuries have complained that it contains numerous incidents of heterosexual and lesbian sexual activity, female masturbation, flagellation and voyeurism. Typical of the criticism leveled at the novel is that of United States

Supreme Court Justice Thomas C. Clark, who observed in a dissenting opinion in 1966,

> In each of the sexual scenes the exposed bodies of the participants are described in minute and individual detail. The pubic hair is often used for a background to the most vivid and precise descriptions of the response, condition, size, shape, and color of the sexual organs before, during and after orgasms.

Such criticism ignores the many instances in which the language is ornate and metaphorical as Cleland refers to genitalia through such euphemisms as "engine," "champion" and the "machine," as well as "the tender small part framed to receive it," the "pit" and the "wound." Although the novel may be "essentially a guidebook to erotic variations," the author presents them with humor. The author uses none of the "four-letter" words that are usually labeled "obscene," although he does use such candid terms as "maidenhead" and "defloration." The frequent labeling of the novel as priapic is also evident in the fascination that Fanny shows with the male anatomy, as in the scene in which she and her first lover Charles have sex:

> a column of the whitest ivory, beautifully streak'd with blue veins, and carrying, fully uncapt, a head of the liveliest vermilion: no horn could be harder or stiffer; yet no velvet more smooth or delicious to the touch. . . . a pair of roundish balls, that seem'd to pay within, and elude all pressure but the tenderest, from without.

At the end of the novel, after having experienced every variation of sexual intimacy, Fanny leaves her life of sin and marries Charles, providing the reader with her observation that "looking back on the course of vice I had run, and comparing its infamous blandishments with the infinitely superior joys of innocence, I could not help pitying even in point of taste, those who, immers'd in gross sensuality, are insensible to the so delicate charms of VIRTUE."

CENSORSHIP HISTORY

In 1749, less than one year after publication of *Fanny Hill, or The Memoirs of a Woman of Pleasure*, John Cleland was imprisoned on the orders of Lord Newcastle, the British secretary of state, on a charge of "corrupting the King's subjects." The action was taken after high-ranking officials of the Church of England had protested the nature of the book and demanded the arrest of Cleland, his publisher and his printer. The bishop of London had personally contacted Newcastle, asking him to "give proper orders, to stop the progress of this vile Book, which is an open insult upon Religion and good manners, and a reproach to the Honour of the Government, and the Law of the Country."

The trial of *Fanny Hill* in 1821 in Massachusetts was the first obscenity case involving a book to be heard in the United States. The novel had been surreptitiously published in the United States for many years, beginning with several expurgated editions of the novel published by Isaiah Thomas between 1786 and 1814, but not until Peter Holmes published the first edition of the novel in its original form in 1821 did censors take notice. The publisher was convicted for publishing and printing a "lewd and obscene" novel. Holmes appealed to the Massachusetts Supreme Court, claiming that the court had not seen the book and that the jury had only heard the prosecution's description. In delivering a decision on the appeal, Chief Justice Isaac Parker observed that the publisher was "a scandalous and evil disposed person" who had contrived to "debauch and corrupt" the citizens of the commonwealth and "to raise and create in their minds inordinate and lustful desires." Of the novel, he stated that "said printed book is so lewd, wicked and obscene, that the same would be offensive to the court here, and improper to be placed upon the records thereof." In short, Holmes lost his appeal because the judge refused to review the book, to have the jury read the book and to enter passages from the book into the court record for to do so "would be to require that the public itself should give permanency and notoriety to indecency, in order to punish it."

In 1930, while the Massachusetts legislature debated a revision of censorship laws, *Fanny Hill* was among 300 books seized in a raid on a Philadelphia bookshop. The city district attorney led the raid and announced at the same time that Philadelphia officials would undertake an extensive campaign to curb sales of "obscene" literature.

In 1963, G.P. Putnam's Son's announced that it would issue an unexpurgated edition of *Fanny Hill*. New York City prosecutors with city attorney Leo A. Larkin decided to take legal action against the publisher. Because Putnam had a reputation as a responsible firm with book sales in many of New York City's largest bookstores, the city decided against arrests and criminal charges. Instead, city officials utilized the state injunctive procedure that allowed them to order the listing of inventories and to freeze stocks to prevent further sales until *Larkin v. G.P. Putnam's Sons*, 40 Misc. 2d 25, 243 N.Y.S2d 145 (Sup. Ct. N.Y. Co. 1963) was decided. A further advantage to the prosecution in proving the book was pornographic was that the injunctive procedure required the lesser proof of a civil case rather than the proof beyond a reasonable doubt of a criminal case. Judge Charles Marks issued an order to restrain sales of the novel. The case then went before the state supreme court and was tried without a jury before Justice Arthur G. Klein in *Larkin v. G.P. Putnam's Sons*, 14 N.Y.2d 399, 200 N.E.2d 760 (1964). Expert witnesses argued that the novel portrayed the economic realities of the times and emphasized its literary merit. The reporting of the British Profumo scandal, a sex-and-spy scandal that threatened to topple the British government, occurred while Justice Klein was deliberating. He dissolved the restraining order and dismissed the city's action, asserting that

> if the standards of the community are to be gauged by what it is permitted
> to read in its daily newspapers, then Fanny Hill's experiences contain little

more than the community has already encountered on the front pages of many of its newspapers in the reporting of the recent "Profumo" and other sensational cases involving sex.

The prosecution appealed the decision in 1964, and in a 3 to 2 split decision in *Larkin v. G.P. Putnam's Sons*, 20 A.D.2d 702, case no. 2, 247 N.Y.S.2d 275 (1st Dep't 1964) the New York State intermediate appeals court reversed Justice Klein's action and ordered Putnam to refrain from selling the novel in the state of New York. Putnam then took the case to the New York Court of Appeals, which in a 4 to 3 decision reversed the decision of the lower court and granted final judicial amnesty to *Fanny Hill* in New York.

In 1963 the United States Supreme Court considered the validity of a Massachusetts Supreme Judicial Court decision that the novel was "pornographic" in *A Book Named "John Cleland's Memoirs of a Woman of Pleasure" v. Massachusetts*, 383 U.S. 413 (1966). The court cleared *Fanny Hill* of obscenity charges in a conditional decision. Justice William J. Brennan stated in the majority decision that historical importance is a factor and "the circumstances of production, sale and publicity are relevant in determining whether or not the publication and distribution of the book is constitutionally protected."

In London in 1963, the publication of unexpurgated paperback versions of the novel motivated the director of public prosecutions to secure a seizure order for all copies of the novel that were currently displayed in the window of a small Soho bookstore. The store proudly proclaimed on a sign in the window that the novel was "Banned in America." The trial was held early in 1964; after four days of testimony, the novel was determined to be obscene and the seized copies were ordered to be destroyed.

In 1965, Paul's Book Arcade of Auckland, New Zealand, sought to avoid censorship and applied to the Indecent Publications Tribunal for a determination regarding the expurgated paperback edition of the novel, published by Mayflower Books Limited of London in 1964. In a decision rendered on May 20, 1965, the tribunal ruled:

> The book has no substance other than to relate the experiences of a prostitute and we think that it might arouse interest in the one form of perversion it describes. . . . We accordingly make a ruling which the statute permits classifying it as indecent in the hands of persons under eighteen years of age, though we feel considerable doubt as to how far, if at all, such a classification will have the effect sought.

FURTHER READING

Cooper, Morton. "Fanny Hill vs. the Constitution." *Pageant* 14 (June 1964): 14–20.
Foxon, David F. "John Cleland and the Publication of *Memoirs of a Woman of Pleasure*." *Book Collector* 12 (Winter 1963): 476–87.

Kuh, Richard H. *Foolish Figleaves? Pornography In and Out of Court.* New York: Macmillan, 1967.

Rembar, Charles. *The End of Obscenity: The Trials of "Lady Chatterley's Lover," "Tropic of Cancer" & "Fanny Hill" by the Lawyer Who Defended Them.* New York: Random House, 1968.

Rolph, Cecil Hewitt. *Book in the Dock.* London: Deutsch, 1961.

Sebastian, Raymond F. "Obscenity and the Supreme Court: Nine Years of Confusion." *Stanford Law Review* 19 (November 1966): 167–89.

Stuart, Perry. *The Indecent Publications Tribunal: A Social Experiment.* Christchurch, New Zealand: Whitcombe and Tombs, 1965.

Wald, Emil W. "Obscene Literature Standards Re-Examined." *South Carolina Law Review* 18 (Spring 1966): 497–503.

FOREVER

Author: Judy Blume
Original date and place of publication: 1975, United States
Original publisher: Bradbury Press
Literary form: Young adult novel

SUMMARY

Forever is a novel about first love and the chaotic feelings that accompany the romance and the sexual desire of teenagers Katherine and Michael. After meeting at a New Year's Eve party, the two date for several weeks, becoming closer and more sexually aroused each time that they meet. Katherine is a virgin and hesitant to "lose control," but Michael's passionate overtures eventually overcome her doubts. Their first few times having sex are unremarkable for Katherine because Michael reaches orgasm before she is completely aroused. After they finally synchronize their desire, Katherine becomes an enthusiastic aggressor, enjoying their lovemaking and seeking times to be alone with Michael. They pledge to love each other "forever," and for her 18th birthday, Michael gives Katherine a silver necklace on which her name is inscribed on one side of a disk with the words "forever, Michael" inscribed on the other.

Both partners act in a responsible manner, discussing their concerns regarding birth control and the prevention of sexually transmitted diseases and substituting mutual masturbation for sexual intercourse until birth control is available. Their encounters are detailed for the reader who can trace the growing intensity of their desire from Michael's sensitive exploration of Katherine's breasts to their later frequent and varied lovemaking. Sexual activity is also integral to the subplots involving several friends. Sibyl who "has a genius I.Q. and has been laid by at least six different guys" has a baby whose father she cannot identify. Erica seeks to help talented high school actor Artie determine if he is gay or not by having sex with him, but her efforts push him to attempt suicide.

Concerned that Katherine is too young to make a lifetime commitment to Michael, her parents urge her to date others and eventually demand that she work at a summer camp several hundred miles away to test the relationship. When her grandfather dies, Katherine rushes into the arms of fellow counselor Theo, who wisely tells her he wants her but "not with death for an excuse." This makes Katherine realize that she really will not love Michael "forever." When they next meet, she breaks off the relationship, leaving Michael angry and embittered.

CENSORSHIP HISTORY

Forever has been repeatedly challenged and banned in schools and libraries because of the detailed sexual descriptions and the perceived frequency of the sexual activity in the novel. In 1982, the parents of students attending Midvalley Junior-Senior High School in Scranton, Pennsylvania, challenged the book, charging that it contained "four-letter words and talked about masturbation, birth control, and disobedience to parents." It was also challenged that year in the Orlando, Florida, schools and at the Park Hill (Missouri) South Junior High School library where librarians were required by the school board to place the book on the "restricted" shelves. In 1983, parents called for the removal of the book from the Akron, Ohio, school district libraries and from the Howard-Suamico (Wisconsin) High School library because "it demoralizes marital sex." In 1984, challenges to the book by parents resulted in its removal from the Holdredge (Nebraska) Public Library young adult section to the adult section because of claims that the "book is pornographic and does not promote the sanctity of family life." That same year, parents challenged inclusion of the book in the Cedar Rapids (Iowa) Public Library because it was "pornography and explores areas God didn't intend to explore outside of marriage."

The Patrick County (Virginia) School Board, responding to parent complaints in 1986, ordered the novel placed on a "restricted" shelf in the high school library, and challenges were raised against its inclusion in the Campbell County (Wyoming) school libraries because it is "pornographic" and would encourage young readers "to experiment with sexual encounters." Parents of students in the Moreno Valley (California) Unified School District sought to remove the novel from the school libraries in 1987 and claimed that it "contains profanity, sexual situations, and themes that allegedly encourage disrespectful behavior." In 1987, charging that the "book does not paint a responsible role of parents," that its "cast of sex-minded teenagers is not typical of high schoolers today" and that the "pornographic sexual exploits are unsuitable for junior high school role models," parents of students attending Marshwood Junior High School in Eliot, Maine, demanded its removal from the classroom library. In 1988, the principal of West Hernando (Florida) Middle School yielded to parents' complaints that the novel was "inappropriate" and asked that it be removed from the school library shelves.

The challenges to *Forever* continued in the 1990s. In 1992, the novel was placed on the "reserve" shelf at the Herrin (Illinois) Junior High School library because it was "sexually provocative reading," and students could only check out the book if they had written permission from their parents. In 1993, the novel was removed from the Frost Junior High School library in Schaumberg, Illinois, after parents charged that "it's basically a sexual 'how-to-do' book for junior high students. It glamorizes sex and puts ideas into their heads." Also in 1993, the superintendent of schools in Rib Lake, Wisconsin, filed a "request for reconsideration" of the book after determining that it was "sexually explicit." The novel was placed on the "parental permission shelf," then later confiscated by the high school principal. A high school guidance counselor who spoke out against the district book policy and criticized the actions of the principal in restricting student access to the novel was not rehired for the following academic year. He sued the school district and a federal jury in Madison, Wisconsin, awarded him $394,560 in damages and lost wages. In 1994, school officials in Mediapolis, Iowa, responded to parent complaints about the novel and removed it from the school libraries because it "does not promote abstinence and monogamous relationships and lacks any aesthetic, literary, or social value." The book was returned a month later, but only to the high school library.

FURTHER READING

Forman, Jack. "Young Adult Books: 'Watch Out for #1.'" *Horn Book* 61 (January/February 1985): 85.

Maynard, Joyce. "Coming of Age with Judy Blume." *New York Times Magazine* (December 3, 1978): 80+.

Newsletter on Intellectual Freedom (July 1982): 124, 142; (May 1982): 84; (May 1983): 85–86; (March 1984): 39; (May 1984): 69; (March 1985): 59; (September 1985): 167; (March 1986): 39; (March 1987): 66–67; (July 1987): 125; (November 1987): 239; (March 1988): 45; (May 1992): 80; (May 1993): 70; (July 1993): 98, 104–5; (September 1993): 146–47; (May 1994): 83, 86; (July 1994): 109; (March 1995): 56.

Thompson, Susan. "Images of Adolescence: Part I." *Signal* 34 (1981): 57–59.

FOREVER AMBER

Author: Kathleen Winsor
Original date and place of publication: 1944, United States
Original publisher: The Macmillan Company
Literary form: Novel

SUMMARY

Forever Amber relates the career of Amber, an illegitimate child born of noble lineage in 1644, from her rustic upbringing through her adventures in London when she becomes a duchess and the mistress of Charles II. She has numerous lovers and gives birth to three children by three different lovers. She does marry four times, but only her first marriage is legal, and she fails to marry one man whom she truly loves.

The novel contains historically accurate detailed descriptions of the Restoration period, including Newgate Prison, the Great Plague and the Great Fire in London, as well as numerous notable Restoration figures. The author achieves accuracy in recreating the court of Charles II, as well as the costumes and the stage of the period. Amber loves forever Bruce, the first man who seduces her, but she is proud to become the mistress of King Charles II, assuring herself after their first encounter, "I'm somebody now! I've lain with the King!" After being moved into the palace, where she bears the king several children, she also makes several advantageous marriages, one to the older Lord Radclyffe whose grown son she also seduces. Throughout the novel, Amber uses her sexuality to achieve her aims, actions befitting the times as portrayed in the novel in which most of the characters ignore traditional morality and use any means to achieve their ambitions.

Despite the disapproval of critics, anatomical references are limited to descriptions of Amber's breasts, as "full and pointed, and upward tilting," and the sexual scenes are presented in general terms. Typical of such vague description is Amber's first seduction:

> At last his arm reached out, went around her waist, and drew her slowly toward him; Amber, tipping her head to meet his mouth, slid both her arms about him.
> The restraint he had shown thus far now vanished swiftly, giving way to a passion that was savage, violent, ruthlessly selfish. Amber, inexperienced but not innocent, returned his kisses eagerly. Spurred by the caressing of his mouth and hands, her desire mounted apace with his. . . .
> Amber, crying, half-mad with passion and terror, suddenly let herself relax.

CENSORSHIP HISTORY

Literary critics generally condemned the value of the novel; and the condemnation by *Atlantic* reviewer Frances Woodward that *Forever Amber* was "without any literary distinction" was typical. In 1946, the United States Department of the Post Office declared *Forever Amber* "obscene" and banned it from the mails, in theory until 1957, when the ban was officially lifted. The ruling had no significant effect upon sales of the book because mail distribution did not represent an important means of sales, although suggestive advertising materials sent through the mail had motivated the banning.

Forever Amber had been in print for four years, with 1.3 million copies sold in the United States and more than 100,000 copies in England, when it became the target of censors in the Commonwealth of Massachusetts in 1948. The case went to the highest court in the state as a civil rather than a criminal action under a new law that provided that whenever there was reasonable cause to believe that a book was "obscene, indecent or impure" the attorney general or any district attorney could ask a justice of the Superior Court to rule on the book. State Attorney General George Rowell charged that the book contained "70 references to sexual intercourse; 39 to illegitimate pregnancies; 7 to abortions; 10 descriptions of women undressing, dressing or bathing in the presence of men; 5 references to incest; 13 references ridiculing marriage; and 49 miscellaneous objectionable passages." The decision in *Attorney General v. Book Named "Forever Amber"*, 323 Mass. 302, 81 N.E.2d 663 (Sup. Jud. Ct. 1948) went against Rowell. Judge Donahue of the Massachusetts Supreme Court acknowledged the historical accuracy of the novel and stated that "these matters indicate a certain amount of study and research . . . that *Forever Amber* is sufficiently accurate for the purpose of representing a portrait of the period and its customs and morals; that it does not exaggerate or falsify any traits of the Restoration." The judge also noted that "sexual episodes abound to the point of tedium" and observed that they "are lacking in realistic detail, although some are coarse." Judge Donahue noted in closing statements that the book was "a soporific rather than an aphrodisiac" and noted that "while the novel was conducive to sleep, it was not conducive to a desire to sleep with a member of the opposite sex."

In 1952, the novel was banned in New Zealand after the Honourable Walter Nash, Minister of Customs, reviewed a copy seized by Customs officers. Applying powers granted him by the Customs Act of 1913, Nash acted as censor and made the final decision banning further importation of the novel. Perry notes that the law also allowed for the importer to "dispute the forfeiture, for the Attorney-General to lay an information against the importer for the condemnation of the book, to which the importer would file a defence . . . I can, however, find no record in the *New Zealand Law Reports* of a case relating to books prohibited on grounds of indecency having been dealt with in this way." Only the Dunedin members of the New Zealand Library Association Fiction Committee raised a protest against the censoring of *Forever Amber*. Although they criticized the novel as "trivial and naive," they found the way in which the Minister of Customs had dealt with the work to be objectionable and they made the public statement that "the operation of censorship in New Zealand was 'casual, arbitrary and ill informed'." Their views had no effect on the ban.

FURTHER READING

Ernst, Morris L., and Alan U. Schwartz. *Censorship: The Search for the Obscene*. New York: Macmillan, 1964.

Gillotti, Chris F. "Book Censorship in Massachusetts: The Search for a Test of Obscenity." *Boston University Law Review* 42 (Fall 1962): 476–91.

Morse, J. M. "*Forever Amber*: Defendant at Trial in Suffolk County Superior Court, Boston." *New Republic* (January 6, 1947): 39–40.

Paul, James C. N., and Murray L. Schwartz. *Federal Censorship: Obscenity in the Mail.* New York: Free Press, 1961.

Perry, Stuart. *The Indecent Publications Tribunal: A Social Experiment.* London: Whitcombe and Tombs, 1965.

Woodward, Frances. "*Forever Amber*." *Atlantic* (December 1944): 137.

THE GROUP

Author: Mary McCarthy
Original date and place of publication: 1963, United States
Original publisher: Harcourt, Brace & World
Literary form: Novel

SUMMARY

The Group relates the story of eight women, graduates of the Vassar College class of 1933, who formed a clique while undergraduates. Six of the group are from wealthy Eastern families, one of the remaining two is the daughter of a wealthy self-made man whereas the other is of middle-class background and raised in the West. All members of the group are determined to make their mark in the world and to have careers that will give them lives far different from those of their mothers. Inspired by the progressive thinking that they enjoyed at Vassar, the young women approach life with enthusiasm and with the expectations of those who have experienced privileged educations.

Comic and ironic at turns, the novel begins a week after commencement, as the group gathers to celebrate the first wedding of one of their numbers, Kay Strong, who had daringly lived with Harald [sic] beforehand. As the other members of the group, whose nicknames include "Pokey," "Lakey" and "Priss" as well as Dottie, Libby, Polly and Helena, assess the possible success of the marriage, they reveal their shallow personalities and equally shallow values. In the 10 years that follow, the group members dabble in "Trotskyite" politics, join the bohemian theater world, engage in numerous love affairs and deal with abusive boyfriends and husbands. Lakey spends years in Europe, later bringing home her lesbian lover, the baroness, whose demeanor leaves the others insecure that "Lakey would now look down on them for not being Lesbians."

The novel ends with the funeral of Kay, said to have lost her balance and fallen from a window on the 20th floor of the Vassar Club in New York City while airplane-spotting only a few weeks before the United States enters World War II. Mrs. Davison, an older Vassar graduate present in the lounge when the incident occurs, refutes suggestions of suicide. She claims that Kay appeared to be in good spirits and "had left a cigarette burning in the ashtray by her bedside. She states that "'no young woman who was going to kill herself would do it in the middle of a cigarette.'"

References to sexual situations and graphic descriptions of the group's affairs aroused criticism when the novel was published. Later, the following passage was labeled "disgusting" in the 1970 President's Committee Report on Obscenity and Pornography:

> Down there, she felt a quick new tremor. Her lips parted. Dick smiled. "You feel something?" he said. Dottie nodded. "You'd like it again?" he said, assaying her with his hand. Dottie stiffened; she pressed her thighs together. She was ashamed of the violent sensation his exploring fingers had discovered. But he held his hand there, between her clasped thighs, and grasped her right hand in his other, guiding it . . . over that part of himself, which was soft and limp, rather sweet, really, all curled up on itself like a fat worm. Sitting beside her, he looked into her face as he stroked her down there and tightened her hand on him. "There's a little ridge there," he whispered. "Run your fingers up and down it." Dottie obeyed, wonderingly. She felt his organ stiffen a little, which gave her a strange sense of power.

CENSORSHIP HISTORY

The Group was banned in Ireland on January 21, 1964. A prohibition order was published in the *Iris Oifigiuil*, "the only official source from which booksellers [and readers] might learn of a new prohibition order," in which all articles blacklisted by the Irish Board of Censors were listed. According to the Censorship of Publications Bill of 1928, "the notice in *Iris Oifigiuil* should be sufficient evidence in the courts of summary jurisdiction as to the character of the publication," despite the acknowledgment by justices quoted in Adams's thorough study of Irish censorship laws that "this gazette is not a publication which booksellers are addicted to reading." The Irish Board of Censors found the work "obscene" and "indecent," objecting particularly to the author's handling of the characters' sexuality, suggestions of homosexuality and "promiscuity." The work was officially banned from sale in Ireland until the introduction of the Censorship Publications Bill in 1967 reduced to 12 years the duration of a prohibition order, and the work was among 5,000 titles released from the list of banned books.

In March 1964, New Zealand Customs placed the novel on its "Publications Restricted or Prohibited" list, classifying it under Category VI, reserved for "publications which, if imported, should be detained and copies referred for decision." The principal distributors' associations in New Zealand as well as the New Zealand Library Association quickly expressed their disapproval of the censorship. On May 20, 1964, the New Zealand Library Association wrote to the Ministry of Justice, reminding officials that the novel had been freely circulating for months and asking the Justice Department to refer the work to the Indecent Publications Tribunal for a decision rather than to allow the Customs department to have the final word. Newspaper reports ridiculed the Wellington Customs department's claim that they had delayed referring the work to the tribunal until they could obtain copies of the book, because libraries had received copies the previous year and the books were still being sold in bookstores. Faced with public disapproval, the comptroller of Customs announced on June 24, 1964, that the book would neither be referred to the tribunal nor would future imports of the book be detained.

FURTHER READING

Adams, Michael. *Censorship: The Irish Experience*. University: University of Alabama Press, 1968.

Brightman, Carol. *Writing Dangerously: Mary McCarthy and Her World*. New York: Clarkson Potter, 1992.

Gelderman, Carol. *Mary McCarthy: A Life*. New York: St. Martin's, 1988.

Perry, Stuart. *The Indecent Publications Tribunal: A Social Experiment*. London: Whitcombe and Tombs, 1965.

United States President's Commission on Obscenity and Pornography. *The Report of the Commission on Obscenity and Pornography*. New York: Random House, 1970.

JUDE THE OBSCURE

Author: Thomas Hardy
Original date and place of publication: 1895, England; 1895, United States
Original publisher: Osgood, McIlvaine; Harper
Literary form: Novel

SUMMARY

Jude the Obscure is the story of a man whose ambition and desire for prestige war with his personal desires. Jude Fawley, a restless young man whose wanderings reflect his unsatisfied longings, works painfully to educate himself and to learn the classics and theology after his schoolmaster, Richard Phillotson, leaves for the great university town of Christminster. To earn his living, he becomes a stonemason and leaves Wessex for Christminster, where he hopes to advance his education as he works. His relationships with two significantly different women impede his progress.

Jude meets Arabella Donn, the daughter of a pig farmer, before he reaches Christminster. She and other young women are washing pig parts after slaughtering, and she captures Jude's attention by throwing a pig's "pizzle" (penis) at his head. Attracted by her appearance, Jude returns the missile of cold flesh to her and the two engage in a romantic dalliance while the "pizzle" lies draped over the nearby bridge railing. A short while later, Arabella seduces

Jude and they marry. Unsuited for each other beyond their initial physical passion, the two eventually separate, though not before having a child.

Free again to pursue his goal of education, Jude goes to Christminster and meets his cousin, Sue Bridehead, an androgynous woman whose intellect and efforts for women's rights and the equality of the sexes make her a "new woman." Although the two are in love, Sue chooses to marry Jude's old schoolmaster, Phillotson. The marriage is not happy and, after Sue leaves Phillotson, she and Jude live together. They have two children who are murdered by Father Time, Jude's child with Arabella, and Father Time then commits suicide. When Sue leaves Jude, he returns to Arabella but does not live for long. Jude dies at the age of 30, wasting away within sight of the college that he had so desperately wanted to attend but which had rejected him. After discovering his dead body, Arabella decides to wait until the next morning to tell anyone, in order to enjoy a night at the festival with Jude's friends.

CENSORSHIP HISTORY

Hardy consented to the bowdlerization of several of his works before they reached the public, thus removing much of the potential controversy. Malcolm Cowley writes that because Hardy "adapted himself to the public" he became "a scandal even in academic circles." *Jude the Obscure* was serialized by *Harper's New Monthly* magazine in the United States but only after the author was willing to make changes in the novel. Pinion records that editor H. M. Alden reminded Hardy that "the Magazine must contain nothing which could not be read aloud in any family circle." Before the monthly installments were published, Hardy had to change the title to *Hearts Insurgent* and present as adopted orphans the two children who are born outside of marriage to Jude and Sue.

The excised material was restored when the novel was published in 1895, and *Jude the Obscure* was more savagely attacked by reviewers than any of Hardy's other works. Martin Seymour-Smith noted that reviewers called it a "grimy story" that was "steeped in sex" and accused Hardy of "wallowing in the mire." The London *World* labeled him "Hardy the Degenerate," and the *Guardian* condemned the novel as "a shameful nightmare to be forgotten as soon as possible." Novelist Mrs. Oliphant wrote in *Blackwood* that *Jude the Obscure* was "foul in detail" and claimed never to "have read a more disgusting book." Bishop How of Wakefield professed that he burned his copy of the novel and urged others throughout England to do the same. The bishop objected to the "crude image" of Arabella's means of introducing herself to Jude, as well as the hanging suicide of little Father Time. How was also successful in having the novel withdrawn from W. H. Smith's circulating library. The popular circulating libraries had significant influence on book sales during the second half of the 19th century. Novels were expensive and authors made little money in sales unless the circulating libraries accepted their books.

In 1903, Hardy revised the novel before it was published by his new English publishers, Macmillan and Company. The scene of the thrown pig pizzle was greatly modified out of fear for future sales. The references to the "clammy flesh" of the pizzle are deleted, as are references to it as the "indecent thing," "the lump of offal," "the fragment of pig" and "the limp object." He also toned down Arabella's seductive behavior and sensual nature.

Although Hardy lived for 33 years after *Jude the Obscure* was first published, it was his final novel. He lost heart when Bishop How burned the book, "the experience completely curing me of further interest in novel-writing." He acknowledges in the 1890 essay "Candour in Fiction" that presenting morally imperfect characters who work out their destinies in a natural manner might result in a novel that contains cruelty, envy or other evils, but that is merely reality. That such writing might have a negative influence on the weak minded is also reality. As Hardy wrote in "Candour in Fiction":

> Of the effects of such sincere presentation on weak minds, when the courses of the characters are not exemplary, and the rewards and punishments ill adjusted to deserts, it is not our duty to consider too closely. A novel which does moral injury to a dozen imbeciles, and has bracing results upon a thousand intellects of normal vigor, can justify its existence; and probably a novel was never written by the purest-minded author for which there could not be found some moral invalid or other whom it was capable of harming.

He also blames the libraries and the magazines for censorship, because they claimed that their readers were younger members of the family and felt it necessary to take precautions that would not be needed for adults. Inevitably, he concedes that satisfying "the prudery of censorship" is "the fearful price" that he has to pay "for the privilege of writing in the English language—no less a price than the complete extinction, in the mind of every mature and penetrating reader, of sympathetic belief in his personages."

FURTHER READING

Cowley, Malcolm. *After the Genteel Tradition*. Rev. ed. Carbondale: Southern Illinois University, 1964.

Hardy, Thomas. "Candour in Fiction." In *Thomas Hardy's Personal Writings: Prefaces, Literary Opinions, Reminiscences*, edited by Harold Orel. Lawrence: University of Kansas Press, 1966.

Pinion, F. B. *Thomas Hardy: His Life and Friends*. New York: St. Martin's, 1992.

Seymour-Smith, Martin. *Hardy: A Biography*. New York: St. Martin's, 1994.

Yevish, I. A. "Attack on *Jude the Obscure*: A Reappraisal Some Seventy Years After." *Journal of General Education* 18 (January 1967): 239–48.

THE *KAMA SUTRA* OF VATSYAYANA

Author: Vatsyayana (translated by Richard F. Burton and F. F. Arbuthnot)
Original date and place of publication: 1883, Switzerland; 1962, United States
Original publisher: Kama Shastra Society; E. P. Dutton
Literary form: Marriage manual

SUMMARY

The *Kama Sutra* of Vatsyayana is a Sanskrit classic written in India, circa 300 B.C., and it was well known among the educated classes. English traveler and adventurer Sir Richard Burton translated the work into English in 1883, but the nature of the work limited publication to private editions.

The origin of the work is complicated. Also known as the *Kama Shastra* and the *Ananga Ranga*, the work is an Indian marriage manual. The manuscript used by Burton for translation was actually written by a 16th-century poet named Kalyana Malla, who drew much of his material on erotic subjects from earlier writers, particularly the sage Vatsyayana, who was largely credited as being the ancient author of the *Kama Sutra*. In the Indian vernacular, Kama was the love god, and Vatsyayana's writings were contained in a text known as the *Kama Sutra*, or "Love Verses," a manual of erotic instruction.

Burton had corresponded with Foster Fitzgerald Arbuthnot, who had possession of a copy of the work and had decided to have the erotic classic translated into English. They hired an Indian scholar named Bhagvanlal Indraji to create a rough draft in English, then Burton polished the text and imposed his own view of how a man must treat a woman. As Rice observe, "Thus, many sections of the English version of the *Kama Shastra* come not from Kalyana Malla's Sanskrit but from Burton's fertile brain, developing and improving upon a text that some Western scholars believe is poorer and more pedantic than its translation."

The work contains charts of how and where the man is to touch the woman, from forehead to big toe (the latter assuming the symbolic role of the clitoris) to provide "the touches by which passion is satisfied." The manual also contains significant use of scratching, biting, kissing and chewing, actions that Burton justified by pointing out that the marriages in India often took place between children, so such "play" occurred in the process of becoming familiar with each other.

The following passage from the *Kama Sutra* has been cited by critics as being "a startlingly apparent" example of material that results in psychological disintegration:

> On the occasion of a "high congress" the Mrigi (Deer) woman should lie down in such a way as to widen her yoni, while in a "low congress" the Hastini (Elephant) woman should lie down so as to contract hers. But in an "equal congress" they should lie down in the natural position. What is said above

concerning the Mrigi and the Hastini applies also to the Vadawa (Mare) woman. In a "low congress" the woman should particularly make use of medicine, to cause her desire to be satisfied quickly.

The Deer-woman has the following three ways of lying down:

The widely opened position.

The yawning position.

The position of the wife of Indra.

When she lowers her head and raises her middle parts, it is called the "widely opened position." At such a time, the man should apply some unguent, so as to make the entrance easy.

In addition to providing instructions for various sexual positions, of which Burton commented that "one has to be an athlete to engage in," the work also provides women with instructions in how they may use men. The final sections relate "On the Means of Getting Money" and "Subjugating the Hearts of Others."

CENSORSHIP HISTORY

Burton and his collaborators in the Kama Shastra Society anticipated attempts of censorship as they approached the publication of the *Kama Sutra*. Their pretense was that the book was printed outside of England and that it was intended for scholars who wished to study "the great unknown literature of the East." Furthermore, by pricing the books at the equivalent in today's money of $200 each, the publishers also guaranteed that their readers had to be wealthy. The cover contained the words "For Private Circulation Only," and the place of publication was listed as Benares. After their problems in 1875, when the English printers refused to complete production of the book, Burton and his partners used two different printers to prevent confiscation of all copies should the authorities stage a raid. Soon after the first copies appeared in 1883, pirated copies appeared in Paris, Brussels and the English Midlands.

The *Kama Sutra* was not sold openly in England, but pirated copies did appear in the United States. After spending 60 days in jail in 1930 for distributing unexpurgated copies of *ULYSSES*, Samuel Roth turned to more profitable publications and produced editions of the *Kama Sutra* and *The Perfumed Garden*. Agents of the New York Society for the Suppression of Vice brought complaint against Roth, who was prosecuted and sentenced to 90 days in jail for selling those books.

In hearings before the Subcommittee on Postal Operations of the Committee on Post Office and Civil Service in 1962, Robert W. Edwards, Deputy Collector of Customs, United States Customs Mail Division in Boston, testified that the *Kama Sutra* "bears the dubious distinction of being the filthiest book published today. . . . In my opinion, the human mind is scarcely able to withstand the impact of the overwhelming obscenity and sexually based desire for torture in the *Kama Sutra*." The President's Commission on Obscenity and Pornography recommended that books of its sort be "banned from the mails."

FURTHER READING

Lockhart, William B., and Robert C. McClure. "Censorship of Obscenity: The Developing Constitutional Standards." *Minnesota Law Review* 45 (November 1960): 19.

Rice, Edward. *Captain Sir Richard Francis Burton.* New York: Scribner's, 1990.

Thomas, Donald. *A Long Time Burning: The History of Literary Censorship in England.* New York: Praeger, 1969.

United States President's Commission on Obscenity and Pornography. *The Report of the Commission on Obscenity and Pornography.* New York: Random House, 1970.

LADY CHATTERLEY'S LOVER

Author: D. H. Lawrence
Original date and place of publication: 1928, Italy; 1959, United States
Original publisher: Orioli; Grove Press
Literary form: Novel

SUMMARY

Lady Chatterley's Lover conveys Lawrence's bitter and deep dissatisfaction with the stultifying effects of industrialization and modern sterile society upon the natural life of all English classes. In general, he portrays the manner in which the upper classes have become devitalized and the lower classes debased by the increasing artificiality of their emotional and physical relationships. The novel relates the experiences of a young woman named Connie Chatterley, married to a baronet who is paralyzed from the waist down after severe injuries incurred fighting in World War I. She is sexually frustrated and becomes increasingly dissatisfied with the artificial and sterile nature of the society in which she lives. A brief affair with a man within her husband Clifford's social circle proves to be unsatisfying and leaves her even more restless and unhappy.

Repelled by her husband's suggestion that she become pregnant by another man and produce a child whom he might make his heir, Connie turns further away from him. Instead, she feels attracted to their gamekeeper, Mellors, Lawrence's example of the "natural man," whom society has neither devitalized nor debased. His coarse exterior and verbal expression mask a highly developed spiritual and intellectual independence, and the two become lovers. Their affair is deeply passionate and their lovemaking extremely tender, as Mellors gradually leads Connie to abandon her preconceived views of propriety and inhibitions. A number of passages contain detailed and candid descriptions of their sexual pleasures and their uncensored utterances and descriptions of both genitals and bodily functions.

"Th'art good cunt, though, aren't ter? Best bit o'cunt left on earth. When ter likes! When tha'rt willin'!"

"What is cunt?" she asked.

"An' doesn't ter know? Cunt! It's thee down theer; an' what I get when I'm i'side thee; it's a' as it is, all on't."

"All on't," she teased. " Cunt! It's like fuck then."

"Nay, nay! Fuck's only what you do. Animals fuck. But, cunt's a lot more than that. It's thee, dost see: an' tha'rt a lot besides an animal, aren't ter? even ter fuck! Cunt! Eh, that's the beauty o' thee, lass."

Such passages, although relevant to the plot and to the development of the characters, became the basis for numerous attempts to ban the novel.

At the end of the novel, Connie is pregnant with Mellors's child and plans to marry him after obtaining a divorce from Clifford.

CENSORSHIP HISTORY

Lady Chatterley's Lover was suppressed long before the case of *Grove Press v. Christenberry* went to trial in 1959. The decision was made to publish the novel in Italy in 1928, then to send copies to subscribers in England to avoid censors. Publishing in this way made it impossible for Lawrence to obtain an international copyright, so the author lost substantial money through the appearance of numerous pirated editions. The United States government had declared the novel obscene in 1929, and the post office ruled the novel barred from the mails. Travelers returning from Europe with copies of the novel faced having the book confiscated by United States Customs. Objections to the novel arose over both the explicit sexual description in the novel and the language used by the characters. As Charles Rembar, the lawyer who defended the novel in the 1959 trial, observed in his account of the case,

> not only did the Lawrence novel devote more of its pages to the act of sex and deal with it in greater detail than anything ever before sold over the counter; it had language that had never been seen in a book openly circulated, except when used for tangential and occasional purposes, and not often then. . . . *Lady Chatterley's Lover* presented the forbidden acts in forbidden detail, and described them in forbidden language.

In 1929, John Sumner, secretary of the New York Society for the Suppression of Vice, alerted officials at the Boston Watch and Ward Society that bibliophile and former Yale librarian James A. DeLacey, now proprietor of Dunster House Bookshop, had ordered five copies of the novel. An agent went to the bookstore to purchase the book and, after repeated refusals, finally obtained a copy. The society then instituted legal proceedings against DeLacey and his clerk, Joseph Sullivan, who were found guilty on November 25, 1929, by Judge Arthur P. Stone in Cambridge district court. DeLacey was fined $800 and sentenced to four months in jail, and Sullivan was fined $200 and sentenced to two weeks in jail. The convictions were appealed, but, despite strong community support for the two men and attestations to their character, on December 20, 1929, Judge Frederick W. Fosdick upheld the lower court conviction. The case was then taken to the state supreme court.

A year later, the novel was the key element of the "Decency Debates" that raged in the United States Senate between Senator Bronson Cutting of New Mexico and Senator Reed Smoot of Utah. Cutting worked to modify the censorship laws while Smoot opposed reform ("Senator Smoot Smites Smut," read one newspaper headline). That same year, a Philadelphia prosecutor authorized a raid on a bookshop and the seizure of 300 books, among them *Lady Chatterley's Lover*, FANNY HILL and *The Perfumed Garden*, marking the beginning of an extensive campaign to eliminate the sale of "obscene literature" in that city. Also in 1930, the Massachusetts supreme court affirmed DeLacey's conviction, and he was sentenced to four months in jail.

In 1944, John Sumner, acting in the name of the New York Society for the Suppression of Vice, seized copies of *The First Lady Chatterley*, and the book remained on the blacklist of the National Organization of Decent Literature until 1953.

The novel had appeared in expurgated form over the 30 years since it had first appeared, but the Grove Press edition was the full edition with all of the "four-letter words" and sex scenes created by Lawrence. As soon as the novel was published by Grove, Postmaster General Christenberry issued an order to ban the novel from the mails. The publisher went to court and *Grove Press Inc. v. Christenberry*, 175 F. Supp. 488 (S.D.N.Y. 1959) was heard in federal district court by Judge Frederick van Pelt Bryan, who agreed with the publisher and lifted the ban. He stated in his opinion that the application of a rule of contemporary community standards to the case signals acceptance of the book throughout the country:

> the broadening of freedom of expression and of the frankness with which sex and sex relations are dealt with at the present time require no discussion. In one best selling novel after another frank descriptions of the sex act and "four-letter" words appear with frequency. These trends appear in all media of public expression, in the kind of language used and the subjects discussed in polite society, in pictures, advertisements and dress, and in other ways familiar to all. Much of what is now accepted would have shocked the community to the core a generation ago. Today such things are generally tolerated whether we approve or not.
>
> I hold that at this stage in the development of our society, this major English novel does not exceed the outer limits of tolerance which the community as a whole gives to writing about sex and sex relations.

In *Grove Press Inc. v. Christenberry*, 276 F.2d 433 (2d Cir. 1960), the circuit court of appeals agreed with Judge Bryan's decision.

In 1959, Postmaster General Summerfield made the decision to continue to suppress copies of *Lady Chatterley's Lover* from the mail, declaring that the book was filled with "filthy," "smutty," "degrading," "offensive" and "disgusting" words, as well as with descriptions of sexual acts. He claimed that such "filthy words and passages" outweighed any literary merit that the book might have.

In England in 1960, the director of public prosecutions brought a criminal action against Penguin Books, Ltd., when the publisher announced its intention to openly publish the first unexpurgated British edition of *Lady Chatterley's Lover*. The prosecutor, Senior Treasury Counsel Mervyn Griffith-Jones, asked jurors to test the obscenity of the book themselves by answering these two questions: "Is it a book that you would have lying around your house? Is it a book that you would even wish your wife *or your servants* to read?" The defense attorneys argued that the novel as a whole was not obscene, despite language and sexual content in various passages. Thirty-five defense experts stressed the literary merit of the work, and the jury deliberated for three days before acquitting Penguin Books of all charges. Kuh relates that when the House of Lords debated the trial that cleared the novel, with its sexual episodes between a lady and her gamekeeper, a peer who agreed with the decision was asked, "Would you want your wife to read it?" He replied, "I would not object to my wife reading it, but I don't know about my gamekeeper."

In 1965, the Indecent Publications Tribunal of New Zealand reviewed the paperback edition of *Lady Chatterley's Lover* to determine if it was indecent, despite an earlier decision that no action would be taken regarding the import or sale of the cloth-bound edition of the novel. At the time, the cloth-bound edition sold in New Zealand for 16 shillings and the paperback edition for 5 shillings. The tribunal acknowledged that the novel "is a seriously written work by an author who has an established place in the field of English literature" and that "the text of the story is in the case of each identical; there is no difference between the two editions save in regard to the preface of the one and the introduction of the other and the form of each respectively."

Nonetheless, tribunal members considered if the novel should be kept out of the hands of persons under 18 years of age, and the issue became the difference in cost between the cloth-bound and the paperback editions, the low price of the paperback making it easily available to minors. This consideration motivated dissent among the members of the tribunal, two of whom asserted that "the sale of the Penguin [paperback] edition should be restricted to persons of seventeen years or over. . . . They think it is a matter for regret that the free circulation of the hardcover edition should have prejudiced the issue, embarrassed the Tribunal and made it virtually impossible in a particularly clear instance to invoke the provisions of the statute." The other three tribunal members felt that, given the unrestricted circulation of the hardcover edition, "it would be futile to classify the paperback edition as indecent in the hands of juveniles." Viewing any restrictive action against the paperback edition as futile, the majority view of the tribunal determined on April 7, 1965, that "the paperback edition of *Lady Chatterley's Lover* published by Penguin Books is not indecent within the meaning of the Indecent Publications Act of 1963."

FURTHER READING

Boyer, Paul S. *Purity in Print: The Vice-Society Movement and Book Censorship in America.* New York: Scribner's, 1968.

Grant, Sidney S., and S. E. Angoff. "Censorship in Boston." *Boston University Law Review* 10 (January 1930): 36–60.

———. "Recent Developments in Censorship." *Boston University Law Review* 10 (November 1930): 488–509.

Maddox, Brenda. *D. H. Lawrence: The Story of a Marriage.* New York: Simon & Schuster, 1993.

Paul, James C. N., and Murray L. Schwartz. *Federal Censorship: Obscenity in the Mail.* New York: Free Press, 1961.

Perry, Stuart. *The Indecent Publications Tribunal: A Social Experiment.* London: Whitcombe and Tombs, 1965.

Rembar, Charles. *The End of Obscenity: The Trials of Lady Chatterley's Lover, Tropic of Cancer & Fanny Hill by the Lawyer Who Defended Them.* New York: Random House, 1968.

Roeburt, John. *The Wicked and the Banned.* New York: Macfadden Books, 1963.

United States President's Commission on Obscenity and Pornography. *The Report of the Commission on Obscenity and Pornography.* New York: Random House, 1970.

LOLITA

Author: Vladimir Nabokov
Original date and place of publication: 1955, France; 1959, England; 1958, United States
Original publisher: Olympia Press; Weidenfeld and Nicholson; G. P. Putnam's Sons
Literary form: Novel

SUMMARY

Lolita is structured as a psychiatric case study of the pedophiliac protagonist, Humbert Humbert, the middle-aged lover of 12-year-old Lolita. The book traces Humbert's sexual obsession with young girls, his marriage to Lolita's mother, Charlotte, and the long cross-country trip that he takes with Lolita after her mother's death. Near the end of the novel, the nymphet, now 16, married, pregnant and physically worn out, writes and asks for money. Still obsessed with the image of the young Lolita, Humbert hysterically begs her to leave with him but she refuses. In desperation, he offers her a check for $3,600 and $400 in cash if she will reveal the name of the man with whom she ran off. That man is Quilty, a friend of her late mother's and Lolita's old lover from the time when Humbert was still ogling and desiring the 12-year-old. Revenge is his aim, and Humbert is later incarcerated for shooting and killing Quilty.

Humbert's obsession dominates his adult life as he sees every attractive adolescent as a seductress. As he intellectualizes his lust, Humbert places the blame for his obsession on the girls whom he feels lead him on deliberately. Sitting in parks, he "throbs with excitement," "pulses with anticipation," struggles to control the feelings that make him "race with all speed toward my lone gratification." Before meeting 12-year-old Dolores ("Lolita") Haze and her mother, Humbert has had three breakdowns and confinements in sanitariums. He refers to adventures with a succession of girllike prostitutes and relates that he frequents brothels looking for young girls.

The initial meeting with Lolita is sexually charged as Humbert notes each sensuous detail of the childlike body, then becomes obsessed with determining how to appease his sexual desire. In one early scene, he teases Lolita by taking her apple as she sits beside him on the couch. Humbert experiences "a glowing tingle" that develops into a "deep hot sweetness" that he can barely control. He feels that "the nerves of pleasure had been laid bare" and "the least pressure would suffice to set all paradise loose." As he sits "suspended on the brink of that voluptuous abyss," he moves his hand up Lolita's leg "as far as the shadow of decency would allow."

After Humbert marries Charlotte, with the aim of having freer access to Lolita, he daydreams of "administering a powerful sleeping potion to both mother and daughter so as to fondle the latter through the night with perfect impunity." Charlotte dies when she runs into traffic after reading Humbert's secret diary that details his fantasies, and Humbert tries out his sleeping pill scheme when he retrieves the orphaned Lolita from camp. The pills don't make her comatose as he had planned, but he seduces her anyway. That begins their two years of travel, posing as father and daughter as they go from motel to motel, encountering the seedy side of the American landscape. After Lolita runs away, Humbert once again has a breakdown and enters a sanitarium, which he later leaves with the intent of finding Lolita and avenging his loss.

CENSORSHIP HISTORY

Lolita was denounced as "filth" and "sheer unrestrained pornography" when it was first published. Author Nabokov claimed that *Lolita* was a comedy and disagreed with those who considered it erotic writing, yet he argued strenuously to have the novel published anonymously in order to protect his career as a professor at Cornell University. American publishers were similarly reticent about an association with the topic, and the novel was promptly refused by many when Nabokov's agent circulated it in 1954. Pascal Covici of Viking Press and Wallace Brockway of Simon and Schuster thought it would strike readers as "pornographic." James Laughlin of New Directions refused the book because "we are worried about possible repercussions both for the publisher and the author" and suggested publication in France. Before giving up, Nabokov sent the manuscript to Roger Straus of Farrar, Straus & Young and to Jason Epstein of Doubleday, who also rejected the manuscript. When the novel failed to find a publisher in the United States, Nabokov's agent took it to Olympia Press in Paris, which published it in two volumes.

After Olympia Press published *Lolita* in English in 1955, France banned the book in December 1956. The publisher, Maurice Girodias, asked Nabokov for help in fighting the ban, but the author replied, "My moral defense of the book is the book itself." He also wrote an essay entitled "On a Book Entitled Lolita" that was a lengthy justification, later attached to the American edition, in which he claimed that readers who thought the work erotic were misreading his intentions. Rather, Nabokov stated, "That my novel does contain various allusions to the physiological urges of a pervert is quite true. But after all we are not children, not illiterate juvenile delinquents, not English public school boys who after a night of homosexual romps have to endure the paradox of reading the Ancients in expurgated versions."

Olympia Press won its case in 1957 in the Administrative Tribunal of Paris, and the novel was back on sale in January 1958. When the Fourth Republic fell in May 1958 and General Charles de Gaulle assumed power, the French minister of the interior appealed to the Conseil d'Etat, the highest court in France. By December of that year, the book was again banned in France after the government successfully appealed the initial judgment. No appeal was possible, but the publication of the novel in French by the prestigious French publisher Gallimard in April 1959 gave Olympia Press foundation for a suit. The publisher sued the French government on the basis that the legal principle of equality between French citizens had been violated by the banning of the Olympia Press edition of *Lolita* and not the Gallimard edition. The English version was placed back on the market in France in September 1959.

British Customs banned the book in 1955, the same year that Graham Greene, in the *Sunday Times*, nominated *Lolita* as one of his three favorite books of the year. Greene's article led John Gordon to remark in the *Sunday Express*: "Without doubt it is the filthiest book I have ever read. Sheer unrestrained pornography." Several British publishers were eager to bid for the rights to the novel, but they waited for the enactment of the Obscene Publications Bill in 1959, which would permit literary merit to be taken into account should the book be placed on trial. They expected prosecution because reviewers were already waging a war against the novel, several stating that the novel should be suppressed in England if it could be proven that "even a single little girl was likely to be seduced as a result of its publication." Conservatives in Parliament urged Nigel Nicholson, a member of Parliament as well as a publisher, not to publish the book, claiming that it would be detrimental to the party image. He lost his next bid for reelection, partly because of *Lolita*.

In contrast, United States Customs determined in February 1957 that the book was not objectionable and could be admitted into the country. Therefore, the book could not be legally exported from France, but people who smuggled the book out could import it legally into the United States. Despite its admissibility by Customs, United States publishers refused to publish *Lolita* until G. P. Putnam's Sons took the chance in 1958. A year later, the bans in England and France were lifted and the book was published openly in those countries. In the United States, however, the Cincinnati Public Library banned the book from its shelves after the director observed that "the theme of perversion seems to me obscene."

The novel was also banned in 1959 in Argentina, where government censors claimed that the book reflected moral disintegration. In 1960, the minister of commons in New Zealand banned import of the novel under the Customs Act of 1913 that prohibited importing books deemed "indecent" within the meaning of the Indecent Publications Act of 1910. To fight the ban, the New Zealand Council of Civil Liberties imported six copies of the book and successfully challenged the Supreme Court. Mr. Justice Hutchin delivered the judgment, noting that the book had been written with no pornographic intent and for the educated reader. Basing his decision on the recommendation of a ministry advisory committee that individual orders should be permitted, the justice observed that New Zealand Customs did admit certain books addressed to authorized individuals or intended to be sold to restricted classes. The ban on *Lolita* in South Africa, instituted in 1974 because of the "perversion theme" of the novel, was lifted in 1982, and the South African Directorate of Publications gave permission for its publication in paperback form.

FURTHER READING

Baker, George. "*Lolita*: Literature or Pornography." *Saturday Review* 40 (June 22, 1957): 18.

Centerwall, Brandon S. "Hiding in Plain Sight: Nabokov and Pedophilia." *Texas Studies in Literature & Language* 32 (Fall 1990): 468–84.

Dupee, F. W. "*Lolita* in America." *Encounter* 12 (February 1959): 30–35.

Feeney, Ann. "*Lolita* and Censorship: A Case Study. *References Services Review* 21 (Winter 1993): 67–74, 90.

Hicks, Granville. "Lolita and Her Problems." *Saturday Review* 41 (August 16, 1958): 12, 38.

Levin, Bernard. "Why All the Fuss?" *Spectator* 202 (January 9, 1959): 32–33.

"Lolita in the Dock." *New Zealand Libraries* 23 (August 1960): 180–83.

Patnoe, Elizabeth. "Lolita Misrepresented, Lolita Reclaimed: Disclosing the Doubles." *College Literature* 22 (June 1995): 81–104.

Roeburt, John. *The Wicked and the Banned*. New York: Macfadden Books, 1963.

Scott, W. J. "The *Lolita* Case." *Landfall* 58 (June 1961): 134–38.

MADAME BOVARY

Author: Gustave Flaubert
Original date and place of publication: 1857, France; 1888, England

Original publisher: Michel Levy; Henry Vizitelly
Literary form: Novel

SUMMARY

Madame Bovary relates the story of Emma Roualt, a young French woman married to hardworking doctor Charles Bovary, and the manner in which she allows impossible romantic ideals to destroy her marriage and her life. Despite her husband's infatuation with her, Emma feels little for him and, instead, seeks the passionate love she has read about in romance novels. When the couple attends a fancy dress ball at the estate of a marquis, Emma dances with royalty and mingles with the rich, then leaves believing that this was the life she was born to lead.

She becomes extremely unhappy, and Charles decides that she needs a change of scenery. As they move from Tostes to Yonville, Emma learns that she is pregnant. This knowledge and the attentions of notary clerk Leon, who shares her interests in art and literature, distract her at least until the baby is born. Having hoped for a boy, Emma is disappointed when a daughter is born, and she begins to borrow money from dry goods merchant Lheureux to buy luxury items that she believes she deserves.

As Emma becomes increasingly unhappy, she gravitates toward Leon and the two profess their love but do not begin an affair. Instead, to avoid temptation, Leon moves to Paris. Emma, however, begins an affair with a patient of her husband's, the wealthy Rodolphe Boulanger, who wants only to add her to his list of conquests. Emma obsessively rushes to Boulanger's estate each morning where the two make passionate love and meets him some evenings after Charles is asleep.

After the novelty wears off and Boulanger ends the affair, Emma sinks into a deep depression, staying in bed for two months. When she recovers, Charles takes her to Rouen to enjoy the opera, but she secretly meets Leon and they begin an affair. She lies to Charles, telling him that she will take weekly piano lessons in Rouen, but she meets Leon in a hotel room each week to continue their affair.

At the same time, her debt to Lheureux increases, and she begins to borrow money elsewhere to pay him back. She becomes desperate when he confronts her and threatens to confiscate all of her property unless she immediately pays him 8,000 francs. Unable to raise the money, Emma commits suicide by ingesting arsenic after writing a letter of explanation to Charles. Her death weakens Charles, who dies soon after, leaving their daughter Berthe to work in a cotton mill to earn her living.

CENSORSHIP HISTORY

Madame Bovary was censored before publication as a novel, when it appeared in installments in *Revue de Paris*, a literary publication run by Flaubert's friend,

Maxime DuCamp. Before agreeing to publish the work, DuCamp asked to excise a single passage about a page and a half in length near the end of the novel. The passage relates Emma's extended tryst with Leon behind the closed curtains of a cab, and DuCamp felt that getting it past the censors would be "impossible." Flaubert agreed, but he was not prepared for the following editorial note inserted by the editors in place of the passage: "Here the editors found it necessary to suppress a passage unsuitable to the policies of the *Revue de Paris*; we hereby acknowledge this to the author." The editors later requested that cuts be made in the sixth and final installment of the novel, a move that Flaubert first fought, then reluctantly accepted and to which he added his own disclaimer regarding the quality of the now-fragmented work.

The omission of the offensive passages did not prevent government action being taken against *Madame Bovary*, a move that Flaubert felt was aimed more at the overly liberal *Revue* than his novel. *Madame Bovary* went on trial on January 29, 1857, in highly formal court proceedings in which Imperial Advocate Ernest Pinard admitted that the language of the law of 1819 was "a little vague, a little elastic." He also asserted that the prosecution faced "peculiar difficulty" because reading the entire novel to the jury would be too time consuming, but reading only the "accused passages" would be too restrictive. To solve the problem, Pinard summarized the novel in detail and read verbatim the offending passages. When his version reached the appropriate point in the narrative, Pinard called upon the jury to apply "limits and standards" and noted, "Yes, Mr. Flaubert knows how to embellish his pictures with all the resources of art, but without art's restraints. No gauze for him, no veils—he gives us nature in all her nudity and crudity!"

In defense, Flaubert's lawyer portrayed the novel as a handbook of bourgeois respectability, noting that it taught the consequences of straying from moral behavior. The jury, which waited a week to deliver a verdict, acquitted the author, publisher and printer without costs on the basis that their guilt had been "insufficiently established." In essence, the jury asserted that Flaubert "committed the wrong of occasionally neglecting the rules which no self-respecting writer should transgress, and of forgetting that literature, like art, must be chaste and pure not only in its form but also in its expression, in order to accomplish the good effects it is called upon to produce." A few months later, the novel was published in its entirety, all cuts restored, and sold 15,000 copies in two months.

In 1888, Flaubert's English publisher, Vizitelly, came under attack by the National Vigilance Association (NVA), a group composed mainly of clergymen founded in 1886 to continue the work of the Society for the Suppression of Vice, which had ceased operations a few years before. *Madame Bovary*, translated from French into English by the publisher's son, was specifically cited, as were works by Zola, Goncourt, Maupassant, Daudet and Bourget. The NVA gained the attention of House of Commons member Samuel Smith, M.P., who spoke in May 1888 against Vizitelly, "the chief culprit in the spread of pernicious literature." The House passed a motion that "the law against obscene publications and indecent pictures and prints should be vigorously enforced and, if necessary, strengthened." The government would leave the initiation of proceedings to private individuals.

Other politicians and the newspapers joined the campaign against pornography, widening the scope of the battle. The Roman Catholic newspaper *Tablet* attacked him as a "pornographer." The law firm Collette & Collette, retained by the NVA, obtained a summons on August 10, 1888, against Henry Vizitelly. The defense argued that Vizitelly had carefully expurgated the books while translating them into English and pointed out that the unexpurgated French versions were being freely circulated and sold in England at the same time. The prosecution declared the fact irrelevant, and the publisher went to trial at the Old Bailey in October 1888 where a jury charged him with "uttering and publishing certain obscene libels." Vizitelly was fined and ordered to desist publishing the offensive works. When he repeated the offense in 1889, the publisher received a four-month prison sentence, despite impaired health.

In 1893, the American Library Association for the first time offered a 5,000-title book guide for small popular libraries and branches, calling it a collection that "one could recommend to any trustee." No works by Flaubert were included in the list.

FURTHER READING

Elliott, Desmond. "The Book That Shocked Paris: The Strange Story of *Madame Bovary*." *Books and Bookmen* 5 (June 1960): 11, 46.
Geller, Evelyn. *Forbidden Books in American Public Libraries, 1876–1939*. Westport, Conn.: Greenwood, 1984.
Kendrick, Walter. *The Secret Museum*. New York: Viking, 1987.
Mancuso, Ludwig. *The Obscene: The History of an Indignation*. London: MacGibbon & Key, 1965.
Steegmuller, Francis. *Flaubert and Madame Bovary*. Boston: Houghton Mifflin, 1970.

MEMOIRS OF HECATE COUNTY

Author: Edmund Wilson
Original date and place of publication: 1946, United States
Original publisher: Doubleday & Co.
Literary form: Collection of short stories

SUMMARY

Memoirs of Hecate County consists of six interconnected stories that relate the lives of the well-to-do residents of a New York suburb. All of the short stories—"The Man Who Shot Snapping Turtles," "Ellen Terhune," "Glimpses of Wilbur Flick," "The Milhollands and Their Damned Soul," "Mr. and Mrs. Blackburn at Home"—and the novella entitled "The Princess with the Golden Hair" are related by an unnamed male narrator, but only the novella contains candid accounts of sexual relations.

"The Princess with the Golden Hair" relates the narrator's experiences with two women: the "princess" of the title, Imogen Loomis, the beautiful, sheltered wife of a wealthy advertising magnate, and Anna Lenihan, a young working-class woman of immigrant background who is separated from her emotionally unstable husband. He relates through diary entries his efforts to seduce Imogen while he conducts a satisfying sexual relationship with Anna. Using frank language, the narrator describes how he "liberated one little breast" of Anna's and relates that she becomes "so responsive to my kissing her breasts that I can make her have a climax in that way." After he contracts gonorrhea from Anna, the narrator sees a doctor and renews his efforts to seduce Imogen.

When the narrator and Imogen finally have an assignation, he learns that she wears a brace on her back. She claims to have tuberculosis of the spine, but the narrator later learns that her ailment is only in her imagination. Nonetheless, their sexual encounter is described at length. In a prolonged passage, the narrator describes Imogen's thighs and genitals:

> all that lay between them was impressively beautiful, too, with an ideal aesthetic value that I had never found there before. The mount was of classical feminin- ity: round and smooth and plump; the fleece, if not quite golden, was blond and curly and soft; and the portals were a deep tender rose.

She does "something special and gentle" to him, then has an orgasm, "a self-excited tremor . . . brimming of female fluid."

The narrator visits Anna, who is hospitalized to undergo surgery to correct the damage of the gonorrhea to her reproductive system. While she is at home recuperating, he urges her to marry another man whom she does not love. The novella ends as the narrator receives a letter from Anna telling him that she has taken his advice, and he now realizes that he will "never make love again."

CENSORSHIP HISTORY

The literary merit of *Memoirs of Hecate County* was established before the work was taken to court and found "obscene" in both California and New York. The *New York Times Book Review* called it "a good, distinguished book," and *Time* magazine named it "the first event of the year which can be described as 'literary.'" A further unusual aspect of the litigation is that the book was ruled "obscene" based only on one of the six stories, despite the increasing agreement of legal authorities to judge a work in its entirety and not according to specific sections that have been determined to be obscene. Wilson's fellow writers asserted that the sexual descriptions were boring rather than arousing. Raymond Chandler observed that Wilson had "made fornication as dull as a railroad time table," while Malcolm Cowley described the sex scenes as "zoological."

In 1946, booksellers in San Francisco and New York City were arrested for selling the work and taken to trial. That same year, copies of the book were confiscated in Philadelphia and the publishers ceased shipment to Massachusetts because of its censorship laws. In San Francisco, a bookseller was charged with selling an "obscene" book, but the first trial was dismissed because it resulted in a hung jury. In the second trial of *People v. Wepplo*, 78 Cal. App. 2d 959, 178 P.2d 853 (1947), the jury acquitted the bookseller.

In New York City, the New York Society for the Improvement of Morals, formerly the New York Society for the Suppression of Vice, brought suit against Doubleday & Co. for violating section 1141 of the New York State Obscenity Statute. Police confiscated 130 copies of the work from four Doubleday bookstores after society secretary John Sumner charged that the book was the "most salacious and lascivious work issued for indiscriminate circulation." The next day, major bookstores such as Brentano's, Scribner's and Hearn's had removed all copies from their shelves. Since its publication a few months earlier, 50,000 copies of the book had been sold. The publisher went to court and was convicted of obscenity for publishing *Memoirs of Hecate County* in *People v. Doubleday & Co., Inc.*, 272 App. Div. 799, 71 N.Y.S.2d 736 (1st Dep't). Literature professor and critic Lionel Trilling testified at the New York trial at the Court of Special Sessions and emphasized that the stories are related and constitute a study of good and evil. He also observed that the sexually frank passages contribute heavily to the "very moral" theme of the book. The district attorney, Frank Hogan, countered with evidence that the book contained "the most intensive concentration of sex episodes, with nothing omitted in the way of bare-skinned description." He asserted in the brief that

There are 20 separate acts of sexual intercourse. . . . These take place between the protagonist and four different women. Eighteen of the acts occur in the space of an hour or two with two different women. Three of the acts occur with two married women.

The brief cited specific pages on which these acts occur and detailed further attempts at sexual intercourse, nocturnal dreams of intercourse, daydreams of intercourse and "filthy conversations about sex" in the book. The decision was affirmed by the State Supreme Court Appellate Division in *People v. Doubleday & Co., Inc.*, 297 N.Y. 687, 77 N.E.2d 6 (1947) and the publisher was fined $1,000. The state district attorney also warned that booksellers who sold the book would be sentenced to a year in prison. Writing about the decision, *Time* magazine observed that "the decision made thousands of citizens more impatient than ever to get their morals ruined. It also proved again that finding a yardstick for proving a serious book indecent is as difficult as weighing a pound of waltzing mice."

In 1948, the case then went to the United States Supreme Court, which refused to overturn the decision of the lower court and, instead, rendered a 4 to 4 curiam decision that the book was obscene after Justice Felix Frankfurter chose to not participate. The conviction remained but the 4 to 4 decision meant that no opinion was written in *Doubleday & Co. v. New York*, 335 U.S. 848 (1948).

The book was not published in England until 1951 because publisher Frederic Warburg knew of the case against Doubleday & Co. in the United States and wanted to avoid the same action. He tried to have the text set in England but could not find a willing printer, so he begged Wilson to edit the text. Wilson refused, so the work was not published until 1951 by W. H. Allen.

In 1961, New American Library published the paperback edition of the work with the following legend on its cover: "Not for Sale in New York State." When Ballantine Books issued a paperback edition in 1966, the book was described on the cover as "authentic and unexpurgated" as well as "still banned in the State of New York."

FURTHER READING

Bates, Ralph. "Mr. Wilson's Visit to Suburbia." *New York Times Book Review* (March 31, 1946): 7,16.
"Evil in Our Time." *Time* 48 (March 25, 1946): 102.
Lockhart, William B., and Robert C. McClure. "Literature, the Law of Obscenity, and the Constitution." *Minnesota Law Review* 38 (March 1954): 295–395.
Moskin, Morton. "Inadequacy of Present Tests as to What Constitutes Obscene Literature." *Cornell Law Quarterly* 34 (Spring 1949): 442–47.
"Pound of Waltzing Mice." *Time* 48 (December 9, 1946): 24–25.

MOLL FLANDERS

Author: Daniel Defoe
Original date and place of publication: 1722, England
Original publisher: Privately printed
Literary form: Novel

SUMMARY

Moll Flanders is subtitled "The Fortunes and Misfortunes of the Famous Moll Flanders, who was born in Newgate, and during a Life of continu'd Variety, for Threescore Years, besides her Childhood, was Twelve Year a *Whore*, five times a *Wife* (whereof once to her own Brother), Twelve Year a *Thief*, Eight Year a Transported *Felon* in *Virginia*, at last grew *Rich*, liv'd *Honest*, and died a *Penitent*." The author, thus, aptly summarizes his book and provides readers with advance warning about the heroine they will encounter.

The author relates in the Preface that this is "a private history . . . where the names and other circumstances of the person are concealed." Taking the charade farther, Defoe seeks to appease potential critics by acknowledging that the story of a woman so "debauched" and "wicked" makes it difficult "to wrap it up so clean as not to give room, especially for vicious readers, to turn it to his disadvantage." Still, Defoe warns that, to be a true lesson in morality, "the wicked part should be made as wicked as the real history of it will bear."

In this spirit, Moll's adventures and philosophy are presented. She "kept true to this notion, that a woman should never be kept for a mistress that had money to make herself a wife," a state that she enters repeatedly. Sexual relationships are Moll's means to marriage. She is widowed in several instances, and marries her brother in one; thus, nothing is left for "a poor desolate girl without friends" but to try again. When the novel ends, Moll appears comfortable and ready to enjoy a secure old age.

CENSORSHIP HISTORY

Moll Flanders was popular when it first appeared, running to three editions in the first year and another edition annually for the next 60 years. The book then disappeared from publication as a single entity until 1896, when it resurfaced in an edition published in Holland. Perrin states, "It was not expurgated; it was also not reviewed." The highly popular novel was, thus, informally banned by acts of omission, but wealthy fans of the work were able to obtain copies if they were willing to buy expensive entire sets of Defoe's works. This strategy was used by the Victorians to allow "wealthy 'strong' readers" to read forbidden works. Thus, both *Moll Flanders* and the similarly racy *Roxana* (1724) were included unexpurgated in several sets of Defoe's works during the 19th century. Buyers of these volumes secondhand would find one or both novels missing for, as Desmond MacCarthy stated in *Criticism*, "When I was a boy, it [*Moll Flanders*] was not an easy book to come by. . . . From second-hand sets of Defoe's worlds that volume was frequently missing."

In 1892, when Viking Portables decided to issue an anthology entitled *Selections from Defoe's Minor Novels*, meaning everything but Robinson Crusoe, editor George Saintsbury expurgated *Moll Flanders* freely. Perrin describes the expurgation:

> But first he got out his gelding knife. Having picked a group of the blander scenes, he lopped out all racy paragraphs. . . . Then he went through again, cutting out individual sentences. . . . Finally he poked through word by word—and fell abruptly to the ranks of the lower-grade bowdlerists.

Even Defoe's subtitle created consternation among Victorians. In his comprehensive 1878 *Dictionary of English Literature*, W. Davenport Adams summarizes the subtitle as follows: "The title of a novel written by Daniel Defoe; the heroine of which is a female of questionable reputation, who afterwards becomes religious." As Perrin observes, "The one thing Moll's reputation isn't, of course, is questionable."

Through the first three decades of the 20th century, *Roxana* and *Moll Flanders* were among books regularly seized by local United States Customs inspectors for being "obscene," the last time in 1929 in New York City. The ban was lifted when the passage of the 1930 amendment to the Tariff Act eased restrictions on the importation of classics.

FURTHER READING

Alkon, Paul. *Defoe and Fictional Time*. Athens: University of Georgia Press, 1979.

MacCarthy, Desmond. *Criticism*. London: J. Dent, 1932.

Moore, John R. *Daniel Defoe: Citizen of the Modern World*. Chicago: University of Chicago Press, 1958.

Perrin, Noel. *Dr. Bowdler's Legacy*. New York: Atheneum, 1969.

Sutherland, James. *Defoe*. Philadelphia: Lippincott, 1938.

"Defoe's Works Banned." *Publishers Weekly* 116 (October 19, 1929): 1,938.

PAMELA, OR VIRTUE REWARDED

Author: Samuel Richardson
Original date and place of publication: 1740, England
Original publisher: Privately printed
Literary form: Epistolary novel

SUMMARY

Pamela, or Virtue Rewarded is concerned with a domestic middle-class and predominantly feminine world of "domestic politeness." The novel grew out of a project that several booksellers commissioned of Richardson, a book of letters to be used as models by the less educated when they needed to write on special occasions. Among these models was a letter written by parents to their daughter, a servant whose master had tried to seduce her. Richardson's imagination was piqued by the idea and he expanded it into the series of letters that became *Pamela*.

The letters from Pamela to her parents dramatize her sexual ordeal, as she describes the manner in which Mr. B first attempts to seduce and then rape her. The story pits pure female innocence against ruthless and powerful male lust in letters that are frequently written by Pamela on the run, as she escapes one trap after another. Writing in her room, Pamela hears Mr. B at her door, so she hurriedly grabs her paper and pen and continues to scribble while slipping out through an open window. She runs from him, but not so quickly that he will not catch her.

Despite all protestations of innocence, Pamela provides her readers with detailed descriptions of her ravishment. Nearly swooning, she has the presence of mind to write, "he then put his hand in my bosom," before she "fainted away with terror." She repeatedly locks herself in a closet or her room but never takes any of the many opportunities to leave the estate. Finally, Mr. B. marries Pamela.

CENSORSHIP HISTORY

Pamela's behavior motivated both praise and censure for the novel. Although Richardson's proclaimed intention was to show the reward (marriage) to be gained when a girl preserves her virtue, his contemporaries were skeptical. Author Henry Fielding attacked in a parody named *Shamela* (1741) what he viewed as the facile opportunism of Pamela. His view was that, rather than an innocent victim, the servant girl was a coy temptress who, with bold calculation, constantly put herself in Mr. B's line of vision. Another contemporary, Charles Povey, blasted Richardson's "inflammatory novel" in his work *Virgin in Eden* (1741), stating, "What can youths and virgins learn from *Pamela*'s letters, more than lessons to tempt their chastity." The outraged moralist asserted that Pamela showed a lack of the very modesty for which Richardson had praised her when she exposed herself a second time to Mr. B's advances.

Pamela was condemned by the Roman Catholic Church in 1744 and was prohibited reading for Catholics. It appeared on the Index Librorum Prohibitorum mainly because it was a novel that related a suggestively romantic relationship, despite Richardson's pretense of presenting a moral. The work appears on the Index of Benedict XIV, issued in 1758, and the Indexes of Pope Leo XIII, issued in 1881 and 1900 and still in force in 1906. As Putnam observes, the selection of fiction that appears on various editions of the Index is "curiously disproportionate, and in fact almost haphazard in its character."

Both *Pamela* and Richardson's *Clarissa Harlowe* (1747) were published as long chapbooks in the United States in 1772, when Reverend Jonathan Edwards warned the young against reading both books more because they were fiction, "considered a sinful form of writing, than because of any intrinsic sin."

In 1893, the American Library Association created for the first time a 5,000 title book guide for small popular libraries and branches, claiming it to be a collection that "one could recommend to any trustee." *Pamela* and *Clarissa Harlowe* were omitted from the list, although works by Henry Fielding were included. When the ALA released its *Catalog* in 1904, *Pamela* and *Clarissa Harlowe* were still excluded from the list, leading to the implication of censorship via omission. Many individuals agreed with Corinne Bacon, first a librarian at the Newark (New Jersey) Public Library and later the editor of the H. W. Wilson *Fiction Catalog*, in criticizing the heroine who "held out for a 'higher price' (marriage), as more immoral than Hester Prynne of *The Scarlet Letter*."

FURTHER READING

Bacon, Corinne. "What Makes a Novel Immoral?" *Wisconsin Library Bulletin* 6 (August 1910): 83–95.

Geller, Evelyn. *Forbidden Books in American Public Libraries, 1876–1939*. Westport, Conn.: Greenwood, 1984.

Thomas, Donald. *A Long Time Burning: The History of Literary Censorship in England.* New York: Praeger, 1969.

PEYTON PLACE

Author: Grace Metalious
Original date and place of publication: 1956, United States
Original publisher: Julian Messner
Literary form: Novel

SUMMARY

Peyton Place opens with some of the most provocative lines in literature: "Indian summer is like a woman. Ripe, hotly passionate, but fickle, she comes and goes as she pleases so that one is never sure whether she will come at all, nor for how long she will stay." The novel is devoid of blatantly sexual passages, except in one instance near the end, but the aura of illicit sexuality remains, as does the reminder that it is the book that "lifted the lid off a small New England town." At its most basic, *Peyton Place* is the melodramatic story of the greed, revenge, destructive pettiness and simmering sexuality that pervade many small towns. Neighbors spy on neighbors, people pry into each other's lives and townspeople try strenuously to hide their own faults and desires.

The story revolves around Allison MacKenzie, whose mother, Constance Standish, had left the town years before to make a career in New York City. Constance had returned with her infant daughter, fathered by a married man, and the story of having been married and widowed. Unaware of the circumstances of her birth, Allison dreams of similarly escaping from Peyton Place and its pettiness after high school graduation and becoming a writer in New York City. Selena Cross, the third main female character and a product of the poor neighborhood, is sexually victimized by her stepfather, but she becomes a strong and independent woman. The novel contains characters who engage in adultery and incest, and the women in the novel are among the first in popular fiction to seek sex rather than to act merely as pawns in sexual activity. Near the end of the novel, as Allison briefly becomes the lover of a married literary agent, she hesitates and states to him, "Then you think that sex between unmarried persons is excusable." Moments later, she is in his arms and "began to make moaning, animal sounds, and even then he continued his sensual touching and stroking and waited until she began the undulating movements of intercourse with her hips." She does not lose her virginity until 500 pages into the novel and seven pages before its end. Disappointed to learn that her lover is married, she returns to Peyton Place, no longer awed by its power over her.

CENSORSHIP HISTORY

Peyton Place created a sensation even before it was published; Allan Barnard, the editor at Dell Books, which bought the reprint rights in advance of publication, realized that publishing company head Frank Taylor might refuse to take a chance on the book so he told Taylor, "I have something I want to buy, but I don't want you to read it." Taylor agreed, but when he later asked about Barnard's earlier request, Barnard replied, "Because you wouldn't have let me buy it." The novel sold three million paperback copies in 1957, and more than 10 million paperback copies by 1967. Throughout years of enormous sales, the novel retained a notoriety that appeared to fuel sales.

In 1957, the city of Knoxville, Tennessee, activated a city ordinance that permitted the Knoxville City Board of Review to suppress any publication that it considered to be obscene. The target was *Peyton Place*; local dealers were forbidden to sell it. When one indignant newsstand owner tested the ordinance, it was ruled unconstitutional.

Peyton Place was banned in Ireland on May 6, 1958. A prohibition order was published in the *Iris Oifigiuil*, "the only official source from which booksellers [and readers] might learn of a new prohibition order," in which all articles blacklisted by the Irish Board of Censors were listed. According to the Censorship of Publications Bill of 1928, "the notice in *Iris Oifigiuil* should be sufficient evidence in the courts of summary jurisdiction as to the character of the publication," despite the acknowledgment by justices quoted in Adams's thorough study of Irish censorship laws that "this gazette is not a publication which booksellers are addicted to reading." The Irish Board of Censors found the work "obscene" and "indecent," objecting particularly to the author's handling of the characters' sexuality, acts of incest and "promiscuity." The work was officially banned from sale in Ireland until the introduction of the Censorship of Publications Bill in 1967 reduced to 12 years the duration of a prohibition order, and the work was among 5,000 titles released from the list of banned books.

Also in 1958, a shipment containing copies of *Peyton Place* was confiscated by Canadian Customs officers and further copies of the book were refused entry. To determine if the novel was obscene, the Canadian Tariff Board held a hearing at which a professor of English and a former professor of history gave testimony on behalf of the book. Based on their testimony, the tariff board handed down a ruling that permitted the entry of *Peyton Place* into Canada. In its statement, the board observed that the statements of the witnesses give "a distinction between obscenity and realism in literature and an interpretation of modern fiction."

The novel was one of several paperback books considered objectionable for sale to youths under 18 in *State v. Settle*, 156 A.2d 921 (R.I. 1959). In 1959, the Rhode Island Commission to Encourage Morality in Youth brought action against Bantam and three other New York paperback publishers whose books were distributed throughout the state of Rhode Island by Max Silverstein &

Sons. The commission notified Silverstein that the Bantam Books paperback editions of *Peyton Place* and *The Bramble Bush* were on their list of "objectionable" publications that they circulated to local police departments. Unwilling to risk court action, the distributor retrieved unsold copies of the books and returned them to the publishers, who appealed first to the Rhode Island Superior Court, which upheld the ban, then to the United States Supreme Court, which reversed the decision. In rendering a decision, in *Bantam Books, Inc., et.al., v. Joseph A. Sullivan et al.*, Supreme Court Justice William J. Brennan stated that "informal censorship may sufficiently inhibit the circulation of publications to warrant injunctive relief . . . [but] criminal sanctions may only be applied after a determination of obscenity has been made in a criminal trial." Although the commission had no legal means of extracting compliance from Silverstein, their means of intimidation and the threats to institute criminal proceedings followed by police visits "plainly serve as instruments of regulation independent of the laws against obscenity." The Supreme Court reversed the lower court ruling.

FURTHER READING

Adams, Michael. *Censorship: The Irish Experience*. University: University of Alabama Press, 1968.

Beattie, A. M., and Frank A. Underhill. "Sense and Censorship: On Behalf of *Peyton Place*." *Canadian Library Association Bulletin* 15 (July 1958): 9–16.

Booth, Wayne C. "Censorship and the Values of Fiction." *English Journal* 53 (March 1964): 155–64.

Davis, Kenneth C. *Two-Bit Culture: The Paperbacking of America*. Boston: Houghton-Mifflin, 1984.

Ernst, Morris L., and Alan U. Schwartz. *Censorship: The Search for the Obscene*. New York: Macmillan, 1964.

Loth, David. *The Erotic in Literature*. New York: Dorset, 1961.

Pearce, Lillian. "Book Selection and Peyton Place." *Library Journal* 83 (March 1958): 712–13.

RABBIT, RUN

Author: John Updike
Original date and place of publication: 1960, United States
Original publisher: Alfred A. Knopf
Literary form: Novel

SUMMARY

Rabbit, Run relates the story of onetime high school basketball star Harry "Rabbit" Angstrom, 26, who impulsively deserts his pregnant wife. The novel is set in the small town of Mt. Judge, a "suburb of the city of Brewer, fifth largest city in Pennsylvania," in the spring of 1959. Rabbit feels trapped in his life as a lower-middle-class family man who now demonstrates "a penny's worth of tin called a friggin' MagiPeeler in five-and-dime stores." His wife, Janice, pregnant with their second child, spends her days in an alcoholic stupor, watching television. Despite his contempt for her, Rabbit sometimes finds wisdom in the "Mickey Mouse Club," especially in the daily advice offered by head Mouseketeer, Jimmy.

Little in Rabbit's life is what it appears to be. The fame and success of his high school basketball career have left him with an idealized view of those years that extends to his old coach, Marty Tothero, now unemployed and living in a tenement. As Rabbit tries to recapture some of the order and certainty of his earlier life, he realizes that Tothero is only a broken old man with a penchant for being beaten by his stern lover, Margaret, who refers to him as "an old bloated bastard." The young minister, Jack Eccles, sent to find Rabbit and return with him to Janice and her family, is ineffective. Unable to make Rabbit return, Eccles suggests that they play golf sometime. When Rabbit arrives at the Eccles' house and finds the minister's young wife in tight orange shorts, he cannot resist slapping "her sassy ass," then ruminating on its firmness. When Rabbit eats in a Chinese restaurant, the waiters speak in heavily accented English as they take his order but speak in perfect English once he leaves.

Throughout the novel, Rabbit remains constantly aware of his sexuality. When he first runs off, he thinks of finding "hard-bodied laughers" in West Virginia and remembers the "young whores in Texas," whom he frequented when in the army. Through Tothero, Rabbit meets Ruth, a warmhearted, voluptuous prostitute into whose apartment he moves. He rhapsodizes about her body and their sexual relationship in specific detail at various points in the novel.

When Janice goes into labor, Rabbit moves home, but he moves out again when Janice rejects his sexual advances as signs of "his whore's filthiness." She accidentally drowns their baby while drunk. The day of his baby's funeral, Rabbit sees "two teenage girls in snug shorts" and is unable to resist ogling "their perky butts and expectant sex." After the funeral, Rabbit returns to Ruth, pregnant with his child, but she refuses to resume their relationship unless he chooses between his wife and her. The novel ends with the panicked Rabbit running blindly down the street.

CENSORSHIP HISTORY

Rabbit, Run was banned in Ireland on February 20, 1962. A prohibition order was published in the *Iris Oifigiuil*, "the only official source from which book-sellers [and readers] might learn of a new prohibition order," in which all articles blacklisted by the Irish Board of Censors were listed. According to the Censorship of Publications Bill of 1928, "the notice in *Iris Oifigiuil* should be sufficient evidence in the courts of summary jurisdiction as to the character of the publication," despite the acknowledgment by justices quoted in Adams's thorough study of Irish censorship laws that "this gazette is not a publication which booksellers are addicted to reading." The Irish Board of Censors found the work "obscene" and "indecent," objecting particularly to the author's handling of the characters' sexuality, the "explicit sex acts" and "promiscuity." The work was officially banned from sale in Ireland until the introduction of the revised Censorship Publications Bill in 1967.

In 1976, parents of students in six community high schools in Aroostock County, Maine, challenged the inclusion of *Rabbit, Run* in the high school libraries because of its references to sex and to an extramarital affair. Parents cited as one of several objectionable scenes Rabbit's first sexual encounter with Ruth, in which Updike first describes Rabbit caressing her breasts, then provides a detailed description of them having sex:

> He kneels in a kind of sickness between her spread legs. With her help their blind loins fit. . . . she reaches her hand down and touches their mixed fur and her breathing snags on something sharp. Her thighs throw open wide and clamp his sides and throw open again so wide it frightens him. . . . His sea of seed buckles, and sobs into a still channel. At each shudder her mouth smiles in his and her legs, locked at his back, bear down.

They also raised objections to Rabbit's constant fantasizing about sexual experiences with most of the women he meets and the language in which he expresses such desires. His two-month affair with Ruth, after he leaves Janice for the first time, motivated further objections because the book "seems to make his wife at fault for the affair."

The county school board established a review committee to consider the complaints and recommended that the book be retained. In making the final decision on the book, the school board voted 8 to 6 against banning the book from the libraries but determined that some restriction was required. In a vote of 7 to 6, with one abstention, the board decided that the novel should be placed on the reserved shelf in each of the six county high school libraries and only charged out to students who brought signed permission slips from their parents.

In 1986, the novel was removed from the required reading list for the high school English classes at Medicine Bow, Wyoming, because of the sexual descriptions and profanity in the book. In their complaint to the school board, parents cited Rabbit's cursing, including "shit," "bastard" and "son of a bitch," and Tothero's use of the word "cunt." They also identified the sexually explicit passages between Ruth and Rabbit and his "sexually explicit fantasies."

FURTHER READING

Adams, Michael. *Censorship: The Irish Experience.* University: University of Alabama Press, 1968.

Galloway, David D. *The Absurd Hero in American Fiction*: 21-50. Rev. ed. Austin: University of Texas Press, 1970.

Hunt, George W. *John Updike and the Three Great Secret Things: Sex, Religion, and Art.* Grand Rapids, Mich.: Eerdmans, 1980.

Markle, Joyce. *Fighters and Lovers: Theme in the Novels of John Updike.* New York: New York University Press, 1973.

Newsletter on Intellectual Freedom (March 1977): 36; (March 1987): 55.

Updike, John. "The Plight of the American Writer." *Change* 9 (April 1978): 36–41.

Wright, Derek. "Mapless Motion: Form and Space in Updike's *Rabbit, Run.*" *Modern Fiction Studies* 37 (Spring 1991): 35–44.

SANCTUARY

Author: William Faulkner
Original date and place of publication: 1931, United States
Original publisher: Cape & Smith
Type: Novel

SUMMARY

In brief, *Sanctuary* tells the story of sexually provocative 17-year-old Temple Drake, a socially prominent judge's daughter and college student, who accidentally becomes a witness to murder, then falls victim to a sadistic rape. Taken to the isolated house of ex-convict Lee Goodwin and his common-law wife, Ruby, one evening by her date, Gowan Stevens, after the two have had too much to drink, Stevens wants to buy bootlegged liquor. While there, he remains drunk for three days. When he finally sobers up and realizes that he is outnumbered he runs off and leaves Temple. Temple is sexually harassed, then raped with a corncob by an impotent bootlegger named Popeye, who also kills Tommy, a mentally retarded gang member who witnessed the act. Afterward, Popeye confines Temple in a Memphis brothel, where she is forced to engage in sexual acts with a stranger named Red while Popeye watches. When Temple begins to enjoy her involvement with Red, Popeye shoots him, then disappears.

Temple is located at the brothel by the lawyer assigned to defend Goodwin on the charge of murdering Tommy, but she falsely identifies him as the killer to protect her reputation. Both she and her prominent father want to hide her sexual involvement with Red and her experiences at the brothel, so they guarantee that her testimony and the trial will be over quickly by implicating Goodwin. Without remorse, Temple is escorted from the courtroom after testifying and leaves for vacation in Luxembourg. The innocent Goodwin is burned to death by a lynch mob.

Despite the persistent sexual undercurrent of much of the novel, none of the sexual acts is described in detail. Even the rape by corncob is referred to and only Temple's bleeding afterward is described. Throughout, anatomical references are limited to the thighs or the loins. The erotic passages emerge in images of Temple's appearance, with her short dress that reveals "fleet revelations of flank and thigh," and the voyeurism in the brothel. Popeye's advances are detailed: "Then it touched me, that nasty little cold hand, fiddling around inside the coat where I was naked. . . . his hand was going inside the top of my knickers." Later in the novel, after becoming eroticized by Red, Temple sits "in a floating swoon of agonized sorrow and erotic longing, thinking of Red's body," then begs him to have sex with her: "Please. Please Please. Don't make me wait. I'm burning up." The novel was unusual for its time in its topics of rape and voyeurism as well as for the brothel setting, in which a major part of the action takes place.

CENSORSHIP HISTORY

William Faulkner's sixth novel, *Sanctuary* gained notoriety as much for its erotic passages and inclusion of rape, voyeurism and prostitution as for the author's claim in his introduction to the 1932 Modern Library edition that he had written about these topics for financial rather than artistic reasons.

In 1948, *Sanctuary* was one of nine novels identified as obscene in criminal proceedings in the Court of Quarter sessions in Philadelphia County, Pennsylvania. Indictments were brought by the state district attorney, John H. Maurer, against five booksellers who were charged with possessing and intending to sell the books. The other allegedly obscene novels were Harold Robbins's *Never Love a Stranger*, James Farrell's *Studs Lonigan Trilogy* (*Young Lonigan, The Young Manhood of Studs Lonigan* and *Judgment Day*), Farrell's *A World I Never Made*, Erskine Caldwell's *God's Little Acre*, Calder Willingham's *End as a Man* and Faulkner's *Wild Palms.*

In his March 18, 1949, decision in *Commonwealth v. Gordon*, 66 D. & C. 101 (1949) that *Sanctuary* is not obscene, Judge Curtis Bok stated: "There are no vulgar Saxon words in the book, but the situations are stark and unrelieved. It makes one shudder to think of what can happen by misadventure." Bok refused to declare *Sanctuary* "obscene" because the definition in cases that he cited in his decision restricted the meaning of the term "to that of sexual impurity, and with those cases that have made erotic allurement the test of its effect." The work also failed to meet Bok's definition of sexual impurity in literature, which he defined "as any writing whose dominant purpose and effect is erotic allurement—that is to say, a calculated and effective incitement to sexual desire."

Faulkner was awarded the Nobel Prize for literature in 1950. Although *Sanctuary* did not go to court again, by 1954, it was again condemned as obscene by numerous local censorship groups throughout the United States, and the National Organization of Decent Literature placed it on the disapproved list. Also in 1954, Ireland banned *Sanctuary*, along with most of the author's other works, because of the language such as "son of a bitch," "whore," "slut" and "bastard" combined with the brutal violence of the story. Irish and U.S. censors also objected to the character Ruby, who prostituted herself to obtain money to free her common-law husband from jail, to obtain legal fees and to pay their expenses. Changes in society have removed most objections to the book, although scattered local censorship continues throughout the United States.

FURTHER READING

Gladstein, Mimi. *The Indestructible Woman in Faulkner, Hemingway, and Steinbeck*. Ann Arbor, Mich.: UMI Research Press, 1986.

Heller, Terry. "Mirrored Worlds and the Gothic in Faulkner's *Sanctuary*." *Mississippi Quarterly* 42 (Summer 1989): 247–59.

Loe, Mary Hong. "Case Studies in Censorship: William Faulkner's *Sanctuary*." *Reference Services Review* 23 (Spring 1995): 71–84.

Page, Sally R. *Faulkner's Women: Characterization and Meaning*. De Land, Fla.: Everett/Edwards, 1972.

Tanner, Laura E. "Reading Rape: *Sanctuary* and the Women of *Brewster Place*." *American Literature* 62 (December 1990): 559–82.

Williams, David. *Faulkner's Women: The Myth and the Muse*. Montreal: McGill-Queen's University Press, 1977.

Wilson, Andrew J. "The Corruption in Looking: William Faulkner's *Sanctuary* as a Detective Novel." *Mississippi Quarterly* 47 (Summer 1994): 441–60.

TROPIC OF CANCER

Author: Henry Miller
Original date and place of publication: 1934, France; 1961, United States
Original publisher: Obelisk Press; Grove Press
Literary form: Novel

TROPIC OF CAPRICORN

Author: Henry Miller
Original date and place of publication: 1939, France; 1962, United States
Original publisher: Obelisk Press; Grove Press
Literary form: Novel

SUMMARY

Tropic of Cancer relates the loneliness, futility, shallow pleasure-seeking, degradation and squalor of one American's life in France in the early 1930s. Begun as Miller's autobiography and written in the form of a diary, with a main character named for the author, the novel relates Miller's life in Paris and includes portraits of his many friends and acquaintances there. Despite the link to his life, the novel is neither chronologically organized nor specific as to dates and places. Rather, Miller uses a technique of free association in recalling events and creates an impressionistic rather than reportorial interior monologue.

An American expatriate in Paris who depends upon his friends for meals and lodging, the main character enjoys sexual adventures with a diverse number of women. His erotic life is graphically described, although the frequent use of exaggeration turns the seemingly erotic material into outlandish situations that point up the absurdity of human existence more than they arouse.

The sexual imagery and the language used to relate Miller's views are blunt throughout the novel, as the following passage that appears early in the novel illustrates:

> O Tania, where now is that warm cunt of yours, those fat, heavy garters, those soft, bulging thighs? There is a bone in my prick six inches long. I will ream out every wrinkle in your cunt, Tania, big with seed. I will send you home to your Sylvester with an ache in your belly and your womb turned inside out. Your Sylvester! Yes, he knows how to build a fire, but I know how to inflame a cunt. . . . I am fucking you, Tania, so that you'll stay fucked. And if you are afraid of being fucked publicly I will fuck you privately. I will tear off a few hairs from your cunt. . . . I will bite into your clitoris and spit out two franc pieces.

Miller also includes numerous emetic references in the work. In one instance, he describes the continuous droning speech of a dinner companion as feeling "exactly as if he had taken out that circumcised dick of his and was peeing on us." In another instance, he offers social criticism and notes, "for a hundred years or more the world, *our* world has been dying. And not one man, in these last hundred years or so, has been crazy enough to put a bomb up the asshole of creation and set it off."

Tropic of Capricorn is also semiautobiographical. The novel covers the years from 1920 to 1924 in Miller's life, before he left America for Europe. During this period, he worked for Western Union, called the Cosmodemonic Telegraph Company of North America in the work. Once again, as in the earlier novel, Miller recounts his agony in trying to "find" himself and to be true to himself despite the pressures to conform brought on artists by an industrial society. Although he was married to his first wife during the years covered by *Tropic of Capricorn*, Miller relates a series of sexual adventures with prostitutes, the wives and sisters of friends, and casual acquaintances.

Strewn throughout the novel are numerous "four-letter" words, not only relating to sexual and emetic incidents but also infused in casually related incidents. At one point, he states, "I had a good time because, as I said before, I really didn't give a fuck about anything." In another section, he notes, "I wasn't a good ass licker." He criticizes America in equally blunt language: "I think of all the streets in America combined as forming a huge cesspool, a cesspool of the spirit in which everything is sucked down and drained away to everlasting shit. . . . In the belly of the trombone lies the American soul farting its contented heart out."

As in *Tropic of Cancer*, Miller uses exceedingly frank language in this novel in referring to bizarre sexual activity with "Mona," who represents his second wife. After spying on Mona, who is masturbating in the bathroom, Miller approaches her:

> She just stood there quietly and as I slid my hand up her legs she moved one foot a little to open her crotch a bit more. I don't think I ever put my hand into such a juicy crotch in my life. . . . I had my whole four fingers inside her, whipping it up to a froth. Her mouth was stuffed full and the juice pouring down her legs. Not a word out of us, as I say. Just a couple of quiet maniacs working away in the dark like gravediggers. It was a fucking Paradise and I knew it, and I was ready and willing to fuck my brains away if necessary. She was probably the best fuck I ever had.

Despite the blunt language, sexual descriptions and emetic references, Miller manages to impart to readers the absurdity of the human condition.

CENSORSHIP HISTORY

Tropic of Cancer was first published in Paris in 1934 and remained officially banned from the United States for three decades, but college students smuggled thousands of copies into the United States in that time until Grove Press published the novel in the United States. Of nearly two million copies of the book distributed, nearly three-quarters of a million were returned to the publisher. The book was involved in at least 40 criminal cases against wholesalers and booksellers, even after the federal government refused to ban the book. An untold number of civil suits to suppress the book have also occurred, as have "voluntary" withdrawals from sale after local intimidation.

In 1950, Ernest Besig, the director of the American Civil Liberties Union in San Francisco, attempted to import both *Tropic of Cancer* and *Tropic of Capricorn* into the United States and initiated the first court case involving the novels. Citing Section 1305 of the United States Code, Customs department officials held the books and Besig sued the government. Before the case went to trial, Besig requested a motion to admit 19 depositions from literary critics testifying to the literary value of the novels and to Miller's stature as a serious writer. The motion was denied by Judge Louis A. Goodman, who stated bluntly:

> In my opinion the dominant effect of the two respondent books is obscene. Both books are replete with long passages that are filthy and revolting and that tend to excite lustful thoughts and desires. While the books also have passages,

and indeed chapters, that may be said to have literary merit, the obscene portions have no literary value; they are directly, completely and wholly filthy and obscene and have no reasonable relation to any literary concept inherent in the books' theme.

The case went to trial without a jury in 1951 with Judge Goodman presiding. Despite the presentation by Besig of literary reviews of Miller's work and the statements from critics describing the literary merits of the books, the judge condemned the books and declared them obscene. In closing statements, Judge Goodman wrote,

> The many long filthy descriptions of sexual experiences, practices and organs are of themselves admitted to be lewd. . . . It is sufficient to say that the many obscene passages in the books have such an evil stench that to include them here in footnotes would make this opinion pornographic. . . . There are several passages where the female sexual organ and its function are described and referred to in such detailed and vulgar language as to create nausea in the reader. If this be importable literature, then the dignity of the human person and the stability of the family unit, which are the cornerstones of society, are lost to us.

Besig appealed the decision to the Ninth Circuit Court of Appeals, and on October 23, 1953, the novels were again declared "obscene" by a unanimous decision in *Besig v. United States*, 208 F. 2d 142 (9th Cir. 1953). In his written decision, Circuit Judge Albert Lee Stephens characterized the books as being the "unprintable word of the debased and morally bankrupt" and claimed that, even taken as a whole, they lacked literary merit. He stated:

> Practically everything that the world loosely regards as sin is detailed in the vivid, lurid, salacious language of smut, prostitution, and dirt. And all of it is related without the slightest expressed idea of its abandon. Consistent with the general tenor of the books, even human excrement is dwelt upon in the dirtiest words possible.

The 1961 Grove Press edition of *Tropic of Cancer* attracted numerous later legal actions because no test case had been heard by the Supreme Court, as there had been in the case of *LADY CHATTERLEY'S LOVER*. Grove Press delayed appealing the earliest cases to the Supreme Court, and the delay in securing a definitive judgment proved costly because the publishing firm committed itself to assisting every bookseller prosecuted. Five state courts declared the novel "obscene" in *State v. Huntington*, no. 24657, Super. Ct., Hartford County, Conn. (1962) (Connecticut); *Grove Press, Inc. v. Florida*, 156 So. 2d 537 (Fla. Dist. Ct. App. 1963) (Florida); *Haiman v. Morris*, Ill. Sup. Ct., June 18, 1964 (opinion not printed; later withdrawn) (Illinois); *Commonwealth v. Robin*, no. 3177, C.P. Phila. Co. Penn. (1962) (Pennsylvania); and *People v. Fritch*, 13 N.Y.2d 119, 192 N.E.2d 713 (1963) (4–3 decision) (New York). Within the same period, California, Massachusetts and Wisconsin declared the novel "not obscene" in *Zeitlin v. Arnebergh*, 31 Cal. 800, 383 P.2d 152 (1963) (unanimous); *Attorney General v. Book Named "Tropic of Cancer,"* 345 Mass. 11, 184 N.E.2d 328 (1962) (4–3 decision); and *McCauley v. Tropic of Cancer*, 20 Wisc. 2d 134, 121 N.W.2d 545 (1963) (4–3 decision).

On June 22, 1964, in a 5 to 4 decision in *Grove Press, Inc. v. Gerstein*, 378 U.S. 577 (1964), the United States Supreme Court reversed the Florida decision of *Grove Press, Inc. v. Florida*, 156 So. 2d 537 (Fla. Dist. Ct. App. 1963). The judgment was reversed by a *per curiam* order in which Justice William J. Brennan Jr. declared that "material dealing with sex in a manner that advocates ideas, or that has literary or scientific or artistic value or any other form of social importance, may not be branded as obscenity and denied the constitutional protection."

Grove Press vigorously defended *Tropic of Cancer* in numerous jurisdictions, but the publisher was forced to issue a statement that it did not have the financial means to defend booksellers in cases regarding Miller's *Tropic of Capricorn*.

FURTHER READING

"Another Furor over Books." *Ohio State University Monthly* 55 (December 1963): 8–12.

Ciardi, John. "*Tropic of Cancer*." *Saturday Review* 45 (June 1962): 13.

De Grazia, Edward. *Girls Lean Back Everywhere: The Law of Obscenity and the Assault on Genius*. New York: Random House, 1992.

Hutchison, E. R. *Tropic of Cancer on Trial*. New York: Grove, 1968.

Kilpatrick, James J. *The Smut Peddlers*. New York: Doubleday, 1960.

Kincaid, Larry, and Grove Koger. "*Tropic of Cancer* and the Censors: A Case Study and Bibliographic Guide to the Literature." *Reference Services Review* 25 (Spring 1997): 31–38, 46.

Kuh, Richard H. *Foolish Figleaves? Pornography In and Out of Court*. New York: Macmillan, 1967.

Moore, Everett T. "*Tropic of Cancer*" (Second Phase). *ALA Bulletin* 56 (February 1962): 81–84.

"Obscenity-Evidence Admission of Contemporary Critical Evaluation of Libeled Book." *Minnesota Law Review* 35 (February 1951): 326–30.

Roeburt, John. *The Wicked and the Banned*. New York: Macfadden, 1963.

Smith, Roger H. "Cops, Counselors and *Tropic of Cancer*." *Publishers Weekly* 180 (October 23, 1961): 35.

United States President's Commission on Obscenity and Pornography. *The Report of the Commission on Obscenity and Pornography*. New York: Random House, 1970.

ULYSSES

Author: James Joyce
Original date and place of publication: 1918, England; 1933, United States

Original publisher: Sylvia Beach's Shakespeare & Co.; Random House
Literary form: Novel

SUMMARY

Written in the stream-of-consciousness style, *Ulysses* takes place on one day, June 16, 1904, and relates the thoughts, feelings, words and actions of Leopold Bloom, his wife, Molly, and Stephen Dedalus. The novel was severely criticized because it explicitly describes physical and sensual pleasures, makes emetic references and depicts sexual incidents in frank terms. In addition, complaints were made about the language, which contains numerous uses of "fuck," as well as frequent genital references such as "vagina," "scrotum," "penis," "hymen," and euphemisms for the genitals.

Most of the erotic references emerge through the characters of Bloom and Molly. Wandering through the city of Dublin and stopping at various bars throughout the day, Bloom reflects the journey of the epic hero Ulysses, who wandered 10 years before reaching his home and family. Bloom, who is obsessed with physical and sensual pleasures, recalls his sexual experiences while on his daylong journey, remembering one instance in which "Wildly I lay on her, kissed her; eyes, her lips, her stretch neck, beating, woman's breasts full . . . fat nipples upright." He is also explicit in emetic references, describing in detail a bowel movement in the outhouse and relating the physical sensations produced. He enjoys eating "grilled mutton kidneys which gave to his palate a fine tang of faintly scented urine."

Molly is equally concerned with emetic matter and sex. When she has run out of a skin cosmetic, she thinks, "I suppose Ill [*sic*] only have to wash in my piss." She thinks of sex with her lover, Blazes Boylan, noting, "I think he made them a bit firmer sucking them like that so long he made me thirsty titties he calls them I had to laugh yes this one anyhow stiff the nipple gets for the least thing Ill [*sic*] get him to keep that up." Molly describes the male sexual organ as a "tremendous big red brute of a thing" and "some kind of a thick crowbar" as she prepares to have sex near the end of the novel. In rhapsodizing about the encounter, she describes taking off her clothes and experiencing "one the size of that to make you feel full up . . . like a stallion driving it up into you. . . . I made him pull it out and do it on me considering how big it is so much the better in case any of it wasnt [*sic*] washed out properly the last time I let him finish it in me." The sexual references are numerous, but the descriptions emerge in a fragmentary manner, most appearing as interior monologues of the characters.

CENSORSHIP HISTORY

In 1922, the United States Department of the Post Office burned 500 copies of the novel when an attempt was made to import the book and court decisions ruled against the book. The first court trial of the book, however, actually occurred in 1921, when John Sumner, the secretary for the New York Society for the Suppression of Vice, and his followers seized an issue of the *Little Review*, which contained one chapter of the serialized version of the novel. The trial took place in the court of general sessions with magazine editors Margaret Head and Jane Heap as defendants. Author John Cowper Powys and playwright Philip Moeller, called as witnesses, testified that Joyce's style was too obscure to be understood by most people, but the court ruled against the *Little Review* and the novel.

Bowdlerized and bootlegged copies of the novel appeared, but no further action occurred until 1932, when the collector of Customs seized a copy of the book sent to Random House and declared it obscene under the Tariff Law of 1930. Random House intervened in the case because the publisher was, at that time, producing copies of the book with the intent to distribute it to the American reading public. The publisher demanded the court hearing required by the tariff law and asked for exculpation of the work. In pleas to the Federal Court of New York, Random House asked that the book be read in its entirety and that the passages declared to contain "the dirtiest language" be viewed in the context of the whole. In *United States v. One Book Entitled "Ulysses,"* 5 F. Supp. 182 (S.D.N.Y. 1933), later affirmed in *United States v. One Book Entitled "Ulysses,"* 72 F.2d 705 (2d Cir. 1934), Judge John M. Woolsey rejected the claims of obscenity, stating that despite the "unusual frankness" of the novel, "I do not anywhere detect the leer of the sensualist. I hold, therefore, that it is not pornographic." He further observed that he viewed the language and actions to be entirely consistent with the types of people whom Joyce describes. As to "the recurrent emergence of the theme of sex in the minds of his characters, it must always be remembered that his locale was Celtic and his season Spring." Judge Woolsey ruled that the book was not obscene when judged by its effect on the average man, l'homme moyen sensuel. He stated the following:

> In many places it seems to be disgusting, but although it contains, as I have mentioned above, many words usually considered dirty, I have not found anything that I consider to be dirt for dirt's sake. Each word of the book contributes like a bit of mosaic to the detail of the picture which Joyce is seeking to construct for his readers.

The government appealed the decision in the circuit court of appeals where, in *United States v. One Book Called "Ulysses,"* Judge Augustus Hand and Judge Learned Hand upheld the earlier decision. In the majority decision, they noted, "We think that *Ulysses* is a book of originality and sincerity of treatment, and that it has not the effect of promoting lust." The government chose not to appeal to the Supreme Court, and thus ended a decade-long struggle with the United States government and local censorship groups. It also provided a step toward freedom in the struggle between the moralists and publishers. In essence, the court ruled that the harm of an "obscene" book must be judged not from reading select passages but as a result of the whole book. Therefore, if the book as a whole had merit and the allegedly obscene parts were germane to the purpose of the book, then the book could not be viewed as obscene. In summing up the new interpretation of the law, Judge Augustus Hand stated:

> We believe that the proper test of whether a given book is obscene is its dominant effect. (I.e., is promotion of lust the dominant effect of reading the whole book?) In applying this test, relevancy of the objectionable parts to the theme, the established reputation of the work in the estimation of approved critics, if the book is modern, and the verdict of the past, if it is ancient, are persuasive pieces of evidence; for works of art are not likely to sustain a high position with no better warrant for their existence than their obscene content.

A significant result of the verdict was that it led judges and prosecutors to examine a book in its entirety rather than according to isolated passages. The decision also admitted the novel into the United States.

FURTHER READING

"Another Repeal: Joyce's *Ulysses* Is Legal at Last." *Nation* 137 (December 20, 1933): 693.

Arnold, Bruce. *The Scandal of "Ulysses": The Sensational Life of a Twentieth-Century Masterpiece*. New York: St. Martin's, 1994.

Bryer, J. R. "Joyce, *Ulysses* and the *Little Review*." *South Atlantic Quarterly* 66 (Spring 1967): 148–64.

Ernst, Morris L., and Alan U. Schwartz. *Censorship: The Search for the Obscene*. New York: Macmillan, 1964.

Marcuse, Ludwig. *The History of an Indignation*. London: MacGibbon & Key, 1965.

Paul, James C. N., and Murray L. Schwartz. *Federal Censorship: Obscenity in the Mail*. New York: Free Press, 1961.

St. John-Stevas, Norman. *Obscenity and the Law*. London: Secker & Warburg, 1956.

United States President's Commission on Obscenity and Pornography. *The Report of the Commission on Obscenity and Pornography*. New York: Random House, 1970.

WOMEN IN LOVE

Author: D. H. Lawrence
Original date and place of publication: 1920, United States
Original publisher: Thomas Seltzer
Literary form: Novel

SUMMARY

Women in Love deals with the psychological explorations and the interrelationships of sisters Ursula and Gudrun Brangwen as they deal with love and life in a small English mining town. Alike in many respects, the sisters mirror the goals and desires of other modern young women of the early 19th century in their reservations about marriage and having children, as well as in their hatred of their middle-class origins. Ursula, however, is different from Gudrun in her ability to respond both spiritually and physically to Rupert Birken, although the two struggle mightily before Ursula and Rupert reach an understanding in which "He wanted sex to revert to the level of the other appetites, to be regarded as a functional process, not as a fulfillment." When they do consummate their relationship, Lawrence blends the physical passion with a spiritual bonding.

> They threw off their clothes, and he gathered her to him, and found her, found the pure lambent reality of her forever invisible flesh. Quenched, inhuman, his fingers upon her unrevealed nudity were the fingers of silence upon silence. . . . She had her desire fulfilled. He had his desire fulfilled.

In another segment of the novel, their sexual interaction is more fully revealed as "Kneeling on the hearth-rug before him, she put her arms around his loins, and put her face against his thighs."

Gudrun, on the other hand, and her lover Gerald are too self-absorbed to establish any true communication, and references to their sexual relationship are brief.

Beyond the sensual passages between Ursula and Rupert, critics have objected to Rupert's desire for intimacy with Gerald Crich. Rupert believes that men are capable of establishing an intimate friendship that a man can never attain with a woman. At one point in the novel when the two men wrestle in the nude, Rupert believes that he and Gerald are about to reach a plateau of trust and understanding, but Gerald appears unable to surrender his feelings entirely to anyone.

CENSORSHIP HISTORY

Overall, although *Women in Love* does not contain language that is usually identified as "obscene," nor are passages graphically sexual, the sexual relationship between Ursula and Rupert and the homoerotic relationship of Rupert and Gerald evoked strong objections from critics. The novel first appeared in 1920 in a limited edition of 1,250, marked "for subscribers only." The title page omitted Seltzer's imprint and carried, instead, the phrase "Privately Printed" to protect the company from attacks by censors. That move alone might have signaled to would-be censors that even the publisher thought the book too erotic to be published as part of the company's usual list. Two years later, Seltzer published the novel in a regular trade edition with the company imprint. In 1922, the limited edition of *Women in Love* became one of three titles, published by Thomas Seltzer, that were involved in a well-publicized censorship case. The other two were Arthur Schnitzler's *Casanova's Homecoming* and the anonymous *Young Girl's Diary*. The magistrate's court ruled in favor of the publisher.

In 1923, Supreme Court Justice John Ford tried to suppress *Women in Love* after his daughter brought the book home from the circulating library that had recommended it to her. Ford founded the Clean Books League and worked with John Sumner, secretary of the New York Society for the Suppression of Vice, to achieve the passage of a "clean books" bill in the New York legislature. He also favored upholding and strengthening existing obscenity laws. Incensed by the action, Lawrence sent Ford a telegram from Taos, quoted on page 580 of the February 24, 1923, issue of *Publishers Weekly*:

> Let Judge John Ford confine his judgment to courts of law, and not try to perch in seats that are too high for him. Also let him take away the circulating library tickets from Miss Ford, lest worse befall her. She evidently needs an account at a candy shop, because, of course, 'Women in Love' wasn't written for the Ford family. . . . Father and mother and daughter should all leave the tree of knowledge alone. The Judge won't succeed in chopping it down, with his horrified hatchet. Many better men have tried and failed.

FURTHER READING

Boyer, Paul S. *Purity in Print: The Vice-Society Movement and Book Censorship in America*. New York: Scribner's, 1968.

"Censorship Beaten in New York Case." *Publishers Weekly* 102 (September 16, 1922): 801–904.

De Grazia, Edward. *Girls Lean Back Everywhere: The Law of Obscenity and the Assault on Genius*. New York: Random House, 1992.

Ford, John. *Criminal Obscenity, a Plea for Its Suppression*. New York: Revell, 1926.

Lawrence, D. H. "On Obscenity." *Publishers Weekly* (February 23, 1923): 580.

Loth, David. *The Erotic in Literature*. New York: Dorset, 1961.

LITERATURE SUPPRESSED ON SOCIAL GROUNDS

The broad nature of obscenity laws has made possible a wide interpretation of what constitutes an essentially "obscene" literary work. The language of American law stresses work that "depicts or describes sexual conduct in a patently offensive manner." The law also specifies that the "average person, taking contemporary community standards, would find that a work, taken as a whole, appeals to the prurient interest." Often what this has meant in reality is that works containing words deemed "vulgar" by specific members of a community or presenting interracial or homosexual relationships that are unacceptable to the standards of a given community acquire the label "obscene." These are social factors, the topic of this section, and they are distinctly different from erotic, religious and political content.

Censors have so frequently applied such general guidelines to published writing that a wide range of literature has been declared "obscene." This section avoids such generalization. Instead, the books discussed here are literary works that have been banned, censored or challenged because of language, racial characterization or depiction of the drug use, social class or sexual orientation of characters, or other social differences, that their challengers have viewed as harmful to readers. thus Mark Twain's *The Adventures of Huckleberry Finn* is included, while D. H. Lawrence's *Lady Chatterley's Lover* is not, even though both have been banned in the past for being "obscene"; the first has attracted the label because of its language and depiction of race, while the second contains graphic sexual description and has been banned for its erotic content. The following books have been censored because their subject matter and characters do not conform to the social, racial or sexual standards of their censors.

The goal of this section is to identify and discuss books that have been censored as obscene, in centuries past as well as in the 20th century, either because the authors or the works did not conform to the social expectations of their censors or because they contain socially unacceptable ideas or speech. Taken as a whole, the entries provide a fascinating view of socially motivated censorship.

—Dawn B. Sova, Ph.D.

THE ADVENTURES OF HUCKLEBERRY FINN

Author: Mark Twain (Samuel Langhorne Clemens)
Original date and place of publication: 1884, London
Original publisher: Self-published
Literary form: Novel

SUMMARY

This novel relates the adventures and struggles of a rambunctious young southern boy in the early 19th century. Told from the first-person point of view, *The Adventures of Huckleberry Finn* portrays river life in a developing America, and young Huckleberry Finn's adventures while on the journey from boyhood to manhood. The story begins with Huck's escape from his brutal father, and follows him up the Mississippi River as he and his slave friend Jim run from authorities and various other scoundrels.

As the novel opens, Huck reminds readers that many of his adventures have already been detailed in Mark Twain's *The Adventures of Tom Sawyer*. He states that the $12,000 that he and Tom had found in the previous novel was invested for them and was earning interest. As the novel opens, Huck, who now lives with the Widow Douglas and Miss Watson, expresses annoyance with the amount of concern placed on making him conform to society. Huck sees no point in this lifestyle and yearns to be a rambunctious youth, as is his nature.

As the narrative progresses, Huck's father, the town drunk and a general burden on society, learns of Huck's recent wealth. He kidnaps Huck and holds him hostage in a shack in a remote area outside the town. While Huck waits to be either freed or rescued, his father repeatedly beats him, leaving Huck convinced that escape is the only feasible solution. To accomplish this, he conjures up a plan to make it appear that he has been murdered. Succeeding in his plan, Huck flees to safety on Jackson's Island, where he is reunited with Miss Watson's runaway slave, Jim. Jim is also hiding, fearful that he will be caught and punished for leaving his mistress. Huck agrees not to speak of Jim to anyone, and the two become partners. Aware that men are looking for Jim, the two decide to leave the island in search of adventure and the free states.

They board a raft that they found on the island and begin their journey. By day they hide on land, and by night they travel on the river. All goes well until one night when, during a violent storm, the raft is torn apart by an oncoming steamship. This experience not only almost ends Huck's young life, but it also separates him from Jim.

Huck swims to shore and finds himself in the midst of a feud between two families, the Grangerfords and the Shepherdsons, and he is immediately attacked by members of the Grangerford family. He states his name as George Jackson and explains quickly that he fell off a riverboat and was washed ashore. He stays with the family for a short time, enjoying their lifestyle and making new friends along the way, and he even manages to be reunited with Jim. When the family feud escalates and Huck and Jim watch numerous members of both families die, they decide to resume their adventure on the river, where they meet two men known as the duke and the king. The unscrupulous men specialize in robbery and deceit, and they do not hesitate to pose as a dead man's next of kin in order to receive a rather large inheritance. The innately moral Huck refuses to cooperate, and he reveals the duke and the king's deceit. The scoundrels flee, but they first sell Jim to Silas Phelps.

Seeking to obtain Jim's freedom, Huck visits the Phelps farm where he is mistaken for Tom Sawyer, who is expected to arrive the same day. Huck allows the deception to continue, then meets with the real Tom, who agrees that Huck will continue to pose as Tom, and Tom will pose as his brother Sid. The two also agree to free Jim as soon as possible. After many attempts, Jim finally escapes, but Tom is accidentally shot in the leg during the effort. Although Jim has been portrayed as ignorant throughout the novel, he is a morally decent man who temporarily puts aside his dreams of freedom to nurse Tom back to health.

The novel closes as Jim and the boys learn that Jim is already a free man, as decreed by the last will and testament of Miss Watson, his former owner. This puts an end to all escape plans, and allows Jim to be the one thing that he has always wanted to be, free. Huck also decides to leave and wander on his own, convinced that the civilized world is no place for him.

CENSORSHIP HISTORY

The novel excited controversy from the outset, when Concord (Massachusetts) Public Library banned the book in 1885, charging that the novel was "trash suitable only for the slums." Conventional morality was offended by the street vernacular spoken by Jim and Huck, as well as by their coarse behavior. Denver (Colorado) Public Library banned the novel in 1902, and Brooklyn Public Library removed it from the children's room on the charge that "Huck not only itched but he scratched, and that he said sweat when he should have said perspiration." In 1930, guards at the U.S.S.R. border confiscated the novel, along with *The Adventures of Tom Sawyer*.

In the United States, the furor quieted down for five decades, as the novel became an American classic and a mainstay of school reading lists. A new challenge emerged in 1957 when the National Association for the Advancement of Colored People protested the racist aspects of the book and demanded that it be removed from high schools in New York City. African-American author Ralph Ellison noted that Huck's friendship with Jim demeaned the stature of black males, because the adolescent Huck is portrayed as equal or superior to the adult Jim in decision-making capability. In 1969 Miami Dade (Florida) Junior College removed the novel from the required reading list, charging that the book inhibited learning in black students by creating an emotional block.

In 1973 the Scott, Foresman publishing company yielded to the demands of school officials in Tennessee and prepared a version of the novel that omitted material to which officials objected. The version omits the passage in Chapter 18 in which the young men of the Grangerford family toast their parents each morning with alcohol. It appears in *The United States in Literature*, a textbook distributed and used nationally.

The most frequent objection to the novel has been its language in reference to African Americans. Yielding to pressures from school districts across the nation, textbook publishers up to 1975 met challenges by substituting euphemisms for the term "nigger." Scott, Foresman rewrote passages to eliminate the word, Singer replaced the term with "slave" and McGraw-Hill replaced the term with "servant." In a 1975 dissertation, Dorothy Weathersby found that Ginn and Company was the only textbook publisher to retain the word, but their textbook included an essay by Lionel Trilling to explain the need to include the word in the novel.

The novel has been frequently banned or challenged by school districts for its language, particularly its racial references and the use of the slur "nigger." A significant number of such challenges have come from well-educated, middle-class, African-American parents who wish to prevent their children from exposure to such insulting references. The Winnetka (Illinois) school district challenged the novel as being racist in 1976, as did school districts in Warrington, Pennsylvania in 1981; Davenport, Iowa in 1981; Fairfax County, Virginia in 1982; Houston, Texas in 1982; State College, Pennsylvania in 1983; Springfield, Illinois in 1984; and Waukegan, Illinois in 1984.

In 1988 Rockford (Illinois) public schools removed the book from their required reading list because it contained the word "nigger." Berrien Springs (Michigan) High School challenged the novel that same year, while Caddo Parish (Louisiana) removed the novel from both its school libraries and required reading lists, charging that it contained racially offensive passages. The following year, the novel was challenged at Sevierville County (Tennessee) High School due to perceived racial slurs and the use of ungrammatical dialect.

The 1990s brought new challenges and continued antagonism to the novel. Citing derogatory references to African Americans, parents challenged its inclusion on the supplemental English reading list in Erie (Pennsylvania) High School in 1990. That same year, the novel was challenged as being racist in Plano (Texas) Independent School District.

In 1991 citing the repeated use of the word "nigger," parents in Mesa (Arizona) Unified School District challenged inclusion of the novel in the curriculum and claimed that such language damaged the self-esteem of young African Americans. For the same reason that year, the novel was removed from the required reading list in the Terrebone Parish public schools in Houma,

Louisiana. Also in 1991 it was temporarily removed from the Portage (Michigan) curriculum after African-American parents charged that the portrayal of Jim and other African Americans made their children "uncomfortable."

In 1992, the school superintendent of Kinston (North Carolina) School District removed the book from the middle school in the belief that the students were too young to read a work containing the word "nigger." Concern with the same word, as well as additional "offensive and racist language," motivated a 1992 challenge to including the novel on the required reading list in Modesto (California) High School. In 1993, challengers charged in the Carlisle (Pennsylvania) school system that the racial slurs in the novel were offensive to both African-American and Caucasian students. In contrast to other areas, the Lewisville (Texas) school board retained the novel on school reading lists in 1994, despite challenges of its racism. The most comprehensive objection to the novel regarded its use in English classes at Taylor County (Butler, Georgia) High School in 1994, when challengers not only claimed that it contained racial slurs and improper grammar, but it also did not reject slavery.

FURTHER READINGS

Bradley, Julia T. "Censoring the School Library: Do Students Have the Right to Read?" *Connecticut Law Review* 10 (Spring 1978): 747–71.

Cloonan, Michele. "The Censorship of the Adventures of Huckleberry Finn." *Top of the News* (Winter 1984): 191–94.

Geller, Evelyn. *Forbidden Books in American Public Libraries, 1876–1939: A Study in Cultural Change*. Westport, Conn.: Greenwood Press, 1984.

Nelson, Randy F. "Banned in Boston and Elsewhere." *The Almanac of American Letters*. Los Altos, Calif.: William Kaufman, 1981.

Newsletter on Intellectual Freedom. (May 1969): 52; (July 1976): 87; (September 1976): 116; (November 1981): 162; (January 1982): 11, 18; (May 1982): 101; (July 1982): 126; (September 1982): 171; (January 1984): 11; (May 1984): 72; (July 1984): 121–22; (November 1984): 187; (January 1985): 38; (September 1988): 152–53; (November 1988): 201; (January 1989): 11; (March 1989): 43; (May 1989): 94; (January 1991): 17–18; (March 1991): 44–45; (May 1991): 90–92; (March 1991): 43, 64; (July 1992): 126; (September 1992): 140; (May 1993): 73; (May 1994): 99–100; (March 1995): 42.

People for the American Way. *Attacks on the Freedom to Learn, 1990–91*. Washington, D.C.: People for the American Way, 1991.

Reichman, Henry. *Censorship and Selection: Issues and Answers for Schools*. Chicago: American Library Association; Arlington, Va.: American Association of School Administrators, 1993. A joint publication.

Weathersby, Dorothy T. *Censorship of Literature Textbooks in Tennessee: A Study of the Commission, Publishers, Teachers, and Textbooks*. Ed.D. dissertation, University of Tennessee, 1975.

ANNE FRANK: THE DIARY OF A YOUNG GIRL

Author: Anne Frank
Original date and place of publication: 1947, The Netherlands
Original publisher: Contact Publishers
Literary form: Diary

SUMMARY

Anne Frank: The Diary of a Young Girl is a compilation of the notebooks and papers left behind by a 15-year-old Jewish girl, Anne Frank, when she and her family were taken from their hiding place in Amsterdam by German soldiers during the Nazi occupation of the Netherlands in World War II. The hiding place was a "secret annex," a group of rooms at the top and back of a building that served as a warehouse and office for a Dutch-owned business. Those hiding remained quiet by day, while business was conducted in the lower part of the building, but they moved freely at night when the building was deserted. After the Frank family was taken, members of the Dutch family that had sheltered them gathered the papers and hid them in a desk without reading them. When Otto Frank, Anne's father and the only one of the family to survive the war, returned from the death camps, he took the papers and sought to publish them. He would thus fulfill his late daughter's dream for her work, and make her live again through her writing.

The final published diary is the combination of Anne's original text with the later edited version that she began, modifying her earlier, more childish phrasing. She also used pseudonyms for the other occupants of the annex, as well as for their protectors, to prevent hurt feelings in instances in which she is critical of them. She writes at several points in the diary that she wants it to live on long after her death and would like it published as *Het Achterhuis* (The House Behind), the title under which the work first appeared.

The small red-checkered diary, which Anne named "Kitty," was a birthday present from her father on her 13th birthday, June 12, 1942, less than a month before they would enter the annex. She began the diary on her birthday, writing in it and in notebooks for the family's 25 months in hiding, from July 5, 1942 through August 1, 1944, three days before Gestapo Sergeant Silverbauer and four soldiers broke in and took them away. In the diary Anne followed the course of the war and recorded her hopes, dreams, fears and desires, as well as her observations of daily life. The increasingly bad news brought by their protectors, as well as what they heard on the English radio, also prompted Anne's reflections.

Anne's observations about her family as well as the dentist, Mr. Dussel, and the Van Daan family (a father, mother and 16-year-old son), who share the annex with the Franks, are followed in the diary. She irritably records Mrs. Van Daan's attempts to flirt with Otto Frank, noting that "she strokes his face and hair, pulls her skirt right up, and makes so-called witty remarks," and registers her relief that her father "doesn't play ball." She also records the idiosyncrasies of the other inhabitants, as well as her coldness toward her mother. The reader also learns that the three young people managed to read a lot during their stay and even completed a correspondence shorthand course. Anne also manages to maintain her sense of humor as conditions worsen, remarking at one point when food becomes scarce, "Whoever wants to follow a slimming course should stay in the 'Secret Annexe'!"

CENSORSHIP HISTORY

Censorship of *Anne Frank: The Diary of a Young Girl* began with its initial publication in the Netherlands. Anxious to spare the feelings of their protectors and the memory of the other occupants, Otto Frank excised details of the squabbling among the occupants of the annex, and sections in which Anne complained about the selfishness or insensitivity of others. Because she viewed the diary as her private writing, Anne frequently expressed unadorned thoughts and concerns, and used the diary as a means of venting her frustrations with the situation. Her father removed such passages without changing significantly the overall representations of the others or their relationships.

Once Otto Frank sought a publisher, additional censorship was required. The Dutch publisher, Contact, required that certain passages that the editors viewed as "tasteless" or "unseemly" be removed. These included Anne's references to her and her sister's menstruation. Anne's growing sexual curiosity was also deemed unacceptable, despite the naturalness of such curiosity in an adolescent. Therefore, a passage in which she recalls a friend's developing breasts and muses about wanting to touch them was removed. The publisher also asked that Otto Frank delete all "offensive" remarks made by Anne about her mother.

In 1950 the German publishing firm of Lambert Schneider commissioned a German translation, and additional censorship occurred. The *Critical Edition* notes that material that would have been especially offensive to German readers was removed. One such passage written by Anne related the rule in the annex that everyone was required "to speak softly at all times, in any civilized language, therefore not in German," which Lambert Schneider changed to "All civilized languages . . . but softly."

The 1952 publication of the diary in England restored most of the excised material. More recent challenges have focused on Anne's growing sexual awareness. In a January 5, 1944, entry Anne recollects sleeping with a girlfriend and having "a strong desire to kiss her," which she did. She states further that she was terribly curious about the other girl's body, "for she had always kept it hidden from me. I asked her whether, as proof of our friendship, we should feel one another's breasts, but she refused. I go into ecstasies every time I see the naked figure of a woman, such as Venus, for example. . . . If only I had a girl friend!" At the same time, she develops a crush on Peter Van Daan, who shows her "the male organs" of a cat, and with whom she experiences her first ardent kiss on the mouth, questioning if she "should have yielded so soon." She also observes increased flirting between the dentist and Mrs. Van Daan and notes that "Dussel is beginning to get longings for women."

In 1982, parents in Wise County, Virginia, challenged the use of the book in school and asserted that Anne's discussion of sexual matters was "inappropriate" and "offensive" and that the criticism of her mother and of the other adults "undermines adult authority." Others have objected to the discussion of "the mistreatment of the Jewish people" and one parent of Arab ancestry objected to the portrayal of a Jewish girl. In 1983, four members of the Alabama Textbook Commission wanted to reject the title for use in the schools because it was "a real downer."

FURTHER READINGS

Frank, Otto. "Introduction." In *Anne Frank. The Diary of a Young Girl: The Definitive Edition.* Ed. by Otto Frank and Mirjam Pressler. New York: Doubleday & Company, 1995.
Newsletter on Intellectual Freedom (March 1983): 39.
Wisse, Ruth. "A Romance of the Secret Annex." *New York Times Book Review* (July 2, 1989): 2.

ANNIE ON MY MIND

Author: Nancy Garden
Original date and place of publication: 1982, United States
Original publisher: Farrar, Straus & Giroux
Literary form: Young adult novel

SUMMARY

Annie on My Mind details what happens to two teenage girls who recognize that they love each other. Students at different schools who start out as friends, Annie and Liza meet at a museum and share a common interest in art and the Middle Ages. Annie is the daughter of minimally educated Italian immigrant parents and attends an inner-city school. In contrast, Liza is from an affluent family. Her parents are professionals and she attends Foster Academy, a private school where she is student council president.

The main setting of the book is Foster Academy, run by a headmistress who demands that even minor infractions of rules be disciplined. The academy is in financial trouble, and a fund drive is in progress, a complication that requires that all hint of scandal be eliminated or the academy will suffer.

The love between Annie and Liza develops gradually. They have difficulty admitting their feelings because of the stigma attached to their love, and there is no place for them to become physically intimate. When two of the academy's best-liked teachers, Ms. Widmer and Ms. Stephenson, who share a house, go on vacation, Liza offers to care for their cats, then realizes that she and Annie can be alone there. Liza also discovers that the two teachers are lovers when she explores the empty house, sees books about lesbians in the master bedroom and notices the bedroom furnishings. During that spring vacation, Liza and Annie meet at the house and explore their sexual relationship. They are discovered by another student and a nosy school secretary who tells the headmistress and exposes the two teachers as well.

Liza is suspended from school and required to attend a disciplinary meeting of the school's board of trustees, who will decide if the incident should be placed on her permanent record and if the board should inform the Massachusetts Institute of Technology, which has accepted Liza as an architectural student. Annie attends another school, so she is spared the humiliation and her parents never learn about the incident. The academy board takes no disciplinary action, but Liza must bear nasty remarks and whispering when she returns to school. The two teachers, however, lose their jobs because the school mistakenly believes that they influenced the girls.

Annie attends the University of California at Berkeley on the West Coast, while Liza remains on the East Coast and attends MIT in the fall. Annie writes Liza a letter, but Liza does not answer it. Finally, after realizing that she does love Annie, Liza telephones her and they decide to get together during Christmas vacation.

CENSORSHIP HISTORY

The novel has frequently been attacked on the grounds that it promotes, idealizes or encourages homosexuality. Challengers who have not read the book mistakenly charge that it contains explicit sex. Other critics cannot accept the positive portrayal of the gay characters, who are not psychological misfits, nor are they condemned. Yet the book makes a compelling point that homosexual behavior risks harsh consequences and may often result in pain and suffering for individuals who dare to challenge the majority.

In 1988, patrons of Cedar Mill Community Library in Portland, Oregon, challenged the book because it portrays lesbian love and sex as being normal. The book was temporarily removed from shelves, then returned. In 1990, a parent in Sedgwick, Maine, became upset when she learned that the novel was included in the seventh- and eighth-grade library. She objected to the lesbian relationship portrayed. The matter was referred to the school board because the school district did not have a complaint policy in place. The board created a review committee consisting of board members, educators and parents, who voted to retain the book in the library.

In 1991 *Annie on My Mind* disappeared mysteriously from two high school libraries in San Ramon, California. The librarians later discovered that the vice principals of the two high schools had taken the book from the libraries, claiming to want to examine them. The copies had been donated by a community member, who publicly accused the vice principals of censorship and stated, "They might as well burn the books; clearly the intent is to deny students books having a gay or lesbian theme." Although the vice principals denied censoring the books, a representative of the American Civil Liberties Union determined that this had been the intent and stated that "a school district cannot exclude the topic of homosexuality from a school library."

In 1992 librarians at Colony (Texas) Public Library received numerous requests to remove the novel because "it promotes and encourages the gay lifestyle." After receiving the first complaint, the library board members voted unanimously to retain the book in the library and issued a statement that it was not the job of the library to tell children what they could read, "it is the parents' job." The board maintained that position when other complaints followed and encouraged parents to evaluate themselves the materials to which their children were exposed.

In 1993 parents of students at Bend (Oregon) High School challenged the book in their school library because it "encourages and condones" homosexuality. The school board considered the complaints and voted to retain the book. That same year the book was also challenged but retained in the Lapeer (Michigan) West High School library. Several Kansas school districts also experienced challenges in 1993 after the schools received a donation of library copies of the novel from a national group that sought to give young adults "fair, accurate, and inclusive images of lesbians and gay men." The book was first removed, then returned to general circulation in the library in Shawnee Mission School District. Copies of the book were doused with gasoline and burned by a minister and his followers in the Kansas City School District, but a copy of the novel was retained in the high school library, and the school district donated the novel to the city's public library.

In 1994 the novel was banned from the libraries of five junior high and three senior high schools in Olathe, Kansas, by the superintendent of schools with the backing of the school board. When the district refused to return the book to the school libraries, six students and their families contacted the American Civil Liberties Union and filed a lawsuit against the school. The case was decided in December 1995, when a U.S. district judge ruled that the school board and superintendent had violated the First Amendment of the United States Constitution by removing the novel from the school libraries. The judge ordered the district to return copies of the novel to the school libraries and to pay legal fees and expenses for the plaintiffs.

The novel was also removed from the Chanute (Kansas) High School library in 1994, after parents challenged the work. Librarians returned the book to a limited-access shelf and made it available only to those who had written parental permission.

FURTHER READINGS

"Annie Goes Back to School." *School Library Journal* 42 (January 1996): 13.

Cart, Michael. "Carte Blanche: Winning One for the First Amendment." *Booklist* 92 (April 15, 1996): 1,431.

Newsletter on Intellectual Freedom (January 1990): 4–5; (January 1992): 5–6; (July 1992): 125–26; (September 1993): 158-59; (November 1993): 191–92; (January 1994): 13; (March 1994): 51–52; (May 1994): 84; (July 1994): 129; (September 1994): 140–41; (March 1995): 40.

Olson, Renee. "Battles over Books Usher in New School Year." *School Library Journal* 41 (October 1995): 10–11.

ANOTHER COUNTRY

Author: James Baldwin
Original date and place of publication: 1962, United States
Original publisher: The Dial Press
Literary form: Novel

SUMMARY

The novel is set in New York City and moves freely from Greenwich Village to Harlem, as it recounts a year in the lives of the seven major characters. *Another Country* spotlights the interrelationships and artistic careers of African-American jazz drummer Rufus and his sister Ida, a singer, with those of five white characters: Vivaldo, Ida's lover and a would-be writer; Yves, a young Frenchman, and his lover, Eric, an actor; Richard, a pulp novelist, and his wife, Cass. Through the often complex interaction of the characters of both races set in the period of the mid-1950s, the author investigates the deep racial wounds suffered by both groups. He experiments with the concept of equality by placing his characters on roughly similar levels, then examines the reasons for their failure to remain at these levels. Baldwin seeks to shatter prevailing social concepts as he erases established color and sex lines, and spends social expectations of the period by the freedom with which he writes of interracial sex and homosexuality.

Written in social-realist style, the novel examines the lives of its characters at a specific moment in time; in so doing, it successfully recreates the people, streets, stores, apartments and sounds of the city, its glory as well as its more sordid aspects. In keeping with the stress on reality, the characters speak as their real-life counterparts speak, expressing their fears, frustrations, desires and emotions in street vernacular and sprinkling their conversations with obscenities. White characters are sexually attracted to African-American characters, men are drawn to men and the surrounding city casts a squalid gloom on all their lives.

From the outset, despite their efforts, the characters are doomed to succumb to a fate beyond their control. Rufus Scott, a talented and successful musician, internalizes the low opinion of African-American men held by the society of his time. When his white lover, Leona, professes her love and seeks his approval, his lack of self-esteem and inability to overcome the pain of former rejections prevent him from returning her love. Instead, he labels her "white trash" for loving a black man, physically abuses her and accuses her of sneaking out with his male friends. Unable to deal with the hopelessness of his fate, Rufus, the most fully developed character in the novel, commits suicide by jumping off the George Washington Bridge in the first fifth of the novel. In the remaining four-fifths, the rest of the characters cope with their loss, recalling from their unique perspectives their relationships with Rufus and their own frustrations in life.

Although reviewers criticized his unconventional sexual pairings in the novel, the public made it a success and *Another Country* became the second-best-selling novel of the year when it came out in paperback in 1963.

CENSORSHIP HISTORY

Upon publication in 1962, the novel caught the attention of the Federal Bureau of Investigation, which viewed it as being similar in many ways to Henry Miller' *TROPIC OF CANCER* and *TROPIC OF CAPRICORN*. The novel was considered of sufficient importance by the Bureau that it warranted a separate file, *FBI HO 145-2625*, apart from their main file on Baldwin. On September 19, 1962, FBI director J. Edgar Hoover sent the novel to the FBI laboratory to be "examined," expressing particular concern regarding its interracial and homosexual sex scenes. The General Crimes Section returned an unexpected decision, declaring that the novel "contains literary merit and may be of value to students of psychology and social behavior."

In 1963 a New Orleans bookseller was arrested for stocking copies of the novel in violation of city ordinances related to the sale of obscene literature, but the Louisiana district attorney dropped the case. That same year, the New Orleans (Louisiana) Public Library asserted that the novel was obscene and banned it. The case went to court and, after a year of litigation, the book was restored.

In 1965, the FBI received a letter from a Fort Worth (Texas) citizen, claiming that the novel contained "sex perversion at its vilest" and demanding action to curtail the sale of the novel, which was available at stores throughout the city. Hoover replied to the writer, assuring him that the FBI appreciated his concern but stated that the author had not yet broken any federal laws. The air of tolerance is subverted by an entry made in the 1969 FBI summary on the author, which included the suggestion of an informant that Ku Klux Klansmen obtain copies of the novel "to determine whether it is suitable reading for college students."

FURTHER READINGS

Campbell, James. *Talking at the Gates: A Life of James Baldwin.* New York: Penguin Books USA, 1991.

Nelson, Emmanuel. "Critical Deviance: Homophobia and the Reception of James Baldwin's Fiction." *Journal of American Culture* 14 (Fall 1991): 91–96.

Robins, Natalie. *Alien Ink: The FBI's War on Freedom of Expression.* New York: William Morrow & Company, 1992.

Rowden, Terry. "A Play of Abstractions: Race, Sexuality, and Community in James Baldwin's *Another Country.*" *Southern Review* 29 (Winter 1993): 41–50.

APPOINTMENT IN SAMARRA

Author: John O'Hara
Original date and place of publication: 1934, United States
Original publisher: Harcourt, Brace Publishing
Literary form: Novel

SUMMARY

Appointment in Samarra, O'Hara's first novel after the successful publication of short stories, covers three days during the Prohibition era in the lives of the country club set in the fictional town of Gibbsville, Pennsylvania. The characters are driven by money, status and sex, and they worry continuously about which clubs, prep schools, colleges and other associations bring high social status.

The main plot concerns the social and moral disintegration of Julian English, son of a woman of means and a respected physician who heads the staff of the Gibbsville Hospital. Wealthy from childhood and well liked by women, Julian is married to Caroline Walker, to all appearances the ideal wife, but their marriage is strained by Julian's drinking and womanizing. The seemingly prosperous head of a Cadillac automobile dealership, Julian has mismanaged funds and must borrow $20,000 from a newly rich member of the country club, Harry Reilly. Resentful of the obligation and drinking heavily one evening, Julian throws a drink in Harry's face, blackening his eye with an ice cube. Rebuffed when he tries to apologize the next day, Julian then drinks even more heavily and commits suicide by sitting in his car in a closed garage with the motor running. Survivors are mystified, because they cannot see that Julian was any more unhappy than they.

Although no graphic sex scenes occur, sexual references are made and offensive ethnic comments appear throughout the novel. A character kids his wife that the newspaper reports that straitlaced Mervyn Schwartz has been "shot in a whorehouse last night." He then teases her that he plans to take his six-and-a-half-year-old son "out and get him laid tonight" and brags "when I was Teddy's age I had four girls knocked up." When a young woman rejects

Julian's sexual advances, he has the desire "to call her all kinds of bitches." Throughout the novel, characters drink liquor heavily and there are numerous instances in which they are drunk. The mobsters in the town are of Italian background, and they are also the grade-school dropouts with long arrest records.

Anti-Semitism is even more pronounced. A character awakens on Christmas morning, thinks disparagingly about Mrs. Bromberg across the street, feels momentarily guilty, then reminds herself that "Jews do not observe Christmas, except to make more money out of Christians, so you do not have to treat Jews any different on Christmas than on any other day." She considers that having the Bromberg family on their street has "hurt real estate values" and expresses concern that others will move into the neighborhood. "Pretty soon there would be a whole colony of Jews in the neighborhood, and the Flieglers and all the other nice children in the neighborhood would grow up with Jewish accents." At the hearing when Julian's death is ruled a suicide by the coroner, Dr. Moskowitz, Julian's father sees the verdict as revenge for having excluded Moskowitz from a dinner at the country club for the County Medical Society and thinks, "let the little kike quack Moskowitz have his revenge."

CENSORSHIP HISTORY

Appointment in Samarra aroused criticism when it was first published from those who believed that it contained "thoroughgoing vulgarity . . . an insufferable vulgarity, which has crept into many of our supposedly advanced novels that someone not squeamish, nor unread in earlier literatures, must protest against. . . ." Aside from sporadic and weakly enforced pressure placed by the Watch and Ward Society on Boston booksellers to curtail sales of the novel because of its risqué language and situations, *Appointment in Samarra* was openly sold for nearly seven years without major protest.

In 1941, the novel was declared not mailable because of "obscene language," after the solicitor to the United States Department of the Post Office reviewed a copy of the novel. He then advised O'Hara's publisher of the ban, the impetus for which was a complaint brought by the New York Society for the Suppression of Vice that charged the book with being "of an obscene character" because of its sexual references and slurs on various ethnic groups. The post office department would not permit the work to be mailed, and the publisher was told that copies of the book would be confiscated. The novel remained on the United States Post Office's index of banned books through the mid-1950s.

The novel also attracted the attention of the National Organization for Decent Literature, a Roman Catholic organization that identified "objectionable" literature and advised members against reading "offensive" and "obscene" novels. In 1953, NODL found the novel to be "objectionable" and placed it with O'Hara's *Ten North Frederick* on their list of blacklisted books.

The list was then sent to cooperating book dealers who agreed to remove the book from their racks. Such NODL blacklists resulted in elaborate collegial pressure among booksellers, although not legal enforcement against the work. Instead, the organization supplied cooperating booksellers with a certificate to display, containing the following notice: "This store has satisfactorily complied with the request of the Committee [the local committee of the NODL] to remove all publications listed as 'OBJECTIONABLE' by the National Organization for Decent Literature from its racks during the above month." As a result of NODL action, the work was banned from sale in St. Cloud, Minnesota; Port Huron, St. Clair County, Michigan; and Detroit. Sales were limited in numerous other cities, through the efforts of local chapters, until the demise of the organization in the late 1950s.

FURTHER READINGS

Bruccoli, Matthew Joseph. *The O'Hara Concern: A Biography of John O'Hara*. New York: Random House, 1975.

Paul, James C. N., and Murray L. Schwartz. *Federal Censorship: Obscenity in the Mail*. New York: Free Press of Glencoe, 1961.

Podhoretz, Norman. "Gibbsville and New Leeds: The America of John O'Hara and Mary McCarthy." *Commentary* (March 1956): 493–99.

Trilling, Lionel. "John O'Hara Observes Our Mores." *New York Times Book Review* (March 18, 1945): 1, 9. Reprinted as the introduction to *Selected Short Stories of John O'Hara*. New York: Random House, 1956.

THE AUTOBIOGRAPHY OF BENJAMIN FRANKLIN

Author: Benjamin Franklin
Original date and place of publication: 1791, France
Original publisher: Buisson
Literary form: Memoir

SUMMARY

The Autobiography of Benjamin Franklin is an honest and sometimes lusty chronicle of a man who lived life fully. Franklin originally began to write his memoirs for his son, William Franklin, from whom he later became estranged. The *Autobiography* relates the author's rise from poverty as the youngest of 17 children of a soap and candle maker through his apprenticeship as a printer and to his role as Pennsylvania's agent in England in 1757. He provides details regarding his constant struggle to improve himself in education and in business and explains his passion for improvement, of both self and the public. The *Autobiography* ends when Franklin's activities reach an international scope, and he becomes a truly public figure.

Despite the emphasis upon moral improvement in much of the *Autobiography*, Franklin also admits to human failings. He acknowledges that the "hard-to-be-governed passion of youth had hurried me frequently into intrigues with low women that fell in my way, which were attended with some expense and great inconvenience, besides a continual risk to my health by a distemper." He also admits that he has been the victim of passionate bouts of indulgence, and that he has not always stood by his beliefs. Instead, he changed "opinions which I had thought right but found otherwise."

In one episode, Franklin speaks of his hasty departure from Boston in 1723 and writes that he left people to speculate that he left because he "got a naughty Girl with Child." In a later episode, Franklin recounts the incident that caused a breach with a friend named James Ralph, who left behind a wife and child when he traveled to England with Franklin to find work. Ralph began an affair with a young Englishwoman, Mrs. T., and they had a child. Unable to find work teaching in London, Ralph left to teach in a country school and asked Franklin to look after Mrs. T. Franklin lent her money and responded to her frequent calls for assistance. On one of those visits, he "attempted familiarities, which she repulsed with proper resentment," and later told Ralph.

The *Autobiography* presents a very human view of a well-known historical figure.

CENSORSHIP HISTORY

Franklin's *Autobiography* is one of the most frequently expurgated books ever published in America, and it was censored from its first publication. In 1789, Franklin sent copies of the manuscript to friends Benjamin Vaughn and Guillaume Le Veillard, the mayor of Passy, France, asking for their advice. After Franklin died in 1790, a pirated edition of the book appeared in France. With the goal of publishing a more "acceptable" version, Franklin's grandson, William Temple Franklin, edited the French version, which he published in 1818 as part of the comprehensive *Works*. This edition made 1,200 changes in the phrasing of the original *Autobiography* with the expressed aim of modernizing the language for the 19th century. Instead, the changes altered Benjamin Franklin's sometimes salty tone and word choice, providing a vastly different view.

In 1886, Houghton Mifflin published an edition of the *Autobiography* that included the story of James Ralph's affair with the young woman but removed Franklin's admission of a sexual advance. Instead, the editor inserted this explanation of the strained relationship between the old friends: "In the mean time other circumstances made a breach." In 1888, Ginn & Company removed the entire episode. Houghton Mifflin retained the expurgated account in its 1892 edition, but the editor, Middlebury College professor Julian Abernethy, changed the substituted statement to read, "In the mean time another matter which gave offense made a breach." The publishers justified these and similar changes in nearly a dozen editions on the grounds that they were meant for high school students, who must be protected.

Franklin published more overtly bawdy works that earned the approval of his peers, but which are not frequently found among suggested readings. In his "Advice to a Young Man on the Choice of a Mistress," Franklin suggests that more pleasure can be found with an older woman than with a younger because "regarding what is below the Girdle, it is impossible of two Women to tell an old one from a young one" and "They [old women] are so grateful!" In "Polly Baker's Speech," printed in *Gentleman's Magazine* in 1747, he purports to speak as a New England woman who defends herself for being brought to trial, yet again, for having another illegitimate child. Franklin takes flatulence as his subject in "To the Royal Academy at Brussels," in which he parodies scientific reports in the suggestion that chemical additives to food might make "Wind from bowels" less offensive and puns using the slang term "fart."

As Chief Judge Clarke noted in *Roth v. United States*, 345 U.S. 476 (1957), the discussed works by Franklin "which a jury could reasonably find 'obscene,' according to the judge's instructions in the case at bar" would also have subjected a person to prosecution if sent through the mails in 1957 and "to punishment under the federal obscenity statute." The judge further noted that Thomas Jefferson wrote approvingly of "Polly Baker's Speech" and that James Madison not only praised Franklin's humor but wrote similarly Rabelaisian anecdotes. That Franklin is popularly known as "the father of the Post Office" (he was designated postmaster general by the First Continental Congress) is ironic, because his own works, with their tongue-in-cheek sexual references, would have been considered too obscene to mail according to federal statutes such as the Comstock Act, which applied to such matters until recent years.

FURTHER READINGS

Haney, Robert W. *Comstockery in America: Patterns of Censorship and Control.* Boston: Beacon Press, 1960.

Larabee, Leonard W., ed. *The Autobiography of Benjamin Franklin.* New Haven, Conn.: Yale University Press, 1964.

Padover, Saul Kussiel. *The Complete Jefferson.* New York: Duell, Sloan & Pearce, 1943.

———. *The Complete Madison.* New York: Harper & Brothers, 1953.

Perrin, Noel. *Dr. Bowdler's Legacy: A History of Expurgated Books in England and America.* Boston: David R. Godine, Publisher, 1992.

Van Doren, Carl. *Ben Franklin.* New York: Bramhall House, 1987.

THE BELL JAR

Author: Sylvia Plath
Original date and place of publication: 1963, United Kingdom
Original publisher: William Heinemann Ltd.
Type: Novel

SUMMARY

The Bell Jar, first published under the pseudonym of Victoria Lucas, is a thinly veiled autobiographical account of the inner conflict, mental breakdown and later recovery of a female college student in the 1950s. The novel covers approximately eight months in the life of Esther Greenwood, the 19-year-old narrator, and the plot is divided into three parts. In the first part, Esther embarks on a one-month residence in New York City as a guest editor for the college issue of a fashion magazine. Once in the city, she recalls key incidents from the past, exhibiting her emotional and mental disintegration as the recollections become more real and meaning-filled to her than incidents in her daily life. Her unsatisfactory relationships with men dominate her thoughts, and the reader learns of her disappointing date with Constantin, who makes no attempt to seduce her, the brutal and woman-hating Marco, who beats her up, and her conventional and ordinary college boyfriend Buddy Willard, who wants marriage and a traditional life. At the end of the first part, her last night in New York, Esther throws all her clothes off the hotel roof in a mock ceremony that reveals her disorientation.

In the second part, covering chapters 10 through 13, Esther's psychological deterioration continues as she returns home to see the "white, shining, identical clap-board houses with their interstices of well-groomed green [that] proceeded past, one bar after another in a large but escape-proof cage." Increasingly depressed, Esther cannot work or sleep, and she refuses to wash her hair or to change her clothes. Shock treatments deepen her depression and increase her obsession with death and suicide. At the end of this part, Esther visits her father's grave, then crawls beneath her house and consumes sleeping pills until she becomes unconscious.

The third section of the novel, chapters 14 through 20, details Esther's slow and painful recovery after the suicide attempt. She resists all efforts to help her when first hospitalized in the psychiatric ward of a public facility, but her move to a private mental hospital produces great progress. During short leaves from the hospital, she goes to Boston and obtains a diaphragm, then experiences her first sexual encounter, a wholly unpleasant experience. Despite this disillusionment, and despite the death of Joan, another mental patient to whom she has become close, Esther looks forward to leaving the mental asylum and returning to college. Yet, she remains unsure if she will have another breakdown: "How did I know that someday—at college, in Europe, somewhere, anywhere—the bell jar, with its stifling distortions, wouldn't descend again?"

CENSORSHIP HISTORY

The Bell Jar has been challenged for its characters' discussions of sexuality and because it advocates an "objectionable" lifestyle. In one instance, the main character observes that her boyfriend's genitals are disappointing because they remind her of "turkey neck and turkey gizzards." The young college women yearn for sexual experience, and the main character purchases a diaphragm and seeks an anonymous sexual encounter. Beyond perceived obscenity, the novel aroused challenges because it openly rejects traditional marriage and mother-hood. Characterizing marriage as a prison of dull domestic duties, Plath describes mothers as drudges with dirty, demanding children, while wives are subservient and inferior to their husbands.

In 1977 in Warsaw, Indiana, Teresa Burnau, a first-year English teacher at Warsaw Community High School, was assigned to teach an elective course entitled "Women in Literature" using texts that had previously been approved and ordered for the course. Before school began in September, the principal ordered Burnau to remove the literary anthology *Growing Up Female in America* and the novel *The Stepford Wives* from the reading list. The books were removed because "someone in the community might be offended by their criticism of traditional roles for women." By mid-October, the principal demanded that *GO ASK ALICE* also be removed from the list, because it contained "dirty" words. In November, the principal directed that Burnau remove *The Bell Jar* from her list, after reviewing the book and determining that it was "inappropriate" because it spoke of a birth control device (the diaphragm) and used "profanity." Burnau's written protest brought the warning that she would be dismissed for insubordination if she included that book. Although Burnau complied with the demand and dropped the book, the principal later wrote in her evaluation that she exhibited "resentment and a poor attitude" when told not to use *The Bell Jar*. The school board did not rehire Burnau, giving only the reason that she failed to meet her responsibilities and displayed "a poor attitude."

A 17-year-old Warsaw Community High School student and her family challenged the decision of the board. In early 1979, Brooke Zykan, her brother Blair and her parents became the plaintiffs in a suit that charged the school district with violating the First and 14th Amendment rights of students and called for the court to reverse the school board decision to remove the books, which also included *The Feminine Plural: Stories by Women About Growing Up* and *The New Women: A Motive Anthology of Women's Liberation*. A group called People Who Care was formed to deal with the controversy and to further the aim of removing "filthy" material from the classroom and to press their agenda. As one member stated, "School decisions should be based on the absolutes of Christian behavior." In *Zykan v. Warsaw (IN) Community School Corporation and Warsaw School Board of Trustees (1980)*, the plaintiffs claimed that the school board had removed the books from classrooms because "words in the books offended social, political, and moral tastes and not because the books, taken as a whole, were lacking in educational value."

The American Civil Liberties Union attorney associated with the case hoped that the state would recognize academic freedom as a First Amendment right. The suit charged that the school officials had violated students' "right to know" and the constitutional guarantee of academic freedom, but on December 3, 1979, the Indiana District Court rejected these claims and dismissed the suit. The plaintiffs appealed the decision, but the Court of Appeals sided with the school board and proclaimed that the school board had not violated anyone's constitutional rights, because the right of "academic freedom" is limited at the secondary school level. On August 22, 1980, Judge Walter J. Cummings of the Seventh Circuit Court determined that "the student's right to and need for such freedom is bounded by the level of his or her intellectual development" and noted that the local school board has many powers to regulate high school classrooms. This case further strengthened the authority of school boards to select and remove books from school libraries and classrooms and provided warning to individuals who sought academic freedom within the school structure.

FURTHER READINGS

Alexander, Paul. *Rough Magic: A Biography of Sylvia Plath*. New York: Viking Press, 1991.
Butscher, Edward. *Sylvia Plath: Method and Madness*. New York: Seabury Press, 1975.
Hawthorn, Jeremy. *Multiple Personality and the Disintegration of Literary Character: From Oliver Goldsmith to Sylvia Plath*. New York: Ballantine Books, 1983.
MacPherson, Pat. *Reflecting in the Bell Jar*. New York: Routledge Kegan Paul, 1991.
Newsletter on Intellectual Freedom (March 1980): 40; (July 1981): 102.

BLACK LIKE ME

Author: John Howard Griffin
Original date and place of publication: 1961, United States
Original publisher: Houghton Mifflin Company
Literary form: Journal

SUMMARY

Written in journal form, the personal narrative presents an introspective look at racism, examining its consequences in a chronicle of the experiences of a Caucasian social scientist who darkens his skin, shaves his head and assumes the life of an African-American man in the Deep South in 1959. The author acknowledges that as the result of this experiment his life and his views of both races must change forever. Griffin learns that, after having immersed himself in black culture and dealt with the white world as an African American, he can never again live completely as a Caucasian, for his views regarding his own race have changed.

In the opening pages of the work, the author identifies the background of his study and explains his reasons for concern with skin pigmentation. He rationalizes that, even though he is considered to be an expert on racial issues, he has no real idea of what it is like to be an African American and to live in the Deep South. After arranging funding with the magazine *Sepia*, the author travels to New Orleans, where he locates a doctor and begins to undergo the skin-darkening treatments that will change his racial appearance.

Griffin examines his anxiety once the dosage is stabilized and he completes his transformation. Wandering the New Orleans streets, he talks to people with whom he had spoken when he was white and observes a difference in their response now that he approaches them as an African American. He identifies the issues and problems that come with his new, nonwhite identity. First and foremost is the unwritten line between the black and the white races that he violates when he mistakenly allows a white woman to sit near his fellow blacks on a bus. His efforts to deal with the sometimes confusing segregation laws involving rest rooms and restaurants offer a strong indictment against a society that rigidly controlled the access of African Americans to necessities that white Americans could take for granted. In contrast, Griffin enjoys the acceptance of his newly adopted race when the one man in whom he confides his secret eases the transition by teaching him the informal rules of "Negro" behavior.

The author observes that life as an African American is difficult and that security and the respect of others are determined by skin color. As an African American, he is a more frequent target of violence and looked upon as little more than trash by society as a whole. By day he hunts for the jobs available to him as a black man, and for a semblance of humanity from the society in which he lives. By night, he roams the New Orleans pavements, falling deeper and deeper into his blackness. The author finds that other blacks treat him with a great deal of respect and kindness, more so than when he was white. But he also finds that white individuals have lost the humanity and respect they showed when he was white.

Griffin's divergent experiences lead him to postulate that the problem of the "Negro" is twofold. African Americans confront the racism and prejudice of white society, and they must also deal with self-hatred, low self-esteem and loss of pride. He suggests that the two races will be able to live in harmony only when these two ills are eradicated from society.

Griffin reports both blatant and subtle differences in the way that white society in New Orleans treats each race. In one instance, a woman who had conversed with him pleasantly when he was white refuses to cash a traveler's check for him when he is black, even though the transaction involves no financial risk. He observes that instances such as this are common for the black man, and learns that most cafés and bathrooms become off limits to him due to his dark skin color.

In order to widen the significance of the study, Griffin extended the setting to other cities in the South. His reported observations show that the response to his new identity remained relatively consistent. Griffin records that he was addressed by whites as "boy" or "nigger," and that the actions of whites grew increasingly difficult to tolerate as he experienced the persecution and bigotry of segregation and racism. In Mobile, Alabama, white men demanded to know his business in the area and threatened him with death should he cause trouble.

Griffin reports that the way in which the threats were expressed strongly suggested that, if he were murdered, nothing would be done to identify his killers because of his race.

Shortly before terminating his one-month odyssey, the author experienced a revealing incident regarding the nature of white liberalism. Griffin visited the Tuskegee Institute for a day and met a visiting white academic who insisted on proving that he was a trustworthy white whom blacks should not fear. Despite good intentions, his ingrained prejudice emerged all too clearly when he suggested that a black man who was legitimately selling turkeys on the street might have stolen them.

The author reports in the final entries of the work that his experiment elicited hostility from people all over the country. He and his family received death threats and were forced to leave their home.

CENSORSHIP HISTORY

The book has been one of the 30 most frequently attacked books in the United States since its first, partial appearance in 1960 as an article in *Sepia* magazine and its publication as a book in 1961. The principal charge, in most challenges, has been obscenity. Researchers, however, postulate that more likely the truth is that those who challenge the book are opposed to books about African Americans or other minorities. As one teacher stated in a 1982 nationwide survey conducted by Lee Burress, "'In a rural community, people don't care to have their children read about Negroes'." This position is supported by an examination of the 20 most frequently attacked titles between 1965 and 1977. One-third depict individuals belonging to a minority group in strong protest against racism.

In 1966, the paperback edition of the novel was widely attacked as being unfit for children to read. In Wisconsin, a man sued the local school board, claiming that the book contained obscene language, that it was integration-centered, vulgar, filthy and unsuitable for any age level. He further charged that his child was damaged by having read the book as an assignment in English class. The court dismissed the case.

In 1967, the parent of an Arizona high school student challenged the use of the book in the classroom because of its obscene and vulgar language and the situations depicted. The school board removed the book from the classroom. Language, particularly "four-letter words," was the charge leveled in 1977 by a Pennsylvania parent and a clergyman, but the challenge was denied. An objection to the subject matter was similarly denied in a 1982 challenge of the book in Illinois. In Missouri in 1982, however, the material was placed on a closed shelf when a parent challenged the book on the grounds that it was obscene and vulgar and "because of black people being in the book."

FURTHER READINGS

Burress, Lee. *Battle of the Books: Literary Censorship in the Public Schools, 1950–1985.* Metuchen, N.J.: Scarecrow Press, 1989.

Farrell, Walter C., Jr. *"Black Like Me*: In Defense of a Racial Reality." In *Censored Books: Critical Viewpoints.* Ed. by Nicholas Karolides, Lee Burress and John M. Kean: 117–24. Metuchen, N.J.: Scarecrow Press, 1993.

Griffin, John Howard. *Racial Equality: The Myth and the Reality.* ERIC Education Document Reprint Series, No. 26 (March 1971).

Sharpe, Ernest, Jr. "The Man Who Changed His Skin." *American Heritage* 40 (February 1989): 44–55.

BRAVE NEW WORLD

Author: Aldous Huxley
Original date and place of publication: 1932, England
Original publisher: Chatto & Windus Collins
Literary form: Novel

SUMMARY

Brave New World is a satire in which science, sex and drugs have replaced human reason and human emotion in the "perfect" society to which Huxley gives the name "Utopia." The novel depicts an orderly society in which scientifically sophisticated genetics and pharmacology combine to produce a perfectly controlled population whose entire existence is dedicated to maintaining the stability of society. People are genetically engineered to satisfy the regulated needs of the government in regard to specific mental and physical sizes and types. Sexual promiscuity is demanded by the state for the sake of pleasure, not procreation, and women are equipped with contraceptive cartridge belts to avoid pregnancy. The only respectable way to enter the world is through incubation in a bottle—people are decanted rather than born—and learning occurs through preconditioning.

Inhabitants are created and conditioned to fit into specific social slots. Thus, in the Hatchery and Conditioning Center, varying amounts of alcohol are placed into the decanting bottles that contain the embryos to stunt mental growth and create a hierarchy of genetic classes.

Those who will be conditioned to do the monotonous and hard labor of this society receive the highest doses of alcohol to create a low mentality. Labeled in descending order of intelligence as Gammas, Deltas and Epsilons, they are the most numerous and are produced by subjecting the fertilized egg to the Bokanovsky Process, a budding procedure that enables division of the egg into as many as 96 identical beings from one egg and up to 15,000 brothers and sisters from a single ovary. The Alphas and Betas, who carry out the work of the government, remain individualized, yet they, too, are manipulated through early conditioning. The concept of family is unknown, and the terms "mother" and "father" are viewed as smut. In this systematically promiscuous world, men and women are encouraged to experience many sexual partners to avoid the development of intimate emotional relationships that might threaten their obsessive loyalty to the state.

The expected ills of human life have all been eliminated, and inhabitants of this brave new world have been freed of the worries of disease, pain, unhappiness, old age and death. Disease has been eradicated through sterilization and pain or unhappiness are easily banished by liberal doses of *soma*, a drug that provides a high without side effects. Smaller dosages are used to counteract depression, while larger dosages are taken to provide a long-term sense of euphoria, described by one character as a two-week vacation. Blind happiness is necessary for social stability, so all emotions are dulled. Even death takes on a new appearance. People are given treatments that keep them youthful-looking until they near the age of 60, at which time their bodies are allowed to experience a brief, soma-controlled period of aging before they disappear into the prominently placed crematoria that turn human bodies into phosphorus to be used in fertilizer.

Huxley exhibits the undesirable aspects of such a world through the characters of the Alpha-class misfit Bernard Marx and the savage John, who lives on the Savage Reservation, a precivilized region that has been preserved for study. John is the son of the director of Hatcheries and Conditioning (DHC) and a Beta woman who was left on the reservation by the DHC. Taken to England by Marx, John is highly uncomfortable in the emotionless and intellectually vacuous Utopia. He wants love and rejects the promiscuity of Lenina Crowne, a Utopian woman to whom he is sexually attracted but whose morals are repugnant to him. Treated as a curiosity by Utopians who clamor to see him and who gawk at him, John finds only misery in this brave new world and decides that suicide is his only solution.

CENSORSHIP HISTORY

Brave New World has evoked a range of responses from those who are made uncomfortable by Huxley's satire of society. The novel has been charged with being sordid, immoral and obscene, and it has been condemned for vilifying the family, for giving too much attention to sex and for encouraging illegal drug use. Many cite the sexual promiscuity of the Utopians, as did the Board of Censors of Ireland when it banned the novel in 1932, yet the novel contains no graphic scenes of sexual behavior. For the most part, people who seek to ban the novel believe that *Brave New World* is "depressing, fatalistic, and negative, and that it encourages students to adopt a lifestyle of drugs, sex and conformity, reinforcing helpless feelings that they can do nothing to make an impact on their world."

The novel has been frequently challenged in schools throughout the United States. In 1965, a teacher of English in Maryland claimed that the local school board had violated his First Amendment rights by firing him after he assigned *Brave New World* as a required reading in his class. The district court ruled against the teacher in *Parker v. Board of Education*, 237 F. Supp. 222 (D.Md) and refused his request for reinstatement in the teaching position. When the case was later heard by the circuit court, *Parker v. Board of Education*, 348 F.2d 464 (4th Cir. 1965), the presiding judge affirmed the ruling of the lower court and included in the determination the opinion that the nontenured status of the teacher accounted for the firing and not the assignment of a particular book.

In 1979, a high school principal in Matthews County, Virginia, requested that a history teacher in the high school withdraw an assignment that included *Brave New World*. The teacher assigned it anyway, and the school board terminated the teacher's contract. No further actions were taken by either party.

Use of the novel in the classroom was challenged in 1980 in Miller, Missouri, where it was removed from the curriculum, and in 1988, parents of students at Yukon (Oklahoma) High School demanded the removal of the book as a required reading because of its "language and moral content." In 1993, parents challenged the novel as a required reading in Corona-Norco (California) Unified School District based on charges that it "centered around negative activity." After consideration by the school board, the book was retained on the list, but students who objected to the novel were given alternative choices.

FURTHER READINGS

"Another Furor over Books." *Ohio State University Monthly* 55 (December 1963): 8–12.

Bedford, Sybille. *Aldous Huxley: A Biography*. London: Chatto & Windus Collins, 1973–74. 2 vols.

Massie, Dorothy C. "Censorship in the Schools: Something Old and Something New." *Today's Education* 69 (November/December 1980): 56–62.

Matter, William W. "The Utopian Tradition and Aldous Huxley." *Science Fiction Studies* 2 (1975): 146–51.

Nahmod, Sheldon H. "Controversy in the Classroom: The High School Teacher and Freedom of Expression." *George Washington University Law Review* 39 (July 1974): 1,031.

Newsletter on Intellectual Freedom (May 1980): 52; (September 1981): 127; (July 1988): 140; (January 1994): 14; (March 1994): 70.

THE CANTERBURY TALES

Author: Geoffrey Chaucer
Original date and place of publication: 1387–1400, England
Original publisher: Unknown
Literary form: Short story collection

SUMMARY

Canterbury Tales is a group of stories, mostly in verse, written in the closing years of the 14th century. Chaucer establishes the framework for the book in a lengthy prologue in which he describes the 29 individuals who meet with their host at the Tabard Inn in preparation for a pilgrimage to the popular shrine of Thomas à Becket at the Canterbury Cathedral. They agree that, to pass the time on the journey, each pilgrim will tell four stories, two on the way to the shrine and two on the way home. The host will judge the best tale, and the winner will receive a sumptuous feast at the inn. Chaucer originally planned a book of 120 tales but died in 1400 before completing the work. Only 24 of the tales remain. Of these, 20 are complete, two are deliberately left incomplete because the pilgrims demand that the tellers cease and two others were left unfinished by Chaucer's death.

The pilgrims extend across all levels of 14th-century English society, from the nobly born Knight, Squire and Prioress to the low-born Miller, Cook and Yeoman. None are spared Chaucer's critical examination of the human condition as he uses his characters and their tales to expose the absurdities and inadequacies of all levels of society. The travelers quarrel, interrupt and criticize each other, become drunk and provoke commentary. Members of the religious hierarchy are shown to be corrupt, women are lusty and the dark underbelly of society is exposed. The tales reflect the tellers, from the gentle Knight, "modest as a maid," who describes an abstraction of womanhood in his pure Emily, to the bawdy Miller, who describes his Alison as a highly provocative physical object.

Risqué language and sexual innuendo pervade most of the tales. "The Cook's Tale" describes "a wife [who] whored to get her sustenance." In "Introduction to the Lawyer's Prologue," provocative images of incest emerge in "Canace, who loved her own blood brother sinfully" and "wicked king Antiochus [who] bereft his daughter of her maidenhead." "The Reeve's Tale" tells of a miller named Simpkin whose wife "was a dirty bitch" and whose daughter was "with buttocks broad and round breasts full and high." "The Wife of Bath's Tale," one of the two most commonly anthologized of all the tales, offers an extraordinary view of women and sexuality. Described in the prologue as having had five husbands, "not counting other company in her youth," the Wife of Bath questions the concern over virginity and asks "Tell me also to what purpose or end the genitals have been made?" She lustily promises, "In wifehood I will use my instrument as freely as my Maker has sent it."

The second of the two most popularly anthologized stories is "The Miller's Tale," a story about adultery. Alison, an 18-year-old woman married to a middle-aged miller, is courted by Absalom the parish clerk, but she is already having an affair with the boarder, a student named Nicholas. Absalom serenades her outside her window and promises to leave her alone only if she will let him kiss her. She agrees and, when he arrives at her window in the dark, she offers "her naked arse," which he kisses. He soon realizes the trick, for "it seem somehow amiss, for well he knew a woman has no beard; he'd felt a thing all rough and longish-haired." Seeking revenge, Absalom returns to the Miller's house carrying a red-hot poker from the fireplace and calls to Alison for another kiss. This time Nicholas, who "had risen for a piss," decides "to have his arse kissed" to carry on the joke. And, "showing the whole bum," he is shocked when Absalom "was ready with his iron hot and Nicholas right in the arse he got." Later, John, the other student boarder, mistakenly climbs into bed with Alison, who thinks it is Nicholas, and he "pricked her hard and deep, like one gone mad."

CENSORSHIP HISTORY

Canterbury Tales has been expurgated from its first appearance in the United States in 1908 in the Everyman's Library edition. Seventeen of the tales were translated into modern English with extensive expurgation, and seven were left intact but in the original Middle English language. In 1953 the tales were innocent victims of the "Red Scare," when critics approached the Texas State Textbook Commission and demanded that the commission bar the Garden City editions of *Canterbury Tales* and *Moby Dick* from their schools. The two works were illustrated by Rockwell Kent, charged by critics with being a communist.

For the most part, however, the off-color references of the original text and blunt "Anglo-Saxon" terms related to the anatomy or to bodily functions have raised concerns among parents and those who select textbooks. Thus, they are routinely omitted from most editions, as are curses or oaths uttered by characters in the original tales. Editing has led to such absurdities as "He caught her by the queynte" being transformed into "He slipped his hand intimately between her legs." Challenges to the inclusion of "The Miller's Tale," "The Wife of Bath's Tale" and even the "Prologue" have sought to remove the readings from classrooms because of the "unhealthy characters" and the "nasty words" of the text. Risqué language and characters have made the tales a ready target for textbook evaluators and community and school watchdogs.

In 1986, a lengthy case arose over the use of a textbook that included "The Miller's Tale" and Aristophanes' play *Lysistrata* in an elective humanities course for Columbia County High School students in Lake City, Florida. The tale appeared in *The Humanities: Cultural Roots and Continuities Volume I*, a state-approved textbook that had been used for 10 years without incident. In 1985, the daughter of a fundamentalist minister had enrolled in the course and objected to the two selections, even though they were not assigned readings but portions referred to and read aloud by the teacher. In lodging a formal complaint, the minister identified "sexual explicitness," "vulgar language" and "the promotion of women's lib" as his reasons for demanding that the text be withdrawn from use. His specific objections identified concern over the inclusion of the terms "ass" and "fart" in "The Miller's Tale," as well as the jocular way in which adultery appears to be treated. An advisory textbook committee made up of Columbia County High School teachers read and discussed the two selections, then recommended that the textbooks be retained and that the two selections not be assigned. The school board rejected their suggestions and voted to confiscate all copies of the book and to lock them in the book room. Anxious to avoid the charge of censorship, board members also voted to allow a copy to remain in the high school library, but it was placed on "the mature shelf."

In 1988, the American Civil Liberties Union submitted an initial brief against the school board in *Virgil v. School Board of Columbia County*, 677 F. Supp. 1547, 1551–51 (M.D. Fla. 1988) and argued that the actions of the board in removing the textbook from the classroom suppressed the free thought and free speech of students. The ACLU based its arguments on decisions made in *Board of Education, Island Trees Union Free School District No. 26 v. Pico*, 457 U.S. 853, 102 S.Ct. 2799, 73 L.Ed.2d 435 (1982), in which the court decided that school boards violate the First Amendment rights of students when they arbitrarily remove books. (See *BLACK BOY*.) The defense attorney for the school board relied on *Hazelwood School District v. Kuhlmeier*, 484 U.S. 260, 108 S.Ct. 562, 98 L.Ed.2d 592 (1988) in presenting the case, although the case applied to the right of school administrators to censor articles in a school newspaper that was produced as part of a high school journalism class.

The case went to court, and in deciding *Virgil v. School Board of Columbia County*, 862 F.2d 1517, 1525 (11th Cir. 1989), the judge determined that the *Hazelwood* case was the relevant precedent. The limited scope of that case in interpreting the First Amendment rights of students influenced the court to decide in favor of the school board. In the *Virgil* decision, the U.S. Court of Appeals for the 11th Circuit concluded that no constitutional violation had occurred and the school board could decide to remove books from the classroom provided that the removal was "reasonably related" to the "legitimate pedagogical concern" of denying students exposure to "potentially sensitive topics." The written contention of the board that the two selections contained "explicit sexuality" and "excessive vulgarity" was judged to be a sufficient basis for the removal of *The Humanities: Cultural Roots and Continuities* from the classroom. The plaintiffs decided to appeal the case to the United States Supreme Court and directed the ACLU attorney to file a Petition for Writ of Certiorari in 1988. After more than a year passed, the plaintiffs learned that the Supreme Court had never received the petition, because a secretary newly hired in April 1989 by the office of the ACLU attorney had never sent it out. The plaintiffs decided not to pursue the matter, because the changed character of the higher court did not promise success even if the motion to argue the case were approved.

FURTHER READINGS

Johnson, Claudia. *Stifled Laughter: One Woman's Fight Against Censorship*. Golden, Colo.: Fulcrum Publishing, 1994.

Scala, Elizabeth. "Canace and the Chaucer Canon." *Chaucer Review* 30 (1995): 15–39.

CATCH-22

Author: Joseph Heller
Original date and place of publication: 1961, United States
Original publisher: Simon & Schuster
Literary form: Novel

SUMMARY

Catch-22 is a comic novel about World War II that literary critics have described as among the best to have come out of that era. The novel concerns the efforts of Capt. John Yossarian, a bombardier with the 256th U.S. Air Force Squadron, to be removed from combat duty after he witnesses numerous friends being killed in action. He acts insane to achieve his goal, but his efforts are thwarted by military regulation number 22, which states that no insane person would willingly go into combat. Thus, anyone who seeks to avoid combat duty must be considered sane.

Set on the fictional Mediterranean island of Pianosa, from which the squadron makes regular bombing runs to southern France and to Italy, the novel contains graphic descriptions of sex and violence and exhibits strong rebellion against authority. Yossarian lies, sabotages military procedures and exhibits gross irresponsibility. He also walks around naked for a few days, even when he is being awarded a medal. Given light duty censoring letters written by enlisted men, Yossarian plays games and blacks out words randomly, sometimes adding the chaplain's signature to romantic letters home. The unpleasant experience of his tent mate Orr in a brothel is carefully detailed, as the "whore" beats him with her high-heeled shoe. Readers learn that the two are naked and of "her wondrously full breasts soaring all over the place like billowing pennants in a strong wind and her buttocks and strong thighs shim-sham-shimmying this way and that way." Another character visits a brothel in the Eternal City, then kills the prostitute because she might damage his reputation should she tell others about their encounter. Throughout the novel, the men casually refer to and address each other as "son of a bitch," "prick" or "bastard." At one point, Yossarian loses his temper and rants, "That dirty goddam midget-assed, apple-cheeked, goggle-eyed, undersized, buck-toothed, grinning, crazy sonofabitchinbastard!"

The women in the novel are largely stereotypes to whom other characters refer as "whore." The woman whom "he had longed for and idolized for months" is "perfect for Yossarian, a debauched, coarse, vulgar, amoral, appetizing slattern. . . . She was interested in fornication." However, he also hopes that "Nately's whore" will find him a woman who is just as eager for sex as she. At the end of the novel, as Yossarian leaves the base to run off to Sweden, "Nately's whore was hiding out just outside the door." She attempts to kill him, but he escapes.

CENSORSHIP HISTORY

Catch-22 is part of the school censorship case that set precedent by supporting the *student's* right to know. In 1972, the Strongsville, Ohio, board of education used its discretionary power over textbook selection to disapprove purchase of *Catch-22* and Kurt Vonnegut's *God Bless You, Mr. Rosewater*, despite faculty recommendation. The board refused to allow teachers to use the books as part of the English curriculum, charging that they were "completely sick" and "garbage." The board then ordered the two books and *Cat's Cradle*, also by Vonnegut, removed from the high school library and "all copies disposed of in accordance with statutory procedure."

Five high school students and their families brought a class action suit against the school district, the school superintendent and the board of education, claiming that their rights under the First and 14th Amendments had been violated. The families argued that the board had not followed proper procedure and had not given good reason for rejecting the novels. In 1974, the United States District Court for the Northern District of Ohio ruled that the board did not violate First Amendment rights because it had followed the law. Ohio law granted school boards the authority to select textbooks, and the board had held open meetings and consulted enough teachers, administrators and citizens to make a reasonable decision. The judge dismissed the complaint of the families regarding the removal of the books from the school library.

The case was then heard in 1976 by the United States Court of Appeals for the Sixth Circuit, and a different decision emerged. The court upheld the right of the school board to determine the choice of textbooks, but it stood firmly against the right of the school board to remove already purchased books from the school library.

> A public school library is also a valuable adjunct to classroom discussions. If one of the English teachers considered Joseph Heller's Catch-22 to be one of the more important modern American novels (as, indeed, at least one did), we assume that no one would dispute that the First Amendment's protection of academic freedom would protect both his right to say so in class and his

students' right to hear him and to find and read the book. Obviously, the students' success in this last endeavor would be greatly hindered by the fact that the book sought had been removed from a school library.

The court also chastised the school board for withdrawing books from the school library. Stating in the decision that "a library is a storehouse of knowledge," the presiding judge warned that libraries are created by the state for the benefit of students in the schools. As such, they are "not subject to being withdrawn by succeeding school boards whose members might desire to 'winnow' the library for books the content of which occasioned their displeasure or disapproval." The judge ordered the Strongsville school board to replace the books in the school library. In response, the school district appealed to the United States Supreme Court, but the court refused to hear the case.

The use of the word "whore" at several places in the novel to refer to women resulted in challenges in the Dallas (Texas) Independent School District in 1974, where parents demanded that the novel be removed from all of the high school libraries. The same objection motivated a challenge in the Snoqualmie Valley (Washington) School District in 1979. Critics observed that the use of "whore" and Heller's failure to name one woman, calling her only "Nately's whore," represented a stereotyping of women that was harmful to students. In attempts to remove the novel from use in the school system as well as from the Mount Si High School library, critics also cited the "overly descriptive passages of violence" and the increasingly bizarre threats by squadron members against each other. The efforts to remove *Catch-22* were unsuccessful.

FURTHER READINGS

Green, Daniel. "A World Worth Laughing At: *Catch-22* and the Humor of Black Humor." *Studies in the Novel* 27 (Summer 1995): 186–96.

Moore, Michael. "Pathological Communication Patterns in Heller's *Catch-22*." *Et Cetera* 52 (Winter 1995): 431–59.

O'Neil, Robert M. *Classrooms in the Crossfire: The Rights and Interests of Students, Parents, Teachers, Administrators, Librarians, and the Community.* Bloomington, Ind.: Indiana University Press, 1981.

Pinsker, Sanford. *Understanding Joseph Heller.* Columbia, S.C.: University of South Carolina Press, 1991.

Newsletter for Intellectual Freedom (January 1975): 6; (July 1979): 85.

Potts, Stephen. *Catch-22: Antiheroic Antinovel.* Boston: Twayne Publishing, 1989.

Potts, Stephen. *From Here to Absurdity: The Moral Battlefields of Joseph Heller.* San Bernardino, Calif.: Borgo Press, 1982.

THE CATCHER IN THE RYE

Author: J. D. Salinger
Original date and place of publication: 1951, United States
Original publisher: Little, Brown and Company
Literary form: Novel

SUMMARY

The Catcher in the Rye tells the story of a middle-class, urban, late-adolescent male in the 1950s who confronts crisis in his own life by escaping into the disordered and chaotic adult world. The story, told from the first-person point of view of a boy named Holden Caulfield, details 48 hours in his life, and describes how he views and feels about society and the world in which he lives. As Holden experiences his misadventures, he muses about sex, society and American values. He seeks to remain idealistic, but he is confronted at every turn by the phoniness of society.

Holden narrates his story while in a rest home in California, and the reader becomes aware that he is relating a story from his recent past. He flashes back to his school days, in particular to Pency Prep, where he was a student until his expulsion. It is just after this expulsion that the action takes place. For most of the novel, Holden appears to search for someone or something in which to believe, but he finds that his generally pessimistic view of human nature and human values is reinforced rather than refuted.

Before Holden makes the decision to leave school, he visits his history teacher for one last time and receives a lecture regarding his lack of motivation and poor scholarship. Mr. Spencer even goes so far as to read Holden the last examination he took. The disappointments accrue, as Holden returns to his room in the dormitory and learns that his roommate, Ward, has a date with a girl whom Holden had wanted to date. To compound the pain, Ward asks Holden to write a composition, which he later criticizes severely. After the ensuing physical fight, Holden packs a bag and leaves the campus.

Holden boards a train bound for New York City and registers at a hotel upon arrival. When loneliness sets in, he makes several telephone calls without success, then visits a crowded nightclub, but he still cannot fill the void he feels inside. When Holden returns to the hotel, he asks the doorman to arrange for a prostitute, but he sends her away unpaid because he is too scared and too depressed to enjoy her. The doorman and prostitute later awaken him and demand the five dollars, and the doorman beats Holden to obtain payment.

After meeting a friend at a bar and indulging in underage drinking, Holden sneaks into his family's apartment to see his younger sister, Phoebe, with whom he discusses his fears that he may "disappear" into himself. He tells her that he has a mission in this world: "I keep picturing all these little kids playing some game in this big field of rye and all. . . . And I'm standing by on the edge of some crazy cliff. What I have to do, I have to catch everybody if they start to go over the cliff." In his further idealism, he becomes upset when he finds "Fuck You" scrawled on the walls of Phoebe's elementary school and on the wall of the museum where Phoebe will meet him.

Holden plans to hitchhike to the West but changes his mind and agrees to return home when Phoebe packs a suitcase and insists on going with him. He later watches Phoebe ride the carousel in Central Park and realizes that he really cannot protect her from all of the world's abuses and that he has to let her take chances without interfering.

By the end of the novel, after fending off the advances of a male former English teacher and reviewing his disappointments with the adult world, Holden appears resigned in the rest home and predicts that he will soon be returning to school.

CENSORSHIP HISTORY

The novel has long ignited disapproval, and it was the most frequently banned book in schools between 1966 and 1975. Even before that time, however, the work was a favorite target of censors. In 1957, Australian Customs seized a shipment of the novels that had been presented as a gift to the government by the U.S. ambassador. The books were later released, but Customs had made its point that the book contained obscene language and actions that were not appropriate behavior for an adolescent. In 1960, a teacher in Tulsa, Oklahoma, was fired for assigning the book to an eleventh-grade English class. The teacher appealed and was reinstated by the school board, but the book was removed from use in the school.

The following year in Oklahoma City, the novel became the focus of a legislative hearing in which a locally organized censorship group sought to stop the Mid-Continent News Company, a book wholesaler, from carrying the novel. Members of the group parked a "Smutmobile" outside the capital building during the hearing and displayed the novel with others. As a result of public pressure, the wholesaler dropped the criticized novels from its inventory. In 1963 a delegation of parents of high school students in Columbus, Ohio, asked the school board to ban *Catcher in the Rye*, BRAVE NEW WORLD and TO KILL A MOCKINGBIRD for being "anti-white" and "obscene." The superintendent of schools and the school board refused the request and expressed confidence in the ability of their teachers and librarians to choose reading material for the school system.

After a decade of quiet, objections again arose in 1975 in Selinsgrove, Pennsylvania, and the novel was removed from the suggested reading list for an elective course entitled "Searching for Values and Identity Through Literature." Based on parents' objections to the language and content of the book, the school board voted 5–4 to ban the book. The book was later reinstated in the curriculum when the board learned that the vote was illegal because they needed a two-thirds vote for removal of the text.

In 1977 parents in Pittsgrove Township, New Jersey, challenged the assignment of the novel in an American literature class. They charged that the book included considerable profanity and "filthy and profane" language that promoted premarital sex, homosexuality and perversion, as well as claiming that it was "explicitly pornographic" and "immoral." The board of education had originally approved the novel for study. After months of controversy, the board ruled that the novel could be read in the advanced placement class for its universal message, not for its profanity, but they gave parents the right to decide whether or not their children would read it.

In 1978 parents in Issaquah, Washington, became upset with the rebellious views expressed in the novel by Holden Caulfield and with the profanity he uses. The woman who led the parents' group asserted that she had counted 785 uses of profanity, and she alleged that the philosophy of the book marked it as part of a communist plot that was gaining a foothold in the schools, "in which a lot of people are used and may not even be aware of it." The school board voted to ban the book, but the decision was later reversed when the three members who had voted against the book were recalled due to illegal deal-making. In 1979, the Middleville, Michigan, school district removed the novel from the required reading list after parents objected to the content.

Objections to the novel have been numerous throughout the 1980s and into the 1990s. In 1980, the Jacksonville-Milton School libraries in North Jackson, Ohio, removed the book, as did two high school libraries in Anniston, Alabama. In 1982, school officials removed the book from all school libraries because it contained "excess vulgar language, sexual scenes, and things concerning moral issues." In 1983, parents in Libby, Montana, challenged the assignment of the book in the high school due to the "book's contents." Deemed "unacceptable" and "obscene," the novel was banned from use in English classes at Freeport High School in De Funiak Springs, Florida, in 1985, and it was removed from the required reading list in 1986 in Medicine Bow, Wyoming, Senior High School because of sexual references and profanity. In 1987, parents and the local Knights of Columbus chapter in Napoleon, North Dakota, complained about profanity and sexual references in the book, which was then banned from a required sophomore English reading list. Parents of students attending Linton-Stockton (Indiana) High School challenged the book in 1988 because it "undermines morality," and profanity was the reason for which the book was banned from classrooms in the Boron, California, high school in 1989.

The challenges to the novel have continued well into the 1990s. In 1991, the novel was challenged at Grayslake (Illinois) Community High School for profanity, and parents of students in Jamaica High School in Sidell, Illinois, cited profanities and the depiction of premarital sex, alcohol abuse and prostitution as the basis for their 1992 challenge. Three other major challenges to the novel occurred in 1992. The novel was challenged and removed from the Waterloo, Iowa, public schools and the Duval County, Florida, public school libraries because of the "lurid passages about sex" and profanity, while a parent in Carlisle, Pennsylvania, objected to the book because it was "immoral" and contained profanity. In 1993, parents in the Corona-Norco (California) School District protested the use of the novel as a required reading, because it was "centered around negative activity." The school board voted to retain the novel but instructed teachers to select alternative readings if students objected to it. The novel was challenged but retained for use in select English classes at New Richmond (Wisconsin) High School in 1994, but it was removed as mandatory reading from the Goffstown, New Hampshire, schools the same year because parents charged that it contained "vulgar words" and presented the main character's "sexual exploits."

FURTHER READINGS

Alvino, James. "Is It Book Burning Time Again?" *The New York Times* (December 28, 1980): 11:18.
"Another Furor Over Books." *Ohio State University Monthly* 55 (4): 8–12.
Booth, Wayne C. "Censorship and the Values of Fiction." *English Journal* 53 (March 1964): 155–64.
Corbett, Edward P. J. "Raise High the Barriers, Censors." *America* 54 (January 7, 1961): 441–44.
Newsletter on Intellectual Freedom (November 1978): 138 ; (January 1980): 6–7; (May 1980): 51; (March 1983): 37–38; (July 1983): 122; (July 1985): 113; (March 1987): 55; (July 1987): 123; (January 1988): 10; (September 1988): 177; (November 1989): 218–19; (July 1991): 129–30; (May 1992): 83; (July 1992): 105, 126; (January 1993): 29; (January 1994): 14; (March 1994): 56, 70; (May 1994): 100; (January 1995): 12.
Oboler, Eli M. "Idaho School Librarians and Salinger's *Catcher in the Rye*: A Candid Report." *Idaho Librarian* 15 (October 1963): 137–39.

A CLOCKWORK ORANGE

Author: Anthony Burgess (John Anthony Burgess Wilson)
Original date and place of publication: 1962, United Kingdom
Original publisher: William Heinemann Ltd.
Literary form: Novel

SUMMARY

A Clockwork Orange is a futuristic warning against both mindless violence and the mechanical reconditioning that is often proposed as society's solution to its ills. It offers a horrifying view of a future England in which gangs of hoodlums, or "droogs," roam the streets freely, robbing, fighting, raping and consuming illegal drugs and alcohol. Society is limp and listless, a socialist world in which no one reads anymore, despite streets named Amis Avenue and Priestley Place. Teenage language, "nadsat," consists largely of English mixed with Russian and half-Russian words, and the current music star is a "Russky" singer named Jonny Zhivago. The rule of society is that everyone "not a child nor with child nor ill" must work, yet the prisons are overcrowded and officials work to rehabilitate criminals to make room for the large number of expected political prisoners. Even with regular elections and opposition, the people continue to re-elect the current government.

Alex, the 15-year-old cocky and self-indulgent main character, is both a product of and a reason for the continued breakdown of social institutions. Deteriorating urban life, ineffective law enforcement, the failure of officials to create order from the chaos and sexual violence characterize this world, in which social ills perpetuate the violent behavior and prevent cohesion. It is a nightmarish place in which the droogs drive over a big, snarling, toothy thing and "odd squealing things" in the road throughout the night, accompanied by screams and squelches. The young hoodlums drink doped milk, and before committing robberies Alex and his fellow droogs put on their "maskies," faces of historical personalities: Disraeli, Elvis Presley, Henry VIII and "Peebee" Shelley. Women exist for the droogs only as objects of rape and other violence, and sex has also taken on a mechanical characteristic that is reinforced by the term to describe the sex act, "the old in-out in-out." Even classical music, usually viewed as a sign of civilized taste, gains a new character in the novel. Symphonic music is Alex's passion, and he retreats frequently to his speaker-filled room to lie naked on his bed and listen to the music of Mozart, Beethoven or Bach. As the music swells, he fantasizes raping and terrorizing young girls and grinding his boot heel into the faces of helpless victims.

The novel is divided into three parts. In the first third, Alex simply does whatever he wants without guilt or concern for others, and he experiences joy in violence of every kind, from destruction or theft of objects to every form of sexual and nonsexual assault. He is free to choose whatever pleasures he desires, however destructive to society they might be. However, because his choices are harmful, society asserts its right to deprive Alex of his freedom. Sentenced to 14 years for the murder of an old woman during a burglary, Alex is placed into prison, where he kills a fellow inmate. This ushers in the second part of the novel. The murder focuses attention on him and makes him the likely choice for an experimental treatment that will leave him "transformed out of all recognition" and make him unable to choose any socially deleterious course of action afterward. In essence, he is injected with a drug, strapped into a chair and forced to watch films of Japanese and Nazi atrocities during World War II, as well as specially made films that combine with the drug to condition him against all thoughts of violence. His progress is measured with electronic devices that are wired to his body. The conditioning works, and the doctors declare Alex cured of his violent desires and now "your true Christian . . . ready to turn the other cheek, ready to be crucified rather than crucify, sick to the very heart at the thought even of killing a fly."

In the third part of the novel, the rehabilitated Alex, now a harmless citizen, returns home to find that his parents have rented out his room to a lodger and that his stereo equipment has been confiscated by the police and sold to provide food for the cats of the woman he murdered. He is attacked by a group of old men whom he had victimized earlier, then rescued by three policemen, two of whom are former gang members who tell him that the government has been cleaning up the streets and hiring former hoodlums as police. Rather than help Alex, they beat him severely, leaving him to crawl to a nearby cottage. There, he is bandaged and fed by a man whom he had once attacked and whose wife he had brutally raped and beaten, but the man does not recognize him at first. Instead, F. Alexander sees in Alex an opportunity for propaganda against the government. Professing that "a man who cannot choose ceases to be a man," he calls together his friends but soon realizes that Alex is his wife's murderer. He tortures Alex by playing symphonic music loudly, and Alex tries to commit suicide by jumping out a window. Days later, he awakens in the hospital, completely swathed in bandages, and realizes that he has regained his violent nature. The doctors and government officials are happy because they are now free of the charges that they had perpetrated a criminal reform scheme and violated Alex's rights. While he was in a coma, they used "deep hypnopaedia or some such slovo" to restore his former depraved nature and his appetites for Beethoven and violence. As the old thoughts of violence fill Alex's head, he declares himself "cured all right."

CENSORSHIP HISTORY

A Clockwork Orange has motivated debate since its publication, and the controversy has centered on the language of the book as well as on the brutality and sexual violence of the first third of the novel. In 1973 a book dealer in Orem, Utah, was arrested for selling three purportedly obscene books: *Last Tango in Paris* by Robert Ailey, *The Idolators* by William Hegner and *A Clockwork Orange*. Using the 1973 Supreme Court "local standards" decision, *Miller v. California* (June 21, 1973), the town passed a very specific obscenity ordinance under which police charged bookstore owner Carole Grant. The charges were later dropped, but Grant was forced to close the store and relocate to another city.

In Aurora, Colorado in 1976, the school board at a regularly scheduled meeting approved 1,275 books for use in the high school, but they disapproved *A Clockwork Orange* and the following nine books: *The Exorcist* by William P. Blatty; *The Reincarnation of Peter Proud* by Max Ehrlich; *New American Poetry 1945–1960* by Donald Allen; *Starting from San Francisco* by Lawrence Ferlinghetti; *The Yage Letters* by William Burroughs and Allen Ginsberg; *Coney Island of the Mind* by Lawrence Ferlinghetti; *Kaddish and Other Poems, 1958–1960* by Allen Ginsberg; *Lunch Poems* by Frank O'Hara and *Rosemary's*

Baby by Ira Levin. The books had already been included by teachers in their course reading lists, but on January 13, 1976, the school board issued a statement to teachers directing that the books "will not be purchased, nor used for class assignment, nor will an individual be given credit for reading any of these books." The school board did not rule that the books were legally obscene nor did it remove the books from the school libraries. The teachers challenged the decision of the board and the case went to court, where, in *Bob Cary, et al. v. Board of Education of Adams-Arapahoe School District 28-J, Aurora, Colorado,* 427 F. Supp. 945, 952 (D. Colo. 1977), they argued that the decision had impinged on their academic freedom. In his decision, Judge Matsch observed that the board had committed itself to offering students "an opportunity to engage actively in the free exchange of ideas" by offering the courses as electives. He stated, "It is enough to conclude that having granted both teachers and students the freedom to explore contemporary literature in these high school classes, the school board may not now impose its value judgments on the literature they choose to consider." Despite his stated position, the judge was forced to rule against the teachers because the teachers had bargained away their rights to academic freedom in this matter with a specific clause in their master contract.

In Westport, Connecticut, in 1977, parents approached members of the school board to protest the use of the novel in the high school classroom. They cited "objectionable" language in their complaints. The work was removed from the classroom. In Anniston, Alabama, in 1982, protests resulted in the temporary removal of the novel from the school libraries, but the work was later reinstated with the restriction that students would need parental permission to take out the book.

FURTHER READINGS

Aggeler, Geoffrey. *Anthony Burgess: The Artist as Novelist.* Birmingham: University of Alabama Press, 1979.
Coale, Samuel. *Anthony Burgess.* New York: Frederick Ungar Publishing, 1981.
Modern Fiction Studies (special Burgess issue) 27 (Autumn 1981).
Newsletter on Intellectual Freedom (May 1976): 70; (January 1977): 8; (March 1983): 37.
Pace, Eric. "Fears of Local Censorship Haunt the Book Trade." *New York Times* (January 8, 1974): 26.

CUJO

Author: Stephen King
Original date and place of publication: 1981, United States
Original publisher: Viking Press
Literary form: Novel

SUMMARY

Cujo is the story of a 200-pound Saint Bernard, a placid and typical "good dog" who becomes a source of terror to the family that loves him and to the inhabitants of the small town of Castle Rock, Maine. The Camber family pet, Cujo is the best friend of 10-year-old Brett Camber. The dog is bitten by rabid bats when he bolts into a cave while chasing rabbits. As Cujo slowly and painfully succumbs to rabies, King introduces his readers to the inhabitants of Castle Rock, some of whom will be attacked violently by Cujo and die.

Joe Camber, an auto mechanic and an abusive husband, makes a strong effort to indoctrinate his son Brett in his brutal ways, an effort that his wife, Charity, tries to counteract. Vic Trenton, a New York advertising executive who has moved with his wife, Donna, and son, Tad, to enjoy the peaceful Maine surroundings, strives to keep his marriage together even as Donna has an affair with local poet Steve Kemp, who cannot resist writing to Vic, "I enjoyed fucking the shit out of her." After receiving the note, Vic imagines their sexual encounter in detail. Aunt Evie, at 93 the oldest inhabitant, foretells the weather and has been labeled "that old loudmouth bitch" by postman George Meara, who is called "an old fart" by Aunt Evie. Gary Pervier, "meaner than a bull with a jackhandle up its ass," turned his Distinguished Service Cross into an ashtray in 1968. When hippies sought him out to tell him that he was "too fucking much," Gary threatened them with his rifle, for he considered them "a bunch of long-haired muff-diving crab-crawling asshole pinko fucksticks," and "told them he didn't give a shit if he blew their guts from Castle Rock to Fryeburg." The novel also contains "country club cunts" and several characters who routinely tell each other, "Fuck you."

Tad Trenton begins to see a monster in his closet each night soon after Cujo is bitten, and the two events are left for the reader to connect as representative of the evil that pervades ordinary life. The monster, "its eyes amber-glowing pits" that seem to follow him, frightens him and leaves "his scrotum crawling." He hears the monster's "purring growl" and smells "its sweet carrion breath." The monster disappears when Tad's parents enter the room, but reappears after they leave and warns Tad that his name "was Frank Dodd once, and I killed the ladies and maybe I ate them, too." He also warns Tad that someday soon he will pounce on the little boy and eat him.

The narrative continues, lapsing occasionally into Cujo's consciousness as he relates his physical deterioration, notes his muscle aches and festering muzzle and puzzles over his growing desire to kill the humans around him. The suspense builds with each kill, until Cujo traps Donna and Tad in their car, which she has taken to Camber's garage for repairs. For nearly two days, Donna struggles to keep her son safe from Cujo until she is forced into a physical confrontation with the dog and eventually kills him, using a baseball bat as her defense. Donna survives, although her deep bites bleed profusely and she must be treated for rabies, but Tad dies of dehydration despite her efforts to save him. As the novel ends, Vic and Donna reconcile, and Charity and Brett Camber begin a new life, free of Joe's brutality.

CENSORSHIP HISTORY

Many works written by Stephen King have been challenged or removed from school and community libraries, and they include the following: *Carrie, Christine, The Dark Half, The Dead Zone, Different Seasons, The Drawing of the Three, The Eyes of the Dragon, Firestarter, Four Past Midnight, It, Night Shift, Pet Sematary, Salem's Lot, The Shining, The Skeleton Crew, The Stand, The Talisman, Thinner* and *The Tommyknockers*. The most frequently challenged of King's works is *Cujo*, which has been charged with "age inappropriateness," "unacceptable language" and being "violent."

In 1984, parents of students in the Rankin County (Mississippi) School District challenged the appearance of the novel in the school libraries, claiming that it is "profane and sexually objectionable." The school board voted to retain the book in the libraries. In 1985, the novel was removed from the high school library in Bradford, New York, after parents complained that it is "a bunch of garbage." Also in 1985, the school trustees in Hayward, California, refused to approve a purchase order for the book because of the "rough language" and "explicit sex scenes." That same year, the Washington County, Alabama, board of education made a unanimous decision to remove the novel from all school libraries in the county, based on their perception that the novel contains "unacceptable language" and is "pornographic." In 1987, school officials removed the novel from the high school library after parents in Durand, Wisconsin, objected to it because of "violence" and "inappropriate language." The school board appointed a nine-member panel composed of school personnel and community members to review the book, and the issue was not pursued further.

In 1992, parents complained to the school superintendent in Peru, Indiana, that the novel and two other King novels, *The Dead Zone* and *Christine,* contained "filthy language" and were "not suitable for high school students," and they asked for its removal. The superintendent recommended to the school board that the novels be kept in the school library and made available to students who have parental permission. The school board refused to consider the suggestion and voted 5–1 to ban the books entirely from the high school library. Also in 1992, parents of middle school students in South Portland, Maine, requested that the school board remove the novel from the middle school library because of its "profanity" and sexual references. A review committee appointed by the school board to consider the request recommended its retention in the library collection. That same year, parents of students in Sparta, Illinois, appeared before the board of education and requested the removal of all books by Stephen King from the school libraries, claiming they are "violent" and "contain sex and explicit language." The board honored the parents' request to bar their children from using the book, but refused to ban the books.

In 1994, a local minister and a school board member in Bismarck, North Dakota, claimed that *Cujo* and eight other King novels (*Carrie, Christine, The Dead Zone, The Drawing of the Three, The Eyes of the Dragon, Pet Sematary, The Shining* and *Thinner*) should be removed from the school libraries. They challenged the novel on grounds of "age appropriateness."

FURTHER READINGS

Egan, James. "Sacral Parody in the Fiction of Stephen King." *Journal of Popular Culture* 23 (Winter 1989): 125–41.

Hohne, Karen A. "The Spoken Word in the Works of Stephen King." *Journal of Popular Culture* 28 (Fall 1994): 93–103.

King, Stephen. "Banned Books and Other Concerns: The Virginia Beach Lecture." In *The Stephen King Companion.* Ed. by George Beahm, 51–61. Kansas City, Mo.: Andrews & McMeel, 1989.

Newsletter on Intellectual Freedom (May 1984): 69; (January 1985): 8; (May 1985): 75, 77; (July 1985): 111; (January 1986): 7; (January 1987): 12; (March 1987): 54–55; (May 1987): 86; (July 1987): 125; (November 1987): 225, 226; (September 1988): 152; (January 1989): 11; (March 1989): 4; (May 1989): 75; (January 1990): 4–5; (January 1991): 12; (March 1992): 40; (May 1992): 79, 80; (July 1992): 105; (July 1992): 106; (March 1993): 41, 56; (July 1993): 124; (May 1994): 84–85; (September 1994): 166–67.

FAHRENHEIT 451

Author: Ray Bradbury
Original date and place of publication: 1953, United States
Original publisher: Ballantine Books
Literary form: Novel

SUMMARY

Fahrenheit 451 relates the story of an oppressive society in which books are forbidden objects and firemen are required to burn all books they encounter. The novel, an expanded version of a 1950 story entitled "The Fireman," takes its title from the temperature at which paper ignites: 451°F. One of a number of dystopic novels published after World War II, the work portrays humans as having lost touch with the natural world, with the world of the intellect and with each other. As the fire captain observes, "the word 'intellectual' became the swear word it deserved to be."

People hurry from their homes to their workplaces and back, never speaking of what they feel or think but only spouting meaningless facts and figures. At home, they surround themselves with interactive picture walls, wall-size television screens on three walls (four walls if one can afford them) containing characters who become accepted as family in an otherwise unconnected life. The streets have become dangerous as *minimum* speed limits of 55 miles per hour must be maintained, and speeds well over 100 miles per hour are more common. Teenagers and daring adults race their cars through the streets without concern for human life. War with an unnamed enemy is imminent.

For one fireman, the realization that there is a better life comes in the form of a 17-year-old girl named Clarisse, whose appreciation of nature, desire to talk about feelings and thoughts and appreciation for simply being alive mark her as an "odd duck." Guy Montag likes his job as a fireman, but he has clandestinely taken books from several sites where he and his fellow firemen have burned books and the houses in which they were hidden. Clarisse's questions as to why Montag became a fireman and her observations that the job does not seem right for him are disconcerting. A call to burn the books and house of a woman who refuses to leave the premises and, instead, ignites herself with the books increases Montag's discontent. He tries to speak with his wife Mildred, but she blocks him out with her Seashell ear thimbles, tiny radios worn in the ear that play continuously, and her involvement with her "family" on the picture walls.

Montag learns that the major reason for the abolition of books was to keep everyone happy. His fire captain explains that without books there is no conflicting theory or thought, and no one learns anything more than anyone else. With books, "Who knows who might be the target of the well-read man?"

After his wife reports that Montag has books in the house and their home is destroyed by the firemen, he seeks the help of former English professor Faber, who is part of a broader movement to preserve the knowledge of the past. Following Faber's directions, Montag goes to the railroad yards where he meets a group of old men, all former university professors who have each memorized specific literary works. They claim to be part of a network of thousands of individuals who will keep literature alive in their heads until the time when the oppression ceases and they can set the literature in type once more. Montag, who has memorized several books of the Old Testament, joins them, and the novel ends on a hopeful note.

CENSORSHIP HISTORY

Fahrenheit 451 is an indictment of censorship and expurgation, so the fact that this book was expurgated and marketed by the publisher that way for 13 years before the author became aware of the abuse is particularly ironic. In 1967, Ballantine Books published a special edition of the novel to be sold in high schools. Over 75 passages were modified to eliminate such words as "hell," "damn" and "abortion," and two incidents were eliminated. The original first incident described a drunk man who was changed to a sick man in the expurgated edition. In the second incident, reference is made to cleaning fluff out of the human navel, but the expurgated edition changed the reference to cleaning ears. No one complained about the expurgation, mainly because few people were aware of the changes, and many had not read the original. The copyright page made no mention of the changes, but thousands of people read only this version of *Fahrenheit 451* because the edition ran to 10 printings. At the same time, Ballantine Books continued to publish the "adult" version that was marketed to bookstores. After six years of the simultaneous editions, the publisher ceased publication of the adult version, leaving only the expurgated version for sale from 1973 through 1979, during which neither Bradbury nor anyone else suspected the truth.

In 1979, a friend alerted Bradbury to the expurgation, and he demanded that Ballantine Books withdraw completely the expurgated version and replace it with his original. The publisher agreed, and the complete version has been available since 1980.

This act of censorship had far-reaching effects for authors in regard to the school book clubs. The incident set in motion the American Library Association (ALA) Intellectual Freedom Committee, Young Adult division. In 1981, the committee looked into expurgation by school book clubs, such as Scholastic, and found that all of them expurgated books to some extent. Using its clout, the ALA reminded the book clubs that it awards the Newberry and Caldecott medals for children's books, and the ALA also noted that buyers are attracted to books designated as "ALA Best Books." The organization warned that it would strip the award announcements from expurgated books. The ALA also alerted teacher groups to demand that an expurgated book in a school book club be clearly identified on the copyright page as an "edited school book edition."

In a "Coda" that now appears in editions of *Fahrenheit 451*, Bradbury states, "I will not go gently onto a shelf, degutted, to become a non-book."

The "adult" version still has its critics. In 1992, students at Venado Middle School in Irvine, California, were issued copies of the novel with numerous words blacked out. School officials had ordered teachers to use black markers to obliterate all of the "hells," "damns" and other words deemed "obscene" in the books before giving them to students as required reading. Parents complained to the school and contacted local newspapers, who sent reporters to write stories about the irony of a book that condemns bookburning and censorship being expurgated. Faced with such an outcry, school officials announced that the censored copies would no longer be used.

FURTHER READINGS

Johnson, Wayne L. *Ray Bradbury*. New York: Frederick Ungar Publishing Company, 1980.

Moore, Everett T. "A Rationale for Bookburners: A Further Word from Ray Bradbury." *ALA Bulletin* 55 (May 1961): 403–4.

Newsletter on Intellectual Freedom (July 1992): 108–9.

Seed, David. "The Flight from the Good Life: 'Fahrenheit 451' in the Context of Postwar American Dystopias." *Journal of American Studies* 28, pt. 2 (August 1994): 225–40.

GO ASK ALICE

Author: Anonymous
Original date and place of publication: 1971, United States
Original publisher: Prentice-Hall
Literary form: Novel

SUMMARY

Go Ask Alice is a fictionalized account said to be based on the actual diary of a middle-class, 15-year-old drug user, the daughter of a college professor. The publisher only identifies "Anonymous" as the author. At the outset, the author has very low self-esteem and expresses dissatisfaction with her appearance. She dislikes her hair, hates the condition of her skin and feels fat, and she has just broken up with her boyfriend. She learns that her family will soon move because her father has received an appointment as dean of political science at another university, and she is excited at the prospect. When school is out for the summer in her new place of residence, the author returns to her old friends while spending the summer with her grandparents.

Bored with her summer, the author jumps at the chance to attend a party given by one of the "top echelon," a girl who ignored her before but who wants to attend the university where the author's father is a dean. The partygoers play a variation on the children's game, "Button, Button, Who's Got the Button?" but the author is not aware that 10 of the 14 colas are spiked with LSD and the "lucky" winners are those who unwittingly select the acid-laced soda. This is her first experience, and she is both fearful and pleased afterward. In her entry a few days later, she writes, "I simply can't wait to try pot." She has also decided that LSD is not so bad, and that "all the things I've heard about LSD were obviously written by uninformed, ignorant people like my parents who obviously don't know what they are talking about." Her drug use experiences escalate to "speed" and to stealing her grandmother's sleeping pills and tranquilizers. During her second acid trip, the author has sex, then worries afterward that she might become pregnant. She vows to stop using drugs, but she keeps her grandmother's sleeping pills.

The author returns home and becomes caught up in a vicious cycle of "Bennies," "Dexies" and hashish. She takes pills to give her bursts of energy during the day and pills to calm her down and let her sleep at night. She and a female friend become involved with two male college students who convince the girls to sell pot, which the girls do gladly, because the boys do not have time to sell and fewer girls than boys are "busted" for selling. Further, the author views herself as "Rich's chick all the way" so she has to do what she can to help him. That includes selling marijuana, LSD and barbiturates to not only high school students but junior high and grade school students as well. Rich only allows her to visit the apartment that he shares with Ted when he restocks her supply of drugs. She finds that she has been used when she and Chris arrive unexpectedly at the apartment and find the two young men having sex. The author berates herself for all that she did for Rich, and she and her friend decide that they will "stay clean," which means running away to San Francisco. Introduced to heroin, she and Chris are sexually and sadistically abused. They return to their parents and high school, but the drug use does not stop. The author is eventually sent to a psychiatrist to deal with the drug use, but she runs away to Denver. She shares a hovel with several others who remain constantly stoned, but the dirt and depressing surroundings convince her to return home again.

Once home, the author decides to finally stop her drug use, but her former friends refuse to allow that. When she has remained drug-free for a time, others begin to threaten her. While babysitting, she unknowingly consumes a batch of homemade candy that has been laced with LSD, which results in a placement in the state mental hospital. Upon her release, the author seems determined to remain free of drugs, and her diary entries are all upbeat. In the final entry, she decides not to keep another diary because she now feels strong enough not to need that crutch. An afterword reveals that only three weeks later she is found dead of a drug overdose that may or may not have been accidental.

CENSORSHIP HISTORY

Go Ask Alice has been the target of numerous challenges and attempts to ban it because of the language, the drug use and the sexual violence and promiscuity contained within. In the 1970s, schools cited the "objectionable" language and explicit sexual scenes as their reasons for removing it from their libraries in Kalamazoo, Michigan (1974); Saginaw, Michigan (1975); Eagle Pass, Texas (1977); and Trenton, New Jersey (1977). Written parental permission was required to take the book out of the library in Marcellus (New York) School District (1975), Ogden (Utah) School District (1979) and Safety Harbor Middle School Library in St. Petersburg, Florida (1982).

The work was one of 11 books banned by the school board in Island Trees Free School District No. 26 in New York in 1982. The court record specified the following passage as "objectionable" and representative of the reason for the ban: "shitty, goddamned, pissing, ass, goddamned beJesus, screwing life's, ass, shit. Doris was ten and had humped with who knows how many men in between/but now when I face a girl it's like facing a boy. I get all excited and turned on. I want to screw with the girl." The novel was returned to the library after the U.S. Supreme Court ruled in *Board of Education, Island Trees Union Free School District No. 26 et al. v. Pico et al.*, 457 U.S. 853 (1982) that the First Amendment rights of students had been violated in the banning.

In 1983, the book was removed from the school libraries because a school board member in Osseo School District in Brooklyn Park, Minnesota, found the language in the book to be "personally offensive," and the same occurred in the Pagosa Springs, Colorado, schools when a parent objected to the "graphic language, subject matter, immoral tone, and lack of literary quality found in the book." The book was challenged in 1984 in Rankin County (Mississippi) School District because it was "profane and sexually objectionable" and at the Central Gwinnett (Georgia) High School library in 1986 because "it encourages students to steal and take drugs."

Go Ask Alice was removed from the school library bookshelves in Kalkaska, Michigan, in 1986 because of "objectionable language," and that same year the Gainesville (Georgia) Public Library prohibited young readers from checking out the book by keeping it in a locked room with other books on the topics of drug use, sexual dysfunction, hypnosis and breast-feeding.

In 1993, the superintendent of schools of Wall Township, New Jersey, ordered the book removed from the intermediate school library because of "inappropriate" language and claims that it "borders on pornography." He expressed shock that the book was still available, because he had ordered the book removed from all reading lists and classroom book collections five years previously after receiving an anonymous letter that condemned the work. Also in 1993, the work was removed because of "graphic" language from an English class at Buckhannon-Upshur (West Virginia) High School and challenged as a required reading assignment at Johnstown (New York) High School because of "numerous obscenities." In 1994, Shepherd Hill High School in Dudley, Massachusetts, banned the book from its ninth-grade reading list due to "gross and vulgar language and graphic description of drug use and sexual conduct."

FURTHER READINGS

Hurwitz, Leon. *Historical Dictionary of Censorship in the United States.* Westport, Conn.: Greenwood Press, 1985.

Massie, Dorothy C. "Censorship in the Schools: Something Old and Something New." *Today's Education* 69 (November/December 1980): 56–60.

Newsletter on Intellectual Freedom (January 1975): 6; (March 1975): 41; (May 1975): 76; (July 1977): 100; (May 1977): 73; (May 1979): 49; (March 1980): 32; (July 1982): 142; (March 1983): 52; (March 1984): 53; (May 1984): 69; (July 1986): 117; (September 1986): 151–52; (November 1986): 207; (January 1987): 32; (March 1989): 39; (May 1993): 71; (July 1993): 109–10; (March 1994): 54; (September 1994): 150.

HOWL AND OTHER POEMS

Author: Allen Ginsberg
Original date and place of publication: 1956, United States
Original publisher: City Lights Books
Literary form: Poetry collection

SUMMARY

Howl and Other Poems contains 11 poems that explore what poet William Carlos Williams called "a howl of defeat." Dedicated to fellow Beat writers Jack Kerouac, William Seward Burroughs and Neal Cassady, of whose works Ginsberg claims "all these books are published in Heaven," the work contains the poet's passionate expressions on numerous taboos of the time. The title poem opens with the following lines: "I saw the best minds of my generation destroyed by madness, starving hysterical naked, / dragging themselves through the negro streets at dawn looking for an angry fix." He continues to speak of similarly unsavory topics, including "angelheaded hipsters . . . hollow-eyed and high sat up smoking in the supernatural darkness of cold-water flats . . . staggering on tenement roofs illuminated . . . publishing obscene odes on the windows of the skull." The veiled, symbolic references in these lines kept the poems relatively safe from prosecution, but his distinct references to homosexuality and to anal and oral sex in such lines as "Who let themselves be fucked in the ass by saintly motorcyclists, / and screamed with joy, / who blew and were blown by those human seraphim, the sailors" have been more easily singled out by censors as obscene. References to drug use abound in the poems, as do Ginsberg's private sexual fantasies and excretory images.

Although the title poem has been most heavily criticized for its obscene imagery and language, other poems in the collection celebrate Ginsberg's loss of virginity ("Transcription of Organ Music"), his disillusionment with America and the declaration that "I smoke marijuana every chance I get" ("America") and reference to the "fairy Sam" ("In the Baggage Room at Greyhound"). Taken in total, *Howl and Other Poems* explores the horrors of the poet's life and, as William Carlos Williams states in the final lines of his introduction to the collection, "Hold back the edges of your gowns, Ladies, we are going through hell."

CENSORSHIP HISTORY

Howl and Other Poems was first printed in England by Villiers and passed through Customs without incident to be published by City Lights Bookstore in the fall of 1956. On March 5, 1957, a second printing was seized in San Francisco by United States Customs officials, who confiscated 520 copies with the excuse that "the words and the sense of the writing is obscene. . . . You wouldn't want your children to come across it." Lawrence Ferlinghetti, owner of the City Lights Bookstore, had the forethought to contact the American

Civil Liberties Union before sending the work to England to be printed and had received assurance that the ACLU would defend him if the book were challenged. Thus, when the local U.S. attorney's office requested permission from a federal judge to destroy the book, the ACLU notified the collector of Customs and the U.S. attorney that it would defend the book. The U.S. attorney decided to drop proceedings.

Despite clearance from U.S. Customs, copies of the book were later seized by the San Francisco police who claimed that the material was not suitable for children, even though the City Lights Bookstore did not carry books for children. Ferlinghetti was booked and fingerprinted in the San Francisco Hall of Justice, after being arrested by two juvenile squad police officers.

The case went to trial and nine literary experts were called to defend the "social importance" of Ginsberg's poem: Mark Schorer, Leo Lowenthal, Walter Van Tilburg Clark, Herbert Blau, Arthur Foff, Mark Linenthal, Kenneth Rexroth, Vincent McHugh and Luther Nichols. The experts identified the work as "social criticism . . . a literary work that hurled *ideological* accusation after accusation against American society." Prosecuting attorney Ralph McIntosh repeatedly attempted to coerce the witnesses into translating the poetry into prose, reading aloud passages from *Howl* that contained what he classified as "dirty" words and sexual images. He also baited the experts by asking if the terms that he deemed to be obscene could have been worded differently by Ginsberg, but presiding Judge Horn stopped him, saying "'it is obvious that the author could have used another term'" but that it was "'up to the author'" to decide.

In handing down his decision on *Howl and Other Poems*, the judge cited the decision of Justice William J. Brennan only four months earlier in *Roth v. the United States*, 354 U.S. 476 (1957), stating that "unless the book is entirely lacking in 'social importance' it cannot be held 'obscene.'" He added further that, while the poem contained "unorthodox and controversial ideas" that were expressed at times through "coarse and vulgar" words, including "cock," "fuck," "ass," "cunt," "gyzym" and "asshole," the work was protected by the constitutional freedoms of speech and press. Horn stated, "An author should be real in treating his subject and be allowed to express his thoughts and ideas in his own words."

Although Judge Horn's decision freed *Howl and Other Poems* in 1957, the poem has remained controversial. In 1988, the listener-supported Pacifica Radio Network did not carry a broadcast of the poem that was set to be read on radio stations nationwide on the evening of January 6, 1988, as part of a weeklong series about censorship called "Open Ears/Open Minds." The network made the decision after being threatened with possible obscenity prosecution by the Justice Department a few months before for broadcasting a play about homosexuality. The decision was also made based on an April 1987 ruling by the Federal Communications Commission stating that stations faced possible penalties for broadcasting "material that depicts or describes, in terms patently offensive as measured by contemporary community standards for the broadcast medium, sexual or excretory activities or organs." In response to Pacifica's decision, the author said, "The Government now has set out rules which have had an intimidating and chilling effect on broadcasters. . . . it's the last desperate gasp of the Reagan neo-conservatives."

FURTHER READINGS

D'Emilio, John, and Estelle B. Freedman. *Intimate Matters: A History of Sexuality in America*. New York: Harper & Row, Publishers, 1988.

Robins, Natalie. *Alien Ink: The FBI's War on Freedom of Expression*. New York: William Morrow and Company, 1992.

Yarrow, Andrew L. "Allen Ginsberg's 'Howl' in a New Controversy." *The New York Times* (January 6, 1988): C2.

LAST EXIT TO BROOKLYN

Author: Hubert Selby Jr.
Original date and place of publication: 1964, United States
Original publisher: Grove Press
Literary form: Novel

SUMMARY

Last Exit to Brooklyn consists of six linked episodes, each preceded by a quote from the Old Testament, that form a novel detailing the brutal and violent lives of a group of lower economic class Brooklyn youths in the late 1940s through the 1950s. The squalor of the environment and the hopelessness of their drug- and violence-dominated lives leave them devoid of human compassion and lacking in conventional morality. Married and single, gay and straight, the men are portrayed as relentlessly brutal, opportunistic and cruel to other men, to women and to the children whom they conceive. Women, powerless for the most part, accept their limited roles, exacting revenge on those weaker than them whenever possible. Children are conditioned to live life as a daily struggle and to accept abusive behavior as normal. For everyone in this novel, crime is an everyday fact of existence.

The novel takes its title from the sign "Last Exit to Brooklyn" that appears on the Gowanus (New York) Expressway, just before the entrance to the Battery Tunnel. That expressway exit is an entrance into a hell composed of waterfront docks, dirty factory buildings, slum housing, cheap bars and subsidized city apartment projects for the poor, with empty, bottle-strewn lots and concrete playgrounds. The language throughout the work is in the vernacular, and the author omits the use of apostrophes in contractions or to indicate the possessive form of nouns and he often runs words together to reflect the characters' states of mind. Four young criminals, each of whom boasts of his prison record, spend their lives "hanging out" at "the Greeks" diner, mocking the prostitutes such as Tralala and boasting of recent 'scores," having "lushed a drunk" or "pulled a job." Opportunistic, they claim to be completely hetero-sexual but become involved with a crowd of male transvestites whom they pretend to view as women in order to take advantage of the free gin, abundant benzedrine tablets and cheap thrills. The young hoodlums pretend to care about the transvestites but their resulting cruelty leads one to overdose on benzedrine tablets. The friends move in different directions, and each later faces his or her own disaster.

Tralala descends into a nightmare of alcoholism and drug addiction, trading her body for drinks and even giving it away for free just to feel wanted. She dies after being taken to a vacant lot filled with broken bottles and rusty cans and raped by 50 or more men from several area barrooms. Afterwards, as Selby writes in a stream-of-consciousness tone,

> . . . the kids who were watching and waiting to take a turn took out their disappointment on Tralala and tore her clothes to small scraps put out a few cigarettes on her nipples pissed on her jerkedoff on her jammed a broomstick up her snatch then bored they left her lying amongst the broken bottles rusty cans and rubble of the lot and Jack and Fred and Ruthy and Annie stumbled into a cab still laughing and they leaned toward the window as they passed the lot and got a good look at Tralala lying naked covered with blood urine and semen and a small blot forming on the seat between her legs as blood seeped from her crotch and Ruth and Annie happy and completely relaxed now that they were on their way downtown. . . .

Later sections explore the brutality of Harry Black, now a union organizer, who repeatedly blames and physically abuses his wife to compensate for his disgust with all women. A braggart and bully who drinks heavily, he has frequent violent dreams in which he sees himself torn to shreds. The dreams end and he achieves temporary happiness and even softens toward all but his wife once he begins a passionate affair with a male transvestite upon whom he lavishes money taken from his union strike expense account. Black believes that he has found true love, but his lover leaves when the strike account closes and the flow of money stops. In a confused state, Black attempts to perform oral sex on a 10-year-old boy in his neighborhood, and his former friends brutally beat him as punishment.

The two sections that deal with marriage, "And Baby Makes Three" and "Landsend," continue the pervasive theme of despair. None of the marriages are happy, because all of the husbands and some of the wives appear to remain eager for extramarital sex. Husbands who work are physically abusive and grudgingly give their stay-at-home wives money to buy food for their children; husbands who do not work but who depend on their wives' paychecks are also abusive and refuse to assume any household or child-care responsibilities.

Capital letters dominate the conversations as Selby indicates the continued arguments that pass for marital communication. Children are neglected and subjected to the constant fighting of their parents. The novel portrays a hellish existence that appears to continue as the characters age.

CENSORSHIP HISTORY

Last Exit to Brooklyn has been censored on both sides of the Atlantic. Several of the chapters had appeared separately in *Black Mountain Review*, *New Directions #17*, *Provincetown Review* and *Swank*. The section entitled "Tralala" first appeared as a play that was banned from off-Broadway production in 1957. In 1965, in Boston, Massachusetts, a local city attorney sought an injunction against the book, but the complaint was dismissed. The following year, a circuit court in Connecticut issued a temporary injunction against sale of the book, now published by both Grove Press and Dell Publishing, charging that it was "obscene and pornographic." The injunction was overturned and sales were again permitted. The novel has also been banned in Italy and Ireland, and placed on a restricted list in Russia.

The most extensive censorship case occurred in England, where the novel was published by Calder and Boyars. In late 1966, Conservative Member of Parliament Sir Charles Taylor received a copy of the novel, sent to him by Sir Basil Blackwell, member of an Oxford bookselling family and a man in his seventies who claimed that his few remaining years had been "defiled" by reading *Last Exit*. Disgusted by the book, Taylor alerted the attorney general in June 1967 to register a complaint with the Office of the Director of Public Prosecutions (DPP). That office replied that Taylor was too late to make an effective complaint because over 11,000 copies of the book had already been sold, and sales were slowing. Attorney General Sir Elwyn Jones stated further that "Literary Criticism was almost unanimous that it had literary merit." The publisher taunted Taylor by including his name in their advertisement in *The Sunday Times*, stating: "Sir Charles Taylor, MP has described *Last Exit* as filthy, disgusting, degrading. It is one of the most important novels to come out of America. . . ."

The audacity of the publisher angered another member of parliament, Sir Cyril Black (Conservative), who used the private prosecutions feature of Section 3 of the *Obscene Publications Act of 1959* to challenge the publishers. He brought a formal complaint against the book in July 1966, calling upon the publisher to prove that the book had value and to establish why it should not be banned. The magistrate who granted the application was Sir Robert Blundell, a chief opponent of *FANNY HILL*, who issued a search warrant for members of law enforcement to seize all copies from area bookshops. The trial was held at Marlborough Street Magistrates Court in November 1966, and the numerous prosecution witnesses were consistent in expressing their disgust with the scenes depicted in the novel, especially with the brutal rape and humiliation of

Tralala. This section has drawn the greatest objection in proceedings against the book because of the horrifying picture that Selby creates of the humiliation and death of Tralala and the cold indifference of onlookers. The presiding magistrate rejected the book, observing that "this book in its descriptions goes beyond any book of a merely pornographic kind that we have seen in this court [and] . . . is more likely to deprave and corrupt than any of those cyclostyled horrors."

Buoyed by the published opinion of several critics that Britain "had made herself the laughing stock of the civilized world," Calder and Boyars announced that they would continue publication. In response, the DPP announced that it would prosecute, using section 2 of the 1959 act that prohibited "possessing an obscene article for gain." The trial was set for November 1967, and an all-male jury was selected to spare women the embarrassment of reading the material. The trial lasted nine days and brought together numerous prominent witnesses. The prosecution spotlighted David Shepherd, a former cricket star who had taken religious orders and would later become a bishop, who claimed that he had emerged "not unscathed" by reading the novel, although as a social worker in the East End of London he could identify many of the character types among his clients. To counter this testimony, Calder and Boyars assembled a list of nearly 30 writers, critics, professors and members of the media who praised Selby's work and his expression of theme. The effort was fruitless for, after deliberating five and a half hours, the jury declared the book guilty of being obscene and that "the effect of reading the book was to horrify, shock, disgust, and nauseate." Although the judge determined that the book had been published in good faith by a respectable publishing house, he fined Calder and Boyars £100 and ordered them to pay £500 in court costs.

The publishers once again appealed the decision, represented this time by John Mortimer, who convinced the appeal judges that the judge in the earlier trial had not sufficiently explained the complexities of the 1959 act to the jury and had left too much to "commonsense" and not enough to law. As a result, the conviction was overturned and *Last Exit* was free to appear in a complete and unexpurgated edition. To avoid further embarrassing litigation based on private prosecution, Section 3 of the *Obscene Publications Act of 1959* was changed. *Last Exit* holds the distinction of being the last serious novel, poem or play prosecuted under the 1959 act.

FURTHER READINGS

Kermode, Frank. "'Obscenity' and the 'Public Interest'." *New American Review* 3 (April 1968): 229–44.

Lane, James B. "Violence and Sex in the Post-War Popular Urban Novel: With a Consideration of Harold Robbins's *A Stone for Danny Fisher* and Hubert Selby, Jr.'s, *Last Exit to Brooklyn*." *Journal of Popular Culture* 8 (Fall 1974): 295–308.

Sutherland, John. *Offensive Literature: Decensorship in Britain, 1960–1982*. Totowa, N.J.: Barnes & Noble Books, 1983.

Wertime, Richard A. "Psychic Vengeance in *Last Exit to Brooklyn.*" *Literature and Psychology* 24 (November 1974): 153–66.

LEAVES OF GRASS

Author: Walt Whitman
Original date and place of publication: 1855, United States
Original publisher: Self-published
Literary form: Poetry collection

SUMMARY

Leaves of Grass appeared in 1855 as a quarto of 95 pages that had been typeset by Whitman in the Brooklyn print shop of Andrew and James Rome. Whitman's name did not appear on the title page, nor did the name of a publisher or printer appear. He did not hide his authorship, however, for the copyright notice was credited to "Walter Whitman" and his portrait faced the title page. The 12 poems in the 1855 edition had no titles, but Whitman created titles for them, with which we are now familiar, in later editions: "Song of Myself," "A Song for Occupations," "To Think of Time," "The Sleepers," "I Sing the Body Electric," "Faces," "Song of the Answerer," "Europe the 72d and 73d Years of These States," "A Boston Ballad," "There Was a Child Went Forth," "Who Learns My Lesson Complete" and "Great Are the Myths." The collection went through five more editions in Whitman's lifetime. The third edition of the collection, published in 1860, contained more than 100 additional poems, many of them with homosexual overtones that brought more notoriety to the work.

The first edition fulfilled Walt Whitman's goal to write a serious work in a clearly sensuous manner. His subject is the common man, unlike other writers of his time who wrote about and for an educated elite. He chose to draw attention to the ordinary people who made up American society. He also had another purpose to his poetry. Whitman stated in the preface to the 1855 edition of *Leaves of Grass* his purpose of uniting the physical aspect of the human with the spiritual, and this purpose appears in the poetry, as in "Song of Myself," which contains the line "I am the poet of the body, / And I am the poet of the soul."

In developing his theme of accepting everything in life equally, excluding nothing, Whitman included blunt anatomical references that offended many of his readers for whom such references remained taboos for many decades into the future. In accepting all of nature, he wrote of "the litter of the grunting sow as they tug at her teats" and "where the bull advances to do his masculine work, and the stud to the mare, and the cock is treading the hen." He similarly accepted people in all stations and situations of life, as he wrote that "the keptwoman [sic] and sponger and thief are hereby invited—the heavy-lipped slave is invited—the veneralee is invited." He offered friendship and brother-hood "to a drudge of the cottonfields or emptier of privies . . . on his right cheek I place the family kiss."

Throughout the poems, Whitman speaks of the physical actions and realities that his contemporaries strained to keep hidden as not being "nice" or "appropriate" to speak of:

> Copulation is no more rank to me than death is.
> I believe in the flesh and the appetites,
> Seeing hearing and feeling are miracles, and
> each part and tag of me is a miracle.
> . . . .
> The scent of these arm-pits is aroma finer than prayer, . . .
> . . . .
> I turn the bridegroom out of bed and stay
> with the bride myself,
> And tighten her all night to my thighs and lips.
> . . . .
> Darkness you are gentler than my lover—
> his flesh was sweaty and panting,
> I feel the hot moisture yet that he left me.

In numerous lines throughout the collection, Whitman celebrated sensuality and reminded people of their most primitive desires.

CENSORSHIP HISTORY

Leaves of Grass was declared obscene from its first publication. The first bookseller to whom Whitman took his book refused to sell it, claiming that it was "too sensual." Whitman met Lorenzo and Orson Fowler, who agreed to distribute the book, but sales were low and Whitman gave away many copies of the first edition. As cries of "immorality" were raised against the work, the Fowler brothers became frightened and gave existing copies of the second edition of the work to Whitman and resigned the whole edition. Libraries refused to buy the book; the Library Company of Philadelphia is the only one on record in America to have bought a copy when it was first published. Thus, other libraries effectively censored the book by their refusal to buy it.

Critic R. W. Griswold, writing on November 10, 1855, in *The New Criterion*, observed, "Thus, then we leave this gathering of muck to the laws which, certainly, if they fulfill their intent, must have power to suppress such obscenity." A review in the English magazine *Saturday Review* also condemned the collection and stated in March 1856: "After every five or six pages . . . Mr. Whitman suddenly becomes very intelligible, but exceedingly obscene. If the *Leaves of Grass* should come into anybody's possession, our advice is to throw them immediately behind the fire." In 1865, Walt Whitman lost his job with the United States Department of the Interior because Chief Secretary James Harlan found an annotated copy of the poetry collection in Whitman's desk drawer and determined that he was "the author of an indecent book." In 1870, Noah Porter, president of Yale University, wrote in *Books and Reading* that "a generation cannot be entirely pure which tolerates writers who, like Walt Whitman, commit, in writing, an offense like that indictable at common law of walking naked through the streets."

Many people, among them Ralph Waldo Emerson, who had praised the book in a letter that Whitman arranged to have published in the *New York Times*, urged Whitman to permit an expurgated version of the collection. He remained staunchly opposed to expurgation and American copyright law protected him unless he consented to it. From the time that the collection appeared in 1855, his editors suggested that a bowdlerized version for the general public would be good for sales. Whitman violently opposed expurgation, viewing such books as "the dirtiest book in all the world." Not until 1892, not long before his death, did he finally agree to an expurgated version as a gesture of friendship for Arthur Stedman, whose father, Edward Clarence Stedman, had done many favors for Whitman.

Leaves of Grass was not expurgated in the United States until 1892, but it was banned entirely, if informally, in New York and Philadelphia bookstores in the 1870s and legally in Boston in the 1880s. As per their usual practice, the Watch and Ward Society in Boston and the New York Society for the Suppression of Vice placed pressure on booksellers to suppress the sale of the book in their shops. Booksellers agreed not to advertise the book nor to suggest its sale to customers.

In 1881, the Society for the Suppression of Vice sought to obtain a legal ban of a proposed new edition of *Leaves of Grass* in Boston. At the urging of the society, the district attorney threatened criminal action against a publisher who had planned a new edition of the work unless it were expurgated. The edition was withdrawn.

In 1883, author, publisher and free-love advocate Ezra Heywood was arrested by Anthony Comstock, the head of the New York Society for the Suppression of Vice, on the charge of sending obscene matter through the mail. The material consisted of *Cupid's Yokes*, a pamphlet that contained "unconventional social and sexual views," and an anthology entitled *The Word Extra* that contained two poems from *Leaves of Grass*, "To a Common Prostitute" and "A Woman Waits for Me." When the case went to trial, the grand jury declared the Whitman poems "too grossly obscene and lewd to be placed on the records of the court." This meant that members of the jury would decide Heywood's fate without being permitted to review copies of the poem nor to hear lines from the poem read before making their decision; they were expected to accept the decision of the prosecution that the works were obscene. Judge T. L. Nelson, presiding in the United States Circuit Court in Boston, threw out the case, "on the grounds that the allegation in the indictment was untrue."

The English bowdlerized the collection from its first appearance in England in 1868. Pre-Raphaelite ex-bohemian William Michael Rossetti, the editor of the expurgated collection, explained in the preface that he had omitted about half the poems of the 1860s edition because he and Whitman lived in "this peculiarly nervous age." He also proudly proclaimed that he was not bowdlerizing the work, because "I have not in a single instance excised *parts* of poems." Perrin observed, "it is the sort of preface a liberal poet might write if he happened to get involved in bowdlerism." Although Rossetti did not excise parts of any poems, he did make numerous changes in Whitman's preface to the original 1855 edition of the collection, excising even the term "prostitute." The expurgated version of *Leaves of Grass* became part of the Everyman Library in 1886 and existed well into the twentieth century. Ernest de Selincourt used that version for Oxford's "World Classics" series in 1920, removing several more poems. Late in life, Whitman considered his work and expressed his dissatisfaction with the English editions, noting that "I now feel somehow as if none of the changes should have been made: that I should have assumed that position: that's the only possible, final, logical position."

FURTHER READINGS

Blodgett, Harold. *Walt Whitman in England*. Ithaca, N.Y.: Cornell University Press, 1934.

Broun, Heywood, and Margaret Leech. *Anthony Comstock*. New York: Albert & Charles Boni, 1927.

Cavitch, David. *My Soul and I: The Inner Life of Walt Whitman*. Boston: Beacon Press, 1985.

Cowley, Malcolm, ed. *Walt Whitman's Leaves of Grass: The First (1855) Edition*. New York: Viking Press, 1959.

Everson, William. *American Bard: The Original Preface to "Leaves of Grass."* New York: Viking Press, 1982.

McCoy, Ralph E. *Banned in Boston: The Development of Literary Censorship in Massachusetts*. Urbana, Ill.: University of Illinois, 1956.

Mordell, Albert. *Notorious Literary Attacks*. New York: Boni & Liveright, 1926.

Perrin, Noel. *Dr. Bowdler's Legacy*. Boston: David R. Godine, Publisher, 1969.

MANCHILD IN THE PROMISED LAND

Author: Claude Brown
Original date and place of publication: 1965, United States
Original publisher: The Macmillan Company
Literary form: Autobiographical novel

SUMMARY

Manchild in the Promised Land is a fictionalized account of Claude Brown's maturation from drug-dealing gang member to one of America's most powerful writers about the African-American experience. The work bears the following dedication: "To Eleanor Roosevelt, who founded the Wiltwyck School for Boys. And to the Wiltwyck School, which is still finding Claude Browns." Throughout the work, Brown uses the vernacular of the Harlem streets in recounting the drug addiction, prostitution and murders that threatened to destroy the generation of young black boys and girls struggling in the 1940s and 1950s to survive in a hostile environment.

The book is narrated by "Sonny," Claude Brown's persona, who tells his story of growth and endurance in Harlem, where survival depends upon an individual's ability to outfight and outmaneuver everyone and everything. He is unhappy at home, disdainful of his complacent mother and angry with his abusive father, and he makes the streets his home. Just 13 when the book opens, he has been shot while stealing bedsheets from a clothesline and is about to be sent away. Already experienced with heroin use, like many of his friends he is headed for a life of poverty, addiction and early death.

After recovering from his wound, Sonny is sent to the Wiltwyck School for socially maladjusted boys, founded by Eleanor Roosevelt, whom he meets when he sees "this rich old lady hanging around Wiltwyck . . . she used to be married to a cat who was President of the United States." At the school, Sonny is impressed by the school administrator, Mr. Papanek, who commands respect through his knowledge and authoritative personality, and who recognizes Sonny's potential to overcome his environment. For the first time, the young boy realizes that a man does not have to use a gun, a knife or a fist to exert power over others; education and intelligence are far more powerful weapons. That awareness stays with him throughout the years ahead.

Once he is back in Harlem, the abuse at home sends him back onto the street, where he continues to deal drugs and to steal. At 14, he is arrested again and sent to a reformatory. This cycle of crime and arrests lasts through most of his teenage years, but the brief experience at Wiltwyck gives him the power to realize that he is going to be just another Harlem statistic who will die of heroin addiction or a gunshot wound unless he makes some changes. The only course is to get a college education. He begins by leaving Harlem to work and to earn a high school diploma.

Once out of Harlem, Sonny takes any job available to pay for his classes. He explores African-American culture as he becomes involved in the Beat movement in art and literature, and new opportunities to grow and learn appear as he becomes friends with musicians who are proud and passionate in exploring their African heritage. He also learns that drugs become unnecessary when life has purpose as he experiments with spiritual movements. For a time, he is drawn to the Coptic faith, more for its African roots than for the religious aspect; then he becomes deeply involved in the Muslim faith. His belief in formal education also strengthens, and he makes plans to leave New York to attend college. Before making this move, he returns to Harlem, walks the streets and assesses what has happened to the people whom he has known. One of his best friends has just died of a drug overdose, his younger brother is in jail for armed robbery and many of his acquaintances are heroin addicts. Only one has had the will to rise above the situation, one of his oldest friends, Danny, who survived heroin addiction and now has a stable marriage and family life and religious convictions. Sonny recognizes that his only hope of escaping the human misery of Harlem is to leave New York behind.

CENSORSHIP HISTORY

Manchild in the Promised Land has been the target of criticism as well as of numerous attempts to remove it from school libraries and the school curriculum since its publication in 1965. Criticized upon its first appearance for what one reviewer called its limited vocabulary that was "not a language at all but an impoverished patois," the work has since been condemned for containing a host of other evils.

Lee Burress reported that *Manchild in the Promised Land* was among the 10 most frequently challenged books in schools between 1965 and 1975. In a 1973 national survey of English department chairpersons, Burress, who does not identify the cities or states in which the bans occurred, only the geographical region of the United States, found that the book was banned across the nation. In the Northeast, a combined group consisting of a parent, clergyman, student and member of the board of education complained that "Trash like this does not belong in the classroom. . . . That hippie English teacher is perverted." The result was that students would not be required to fulfill any reading assignments if a book was judged "graphically realistic." The book was also placed on a closed shelf in the library to which students had no access.

In a case in the West, a parent complained of the "language and content" and the book was again placed on a closed shelf of the library to which students had no access. In a case in the Midwest, a teacher complained that the book was "obscene" and the book was removed from classroom use. In the Southwest, a group calling itself the Committee of Concerned Parents complained to school officials that the book should be removed from the high school library because of "profanity" and sex scenes that are "too explicit." School officials ordered the book placed on a closed shelf to which students had no access.

In 1974, after one parent of a student in the Waukesha, Wisconsin, school system complained about the language in the work as "filth and obscenity," school administrators removed the work from the high school library. Similar charges were leveled by parents in Plant City, Florida, in 1976 and in North

Jackson, Ohio, in 1980; school officials in both these school systems also removed the work from their high school libraries.

A national survey of high school English department chairpersons conducted by Burress in 1977 found that the work had been removed from classroom use in two New York schools because of parents' complaints that the work was "obscene," and it had been removed from the library in a Massachusetts school after the book was brought to the attention of a teacher who found that the book was "not suitable for some grade level students." That same survey reported that a parent's request that the book be removed from classroom use because of objections to the "obscene" language and the masturbation scene was denied in Massachusetts.

In 1977, Concerned Citizens and Taxpayers for Decent Books in Baton Rouge, Louisiana, listed the work with 64 other "offensive" works. Characterizing the book as "pornography and filth," the group called for its removal from the classrooms and the school libraries. The work was removed from classroom use and placed on the restricted shelf in the school library.

In 1987, different complaints were voiced when parents and "concerned citizens" challenged the appearance of the book on reading lists for English classes at Parkrose (Oregon) High School. They protested that the content was "violent, the language offensive, and women are degraded." They further questioned the relevance of the work to the lives of students in Parkrose and claimed that their students "have no need to understand life in a black ghetto."

FURTHER READINGS

Brown, Claude. "Manchild in Harlem." *New York Times Magazine* (April 14, 1996): 111.

Burress, Lee. *Battle of the Books: Literary Censorship in the Public School, 1950–1985.* Metuchen, N.J.: Scarecrow Press, 1989.

Hartshorne, Thomas L. "Horatio Alger in Harlem: Manchild in the Promised Land." *Journal of American Studies* 24 (August 1990): 243–48.

Miller, Warren. "One Score in Harlem—Review of *Manchild in the Promised Land*, by Claude Brown." *Saturday Review* (August 28, 1965): 49.

Newsletter on Intellectual Freedom (September 1974): 111; (May 1980): 51; (September 1987): 176; (November 1987): 240.

NAKED LUNCH

Author: William Seward Burroughs
Original date and place of publication: 1959, France; 1962, United States
Original publisher: Olympia Press; Grove Press
Literary form: Novel

SUMMARY

Begun in Tangier in 1955, *Naked Lunch* is a montage of shocking scenes that combine surreal fantasy and hallucination to create a nightmarish blend of drug addiction, pederasty and cannibalism. The unconventional narrative patterns of shifting point of view and stream-of-consciousness rambling make it less a unified novel than it is a series of images that are linked by their theme of the destructive effects of man's addictions. The lack of a consistent narrative and the frequently changing point of view reflect the nightmare world in which William Lee, the main character, fights himself as often as he must fight with others. Burroughs claimed in his "Introduction" to have illuminated his technique through the title that "means exactly what the words say: NAKED Lunch—a frozen moment when everyone sees what is on the end of every fork."

Three sections make up the work: the account of drug withdrawal in the "Introduction," which is subtitled "Deposition: Testimony Concerning a Sickness"; the paranoid-sexual fantasy of the body of the novel with erratically placed subheadings and the scholarly examination of drug addiction in the "Appendix."

The "Introduction" offers Burroughs' explanation of "The Sickness," his 15-year addiction to opium and opium derivatives. The author scrupulously distinguishes between drugs that create physical dependence and hallucinogens, which he claims are wrongly condemned. Using a sometimes jarring word order, he also describes in painstaking detail the economics of drug dealing and the victimization of the addict. The "Introduction" ends with his apocalyptic warning: "Look down LOOK DOWN along that junk road before you travel there and get in with the Wrong Mob. . . . A word to the wise guy."

The body of the novel is the story of William Lee, a junkie who struggles to free himself of the strictures imposed by drugs, sex, language and bureaucracy. He roams from New York to Mexico to Tangier and beyond, searching for escape from "the heat," which at first is slang reference for the police, but which eventually comes to refer to the pressures of life that have driven him to drug addiction. Space and time fluctuate wildly, and Lee lives in a nightmarish world in which time stretches or constricts according to the amount and type of drug consumed. Locations become interchangeable as Lee travels through a world of sadistic sex, extensive drug use and squalid surroundings. Heterosexual and homosexual acts that emphasize pain and degradation are described in lurid detail, and mutilation imagery abounds in the novel. The names and specific effects of various drugs are detailed, as are the most and least effective means of administering the drugs in order to achieve their maximum effects.

Burroughs juxtaposes seemingly realistic scenes with brutal nightmarish acts that exhibit the degradation of his characters through the violent, bestial acts of others and of themselves. He uses colloquial language to refer to the human body, especially to genitalia, and strives for maximum shock effect in the extended descriptions of drug paraphernalia and use and the forced sexual encounters suffered by men, women and boys.

In the "Appendix," an essay entitled "Letter from a Master Addict to Dangerous Drugs" that was published in *The British Journal of Addiction* (53:2), Burroughs discusses the relative merits and dangers of opiates, cannabis indica, peyote, cocaine and synthetic drugs. He interpolates his own experiences with each substance into an examination of sources and precautions, thus providing a guide to the unwary.

CENSORSHIP HISTORY

The novel has the distinction of being the last literary work to be declared obscene and brought to trial in America. From the 1959 publication of the book until January 1963, Customs agents seized copies of the work entering the United States, justifying their actions under the Tariff Act (1930), which provided for the seizure of allegedly obscene materials. The work was later involved in two legal actions. Although cleared in Los Angeles in 1965 before the case went to trial, it was declared obscene the same year in Boston, where the attorney general argued that the work was "trash." Writers Norman Mailer, Allen Ginsberg and John Ciardi were called as expert witnesses with psychiatrists and academics to testify regarding the literary merit of the work, but Judge Eugene Hudson remained unconvinced. In delivering his verdict, the judge declared the book to be "obscene, indecent and impure . . . and taken as a whole . . . predominantly prurient, hardcore pornography and utterly without redeeming social importance." In response to the claim by the defense that the work held significant social and scientific value, Hudson declared *Naked Lunch* to be trash written by a "mentally sick" individual.

An appeal was made to the Massachusetts Supreme Judicial Court, and *Attorney General v. A Book Named "Naked Lunch,"* 351 Mass. 298, 218 N.E.2d 571 (1966) was heard on October 8, 1965. The Supreme Judicial Court acknowledged that the book was "grossly offensive" and reminded those present that the author had himself described the book as "brutal, obscene and disgusting." They also applied the test of redeeming social value to the work and could find no reason to declare the novel as "not utterly without redeeming social value." Their determination that the work was not lacking in social importance resulted from the many reviews and articles in literary and other publications that discussed seriously the controversial book and showed that a "substantial and intelligent group" within the community believed the book to be of literary significance. On July 7, 1966, the Massachusetts Supreme Judicial Court declared the book not obscene. The four members of the court who delivered the favorable decision and the two dissenting members declared further that the book could be sold in the state, but that people would be subject to prosecution if they "have been or are advertising or distributing this book in this Commonwealth in a manner to exploit it for the sake of its possible prurient appeal."

FURTHER READING

De Grazia, Edward. *Censorship Landmarks*. New York: R.R. Bowker Company, 1969.

Goodman, Michael B. *Contemporary Literary Censorship: The Case History of Burroughs' Naked Lunch*. Metuchen, N.J.: Scarecrow Press, 1981.

Miles, Barry. *William Burroughs: El Hombre Invisible*. New York: Hyperion Publishing, 1983.

Morgan, Ted. *Literary Outlaw: The Life and Times of William S. Burroughs*. New York: Henry Holt & Company, 1988.

Sutherland, John. *Offensive Literature: Decensorship in Britain, 1960–1982*. Totowa, N.J.: Barnes and Noble Books, 1981.

OF MICE AND MEN

Author: John Steinbeck
Original date and place of publication: 1937, United States
Original publisher: Viking Penguin
Literary form: Novel

SUMMARY

Of Mice and Men is the story of two men, big and simpleminded Lennie and small and cunning George, who drift from one ranchhand job to another as they pursue their dream of owning their own place someday. Despite their mismatched intellectual capabilities, the two men are good friends who share the same dream, the simple desire to have their own farm where Lennie will be able to raise rabbits. As they travel from job to job, George becomes frustrated with Lennie's limitations and often loses patience, but he does not desert the childlike giant. George knows that Lennie will inadvertently become involved in a situation from which he will be unable to extricate himself, so vigilance is necessary.

Although the two men are thrilled to be given a ranch job, George must, as usual, cover for Lennie and make him appear to be more capable and intelligent that he really is. The boss's son Curley bullies the childlike Lennie, who finds himself drawn to the bully's lovely young wife. Curley's wife, however, does not treat Lennie fairly and she teases him playfully, unaware of how seriously he perceives her actions. He sees her as being similar to the soft and cuddly puppy that he once had, and he wants only to stroke her soft hair as he had stroked the puppy's soft fur. When Lennie approaches Curley's wife to stroke her hair, she becomes frightened and struggles and starts to scream. He places his hand on her mouth to quiet her, but he is not capable of judging his strength and breaks her neck. When George finds them, Lennie apologizes and cries that he has hurt her just like he had hurt the puppy. George is aware that the ranchhands led by Curley will not have pity for Lennie, so he tells Lennie to pack up so that they can leave. A short time later, as the two sit on a riverbank, George shoots Lennie to death to save him from the more terrifying tortures of a mob.

CENSORSHIP HISTORY

Of Mice and Men has earned the dubious prestige of being the second most frequently banned book in the public school curriculum of the 1990s, second only to the reading anthology *Impressions*, although challenges were frequent in earlier decades as well. Censors claim that the novel contains crude heroes who speak vulgar language and whose experiences exhibit a sadly deficient social system in the United States.

The novel was placed on the banned list in Ireland in 1953 because of "obscenities" and "vulgar" language. It was banned for similar reasons in Syracuse, Indiana, in 1974; Oil City, Pennsylvania, in 1977; Grand Blanc, Michigan, in 1979; and Continental, Ohio, in 1980. In 1977, in Greenville, North Carolina, the Fourth Province of the Knights of the Ku Klux Klan challenged the use of the book in the local school district, for containing "profanities and using God's name in vain." The same reason was given by parents who challenged the book in Vernon-Verona-Sherill (New York) School District in 1980 and in school districts in St. David, Arizona, in 1981 and Tell City, Indiana, in 1982. The school board of Scottsboro, Alabama, banned the novel from Skyline High School in 1983 because of "profanity," and the chair of the Knoxville, Tennessee, school board vowed to remove all "filthy books" from the local school system, beginning with *Of Mice and Men* because of "its vulgar language."

The novel was challenged as "vulgar" and "offensive" by parents in the Christian County, Kentucky, school district in 1987, but it was later reinstated in the school libraries and English classes. "Profanity" was also the reason for the 1988 challenges in Marion County, West Virginia, schools; Wheaton-Warrenville (Illinois) Middle School; and Berrien Springs (Michigan) High School. In 1989, the school board ordered the novel removed from Northside High School in Tuscaloosa, Alabama, because of "profanity," and it was challenged as a reading assignment at a summer youth program in Chattanooga, Tennessee, because "Steinbeck is known to have had an anti-business attitude." That same year, the novel was also removed from all reading lists and all copies were stored away in White Chapel High School in Pine Bluff, Arkansas, because parents objected to the language. "Offensive language" was the reason that parents in the Shelby County, Tennessee, school system challenged the appropriateness of including the novel on the high school reading list.

The 1990s brought an increase in the number of challenges to *Of Mice and Men*. In 1990, a parent in Salinas, Kansas, challenged the use of the book in a 10th-grade English class because it contained "profanity" and "takes the Lord's name in vain." The school board review committee considered the complaint and recommended that the work be retained as a required reading but cautioned that no excerpts from the book should be read aloud in the classroom. That same year, a parent in Riviera, Texas, complained that the novel contained profanities and requested that it be removed from the 11th-grade English classes. At an open school board meeting to consider the request, 50 teachers and administrators and 10 high school students appeared to support continued use of the book. The only person who spoke against the novel was the parent who raised the original challenge. After the parent went through two more levels of appeal, the school board voted to continue assigning the novel.

In 1991, a Fresno, California, parent demanded that the book be removed from the 10th-grade English college preparatory curriculum, citing "profanity" and "racial slurs." The book was retained, and the child of the objecting parent was provided with an alternative reading assignment. In Iowa City, Iowa, a parent complained of the use of *Of Mice and Men* in the seventh-grade literature courses because of the profanity in the book, such as the word "Goddamn." She claimed that her daughter was subjected to "psychological and emotional abuse" when the book was read aloud and expressed the hope that her daughter would "not talk like a migrant worker" when she completed school. The district review committee retained the book. "Profanity," "excessive cursing" and "sexual overtones" were behind challenges to reading of the novel in high schools in Suwanee, Florida; Jacksboro, Tennessee; Buckingham, Virginia; and Branford, Florida.

A large number of challenges arose in 1992. A coalition of community members and clergy in Mobile, Alabama, requested that local school officials form a special textbook screening committee to "weed out objectionable things." Their first target was to be *Of Mice and Men*, which they claimed contained "profanity" and "morbid and depressing themes." No formal complaint was lodged, so school officials rejected the request. Challenges in Waterloo, Iowa, and Duval County, Florida, were made because of "profanity," "lurid passages about sex" and "statements defamatory to minorities." A parent in Modesto, California, challenged the novel on the basis of profanity for the use of the word "nigger," and the NAACP joined in demanding that the novel be removed from the reading list. "Profanity" prompted the challenge at Oak Hill High School in Alexandria, Louisiana, where it was retained.

One of the more detailed complaints emerged in 1992 in Hamilton, Ohio, where the book was temporarily removed from the high school reading list after a parent complained that it contained "vulgarity" and "racial slurs." The parent, vice president of the Parents' Coalition in Hamilton, stated that the novel contained 108 profanities and 12 racial slurs. The school board suggested the use of alternative reading assignments, which the coalition refused, and the novel was temporarily removed from the optional reading list. At the meeting of the board-appointed review committee, 150 parents, students and teachers appeared and enthusiastically supported the book. One student submitted a petition bearing 333 signatures of people who favored retaining the book. A local minister who opposed the book told the board, "Anybody that's got a child shouldn't want them to read this book. It should be burned up, put in a fire." The board of education voted unanimously to retain the book.

Fewer challenges arose in 1993 and 1994. The novel was challenged in 1993 as an appropriate English curriculum assignment by parents of students at Mingus (Arizona) Union High School who were concerned about the "profane language, moral statement, treatment of the retarded, and the violent ending." In 1994, the school superintendent of Putnam County, Tennessee, removed the novel from the classroom "due to the language in it, we just can't have this kind of book being taught." That same year, parents of students at Loganville (Georgia) High School called for a ban of the book because of "its vulgar language throughout."

FURTHER READINGS

Carrington, Ildiko de Papp. "Talking Dirty: Alice Munro's 'Open Secrets' and John Steinbeck's 'Of Mice and Men.'" *Studies in Short Fiction* 31 (Fall 1994): 595–606.

Johnson, Claudia. *Stifled Laughter: Woman's Story About Fighting Censorship.* Golden, Colo.: Fulcrum Publishing, 1994.

Newsletter on Intellectual Freedom (March 1975): 41; (November 1977): 155; (January 1978): 7; (March 1979): 27; (May 1980): 62; (July 1980): 77; (May 1982): 84–85; (July 1983): 198; (July 1984): 104; (May 1988): 90; (July 1988): 140; (September 1988): 154, 179; (November 1988): 201; (January 1989): 28; (November 1989): 162; (January 1990): 10–12; (March 1990): 45; (March 1991): 62; (July 1991): 110; (January 1992): 25; (March 1992): 64; (July 1992): 111–12; (September 1992): 140, 163–64; (January 1993): 29; (March 1994): 53; (March 1995): 46, 53.

Noble, Donald R. *The Steinbeck Question.* Troy, N.Y.: Whitston Publishing, 1993.

ONE FLEW OVER THE CUCKOO'S NEST

Author: Ken Kesey
Original date and place of publication: 1962, United States
Original publisher: Viking Press
Literary form: Novel

SUMMARY

One Flew Over the Cuckoo's Nest is told from the point of view of Bromden, a tall and heavyset schizophrenic Native American called the Chief, who is an inmate of a mental hospital ward. He pretends to be mute as a defense against his surroundings, but the arrival of Randle Patrick McMurphy, a fast-talking con artist who has feigned insanity to enter the mental hospital rather than a prison work farm, gives Bromden confidence and helps him to rebel against the sterile, domineering Miss Ratched. Known to the inmates as Big Nurse, she runs a tightly controlled, efficient ward in which the heavily medicated patients mechanically follow her orders without question and even the orderlies stand at attention, "ready to quell even the feeblest insurrection." McMurphy disrupts her efficiency with his irrepressible high spirits and his goal to create havoc on her well-run ward. The chilling authority of Nurse Ratched appalls McMurphy who provides a direct contrast to the other patients. They "long ago gave up the struggle to assert themselves. Cowed, docile, they have surrendered completely to her unbridled authority."

The boisterous, fun-loving, rebellious McMurphy is a lusty and profane fighter, whose brawling and gambling challenge the rigidly structured world over which Nurse Ratched presides. Against all hospital rules, he initiates gambling among the inmates and smuggles women and wine into the ward. As he openly defies Big Nurse, the other men gradually emerge from their fear-induced inactivity and learn to express happiness, anger and other emotions that have long been repressed. Such behavior becomes dangerous for McMurphy, because he has been committed by the state, not voluntarily as have most of the men, and his behavior will determine the length of his stay. The greater his rebellion against the repressive atmosphere created by Big Nurse, the greater the danger that he will be forced to remain in the hospital for a longer period of commitment.

From taking forbidden cigarettes left at the nurses' station to stealing a fishing boat for an inmates' fishing expedition, McMurphy shows a disregard for the rules that have so long dominated the lives of the other inmates, as his vitality and enthusiasm radically change them. His escapades have sometimes tragic consequences that result from the clash of authority with the inmates' newfound freedom. One man drowns in the therapeutic swimming pool when his fingers become stuck in the grate at the bottom of the pool, while young Billy Bibbit takes his own life after Nurse Ratched threatens to tell his mother that he has had sex with a prostitute whom McMurphy sneaked onto the ward. Even McMurphy must eventually yield to the misguided technology of the mental hospital after he attacks Big Nurse, blaming her brutal treatment and threats for young Billy's death. A few weeks after the attack, McMurphy disappears from the ward for a week. When he returns, the other inmates refuse to accept the changed man and claim that he is an impostor who looks "like one of those department store dummies. . . . a crummy sideshow fake lying there on the Gurney." A lobotomy destroys all that has made McMurphy human and makes him the perfect example of what happens to a man who bucks the system. Unable to bear seeing their friend deprived of his vitality, the remaining inmates decide to provide him with a dignified end. The Chief smothers him with a pillow, then escapes from the hospital to freedom.

CENSORSHIP HISTORY

The novel has been frequently censored and challenged as being racist, obscene and immoral because of its raw language and for its emphasis upon the defiance of authority. The white inmates repeatedly refer to the black orderlies with such racial slurs as "coons," "boys" and "niggers," while the Japanese nurse from the Disturbed ward is spoken of as the "Jap." Numerous obscenities pepper McMurphy's speech, and he appears to purposely taunt the doctors and nurses, as when he challenges their question regarding his psychopathic tendencies: "'Is it my fightin' tendencies or my fuckin' tendencies? Must be fuckin', mustn't it? All that wham-bam-thank-you-ma'am. . . .'" He further describes Nurse Ratched as having "the too big boobs" and as "a bitch and a buzzard and a ballcutter."

Identified as containing "obscene, filthy language," the novel was challenged in 1971 in Greeley, Colorado, where parents in the public school district demanded that it be removed from the non-required American Culture reading list along with *I Never Promised You a Rose Garden* and *Love Story*. In 1974, five residents of Strongsville, Ohio, sued the board of education to remove *One Flew Over the Cuckoo's Nest* and *MANCHILD IN THE PROMISED LAND* from the classroom. Labeling both books "pornographic materials," they charged that the works "glorify criminal activity, have a tendency to corrupt juveniles, and contain descriptions of bestiality, bizarre violence, and torture, dismemberment, death, and human elimination." In 1975, the book was removed from public school libraries in Randolph, New York, and Alton, Oklahoma, and school officials in Westport, Massachusetts, removed the novel from the required reading list in 1977.

In 1978, the novel was banned from St. Anthony Freemont (Idaho) High School classrooms, and the contract of the instructor was not renewed after parents complained about the language in the book. The school superintendent did not read the book, but he collected all copies from students without attempting to determine its literary or scholastic value. The teacher claimed to have sent home a list of books to be read with the condition that alternative titles would be provided for students wko chose not to read a specific assigned book, and no one had objected. The teacher worked with the American Civil Liberties Union to file a complaint in the United States District Court for the District of Idaho, claiming that his rights and the rights of his students under the First and Fourteenth Amendments had been violated. *Fogarty v. Atchley* was filed but not decided. The novel was also challenged in 1982 by parents of students in Merrimack (New Hampshire) High School, where it was removed, but in a 1986 challenge to the novel as part of the honors English curriculum at Aberdeen (Washington) High School, the school board voted to retain the novel.

FURTHER READINGS

Newsletter on Intellectual Freedom. (May 1971): 59; (November 1974): 152; (May 1975): 41; (July 1975): 108; (May 1978): 57; (July 1978): 96, 100; (May 1980): 52; (September 1982): 170; (November 1986): 225.

O'Neil, Robert M. *Classrooms in the Crossfire: The Rights and Interests of Students, Parents, Teachers, Administrators, Librarians, and the Community.* Bloomington, Ind.: Indiana University Press, 1981.

Tebbel, John. *A History of Book Publishing in the United States.* Vol. IV. New York: Bowker and Company, 1981.

THE SCARLET LETTER

Author: Nathaniel Hawthorne
Original place and date of publication: 1850, United States
Original publisher: Ticknor and Fields
Literary form: Novel

SUMMARY

The Scarlet Letter opens with a long, detailed preface entitled "The Custom House: Introductory to *The Scarlet Letter*" in which Hawthorne creates the illusion that the novel following is based on fact. He claims that, while working as a custom house agent, he found a manuscript and a faded and worn red letter "A" in one of the upper rooms. The manuscript, written by Jonathan Pue, a predecessor of his in the Custom House in Salem, Massachusetts, detailed the story of a Mistress Hester Prynne who had been found guilty of adultery in Boston two centuries earlier and punished. In addition to creating the premise for the novel, the section also makes reference to Hawthorne's ancestors and provides insight into his daily work as a civil servant.

The story of *The Scarlet Letter* is that of a romantic triangle. Hester Prynne, the beautiful young wife of an old and introverted scholar, is separated from her husband for two years after being taken from her home in England to the wildlands of the New World. Lonely and without friends, she falls in love with Arthur Dimmesdale, an attractive young minister, and bears his child, whom she names Pearl for she "was purchased at great price." Condemned by the townspeople, especially the women, who feel that jailing Hester, forcing her to stand on a scaffold in the middle of town and wearing the scarlet letter "A," for adultery, for life are not severe enough, Hester carries herself with dignity.

True to her strong character, Hester bears the shame and punishment alone and never reveals her child's father, although to do so would alleviate a great part of her punishment. Instead, Hester creates her own world for Pearl and supports herself by her excellent needlework skills. Her husband appears as a physician just returned from the frontier, but they agree to keep his identity a secret as the bitter and physically misshapen man takes the name Roger

Chillingworth. He treats the physical ailments of Dimmesdale and eventually uncovers the identity of Pearl's father. The evil Chillingworth, feigning friendship, slowly destroys the minister. As Dimmesdale sinks into physical decay and Chillingworth decays morally, Hester wins the respect of the townspeople, who begin to view the "A" as representing "angel" for the many kind deeds she performs.

At the end of the novel, the dying Dimmesdale confesses publicly that he is Pearl's father as he stands holding hands with Hester and Pearl, on the same scaffold on which Hester alone stood soon after Pearl's birth to display her shame to the townspeople. Dimmesdale dies and Hester takes Pearl to Europe, then returns years later to her small cottage. After she dies, Hester is buried under the same grave marker as Dimmesdale.

CENSORSHIP HISTORY

The novel was a success when it was first published, selling out a first printing within a few days. Although critics and literary figures praised the novel, religious journals and clergymen denounced it as "a dirty story" that belonged only in "a Brothel Library." A review in *Brownson's Quarterly* declared that neither Dimmesdale nor Hester exhibited "remorse" or "really repents of the criminal deed" and that "it is a story that should not have been told." In *Church Review*, Rev. Arthur C. Coxe also condemned the two main characters as not being sufficiently repentant and stated that "the nauseous amour" was not appropriate subject matter for fiction. In 1852, Coxe called for the banning of *The Scarlet Letter* as he launched a savage attack, proclaiming that he was against "any toleration to a popular and gifted writer when he perpetrates bad morals—let his brokerage of lust be put down at the very beginning." He stated that he could not tolerate a novel that dealt with an "illicit relationship."

The main complaint of those who wanted to ban the novel at the outset was that Hawthorne sided with Hester and condemned her husband's revenge. Strict morality required that Hester suffer in more painful and obvious ways than Hawthorne provided. The citizens of Salem were so incensed by Hawthorne's novel that he moved his family out of the city to a farmhouse in the Berkshires. In 1852, the novel was banned in Russia by Czar Nicholas I in a "censorship terror," but the ban was lifted four years later when Czar Alexander II came into power.

Little attention was paid to the novel for nearly a century. In 1949, in stating the deciding opinion in *Commonwealth of Massachusetts v. Gordon*, 66 D. & C. 101 (1949), Judge Curtis Bok used the novel as an example of the manner in which public morals change when he noted that when first published, "Hawthorne's *Scarlet Letter* was referred to as 'a brokerage of lust,'" but it has become fully accepted by 1949.

In 1961, parents of students in Michigan objected to the assignment of the novel in high school English classes, claiming that it was "pornographic and obscene." They demanded that the book be taken out of the curriculum, but the request was denied. In a 1966 national sample of school librarians and English department chairpersons conducted by Lee Burress, four challenges were raised in locales unidentified by the investigator. In one, a student challenged the assignment of the book to freshman high school students, but no action was taken on the complaint. In a second challenge, a parent complained that the book was "immoral" because it dealt with a "misbegotten" child. The school board denied the request for removal of the book from the curriculum. In a third request to have the book removed from a reading list because it dealt with adultery, the request was also denied. The only successful challenge reported in the survey occurred when a high school principal declared the book too "frank" and "revealing" and removed it from the recommended reading list. A 1967 survey of high school censorship in Arizona conducted by Kenneth Donelson and Retha K. Foster reported one challenge by a parent who demanded the book be removed as a required reading because it discussed adultery. The request was denied.

In 1977, a parent and a principal in Michigan objected to the inclusion of the novel in the high school English curriculum because it dealt with a clergyman's "involvement in fornication." The book was removed from classroom use and from the recommended reading list. That same year, a parent in Missouri condemned the book for its use of "4-letter words" and "other undesirable content" and demanded its removal from the high school library. The school librarian recognized that the parent had not read the book because no obscenities appeared in the novel, and she convinced the parent of his error. The book was retained.

In a 1982 survey of English department chairpersons in Ohio, James Davis reported one challenge to the novel in which a parent claimed that the book was about "adultery," a "womanizing preacher" and "prostitution" and requested its removal as an assigned reading in a high school English class. The school board denied the request.

FURTHER READINGS

Burress, Lee. *Battle of the Books: Literary Censorship in the Public Schools, 1950–1985.* Metuchen, N.J.: Scarecrow Press, 1989.

Crowley, J. Donald, ed. *Hawthorne: The Critical Heritage.* New York: Barnes and Noble, 1970.

Davis, James E., ed. *Dealing with Censorship.* Urbana, Ill.: National Council of Teachers of English, 1983.

Donelson, Kenneth, ed. *The Student's Right to Read.* Urbana, Ill.: National Council of Teachers of English, 1972.

McClure, Robert C. "Literature, the Law of Obscenity, and the Constitution." *Minnesota Law Review* 38 (March 1954): 325.

Miller, Edwin Haviland. *Salem Is My Dwelling Place: A Life of Nathaniel Hawthorne.* Iowa City: University of Iowa Press, 1991.

Tebbel, John. *A History of Book Publishing in the United States, 1630–1865.* Vol. 1. New York: R.R. Bowker Company, 1972.

Wood, James Playsted. *The Unpardonable Sin.* New York: Pantheon Books, 1970.

TO KILL A MOCKINGBIRD

Author: (Nelle) Harper Lee
Original date and place of publication: 1960, New York
Original publisher: Lippincott and Company
Literary form: Novel

SUMMARY

Harper Lee's only novel touched a nerve in American society when it was first published, becoming a best-seller as well as a critical success that won the Pulitzer Prize in 1961. The author claimed that her story of racial bias in the sleepy fictional Alabama town of Maycomb was pure imagination, but reporters who visited her hometown of Monroeville, Alabama, on the 30th anniversary of the book's publication found remarkable similarities to the novel in both setting and character. In essence, the racial ills chronicled in the novel appear to have been realistically drawn from the author's life.

The novel is told from the point of view of the adult Jean Louise Finch, known as Scout to her friends, who relates the events of three years, beginning with her sixth summer. With her brother Jem, four years her senior, and summer visitor Dill, modeled after a real-life summer playmate who grew up to be the writer Truman Capote, Scout devises a series of projects to make their mysterious next-door neighbor, Arthur "Boo" Radley, emerge from his house. The early chapters of the novel detail the comfortable cocoon of childhood that Scout enjoys, as she enters school, engages in fistfights with boys and shares confidences with her father, lawyer Atticus Finch.

Scout's comfortable world is shattered when her father agrees to take the unpopular defense of black laborer Tom Robinson, accused of raping white Mayella Ewell. The townspeople want Tom to die, but Atticus believes that Tom is innocent and establishes that Tom's withered left arm could not have made the bruises on the right side of Mayella's face.

As bitterness engulfs the town, Atticus must defend his client not only in court but also from a lynch mob. Atticus manages to prove that Tom is physically incapable of committing the crime, yet the jury brings in a verdict of guilty despite the revelation that Mayella had made sexual advances to Tom that he had refused out of fear for his life. In addition, townspeople are angered because Tom expresses pity for a white woman.

Atticus plans to appeal the decision, but Tom is fatally shot while trying to escape during a jail exercise period. The final chapters of the novel contain Bob Ewell's attempted revenge against Atticus for having defended Tom and the emergence of Boo Radley from his house to save Jem and Scout from Ewell's knife.

CENSORSHIP HISTORY

Despite its strong annual sales and appearance on required reading lists in numerous high schools throughout the United States, *To Kill a Mockingbird* has frequently been challenged by parents and groups who object to either the language or the way in which race is represented. The Committee on Intellectual Freedom of the American Library Association lists the novel as being among the 10 most frequently challenged books today. In 1977, Eden Valley (Minnesota) School District temporarily banned the book because the words "damn" and "whore lady" appeared in the text, and parents in Vernon-Verona-Sherill (New York) School District challenged the book in 1980 as being a "filthy, trashy novel." Black parents in Warren Township (Indiana) schools charged in 1981 that passages in the book that portrayed the submissive behavior of Tom Robinson, Calpurnia and other blacks, and the frequent use of the word "nigger" advocated institutionalized racism and were harmful to the integration process. Despite their vehement efforts, the attempt to censor the book was unsuccessful. As a result, three black parents resigned in protest from the town's human relations advisory council.

The novel was also challenged in 1984 in the Waukegan, Illinois, schools for inclusion of the word "nigger," and in 1985 Park Hill (Missouri) Junior High School parents challenged the novel because it contained racial slurs and offensive language. The most recent attempt to ban the novel occurred in 1985 in Casa Grande (Arizona) Elementary School District, where black parents and the National Association for the Advancement of Colored People protested that the book was unfit for use in the junior high school. School officials there changed the status of the book from required reading to retention on a supplemental reading list.

FURTHER READINGS

"Another Furor over Books." *Ohio State University Monthly* 55 (December 1963): 8–12.

Bruell, Edwin. "Keen Scalpel on Racial Ills." *English Journal* 53 (December 1964): 658–61.

Dave, R. A. "*To Kill a Mockingbird*: Harper Lee's Tragic Vision." In *Indian Studies in American Literature*. Ed. by M. K. Naik, S. K. Desai and S. Mokashi, 311–23. Dharwar, India: Karnatak University, 1974.

May, Jill. "In Defense of *To Kill a Mockingbird*." In *Censored Books: Critical Viewpoints*. Ed. by Nicholas J. Karolides, Lee Burress and John M. Kean, 476–84. Metuchen, N.J.: Scarecrow Press, 1993.

Newsletter on Intellectual Freedom (March 1966): 16; (March 1968): 22; (March 1978): 31; (May 1980): 62; (March 1982): 47; (July 1984): 105; (March 1986): 57–58.

Skaggs, Merrill. *The Folk of Southern Fiction*. Athens, Ga.: The University of Georgia Press, 1972.

INDEX

Boldface numbers indicate major treatment of a topic.

Edict of Worms (1521, Germany) 229
Edwards, Jonathan 315
Edwards, Judity 140
Edwards, Robert W. 298
Edwards v. Aguillard 239
Egypt, censorship in 189–190, 207–208, 252, 253, 256
Eisenhower, Dwight D. 109
Eliot, John 180
Eliot, Maine, censorship in 288
Ellison, Ralph 336
El Saadawi, Nawal
    The Hidden Face of Eve: Women in the Arab World **205–208**
    Women and Sex 207
Emerson, Ralph Waldo 388
Encyclopedia of Censorship (Green) 7, 15, 109, 115, 122, 128, 131, 132
Engels, Friedrich, *Manifesto of the Communist Party* **103–110**
England, censorship in 17–19, 115, 175, 178–180, 185–186, 224–225, 229, 284, 286, 295, 302, 305, 308, 384
Ennis, Jim 139
Epperson, Susan 239
Epstein, Sheldon 69
Erie, Pennsylvania, censorship in 337
Erskine, Thomas 132
Escambia County, Florida, censorship in 221
Essays (Montaigne) **200–203**
Estienne, Robert 179, 180
Ethiopia, censorship in 181, 214
Evans, Edgar J. 50
Evans, Robert B., Sr. 157

F

Fabri, Sisto 202
Fahrenheit 451 (Bradbury) **374–376**
Fairbanks, Alaska, censorship in 182, 275
Fairfax County, Virginia, censorship in 337
Fanny Hill, or Memoirs of a Woman of Pleasure (Cleland) 266, **283–286**, 301
Farel, Guillaume 193
Farnum, Forest 52
Farrell v. Hall 73, 76
Faulkner, William, *Sanctuary* **321–323**
Fayer, Larry 78
Federal Bureau of Investigation (FBI)
    and censorship of books 22, 345
    and Indian affairs 79–90
feminism, books dealing with
    The Hidden Face of Eve: Women in the Arab World (El Saadawi) **205–208**
    Lajja (Shame) (Nasrin) **214–218**
Ferlinghetti, Lawrence 380
Fielding, Henry 315
Fitzgerald, Georgia, censorship in 140
The Fixer (Malamud) 24, 25, 26
Flaubert, Gustave, *Madame Bovary* **306–309**
Flood, Charles B. 111
Florence, Italy, censorship in 274
Florida, censorship in 14, 73, 108, 123, 139, 221, 288, 326, 336, 360–361, 367, 368, 378, 391, 396
Foerstel, Herbert N. 141
Foff, Arthur 381
Fogarty v. Atchley 400

Ford, John 332
foreign policy *See* U.S. foreign policy
Forever (Blume) **287–289**
Forever Amber (Winsor) **289–291**
Forrest, Brenda 141
Fort Laramie Treaty (1868) 79
Fort Worth, Texas, censorship in 345
Fosdick, Frederick W. 301
Foster, Retha K. 403
Fouda, Farag 190
Fowler, Lorenzo & Orson 387
Fox, Charles James 131
Fox, John 108
France, censorship in 106, 179, 191–192, 205, 229, 261, 277, 279, 305, 307
Francis I, king of France 180
Franco, Francisco 246, 260
Frank, Anne, *Anne Frank: The Diary of a Young Girl* 67, **339–341**
Frankfurter, Felix 312
Franklin, Benjamin, *The Autobiography of Benjamin Franklin* **348–350**
Franklin, John Hope, *Land of the Free: A History of the United States* **94–103**
Franklin, William Temple 349
Frederick III (of Saxony) 227, 229
Frederick William II, king of Prussia 248
The Freedom of Christian Man (Luther) 228
Freedom to Read Foundation 86
Fresno, California, censorship in 396
Froben, Johannes 228
Fulbright, J. W. 151

G

Gainesville, Georgia, censorship in 379
Galileo Galilei
    Dialogue Concerning the Two Chief World Systems **197–200**
    Dialogue Concerning Two New Sciences 199
    Letters on the Solar Spots 197
    The Starry Messenger 197
Garden, Nancy, *Annie on My Mind* **341–343**
Gastonia, North Carolina, censorship in 182
Geller, Evelyn 280, 282
General Allotment Act (1887) 800
Gentillet, Innocent 128
Georgia, censorship in 14, 47, 140, 338, 379, 396
Germany
    books about 63–70
    censorship in 6, 69, 107, 179, 259
Gesell, Gerhard 164
Ghazzali, Sheik Mohammed, al- 208
Ginsberg, Allen 394
    Howl and Other Poems **380–382**
Girodias, Maurice 305
Go Ask Alice (Anonymous) 24, **377–379**
Goethe, Johann Wolfgang von
    My Life: Poetry and Truth 258
    The Sorrows of Young Werther **257–260**
Goffstown, New Hampshire, censorship in 368
Gone With The Wind (Mitchell) 157
Gonzales, Mario 83
Goodman, Louis A. 325
Gordimer, Nadine, *Burger's Daughter* **27–31**
Gordon, John 305
Goulart, Simon 202
Gournay, Marie de 202